The Unbroken Thread

Ted Grant

FORTRESS

The Unbroken Thread —
the Development of Trotskyism over 40 years

Selected writings of Ted Grant

This selection first published June 1989

Articles, selection and introductions © Fortress Books

British Library Cataloguing in Publication Data

Grant, Ted
The unbroken thread:
the development of Trotskyism over 40 years:
selected writings of Ted Grant
1. Politics. Trotskyist viewpoints
I. Title II. Pickard, John 320.5'312

ISBN 1-870958-06-3
ISBN 1-870958-05-5 Pbk

Published and distributed by Fortress Books
PO Box 141, London E2 ORL

Typeset by Anteus Graphics 222, Tower Street, Century Building,
Brunswick Business Park Liverpool L3 4BJ (051-709-1560) and
Eastway Offset, 3/13 Hepscott Road, London E9 5HB (01-533-3311)

Printed in Great Britain by Biddles Ltd
of Guildford and Kings Lynn

Cover design by Alan Hardman

Contents

Articles marked* are major extracts from the original document.

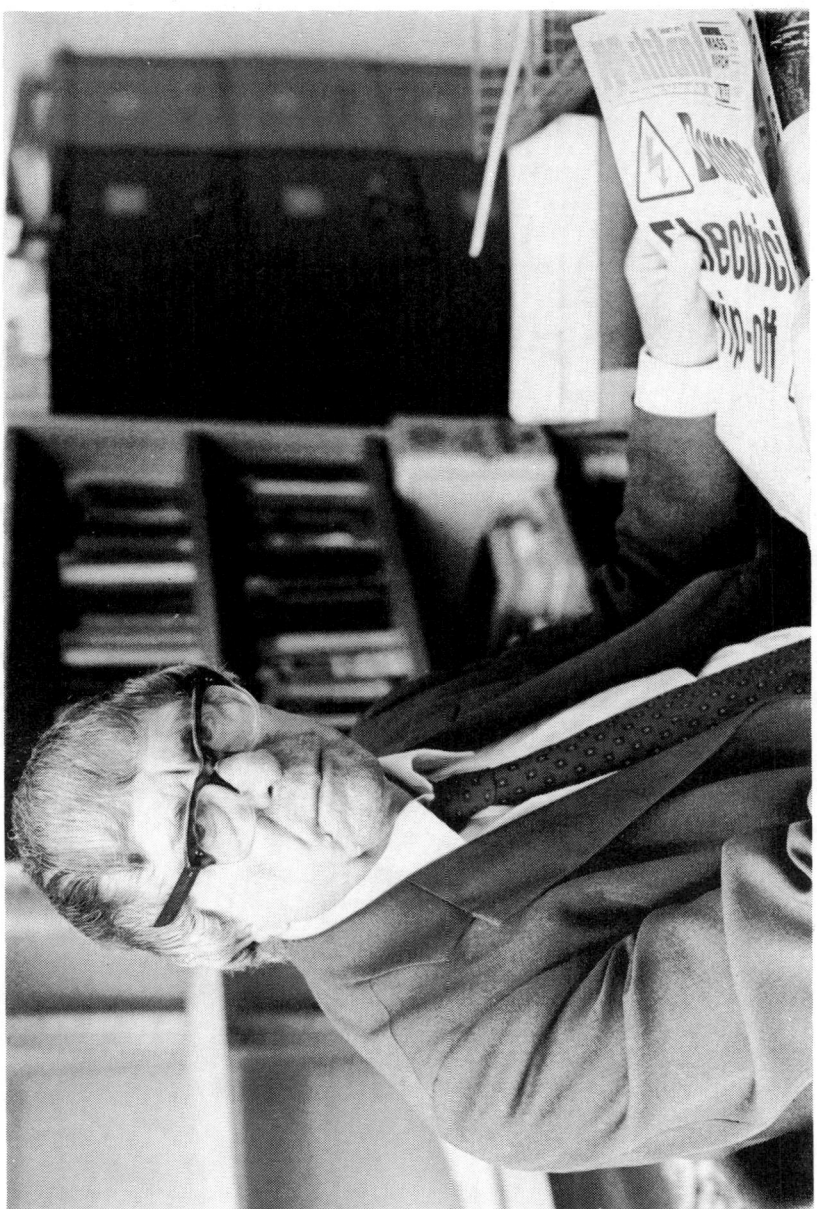

The Unbroken Thread

Introduction

THE PURPOSE of this book is twofold. It is, firstly, to show that the modern ideas of Marxism have their direct roots in the working out of ideas in the previous period. Secondly, it is to show the central and unique role played by Ted Grant in the development of these ideas since the death of Trotsky in 1940.

Ted Grant was born in Germiston, near Johannesburg in South Africa. At the age of eleven, he was introduced to the writings of Bernard Shaw, HG Wells, Maxim Gorky, Jack London and others by Ralph Lee, a member of the Communist Party and a friend of the family. Within a short time, the reading material graduated on to the works of Marx, Engels and Lenin, so that by the time he was fifteen, Ted Grant was a confirmed Marxist.

His association with Trotskyist ideas began with the critique that Trotsky made of the Sixth Congress of the Communist International, in 1928. By a bureaucratic oversight (much regretted by the Stalinists later), Trotsky's criticisms were circulated to delegates. Some American communists smuggled copies out after the Congress and began to organise the distribution of Trotsky's writings, using, among other means, the paper they founded, *The Militant*.

"I think it was in 1928 or 1929", Ted Grant recalls, "when the American *Militant* was sent to radical bookshops in a number of different parts of the world, and a few were sent to Johannesburg. They published all Trotsky's criticisms of Stalinism, including his analysis of the aborted revolution in China in 1925-27. We used to wait eagerly for the arrival of each new batch of papers. We read them avidly from cover to cover, especially the writing of Trotsky himself. These contributions made an enormous difference to our understanding."

Within a few years, Ralph Lee was expelled from the Communist Party and he, Grant and another supporter, Murray Gow Purdy, formed the Workers' International League in South Africa. They regarded themselves as a left opposition to the Stalinist leadership within the Communist Party, as did all the newly-formed Trotskyist groups throughout the world. The WIL around this time organised a strike of black laundry workers in Johannesburg.

In this period, however, the black proletariat was far smaller, with less social weight, in comparison to the situation that developed after the war. It was understandable, therefore, that South African Trotskyists should have looked for inspiration to the many-millioned working class movement in Europe, with its mightier organisations and longer traditions. Not long after Hitler came to power in Germany, in mid-1933, Ted Grant left South Africa, as he put it, for 'broader horizons' in Europe.

The small South African group had already corresponded with the Trotskyist movement in Britain, regularly receiving *Red Flag*, its newspaper. Travelling with another supporter of Trotsky, Sid Frost, Grant went by boat, first to France, then on to London. While they stayed in Paris for a week or two, they met and discussed with Leon Sedov, Trotsky's son and a key organiser of the international Trotskyist movement.

In Britain, Grant joined the Independent Labour Party, but only briefly, and then the Labour League of Youth, the youth section of the Labour Party. With other Young Socialists, he was very prominent in the day-to-day struggles against the Mosleyite blackshirts, including the famous battle of Cable Street.

In 1938, Ralph Lee also came to Britain, and with Grant and others formed a Trotskyist group, once again calling it the Workers International League. Lee was a talented speaker and writer, but within two years returned to South Africa, largely for personal reasons. The continuity of Ted Grant's own political work was saved around this time by 'good fortune': called up in 1940 to serve in the Pioneer Corps, he unfortunately suffered a fractured skull in an accident, and was invalided out of the Forces, without ever having donned the khaki.

The Workers' International League was a marked success in wartime conditions, its theoretical leadership mainly the work of Grant. By 1944, the WIL took over the remnant of the Revolutionary Socialist League, another smaller group, to form the Revolutionary Communist Party. The RCP continued the success, especially in the recruitment of industrial militants. So much so that the War Cabinet was supplied with a secret memo from the Labour Home Secretary, Herbert Morrison, outlining the policies of the RCP, and giving brief biographies of its leaders, including Ted Grant. Although it was not carried through in the end, it is clear that the capitalist class was seriously considering banning the RCP.

Unfortunately, the marvellous momentum of the wartime work was not reflected in the fortunes of the RCP afterwards. This is not the place to give a history of British Trotskyism, but without going into all the background and the causes, it is enough to know that the RCP broke up in 1949-50. Suffice to say that this was in large measure due to bureaucratic interference and outright manoeuvres by the leadership of the Fourth International, of which the RCP was a part.

The International leaders had never been capable of facing up to and explaining the new situation that arose after the war. It was only Ted Grant who had come to terms with developments and described them in Marxist terms. By the time of the demise of the RCP, Ted Grant was the dominant theoretical force within British Trotskyism, and, as the extracts in this volume show, a hundred times more correct than the alleged theoreticians of the International.

After the RCP disintegrated Grant continued to put forward a Marxist view in a variety of journals and magazines. He was editor of *The International Socialist*, a theoretical magazine, and later editor of the paper, *Socialist Fight*. 'When that was coming out duplicated,' he recalls, 'I was doing most of the work for it myself. I wrote most of it. I typed it once, proof-read it and typed it again to justify it (adjust the type to fit evenly between the margins). I even had a hand in working the duplicator from time to time.'

In 1964, he was one of the founders of the newspaper *Militant*, still going strong, twenty-five years later, as 'the Marxist voice for Labour and Youth'. As political editor of the *Militant* he has written regularly on all major political questions, as well as contributing to *Militant International Review*, writing pamphlets and documents, and giving countless speeches and lectures.

Because of the growth in support for the paper, the leadership of the Labour Party began to expel its supporters, beginning with the editorial board, in 1983. After having rejoined the Labour Party in 1950, with thirty-three years continuous membership, Ted Grant was expelled. But to expel the 'head' of a movement, is not to expel the movement itself. The political work of half a century cannot be erased by a flash of the block vote. The fruits of fifty years of work, of an unrivalled contribution to socialist theory are there to be seen: in the development of a Marxist tendency deeply rooted in and inseparable from the labour movement.

Political parties, tendencies and individuals, cannot be judged simply by the formal position they happen to adopt at any one point in time. Even the most limp-brained 'theoretician' can stumble upon a correct idea once in a while. It is better to judge a theory or a set of ideas dialectically, in other words, to examine them in the process of their origin, formation and development.

It was not for sentimental reasons that Lenin and Trotsky urged young comrades to respect the traditions of the socialist movement. It is because in the traditions lie the distilled conclusions of all the theoretical debates and discussions of decades, made sharp by the living experience of the working class. Many young workers today, for example, will take for granted, 'assume', the correctness of certain theoretical concepts, analyses and political methods. Even much of the terminology, the 'jargon' of Marxism, which is more exact and meaningful (as befits a science) than that of the trendy and superficial political sociologists of capitalism, is taken for granted.

But this Marxian theoretical tradition, so often taken as read today, did not appear from nowhere; it had to be fought for. It had to be established and consolidated against all the illusory ideas, the opportunism and ultra-leftism that pervaded the working class movement, including the so-called Trotskyist movement, after the war. And in creating that theoretical tradition, in carrying on the development of Marxism in an unbroken thread from the work of Leon Trotsky, there has been no greater contribution made than that of Ted Grant.

For four decades since the end of the war — nearly five since the death of Trotsky — Grant has defended the method of Marxism against all kinds of alien ideas. What makes this achievement all the more remarkable is that this has been a period, for the most part, of economic upswing and political reaction, at least in the advanced capitalist countries. In the hey-day of the post-war boom, it really did seem to many that capitalism had learnt to overcome the crises and class struggles of the past. The forces of genuine Marxism were reduced, literally, to a handful in one part of the globe. The Stalinist parties became ever more degenerate. The former 'Fourth International' became a circus of middle-class sects, prey to opportunist and ultra-left influences.

It is to one person alone that the credit must go for the maintenance and development of Marxist theory in this most difficult period. Through having an international perspective, and anticipating the limitations of the boom, it was possible to retain complete confidence in the working class and the future of socialism. This, combined with an unbreakable will, ploughed the ground for the later period when the forces of Marxism have been able to grow from tens to tens of thousands. Support for these ideas has spread not only in Britain, but internationally.

In Britain, *Militant* has established Marxism, which in its modern form is Trotskyism, as a bona-fide current of opinion in the labour movement. Stalinism has for decades besmirched the genuine heritage of Marx and Lenin and has thrown up clouds of confusion and doubt in the minds of active workers. More recently, the traditions of Leon Trotsky have been dragged in the mud by a bewildering variety of middle-class ultra-left groups, most of whom have as much connection with workers as with the man in the moon.

But clearly distinguishing themselves from the Stalinists on the one hand and the middle-class 're-re-revolutionaries' on the other, the supporters of *Militant* have worked to build an increasingly significant base of support for their ideas in both the Labour Party and the trade unions. This has been done by debate and discussion, patiently explaining their views with a battery of facts, figures and arguments. Personal attacks, sneers, physical threats, intimidation, stunts: notwithstanding the lies of the capitalist media, these have no place whatsoever in the methods of political work instilled by Ted Grant into *Militant* supporters.

The leaderships of the various unions and the Party — not being able to answer argument and debate — have frequently resorted to organisational measures to rid themselves of the Marxists. In the climate of witch-hunting that presently prevails inside the Labour Party, supporters of *Militant* are being expelled quite blatantly for their ideas. But these expulsions and restrictions will be in vain. Already, the *Militant* has come to represent a powerful Marxist current in a number of the major trade unions and in the Labour Party and it will not be possible for the ideas of the paper to be separated from the labour movement. On the contrary, these will be the ideas of the majority in the future.

The frustration of the witch-hunters arises out of their inability to answer the ideas of *Militant*. The paper has built for itself a reputation of solid attachment to political theory, its supporters taking seriously all the international, historical and theoretical questions that affect the workers' movement. It would not be an exaggeration to say that where the Marxists have an influence in the movement, there always follows a tremendous thirst for theory. The detractors of Marxism frequently sneer at what they perceive as unnecessary baggage, but the value of correct theory has been demonstrated time and time again.

While the Stalinists and the reformists acknowledge events only when they are struck on the nose by them (and even then sometimes not), the Marxists, as scientific socialists, can gain an insight into social processes and the laws that underlie them. It is possible by this means to develop a perspective, a prognosis of the likely out-turn of events, on the basis of a detailed examination of past and present conditions in society, the direction of change, and so on. Marxism can be said to be the science of perspectives, and in political questions, it repeatedly proves the invaluable advantage gained by foresight over astonishment.

Many examples can be given to show the superiority of Marxist methods in relation to current political questions. Just to take one issue, there is at present a great deal of discussion about the 'reforms' of Mikhail Gorbachev in the USSR and the alleged shift of Hungary and Poland towards 'democracy'. This is not the place to go into the question in great detail, but readers of the *Militant* will know that the paper has a well-founded and consistent view on the matter. It has argued that the Stalinist bureaucracy in these states is incapable of yielding any genuine democracy and will not be prepared to share power with any movement or organisation that represents the working class.

This view adopted by *Militant* has not been whistled out of an editor's thumb, but rests upon a long-standing theoretical tradition and an understanding of the social forces and processes in Eastern Europe. It relies upon a scientific appraisal of the origin of the bureaucracy, its role and relationship to the state, and so on.

On the other hand, elsewhere within the labour movement, there are illusions about how far the 'reforming' process can go, some commentators suggesting, for example, that the 'legalisation' of the Solidarity trade union in Poland marks a profound change and a step towards Western-style democracy. Which view is correct?

To answer this it is instructive to go back to 1980, to the period of the origin and growth of the Solidarity union. When the Polish regime signed an agreement at that time, also 'legalising' the union, there were similar illusions, not least within the leadership of the union itself, that the Stalinist state was prepared to tolerate and co-exist with it. *Militant* argued otherwise:

> There can be no half-way house. There will either be totalitarian control under a one-party state, as exists in Eastern Europe and Poland, or there will be control of industry and the state by the workers as

envisaged by Marx, Lenin and Trotsky. An uneasy compromise between the two can exist for only a very short time....the bureaucracy, taking advantage of the inevitable disillusionment amongst the workers, and the ebbing of the movement, will inevitably move to strangle the unions, or incorporate them into the state machine.
(Ted Grant, *Militant* 522, October 3 1980)

Unfortunately, because it gives no pleasure to a Marxist to see a workers' movement suppressed by martial law, the prognosis of the *Militant* was absolutely correct and borne out by events. The illusion — so bluntly and unceremoniously shattered — that Solidarity would be allowed to organise as a free trade union in a totalitarian state was shown to have been based, not on any firm theoretical premise, but on a hope and a prayer.

It is of more than academic interest to show the enormous advantage of scientific method over empirical impressionism. Theory is not counter-posed to political activity, but is dialectically linked to it. If it were only a question of working class self-sacrifice, heroism and a willingness to struggle, then socialism would have been established across the whole globe many decades ago. It is also a matter of organisation, direction, purpose and leadership. All too often, the most courageous workers' movements have been shipwrecked by 'leaders' completely blind to social processes. The huge benefit of foresight, of a grasp of perspectives and developments, lies precisely in the creation of the subjective factor: in building a leadership for the labour movement that matches in understanding what the workers always provide in determination.

But what also has to be understood, and the reason why this brief example is given, is that this Marxist analysis of Eastern Europe, on which could be built a uniquely correct understanding of events and a proven perspective, did not fall overnight from the sky. It represents an extension of a consistent Marxist critique that was established by Ted Grant in the debates and discussions in the first four or five years after the second world war. Moreover, this analysis was itself an extension of the position already worked out by Leon Trotsky before the war.

Taking the works of Marx, Engels, Lenin and Trotsky as a method, rather than as a fixed dogma, Ted Grant has achieved more than any other Marxist theoretician in explaining post-war developments. As the material in this volume shows, the theoretical line that he laid down, especially in the first few years after the war, provided the starting point for an understanding of political and economic developments in the three parts of the world: the advanced capitalist countries, the colonial and ex-colonial countries and the Stalinist states.

No other tendency of the right or the left has had the same honest, earnest and open approach to discussion. In contrast to the Stalinists and the ultra-left sects, all of whom have made an industry out of hiding their previous mistakes and theoretical somersaults, there are none of the writings or speeches of Ted Grant that the author would not now be prepared to re-issue and debate.

That is not to say that there were never any mistakes made, especially in perspectives, in estimating the tempo of events. He who does not make mistakes does not make anything. But the tradition of Marx, Engels, Lenin and Trotsky was always one of openly admitting their errors, explaining them and going forward strengthened, with programme or perspective suitably amended. It is in keeping with this tradition that this selection is offered for those wishing to study the development of Marxism in the post-war world.

★

The selection of material for this single volume has been a very difficult task. There are many, many documents, articles and speeches that have, of necessity, to be left out. In the recent period, there have been major works on Spain and Portugal (mid 1970s), the National Question, the Falklands War, Gorbachev, Iran, the Philippines, Nicaragua, documents on world perspectives, like *The Coming World Revolution* (1984), and many more.

Every one of these works forms part of a consistent whole, linked each to the other, and based on the theoretical roots traced out in this volume. The material on the Falklands War, for example, deals with the fundamental question of war from a Marxist standpoint. It is available in pamphlet form and should be re-read after reading the section in Chapter One on the wartime controversy between the WIL and RSL.

Even in the realm of domestic British politics, there are many issues that are barely dealt with here, if at all. The long-running discussion within the Trotskyist movement about the role of the Labour Party, for example, is hardly done justice here. That may not please some readers, but unfortunately, that would be true whatever the final selection made. A full record of all Ted Grant's political work will have to await a more thorough search and collection than has been possible here. That, in any case, would mean a publication running to many volumes.

In so far as there has been any bias introduced in the selection of documents, it has been towards older material. This is because the earlier articles, many of them not having been reprinted since the original, are less likely to have been seen by the modern reader. But it is also because the theoretical contributions in the immediate post-war decade formed the bedrock upon which an entire tradition was subsequently built.

★

A word or two is necessary in relation to the editing of the material for this volume. The main reason why original articles and documents have been cut has been in an attempt to concentrate as much as possible in a single volume, without vulgarising or simplifying the theoretical constructions. Here and there short points have been taken out where they digress from the main theme, for example in a comment that would have had an immediate relevance at the time of writing, but which has since been lost.

It has been made clear where the material included is incomplete, ie where it is based on extracts from a larger work. But there is no indication in the text (for example,...) where sections, paragraphs, and in some cases even sentences have been left out. There is no ulterior motive for this: the originals are a matter of record and when the collected works are published at some stage in the future the omissions and editing will be made good. The extracts have been closed up, and allowed to run together, simply for the sake of continuity.

The arrangement of the selected material into chapters has been broadly based on the theoretical issues dealt with, apart from the first and final chapters. Although this means inevitably that there are some articles and documents that, strictly speaking, overlap more than one chapter, the editors feel that this arrangement is a better guide to study than one that would have been based, whatever the subject matter, purely on chronological order.

The style of writing has been left as in the original and quotations, for example of Marx, Engels, Lenin and Trotsky, have been checked as far as possible with modern editions. The chapter introductions are intended to provide the reader with some context in which to place the various writings. It would probably be useful to re-read the relevant part of the chapter introduction before beginning to read each new part of a chapter.

It is only to be expected that some of the material included in the book will be difficult to read or understand at the first attempt, especially for readers coming to political theory for the first time. That is unavoidable. Political theory often needs to be thought over, discussed and re-read. It means, in the proper use of the term, having to study, as one would study any other science. As Karl Marx explained:

> There is no royal road to science, and only those who do not dread the fatiguing climb of its steep paths have a chance of gaining its luminous summits.

A careful and diligent study of the material in this volume, combined with discussion and further reading of sources and basic works, will play an indispensible role in the political steeling of future generations of socialists.

For having assisted in the production of this book, sincere thanks are necessary to many comrades. Special mention needs to be made of Anteus graphics for typesetting and lay-out; Helen Watson and John Viner for technical advice on graphics and design; Ginny Armstrong, Soraya Lawrence and Margaret Edwards for proof-reading; Alistair Wilson, Kevin Ramage and Tony Aitman for research, foot-notes and photographs; Alan Hardman for his work on the cover; and Ian Hunter for digging out some of the original works that were so hard to trace.

John Pickard, May 1989.

The War Years

Introduction

BY 1938, while the rest of Europe was hurtling towards another carnage even more bloody than the last, in Spain the civil war was drawing inexorably towards defeat for the Republic.

The Spanish working class had taken the election of the Popular Front government in 1936 as the beginning of the socialist revolution and had moved spontaneously to occupy mines, offices, factories and the land. It was only the movement of the working class, arming itself and mobilising independently of the Popular Front government, that prevented a complete and immediate victory for the rebellion of General Franco in July 1936.

But what began as a civil war between a fascist regime and an incipient socialist revolution was transformed within two years into a conflict between fascism and the capitalist republic. With the enthusiastic backing of the Stalinists the revolutionary movement triggered by the Popular Front was crushed and the capitalist state firmly established. So much so that towards the end of the war there was little to choose between the two governments on either side of the line as far as the workers were concerned.

In Britain, the newly-formed Workers International League (WIL) published a pamphlet by Trotsky, entitled *The Lessons of Spain*. In this 'the Old Man' analysed in particular the failure of the Workers' Party of Marxist Unification (POUM) to play the role of a Spanish Bolshevik Party, providing the clear, decisive and determined leadership that had been available to the Russian workers in 1917.

The intention of the WIL in publishing Trotsky's pamphlet was to draw attention to the need for a Marxist leadership in Britain, in view of the inevitability of a new world war and the revolutionary shocks that would come in its wake. The introduction to the WIL pamphlet, reprinted here, was actually seen and commended by Trotsky himself. Although it was originally signed 'JRS', it was in fact written jointly by Ted Grant and Ralph Lee, both leading WIL members.

When the imperialist war began in Europe, there was at first a period of disorientation in the whole Trotskyist movement. But on the basis of the advice of Trotsky, especially in the most recent writings before his assassination in August 1940, it was possible for the WIL to re-orientate itself to the new situation it faced. Trotsky advocated the adoption of a 'proletarian military policy' based upon the militarisation of everyday life of the working class.

It was not correct, Trotsky argued, to advance the slogan of revolutionary defeatism — of the defeat of 'one's own' imperialism — in a bald and simplistic manner. Lenin, in any case, brought forward the slogan in a different context — where he sought to re-educate the *cadres* of the Marxist movement in the spirit of internationalism, not address the masses directly. It would be wrong, Trotsky insisted, to give the impression to workers that the Marxists favoured support for the 'enemy' imperialism, especially given the loathing that workers in Britain and America felt for the nazi regime which had bloodily crushed the organisations of the German labour movement.

Without, therefore, giving any concession to principles, or giving any support to British capitalism in its alleged war aims, the WIL was able to utilise the genuine fears of the workers of a nazi invasion — especially after the fall of France in 1940 — to raise class demands and to win supporters to the banner of Trotskyism. But in so doing, the WIL drew criticism from the Revolutionary Socialist League (RSL), a largely middle class coalition of Trotskyists without the same decisive working class orientation of the WIL. Both organisations supported the Fourth International, founded by Trotsky in 1938, but the RSL was the official British section, up to 1944.

A whole series of polemical articles and correspondence flowed between the WIL and the RSL over the question of the war: the RSL accusing the WIL of holding a 'defencist' position, the WIL replying by pointing to the petit-bourgeois pacifism of the RSL. When the WIL published their document entitled *Preparing for Power* (see below) the RSL wrote a lengthy criticism of it. The reply of the WIL to this criticism, written by Ted Grant, was a brilliant exposition of the whole question of the military policy, a comprehensive statement that effectively terminated the debate.

Extracts of this WIL document are published here, and although they are dated by the meeting of the Political Bureau of the WIL of June 1943, they are included here as the second item because in a political sense the issues cover the whole period of more than two years up to that point.

The third item in this section is composed of extracts from Preparing for Power written by Ted Grant in June 1942 as the main perspectives document of the WIL, and published in *Workers International News* in September. It especially underlines the historic decline of British capitalism and the inevitability of further decay, even in the event of a victory over nazi Germany: 'Defeat...means the end of British imperialism as a power of the first rank. Victory will mean a less spectacular decline to a second rate position under the patronage of America. This is the best that the British ruling class can hope for.'

Three years before the end of the war, the document anticipates the revolutionary wave that would grip the working class, affecting the shop stewards' committees, the trade union branches and the Labour Party: 'On the basis of the rising wave of discontent with potential revolutionary implications, it is inevitable that the decisive section of the trade union and Labour bureaucrats, including the majority of the parliamentary representatives, will be forced into an open clash with the capitalist class and a breaking of the coalition. In words at least, they will assume an extremely radical attitude.'

It was on the basis of these perspectives that the WIL conducted its war-time work and established a basis in industry far greater than that of other Trotskyist groups, which remained small sects.

For the WIL there was no class 'truce' in the factories and work-places during the war. But after the invasion of the USSR in 1941, the Communist Party of Great Britain did a complete somersault, from being opposed to the war, to being one hundred and twenty per cent in favour. The Party became the most fervent supporter of the Churchill government, vociferously denouncing any strikes or workers' struggles that cut across production.

Unaccustomed to the CP being, in effect, a strike-breaking organisation, many of its best militants left in disgust and quite a few found their way into the ranks of the Workers International League. A considerable part of the political work of the WIL was directed towards winning the best activists of the CP away from the grip of the Stalinist leadership.

When Joseph Stalin dissolved the Communist International in 1943, without any reference to its national sections or the communist rank and file around the world, the WIL immediately rushed out a pamphlet, directed towards Communist Party members, explaining how it could have happened. This document is reprinted in its entirety and forms the fourth part of this chapter on the war years.

In 1944 the WIL formed the Revolutionary Communist Party (RCP), the British section of the Fourth International by, in effect, taking over most of the remnants of the RSL. By this time, when a victory over Hitler seemed certain, the RCP found it necessary to counter the campaign of vicious chauvinism that was being directed against the German nation as a whole, not only by the capitalist press, but even more hysterically, by the 'communist' *Daily Worker*. In fact the nazis had come to power, above all, with the aim of destroying the German labour movement and Hitler's accession to power signalled the wholesale destruction of the flower of the German working class.

In opposing the crude nationalism of the CP, therefore, the RCP repeatedly reminded workers how Hitler had come to power in the first place, and the disgraceful role played by Stalinism. It re-issued a pamphlet written by Trotsky in 1931 entitled *Germany, the Key to the International Situation*.

The introduction to this pamphlet (also printed as an article in the RCP newspaper *Socialist Appeal*), reproduced here, describes the baleful role played by the German Stalinists up to 1933, and the wholehearted support given at the time by the Communist Party of Great Britain. The RCP pamphlet, with much other material published in *Workers International News* and *Socialist Appeal*, educated the best worker-activists about precisely those issues that the CP was trying to cover up —and still tries to cover up to this day.

Lessons of Spain

1938

UNDER THE transparent disguise of the 'Peace Alliance' agitation, the popular front* of Britain now makes its first steps towards entering the political arena. The Liberals cock their ears attentively, the Labour Party heads strenuously oppose the project and the Communist Party, the initiator of the agitation, is utilising every resource it possesses to bring the popular front into being. It now becomes urgently necessary for British workers to draw conclusions from the events in Spain, to examine the experience of popular frontism as it appears in practice in the civil war in order to face up to the problems of tomorrow.

Leon Trotsky, who in a series of articles and pamphlets on the Spanish situation, has consistently pointed the road which the Spanish masses must travel if fascism is to be conquered, has called insistently for the only guide along that road, the revolutionary workers' party, to take up its position at the head of the awakening Spanish masses. Trotsky concludes his pamphlet *The Revolution in Spain*, written in 1931, with these words: 'For a successful solution of all these tasks, three conditions are required: a party; once more a party; again a party.'

The conditions for a workers' victory over reaction, thus epigrammatically summed up, are still unfulfilled: this is the lesson that must be brought to the consciousness of the working class in Britain as in Spain.

While the Spanish fascists openly prepared, with aid from abroad, to strike their blow, the Popular Front government conspicuously failed to make that counter preparation which would have destroyed the enemy swiftly and easily. The army was

*The popular front or people's front was a name given to coalitions between workers' parties and so-called liberal or radical capitalist parties. The Communist International adopted the people's front policy in 1935, after the debacle of Hitler's rise to power.
**The notes briefly explain terms which may be unfamiliar or give background details of parties and individuals. Terms are only notated the first time they occur. Readers may also wish to consult the index at the back of the book. Terms in the index marked by an 'n' are to be found on the page indicated.

left undisturbed in the hands of the reactionaries; under the noses of the Popular Front government they consolidated a powerful basis among the Moors* who, finding the chains of the new government no less galling than those of the monarchy, fell an easy prey to Franco's specious promises. On the other hand, the workers were prevented by their reformist leaders from taking those measures which would have frustrated the fascist plans —the setting up of workers' militia and factory committees. When, in spite of the entreaties of their leaders who begged them not to 'provoke' the reaction, not to 'antagonise' their republican-capitalist partners in the Popular Front, the workers struck and the peasants seized land, the government answered by arresting strikers, breaking up workers' meetings, censoring workers' papers, shooting down peasants. Such is the story related by the press despatches and the official communications in the months of Popular Front power leading up to the civil war. In this way the Popular Front in the months preceding Franco's uprising gagged and tied the masses and drove numbers into the opposite camp to join the Moors in opposing a 'democratic' government that perpetuated their misery and oppression.

Neither the Popular Front nor any other capitalist government could solve the basic problems of modern Spain. Five million peasant families with insufficient land, three million of them with no land at all, were squeezed by taxation and were starving. Only the expropriation of the big landowners and the redivision of the land among the poor peasants could relieve their famine. But this solution was impossible under capitalism, because the whole structure of Spanish banking rests on the land mortgages, so that the ruin of the big landowners would mean the ruin of the capitalists and bankers. Only a Spanish 'October'** could, by dealing a death blow at the capitalist and landowning classes alike, relieve the hunger of the perishing masses of the countryside.

The conditions of the workers in the cities likewise presented a problem insoluble under capitalism. Spanish industry, born too late to compete with the cheap goods which a well-developed foreign industry is able to pour into jealously guarded markets, is unable to find even a home market because of the impoverished peasant population. Marx and Lenin taught that there is no way out for the workers from their prison of meagre wages and growing unemployment except by smashing down the barriers of

---

*The Arab population of NW Africa. They struggled for years in Morocco for autonomy from Spanish rule. Where the Popular Front government did nothing, Franco promised them independence.
**The Russian revolution took place in October 1917 on the old Russian calendar.

capitalism and placing the control of industry into the hands of the working class.

In the first months of the civil war the workers of Spain spontaneously sought this way out as an essential part of their struggle against reaction, for it is not by military method alone that Franco can be defeated. Measures necessary to rouse the masses, by giving them something to fight for, were put into operation: factory, village and shop councils, and workers' tribunals were set up; a workers' police force and militia were initiated. The beginnings of a workers' state thus came into being to conduct a revolutionary war against the fascists, and existed side by side with the Popular Front, challenging its authority and wresting away its functions.

The Communist and Socialist parties came to the rescue of the capitalist government thus threatened with extinction. They entered the Popular Front government and Caballero*, hailed as 'the Spanish Lenin', became the prime minister. Step by step the conquests of the workers were filched back in the name of the 'defence of democracy'. The workers' militia was dissolved into the republican army, workers' courts were eliminated, workers' police corps disbanded.

The same process went on in Catalonia where the POUM entered the coalition government, proclaiming it the workers' government. But the POUM also proclaimed that the civil war was fundamentally a question of socialism versus capitalism, a truth which undermines the very foundations of the Popular Front. Republicans and Stalinists united in a vile campaign of calumny against the POUM accusing it of being in the pay of Franco, driving it from government, suppressing its propaganda and journals, arresting and imprisoning its leaders.

At the begining of May 1937, the government launched its provocative attack on the workers to regain possession of the factories and buildings which were under workers' control. The resistance of the workers was overcome and full control was regained by the bourgeoisie in the economic as in the political and military fields.

The alternatives that confront the Spanish masses today are on the one hand the victory of Franco initiating a totalitarian regime or on the other hand the now problematic victory of a 'democratic' capitalist regime which in a spent and devastated Spain can only rule by a scarcely veiled dictatorship. In either case the chains will

---

*Largo Caballero, leader of a left tendency in the Spanish Socialist Party in the 1930s. Prime Minister from September 1936 – May 1937.

be more securely rivetted on the limbs of the workers, peasants and the colonial people, exhausted and cheated.

From its very inception, the Popular Front disavowed in its programme not only socialist but even semi-socialist measures. It was openly and admittedly the guardian of capitalist property, dangling grandiose plans for future reforms before the eyes of the people to distract their attention from present miseries. The projected popular front in Britain is cut on the same pattern. 'Any idea of real socialism would have to be put aside for the present,' declares Sir Stafford Cripps* in the *Tribune* (14 April, 1938) in pleading for a 'democratic front' government. The *Daily Worker* supports the Liberal candidate in a by-election as against the Labour candidate, and sneered at Labour's 'astonishing "discovery" that Liberals are not socialist, as if Liberals ever made this claim.' (11 May, 1938).

For Britain as for Spain, the struggle against fascism is the struggle for socialism. The arms plans and the food plans, the spy scares and the air raid precautions serve to warn the workers that the 'peace' period draws rapidly to a close. The American recession in industry spreads to Britain; in the first three months of 1938 the decline of new capital issues, £33,000,000 as against £49,505,000 for the corresponding period last year, indicates the dimensions of the coming industrial slump. The increased employment in the armaments industry and the increased recruiting for the army serve for the time being to mask the growth of industrial unemployment, and the shifting centre of gravity in national economy is not visible in the general statistics of trade and industry because the artificial stimulus of war preparations helps to conceal the real process of economic breakdown. The disease that grips the vitals of capitalism in decay produces as its symptom a feverish activity in certain branches of industrial activity, accompanied by that false sense of well-being which must be recognised as pre-war 'prosperity', the delirium before the crisis.

As long as the pre-war boom continues and the British masses continue in a comparatively passive state, the right wing bureaucrats of the trade unions and the Labour Party oppose the popular front. When the masses start to move, as they did in Spain and France, towards a militant socialist solution of their difficulties, the Labour bureaucracy will not scruple to follow the example of its counterparts in Spain and France, to put a bridle on the mass

---

*Stafford Cripps, Labour MP from 1931, expelled from the party for a period in 1939 for campaigning for a popular front. As Chancellor of the Exchequer 1947-50, he introduced an austere economic programme. *Tribune* was the paper of the reformist left in the party which Cripps helped to found in 1937.

movement and lead it into the safe bye-paths of popular frontism. If today they resist the popular front, it is not because it is the open, treacherous abandonment of even the pretence of socialism, but because they are quite satisfied with their own status in capitalist society, because they fear the inevitable exposure to which the taking of political power will subject them. Today they attack the Liberals as non-socialists, tomorrow they will justify and defend them, and work hand in hand with them in the 'strike-breaking conspiracy' of the popular front, as their brother reformists of the Communist Party are already doing.

The Communist Party of Great Britain pleads for the popular front and supports the Liberals on a programme of 'arms for Spain', 'defence of democratic liberties,' 'economic and social advancement of the people.' The French Popular Front in power supplied no arms for Spain; the French colonial slaves of North Africa and Indo-China received as their share of 'democratic liberties' —bullets and prison sentences; the French Popular Front government nibbled at the concessions wrested from the ruling class by the direct strike action of the French workers and frustrated their wage gains by currency manipulation. The Liberals and 'progressive' capitalists offer, in place of reforms, grandiloquent 'plans' for reforms:

The past writings of the Communist Party leaders prove that they are well aware of the treacherous role of the Liberals. Today they are able to exploit the reputation for militancy which has been won by the work of party members in the trade union struggle, in order to lead militant workers along the political path mapped out by their paymasters in the Kremlin. Stalin and company are prepared to sacrifice the socialist aspirations of the British working class for the sake of a war alliance with the British bourgeoisie and to this end they have ordered a popular front in Britain . The Communist Party heads leap to obey; they flatly and brazenly contradict their arguments of a few months back, they consciously and deliberately manoeuvre the workers into supporting a coalition government with the class enemy, they blindfold the worker while the Liberals prepare the dagger which will be plunged into his back.

The Communist Party carries out its traitorous work with loud cries of 'Unity! Unity!' But the British working class constitutes in itself two-thirds of the population, and would draw behind itself the majority of the lower middle class if it pressed forward with a bold programme of socialist demands. The workers have no need for an alliance with any section of the class foe, least of all with the decayed, long ago bankrupt Liberals. They instinctively know that unity is an all-powerful weapon in their struggle —unity of the 'working class'. The popular front is a caricature of unity. The genuine united front on a class basis, binding together the workers, their organisations, their parties on a programme of common struggle is the crying need of today, the only means of defending those rights and privileges which the workers have won in generations of struggle and sacrifice. The successful defence of concessions already gained must lead inevitably to the campaign for full workers' rights, to the struggle for workers' power.

The experience of Spain is a warning and a lesson to the workers of the world, above all to the British workers. Yesterday's drama in Spain is being rehearsed today in Britain. Tomorrow it will be enacted if the British workers have failed to realise the nature of the tasks which history has placed before them. And in preparing to tackle those tasks, the working class has need above all, of 'a party, once more a party; again a party'.

A POUM brigade during the Spanish Civil War. The tall figure at the left is George Orwell.

From: A reply to the RSL. Chauvinism and Revolutionary Defeatism

June 1943

THE BASIC reason for the mistakes of the RSL lies in the fact that the leadership does not understand the revolutionary attitude towards the war. It is this which leads them to the sins against Marxism which they commit. Their position is summed up towards the end of their statement:

> In conclusion, we must state that the basis for all the main political mistakes of WIL is to be found in the defencist position it has adopted with regard to the imperialist war since the fall of France first made the defeat of British imperialism a real possibility. Defencism rarely shows itself in its open form especially in a left-centrist organisation. Concealment is especially necessary in an organisation still professing to stand upon the principles of revolutionary defeatism...

An understanding of this confusion can be obtained by restating the fundamental position of Marxism on the question of war. If we take any of the writings of Lenin during the period of 1914-17, the issue can be clarified. In the little pamphlet *Socialism and War,* for example, we read the following:

> Social chauvinism is adherence to the idea of 'defending the fatherland in the present war'. From this idea follows repudiation of the class struggle in war time, voting for military appropriations, etc. In practice the social chauvinists conduct an anti-proletarian bourgeois policy, because in practice they insist not on the 'defence of the fatherland' in the sense of fighting against the oppression of a foreign nation, but upon the 'right' of one or other of the 'great' nations to rob the colonies and oppress other peoples. The social-chauvinists repeat the bourgeois deception of the people, saying that the war is conducted for the defence of freedom and the existence of nations; thus they put themselves on the side of the bourgeois against the proletariat. To the social chauvinists belong those who justify and idealise the governments and the bourgeois of one of the belligerent group of nations, as well as those who, like Kautsky, recognise the equal rights of the socialists of all

belligerent nations to 'defend the Fatherland'. Social chauvinism, being in practice a defence of the privileges, prerogatives, robberies and violence of 'one's own' imperialist bourgeoisie, is a total betrayal of all socialist convictions and a violation of the decisions of the International Socialist Congress in Basle.

It is clear from this single quotation that the RSL have failed to understand the essence of the meaning of chauvinism. How can any serious party or individual honestly claim that the above quotation characterises the policies and activities of WIL? Our fundamental international thesis *War and the Fourth International* explains:

> In those cases where it is a question of conflict between capitalist countries, the proletariat of any one of them refuses categorically to sacrifice its historic interests, which in the final analysis coincide with the interests of the nation and humanity, for the sake of the military victory of the bourgeoisie. Lenin's formula: 'defeat is the lesser evil' means not that defeat of one's own country is the lesser evil as compared with the defeat of the enemy country; but that a military defeat resulting from the growth of the revolutionary movement is infinitely more beneficial to the proletariat and to the whole people than military victory assured by 'civil peace'. Karl Liebknecht gave an unsurpassed formula of proletarian policy in time of war: 'The chief enemy of the people is in its own country.'

And indeed to pose the problem in any other way would be to become inverted chauvinists: that is, while not supporting the bourgeoisie of one's own country, to fall into the objective position of supporting the bourgeoisie of the enemy country. In his last writings, which are undoubtedly among the finest he ever wrote, the Old Man gave the finest theoretical exposition of the Marxist-Internationalist attitude to imperialist war in general, and the present imperialist war in particular. These fragments will remain for all time the classical exposition of the Marxist approach to the problem and of the dialectical method as a means for determining the policy of the revolutionary party. The readers will forgive us if we quote extensively both from Lenin and Trotsky to establish the position of Marxism on an unassailable basis. Trotsky presents the theoretical basis of our attitude towards the war thus:

> The present war, as we have stated on more than one occasion, is a continuation of the last war. But a continuation does not signify a repetition. As a general rule, a continuation signifies a development, a deepening, a sharpening. Our policy, the policy of the revolutionary proletariat towards the second imperialist war is a continuation of the

policy elaborated during the last imperialist war, primarily under Lenin's leadership. But a continuation does not signify a repetition. In this case too, continuation signifies a development, a deepening and a sharpening. *We were caught unawares in 1914.*

During the last war not only the proletariat as a whole but also its vanguard, and, in a certain sense, the vanguard of this vanguard was caught unawares. The elaboration of the principles of revolutionary policy toward the war began at a time when the war was already in full blaze and the military machine exercised unlimited rule. One year after the outbreak of the war the small revolutionary minority was still compelled to accommodate itself to a centrist majority at the Zimmerwald Conference*. Prior to the February Revolution and even afterwards, the revolutionary elements felt themselves to be not contenders for power but the extreme left opposition. Even Lenin relegated the socialist revolution to a more or less distant future...

In 1915 Lenin referred in his writings to revolutionary wars which the victorious proletariat would have to wage. But it was a question of an indefinite historical perspective and not of tomorrow's task. The attention of the revolutionary wing was centred on the question of the defence of the capitalist fatherland. The revolutionists naturally replied to this question in the negative. This was entirely correct. But this purely negative answer served as the basis for propaganda and for training cadres but it could not win the masses who did not want a foreign conqueror.

In Russia prior to the war the Bolsheviks** constituted four fifths of the proletarian vanguard, that is, of the workers participating in political life (newspapers, elections, etc.). Following the February revolution the unlimited rule passed into the hands of the defencists, the Mensheviks and the SRs. True enough, the Bolsheviks in the space of eight months conquered the overwhelming majority of the workers. But the decisive role in this conquest was played not by the refusal to defend the bourgeois fatherland but the slogan: 'All power to the Soviets!' And only by this revolutionary slogan! The criticism of imperialism, its militarism, the renunciation of the defence of bourgeois democracy and so on could never have conquered the overwhelming majority of the people to the side of the Bolsheviks... (*Bonapartism, Fascism and War*, an unfinished article by Trotsky, dictated just prior to his assassination.)

And following on this analysis, the basis is laid for the Marxist approach to the problems of the war today. The collapse and

---

*Internationalist opponents of the First World War met in 1916 in the Swiss village of Zimmerwald. The February revolution in Russia 1917 saw the fall of the Czar and brought to power a provisional government of reformist and capitalist parties.

**The Bolsheviks and Mensheviks were, respectively, the revolutionary and reformist wings of the Russian Social Democratic and Labour Party, at first as factions and, later, as separate parties. The SRs (Social Revolutionaries) were a reformist party with a large influence among the peasantry.

betrayal of the great parties of the Second International*, by their support of the capitalist fatherland, came as a terrible shock and a great blow to the whole socialist movement. It was no accident, for example, that when Lenin in Switzerland received the issue of *Vorwaerts*, organ of the German Social Democracy, voting war credits to the Kaiser's government, he believed at first that it must have been a forgery of the German general staff. In this little episode is mirrored the confusion and disorientation of the revolutionary vanguard.

The internationalists of all countries remained as isolated individuals and groups, most of whom merely opposed the war in a confused pacifist and semi-pacifist way. As late as the middle of 1915, at the Zimmerwald Conference, only a handful of delegates assembled. Yet even among this vanguard of the masses, confusion and lack of theoretical understanding of the war and of revolutionary policy were clearly displayed. The main task of Lenin during this period was not at all to win the masses to his banner, but to educate the vanguard, and even the vanguard of the vanguard. As Trotsky expresses it, Lenin had to concentrate his attention exclusively at this period on the question of 'defence of the capitalist fatherland'.

If we would examine all the extensive writings of Lenin from the beginning of the war to the outbreak of the February Revolution, we would find that they concentrate on theoretical questions as to the nature of the war and the betrayal by the Second International of the international proletariat. Lenin's basic task was the struggle against what he characterised as social chauvinism and social opportunism. Lenin's role then was to demonstrate that the class struggle remains the basic law of class society in peace time as in war time. Luxemburg and Liebknecht in Germany, and in a confused way the ILP** pacifists and opposition groups in other countries all groped in the same direction. All at that time conducted their work around the theoretical struggle on the question of the 'defence of the fatherland'. So it was that even after the February Revolution, this question occupied a predominant place. It is here that the confusion of the RSL on the question of 'revolutionary defencism' arises.

---

*Established in 1889 bringing together social democratic (socialist) and Labour parties. It effectively collapsed in 1914 when virtually all its sections voted to support their own capitalist governments in the war. It was revived in 1923 as a completely reformist organisation becoming known as the Socialist International.
**Independent Labour Party. Usually on the left, it split from the Labour Party in 1932. Most of its leaders returned to the Labour Party after the war, leaving it to a prolonged period of sectarian isolation until it was wound up in the late 1970's.

Lenin would not tolerate the slightest concession to social patriotism and support of the bourgeoisie. After the overthrow of the Czar, the Mensheviks and SRs became social patriots and supported the Russian bourgeoisie. Lenin condemned the position of Kamenev and Stalin who, in *Pravda,* came out in support of the Provisional government, and in an unclear fashion even supported the war by saying that they would defend the bourgeois revolution against the attacks of the armies of the Kaiser. The revolutionary defencism which Lenin condemned was that of the Mensheviks and SRs who supported the war, who supported the capitalist state, and who supported the ruling class, as the method of defending the gains of the February Revolution. By revolutionary defencism is meant no more, no less, than social chauvinism. Lenin's speech to the delegates of the Bolshevik faction of the soviets clearly put the position:

> The masses approach this question not from the theoretical but from a practical viewpoint. Our mistake lies in our theoretical approach. The class conscious proletarian may consent to a revolutionary war that actually overthrows revolutionary defencism. Before the representatives of the soldiers the matter must be put in a practical way, otherwise nothing will come of it. We are not at all pacifists. The fundamental question is: Which class is waging the war? The capitalist class, tied to the banks cannot wage any but an imperialist war. The working class can... (*Collected Works,* Vol. 20, page 96. International Publishers, New York, 1929).

Let us take an example from another sphere in which the Marxian attitude has been worked out theoretically and demonstrated practically. Marxism has demonstrated the superiority of the Soviet system to parliamentarism. But the position of the anti-parliamentarians, basing themselves on this correct idea, is hopelessly sectarian. It is necessary to lay this down theoretically, but in our day-to-day agitation we still conduct our work through parliamentary elections and convince the masses by their own experience of our point of view; not by the mere repetition, parrot-fashion, that soviets are the sole means of salvation for the working class. The mistakes of the RSL are of the same character.

Trotsky throws a penetrating light on one of the most important reasons for the impotence of the revolutionary left during the last war. Trotsky has emphasised better than anyone else the outlived character of the national state and its reactionary role in our epoch. Our attitude is based on that criterion. Our opposition towards war waged by imperialist states lies precisely on their outmoded character and the fact that support for any imperialism cannot assist the development of the productive forces −on which all human progress depends. From this stems the profoundly dialectical approach of Trotsky to the problems of the revolutionary movement in the last war. Russia was the country where the proletariat was freshest and most revolutionary. Bolshevism had conquered the overwhelming majority of the organised and politically awakened workers before the commencement of the last war.

On the eve of the war, barricades were already appearing on the streets of St Petersburg. Yet in the first period of the war the Bolsheviks were smashed by police repression without protest on the part of the masses, and even sections of the workers participated in patriotic demonstrations in favour of the Czar. The war weariness and disillusionment of the masses led to the February Revolution. Yet despite the traditions of Bolshevism within Russia, the Mensheviks and SRs gained overwhelming preponderance among the masses, including the workers. The war weary masses placed in power, not those who consistently opposed the war, but social chauvinists!

In Germany, where Liebknecht and Luxemburg conducted an internationalist opposition to the war, the German revolution placed the rotten social democracy and not at all the Spartacists* in power. Yet the socialist traitors had supported the Kaiser and the imperialist war to the limit and even figured in the cabinet of his government. The social democrats fought and opposed the revolution with all their strength and even attempted to save the monarchy. Yet by the irony of history they usurped the power in the revolution.

In Britain where the Labour leaders were supporting the war as members of His Majesty's government, the radicalisation and revolutionary upsurge of the British workers saw a tremendous increase in the support and influence of the Labour Party. The revolutionary international remained isolated from the working class −this despite the disillusionment of the masses of the people in the war and its results.

In all other countries the same phenomenon can be observed. One of the reasons for this (of course there are other fundamental reasons into which we cannot enter here) was precisely the issue which Trotsky raises. The correct criticism by the internationalists (by itself), 'of imperialism, its militarism, the renunciation of the defence of bourgeois democracy, and so on, could never have

---

*Grew from the revolutionary wing first in the German SPD, then the Independent Social Democratic Party (USPD). Formed the basis of the Communist Party (KPD) in 1918. Its leaders included Rosa Luxemburg and Karl Liebknecht.

conquered the overwhelming majority of the people to...their side'.

It has been shown that the attention of the revolutionary vanguard was concentrated on the renunciation of the defence of the capitalist fatherland. This could not be a basis to win the masses who do not want a foreign conqueror. 'True enough,' Trotsky wrote, 'the Bolsheviks in the space of eight months conquered the overwhelming majority of the workers. But the decisive role in this conquest was played not by the refusal to defend the bourgeois fatherland but by the slogan "All power to the Soviets!"And only by this revolutionary slogan!'

An examination of the Bolshevik agitation in the period between February and October demonstrates this irrefutably. Not only this. If we examine Lenin's approach to the masses on the question of the war *before* February 1917, and *after*, there is a striking difference. In the first period as we have shown, it is purely of an oppositional character; in the second, the period of revolution, all agitation and for that matter, propaganda and theory, is directed towards the goal of the seizure of power. With the imminence of the goal before him, Lenin links up the question of the war with the problem of which class possesses power. In this he is not at all contradicting his stand during the early period of the war, and in fact remains watchful that the leadership of the Bolsheviks does not stray from the internationalist position. But now, from theoretical clarification, he is carrying the policy into action. From training the cadres, he is advancing towards the solution of the problem of winning the broad masses. In both positions he remains true to the stand of Marxism. There is no need to quote extensively for this.

The RSL has stated (quite incorrectly) that the WIL bases its agitation on the war on Lenin's *Threatening Catastrophe*. However, this pamphlet itself is an annihilating reply to the sectarian criticism of Trotskyism and its attitude towards the war. In attempting to dodge the issue the RSL states: 'In practice the WIL claim that, for instance, Lenin's remarks on the *Threatening Catastrophe* [written on the eve of the seizure of power!] apply today, and such is the basis of their propaganda.' We might draw the attention of the leadership of the RSL to the fact that even if we did base ourselves on the perspective of the immediate seizure of power, it solves nothing of the question of whether or not we are chauvinist. It would indicate only, in the worst event, *an error of perspective*.

The fact that Lenin wrote on the eve of the seizure of power could not excuse him *if he were guilty of chauvinism*. Nor would it excuse the WIL today. Twenty-five years after they are willing to

forgive Lenin his 'chauvinism' because it led to the successful
revolution, but without having learned that had Lenin adopted
their method, there would have been no revolution. In our view,
chauvinism 'on the eve of the seizure of power' would be a hundred
times more unpardonable than at any other time. However, let us
examine what Lenin really did say. In *Threatening Catastrophe*,
under the section, *The war and the fight against economic ruin:*

> All the above measures of fighting the catastrophe would, as we have
> already pointed out, immeasurably strengthen the defensive power or,
> in other words, the military strength of the country. This on the one
> hand. On the other hand these measures cannot be introduced without
> transforming the predatory war into a just war, without transforming
> the war waged by the proletariat in the interests of all the toilers and
> exploited.

And again:

> It is impossible to lead the masses into a robbers' war in accordance with
> secret treaties and still expect them to show enthusiasm. The foremost
> class of revolutionary Russia, the proletariat, realises ever more clearly
> the criminal character of the war, while the bourgeoisie not only has
> failed to shatter this conviction of the masses, but on the contrary, the
> consciousness of the criminal character of the war is growing. The
> proletariat of both capitals of Russia has become definitely
> internationalist. How can anyone talk about mass enthusiasm here in
> favour of the war? One thing is inseparably bound up with the other;
> internal politics with foreign politics. It is impossible to render the
> country capable of defending itself without the greatest of heroism on
> the part of the people in courageously and decisively carrying out great
> economic transformations. And it is impossible to appeal to the heroism
> of the masses without breaking with imperialism, without offering to all
> the peoples a democratic peace, without thus transforming the war
> from a war of conquest, a predatory criminal war, into a just, defensive,
> revolutionary war.

The RSL triumphantly exclaims, as if it had discovered a
crime:-

> ...their [the WIL] slogan, nowhere explicitly stated in the document it is
> true, but implicit in it and in their other propaganda is 'turn the
> imperialist war into a workers' anti-fascist war'. In other words their
> main attack is directed not against the British bourgeoisie, but its rivals,
> the fascist regimes.

If the argument contained in the first part of this 'charge' can be
levelled against us, then it applies a hundred times more to
Lenin...because Lenin's propaganda for changing the imperialist

war into a workers' war is not implicit, but explicitly stated. In any event, how can the war be changed into an anti-fascist war without the workers having conquered power? So far as we are concerned, we prefer to remain in the 'chauvinist' company of Lenin. The latter part of this criticism, that our 'main attack is directed against the fascist regimes' is absolutely false and cannot honestly be held by anyone who reads our press and documents.

On the question of slogans too, Lenin answered the RSL long in advance. They complain that WIL does not raise the slogan of turning the imperialist war into a civil war, though the WIL has proclaimed often enough that it stands on the principles and methods of the Fourth International. It would be nothing short of lunacy to raise this as an agitational slogan in the period ahead. As senseless as raising the slogan of the insurrection for the week after next.

There is a time and a place for every slogan. Just think, in the middle of the revolution, Lenin proclaims: 'To speak of civil war before people have come to realise the need of it, is undoubtedly to fall into Blanquism*.' (*CW*, Vol. 24, page 236). And to give some advice that ultra-lefts would be wise to pay some attention too: 'It happens only too often that, when history makes a sharp turn, even the most advanced parties cannot get used to the revolutionary situation for some time, and repeat slogans that were correct yesterday, but have no more meaning today, having lost it as suddenly as the sharp turn in history "suddenly" occurred.'(*CW*, Vol. 21, page 43. International Publishers, New York, 1929). At a certain stage in the revolution, Lenin even denounced those who claimed that he stood for civil war, quite correctly laying the responsibility on the shoulders of the bourgeoisie for anything of the sort.

The Conquest of Power is the Axis of our Propaganda.

Our policy in relation to the problems of the epoch remains on the granite foundation laid down by Lenin. Our attitude towards imperialist war remains that of irreconcilable opposition. We continue the traditions of Bolshevism. But in the epoch of the decline and disintegration of capitalism a continuation, as Trotsky points out, does not mean a mere repetition. In the quarter century that has passed, the objective conditions for the socialist revolution have reached maturity and the decay and disintegration of

---

*After Louis Blanqui (1805-81). French revolutionary socialist whose name became linked with the theory of armed insurrection by small conspiratorial groups, as opposed to the Marxist concept of mass struggle.

capitalism have revealed themselves in the abortive attempts at revolution on the part of the masses, in fascism, and now in the new imperialist war. All the objective conditions of the past epoch render the proletariat responsive to the posing of the problem of the conquest of power by the working class.

As distinct from 1914-18, the cadres of Bolshevism have been trained and educated in the Leninist approach towards imperialist war. The social-chauvinism on the part of the Social Democrats and the Stalinists was anticipated and predicted by the Trotskyists long in advance. The theoretical exposure of social chauvinism is not a live issue for Bolshevism today. We build and construct our party on the Leninist internationalist basis, not least on the fundamental question of war.

As Trotsky once pointed out, war and revolution are the fundamental test for the policy of all organisations. On both these questions we continue the Leninist tradition. But Marxism does not consist in the repetition of phrases and ideas, however correct these may be. Otherwise Lenin could not have developed and deepened the conceptions first formulated by Marx. And Trotsky could not have propounded the theory of the Permanent Revolution. If all that was required of revolutionaries was to repeat *ad nauseam* a few phrases and slogans taken from the great teachers of Marxism, the problem of the revolution would be simple indeed. The SPGB* would be super-Marxists instead of incurable sectarians. As Trotsky remarked of the ultra-lefts, every sectarian would be a master strategist.

In the last analysis, the basic principles of Marxism, as developed theoretically by Marx himself, have remained the same for nearly a century. The task of his successors consists, not at all in repeating a few half-digested ideas, parrot fashion, but of using the *method of Marxism* and applying it correctly to the problems and tasks posed at a particular period. It is now necessary to approach the problem of war, not only from its theoretical characterisation by Lenin, but in the task of winning the masses to the Leninist banner. For the past epoch the cadres of the Fourth International have been educated in the spirit of internationalism. We look at the war from the principled basis established by Lenin, but now from a more developed angle. We do not conduct our propaganda from the standpoint of analysing the nature of the defence of the capitalist fatherland *alone* but from the standpoint of the conquest of power by the working class and the defence of the proletarian fatherland.

*The Socialist Party of Great Britain (SPGB), established in 1905, was, and remains, a small sect with its own peculiar 'interpretation' of Marxism.

As Trotsky posed the problem:

> That is why it would be doubly stupid to present a purely abstract pacifist position today; the feeling the masses have is that it is necessary to defend themselves. We must say 'Roosevelt says it is necessary to defend the country: good, only it must be our country, not that of the 60 families and their Wall Street.' (*American Problems.* August 7, 1940.)

Only hopeless formalists and sectarians, incapable of appreciating the revolutionary dynamic of Marxism, could see in this a chauvinist deviation or an abandonment of Leninism. Our epoch is the epoch of wars and revolutions, militarism and super-militarism. To this epoch must correspond the policy and approach of the revolutionary party. War has come as a horrible retribution for the crimes of Stalinism and reformism. It came through the fact that the traitors in the workers' leadership frustrated the striving of the masses in the direction of the socialist revolution. It is a reflection of the blind alley in which imperialism finds itself, and of the historical ripeness and over-ripeness for the socialist revolution.

The last world war was already an expression of that fact that on a world scale capitalism had fulfilled its historical mission. This objective fact leads rapidly to the subjective position where the masses of the workers are ripe for the posing of the problem of the socialist revolution, that is the problem of power. The events of the past epoch have left the working class with a psychology of frustration and bewilderment. They regarded with apprehension and horror the coming of the second blood-bath in which they would expect nothing but suffering and misery. In this war, right from its inception, among the British workers, especially among the Labour workers, there has been an absence of hatred towards the German people. Even in America, where the masses are far less politically conscious than in Britain, in a recent Gallup Poll, two thirds of the people interviewed differentiated between the German people and the nazis on the question of responsibility and punishment after the war. This, despite all the propaganda of the bourgeoisie. If this is the case in America, it is a hundred times more true of Britain.

It is perfectly true, however, that especially among the working class there is an unclear, but deep-seated hatred of Hitlerism and fascism. But with all due respect to the leadership of the RSL, this hatred is not reactionary and chauvinist but arises from a sound class instinct. True, it is being misused and distorted for reactionary imperialist ends by the bourgeoisie and labour lackeys. But the task of revolutionaries consists in separating what is progressive and what is reactionary in their attitude; in winning away the workers from their Stalinist and Labour leaderships who misuse these progressive sentiments. And there is no other way than that mapped out by Trotsky in his last articles, of separating the workers from the exploiters on the question of war.

The decay and degeneration of British imperialism render the masses responsive to the posing by the revolutionaries of the problem of power; to the problem of which class holds the power. Every issue which arises must be posed from this angle. Our position towards war is no longer merely a policy of opposition, but is determined by the epoch in which we live, the epoch of socialist revolution. That is, as contenders for power. Only thus can we find an approach to the working class. On paper, and in the abstract, the RSL accepts the Transitional Programme as the basis for our work in the present period. Trotsky points out that the objective situation demands that our day to day work is linked through our transitional demands with the social revolution. This applies to all aspects of our work. The plunging of the world into war does not in the least demand a retreat from this position, but on the contrary gives it an even greater urgency. But the same theoretical conception which forms the basis of the Transitional Programme* and dictates the strategical orientation of all our activists forms the basis of the strategical attitude towards war in the modern epoch.

War is part of the life of society at the present time and our programme of the conquest of power has to be based, not on peace, but on the conditions of universal militarism and war. We may commiserate with the comrades of the RSL on this unfortunate deviation of history. But alas we were too weak to overthrow imperialism and must now pay the price. It was necessary (and, of course, it is still necessary) to educate the cadres of the Fourth International of the nature and meaning of social patriotism and Stalino-chauvinism and its relation towards the war. Who in Britain in the left wing has done this as vigorously as WIL? But we must go further. The Transitional Programme, if it has any meaning at all, is a bridge not only from the consciousness of the masses today to the road of the socialist revolution, but also for the isolated revolutionaries to the masses.

The RSL convinces itself of the superiority of its position over that of Stalinism and reformism. It comforts itself that it maintains the position of Lenin in the last war. This would be very good...if the RSL had understood the position of Lenin. However, for Trotsky and the inheritors of Bolshevism, *we start* (even if the RSL

---

*Adopted by the Fourth International at its founding in 1938. Transitional demands are intended to bridge the gap between the existing level of conciousness of the working class and the need for socialist revolution.

correctly interpreted Lenin, which it does not) where the RSL leadership finishes! We approach the problem of war from the angle of the imminence of the next period of the social revolution in Britain as well as other countries. The workers in Britain, as in America 'do not want to be conquered by Hitler, and to those who say, "let us have a peace programme" the workers will reply: "but Hitler does not want a peace programme." Therefore we say, we will defend the United States with a workers' army with workers' officers, and with a workers' government, etc.' (Trotsky, *American Problems*).

Those words of the Old Man are saturated through and through with the spirit of revolutionary Marxism, which, while uncompromisingly preserving its opposition towards the bourgeoisie, shows sympathy and understanding for the attitude of the rank and file worker and the problems which are running through his mind. No longer do we stop at the necessity to educate the vanguard as to the nature of the war and the refusal to defend the capitalist fatherland, but we go forward to win the working class for the conquest of power and the defence of the proletarian fatherland.

A Petty-Bourgeoise Pacifist Tendency

The harping on the theme of 'peace' runs like an ever recurring thread through the RSL document, and indeed, provides the key to the development of the RSL and their present position. Commenting on a sentence in *Preparing for Power*, 'The corruption and incompetence, industrially and militarily, raises sharply in the minds of the workers the question of the regime,' the RSL writes:

> There is no question of misunderstanding this sentence. It means that the workers are questioning the right of capitalism to continue as the system of this country. This before the workers have even begun to display a mass sentiment for peace, while they still support the imperialist war and are, in fact, anxious to see it more efficiently and offensively conducted.

This recurring theme of 'peace' indicates the hopelessly petit bourgeois position of the leadership of the RSL. And it does not rise accidentally either. It is the continuation and culmination of a whole series of mistakes on the question of the revolutionary attitude towards militarism and war. At the time when conscription was imposed in Britain a few months before the outbreak of the war, the RSL in the *Militant** correctly condemned conscription for

*Journal of the RSL. Not linked to the paper *Militant* established in 1964.

imperialist ends. But as a means of fighting against this they found themselves in the company of the Peace Pledge Union, the ILP and other pacifist and semi-pacifist bodies in advocating the futile, and from a revolutionary point of view, the dangerous policy of refusal to accept conscription into the militia. This at a time when it was obvious that the overwhelming majority of the workers would enter into the militia. In the *Militant* of June 1939, the RSL wrote, under the heading 'What to do':

> Conscription must be smashed! Demand that the TUC prepare a General Strike. Demand that the Labour Party force a General Election. Demand that the Executive Committee of your Trade Union instructs all its members of conscription age to refuse to register, and defend them if they are prosecuted for refusing. Only by mass action can conscription be smashed!

This revolutionary-sounding alternative had an entirely social pacifist orientation, characteristic of centrism and petty bourgeois socialism. From the standpoint of the traditional Leninist position it was a false general directive: and as the attitude towards conscription adopted by comrade Trotsky demonstrates, it was also false from the standpoint of modern Leninism-Trotskyism. It left the members and sympathisers of the RSL without the slightest directive on what to do when faced with the concrete position: Register.

Indeed, so utopian was this that the directive to refuse to register was given, yet the members of the RSL registered. It is indeed somewhat embarrassing to even have to argue over such questions among people who claim to be supporters of Lenin. But as the RSL leaders seem to have a hankering for posing as defenders of 'old fashioned' ideas, perhaps it will settle the matter if we give a good quotation from Lenin on this question. Incidentally, the revolutionary attitude on this issue goes way back to Marx, and even the old social democracy on the continent had a correct and revolutionary attitude when compared with that of the RSL:

> At the present time the whole of social life is being militarised. Imperialism is a fierce struggle of the great powers for the division and re-division of the world, therefore it must inevitably lead to further militarisation in all countries, even in the neutral and small countries. What will the proletarian women do against it? Only curse all war and everything military, only demand disarmament? The women of an oppressed class that is really revolutionary will never agree to play such a shameful role. They will say to their sons: 'You will soon be big. You will be given a gun. Take it and learn to use it. The proletarians need this knowledge not to shoot your brothers, the workers of other

countries, as they are doing in the present war, and as you are being advised to do by the traitors to socialism, but to fight the bourgeoisie of your own country, to put an end to exploitation, poverty and war, not by means of good intentions, but by a victory over the bourgeoisie and by disarming them.' (Lenin, *CW*, Vol. 23, page 82.)

Immediately the war began, the RSL joined up in an unprincipled alliance with the pacifists in the 'Socialist Anti-War Front'. Hardly had they recovered breath from the exertions in this direction than they immediately fell into an even worse petit-bourgeois pacifist position. At a time when both the Stalinists and the ILP came out with the slogan 'Stop The War', the RSL made haste to follow in the same pacifist strain. In one of the issues of the *Militant* this was blazoned as the main headline! There is no need to polemicise against this position today, as events drove it into oblivion.

Not even the RSL, which dropped this slogan without explanation, would argue in its favour now. In fact even the centrists of the ILP would not do so. From this error, the RSL leadership naturally and automatically slid into the next. The Executive Committee of the RSL issued a special statement repudiating the section of the *Manifesto of the Fourth International —Imperialist War and the World Revolution, 1940,* under the heading: 'Workers must learn the Military Arts' as being inapplicable to Britain. In private the leaders of the RSL pooh-poohed the idea that comrade Trotsky could have been the author of such 'chauvinist' statements, which corresponded to the WIL's position. This is what they said:

> Under the heading 'Workers must learn the Military Arts', the Manifesto demands that the state immediately provide the workers and the unemployed with the possibility of learning how to use arms. This might be construed by some as support for the opportunist demand put forward by certain organisations in this country for the arming of the workers. The slogan 'arm the workers' put forward in a belligerent country at a time when the masses are at a white heat of patriotism and in immediate fear of invasion is purely defencist and patriotic in character. The masses at such a time desire arms in order to repel the invader, ie in order to defend their 'own' capitalist state. Such a slogan is used by the imperialists for recruiting purposes....The British Section therefore states that the demand in the international manifesto has no validity in the existing conditions in this country...

Their position on this question flowed from the incorrect policy they held previously on the question of conscription. And finally, as the culminating point of this whole process, they finish up with the position of...peace in the present period! Well might an ordinary worker retort to such a position: 'They say "Peace, Peace", and there is no peace!' Lenin undoubtedly pointed out the necessity to utilise at a certain stage the desire of the masses for peace. But he pointed out that such a position had nothing in common with pacifism. The RSL's position, on the contrary, is pacifist and has nothing in common with Leninism. All Lenin's writings on this question were aimed not only against the social patriots, but also against those who toyed with the slogan of peace without reference to time and place and the conditions under which peace could be obtained:

> We do not want a separate peace with Germany, we want a peace among all peoples, we want the victory of the workers of all countries over the capitalists of all countries. (*CW*, Vol. 24, page 125).
>
> The slogan 'Down with the War' is correct, to be sure, but it does not take into account the peculiarity of the tasks of the moment, the necessity to approach the masses in a different way. It reminds me of another slogan, 'Down with the Czar', with which an inexperienced agitator of the 'good old days' went directly and simply to the village —to be beaten up. Those from the masses who are for revolutionary defencism are sincere not in a personal but in a class sense, ie they belong to such classes as really gain nothing from annexations and the strangling of other peoples. They are quite different from the bourgeoisie and the intelligentsia who know very well that it is impossible to give up annexations without giving up the rule of capital, and who unscrupulously deceive the masses with beautiful phrases, with no end of promises, no end of assurances.
>
> The average person who favours revolutionary defencism looks upon the thing in a simple matter-of-fact way: 'I for one, do not want any annexations, but the German "presses" me hard, that means that I am defending a just cause and not any imperialist interests.' To a man like this it must be explained very patiently that it is not a question of his personal wishes, but of mass, class, political relationships and conditions, of the connection between the war and the interests of capital, the war and the international network of banks etc. Only such a struggle against defencism is serious and promises success, perhaps not very quick, but real and durable. The war cannot be ended 'at will'. It cannot be ended by the decision of one side. It cannot be ended by 'sticking the bayonet into the ground', to use the expression of a soldier defencist. (*CW*, Vol. 24, page 65).

Lenin defines the position on war further:

> To terminate the war in a pacifist manner is sheer Utopia. It may be terminated by an imperialist peace. But the masses do not want such a peace. War is a continuation of the policies of a class; to change the character of the war, one must change the class in power. (*CW* Vol. 24, page 150).

This clear and simple position constitutes an annihilating reply to the position of the RSL on peace. In following all the major errors of the leadership of the RSL during the last few years on this question, there is revealed indubitably the existence of a petit-bourgeois pacifist or semi-pacifist tendency. But the *quantity* of the mistakes develops into a new *quality*. The RSL leadership is now revealing a fundamental breach with the ideas and methods of Leninism, with the ideas and methods of the Fourth International. Trotsky answered this particular argument on 'peace' for us in his criticism of Shachtman* in August 1940:

> We should understand that the life of this society, politics, everything, will be based on war, therefore the revolutionary programme must also be based on war. We cannot oppose the fact of the war with wishful thinking; with pious pacifism. We must place ourselves upon the arena created by this society. The arena is terrible, it is war, but in as much as we are weak and incapable of taking the fate of society into our hands; in as much as the ruling class is strong enough to impose upon us this war, we are obliged to accept this basis for our activity.
>
> I read in a short report of a discussion that Shachtman had with a professor in Michigan, and Shachtman formulated this idea: 'let us have a programme for peace, not war; for the masses not for murder,' etc. What does this mean? If we do not have peace, we cannot have a programme for peace. If we have war, we must have a programme for war, and the bourgeoisie cannot help but organise the war. Neither Roosevelt** nor Willkie are free to decide; they *must* prepare the war, and when they have prepared it they will conduct it. They will say they cannot do otherwise, because of the danger of Hitler, etc., of the danger from Japan, etc.
>
> There is only one way of avoiding the war —that is the overthrow of this society. However, we are too weak for this task, the war is inevitable. The question then, for us, is not the same as in the bourgeois salon —'Let us write an article on peace, etc.', which is suitable for publications like *The Nation*. Our people must consider it seriously; we must say: the war is inevitable, so let us have an organised workers' programme for the war. The draft of the youth is part of the war and becomes part of the programme. (*American Problems*)

Comrades of the RSL, there is nothing chauvinist in this! It is the revolutionary internationalist and Marxist approach to war and the militarism of our epoch. It is not at all excluded that at a certain stage, there will arise a mass feeling for peace resulting from the

*Max Shachtman. One of the founders of the American Left Opposition, he split from the official Fourth International in 1940.
**Franklin D Roosevelt, a Democrat, was American President from 1933-45. Introduced the 'New Deal' programme of state intervention intended to deal with economic recession while heading off the radicalisation of the working class. Wendell Willkie was the Republican Party Presidential candidate in 1940.

mass slaughter, stalemate on the military fronts, the suffering of the
masses reaching an unbearable intensity. However, even if this arises,
our approach would still have nothing in common with the pacifist
position of the RSL leadership. We would approach the question
from the angle, that just as we cannot leave the problem of the war in
the hands of the capitalists, so it would be fatal to leave the problem of
peace in their hands. Peace in the modern epoch, if imperialism still
survives, will not be much different from war. Peace under capitalism
cannot be of long duration, but merely an interlude.

The sole road for ensuring peace would lie in the overthrow of
imperialism in Europe and the world. In effect then our emphasis
might shift in our agitation from the difference between war waged
in the interests of the masses and war waged by the capitalists, on
the one hand, to peace in the interests of workers, and peace in the
interests of the capitalists, on the other. The axis of our agitation
would remain the same: *the problem of power: which class holds and
wields the power in its own interests.*

In order to strengthen their case, the RSL quotes from *War and
the Fourth International:* 'The revolutionary struggle for peace which
takes on ever wider and bolder forms is the surest means of
"turning the imperialist war into a civil war"...' This conditional
prognosis of the possible development of events is used merely as a
cover for a pacifist or semi-pacifist position. However, even in the
Russian Revolution, which is deemed 'typical' of the events which
will take place in other countries, the slogan of 'peace' was not
separated by Lenin from the idea of revolutionary war. On the
contrary, Lenin waged a struggle, especially in the first months of
the revolution, precisely around the question of 'revolutionary war'
being possible only if the proletariat held state power. However, he
never considered it in the bald way in which the problem is
conceived by the RSL.

True it is, that the slogan of peace was one of the mightiest
weapons in the arsenal of Bolshevism. However, this conditional
formula does not necessarily have to be put forward at all stages of
the war, possibly not at all at certain periods. Slogans such as 'peace'
are based on the consciousness of the masses. At the present time
the masses in Britain are what the RSL chooses to call 'chauvinist'.
Faced with a choice between peace with a victory for Hitler, or even
a compromise with the nazis, and the continuance of the war, 99
per cent would favour a continuance of the war. The Labour
leaders justify their support for the capitalist government by the
necessity to fight Hitlerism. What can the RSL reply to this? To
refer to the enemy at home is very good and correct, but does
not constitute a reply to the worker. For he does not desire a
foreign conqueror and a fascist one at that. Instead of looking

down with scorn and disgust at the 'chauvinist' masses, the RSL leaders should try and learn something from the workers as well as attempt to be their 'teacher'.

An instructive episode occurred in the early stages of the war in 1939, before the fall of France. The Stalinists, during their 'anti-war' period, launched a campaign in their stronghold of South Wales. They secured a referendum among the South Wales miners on the question of war. This among one of the most militant and class conscious sections of the workers in Britain. A great deal of discontent and uneasiness existed among the miners on the question of the war. They were suspicious of the aims of the ruling class. Under these conditions, the Labour and reformist bureaucrats had to execute a manoeuvre to prevent the Communist Party from gaining big support among the miners on the ballot vote. They placed the question on the following basis: 'Against the war' or 'For the war with a Labour government'. As was to be expected they secured an overwhelming majority of the votes for the latter. And this was at a time when Hitler had not gained his tremendous victories and the masses did not feel directly threatened by the totalitarian heel of the nazis.

To reach these workers we must have a programme that can face up to the problem squarely of the defeat of reaction both at home and abroad. It is significant in this connection that the pacifists have lost a great part of what little support they had at the beginning of the war. Even the ILP has been compelled to modify its pacifist outlook. And even from the intransigent and isolated RSL leadership, while retaining basically its pacifist outlook, no more is heard of the pathetic slogan 'Stop the War'. All this, of course, has been due to the unparalleled victories of German imperialism. The leadership of the RSL has been unable to orient themselves to events and apply the *revolutionary method* which a theoretical understanding of the past would demand. For them everything must be an exact replica of the past. Revolution in war-time must follow the exact pattern of the Russian Revolution. In reality history proceeds in a far more complex way. The events of all revolutions are decided by the fundamental structure of class society, and that is why the basic laws of all revolutions can be formulated and predicted in advance. But to lay down an absolute blueprint, from which events cannot deviate, would be scholastic nonsense. There are too many factors involved which are completely incalculable. The Paris Commune* developed on different lines from the Russian Revolution; the Russian from the

---

*The Short-lived workers' government established after the uprising of the Paris workers on 18 March 1871. It was crushed on 28 May 1871, with over 20,000 workers murdered. Fully dealt with in Trotsky's *On the Paris Commune* and Marx's *The Civil War in France*.

Chinese and Spanish, etc, etc. On questions of this character, the lines of development can be indicated only algebraically.

The Situation in Britain Today

Let us examine how the RSL sees the present situation in Britain today:

> Nor are these false policies long in merging. 'The corruption and incompetence, industrially and militarily, raises sharply in the minds of the workers the question of the regime.' There is no question of misunderstanding this sentence. It means that the workers are questioning the right of capitalism to continue as the system of this country. This before the workers have even begun to display a mass sentiment for peace, while they still support the imperialist war and are, in fact, anxious to see it more offensively conducted.
>
> Either all previous history was accidental and from it no lessons can be learned or else the WIL utterly misunderstands and distorts not only the present position of British imperialism, but also the present stage of development of working-class consciousness. We incline to the latter theory. The mood of the masses is still predominantly in support of the imperialist war and the British bourgeoisie are conducting the war as efficiently as the limitations of 'democratic capitalism' permit. These factors do not provide for the 'rapid maturing' of 'all the conditions for social explosions'. When social explosions come, as come they will, they will not arise upon the basis of demands by the workers for a more efficient prosecution of the war. No class struggles can arise on this issue because it is not a class issue as far as the workers are concerned. This is not their war and they have no class interest in victory in it.
>
> At present the masses are under the ideological leadership of the bourgeois and petit-bourgeois and hence support the imperialist war. Many defeats have been suffered by the British bourgeoisie in this war and sections of the workers have as a result criticised the leadership of the bourgeoisie and demanded a more efficient prosecution of the struggle. But this is not a proletarian class reaction to the situation, it is a petty bourgeois reaction and is possible only because the workers are still imbued with alien class ideology. Such working class discontent will stop at grumbling, in the same way as the similar and even more vocal discontent of the petty bourgeois does, and may even be transformed by British victories into greater support for the imperialist government.
>
> It cannot lead to working-class action, just because the demand for a more efficient prosecution of the imperialist war is not a class demand for the workers. Moreover class action by the workers, as they know, would yet further impair the efficiency of British imperialism. British defeats can lead to social explosions, but they will be explosions caused by war weariness, by a desire to end the fruitless slaughter, to escape from the economic hardships of war and to bring an enduring peace and prosperity to the world.

These lines indicate a complete lack of comprehension of the position in Britain today. They constitute an indictment of the stagnant position in which the RSL finds itself. Any organisation with the remotest connection with the working class in Britain would realise that this is hopelessly incorrect as an appraisal of the actual situation. The development of mass consciousness in Britain during the war has been in the direction of a 'socialist' and, yes...even a 'communist' consciousness. Among the workers, within the ranks of the armed forces, among wide strata of the middle classes, a growing ferment and a process of radicalisation has been taking place.

There has not been a period in Britain for many decades in which the minds of the masses have been so receptive to revolutionary ideas and revolutionary perspectives. The objective, and even in a sense, the subjective conditions for the socialist revolution are already maturing in Britain. It can be stated without exaggeration that the ground is more favourable for the swift growth of Trotskyism within the British working class than at any time in the history of our movement. There is a growing and widespread criticism and lack of confidence in the ruling class. The present relationship of forces between the classes has been completely undermined. This, in its turn, has its effect within the ranks of the ruling class, where differences and fissures have been opening out.

We are in a pre-revolutionary situation. With a correct policy we can gain a good springboard for a great leap in influence in the coming period. Here we see why it is that the WIL has made substantial if modest gains in the present milieu, while the RSL has declined and disintegrated. But in order to take advantage of the situation it is necessary to understand the process that is taking place and the way in which the mass consciousness will develop.

With an air of smug incredulity, the RSL proclaim 'there is no question of misunderstanding this sentence. It means that the workers are questioning the right of capitalism to continue as the system of this country...' If this means that we say that the workers seriously desire a socialist revolution now, it is nonsensical. But that the workers are unconsciously moving in this direction, is true beyond a doubt. Yes, comrades, we definitely assert that the workers are *beginning* to challenge the right of capitalism to continue as the system of this country.

Only hopeless scholastics would attempt to lay down a rigid pattern from which events do not deviate. The RSL pictures the workers as if they were in a state of violent and hysterical chauvinism. They triumphantly point to the undoubted fact that the overwhelming majority of the masses still support the war. But they do this because of a desire to defend their rights and their

organisations from destruction, and not at all from a desire to
defend the capitalist class. It is a pity that the RSL never asks the
question: why if their mechanical schema is correct, the defeats of
British imperialism in the past did not lead the masses to demand
'peace' but on the contrary, led them to desire to see the war 'more
efficiently and more offensively conducted'? Nor do they explain
why the workers, who support the war, have become more and
more critical of the ruling class *despite the victories,* as is shown from
the by- election results and the increased number of strikes. Any
pseudo-socialist programme has secured big support against
government candidates in by-elections.

The Common Wealth*, reflecting the move of the
petit-bourgeoisie towards the proletariat has secured successes in
traditional Tory strongholds. *The Times* sees in this an ominous
'portent' of the feeling of the masses. The 'revolutionary Marxists'
of the RSL are incapable of making this correct evaluation.
Literally, there is not a single firm social prop within the
population upon which the bourgeoisie could be certain of relying
in a social crisis. The civil servants in one union after another are
violating the Trades Disputes Act. Even the police have not been
unaffected by the prevailing mood within the population. It is
precisely in an attempt to sidetrack this mood among the masses,
that the Beveridge Scheme** has been brought forward. Millions
of workers are sceptical of the aims of the ruling class in the war
and of the results of a British victory. But they still support the war.
Is it because they have a hatred of the 'Huns' as the RSL would
have us believe? On the contrary, among the broad masses,
especially those organised in the labour and trade union movement
such a feeling is non-existent.

As if to mock the position of the RSL *the victories of the British
armies in North Africa have coincided with strikes and unrest throughout
the country on wage questions.* According to the RSL's version, the
opposite should have taken place. In reality there is no
contradiction here. The masses support the war because they
cannot see any alternative. In the meantime, the class struggle does
not wait. Here is the key to the mood in Britain which the Old Man
so clearly visualised.

The masses are becoming critical of capitalism and imperialism,
but feel themselves paralysed by fear of the consequences

*The Common Wealth party was formed in Britain during the war. Advocating
radical policies including nationalisation, and opposing the wartime electoral truce,
it won substantial votes and two bye-elections.
**The report on 'Social Insurance and Allied Services', published in December
1942. Its main proposals, a National Insurance Scheme and a National Health
Service, were implemented by the 1945 Labour government.

of a nazi victory. The military policy and the Old Man's writings give us the weapon that provides the answer to the questions which are troubling the masses. The leadership of the RSL still supports the idea of agitating for Labour to take power. How does it happen that they support what, according to their method of reasoning, should obviously be a 'chauvinist' demand? And they have done so right throughout the course of the war. Far from the Labour leadership desiring 'peace', even the so-called left wing of the type of Shinwell and Bevan are more zealous than anyone else in their support of the war. The RSL talks of the big swing in the direction of Labour that will take place in the next period. This is correct, but they have not understood or explained why this is so.

The first big swing of the workers to the left, a process which is in its beginnings already, will come because of the dissatisfaction with the contrast between their own conditions and the profits and privileges of the capitalist class. It will not be an anti-war movement as such at all. In spite of the Labour Party's whole-hearted support of the war, the masses will inevitably move towards the Labour Party. A revolutionary situation does not arise with the masses as hysterical patriots one day, and deliriously demanding peace the next. Their demands will reflect themselves in pressure on the leadership of the mass organisations. Today that pressure is being reflected in the movement towards the ending of the political truce. But the growth of the mass feeling for the ending of the coalition is expressed as a reaction against support for the bourgeoisie, not against support for the war.

What programme does the RSL suggest we should develop among the masses as the programme for the Labour government? A programme for immediate peace? As fear of a Hitler victory subsides, the demands of the masses for improvements and concessions grow. This is especially so, as the broad strata realise, that victory and the ending of the war will not improve their conditions, but will result in mass unemployment and widespread distress. In spite of the ideas of the RSL, the experiences of the last war and its aftermath have not gone without leaving traces on the consciousness of the working class. The need for Marxists is to dissect and find what is progressive in the contradictory moods and to understand the changes in the psychology and movement of the masses.

The attempt of the labour and trade union leaders to demagogically intensify their promises to the working class of the glorious prospects after the war is far from achieving startling success. The Stalinists are beginning to reap the rewards of their strike-breaking and anti-working-class activity in the shape of increasing antagonism towards them on the part of the workers. And this, in spite of their attempts to whip up and intensify chauvinist feelings, and in spite of the widespread sympathy for the Soviet Union.

Strikes last year were the highest in many years in the face of innumerable difficulties and obstacles placed before the workers by the Stalinist and Labour bureaucrats. Hardly an indication of tranquil relationships in Britain! But in one factor, we see the amazing maturity of the working class demonstrated better than anything else: the widespread critical attitude not only towards the bourgeoisie, *but towards the Labour leaders*. This is not an isolated phenomenon, but embracing large sections of the workers, organised and unorganised, in industry and in the armed forces. Broad sections of the workers have no illusions about the trade-union bureaucrats, yet their class instinct and solidarity makes them cling to their organisations despite this. For the present they tolerate them for lack of an alternative.

The whole situation imperiously demands that we prepare for the explosions that are developing by understanding what is taking place in the objective development of events and their subjective reaction within the consciousness of the working class. The revolutionary minority can play a role even now, and can make certain of a powerful influence on the coming revolution. That we are in a period of black reaction and chauvinism within the working class can only be the opinion of sectarians who are completely out of touch with the working class.

From: Preparing For Power

June 1942

THE WHOLE world is now involved in the agonies of the imperialist conflagration. The few remaining 'neutrals' are neutral in name only. They have been compelled to restrict consumption of the very essentials of life just in the same way as the actual belligerents —and sometimes to an even greater extent. Besides this, most of them are turning out armaments to the peak of their capacity for one or another of the great powers —with all that this implies. Few of them will avoid the actual shedding of blood. Ireland, Spain, Portugal, Turkey, and even Vichy France* will all be involved in the war in one way or another.

The Fourth International predicted long in advance that wherever the war started, it would inevitably and very rapidly, envelop the whole world. Everything had pointed to this: the contradictions of capitalism which the growth of the productive forces had intensified and aggravated; the sharpening imperialist antagonisms throughout the world; the incapacity of the leadership of the Second and Third Internationals to solve these contradictions. Between the first and second world imperialist wars, terrible national and social antagonisms were engendered and aggravated. With the failure of the workers' leadership to take power out of the hands of the bourgeoisie, these led inevitably to world war.

But the developments which have given the war its universality have at the same time, far from strengthening imperialism, weakened it in the extreme. The very contradictions which led the imperialists to seek a way out in war will lead directly to revolutions. It is no longer a question of attempting to estimate where the weak link in the chain of capitalism might be. There are no strong links.

*In June 1940 the French Prime Minister, Petain, signed an armistice with Hitler which allowed one third of France to remain unoccupied, with a government based at Vichy. The Vichy regime collaborated with the nazis.

There is not a single country, not even mighty America, which has the possibility of escaping terrific social convulsions and even civil war. Just as no one could state for certain where the war would begin, so it is with the social revolution. It may be Japan, China, Germany, the continent of Europe, Britain, or perhaps a colonial revolt in Africa. But just as the war had to spread inevitably throughout the world, so will the social revolution spread from country to country and continent to continent – and at an even greater speed.

Britain's Decline as a World Power

The decline of Britain as the invincible mistress of almost half the world is best seen in the loss of her position on the seven seas. Britannia has ceased to rule the waves. America, even before she had fired a shot in either hemisphere, announced a programme of naval expansion which would alone assure her unchallengeable superiority in a sphere which Britain has for centuries considered her own exclusive preserve; and a sphere too, in which the loss of first position exposes Britain to particular vulnerability in any conflict with the new master. Britain is thus at the mercy of her transatlantic 'saviour'.

Not only metropolitan Britain, but the empire too is in this position. Australia has already passed under the direct domination of America. The Australian Premier has openly proclaimed that they must look to America for succour. The pooling of the industry of the United States and Canada is but a pale reflection of the penetration of American finance capital into what is now but a province of the USA. New Zealand and South Africa, although not so far on the road, are already travelling in the same direction.

South America, which in the past provided one of the biggest fields for British investments, has now become an American preserve. In the Far East, the situation is just as gloomy for the British bourgeoisie. Not only have Malaya and Burma fallen to the Japanese, but China now looks to America for arms and subsidies in her war against Japan. And in India, American influence makes itself felt more and more.

The British bourgeoisie and their man of the hour, Churchill, are compelled to accept this overlordship of American imperialism. There is nothing else they can do. Defeat in the present war at the hands of Germany means the end of imperialist Britain as a power of the first rank. Victory will mean a less spectacular decline to a second rate position under the patronage of America. This is the best that the British ruling class can hope for. In reality the process of decline has been going on for many years before the war. The altering relationship of forces between the powers was bearing less and less relationship to Britain's nominal position. The shattering blows of German and Japanese imperialism have served to reveal the true position and exposed the senility and decay of British imperialism.

The revelation of this weakness, particularly through the Japanese advance, to the hundreds of millions of colonial slaves in the British empire will lead to action on their part on the morrow. The colonial masses are being stirred by mighty events out of their apathy and indifference. It will be impossible for the paralytic hand of Whitehall to keep them in continued enslavement.

In addition, the working class in Britain is becoming more conscious and critical of the old school tie blimps in the colonial service and the armed forces, whose stupidity and incompetence is but a reflection of the fact that the British bourgeois system has completely outlived itself. A realisation of the enfeeblement and decline of the ruling class is beginning to crystallise itself in the consciousness of the masses. A mood of criticism on the basis of the past defeats has penetrated all strata of the population.

Britain's Internal Situation

Even before the crisis of world capitalism had resolved itself into the agony of a protracted death struggle between the imperialist rivals for world domination, the ruling class had perceived the necessity for a violent settlement with the British workers. The whole policy of the guiding layer of the bourgeoisie in the years before the war, was conditioned by a preoccupation with the problems and tasks of *civil war*.

While the leadership of the mighty mass organisations — trade unions, Labour Party, Communist Party, not to speak of the Independent Labour Party (ILP) — was lulling the masses with the soothing routine of parliamentarism, the leadership of finance capital, soberly assessing the situation, was overhauling its plans for an armed struggle with the masses.

In the two years preceding the present war, army manoeuvres were, for the first time, based on the assumption that civil war was raging in Britain.

All these plans of the ruling class (utopian in any event except in the case of the complete paralysis of the leadership of the workers' vanguard) have been shattered by the course of events. The war has resulted in the fusion of the army with the working class far more than in any other period in history. (It may be remarked in passing, that it is in an effort to minimise or overcome this that the bourgeoisie has spent so much effort in attempting to incite the soldiers against the workers by demogogically contrasting 'high' wages of the workers with low rates of pay in the army.)

The almost complete destruction of the European labour movement in the past eight or nine years has been accompanied by an apparently inexplicable strengthening of the British labour and trade union bureaucracy. Alone on the European continent (with the unimportant exceptions of Switzerland and Sweden, which exist by gracious consent of Hitler) the British labour organisations remained intact. This is explained by the fact that while her rivals were preoccupied with internal social conflict or intensive preparations for the coming war, Britain managed, for the last time perhaps, to increase her trade to nearly all markets. By these means she was enabled to grant slight illusory concessions to the working masses. As a result the few years preceding the war were among the most peaceful in the history of British capitalism. The class struggle suffered a lull with far fewer and less bitter strikes on the industrial field. The labour and trade union bureaucracy became more than ever associated with the interests of the employers as obedient and interested servants.

Because of the super-exploitation of the colonial masses the British imperialists were enabled to grant concessions to a privileged stratum of the British working class, and even to a certain extent, to raise the level of the whole of the British workers above that of the European workers. Basing herself on this, Britain's industries became archaic and outdated, instead of advancing as in Germany and America, on the basis of modern technique. Hopelessly outmoded from a technical standpoint, she has been fighting on the shoulders of the colonies. But the war is having its full effect on the British economy.

In the first nine months of 1941 Britain spent £3,495,761,703, while her ordinary income during that period was only £1,221,567,147. Less than a decade ago in 1931, the financial oligarchy engineered a crisis in order to throw out the Labour government ostensibly because of its refusal to cut unemployment benefit by £2,000,000 per year. Today the deficit amounts to more than this sum in a fortnight, and all the burdens of this are laid on the shoulders of the workers.

In every sphere the ruling class has revealed its complete senility and incapacity to even conduct its *own* war. The corruption and incompetence industrially and militarily, raises sharply in the minds of the workers *the question of the regime.* In the factories, chaos, waste and mismanagement, the incapacity to organise production because of the fetters of the profit system, assume a particularly baleful character when counterposed to the ever-increasing exhortations for the workers to 'go to it'. This is especially so when military defeats are justified by the 'lack of equipment'. Meanwhile the combines and big monopolies are assuming a stranglehold on the economic life of the nation. An unbridled clique of monopoly capitalists who control the banks, armaments manufacture and food combines are drawing greater dividends today more than ever before. It is not merely the despoliation of the working class, but the middle class is being completely ruined. The small shopkeepers and business people, professionals and clerks have been hard hit by the war.

The decay of the ruling class is so great that big sections are beginning to lose confidence in themselves. For the moment they have no substitute for Churchill. The complaints of Conservative members of Parliament of the inefficiency in industry and the army are but a glimpse of the fissures and internecine strife which are opening out within the ranks of the ruling class. And this at a time when the masses are not yet moving into action! All these symptoms are a reflection of the profound processes taking place within British society. Deep disillusionment and discontent at the moment find no outlet, but are simmering deep within the masses. All the conditions for social explosions are rapidly maturing

The Possibilities of Fascism in Britain

The reluctant taking up of arms by British imperialism to defend her interests, compelled her to base herself on the hatred of the population for fascism —and even demagogically and confusedly, to intensify this hatred. Automatically this compelled the ruling class to dispense with its reserve weapon —the organisation of Mosley* fascists. Robbed of his basis, like the fascists in occupied Europe, Mosley logically became an agent for German imperialism —a British Quisling. Under these circumstances he could not hope to retain what small support he had gained prior to the war. Fascism finds its mass basis essentially among the petty

*Oswald Mosley entered British politics as a Tory, switched to Labour, then split to form the New Party, which he transformed into the British Union of Fascists in 1932. Thereafter he organised various fascist groups. The term Quisling came from Vidkun Quisling, a Norwegian army officer and nazi collaborator, who became 'minister president' in nazi occupied Norway from 1940.

bourgeoisie and the most backward strata of the population. British fascism had not penetrated the decisive sections of the petty bourgeoisie, not to speak of the backward strata of the working class. Mosley's position was untenable and the capitalists were compelled to put him in a safe place (comfortably, to be sure) behind bars as a protection against the working class and a sop to public opinion. Not to have done so would have led to his being torn to pieces by an infuriated British working class. His organisation vanished from the scene. It can be seen therefore, that there can be no question of fascism in Britain in the period opening up. Mosley could only come to power on the basis of German bayonets.

The bourgeoisie has no reserve weapons at the present time. The ruined middle class; the dissatisfied workers; the lack of confidence of the rulers themselves: all lay the basis, not for a turn in the direction of fascism, but for the most revolutionary period in British history. The fragile basis for the rule of the bourgeoisie rests in the failure of the leadership of the workers to offer an alternative to capitalist rule, which they justify by the threat from 'foreign fascism'.

Nevertheless the distrust and hostility towards the ruling class is increasing within all strata of the population. The eyes of the workers cannot remain closed to the incapacity and corruption of bourgeois rule. It confronts them in every sphere of their daily lives. This awakening is preparing for a revolutionary wave of such titanic proportions that even the great struggles of Spain and France will appear Lilliputian.

Fascism could only arise in the event of the defeat of this movement resulting from the betrayal of the Labour and Stalinist parties, and if we do not succeed in gaining the support of the decisive section of the British workers. On the basis of such a defeat the bourgeoisie would gradually regain confidence and prepare for its revenge. Basing itself on the despairing middle class and even backward sections of the workers disappointed in the failure of the revolutionary wave, the bourgeoisie could, in a short space of time organise a fascist movement — a 'British Empire Protection Society,' or some such organisation — and attempt to establish a precarious rule by a bloody and horrible repression of the working class. Lacking a social base, faced with the fact that the working class is the decisive section of the population —75 per cent —a fascist regime in this country would of necessity be even more ruthless than Franco's.

The Role of the Labour Party in British Society

Immediately after the declaration of the war, the cloven hoof of the bourgeoisie was revealed. Draconic legislation, which if carried out would turn Britain into a totalitarian state on the approved model, was placed on the statute book with the tacit support of the Labour leaders. Nevertheless, in contradistinction to the 'democratic' ally, France, no immediate attempt was made to put these laws into effect. The French bourgeoisie was compelled by the severity of the social crisis and the bitter mood of the workers to carry its repressive legislation into immediate effect, and, in the last analysis, at the decisive moment — as a safeguard against their own masses — to surrender to Hitler.

The same military crisis which resulted in the obliteration of Blum, Jouhaux* and company in France, placed the Labour leaders in Britain more firmly in ministerial positions. Much more than in the last war the capitalists lean for support upon their Labour agents. The course of the struggle on the continent; the chains which German imperialism has riveted upon the conquered and subject peoples, enabled the Labour bureaucracy to move confidently and surely to the path of open surrender to the bourgeoisie. The working class, not without some murmuring, faced with no alternative that they could see other than nazi totalitarianism or support for their 'own' government, supported the entry of the Labour ministers into the government. Thus the worsened international position and the difficulties of British imperialism strengthened the role of the Labour bureaucracy in the internal calculations of the bourgeoisie. Morrison and Bevin have been placed in those posts where the bourgeoisie expected there would be the most pressure from the masses —Home Security and Labour. Under the sign-post 'Against Hitlerism' the Labour leaders have called for the utmost exertion on the part of the workers as exemplified by the 'inspiring' 'GO TO IT' slogan of Morrison.

In the last war the ministerial coalition of Labour with the bourgeoisie which commenced in 1915, was ended in 1917 through the pressure of the disillusioned workers exasperated by the privations at home and the predatory imperialist policy abroad. A tremendous effect was created by the Russian Revolution which had immediate repercussions in Britain. The widespread swing to the left was reflected in the attitude of the Labour leaders, who, scenting danger, were compelled to put forward pseudo-revolutionary speeches to maintain their hold on the rank and file.

The revolutionary left, which later crystallised into the

*Leon Blum Socialist Party Prime Minister in the 1936-7 Popular Front government, Leon Jouhaux general secretary of the trade union federation, the CGT (1909-40).

Communist Party of Great Britain, destroyed its chance of winning a mass basis, precisely because it failed to understand the necessity of keeping in close touch with the unclear feelings and aspirations of the masses, which in their beginnings could not but be in the direction of the Labour Party. As Lenin had occasion to lecture the ultra-lefts: it is very useful to chronicle the crimes of the Labour bureaucracy but that is not sufficient to win the masses. This was the key to the weakness of the revolutionary forces in the first years. It is the key to all the subsequent developments, coupled of course, with the betrayal of Stalinism.

The experience of the first Labour government once again demonstrated the strong roots which reformism has within the working class. The Communist Party, at that time not yet completely degenerated, failed to gain a mass support, despite the fact that Labour had shown itself utterly incapable of introducing even one major reform in the interests of the masses. The embittered toilers turned from the political to the industrial struggle. A revolutionary radicalisation of the masses began. It reached its culmination and greatest expression in the general strike of 1926. The trade union wing of the Labour bureaucracy were compelled by the upward swing to place themselves at the head of the movement which they hated and dreaded, if that movement was not to get completely out of their control. In order to cloak their activities they utilised the Russian trade unions through the Anglo-Russian Committee*. This they were enabled to do because of the policies of Stalin.

The defeat of the general strike, instead of 'finally' exposing the role of the Labour and trade union leaders to the organised workers, led to the reinforcement of the Labour bureaucracy. The striving of the masses found its outlet in the formation of the second Labour government. The debacle of 1931 soon followed; the leadership revealed its true colours and went openly over to the camp of the class enemy. Yet, despite this, the masses of workers, with ranks almost intact, remained under the banner of Labour. Not of course without inner convulsions; the pressure from within forced a split of the left-wing —the ILP broke away from the Labour Party.

The Swing to the Left of the Labour Bureaucracy

Since the crisis of 1931, even before the outbreak of the war, the

*Formed in 1925 as a bloc of the trade union leadeships, it helped to give left wing credentials to the British TUC leaders who were to betray the general strike in 1926. The committee folded when they walked out from it in 1927.

top stratum of the Labour and trade union bureaucracy has completely degenerated and become more closely integrated with the bourgeois state machine. Simultaneously, they have taken to the outlook and ideology of the bourgeoisie. While the capitalists lean more heavily upon this strata, the dialectic of the process reveals that under the pressure of events a section of the bureaucracy is becoming completely separated from any mass basis. The deeper this process evolves, the more will the bourgeoisie find itself leaning on a vacuum. It is only the temporary inertia and inaction of the workers which enables these leaders to play their present role. But the reawakening of the masses will destroy their basis completely. The Labour bureaucracy has always operated the Labour Party as an electoral machine. It was purely for this purpose that a certain amount of activity was tolerated. But with the outbreak of the war and the fusion of the bureaucracy with the bourgeois state, there is no activity for the Labour Party branches as such. Moreover, the bureaucracy finds any sign of life within the party irksome, as it can only bring the tops into collision with the rank and file. On the other hand the trade unions, which have always been the backbone of the Labour Party, are continuing their existence and becoming more lively. This is reflected in the move of millions of workers to become organised.

But the unions too are becoming alienated from the stratum of the bureaucracy which has entered the government and upon whom the bourgeoisie lean most heavily, thus forcing them to come into sharp collision with the workers. This is leading directly and inevitably to a split within the trade union and Labour bureaucracy. The MacDonald experience* will at a later stage, be enacted once again, but now with different social implications. This tendency is already visible in the preliminary skirmishes between Citrine and Bevin** on the one hand, and more glaringly in the development of a left wing within the Labour Party. Even in the distorted reflection of parliament, the pressure of the rank and file is evidenced. Aneurin Bevan, Shinwell, Laski, etc, represent this tendency. The 'revolt' on the issue of conscription of the masses but

*Ramsay MacDonald was Prime Minister in the 1929-31 Labour government. When he was unable to gain support for cuts in unemployment benefit in 1931, he split from Labour to form a National Government with the Tories and Liberals.
**Walter Citrine was TUC general secretary 1925-47, Ernest Bevin general secretary of the TGWU 1921-40 and Minister of Labour in Churchill's wartime coalition. Aneurin Bevan was regarded for years as the leader of the left in the Labour Party (hence the term Bevanites used for lefts in the party in the 1940's and 1950's), editor of *Tribune* 1940-45. Harold Laski was chairman of the party 1945-50. Emanuel Shinwell was a cabinet minister 1945-51.

not of wealth is a first indicaton of what is to come. Although the 'lefts' made haste to come to peace on the welcome pretext given by Japan's entry into the war, tomorrow the differences within the working class will assume wider and more bitter proportions.

A split in the Labour Party is inevitable. The thoroughly rotten and decayed elements of the extreme right wing will step over into the camp of the ruling class as did MacDonald. The left will be driven to break the coalition and form an open opposition in Parliament, and what is more, they will almost certainly gain a majority. In 1931, in spite of the demoralisation among the masses, only the most degraded and corrupt of the Labour bureaucracy went openly over to the camp of the class enemy.

Already at the first signs of a critical spirit awakening, the Labour 'lefts' have been forced into opposition. On the basis of the rising wave of discontent with potential revolutionary implications, it is inevitable that the decisive section of the trade union and Labour bureaucrats, including the majority of the parliamentary representatives, will be forced into an open clash with the capitalist class and a breaking of the coalition. In words at least, they will assume an extremely radical attitude. This process will depend to a large extent on a number of factors; especially the events which take place on the military fronts. These will have a greater or lesser effect on the subjective consciousness of the British masses, heightening or lowering the growth of the mass movement. For example, continued defeats in the Far East on a background of Russian successes will incense the workers and hasten their differentiation and regroupment towards the left. On the other hand, a defeat of the Soviet Union would temporarily have profound repercussions on the British as well as the international working class. Under these circumstances the workers would see no alternative but to cling to the coat-tails of the bourgeoisie. The activity of the Stalinists will delay the more extreme manifestations among the workers, nevertheless the processes taking place have an inexorable logic in their development and direction.

Whatever delays may be imposed, these cannot be of any great duration —even in the event of the greatest catastrophe the working class movement of the world has ever suffered, the defeat of the Soviet Union. Despite all the efforts of the Labour leaders to canalise and give a parliamentary expression to the movement of the workers, it will be impossible for them to succeed. In this period the *Tribune* group of left social patriots will in all probability step forward as the main organising centre of the leftward swing.

The Communist Party

Despite the handicaps of Stalinist policy, the revolutionary traditions of the October Revolution and the militant activity conducted by the party over a period of years, resulted in the key militants in a number of areas turning to the Communist Party. Nevertheless, the Stalinists succeeded in penetrating only the advanced layer of the working class without gaining a widespread support among the masses.

During the 'anti-war' period, despite their adventurous industrial policy they succeeded in extending their influence among the advanced sections of the industrial workers. It is a fact that the untiring work of the best CP militants (without any real lead from above) redounded to the credit and prestige of the Communist Party. In South Wales and in some parts of Scotland they succeeded in capturing leading positions among the miners.

On Clydeside, among the most class conscious sections of the British workers, their roots extend deep into the ship-building and engineering industry. In other parts of the country they have succeeded in gaining influential points of support. The National Council of Engineers and Allied Shop Stewards came completely under the domination of the CP. With the extension of the aircraft industry they bade fair to completely dominate the leadership of the workers. Indeed in the event of a big upsurge among the workers, the Communist Party had the opportunity to capture a leading role, as did the French Communist Party at the beginning of the stay-in strikes in France.

However, with the new turn to class collaboration and strike-breaking, some sections of the party, already disillusioned with the rapid shifts in the policy of the tops, have become bewildered and disoriented. Hundreds of the best militants in the local areas have been driven from the party as 'Trotskyists' and 'agents of Hitler'. Meanwhile wide sections in the factories and unions which followed in the wake of Stalinism because of past militancy in the industrial field, have become alienated. This strike-breaking policy has made it possible, by bold and militant leadership in the factories and unions, to win over those politically unclear militants who followed in the wake of Stalinism in the past.

The prospects of the Communist Party are dependent greatly on the fortunes of the Soviet Union. The peculiar situation is developing by the logic of the struggle, that where the party has its greatest grip —among the advanced workers —here it is fast losing ground. But from the backward strata now coming into political activity partly on the basis of their chauvinism and partly by their association with Russia, the CP is recruiting a new membership up and down the country. This shift was particularly noticeable in the composition of the delegates to their 1942 Conference where more than half the delegates had been in the party not more than three years. The new element replaces in greater numbers those who have dropped out in disillusionment or attempted opposition to the 'new' policy. But of course these are not so active as those they are replacing. However, despite the turn, large numbers, with secret misgivings perhaps, even the big majority of former members, remained within the party.

Big successes for the Soviet Union or the failure of Hitler's offensive cannot but lead to more support for 'communism' which will find distorted expression in the Communist Party. Stalemate on the Eastern front will have a similar result.

A complete destruction of the Soviet Union on the other hand would lead to the obliteration of the Stalinist tendency, the most corrupt section of the apparatus, as with Doriot* in France, going over directly to the bourgeoisie; another section fusing with the Labour and trade union bureaucracy; while the remainder will drop out of politics altogether.

Given the continued resistance of the Soviet Union, the revolutionary wave will lead inevitably to a temporary strengthening of the CP. But this influence could not be of long duration. The strike-breaking policy which is already repelling a section of the advanced strata of the workers will force the workers away from the Stalinists.

Despite the expulsions and attempts to stifle criticism by the use of a police regime within the party, the discontent of the workers is reflected in the ranks of the party. A reflection of this is in the statement of the Political Bureau issued in mid-1942 which admits to the fact that more energy is expended by the party membership in discussing the electoral policy of support for the Tories than in carrying out the party's agitation for the 'second front.' This criticism, which extends to all aspects of party policy has forced the leadership to allege that the Trotskyists have become members of the Young Communist League and Communist Party and are doing serious harm to the party. This opposition, which is essentially revolutionary, must be reached and gained as adherents to the Fourth International. From here some of the best forces of

*Jacques Doriot, a leading CP member was expelled in 1934. He moved sharply to the right and founded the pro-fascist French People's Party.

the Fourth International will be recruited.

The Independent Labour Party

After years of complete isolation from the masses, the ILP is beginning to revive. Numbers of workers, especially from the youth, disgusted with the policy of the Labour Party and hostile to Stalinism, particularly in its present shameless phase of support for Churchill, are moving towards the ILP. The 'left' policy, veiling centrist confusion, has resulted in a definite increase in membership. Whereas in the last few years it had completely lost touch with the workers in the trade unions and industrial movement, it is now beginning to penetrate the fringes of the movement. As the only opposition force at by-elections of national importance, it has gained a certain standing among the workers who are becoming disillusioned with the present government.

In addition, the long-standing tradition of the ILP within the working class as the left wing of the workers' movement makes it inevitable, that without any other organisation in sight, leftward moving workers should gravitate almost automatically towards the ILP.

A steady growth within the coming months and years will be inevitable. Revolutionary repercussions will push the more 'left' section of the workers towards the ILP. Under these conditions the ILP will be one of the most important recruiting grounds for the revolutionary party. It is not excluded in the event of a mass upsurge, that a fusion of the extreme left of the Labour Party with the ILP will take place to form a new centrist organisation. But even if it became a mass party, the ILP could not exist as such for long. The conflicting currents within it would break out in fractional struggles; splits and disintegration would take place and speedily shatter it to pieces. Even the relative stability which was achieved by the POUM in the Spanish revolution could not be attained by the ILP. The present cohesion in the ILP, is based on its divorce from the necessity of any real activity. Its entry into the arena of mass politics would doom it to complete destruction.

On the other hand, a change in the weather-cocks of the Labour Party, always sensitive to the mood of the masses, might lead the ILP leadership to drag at the tail of the Labour Party. But on whatever course events drive the ILP, it is necessary that the organisation prepare now to influence the worker revolutionaries in that party. A great part of our activity must be devoted towards the ILP. Even now in large numbers of branches there are workers who are thoroughly dissatisfied with the rotten compromising policy of the parliamentary clique and the whole centrist leadership. They are looking for a way out, honestly and sincerely seeking the revolutionary policy of Bolshevism.

The older layer of confirmed and crusted centrists has been supplemented by a younger and fresher layer entering politics in large numbers of cases for the first time. Numbers have entered since the war and are not anchored to the ILP like the older and more conservative elements. Especially necessary is the supplementing of the pressure of the revolutionaries within by pressure on the ILP from the outside. Proposals for joint activity against the bourgeoisie as well as against the Stalinist slander campaigns, etc, can break down the hostility which the leadership attempts to foster towards the Trotskyists.

The tactic of our organisation up to and including the first eighteen months of the war was to place the main emphasis on the Labour Party and especially the Labour League of Youth. That this was correct up to the outbreak of the war was indicated by the orientation of the ILP. Finding themselves isolated from the mainstream of the workers' movement and falling into complete decay, the ILP was compelled by the force of events, to turn towards the mass organisation of the working class. The leadership entered into discussions and conducted negotiations for re-entry into the Labour Party.

That advice of Trotsky which they so carelessly rejected in 1934, to turn to the Labour Party, they tardily adopted before the outbreak of war, giving it an opportunist tinge, and found no other course except capitulation to the Labour leaders. At that stage it seemed the most likely course of events that the political awakening of the masses would move completely on the traditional course and pass through the Labour Party.

But the outbreak of the war cut across the development of events and produced a different pattern. Far from growing in activity and political membership, the Labour Party machine in most areas has fallen to pieces. Branches and wards, executives of divisions and towns do not meet for months on end.

At the present time, political life within the working class exists in the unions and in the factories. Most of the members of the Labour League of Youth have been called up to the armed forces or work long hours in industry. Already enfeebled by the heavy hand of Transport House*, the League of Youth has disappeared as a political force, it is in the trade unions, factory and shop committees where the militant workers are to be found in a mood receptive to revolutionary ideas.

*Transport House, the headquarters of the TGWU, was also the head office of the Labour Party for many years.

The situation dictates that our tasks lie in making known our banner among the widest strata of the working class; and struggling for leadership amongst the reactionary and reformist organisations.

The present period is characterised by a radicalisation and ferment within the working class without a mass *political* vent for this dissatisfaction. Insofar as the workers are moving at all at present, they are expressing themselves on the industrial field.

Careful attention must be paid to the processes taking place within the working class, but the necessity remains for the main activity round the general agitational and transitional demands, including the demand that Labour break with the capitalists and take power on a socialist programme.

Trade Unions and Factory Committees

In Britain, more perhaps than in any other country in the world, a correct policy towards the trade unions and factory committees is necessary for a young revolutionary party. Without a correct attitude on this question, our organisation would doom itself to vegetate in sectarian isolation. This is especially the case today when the workers are beginning to stir and awaken ·from the period of relative 'peace' in industry which followed the debacle of the Labour Party in 1931, and when the whole of the working class is undergoing a transformation in its outlook.

This awakening of the working class is shown by the number of strikes that are taking place in formerly backward areas which were only partially organised before the war. Commencing with Betteshanger Colliery, the unrest among the miners – always a barometer of the temper of the British workers – has been followed by strikes on one coalfield after another. Small strikes have taken place among the dockers, railwaymen, engineers and ship-building workers. All these have for the present been limited to a local scale. But they are the first rumblings that give warning of the coming eruption.

The bourgeoisie and the Labour bureaucracy are looking with alarm on these signs of discontent among the workers, and have been compelled to retreat and compromise. They are afraid that by too stubborn opposition, they might release forces beyond their power to control. This process, however, is developing in a contradictory fashion. It can be seen, for example, that despite the terrific discontent among the highly class conscious workers in South Wales and Clydeside, no big movement is taking place in these traditional storm centres. The reason for this has not been unwillingness on the part of the workers to fight. It is the stranglehold exercised by the Stalinists over the shop stewards and leading militants in these districts. Undoubtedly, but for this feature, there would already have been a general strike on the Clydeside, at least among the ship-building workers. Had the Stalinists been pursuing their pseudo-left line of the 'people's government' period, they would today be at the head of a mass movement throughout the country. It is no exaggeration to say that they would probably have captured the rank and file militants in every union in industry. But the changing of the party line after Hitler's attack on Russia, revealed the true face of Stalinism: the Communist Party has come forward as the principal strike-breaking force at the service of the ruling class.

This offers a tremendous opportunity to the Fourth International, and one which must be utilised to the fullest possible extent. Once again it must be emphasised —face to the factories, the unions, the factory committees!

It is impossible for the Stalinists to dam up the tide of militancy of the British workers for any length of time. Their attempts to divert it into Joint Production Committees will merely serve to discredit them at a later stage. The workers will learn from experience that this road leads not so much to increased production as to increased slavery. Revolutionaries must take into account the attitude of the workers to the question of production. In a false and distorted fashion the Stalinists have themselves raised the question of 'control' of production through these committees. Their failure to achieve results will lead the workers to draw the conclusions of workers' control on the morrow.

In is noteworthy that already throughout the country militants in the factories and trade unions are becoming aware of the role of Joint Production Committees and the strike-breaking role of the Stalinists. This is especially so where we have members who can crystallise this opposition mood.

In the past, the best workers who sought a militant industrial policy were almost automatically dragged in the wake of Stalinism — even where they did not support the whole policy of the Communist Party. Now, many of them are instinctively refusing to accept the Communist Party's class collaboration policy. Such workers can be won to the programme of the revolution. They must be won to that programme and to the banner of the Fourth International!

Today our Transitional Programme takes on flesh and blood before our eyes. The response to our industrial slogans and propaganda has underlined the vital importance of partial, transitional demands. Our tiny voice and our inadequate forces have received a wonderful response from that part of the working class we have been able to reach. With an energetic application of our Transitional Programme this influence can be increased a hundred-fold in the period which lies immediately ahead.

The Stalinists have added their shrieks to the hallelujah of the Labour leaders' chorus of 'go back to work' just at the time when the workers are becoming increasingly opposed to the treachery of Transport House. The Stalinist demagogues are, of course, much more skilful in putting over their blackleg policy, but, armed with a correct programme and attitude, these gentlemen can be dealt with by our comrades on the spot.

The struggle must be waged against the trade union bureaucracy no less than against Stalinism. The propaganda to remove strike-breakers from the leadership of the trade unions, now comes to the fore. Within the unions there is developing a critical attitude towards the leadership. Some of the local officials of the unions are becoming radicalised and are pushing forward as militant leaders. Others of the local officials have remained with the bureaucracy through inertia. Either they will learn, or they will have to be thrust aside. What is outstanding at the present time is that the rank and file are to the left of even the militant elements among the leadership. But only a tiny section of workers have drawn the logical conclusions from the sabotage of the leadership. The majority are in opposition to the strike-breaking officialdom, but are not fully conscious of the next step in the struggle. It is our task to provide that consciousness. We must fight to renew even the topmost strata of the trade-union leadership; we must fight to convert the unions into organs of the revolution.

Even more vital than work in the unions, is work among the shop stewards in the factories. These are directly under the pressure of the workers on the job, and this is assuring that old reformist elements (and now the Stalinists) are being replaced by a fresh layer of militants. Workers who previously took no active interest in union affairs are today being pushed to offer themselves as alternative 'unofficial' stewards.

As the struggle develops it will extend through the efforts of the local leaders, to other factories; from single localities to a regional and finally to a national scale. Spontaneously the workers will create fighting committees on a local and national scale which will embrace not only one industry but all the industries in the areas affected. This movement will give expression to the long dormant energies and power of the British proletariat and will assume tremendous scope. The Stalinists and Labour leaders will use 'left' phrases in attempts to divert these energies into the channels of the bourgeoisie. They will only succeed in this if we fail to play our part in the struggle.

The leadership of this movement can be won if our key militants in the decisive areas can give a lead to the workers. Our small forces must be trained and prepared to give leadership to the workers on all problems that face them in industry. Our opportunities in the factories are unlimited. With a correct policy and a true orientation we can grow at a tremendous pace, a pace that will enable us to face the gigantic tasks which confront us, with confidence.

Britain Entering a Pre-Revolutionary Period

Among the backward elements in the ranks of both civilians and soldiers there is to be observed an undercurrent of reactionary and anti-semitic moods. The bourgeoisie has attempted to canalise these tendencies to suit its own interests, particularly by giving its campaign against the black market, a veiled anti-semitic slant. But these moods are not based on, and do not represent, the dominant current, which is to the left.

Under the influence of the war and of Britain's changed position in the world, profound processes are taking place in the consciousness of broad sections of the working class. The age-old 'conservatism' of the British masses had its real basis in the privileged position of Britain in the markets of the world, and the super-exploitation of the colonial masses. Now with that foundation crumbling, so also is the outlook, upon which it had been built. The main burdens of the war are now being shifted on to the shoulders of the British workers. Millions of them have been violently torn out of their customary routine and inertia by the war. The basis of 'family life' has been shattered.

Women, the most oppressed and backward strata of the working class, as well as the youth, have been forced into industry and the armed forces. The old conception of a 'tranquil' and 'ordered' existence is being shattered by events. And as the conditions of the masses have changed, so has their consciousness. They have become responsive to new ideas and perspectives. The old faith in the ruling class and the acceptance of the continued co-existence of classes has virtually vanished. The unemployed have become re-proletarianised and the demoralised elements placed under the discipline and organisation of the army and industry. Large sections of the middle class have been reduced to the level of proletarians and forced into the factories.

The mood of discontent simmering among the workers and middle class has had no outlet yet. In fact, a great deal of it has been diverted, for the present, even into patriotic channels.

Aroused principally by the incompetence of the ruling class in 'fighting fascism' and backed up by the lessons of France where the capitalist class acted as direct capitulators to Hitler, this discontent has found no channel which leads to a genuine fight against fascism. The Labour and Communist Parties accept the continued rule of the capitalists, and utter shrill warnings that any break in 'national unity' will mean victory for Hitler! The ILP offers only pacifism.

In spite of this, the molecular changes within the ranks of the workers have proceeded apace. The 'Churchill myth' has passed its apogee and is now on the downward grade. The mood of the masses has become increasingly critical and its waves are beating ceaselessly against the walls of class collaboration. Despite the efforts of the Bevins and the Pollitts* to stop the first little gaps in the dyke with their fists, the mighty mass pressure cannot for long be resisted. In a short space of time the wall must crumble.

If the ruling class, under the threat of revolution, were to attempt to capitulate to Hitler as the French bourgeoisie did, they would immediately provoke an uprising among the masses. Such an attempt at capitulation would compel the Labour leaders to place themselves at the head of the masses in order to continue the war. Because of the feeling that would be aroused among the masses, and because their own heads would be at stake, they would be compelled to wage a struggle to take control into their own hands. At least the left wing would do so. This would immediately precipitate the socialist revolution. But such a development is improbable in the extreme.

If, on the other hand, complete victory over Germany and Japan were to be gained by Britain (in reality the USA) this too could not prevent revolutionary repercussions among the masses. The programme of finance capital is utopian and insane. The idea that the British masses would tolerate the forcible holding down of the continent of Europe and Asia, not to mention Africa, is absurd. Once the masses compare the glittering promises about 'after the war', of which they are sceptical even today, their indignation will rise to unprecedented heights when confronted with reality.

Freed from the nightmare of victory for the nazis, neither the workers nor the soldiers would tolerate for long the outcome of the conflict which the capitalist class is preparing. Revolutionary explosions would be inevitable.

The prospect of stalemate and a compromise peace is even more

*Harry Pollitt was general secretary of the British Communist party 1929-56, except during the period of the Stalin-Hitler pact, when he favoured a Soviet agreement with British instead of German imperialism.

remote. The antagonisms which brought about the war and have
been sharpened by it, have now reached an unbearable tensity.
Compromise could only come after the contestants were
completely exhausted and the whole world was drained dry. This
could only lead to further explosions. Long before the war had
reached such a stage, and it would require several years, the
endurance of the masses would have reached breaking point and
the stability of the imperialist regimes would be put to the test.
Revolution would begin in Europe or Asia and alter the whole
balance of forces.

All three possibilities in regard to the war, therefore, lead to the same
conclusion. The struggle between the classes in Britain must
inevitably lead to the socialist revolution.

In the event of the failure of the working class to show a way out
of the crisis in which the bourgeoisie has placed society, a terrible
social and political reaction would rage in Britain. The worsened
position of British imperialism in the world market would dictate
the need for the bourgeoisie to destroy all working class resistance
to its imposition of lower standards of living, etc. A failure of the
coming revolutionary wave would provoke outbursts of despair
and hopelessness among the petty bourgeoisie and the backward
strata of the working class. Basing itself on this mood, the
bourgeoisie would, within the shortest space of time, create a fascist
party and attempt to obliterate the organisations of the working
class. *But this reaction would only arise after a defeat of the inevitable
revolution.*

Taking the situation as a whole, it can be seen that more
favourable opportunities exist for the British Trotskyists and for
the success of the socialist revolution in Britain than for almost any
other country.

The British working class has not suffered a severe defeat since
the general strike of 1926 and the debacle of Labour in the general
election of 1931. No big class struggles were waged in the last years
before the outbreak of the war. The British workers are fresh and
unjaded. They possess an overwhelming weight in British society.
Concentrated as it is in big industrial cities, London, Glasgow,
Birmingham, Liverpool, Leeds, Manchester, Swansea, etc, the
working class finds its preponderating social weight still further
increased.

That two and a half years after the outbreak of the most
sanguinary battle for survival among the imperialist powers, most
of the democratic rights of the working class, although formally
abolished, are still intact, is a testimonial not of the strength of
British imperialism, but indicates its Achilles' heel.

The ruling class is compelled to seek salvation in deceit and demagogy rather than in force. The continued, if precarious, existence of democratic rights gives us possibilities of growth in the most favourable of conditions. It arises out of the necessity on the part of the ruling class to disguise their imperialist war as one between democracy and dictatorship. It also arises, of course from the present dependence of the bourgeoisie on the shell of the organisations of the working class. All this gives us a unique opportunity of conducting our work legally, unhampered by the trammels which fascism and occupation have attached to our comrades on the continent.

The Future is Ours

The possibility exists for an unprecedented growth in influence and numbers in the shortest possible time. Today the problem consists mainly in preparing the basis for a rapid increase in growth and influence. The Workers International League will grow with the growth of the left wing. It is necessary to break sharply and consciously, as the group is already doing, with the psychology and perspectives of the past. The most difficult period is in the past —isolated membership and the hostility or indifference of the masses. Big movements and big events *which we can influence* are on the order of the day. The group must not be caught unawares by the development of events.

It is necessary that the membership systematically face the workers and penetrate among the masses. Above all, it is necessary to bring the Fourth International before the masses of the workers as an independent tendency.

It is necessary that the organisation face up critically to the most vital of all factors: the leadership and the organisation are lagging behind the development of events. Objectively, conditions are developing and have already developed, which make for the speediest and most favourable growth and entrenchment of our organisation. But the basic weakness lies in the lack of trained cadres. The membership is for the most part young and untrained and lacks theoretical education. The organisation, despite the leap in influence, still maintains for the most part the habits and attitude of mind of the past — that is, of propaganda circles rather than of branches for agitation among the masses. The difficulties and tasks of the past period of the group's life are still reflected in its ideas and work. On the basis of the new perspective a sharp break must be made with the past.

It can be stated without exaggeration that the decisive question of whether the organisation will be able to face up to events will be determined by whether the leadership and membership can base themselves thoroughly in the shortest space of time, on these perspectives and face up to implementing them in the day to day work of the organisation. To develop deep and firm roots and to become known as a tendency and organisation throughout the country, and above all, among the advanced workers in the factories is the basic task of the organisation.

The disproportion in the situation in Britain lies in the lack of relationship between the ripeness of the objective situation and the immaturity and weakness of our organisation. Prospects of a swift impulsion of the masses leading to a spectacular growth of the organisation on the lines of the POUM in the Spanish revolution, are rooted in the situation. But only if we realise the scope of the tasks and possibilities which history has placed before us. We will rise to the situation *only if in the interim, skeleton cadres are built throughout the country*. These cadres would serve as the bones on which the body of a powerful organistion could be built up from the new and fresh recruits who will come towards us as the crisis develops.

These tasks must be accomplished. Our untrained and untested organisation, will, within a few years at most, be hurled into the turmoil of the revolution. The problem of the organisation, the problem of building the party, goes hand in hand with the revolutionary mobilisation of the masses. Every member must raise himself or herself to the understanding that the key to world history lies in our hands. The conquest of power is on the order of the day in Britain —but only if we find the road to the masses.

Revolutionary audacity can achieve everything. The organisation must consciously pose itself and see itself as the decisive factor in the situation. There will be no lack of possibilities for transforming ourselves from a tiny sect into a mass organisation on the wave of the revolution.

The Rise and Fall of the Communist International

June 1943

THE THIRD International has been officially buried. In the most undignified and contemptible fashion it would be possible to conceive, it has passed off the stage of history. Hurriedly and without consultation with all the adhering parties, not to speak of the rank and file throughout the world, without any democratic discussion and decision, as the result of the pressure of American imperialism, Stalin has perfidiously abandoned the Comintern.

To understand how it is that this organisation which aroused the terror and hatred of the whole capitalist world has come to such an inglorious end at the bidding of capitalism, it is necessary to review briefly the stormy rise and even stormier decline of the International. The decree for its dissolution was merely an acknowledgement of what has long been known to all informed people; that the Comintern as a factor making for world socialism was dead and had departed forever from its original aims and purposes. Its demise was predicted and foreseen long in advance.

The Third International grew out of the collapse of capitalism in the last war. The Russian revolution sent a wave of revolutionary fervour through the ranks of the working class throughout the world. To the war-weary, disillusioned and embittered masses, it came as a message of hope, of inspiration and courage, it showed the way out of the bloody chaos into which capitalism had plunged society. It was born as a direct consequence of the betrayal and breakdown of the Second International which supported the ruling classes in the last war.

The breakdown of imperialism and capitalism was signalled by the revolutions in Germany, Austria, Hungary, revolutionary situations in Italy, France and even Britain. The spectre of socialist revolution hung all over Europe. The memoirs and writings of nearly all the bourgeois politicians of that time bear witness to the despair, the lack of confidence of the bourgeoisie in the face of the fact that they had lost control of the situation. Social democracy saved capitalism.

The powerful trade-union and socialist bureaucracies placed themselves at the head of the upsurge of the masses and diverted it into harmless channels. In Germany, Noske* and Scheidemann conspired with the Junkers and capitalists to destroy the revolution. The soviets of workers, soldiers, sailors, peasants and even students, which had issued from the November revolution of 1918, held power in their hands. The social democrats handed the power back to the capitalists.

Gradually, slowly, peacefully, as their theoretical conceptions explained it, they would transform capitalism into socialism. In Italy, by 1920 the workers had seized the factories. Instead of leading the workers to the conquest of power, the Socialist Party bade them cease 'unconstitutional' procedure. So it was throughout Europe. The results of this programme are evident today. The worst tyranny and the bloodiest war in the history of capitalism. But precisely because of the breakdown of international socialism in the Second International, which had betrayed Marxism, the Third International was formed.

As early as the beginning of the last war (First World War) Lenin had courageously issued the call for the Third International. The Third International was formally inaugurated in March 1919. Its declared aims and objects were the overthrow of world capitalism and the construction of a world chain of united soviet socialist republics to join up with the USSR, which itself was not conceived as an independent entity but merely as the base for the world revolution. Its fate would be determined and was bound up with the fate of the world revolution.

The formation of the Third International swiftly led to the creation of mighty communist parties throughout the most important countries in the world. In Germany, France, Czechoslovakia and other countries, communist parties with a mass membership were created. In Britain a small communist party was formed which wielded considerable influence. The success of the world revolution in the next period seemed assured by the development of events. The communist parties in Europe were steadily increasing in numbers and influence at the expense of the social democracy.

*Right wing SPD leaders. Gustav Noske, as minister of war, organised suppression of the January 1919 uprising of the German workers and sanctioned the murder of Luxemburg and Liebknecht. Philipp Scheidemann became Chancellor in 1919. The Junkers were reactionary Prussian aristocrats who dominated the military and civil service until the 1930's. See: *Germany — From Revolution to Counter-Revolution* by Rob Sewell (Fortress).

Front cover of the WIL pamphlet Lessons of Spain with Ted Grant's introduction.

Londoners sleep in the Underground during the war. It was the WIL's demand that the stations be opened up to be used as air-raid shelters that led the petit-bourgeois RSL to dub them 'chauvinists'! (See 'A Reply to the RSL').

The last war had not succeeded in solving any of the problems of world capitalism. In fact it had aggravated them. Capitalism had broken down at its 'weakest link' as Lenin expressed it. The attempts to destroy the young Soviet Republic by the wars of intervention had completely failed. German capitalism, the mightiest in Europe, found itself stripped of its resources, part of its territory, burdened with staggering reparation payments, and generally placed in an impossible position. British and French imperialists, the 'victors' in the last world war, were in a position fundamentally not much better.

Encouraged by the Russian revolution, the colonial and semi-colonial masses were stirring and preparing to revolt. The masses at home were restless and uneasy and the economic position of Anglo-French imperialism had worsened considerably in comparison with that of Japanese and American capitalism. It was on this international background that the crisis broke out in Germany in 1923. Germany with her high productive capacity was crippled by the restrictions imposed by Versailles* and had now become the weakest link in the chain of world capitalism.

The failure of Germany to pay the instalments on the reparations resulted in the French capitalists marching into the Ruhr. This helped to complete the collapse of the German economy, and the German bourgeoisie endeavoured to unload the burdens onto the shoulders of the working and middle classes. The mark fell in value from 20 to 40 to the pound in January, to 5 million in July and 47 million at the end of August. The indignant German masses turned towards communism.

As Brandler, the then leader of the Communist Party, stated at the meeting of the Executive Committee of the Comintern: 'There were signs of a rising revolutionary movement: We had temporarily the majority of the workers behind us, and in this situation believed that under favourable circumstances we would proceed immediately to the attack...' But unfortunately the leadership of the International failed to stand up to the test and take advantage of the opportunity. Success in Germany would inevitably have led to victory throughout Europe. But as in Russia of 1917, so in Germany of 1923, sections of the leadership vacillated.

Stalin, with his organic opportunism, urged that the German party be 'curbed' from taking any action. The result was that the favourable opportunity to take power in Germany was missed and the communists in Germany suffered defeat. For similar reasons

*The Treaty of Versailles signed in 1919 imposed harsh terms on Germany at the end of the First World War.

the revolution in Bulgaria also suffered shipwreck. But the defeats of the revolution in Europe caused by the failure of the leadership inevitably led to serious consequences. As Lenin had written, urging the necessity to prepare for the insurrection, in Russia in 1917: 'The success of the Russian and world revolution depends upon two or three days' struggle.'

The failure of the world revolution and the isolation of the Soviet Union, taken in conjunction with its backwardness, the weariness and apathy of the Soviet masses who had gone through years of war, terrible privations and suffering during the course of the civil war and the intervention, their disillusionment and despair at the failure of their hopes of aid from the workers of Europe: all this led inevitably to reaction within the USSR.

Reflecting at the time, perhaps unconsciously, the interests of the reactionary and conservative bureaucracy which was just beginning to raise itself above the Soviet masses, Stalin for the first time in 1924 came forward with the utopian and anti-Leninist theory of 'socialism in one country'. This 'theory' sprang directly from the defeat which the revolution had suffered in Germany. It indicated a turning away from the principles of revolutionary internationalism on which the Russian revolution had been based and on which the Communist International was founded.

Stalin, at the funeral of Lenin in January 1924, from force of habit following in the tradition of the Russian revolution declared: 'In leaving us Comrade Lenin enjoined on us fidelity to the Communist International. We swear to thee, Comrade Lenin, to devote our lives to the enlargement and strengthening of the union of workers of the whole world, the Communist International.' At that time he had not the slightest notion of whither the theory of socialism in one country would lead the Soviet Union and the Comintern.

The history of the Comintern since those days has been largely bound up with the fluctuating policies of the bureaucracy of the USSR. Lenin had insistently linked the fate of the Soviet Union with that of the world working class, and principally of its vanguard the Comintern. Even the oath of the Red Army pledged the red soldiers to loyalty to the international working class. Indeed the Red Army was not regarded as an independent 'national' force, but as one of the instruments of the world revolution.

Of course, all this has long since been altered by Stalin. Trotsky, in conjunction with Lenin who, in his last years, viewed the developing situation with alarm, had already begun the struggle against the bureaucratisation of the Bolshevik Party and the Soviet State in 1923. Lenin was warning of the dangers of degeneration which threatened the Soviet state.

On the background of the growing reaction, nationally and internationally, the struggle between the internationalists and the Thermidorians* entered into an acute stage. Trotsky, in alliance with Lenin, had demanded the restoration of complete democracy within the Bolshevik Party and the soviets. Lenin, in pursuit of this objective, had demanded the removal of Stalin from the post of General Secretary of the party because he had become the focal point around which the bureaucracy was crystallising.

After Lenin's death, Zinoviev, Kamenev** and Stalin, 'the troika' secured a decision disregarding Lenin's advice by the Central Committee and commenced a campaign against Lenin's ideas which were being put forward by Trotsky, with the spurious invention and legend of 'Trotskyism'. The fate of the Comintern was linked with the fate of the Bolshevik Party of the Soviet union which, through its prestige and experience, was naturally the dominant force in the International.

The transition from the policy of world revolution to that of socialism in one country expressed a sharp turn to the right in the Comintern. In Russia, Zinoviev and Kamenev were forced into opposition by the anti-Marxian policy now being developed by Stalin. They were thrust into an alliance with Trotsky and his supporters. Stalin, together with Bukharin, opposed the policy of industrialising Russia through a series of five year plans suggested by the Left Opposition led by Trotsky and came out with his famous aphorism at the plenary meeting of the Central Committee in April 1927 that 'to attempt to build the Dnieperstroy hydro-electric station would be the same thing for us as for a muzhik*** to buy a gramophone instead of a cow'.

As late as the end of 1927, during the preparations for the Fifteenth Party Congress, whose task was to expel the Left Opposition, Molotov said repeatedly: 'We must not slip down into poor peasant illusions about the collectivisation of the broad masses. In the present circumstances it is no longer possible.' Inside Russia the policy was to allow the kulaks (rich peasants) and the Nepmen (capitalists in the towns —so-called after the New

*From Thermidor: a term used to describe political reaction without a social counter-revolution. Derived from analogy with the shift of power in the French revolution in the month of Thermidor (July) 1794 when the radical Jacobins led by Robespierre were overthrown by a right wing coup, whilst leaving the fundamental gains of the (capitalist) social revolution intact. Thus Thermidorians: supporters of political reaction in Russia.

**Grigori Zinoviev and Lev Kamenev were Old Bolsheviks. The former was the first president of the Communist International, the later was one-time deputy to Lenin. Both were opposed at the time to the Soviet seizure of power in October 1917. Later, together with Stalin, they blocked the implementation and denied the existence of Lenin's Testament, which called for Stalin's removal as General Secretary. Both were executed in the 1936 purge trials.

***A Russian term for peasants.

Economic Policy of 1921), full scope for economic development. This policy was perfectly typified by the slogan coined by Bukharin with the full support of Stalin, given out to the peasantry: 'Enrich yourselves!'

The policy of the Comintern was now pushed far to the right with the preoccupation of Stalin to find allies to 'defend the Soviet Union from attack'. The Comintern was already being reduced to the role of a border guard. The disagreements within the Bolshevik Party and the International flared up over the question of the Chinese revolution and the situation in Britain. In China during 1925-7 the revolution was stirring up the millions of Asia into action. The Comintern, instead of relying on the workers and peasants to carry through the revolution, as was the Leninist policy in Russia, preferred to rely on the Chinese capitalists and generals.

The Left Opposition warned of the consequences of this policy. The Chinese Communist Party was the sole workers' party in China and had a dominating influence over the working class; the peasantry were looking towards the example in Russia to show them the way out of their centuries-long suffering at the hands of the landlords, through the seizure of the land. But the Comintern stubbornly refused to take the road of working-class independence which Lenin had insisted on as the prerequisite for communist policy in relation to the bourgeois-democratic and anti-imperialist revolutions in the East.

Meanwhile a similar policy was pursued in Britain where the masses were undergoing a process of intense radicalisation. As a means of struggling against intervention against the Soviet Union the Russian trade unions made an agreement with the General Council of the TUC. The tendency towards revolutionary developments in Britain is seen in the fact that a million members, a quarter of the trade-union membership, were organised in the Minority Movement*. Trotsky, analysing the situation in Britain, had predicted the outbreak of a general strike.

The task of the Communist Party and the Communist International should have been to prepare the workers for the inevitability of a betrayal on the part of the trade-union leadership. Instead, they sowed illusions in the minds of the workers, especially as the trade-union bureaucrats had covered themselves with the agreement with the Russian trade unions, whose prestige they utilised as a cloak. After the betrayal of the 1926 general strike by the trade-union bureaucracy, Trotsky demanded that the Russian trade unions should break off relations with the TUC. This Stalin and the Comintern refused to do.

*An organisation that brought together the left in the British trade unions in the 1920's. It was initiated and largely led by the Communist Party.

WORKERS' INTERNATIONAL LEAGUE
(Fourth International)

A MEETING

To Commemorate the 24th Anniversary of the

RUSSIAN
REVOLUTION

WILL BE HELD AT

LUNDIE HALL

(BEECH STREET)

SATURDAY, NOVEMBER 22nd.

TROTSKY SPEAKS

(Gramophone Records — English Speaking)

SPEAKERS :—

TED GRANT   A. ROY

CHAIRMAN :—

R. BRISCOE

Doors open 2-0 p.m.   Meeting starts 3-0 p.m.
RESERVED SEATS 6d.

Nicol & Sons, Printers (T.U.), 37 Norton-st., Liverpool

A 1941 leaflet advertising a meeting in commemoration of the Russian Revolution.

THE 3RD INTERNATIONAL IS BURIED! LONG LIVE THE 4TH INTERNATIONAL

SOCIALIST APPEAL — WORKERS OF THE WORLD UNITE!

ORGAN OF WORKERS INTERNATIONAL LEAGUE, FOURTH INTERNATIONAL.

VOL. 5. No. 12. JUNE, 1943. TWOPENCE.

END THE TRUCE

LABOUR TO POWER

THIS LABOUR PARTY CONFERENCE MEETS WHEN THE WORLD WAR HAS BEEN ON FOR NEARLY FOUR YEARS AND THE LABOUR MINISTERS HAVE BEEN IN THE GOVERNMENT FOR MORE THAN THREE OF THOSE TERRIBLE YEARS. IT IS A SUITABLE TIME TO DRAW UP A BALANCE SHEET OF THE RESULTS THIS HAS HAD FOR THE WORKERS OF BRITAIN, AND OF THE WORLD.

The Labour and Trade Union leadership entered the Government claiming that this action was necessary in order to destroy fascism and in order to exert the maximum pressure to ensure social advance, both now and in the better world that should come after the war.

Every worker naturally wants to see the wiping out of fascism from the face of the earth once and for all. But can this be obtained by support of the Government?

What are the results of the coalition? At the present time the armies of Britain and America are being prepared for the terrible slaughter that still lies ahead. Millions of lives will inevitably be lost in the battles that are to come. The destruction and the carnage of the war are causing more devastation and suffering than even in 1914-1918.

The Labour leaders have pointed to the atrocities and horrors that have been committed by the Nazis, and the Japanese militarists, which have aroused the justified horror and indignation of the working class throughout the world. But we see that by their actions the Anglo-American imperialists have demonstrated irrefutably their aims and objects are entirely different from the aims of the working class. Churchill and Roosevelt at the time of the "liberation" of N. Africa installed in power some of the gang of quislings and gangsters who betrayed France into the hands of the Nazis and who

Continued on page 2

3,500 CLYDE AERO STRIKE

By TOM BURNS

For quite a while the workers in the foundry at a large West of Scotland Aircraft Factory, have been smarting under a number of grievances. Not only were the general conditions below standard, but to bring it home to the workers the manager controlled affairs in a ruthless fashion. One pin-pricking measure of his was to fix wire netting to a part of the lavatory doors, so that the workers could be watched!

On Thursday, May 20th and the following day, a total of 3,500 workers in the foundry stopped work in sympathy with the furnace men who had received a wage reduction. 22 furnace men were involved.

Due to pressure from the furnace men, who demanded more time for each "heat", a temporary agreement to last 3 months, was made between the Union and the employers, extending the period for each "heat" from 82 minutes to 97 minutes. Even on these terms the worker had a task to make a suitable wage. Now that the agreement has expired, the boss is attempting to enforce the men to revert to the old conditions. It is this attack of the management which was the cause of the big strike.

If the Manager's time limit is enforced it would mean a loss of approximately £1 1. 0 per week.

The workers have learned the hard way what "Production Weeks" have meant to them. The manager's promise of **"the sky is the limit for earnings"** is now shown to be nothing else but a manoeuvre to force down the wage rates. The firm now throws it to the workers: **"You did so many castings on such and such a time—why not regular?"** It is evident that the General Works Manager will apply this principle to all blocks. Already the prelude of more rigid shop discipline is being pushed through the works which is simply paving the way for a drive against piece-work earnings.

WORKERS: DEMAND THE WITHDRAWAL OF THE PROSECUTIONS AGAINST THE 22 FURNACEMEN! END THE VICIOUS ESSENTIAL WORKS ORDER!

TO THE WORKERS OF BRITAIN—

MANIFESTO OF WORKERS INTERNATIONAL LEAGUE (FOURTH INTERNATIONAL).

COMRADES!

THE THIRD INTERNATIONAL, LONG DEAD AS AN INTERNATIONAL REVOLUTIONARY FORCE HAS BEEN FORMALLY BURIED. THE ORGANISATION WHICH LENIN AND TROTSKY FOUNDED IN 1919 TO ACHIEVE THE EMANCIPATION OF THE WORKING CLASS AND TOILING MASSES THROUGH THE WORLD SOCIALIST REVOLUTION, HAS BEEN DISSOLVED IN IGNOMINY AND DISGRACE.

THIS EVENT, WHICH INEVITABLY RESULTED FROM THE INTRODUCTION OF THE CONSERVATIVE AND NATIONALIST THEORY OF "SOCIALISM IN ONE COUNTRY," WAS FORESEEN AND PREDICTED BY THE TROTSKYISTS WHO REMAINED TRUE TO THE INTERNATIONAL SOCIALIST IDEAS OF MARX, ENGELS, AND LENIN.

The founding of the Comintern took place in face of the organised terror and hatred of the ruling classes of all countries of the world. Its leaders were hounded and branded as "terrorists" and "murderers" who sought to destroy civilisation.

To-day the jackals howl with glee over the corpse of the Comintern. They hail the capitulation of Stalin and his blow against internationalism, as a magnificent and statesmanlike act. By this victory, the capitalists know that a great blow has been struck at the international working class. They believe that they have laid the spectre of Communism, which Marx proclaimed was already haunting Europe in 1848. They know that Stalin has dealt a blow to the Soviet Republic, where the spectre took flesh and blood through the October Revolution in 1917.

BUT THE HOWLS OF THE CAPITALISTS ARE PREMATURE. LONG BEFORE THE OFFICIAL BURIAL OF THE COMINTERN, THE FOURTH INTERNATIONAL HAD ALREADY BEEN BORN.

By its international socialist programme and actions, the Third International under Lenin and Trotsky continued the great traditions of Marx and Engels, who founded the First International; it continued the great traditions of the Second International when it collapsed, having besmirched the banner of internationalism by support of their own capitalist governments by its national sections in the first world imperialist war.

Continued on Back page.

THE FOUNDERS OF THE COMINTERN—STALIN THE EXECUTIONER ALONE REMAINS!

RYKOV
Executed
BUKHARIN
Executed
SVERDLOV
Dead
STALIN
Survivor
ZINOVIEV
Executed
KAMENEV
Executed
LOMOV
Disappeared
SHOMYAN
Dead
BERZIN
Disappeared
MURANOV
Disappeared
ARTEM
Dead
STASSOVA
Disappeared
KRESTINSKY
Executed
URITSKY
Dead
NOGIN
Dead
DZERZHINSKY
Dead
BUBNOV
Disappeared
SOKOLNIKOV
Imprisoned
KOLLONTAI
Sweden
SMILGA
Executed
TROTSKY
Assassinated
LENIN
Dead
MILIUTIN
Disappeared
JOFFE
Suicide

LENIN'S GENERAL STAFF — THE BOLSHEVIK CENTRAL COMMITTEE OF 1917

These pictures depict the General Staff of the Bolshevik Party which, under the leadership of Lenin, led the victorious October Revolution of 1917. Stalin destroyed the entire generation of the Old Guard. Not only that. He also decapitated the entire leadership of the Red Army, the trade unions, the Youth organ-isations. Lenin attached tremendous significance to the Old Guard of Bolshevism. He regarded these men—the living embodiment of the experience of three revolutions (1905, February 1917, October 1917), of the struggle against World War I, the Civil War, the post war period of reconstruction, as the only guarantee of correct policies. "If we do not close our eyes to reality, then it must be recognised," Lenin wrote in March 1922, "that at the present time the proletarian policy of our party is determined not so much by its social composition as by the enormous and unlimited authority of that thin layer which may be called the Old Guard. Even a minor internal struggle within this layer would suffice if not to undermine, then, in any case, to weaken its authority to such an extent that the decisions would thereafter no longer depend upon it."

Stalin and the bureaucracy have not stopped at "weakening its authority". They have annihilated it, and with it the programme of international Socialism for which it stood. Having destroyed the whole generation of Communist leaders, and having destroyed the Communist International which these outstanding revolutionaries were responsible for launching as an instrument of world Socialist Revolution, Stalin has now formally buried the corpse of the Comintern, which has befouled the international labour movement for the past 10 years.

STATEMENT OF THE BARNSLEY TRANSPORT STRIKE COMMITTEE

The nation-wide discontent among the transport workers at the insulting and provocative findings of the "Arbitration" Court with reference to their recent wage claim is now beginning to show up clearly from the barrage of strikes which accompanied the decision.

As the following statement by the Barnsley workers shows, the strike is two fold. The most important reason is the obtaining of the demands. The other is the failure of "arbitration courts" and other machinery.

"The dispute originates from a claim staked on January 4th, 1943, which the employers rejected completely. The claim was for a flat 15/- per week increase, which, considering the wages paid, is not an excessive demand. A top rate man receives £4 2s. 0d., without deductions, and takes home a little over £3 usually. It must be remembered that transport workers get no overtime pay of any type: that because of lengthy "split" duties they are often compelled to spend some 62 hours in working a normal week of about 30 hours. It must also be pointed out that, unlike other industries, the transport workers are "at it" nearly all the time; they start before other workers and finish later. They are working on holidays and Sundays. Despite these conditions, which are only a few of the many bad ones, they are among the very lowest paid sections of the workers.

In these circumstances, the Union took the claim from negotiation to arbitration. After a lengthy sitting, which lasted some 19 weeks, due in part to the Chairman's illness, the answer was still negative. The temper of the men had meanwhile risen to boiling pitch and they were clamouring to stop the wheels. When the vehicles were run in, last Tuesday night, the decision was taken. At almost the same time, similar decisions were taken by the Wakefield and West Riding Company, the South Yorkshire Motors, Pontefract, and Bullock & Sons, of Featherstone. This proves that the issue is no local one.

The strike is "unofficial" and the Barnsley workers wish to emphasize that it is not against the principles of trade-unionism that they have struck, but rather to strengthen it. The official channels have been tried and failed; the men have no further confidence in them and believe that direct action is the only way left open. A dispute committee, democratically elected by the mass of employees, has been formed to safeguard the local union officials, and to ensure co-ordinated action.

This committee has contacted the local M.P.s and asked them to intervene on the workers' behalf. It has also telegraphed Mr. Bevin demanding that he immediately open an enquiry into the dispute.

The Barnsley workers emphasise that they are out solid, no matter who goes back, and believe that solidarity with them would bring results in a matter of days.

They are pleased to record contributions of some £18 which have been welcome in view of the expense of pre-paid wires, etc.

In reply to the criticisms and arguments of certain individuals about "patriotism," the Barnsley workers consider that they have efficiently and loyally "done their bit." They have brothers, sons and sweethearts in the front line, who will have to return to the conditions the workers have fought for. It is, further, their opinion that refusal to grant just demands, and thereby provoking a disruption of industry, is the employers' own method of assisting their Nazi class-brothers."

SOLIDARITY WITH THE BARNSLEY WORKERS.
FOR THE YEARLY RE-ELECTION OF ALL UNION OFFICIALS, IN ORDER TO PRESERVE THE MILITANT INDEPENDENCE OF THE TRADE-UNIONS.
FOR THE WITHDRAWAL OF THE T.U.'s FROM THE ARBITRATION MACHINERY AND THE RE-INTRODUCTION OF INDEPENDENT BARGAINING.

Send your financial help to:—

Mr. Brown, The Treasurer, 5, Wesley Street, Barnsley. Don't forget a resolution of support at your T.U. Branch Meeting.

Front page of the WIL's Socialist Appeal from 1943 reporting the winding-up of the Third International (see The Rise and Fall of the Communist International).

After using the Anglo-Russian Committee for as long as they needed, more than a year after the General Strike, the British trade-union leadership broke off relations. The Comintern let out a howl that they had been betrayed. But meanwhile the young Communist Party of Great Britain which should have increased its membership by leaps and bounds as a result of these great events, was paralysed and disorientated by the policy of the International, was completely discredited and dwindled in influence among the masses. These further defeats of the International, due directly to the policy of Stalin and the bureaucracy, at first sight paradoxically, increased the power of the bureaucracy within the Soviet Union.

The Soviet masses were further disheartened and disillusioned by these new defeats of the international proletariat and suffered a further decline in spirits. The defeats which had been a direct consequence of the policy of Stalin and the bureaucracy further strengthened its hold on the Soviet Union. The Left Opposition led by Trotsky which had correctly analysed and forecast these developments was now expelled from the Bolshevik Party and from the International.

The internal results of Stalin's policy now began to bear fruit in the alarming growth of the strength and influence of the kulaks and of the Nepmen. The Soviet Union stood on the brink of disaster. In panic and terror Stalin and the bureaucracy were compelled to adopt a caricature of the very policy for which Trotsky and his co-thinkers had been expelled. In Russia the Five Year Plans against which Stalin had so strenuously fought were introduced.

It is on the basis of this planned production that the Soviet Union achieved its greatest successes and on which the present day USSR bases itself in war. Meanwhile the panic turn to the left internally was reflected in a panic turn to the left internationally. Stalin had burned his fingers badly in his attempts to lean on capitalist elements in China and to conciliate social democracy. Now he veered the International sharply in the opposite direction. In violation of its statutes the International did not hold a conference for four years. A new conference was called which introduced officially the programme of the Communist International. It also proclaimed the end of capitalist stability and the beginning of what was termed the 'Third Period'. This was supposed to usher in the period of the final collapse of world capitalism. At the same time the social democracy, according to the once-famous (but now buried) theory of Stalin, was supposed to have transformed itself into 'social fascism'. No agreements were now possible with 'social fascists' who constituted the main danger confronting the working class and must be destroyed.

It was just at this period that the unprecedented slump of 1929-33 affected the world. In particular it hit Germany. The German workers were thrust into a position of degradation and misery and the middle classes were ruined. Germany's unemployment figure rose steadily till at the peak it reached 8,000,000. The middle class, having failed to receive anything from the revolution of 1918, and disappointed with the failure of the communists in 1923 to take power, now in anguish and despair began to look for a solution to their problems in a different direction.

Subsidised and financed by the capitalists, the fascists began to secure a mass basis in Germany. In the elections of September 1930, they secured nearly six and a half million votes. Despite their expulsion from the Communist International, Trotsky and his followers still considered themselves as part of it and insistently demanded that they be allowed to return to the ranks. At the same time they subjected the suicidal theory, which had now been adopted by the Comintern, to a sharp criticism. In place of it they demanded a return to the realistic Leninist policy of the united front* as a means of winning the masses in action and through their own experience, to communism.

With the victory of Hitler at the polls Trotsky sounded the alarm. In a pamphlet entitled *The Turn in the Communist International — the Situation in Germany* he issued a signal for a campaign, which was carried on for three years by the International Left Opposition of the Comintern, as the Trotskyists looked on themselves. In Germany, France, USA, Britain, in far away South Africa, and in all countries where they had groups, the Trotskyists conducted a campaign demanding that the German Communist Party set into motion a campaign for a united front with the Social Democrats to prevent Hitler from coming to power.

At the direct instructions and bidding from Stalin and the Comintern, the German Communist Party denounced this policy as a counter-revolutionary 'social fascist' one. They insistently fought against social democracy as the 'main enemy' of the working class and argued that there was no difference between democracy and fascism. In September 1930, the *Rote Fahne*, organ of the German CP proclaimed: 'Last night was Herr Hitler's greatest day, but the so-called election victory of the nazis is the beginning of the end.'

Right throughout these years the Comintern continued its fatal course. When Hitler organised a referendum in 1931 to oust the

*The united front was conceived as a temporary agreement between mass workers' organisations, for action on specific issues, while retaining independence of programmes.

Social Democratic government in Prussia, at the direct insistence of Stalin and the Comintern the German communists voted with the nazis against the social democrats. As late as May 1932, the British *Daily Worker* could proudly indict the Trotskyists for their policy in Germany thus: 'It is significant that Trotsky has come out in defence of a united front between communist and social democratic parties against fascism. No more disruptive and counter-revolutionary class lead could possibly have been given at the time like the present.'

Meanwhile Trotsky had written four pamphlets and dozens of articles and manifestos; everywhere the international Trotskyists explored every avenue to exert pressure on the Comintern to change its policy. In vain. In January 1933 Hitler was enabled to take power without any organised opposition whatsoever in a country with the most highly organised working class and with the strongest Communist Party outside of Russia.

For the first time in history reaction was enabled to conquer power without any resistance on the part of the working class. The German CP numbered 6,000,000 supporters, the Social Democracy numbered 8,000,000 —together they were the mightiest force in Germany. By this betrayal, the German CP was doomed forever.

But the Comintern was far from recognising the nature of the catastrophe. Instead, it solemnly endorsed the policy of the German CP and of the International as having been perfectly correct. An organisation which cannot learn from the lessons of history is doomed. As a force for world socialism, the Communist International was dead. The International Left Opposition broke away and proclaimed the necessity of a new international. But what was apparent to the vanguard who had abandoned the attempt to reform the Comintern, could not be apparent to the broad masses. Only great events could teach them.

The Communist International continued to carry on this false policy right up to 1934. When the fascists in France, encouraged by the successes of fascism in Austria and Germany, conducted armed demonstrations for the overthrow of the Liberal government and parliament, the CP issued orders to demonstrate with them. But now the full danger which Hitler represented to the Soviet Union was apparent to everyone. Stalin and the bureaucracy became panic-stricken. Contemptuous and cynical of the capacity of the Comintern as an instrument of world revolution, Stalin more openly converted it into an instrument of Russian foreign policy.

An organisation in class society which ceases to represent the working class inevitably falls under the pressure and influence of the bourgeoisie. Stalin, in his search for allies, now turned to the bourgeoisie of Britain and France. The 'Popular Front' policy was initiated and endorsed at the last Congress of the International held in 1935.This policy of coalition with the Liberal capitalists is one against which Lenin had struggled all his life. It represented a new stage in the degeneration of the Comintern and the first workers' state.

With the rise of Hitler, again due to the policies of Stalin, the stranglehold of the bureaucracy within the Soviet Union was further increased. Higher over the Soviet masses has the bureaucratic caste raised itself and increased its power. But this progressive degeneration has had qualitative changes. From merely being incapable of insuring anything but defeats for the world working class, Stalinism has become opposed to the workers' revolution in other countries. The Moscow trials, the murder of the old Bolsheviks, the purges, the murder and exile of tens of thousands of the flower of the Russian communist workers, completed the Stalinist counter-revolution within the Soviet Union.

Events in France and Spain* are fresh in every revolutionary's mind. The Comintern played the main role in destroying the revolution which could have been accomplished. Indeed, it revealed itself as the fighting vanguard of the counter-revolution. The defeats of the world working class inevitably led to the new world war. Ironically, the war was ushered in by a pact between Hitler and Stalin. Thus Stalin dealt new blows to the world working class and the Comintern. It now executed a somersault and conducted a campaign for peace in the interests of Hitler, with a skilful counterfeit of a 'revolutionary' policy.

As Trotsky forecast in his prediction of the Stalin-Hitler agreement in an article written in March 1933:

> The fundamental trait of Stalin's international policy in recent years has been this: that he trades in the working-class movements just as he trades in oil, manganese and other goods. In this statement there is not an iota of exaggeration. Stalin looks upon the sections of the Comintern in various countries and upon the liberating struggle of the oppressed nations as so much small change in deals with imperialist powers. When he requires the aid of France, he subjects the French proletariat to the radical bourgeoisie. When he has to support China against Japan, he subjects the Chinese proletariat to the Kuomintang. What would he do in the event of an agreement with Hitler? Hitler, to be sure, does not particularly require Stalin's assistance to strangle the German Communist Party. The insignificant state in which the latter finds itself

---

*Popular front governments were elected in Spain in February 1936 and in France in June 1936. As in Spain, the French workers immediately moved into action, occupying factories, establishing workers' committees. In both countries the popular front government acted as a strike breaking force, in Spain opening the way for Franco's fascist uprising in July 1936.

has moreover been assured by its entire preceding policy. But it is very likely that Stalin would agree to cut off all subsidies for illegal work in Germany. This is one of the most minor concessions that he would have to make and he would be quite willing to make it. One should also assume that the noisy, hysterical and hollow campaign against fascism which the Comintern has been conducting for the last few years will be slyly squelched.

This policy of Stalin and the 'stinking corpse' of the Comintern suffered irretrievable ruin when the nazis invaded the Soviet Union. The Comintern had to execute a right about turn and convert itself once again into a doormat for Roosevelt and British imperialism. But with the increased dependence of Stalin on American and British imperialism, has come the increased pressure on the part of capitalist 'allies'. American imperialism especially has demanded the ending of the Comintern as a final guarantee against the danger of social revolution in Europe after the downfall of Hitler.

The long drawn-out pretence is over. Stalin has dissolved the degenerate Comintern. In doing so he openly announces his stepping over to the side of the capitalist counter-revolution as far as the rest of the world is concerned. But the imperialists, in forcing Stalin to make this trade in return for concessions and bargains on their part, have not understood the consequences this will have. It cannot and will not prevent the coming of new revolutions throughout the world. In the less than two decades since the beginning of its degeneration, the Comintern has ruined many favourable situations in many countries.

The coming decades will witness many revolutions with the breakdown and collapse of capitalism. Even the violently disturbed epoch of the period between the wars will seem comparatively tranquil compared to the period which lies ahead. On this background of storms and upheavals a real instrument of world revolution will be created. What the workers lacked in the last decades, outside Russia, was a workers' Bolshevik Party and a Bolshevik leadership. The great days of the Comintern of 1917-23 will live again. The growth in support for the ideas of Marxism internationally, based on the traditions of Bolshevism, the rich experience of the past, and learning the lessons of defeats of the working class, can once again lead the oppressed to the overthrow of capitalism and to the world socialist republic.

GERMANY

THE KEY TO THE INTERNATIONAL SITUATION

By LEON TROTSKY December, 1931

The background to the rise of Hitler
and the responsibility of the
Labour and Stalinist Leaders.

INTRODUCTION BY TED GRANT

6d.

*Front cover of the RCP edition of Trotsky's Germany the Key to the International
Situation, with Ted Grant's introduction.*

Why Hitler Came To Power

December 1944

THE IMMINENT defeat of Hitler raises many questions as to the past and future of Germany. According to the reports at the Quebec Conference*, *What to do with Germany* once she has been defeated has loomed large as the problem which is worrying the spokesmen of Anglo-American imperialism. They consider this to be as grave and thorny a problem as the destruction of German imperialist power itself. Their fears as to the possibility of maintaining control of Germany by means of Allied armies of occupation has led the imperialists to launch a virulent hate campaign. Now at the head of the gang, spewing forth the foul doctrines of racialism and nationalism, of indiscriminate hatred of the Germans as a nation, thus emulating the worst features of the racial doctrine of the nazis, stands the so-called Communist Party leadership. In the rear, but more cautiously, for fear of their own membership, the Labour leaders, faithfully echo the Vansittart** teaching of their imperialist master.

But the fate of Germany today, as it has been for many decades, remains a key question for the fate of Europe. The reason for the insistence of the ruling class and of Stalin on the formula of unconditional surrender, lies in their fear of the socialist revolution which is rapidly maturing within Germany. Once the heavy hand of the Gestapo and the SS has been removed there will be no organised force capable of maintaining the repression of the German masses. During the rule of Hitler, monstrous crimes and repressions on the part of the nazis have engendered a hatred which has few parallels in history. An enormous explosion is being prepared which threatens not only to blow the Nazi Party to

*Towards the end of the war a series of talks took place, one in Quebec (in 1943), between Churchill and Roosevelt on problems which would emerge for imperialism at the end of the war, especially in the Balkans, central Europe and Germany.
**Robert Vansittart, head of the Foreign Office, opposed the policy of appeasement towards Hitler, but primarily from an anti-German stance, while paying lip-service to anti-fascism.

smithereens but threatens the whole of the capitalist system itself. Every worker in Germany knows that it is the combines, monopolies, trusts and big capitalists who organised Hitler and placed him in control. As Rauschning*, the ex-nationalist, ex-nazi Gauleiter of Danzig has pointed out, the expropriation of the Jews leads inevitably to the posing of the problem of expropriation of all the capitalists. It is not for nothing that Hitler has attempted to give his demagogy a 'socialist' coloration. This reflects the aspirations not alone of the German workers but the overwhelming majority of the German population as a whole. In the past few decades all the forms of capitalist exploitation and political rule have been tried and found wanting. Inevitably the socialist revolution will be automatically posed with the fall of Hitler.

But this is precisely what the ruling class of Britain and America and the traitors in the Kremlin fear more than anything else. The spectre of a Geman revolution −of a new and this time *completed* 1918, is their main pre-occupation now that German militarism is in its death throes.

The instinct of the working class in the Allied countries is, while maintaining implacable hatred for fascism, to distinguish between the fascist thugs and the ordinary German worker. Profiting from their experience after the last world war when all the armies of occupation fraternised with the German masses (who easily convinced them that they were no different from themselves) the ruling class are attempting to place barriers in the way of its reoccurrence. The army staffs of both Britain and America have backed up the ideological campaign of chauvinist incitement by strict orders threatening punishment to any soldiers fraternising with German civilians.

The attitude of the British and American workers to the German workers can decide the fate of the coming German revolution and in so doing, will also decide whether there is to be a new version of fascism and imperialist World War Three. Under these conditions the necessity to enlighten the British masses as to the history and meaning of German events, at least since the last world war, becomes doubly important. It becomes necessary to restate the most elementary propositions of Marxism. Today, those traitors who point the finger of scorn at the German workers pretend that it is the fault of the German workers that Hitler came to power. They attempt to evade their own historic responsibility for this

---

*Hermann Rauschning was a capitalist who initially supported the nazis as opponents of the organised working class but then changed his position when the nazis became out of control, publishing a book, *We Never Wanted This*. In nazi Germany a Gauleiter was a district 'leader'.

catastrophe. In commenting on the murder of Thaelmann* the *Daily Worker* cynically says that he fought for the united front in Germany with all other working class organisations in order to destroy fascism. That is why it is all the more necessary to explain to the British and other workers exactly what did take place. The new generation, in particular, must understand the part Stalinism played in German events prior to Hitler's seizure of power, if they wish to understand its present role.

Thaelmann has been murdered by the nazis together with tens of thousands of other victims of the fascist barbarians. But it is necessary to speak the truth if there are to be no more victims of the system which produced Hitler. Now the Stalinists wish to use Thaelmann's martyrdom as a cover for their crimes against the German people. All the more necessary then, to show the role that Stalinism played in the rise of Hitler.

The truth of the matter is that the Stalinists devoted the major part of their energy to ridiculing the danger of the nazis and concentrated their whole attention on fighting the social democrats as the 'main enemy'. They fought viciously against Trotsky's suggestion that the united front was the only means of smashing Hitler and preparing the way for the victory of the working class. From the lips of Thaelmann himself we get the following:

> Trotsky wants in all seriousness a common action of the Communists with the murderer of Liebknecht and Rosa (Luxemburg), and more, with Mr Zoergiebel** and those police chiefs whom the Papen regime leaves in office to oppress the workers. Trotsky has attempted several times in his writings to turn aside the working class by demanding negotiations between the chiefs of the German Communist Party and the Social Democratic Party. (Thaelmann's closing speech at the 12th Plenum, September 1932, Executive Committee of the Communist International. (*Communist International* No 17-18, Page 1329.)

The Stalinists went even further, openly inciting the communist workers to beat up socialist workers, break up their meetings, etc, even carrying the fight to the school children in the very playgrounds! Thaelmann even put forward openly the slogan '*Chase the social fascists from their jobs in the plants and the trade unions.*' Following on this line of the leader, the Young Communist organ

---

*Ernst Thaelmann joined the German Communist Party in 1920, he became its leader with Stalin's support in 1925. Arrested by the nazis in 1933, he was murdered in 1944.

**Karl Zoergiebel was the Social Democratic commissioner of the Berlin police. Fritz von Papen was appointed Chancellor on June 1 1932. On July 20 he removed the Social Democratic government of Prussia. He became vice chancellor under Hitler.

The Young Guard propounded the slogan: *'Chase the social fascists from the plants, the employment exchanges, and the apprentice schools.'*

But the line has to be carried through to the end. In the organ of the Young Pioneers which catered for the communist children, the *Drum*, the 'unifying' slogan is put forward:

'Strike the little Zoergiebels in the schools and the playgrounds'.

Thaelmann Denounced the United Front

Thaelmann indignantly repudiated the very thought of a united front with the Social Democratic Party. In an article published in *Die Internationale,* —November, December 1931, page 488:

> It (the Social Democratic Party) threatens to make a united front with the Communist Party. The speech of Breitscheid* (whose murder was announced at the same time as Thaelmann's) at Darmstadt on the occasion of the Hesse elections and the comments of *Vorwaerts* on this speech show that social democracy by his manoeuvre is drawing on the wall the devil of Hitler's fascism and is holding back the masses from the real struggle against the dictatorship of finance capital. And these lying mouthfuls... they hope to make them more palatable with the sauce of a so-called friendship for the communists (against the prohibition of the German CP) and to make them more agreeable to the masses.

And again in a vehement attack on Trotsky:

> In his pamphlet on the question, *How will National Socialism be Defeated?*, Trotsky gives always but one reply: 'The German CP must make a bloc with the Social Democracy...' In framing this bloc, Trotsky sees the only way for completely saving the German working class against fascism. *Either the CP will make a bloc with the social democracy or the German working class is lost for 10-20 years.*
> This is the theory of a completely ruined fascist and counter-revolutionary. This theory is the worst theory, the most dangerous theory and the most criminal that Trotsky has constructed in the last years of his counter-revolutionary propaganda. (Thaelmann, closing speech at the 13th Plenum, September 1932: *Communist International*, No.17-18, page 1329.)

But it is not necessary to deal with the dupe. The founthead of this criminal policy was Joseph Stalin. He even put forward the nonsensical theory that the Socialist Party and the fascists were one and the same thing:

> Fascism, said Stalin, is the fighting organisation of the bourgeoisie,

*Rudolf Breitscheid (1876-1945) was a socialist deputy in the Reichstag. He fled to France when Hitler came to power and was handed over to the Nazis by the Vichy regime. *Vorwaerts* was the central organ of the SPD.

which rests upon the active support of the social democracy. Objectively, the social democracy is the moderate wing of fascism. There is no reason to admit that the fighting organisation of the bourgeoisie could obtain decisive successes either in the struggles or in the government of the country without the active support of the social democracy...There is also little reason to admit that social democracy can obtain decisive successes either in struggles or in the government of the country without the active support of the fighting organisation of the bourgeoisie. *These organisations are not mutually exclusive, but on the contrary are mutually complementary. They are not antipodes but twins.* Fascism is a shapeless bloc of these two organisations. Without this bloc the bourgeoisie could not remain at the helm. (Stalin, quoted in *Die Internationale*, February 1932.)

In carrying out this theory the wise Manuilsky* had explained at the 11th Plenum of the Communist International April 1931:

The social democrats, in order to deceive the masses, deliberately proclaim that the chief enemy of the working class is fascism...Is it not true that the whole theory of the 'lesser evil' rests on the presupposition that fascism of the Hitler type represents the chief enemy? (*The Communist Parties and the Crisis of Capitalism*, p. 112.)

It was with this revision of all the teachings of Lenin that the Communist Party of Germany, with the assistance of the social democracy, confused and paralysed the workers and then handed them over without a battle into the hands of the fascist executioner.

The British hypocrites who now slander the German workers applauded this policy of betrayal at the time when the revolutionary socialists were raising their voice all over the world in an effort to prevent the tragedy which was impending in Germany. 'It is significant', jeered the *Daily Worker* of May 26th, 1932, 'that Trotsky has come out in defence of a united front between the Communist and Social Democratic Parties against fascism. No more disruptive and counter revolutionary class lead could possibly have been given at a time like the present'.

At the eleventh hour, just before Hitler's coming to power, Ralph Fox wrote in the *Communist Review* of December 1932:

The Communist Party of Germany has now succeeded in winning the majority of the working class in the decisive industrial areas, where it is now the *first party* in Germany. The only exceptions are Hamburg and Saxony, but even here the Party vote has enormously increased at the expense of the social democrats.

These successes have been won only by the most unswerving carrying through of the line of the Party and the Comintern. Insisting all the

*Dimitri Manuilsky was secretary of the Comintern 1931-43.

time that social democracy is the chief social support of capitalism, the Party has carried on intense and unceasing struggle against the German Social Democratic Party, and the new 'Independent Socialist Labour Party', as well as against the right wing and Trotskyist renegades who wanted the party of the proletariat to make a united front with social fascism against fascism.

It is this suicidal policy of Stalinism against which Trotsky and the International Left Opposition waged a struggle in the critical years 1930-3 when the fate of Germany hung in the balance. Trotsky's works on Germany will remain forever as textbooks on the problem of the united front. They will serve as models for the revolutionary movement of the future. That we commence publication of Trotsky's material on this question in England for the first time, is a reflection on the revolutionary movement in Britain. Every student who desires an understanding of the degeneration of Stalinism will study this material with great care.

Even though *Germany —The Key to the International Situation* was written in 1931, it retains its freshness at the present time. The outline of the situation, not only in Germany, but in the other countries dealt with, indicates clearly Trotsky's profound understanding of the political process of development of our period. Trotsky and the Fourth International alone warned of the catastrophe that the coming to power of Hitler would mean for the workers of Germany, Europe and of the Soviet Union. When the Stalinists refused to learn the lesson of events, and in a most cowardly way, surrendered the German masses to Hitler without a fight, or even a shot being fired; when they even went so far as to proclaim the coming to power of Hitler as a *victory* for the working class —as it expressed the crisis of capitalism and his victory was merely that of the caliph of an hour, boastfully proclaiming 'our turn next' —it was then that Trotsky proclaimed the end of the Comintern as a force making for world socialism.

How pitiful, how despicable are the writings of the pen prostitutes of the Kremlin on Germany, when the real historical events are analysed. These Dutts*, these Rusts, these Ehrenburgs, not satisfied with having betrayed the German workers into the hands of the Nazis, now systematically disseminate chauvinist poison to the Allied workers in order to assist Anglo-American imperialism to enslave the German people. Having proved incapable of leading the German workers to victory, they now actively oppose the socialist revolution in Germany. Thus as always

*Prominent Stalinist publicists, Dutt and Rust of the British CP and Ehrenberg of the Russian bureaucracy.

in politics, ineptness and stupidity, if not corrected, become transformed into treachery.

The German and British workers will yet present their accounts not only to their imperialist oppressors but to their hirelings in the ranks of the working class. Once the working class realises the full depth of their treachery, like the traducers of the Commune, they will forever be held to scorn in the memory of the working class.

It would have been impossible to conceive that elements claiming to represent the working class should stoop to such depths as the Stalinists. From the social democrats nothing more could have been expected −they remained faithful to their past tradition of reformist betrayal. The Stalinists have often enough in the past referred to the murder of Liebknecht and Luxemburg and the betrayal of the revolution of 1918. But nothing in their record could equal the long list of crimes marked up to the account of Stalinism.

Surely, all the gods must have laughed at the spectacle of the Stalinist leaders solemnly intoning that it was necessary to 're-educate' the German workers −and their educators? Allied imperialism and Stalinism! Yes, re-education is necessary! Re-education of the ranks of the working class as to the role of the leadership of the organisations claiming to represent them. Re-education which will assist them to burn out the cancer of Stalinism and reformism which will lead the workers only to further catastrophe. In order to accomplish the task of 'educating' not only the German but the British and world workers, it is necessary that the advanced guard should be trained and armed with a knowledge of the Marxist method and of the history of past defeats. As an indispensible means of understanding the position in Germany today, it is necessary for the workers to conscientiously study the works of Trotsky. *Germany is still the key to the international situation* −with an understanding and with a knowledge of the past and future tasks we will go forward to the building of a new socialist world.

Front cover of the RCP pamphlet setting out their post-war policy (see The Changed Relationship of Forces).

Western Europe after the war

Introduction

FROM 1944, the RCP was the official British section of the Fourth International, the leadership of which, the International Secretariat (IS), was based in the United States during the war. Because of the nazi occupation, the British had been the only European section which had functioned openly in wartime, so that by the time the IS was re-established in Paris, it was the most developed section in the continent politically and one of the most developed organisationally.

The end of the war brought about an entirely novel situation in Europe, presenting the Marxists with difficult and unforeseen theoretical problems. The revolutionary wave in Western Europe did indeed manifest itself in the election of left governments and the strident demands of the workers for concrete reforms and social change. But the full impact of the workers' movement was blunted by the Communist and Socialist Party leaderships, acting as a brake on developments. The precise characterisation of the post-war regimes in Western Europe and the perspectives for these countries were the subjects of intense debate within the Trotskyist movement.

No less controversial were the developments in Eastern Europe. By far the greatest amount of conflict had occurred on the Eastern Front and Germany had only been defeated after a titanic struggle with the Red Army. But the end of the war left the Stalinist bureaucracy in effective occupation of half a dozen countries and a large slice of Germany and controversy soon developed over perspectives for Russia itself — whether the bureaucracy had been strengthened or weakened by the war — and the occupied states.

From the very beginning of its formation, the Revolutionary Communist Party had fundamental differences with the IS on their analysis on all these questions. The post-war leaders of the International were completely incapable of re-adjusting to the new situation and judging developments from a Marxist point of view. They clung dogmatically to the analysis that had been developed by Trotsky in the thirties, repeating sometimes parrot-fashion phrases and formulations which by 1945 were out-dated. Alone among all the Trotskyist groups, the RCP was able, under the theoretical guidance of Ted Grant especially, to apply the method of Marxism to come to terms with events and thus to broaden, deepen and extend the ideas worked out by Trotsky.

The first part of this chapter is a document entitled *The Changed Relationship of Forces in Europe and the Role of the Fourth International*. It was presented by Ted Grant as a policy document at the March 1945 Central Committee of the RCP, approved in August at the national conference and printed in *Workers International News* in September. The resolution presents a broad analysis, an estimation of the political situation coming out of the war and a tentative perspective for the future.

In relation to those parts of Europe occupied by the Red Army, the document was conditional because at this stage of developments it was not clear how events would unfold. It points out that the Stalinists had 'retained capitalism', but it also raises the possibility of the Russian bureaucracy becoming an agency of social change, albeit on the basis of a totalitarian state: 'the bureaucracy will be forced, against its own wishes and at the risk of antagonising its present imperialist allies, to nationalise industry in the permanently occupied countries, acting from above and, if possible, without the participation of the masses.' These developments are dealt with more fully in the next chapter on Eastern Europe.

More significantly, the resolution *The Changed Relationship of Forces*, for the first time acknowledged that there was a relative stabilisation in the political situation in Western Europe. Against the leadership of the IS, who were not prepared to face up to reality, the resolution argued that there had been, thanks to the role of the workers' leaders, a 'counter-revolution in a "democratic" form'. It was a counter-revolution in as much as the capitalist class had been able to ride out the revolutionary moods within the working class – 'given the weakness of the revolutionary vanguard...there is no hopeless position for the bourgeoisie' – but 'democratic' because of the weakness of reaction and the pressure of the mass organisations.

It is important to note that at this point, mid-1945, it was possible to anticipate a relative *political* stabilisation, although that was not to suggest that it would be permanent: 'It is possible on the basis of the support rendered to world imperialism by Stalinism and classical reformism (and this is one of the objective factors to be reckoned with) that world imperialism can succeed, for a period, in "stabilising" bourgeois-democratic regimes in certain countries.'

But what was not apparent at this stage, and could not be, was the fact that Europe, and the West in general, was on the threshold of an historic *economic* upswing which was to last 25 years. What the resolution explains, in effect, are the favourable political conditions which predicated the post-war boom.

The leadership of the International were still repeating old and out-dated ideas. Among such leaders was Pierre Frank, one of the leaders of the Parti Communiste Internationaliste (PCI), the French section of the International. He wrote an article, published in the June/July 1946 *Workers International News*, which argued that in Western Europe, there had been established only Bonapartist governments, ie 'Governments by the Sword', denying, in other words, that 'normal' capitalist democracy existed. The expression coined by the RCP resolution, that there had been a 'counter-revolution in a democratic form', was without meaning according to Frank.

Ted Grant's reply, published in the August 1946 *Workers International News*, and reprinted here for the first time, was a devastating critique of Frank's muddled and un-Marxist approach. To this day, the reply serves as a classic description of Bonapartism, and an explanation of the role of the state in capitalist society. In it, the ideas first put forward in *The Changed Relationship of Forces* are further developed. While the International leadership refused to face up to reality, the RCP inisted on what was increasingly a self-evident truth. that 'everywhere in Western Europe since the "liberation" the tendency has been for a steady movement towards bourgeois democracy', adding that '...at a later stage, this tendency will be reversed.'

This document was one of many major works that drew a line between the method and outlook of genuine Marxism and the increasingly petit-bourgeois and sectarian outlook of the IS. Although it is not the subject of this work, it is worth pointing out that the manoeuvres of the IS —because of its inability to answer the political criticisms of the RCP leadership —eventually led to splits and then the disintegration of the British section between 1947 and 1949. At that point Ted Grant and the British Marxists turned their backs on this international organisation. The fundamental differences in political outlook were never resolved and eventually the so-called Fourth International degenerated to the point where it was no more than an umbrella grouping of tiny ultra-left sects.

One organisation that took the post-war IS position to its logical, and absurd, conclusion was the IKD, an organisation of German and Austrian Trotskyists who had spent most of the war years in exile in Britain. It published a statement in 1943 (*WIN* April 1943), entitled *The National Question — Three Theses*, in which it argued that the occupation of Europe by nazi Germany had led to an economic 'regression', that is, to the destruction of technology and advanced methods of production, in favour of small and even handicraft techniques. At the same time, the democratic rights of the masses had been completely destroyed. The conclusion they drew was that the basic tasks in the post-war period would be the struggle for democracy, not unlike the capitalist revolutions of the nineteenth century. The fundamental aim of the post-war regimes, they argued, was 'basically equivalent to a democratic revolution'.

Further material published by IKD members (*WIN* July-August 1945) reiterated the same ideas adding, for example, that in 'liberated' France, 'the national oppression has remained, only the uniforms of the oppressors have changed.' This was answered by Ted Grant in *WIN* October 1945 (reprinted in *Militant International Review* number 26, Summer 1984). Another contribution by IKD members, published in *WIN* Sept-October 1946, was entitled *Two Balance Sheets*. This repeated, with minor modifications conceded under the pressure of RCP criticisms, the basic ideas already outlined in the *Three Theses*.

Extracts from a second reply by Ted Grant are included here as the third item in this chapter. This was first published in *Workers International News* in January-February 1947 and once again it explains the fundamental character of the revolutionary movement in Western Europe, notably in Greece and Germany, while at the same time pointing to the treacherous role played by the leaders of the mass workers' organisations.

The fundamental hostility that developed between the imperialist powers, dominated by the United States, and the 'soviet' bloc, dominated by Russia, were reflected in the post-war arms race and the so-called cold war. Nowhere was the hostility more clear than in the continued division of Germany. The areas occupied by British, French and American imperialism, on the one side, and the area occupied by the Red Army on the other, were becoming the de-facto, permanently separated states of West and East Germany.

In the British labour movement a controversy began over the question of West Germany's status within the defence agreements of the capitalist powers and especially over whether or not she should be allowed to re-arm. The NEC of the Labour Party, dominated by the right wing, published a statement in July 1954, entitled *In Defence of Europe*, in which it argued in favour of a German contribution within the structure of the European Defence Community. This proposal, for strengthening the armed forces of the capitalist states against the soviet 'threat', was dressed up in the language of 'reconciliation', 'partnership' and so on.

A month later, *Tribune,* then a paper of the left of the Labour Party, published a pamphlet replying to the NEC. It was written jointly by Aneurin Bevan, Barbara Castle, Tom Driberg, Harold Wilson, Ian Mikardo and Richard Crossman, and was called *It Need Not Happen.* It challenged the doctrine that German rearmament was inevitable and argued that within the context of NATO-Warsaw Pact rivalry, a re-armed West Germany, backed by the United States, would be facing a hostile and armed East Germany, backed by Russia. 'Once that is allowed to happen,' the Bevanites claimed, 'World War Three becomes inevitable.'

In a pamphlet published as *Socialism and German Unity*, Ted Grant polemicised against both the position of Labour's right wing and that of the Tribunite left. In particular, it attacked the idea, inherent in both left and right pamphlets, that the German working class were responsible for the war and that there was something inherently different about German (as opposed to French, British or American) capitalism that predisposed it to war. The pamphlet was reprinted in 1980, under the title *Socialism and German Rearmament,* (although wrongly dated as 1953) and extracts are reproduced here.

The last section in this chapter deals with the coming to power of General Charles de Gaulle in France in May 1958, on the back of a political crisis triggered by the beginning of the Algerian national war of independence. De Gaulle, irreverently nicknamed 'Big Asparagus', had been the leader of the 'Free French' government based in London during the war and had led the immediate post-war government. He was followed into office by a succession of unstable governments, the longest of only 16 months duration, reflecting the social crisis in France at the time.

Already by 1958, sections of the capitalist class were preparing to cut across the chronic instability of the French parliamentary government by a shift towards Bonapartism, with de Gaulle cast in the leading role. The general would then be given new

constitutional powers to form a 'strong government' to deal with
the trade unions.

The pretext for this constitutional coup arose over the war in
Algeria. On May 13, the reactionary officers in Algeria carried out
a coup, involving the occupation of the Ministry of Algeria and
other public buildings by paratroops. The officers announced the
formation of a 'Committee of Public Safety' under the
chairmanship of General Massu, commander of the crack
paratroops division. General Salan (Commander-in-Chief, Algeria)
announced on radio that the Army had 'provisionally taken over
responsibility for the destiny of French Algeria'.

From his chateau near Paris, General de Gaulle issued a
statement which, while avoiding any reference to Algeria, made it
clear that he was ready 'to assume the powers of the Republic'. To
keep up the pressure on the incumbent government of prime
minister Pflimlin (referred to at one point in the text by his
nick-name, 'Little Plum'), eight days later paratroops effected a
coup in Corsica, isolating the island from the government in Paris
and linking it to Algiers.

To the labour movement around the world, all these events
recalled the rebellion of General Franco —beginning in Spanish
Morocco —against the Spanish Popular Front government in July
1936. The difference was that the leaders of the French
Communist and Socialist Parties played an even more despicable
role than their counterparts had in Spain 22 years before.

Bearing in mind the end result of the Franco rebellion, it seemed
possible in May 1958 that there was a mortal threat against the very
existence of the workers' organisations in France. Yet in this
situation, the Communist Party refused to mobilise the enormous
support it had within the workers' movement against the
conspiracy of the officers, and the leadership of the Socialists even
supported the handing over of power to de Gaulle as a 'lesser evil'
compared to the generals.

The background to all these events was the subject of a pamphlet,
originally published as *France in Crisis*, written by Ted Grant and
completed only two days before de Gaulle was brought into office.
The pamphlet, extracts of which are published here, was reprinted
in 1980 as *The Rise of De Gaulle and the Class Struggle*. It represents a
further development from the writings on post-war Europe of
1944-8, again elaborating on the theme of Bonapartism.

As the pamphlet anticipated, de Gaulle's accession to power,
forming the twenty-sixth cabinet in 14 years, heralded the
development of constitutional changes in the direction of

Bonapartism. But what it also anticipated were the limits of Bonapartism. Unlike a fascist movement, which is based upon a mass movement of the frenzied petit bourgeois, a Bonapartist movement lacks a stable social base from the very beginning, and therein lies its relative weakness.

Because the power of the trade unions —despite their leadership —remained intact, de Gaulle was never able to assume full and unbridled dictatorial powers. He was always constrained by the pressure of the labour movement and so was not able to do more than hold in check the aspirations of the workers, until they burst into the open in the revolutionary events of May-June 1968.

When he first assumed power he appeased and promoted those who had been responsible for the officers' rebellion of May 1958. But he was nevertheless obliged at a later stage, because of the power of the labour movement, to clip the officers' wings. In typical Bonapartist fashion, after having leaned on the right to strike blows at the left, he now leaned on the left to strike blows to the right. In this way, he was able to extricate France from the unwinnable war in Algeria —against the wishes of the French settlers, the *colons* —and destroy a new generals' conspiracy in the form of the OAS, the Secret Army Organisation.

The pamphlet, *The Rise of De Gaulle*, with the earlier writings of 1944-7, is essential background material for understanding all the subsequent developments in post-war France. It must form part of any serious study of so-called 'Gaullism' or more general studies as to the development and role of Bonapartist regimes.

The Changed Relationship of Forces in Europe and the Role of the Fourth International

March 1945

THE END of the war opens out a new stage of the military, diplomatic, economic and political developments of the world.

The overwhelming economic and military preponderance of the Soviet Union in the East, and of American imperialism with her British satellite in the West, has finally resulted in the reduction of German and Japanese imperialism to dust.

Following in the wake of the victorious 'allied' armies, the 'big three' with their foreign secretaries and advisers meet, discuss, and arrive at secret diplomatic agreements to partition Europe and the world into spheres of influence and zones of exploitation. The satellite states are invited into the councils of the United Nations, but only to create a facade and lend weight to the decisions arrived at by the hard bargaining behind the scenes on the part of the big three.

Overshadowing the military and diplomatic arrangements, however, is the fear of proletarian revolution in Germany and in Europe as a whole; and not only in Europe but in the colonial areas of the East. This cardinal problem, which again and again raises itself for a forceful solution, is rapidly becoming the main preoccupation of the three big powers. Indeed, the cardinal point in the alliance which now cements the 'big three' together, and will do so in the future, is this fear of revolution and the preoccupation with the plans for staving off, or repressing the inevitable revolutionary upheavals in Germany and Europe which will seek to destroy the old capitalist order.

The changed relationship of forces between the world powers since the Treaty of Versailles, hidden in their gradual transformation between the two world wars, is now clearly demonstrated in the military fortunes of the nations.

The destruction of the French army, once the mightiest military force in Europe; the disintegration of the French empire; the miserable role of the ruling class in France during the nazi occupation as Quislings of the conqueror; all these have served to underline the decline of France from the status of a great power to the role of a third rate power in Europe and the world.

The bubble of empire pretensions, widely advertised by the Italian ruling class through their strutting black-shirted legions, has been pricked and shattered. The weak and insufficient economic base, incapable of the slightest strain, cracked at the first test. Italy is reduced to the role of a Balkan country.

Both in the East of Europe and the West, the war has entirely altered the importance of the nations in the new alignment of forces. Poland, Czechoslovakia, the Baltic and Balkan countries, Belgium, Holland, and the Scandinavian lands —all these have a lesser weight and role to play in the 'councils of the nations'.

The collapse of British hegemony of the globe; the inability of Britain to maintain her position on the continent of Europe or to intervene decisively in the military struggles; the subordination of her military leaders on the continent of Europe to those of her Yankee patrons; and her general decline in relation to her Russo-American allies is rapidly placing Britain in her real relationship to the other powers —the 'biggest of the small nations'.

The entry into the world arena of American imperialism with her gigantic economic and military resources, has immediately placed her far in the forefront of the imperialist nations. Both in the East and in the West, the weight of the economic and military forces assures her of a dominant position. The Pacific is fast becoming an 'American lake', while the British dominions gravitate towards the dollar and remain only nominally tied to the motherland.

The Emergence of Russia From The War

But by far the greatest event of world significance is the emergence of Russia, for the first time in history, as the greatest military power in Europe and Asia. The tremendous victories of the Red Army in Europe have forced the majority of the European bourgeoisie to orientate themselves towards the Kremlin; whilst the pro-Soviet movement on the part of the masses, has created a powerful basis of support.

In Europe today there is no continental power left which can effect a challenge to the Red Army. Nor is it possible to create in a few years a military force capable, materially and morally, of undertaking such a challenge. Only on the basis of a complete defeat for the

European working class, the total destruction of its organisations and the introduction of a Yankee black reaction, would it be possible to regroup the forces of European capitalism for an anti-Russian assault.

The weariness of the masses in all countries, especially in Europe, the admiration and support for the Red Army, the sympathy and warm support for the Soviet Union among broad sections of the working class even in the United States —all these factors taken together with the relation of military forces, make it extremely difficult, if not entirely impossible for the Allies to launch an attack on the Soviet Union in the immediate post-war years.

The risks of such an operation are far too great in their political implications, not only in Europe or Asia where the masses would support the Soviet Union, but in Britain and America. Ideologically it would not be possible to mobilise the masses for such a war which would tend to expose the whole nature of the previous struggle against the Axis*. Moreover, such a war would be inevitably protracted because of the military might of the Soviet Union, thus ushering in revolutionary explosions throughout the globe. For the next period, despite the antagonisms, the Allies will be forced to tolerate a deal with the Soviet Union.

The Plans of the Imperialists Went Wrong.

German imperialism confidently anticipated the destruction and disintegration of the Soviet state; the Anglo-American imperialists expected and hoped for the downfall of the Soviet Union, but wished to use Russia simultaneously to break the power of German imperialism, leaving them the victors. They expected at least that the Soviet Union would emerge broken and weakened decisively and thus be unable to resist the demands and impositions they planned to impose upon her.

But their calculations went wrong. An outstanding result of the imperialist war is the definitive emergence of the Soviet Union from a backward state, to the greatest military power on the continent of Europe. This has upset all the calculations of the imperialists of both camps. The results have induced a cold sweat in all the chancelleries of the world.

The war in Europe in great part resolved itself into a war between Germany, armed with the resources of the whole of Europe, and the Soviet Union. And from this decisive test Russia has emerged victorious.

The Stalinist bureaucracy has a two-fold purpose in occupying

*The coalition of Germany, Italy and Japan which originated in 1936.

the countries of Eastern Europe: a strategic defence position against its allies; and the domination, plunder and enslavement of the Balkan and Central European peoples in the interests of the bureaucracy itself. However, the entrance of the Red Army into Eastern Europe provoked a movement among wide strata of the oppressed workers and peasants. The Stalinist bureaucracy has utilised this movement in order to place their puppets firmly in control of the governments. Meanwhile, in order to placate his allies, Stalin has retained capitalism in the areas under his control which have not been incorporated into the Soviet Union, while making concessions in land reforms to the peasants.

Another reason for the retention of capitalism in the occupied areas lies in the fear of the bureaucracy of the inevitable repercussions of setting in motion the forces of the proletarian revolution, even in caricature form in the Balkans and throughout the continent of Europe. The highly explosive situation would mean the spreading of the movement beyond the control of the bureaucracy and would threaten to have tremendous repercussions on the Red Army and the workers and peasants of the Soviet Union.

Thus, the occupation of Germany and Eastern Europe serves, for the bureaucracy, a dual purpose. It aims at defending the Soviet Union by methods which serve the reactionary aims and needs of the Stalinist bureaucracy. Such methods have nothing in common with, in fact are the negation of, Leninism. In relation to the European revolution the Soviet occupation is intended for the purpose of strangling and destroying the revolution of the proletariat.

With the fall of German imperialism the defence of the Soviet Union, which formerly assumed the first importance in the tasks of the proletariat of the Soviet Union in relation to the war, now gives place to the defence of the European revolution against the Soviet bureaucracy. The Red Army is used as a weapon of counter-revolution in the hands of the Bonapartist bureaucracy. For the European proletariat the counter-revolutionary policy of the Stalinist bureaucracy assumes the form of a mortal danger.

Nevertheless, the situation is fraught with mortal danger to the Stalinist bureaucracy. Inevitably the Red Army workers and peasants will fraternise with the workers and peasants of the conquered countries. The soldiers will see the complete falsity of the propaganda of the bureaucracy as to conditions in other countries compared with those in Russia.

In general it can be said that in the coming period *either* the retention of capitalism in the countries of Eastern and Central Europe occupied by the USSR will serve as a starting point for the restoration of capitalism within the Soviet Union itself by providing the bureaucracy with the opportunity of acquiring the ownership of the means of production; *or* the bureaucracy will be forced, against its own wishes and at the risk of antagonising its present imperialist allies, to nationalise industry in the permanently occupied countries, acting from above and, if possible, without the participation of the masses.

The Fourth International, while explaining the nature of the Soviet Union and the necessity of its defence from world imperialism, will expose the counter-revolutionary role of the bureaucracy in relation to the European and world revolution. At the next stage the main task in the defence of the Soviet Union lies in the defence of the European revolution against the conspiracy of the Stalinist bureaucracy with world imperialism. Where the Red Army, which remains under the control of the bureaucracy as an instrument of its policy, is used to crush and destroy the movement of the masses towards revolution, or in the supression of workers' uprisings and insurrections, the Fourth International will call on the workers to oppose the Red Army with all the means in their power, including strikes, armed force, etc, while appealing to the Red Army soldiers to remember the mission of October and come over to the side of the working class. The defence of the Soviet Union can best be served by an extension of October, and the revival of soviet democracy within the Soviet Union.

The Great Russian Stalinist bureaucracy stifles the national aspirations of the national minorities within the Soviet Union. While subordinating the struggle for independence to the defence of the Soviet Union, the Revolutionary Communist Party stands for the *right* of the Ukrainian, Baltic and other Soviet minorities to secede from the Stalinist Soviet Union and form independent socialist states. But the secession is a reactionary utopia unless it is conceived of as part of a struggle for soviet democracy, the overthrow of Stalinism, and for the unification of the democratised USSR with the United Socialist States of Europe.

During the course of the war the separation of the bureaucratic caste from the masses and its elevation above them, has received tremendous impetus. Nothing remains of the gains of October except the basic conquest: nationalised property. Power has passed from the hands of the civil bureaucracy to the military bureaucracy with the galaxy of marshals at its head. Contradictory processes are taking place in the Soviet Union. On the one hand the course of the war has accelerated the proletarianisation of new strata of the population, of women and even children. Thus, the Soviet proletariat today cannot be far short of the number of proletarians in the United States. On the other hand, the differentiation between the bureaucracy and the masses, assumes more and more a capitalist character. Thus, two opposite tendencies are revealed. The capitalist tendencies look more and more to the capitalist West, the vices of which the Soviet bureaucracy has completely assimilated. The Soviet masses are well aware of the crimes of the bureaucracy, of whom they have an intense hatred. The victorious workers, peasants and soldiers will present their account to the Soviet bureaucracy on the morrow. The victories of the Red Army cannot but have imbued the Soviet masses with a tremendous elan and self-confidence. They will not so easily acccept the impositions and excuses of the bureaucracy once the danger from capitalist intervention has declined. The war and the Herculean struggle have thrust the mass of the population out of their despair and apathy. The war has been the means of revolutionising Soviet society no less than that in capitalist countries.

The victories of the Soviet Union are a capital for the world revolution, both in the effects on the masses in Europe and the world, as well as in their preservation of nationalised economy. But it is necessary for the working classes to understand the dual, contradictory process.

On the one hand the victories of the Red Army arouse echoes of the October revolution in the European masses; on the other hand the bureaucracy uses the Red Army and its agencies —the Communist Parties — for the purposes of strangling the proletarian revolution.

From a purely economic point of view, even with bureaucratic excesses and the stifling of the initiative of the masses, the Soviet Union will probably be in a position to restore production within a few years, to the level achieved before the war. Further economic successes could be maintained, but that is not to say that the war has not had profound effects upon Soviet economic life, or that post-war economic developments in the Soviet Union will take place smoothly and without crises. During the past four years the whole economy has been adapted to an almost exclusive production of war equipment. The remarkable productive results which have been obtained, have been won only at great cost —the wearing out of machinery, the elimination of consumers' industries, the physical exhaustion of the workers. Consequently in the future, we can expect sharp crises arising out of the disproportions inside the Soviet economy; crises such as occurred in the pre-war years and which no amount of 'planning' by the bureaucracy can overcome, since they are basically due to the fact that the nationalised economy of the Soviet Union is an isolated and not a world economy.

The already existing disproportions between the various branches of Soviet economy, between light and heavy industry, between industry and agriculture, have all been greatly accentuated as a result of the war. In particular the position of agriculture, which had even by 1941 not yet completely recovered from the ravages of the period of forced collectivisation and which has been largely devastated by the present war, will pose problems not capable of final solution within the framework of the isolated economy of the Soviet Union.

But nevertheless, the advantages of the nationalised economy are such, that despite those economic contradictions, and within their framework, great productive achievements are possible upon a scale and at a speed far beyond the powers of even the most advanced capitalist states.

The differentiation within the Soviet Union has reached such proportions that the perspectives resolve themselves into three possibilities:

1. It is theoretically not excluded that on the basis of an ascending economy, the bureaucracy could maintain itself for a further period of years;

2. The further degeneration of the Soviet bureaucracy would prepare the way for capitalist restoration;

3. The proletarian resurgence would result in the overthrow of the bureaucracy and the restoration of Soviet democracy.

The bourgeoisie of the world, and above all Anglo-American imperialism, is staking everything on the internal degeneration taking place within the Soviet Union. Through economic pressure from without and the reaction within, they are hoping to restore capitalism in the USSR. On the basis of the victory of the reaction in Europe and Asia, they hope eventually to restore capitalism, if necessary by military means. Meanwhile, despite sharp clashes, they are compelled to defer the settlement of this account and to utilise the services of the Kremlin to strangle the revolution, which directly and immediately threatens the very existence of capitalism in Europe and Asia. Thus the bourgeoisie utilise the services of the bureaucracy today in the hour of mortal danger of capitalism, in order to strangle the Soviet Union when the crisis has been surmounted.

But despite the proportions to which the bureaucracy has grown, the situation presents favourable factors for the resuscitation of workers' power. The economic conquests are in contradiction with the stranglehold of the bureaucracy, which becomes an increasing burden on the economy of the country. The power of the traditions of October, even overlaid as it is with the bureaucratic filth, has been shown in the war. Coming events will reveal many surprises for the world bourgeoisie as well as for the Stalinist bureaucracy. Collective ownership, which has revealed its superiority in peace as in war, now finds itself in sharper conflict with the bureaucracy. It will be in the *political crisis* which the aftermath of the war will bring, that the full weakness of the bureaucracy will be shown. Collisions between the workers and peasants, between the soldiers demanding the fruits of victory and the usurpers, are inevitable. It is in these clashes that the mighty Soviet proletariat, and its vanguard the Fourth Internationalists, with its tradition of three revolutions and two victorious wars, will find itself once again.

The National Question in Europe

Despite the ease with which the nazi war machine overran all Europe, but a few years were needed to reveal that the conquest was illusory. The nazis were incapable of holding down the suffering peoples for whom the conquest meant intensified poverty and famine, on top of the insufferable burden of a totalitarian alien yoke. Without a clear class programme as the basis of their struggle, and at the cost of innumerable victims, the masses still succeeded in undermining the nazi domination of Europe.

The ruling class of the conquered countries, willingly or unwillingly, joined hands with the nazi overlords and became managers and junior partners of the conquerors. The champions of 'national dignity' and 'national unity' in the hour of defeat, united with the oppressor against the mass of their own nation. Class interests, like water, find their own level.

If the nazis succeeded with the aid of Quislings, backed by the SS with its torture and terror, in maintaining a precarious hold for a time, this was due to the assistance rendered them by the policies of social democracy and Stalinism. The appeal to national chauvinism could not but aid the German imperialists to draw the German worker and peasant behind them in the 'struggle between the races'; it could not but act as a national cement for the nazi gangsters and the German bourgeoisie. Faced with the choice between national enslavement of others, or themselves becoming nationally enslaved, the German soldiers continued to act as forces of occupation, no doubt with bitterness in their hearts. An internationalist socialist appeal from the mass illegal organisations of the working class, or from the leadership of the Soviet Union, and a systematic campaign of class fraternisation would have echoed, and had results in the far corners of the German Reich and nazi empire. But such an appeal was never made. Systematic class fraternisation and action was never organised.

Our Attitude to the Resistance Movements

Organised resistance to the foreign oppressor was initiated by the Stalinists, social democrats, petty bourgeois parties and sections of the bourgeoisie. Within the heterogeneous groups which formed the resistance, the class contradictions and antagonisms found sharp and organised expression, and in some countries came to the point of civil war.

In Poland, Yugoslavia and in Greece, the sharp division resulted in dual and rival movements of resistance. Zervas* and EDES were representative of the old feudal capitalist reaction, who at certain stages even rested upon the nazis as against Tito and Siantos, who in turn represented the plebian masses. To a lesser extent, this same division was to be found in all the occupied countries; as in France, with the Maquis and the FTP.

In the clashes and armed struggles which took place from time to time, the 'left' wing, or elements of the resistance resting directly on the revolutionary sections of the people, were forced under the pressure of class antagonisms into collisions with the elements representing the bourgeoisie. Despite the 'national', non-class policy of betrayal by the leadership, the movement represented the strivings and pressure of the masses for a class solution, thus, the revolutionary socialists were duty bound to give critical support to the left wing against the right.

But even the left wing of the resistance movement was not based on broad committees, but on an agreement of the parties. As such it was a bloc of parties, and particularly in face of the Quisling role of the bulk of the bourgeoisie, it was a caricature of the popular front. Despite the support of thousands of loyal proletarian fighters, who saw in these left sections of the resistance movement an answer to their class aspirations, the chauvinist petty bourgeois programme, leadership and activity of the resistance bloc, characterised it as a direct agency of imperialism.

---

*Napoleon Zervas was the head of EDES (Greek Democratic National League) which while participating in resistance against the nazis, became a tool of British imperialism and Greek monarchists in the civil war of 1944-49. George Siantos was head of the KKE (Greek Communist Party) 1942-5. Tito (Josip Broz) led the partisan resistance to the occupation of Yugoslavia. The Yugoslav CP broke with Moscow in 1948 (see *Reply to David James* later in this volume). The Maquis were the resistance fighters in the provincial areas of occupied France, while the FTP were the CP-led underground operating mainly in urban areas.

In the midst of the imperialist war, all the objective conditions are such that a genuine struggle for national liberation and a break-up of the alliance with imperialism, could only have been undertaken on the basis of a socialist programme, under the slogan of the Socialist United States of Europe. Organised struggle on any other basis, on the policy of both wings of the resistance was to aid one bloc of imperialists in the midst of the war.

The Trotskyists, therefore, could not dip their banner by entering into the bloc of parties and support this caricature popular front. Whilst supporting and where possible, giving leadership to every real move of the masses: strikes, demonstrations, and armed clashes, the Trotskyists had the duty to denounce the resistance bloc as such, and its leadership as an arm and agency of Anglo-American imperialism, hostile to the class interests of the working class.

In opposition to the military formations of the bourgeois and petty bourgeois-inspired resistance movement the proletarian party has the duty to counterpose, and wherever possible, to organise independent military formations of the working class as well as its own independent military formations.

Implacable hostility to the 'resistance bloc' is supplemented by flexible tactics in the operation of party policy. The organisations of the resistance were important fields for revolutionary activity. The revolutionary party had the duty to send its cadres into the resistance movements counterposing a proletarian to a bourgeois and petty bourgeois programme, helping to destroy the influence of the bourgeoisie over militant sections of the working class, and organising a conscious proletarian opposition to the policy of chauvinism and the chauvinistic leaders.

The 'liberation' of the continent by Anglo-American imperialism posed the problem of the class struggle in an acute form. With the lifting of the heavy hand of totalitarian suppression by German imperialism, the national question tended to be thrust into the background. Only a prolonged military occupation over a period of years by the forces of Anglo-American imperialism and of the Stalinist bureaucracy, could raise the national question to an important place in the politics of the European continent. The indirect oppression and exploitation by the big three powers, the military intervention on the side of the old ruling class against the proletariat would tend rather to raise the *class issues* in the consciousness of the European peoples. It is in the case of Germany that the national problem will assume an acute character with the dismemberment and subjugation of Germany by the Allies.

Classic Conditions for the Proletarian Revolution

The majority of the European bourgeoisie, which has already been badly shaken by the great mass movements of a few years preceding the outbreak of the war, proved incapable of leading the nations which they had summoned to the 'defence of the fatherland'. Further demoralised by the military defeat, without perspective, and filled with hatred for their own working class, almost the entire ruling class of the conquered countries fraternised with the enemy and organised the joint exploitation together with the foreign oppressor, of the mass of their own nation. Thus, as Quislings they earned the hatred of the overwhelming mass of the workers and petty bourgeoisie.

The victory of the Allies now finds the bourgeoisie seeking to play the same role for the 'liberators' as they did for the 'conquerors'. Without stable organs of state oppression, panic-stricken in the face of the mounting wrath of the masses, demoralised and without that confidence which is essential to an exploiting ruling class, they are completely dependent on allied bayonets for the continuation of their rule.

At the other pole, the mass of the working class no longer wants the old regime. The experience of a generation of capitalist rule since the last world war, plus a demonstration of the role of their own ruling class under the nazi occupation; unemployment and starvation, fascism and national humiliation; the recognition that whilst the masses carried the struggle against the foreign oppressor, the ruling class collaborated and enriched themselves; and finally, the gigantic victories of the Red Army with all its associations with the October revolution —all these factors have resulted in a transformation of the outlook of the working masses.

The workers of Europe are breaking with bourgeois parliamentary politics and social democratic reformism and are turning to revolutionary politics and communism —unfortunately at this stage to the Stalinist parties, its caricatured and distorted form.

Total war and the defeat accelerated the concentration of capital and the ruination of the middle class especially in the towns. In their hundreds and thousands the petty bourgeoisie has been rudely pushed down into the ranks of the workers. They have been forced into the factories and slave labour camps; they have been proletarianised. On the background of working class radicalisation a corresponding change has taken place within the ranks of the petty bourgeoisie.

As always, the most oppressed strata of the population — the women and the youth — have had to bear the greatest burdens of the war, and here too, particularly among the youth the desire for a radical change and a communist solution of the problems of the day has taken a firm hold.

Thus all the *objective* conditions for the overthrow of capitalism and the introduction of socialism are clearly in existence. But the *subjective* factors are not yet established. The mass revolutionary parties of the Fourth International have not yet been created. To transform the small Trotskyist groups and parties into the fighting leadership of the working class is the most important question facing our comrades in Europe. Without mass Trotskyist parties the masses, blindfolded by social democracy and particularly by Stalinism will batter their heads in vain against the ramparts of capitalism.

Only the numerical weakness of the cadres of the Fourth International and the isolation of our comrades, gives the ruling class the possibility of a breathing space. The leadership of the bourgeoisie is aware of its own class needs, despite its demoralisation. They must at all costs crush the working class; but they lack the forces to do so at the moment.

The Experience of Greece.

The events in Greece* marked the beginning of a new phase of revolution and counter-revolution within Europe. In this tiny country, where the explosive force of centuries of class antagonism has accumulated and which has been in turmoil for three decades, civil war broke out and was followed by a ruthless and brutal *war of intervention* by the British imperialists.

In the conflict between royalists and republicans during the past generation, the bourgeoisie, incapable of taking decisive action against the feudal landlords, were equally incapable of solving the problems of the democratic revolution and invariably paved the way for monarchist reaction. The restoration of King George** was followed by the dictatorship of

*The German occupation of Greece collapsed in early October 1944, in the face of a full scale war of liberation waged by the Greek workers and peasants organised in ELAS (Greek National Liberation Army), the military wing of the CP-led EAM (National Liberation Front). British troops were only landed after the German forces had evacuated Athens, with the aim of reestablishing the Greek monarchy and preventing power remaining in the hands of the armed masses. Civil war broke out in December 1944 when the British forces began to disarm ELAS. An armistice was signed in February 1945, but the civil war reerupted from 1946 until 1949, leaving 158,000 dead.
**King George II was king of Greece 1913-24. Restored to the throne in 1935, he made Ioannis Metaxas premier. Metaxas assumed dictatorial powers from 1936-41.

Metaxas in an endeavour to restore 'tranquility' and class 'peace'. This 'experiment' was aimed at atomising the Greek working class and peasant movement which threatened to upset the old regime and move in the direction of socialist revolution —as indicated by the strikes of the workers and revolts of sections of the peasantry. The British imperialists, whose financial and strategic interests forced them to regard Greece as a sub-colony, assisted the Greek ruling class in carrying out this reactionary move.

The viciousness of the Metaxas dictatorship had already undermined the basis of the Greek ruling class and created a popular movement of revolt before the war. But the collaboration of the Greek ruling class with the German conqueror as Quislings crystallised the hostility of the masses and thus generated the explosion once the German troops had been withdrawn.

The attempt to foist the old ruling class and even the monarchy upon the masses was not to be tolerated without a struggle. The masses, who had fought a ruthless and bloody war against the S.S. had been largely responsible for the liberation of Greece. *De facto* control was in their hands through the armed organisation, ELAS. Thus, the provocation of the Greek government police in firing on unarmed demonstrators was sufficient to precipitate the armed uprising. Without preparation, organisation, or a clear idea of how to achieve their aims, the valiant Greek proletariat and peasantry went into action. But due to the lack of a revolutionary leadership, the struggle was defeated.

The Stalinist leadership diverted the movement into safe channels on the familiar pattern of the peoples' front, and the movement's social aims were placed in the straight jacket of bourgeois parliamentarism. Thus the ground was laid for defeat and capitulation on the part of the Stalinist leadership.

Once again, the Greek events demonstrated that without a revolutionary party the masses will be led to disaster especially when the class struggle leads to open civil war. Without the party the masses cannot achieve the conquest of power.

However, leaving aside the local peculiarities, Greece represented in itself a model of the problems and lessons for all Europe. Churchill's policy of unrelenting repression was dictated by considerations of imperialist strategy as much as by internal class relationships. With the Stalinist bureaucracy dominant throughout the Balkans by the occupation of the victorious Red Army, it was essential for Britain's imperialist interests in the Mediterranean to have a firm hold over Greece. Even so, in Greece, the imperialists have received an object lesson on the difficulties of an open policy of military repression in Europe. The most sober and realistic section of the ruling class in Britain was opposed throughout to the blundering, adventuristic policy of repression of Churchill. Even in a small country of six million inhabitants, the dangers of such a course of action were revealed by the development of events. British imperialism was compelled to compromise with the petty bourgeois traitors in the leadership of EAM.

The Plastiras* government and its successor the Vulgaris government represent an uneasy attempt to restore the equilibrium of bourgeois society in Greece. Elements of Bonapartism and military dictatorship are undoubtedly present in this set-up. Nevertheless, the compromise arrrived at with the capitulation of the Stalinist leadership, in however attenuated a form (due to the struggle of the masses and the uneasiness of the British proletariat), has left the masses with their organisations, though not completely intact, still far from being destroyed.

This uneasy balance of forces cannot last indefinitely. Either the monarchy will be restored which would inevitably lead to a systematic extermination of the organisations of the proletariat, or the reaction might still feel itself too weak and attempt to manoeuvre with a republic. Even with the latter, however, the present regime could not last long. An impulsion from below would inevitably sweep it aside and the bourgeoisie would attempt to manipulate the political scene again through its popular front agencies. However, developments in Greece will depend to a great extent on events in Western Europe, the Balkans and Britain. Only one thing is predetermined: for the next period the regime in Greece will go through one crisis after another.

The Counter-Revolution in a 'Democratic' Form.

Greece has revealed the heat lightning of the revolutionary storm gathering in Europe. The bourgeoisie of the entire world has assessed these events in correct perspective. The basis of the old system has broken down throughout the whole of ruined Europe. *The disappearance of Hitler and Mussolini means the end of a stable basis for reaction* in Europe, at least for the next immediate period.

---

*General Nicholas Plastiras of the National Progressive Union became the Prime Minister of the puppet pro-British regime in December 1944. Admiral Vulgaris, Commander of the Greek Fleet, was responsible for crushing an anti-fascist mutiny on ships in Alexandria harbour, April 1944. He took over from Plastiras in April 1945.

Under conditions of ferment and radicalisation of the masses, with the rebelliousness of the masses turning directly on the road of insurrection; with the thrice-ruined petty bourgeoisie turning away in hatred and disgust against the combines and monopolies, from the influence of capitalist reaction, the task of Anglo-American imperialism to restore 'order' to Europe, to establish the rule of capital, assumes the shape of complicated and dexterous manoeuvres. To bludgeon the masses will be difficult at this stage and it will be necessary to deceive them with the panaceas of 'progress', 'reforms', 'democracy', as against the horrors of totalitarian rule. In Europe, however, control of the situation has largely slipped out of the hands of the bourgeoisie. It is the mass organisations of the working class which will have the decisive say.

With the fall of Mussolini, the instant appearance of soviet forms of organisation organised by sections of the workers, soldiers and peasants marked the appearance of the proletariat once more on the political arena. Here too, dual power in its elementary stages was immediately apparent. But once again, the main hindrance and drag on the development of the revolution has been the policy of the old workers' parties. The consciousness of the masses is still at an elementary stage; they do not want capitalism and the old regime and have aspirations to follow the example of the Russian workers in the October revolution. But as yet they do not understand the role of the old workers' parties as brakes on the development of the struggle; as yet they do not understand the need for a mass Trotskyist party.

The whole of Western Europe presents a picture of revolutionary crises in their embryonic stages. The lifting of the heavy hand of totalitarian suppression revealed the forces that have been developing beneath the surface. In Belgium, Holland and even Scandinavia the same process of mass resistance to the oppression and the estrangement from the emigre cliques of the old 'governments' is plainly seen.

Eastern Europe presents a similar picture of the development of the molecular process of the revolution. The heroic insurrection of the Warsaw workers* at the approach of the Red Army even though distorted and misled by the London Committee, is

---

*In August 1944, the Warsaw workers rose up against the occupying German army. Within two days they controlled the city. However, the Russian army which was within 15 miles of Warsaw, having been checked by the German army, made no attempt to advance for several weeks, leaving the workers to fight alone. Stalin described the rising as a 'reckless adventure', and a 'mindless brawl led by adventurers'. After 63 days of heroic resistance, which left 93 per cent of the city destroyed and 240,000 Poles dead, the nazis regained control. The London Committee was the Polish government in exile from 1940.

indicative of the mood of the masses of Poland. The calculated betrayal of Warsaw by the Stalinist bureaucracy underlined the counter-revolutionary role which it played in Europe and the world.

It would be true to say that faced with mass revolutionary parties of the working class in Europe, the position of the bourgeoisie would be hopeless. But given the weakness of the revolutionary vanguard, as Lenin explained, there is no hopeless position for the bourgeoisie. Social democracy saved capitalism after the last war. Today there are two traitor 'internationals' at the service of capital —Stalinism and social democracy. They, together with the leadership of the trade union organisations which sprung up once again immediately the pressure of the nazis was lifted, offer themselves as hirelings of capital.

The SS found it an impossible task to control Europe. After their experience, the bourgeoisie realises the impossibility of controlling the masses by similar means at this stage of reawakening. They find a ready and willing tool in the shape of the social democratic and Stalinist organisations to dam the revolutionary upsurge of the masses into safe and harmless channels of class collaboration through an even more degenerate form of popular frontism than existed in the past. Thus, they will combine repressions with illusory reforms. Smashing the embryo organs of workers' rule and disarming the masses, while simultaneously proclaiming their desire for 'representative' government and 'democratic' liberties. There is no other way whereby they can curb the upsurge of the masses towards the overthrow of the capitalist system. True, the counter-revolution of capital in its early stages, will, within a short period of time following the establishment of military government, assume a 'democratic' form. The bourgeoisie will combine the granting of illusory concessions with reprisals and repressions against the revolutionary forces.

The approaching revolution in Europe can be no other than the proletarian revolution. However, in its early stages it is inevitable that the old organisations of the proletariat should succeed in placing themselves at the head of the masses. The masses will learn only through a new experience, however brief, that these organisations represent the interests of the class enemy. And while absolutely clear on *what they do not want,* the masses are not clear about the means by which to achieve their ends. *Thus, all the factors make for a period of Kerenskyism* in the first stages of the revolution in Europe.*

Anglo-American imperialism perceives the inevitability of the fall

---

*From the government of Alexander Kerensky which was in power in Russia from July to October 1917, containing various combinations of reformist and capitalist parties.

of Franco and with it revolutionary disturbances throughout the Iberian Peninsular once Hitler has disappeared from the scene. With the discontent of the masses increasing, Anglo-American imperialism is already negotiating and manoeuvring with sections of the Spanish bourgeoisie, with Franco and with emigre politicians for the purpose of heading off the revolutionary insurrection of the masses. An insurrection in Spain threatens to have too serious effects in the rest of Europe. Hence their search for a Spanish Badoglio* to ensure a 'safe' and 'peaceful' transition from the doomed Franco regime. Whether their efforts are successful or not, the movement of the masses can only be temporarily delayed thereby. However, the serious representatives of finance-capital have learned far more from the experiences of the past decades than the perfidious 'leaders' of the working class. To them the problem of transition from one regime to another is determined by how best the interests of the ruling class can be served and safeguarded.

It is clearly impossible for the bourgeoisie of Britain and America to impose an alien totalitarian yoke on the peoples of Europe for any length of time. Especially important in this connection is the role of the Kremlin. While deadly afraid of the victory of the proletarian revolution, the Kremlin is interested in preserving, wherever possible, the maximum freedom of movement for their agencies, the local Communist Parties. The victory of reaction throughout Europe spells a new and greater danger of imperialist intervention against the Soviet Union on a continental scale. Thus, the policy of the Soviet bureaucracy is that of *ensuring the rule of capital, but with the existence of the workers' movement as a safeguard against the bourgeoisie.* The broad mass of the peoples of Europe look towards the Soviet Union as the banner-bearer of socialism. The capitalist democracies for the present, are compelled to reconcile themselves to this factor, and on the basis of the preservation of capitalism in Europe, are willing —and indeed have no other choice —than to compromise with the Soviet bureaucracy.

The experience of the Russian revolution, of the German Revolution of 1918, of the Spanish revolution of 1931, all reinforce these conclusions. The upsurge of the masses led to the fall of the monarchy in Spain and the proclamation of the Republic by the bourgeoisie. A coalition government of bourgeois republicans and

*Pietro Badoglio, Italian general, became prime minister after Mussolini's fall in 1943. He negotiated an armistice with Allies in Southern Italy, while disarming the workers in the north who had occupied the factories in opposition to the German occupation.

socialists proclaimed radical programmes on paper, while conducting repressions against workers and peasants. Such a government could not be long lasting. The regime of the Spanish republic was a regime of crises. A period of ebbs and flows, of reaction and radicalisation, culminating finally in half a decade in the bourgeoisie and proletariat attempting to find a solution in sanguinary and desperate civil war.

The Spanish pattern of events will be manifested on an all-European scale in the coming period. Backward as well as advanced countries are faced, in some degree or other, with the same crisis. From the Volga to the North Sea, from the Black Sea to the Baltic, nearly all Europe has been reduced to ruins and chaos. A stable basis for bourgeois democracy is thus excluded. Even the relative 'stability' of the Spanish republic will not be achieved. The most revolutionary period in European history is heralded by the events in Italy and Greece.

The Allied Programme for Europe

The Allied programme for Europe, because of the deeper crisis of capitalism, is far more terrible in its provisions than even the Versailles Treaty. Instead of the forcible unity of one gigantic concentration camp which was the aim of the nazis, the Allies wish to atomise and split up Europe on the lines which so signally led to catastrophe after the last war. Europe is to become the prey of British and American imperialism, with sections of Europe as satellites of and within the sphere of the Soviet bureaucracy.

Even under capitalist auspices, a united Europe would loom as too formidable a rival and threat for British and American imperialism. The Soviet bureacracy is unalterably opposed to the prospect of the unification of even part of the continent in capitalist federations, because it would inevitably become the basis for a new war against the Soviet Union in the future. Hence Stalin, together with Truman* and Churchill, is committed to the Balkanisation of Europe and the dismemberment of Germany as the only possible formidable foe in a future war on the continent of Europe.

American imperialism with its huge resources and productive capacity, is driven to attempt the 'organisation' of the entire world in an endeavour to escape the consequences of the insoluble

---

*Harry Truman, Democrat president of USA 1945-53. He developed the Truman Doctrine which gave economic and military 'aid' to countries threatened with 'interference'. He introduced the Marshall Plan of economic aid to prevent revolution in Europe in 1948.

contradictions between the capacities and limitations of even the great American market. America seeks to usurp the age-old dominance of Europe —above all of decaying and enfeebled British imperialism —and to grab the markets of the entire world. Not satisfied with the markets of the colonial countries, America wishes to establish a stranglehold on the markets and industries of Europe as well. She wants the dollar to reign over the the currencies and economy of Europe. Taking advantage of the chaos and disorganisation of Europe caused by the war, American finance capital hopes to put Europe on rations by means of loans and the weapon of food, supplies and equipment, while simultaneously at moments of stress and turmoil, blackmailing and buying off the revolutions by the same means.

The savagery of Anglo-American imperialism in relation to Germany is dictated not only by the programme of subjugation and exploitation, but by fear of the proletarian revolution in Germany. The German people have had the experience of all the regimes of bourgeois rule within a few decades. The proletariat and the petty bourgeoisie will inevitably turn in the direction of the socialist revolution.

It is in Germany that the bourgeoisie will discover the utopian character of their schemes to retain the old system. All attempts to punish fraternisation will collapse with the occupation of Germany for any length of time. The Tommies* and the Doughboys will consider their mission in Europe completed. They will demand demobilisation and a return home to the better world promised them by the bourgeoisie. The struggle of the German proletariat against the occupation forces, against the national humiliation and dismemberment of Germany, the struggle for national and social freedom, will prepare the way, under the very heel of the occupying forces, for a tremendous resistance on the part of the masses.

With their reactionary programme of national enslavement, the Stalinists can hope to bamboozle the German masses for only the briefest of periods. The way is being prepared for a rapid regroupment of forces of the German proletariat in a revolutionary direction. The experience of Italy is an object lesson on how quickly the masses can recover from the effects of terrible defeats under the impact of historic events. The resources and capacity for struggle of the proletariat seem virtually inexhaustible.

The Balkanisation of Germany and Europe, the Anglo-American domination of Western Europe, the claims of France, the domination of Eastern Europe by the Kremlin through bourgeois

*Slang term for British and American soldiers.

puppets, will have even more frightful consequences than the 'peace' of Versailles on the tortured continent. In the epoch of aeroplanes and panzer divisions, the absurdity of national frontiers, customs barriers and armies, of small and large states in Europe, assumes a particularly baleful character for the slow and painful strangulation of the productive forces and the decline of European culture. Particularly as the great powers —included among which are none of the European powers, for the first time —will bleed all Europe for their own ends. The next stage will become the classic period of the epoch of wars, revolutions and counter-revolutions, deepened and intensified by the history of the past decades.

It is possible, on the basis of the support rendered to world imperialism by Stalinism and classical reformism (and this is one of the objective factors to be reckoned with) that world imperialism can succeed, for a period, in 'stabilising' bourgeois democratic regimes in certain countries. Stalinism must offer the masses some gains in the shape of restoration of the trade unions, free (relatively, as in Spain in 1931) press, speech, voting, etc, in however attenuated a form. The imperialists need a 'democratic' interlude before taking the road of reaction. Moreover, they have no other choice. The shocks of the war and the debacle of fascism *leave no mass basis for reaction* in the immediate period ahead. The attempt to set up military dictatorships without social support would be very difficult. Moreover, such regimes could not survive for very long once the British and American troops were compelled to withdraw. The stormy impulsion of the masses compels them to bring forward their reserve weapon in the shape of the labour organisations.

It is possible, on the other hand, that in isolated instances the Anglo-American imperialists and the national bourgeoisie will succeed in immediately introducing military dictatorships. But without a social basis among the masses, these could not be long enduring. On the background of European and world social unrest and clashes such regimes would be faced with crises and convulsions.

Our estimate of the development of events does not mean that we draw pessimistic conclusions. Rather the contrary. But it does demand that the Fourth International utilise the situation in order to prepare for the shocks that await the imperialists. Ours is an epoch of sharp turns. The changes in the situation in Spain following the revolution of 1931* developed with tremendous

*The events following begin with municipal elections in April 1931, where a clear victory for the republican parties led to the abdication of King Alfonso. This was followed by a massive strike wave. The insurrection in Asturias took place in October 1934. The Popular Front was elected in February 1936. Franco's uprising took place in July 1936.

rapidity: upsurge of the masses, sell-out of the reformists, incapacity of the anarcho-syndicalists and Stalinists to give a revolutionary lead (particularly on the democratic and transitional demands). The short period of lull in which reaction prepared its forces to settle with the masses on the basis of disillusionment and despair engendered by their leadership; the masses respond to the whip of the counter-revolution by general strike and insurrection in Asturias and Catalonia; the reaction is unable to consolidate itself; the masses revive, the formation of the People's Front as a bridle for the masses; the February elections; stormy movements of the workers and peasants which the Stalinists and reformists are unable to control; a movement in the direction of the socialist revolution; the July coup of Franco and the answering insurrection of the masses.

Here we have a glimpse of the next period in Europe. The cadres of the Fourth International must study with great care the lessons of these events. To each stage correspond different slogans and tactics, different methods of agitation and propaganda, different actions on the part of the masses.

On this background of crises which extends more or less over the entire continent, spreading across the archaic national boundaries, the objective conditions are created for the establishment of a Socialist United States of Europe as the only solution to the problems which rack every country.

The implications of the war, the struggle of the peoples against Nazi domination, the example of the federation of the USSR, the coming reaction against the Allied domination, the inevitable reaction against nationalist intoxication and chauvinism, the radicalisation of the European masses —all these factors supply also the subjective basis for propaganda for the Socialist United States of Europe to which the masses will respond. As the cord which binds the programme of the Fourth International together, the main strategic slogan will be the United Socialist States of Europe as the only alternative to national decay and disintegration, decline of culture and civilisation in all the countries of Europe.

Our Tasks in Europe

The Fourth International will penetrate the broad masses and build the party of socialist revolution only with a correct tactical approach to the changing situations and moods.

It would require *a whole series of terrible defeats* before the bourgeoisie could establish an open dictatorial rule on the lines of the fascist regimes of Hitler and Mussolini. The cycle begins all over again, but on a new basis. The decay of the capitalist system weakens the bourgeoisie and renders it less capable of firmly rivetting its rule on the masses. It is 1917-21 with which the world is faced −but on a higher level. The degeneracy of the rotted workers' organisations gives capitalism a breathing space. *Only if the series of revolutions fails* can the bourgeoisie hope to save its system once again by resorting to a neo-fascism of monstrous reaction and repression. Before then the masses will have been put to the test. The proletariat will discard its old organisations if the Fourth International in its strategy and tactics is capable of integrating itself with the mass movement of the workers.

The basic task in this period is the building of the mass revolutionary parties of the Fourth International. While striving for and advocating the setting up of *ad hoc* organisations of struggle wherever the opportunity arises, while struggling for and advocating the dictatorship of the proletariat as the only solution, our European comrades cannot hope to achieve this in the first stages of the struggle. True, the masses are seeking the socialist solution; but they will have to go through the experience in action of the policy of betrayal of Stalinism and social democracy in order to learn that even the old standards of life can be obtained only by the rule of the working class.

The struggle for democratic, economic and transitional demands, far from being superceded or obsolete during the course of the revolutionary epoch ahead, assumes tremendous importance for the building of the framework of our movement. Thus, side by side with the propaganda for soviets and workers' government, at this stage there must be waged an agitation for the old organisations of the workers which still maintain the confidence and support of the masses, to break their alliance with the decadent bourgeoisie and Allied imperialism, and for the leaders to match their words with deeds. Our comrades will demand that the mass organisations which claim to represent the workers, wage a struggle to take power into their own hands. 'A Government of Socialists and Communists!' This will be the rallying cry which will be utilised by the Fourth International to mobilise the social democratic and communist workers to wage a struggle against the capitalist class.

Together, and side by side with this, must go the demand for general elections on the basis of universal suffrage from the age of eighteen years. The bourgeoisie and the reformist organisations are prattling about democratic rights, but they have allowed power to remain in the hands of bourgeois cliques, for the most part under the protection of Allied bayonets, without consulting the masses or receiving a mandate from them. Thus, the demand for a general election and the convening of a constituent assembly must play a great role in the agitation of our comrades in the first stages of the revolutionary mobilisation of the masses. Together with these will be linked the transitional slogans in various industries at varying stages of the struggle: Nationalise the banks without compensation! Take over the mines, railways and big combines and industry, and operate them under workers' control! Expropriate the trusts which yesterday collaborated with Hitler and today collaborate with the Allied imperialists! A plan of public works! A sliding scale of hours and wages! The arming of the workers and the organising of workers' militias! There is no need to detail all the demands which will be put forward, according to the development of the situation as laid down in the policy of the Fourth International in its Transitional Programme. These demands are not in contradiction with the programme of soviets, of workers' committees in the factories and streets. But without them there is a danger that the groups of the Fourth International would degenerate into sectarian sterility and isolation. They represent a bridge to the broad masses and without them the problem of organising the vanguard is rendered doubly difficult.

It is in periods such as this that the party of the Fourth International will build itself. The Stalinist and social democratic parties will not attain the stability they achieved in the pre-war era. They will be faced with a constant series of crises and splits. Given correct tactics the parties of the Fourth International will grow at their expense. However, ephemeral, centrist currents and groupings are bound to make their appearance in many countries owing to the weakness of the organisations of the Fourth International and their lack of authoritative spokesmen, such as Leon Trotsky. Authority will be built up on the basis of the ability of the young cadres of the International to learn for themselves in the course of the struggles, and on the basis of the masses' experience of the application of the programme of the Fourth International.

Democracy or Bonapartism in Europe
(A Reply to Pierre Frank)

August 1946

LENIN'S aphorism that we live in an epoch of wars and revolutions —to which Trotsky added 'and counter-revolutions' —has been amply demonstrated by the history of the last three decades. Few periods in history have been filled with such terrific convulsions and clashes between the nations and classes and such kaleidoscopic changes and manipulations of the political regimes whereby finance capital maintains its domination over the peoples. Thus, it becomes doubly important for those who carry on the scientific teachings of Marxism, and who alone can lay claim to make a theoretical analysis of events, to keep a scrupulous and careful check on the changes which are taking place if they are correctly to orientate the advance guard and give guidance to the masses.

In criticising the barren conceptions of Stalinism, which identified all regimes to fascism at the time of the 'third period', Trotsky brilliantly characterised the essence of the epoch as one of *change and fluctuations,* in which generalisations would not suffice. Each stage must be *examined concretely* by the vanguard who could thus understand and interpret events and draw the correct practical conclusions for activity therefrom. He wrote:

> The vast importance of a correct theoretical orientation is most strikingly manifested in a period of acute social conflict, of rapid political shifts, of abrupt changes in the situation. In such periods, political *conceptions* and *generalisations* are rapidly used up and require either a complete replacement (which is easier) or their concretisation, precision and partial rectification (which is harder.) It is in just such periods that all sorts of *transitional, intermediate* situations and combinations arise, as a matter of necessity, which upset the customary patterns and doubly require a sustained theoretical attention. In a word, if in the pacific and 'organic' period (before the war) one could still live on the revenue from a few ready-made abstractions, in our time

each new event forcefully brings home the most important law of the dialectic: *the truth is always concrete. (Bonapartism and Fascism,* July 1934)

Among the cadres of the Fourth International, there are comrades who have not sufficiently understood this lesson. They continue to live on the 'revenue from a few ready-made abstractions' instead of concretising or partially rectifying previous generalisations. An outstanding example of this is the article of Pierre Frank.

Frank attempts to equate all regimes in Western Europe to 'Bonapartism.' His generalisations go even further: he argues that there have been Bonapartist regimes in France since 1934; that it is impossible to have any but Bonapartist or fascist regimes until the coming to power of the proletariat in Europe. This, if you please, in the name of 'the continuity of our political analysis for more than ten years of French history'! Such complacency reduces theory to formless abstractions and conceals inevitable and episodic errors, thus making them into a system. It has no place in the Fourth International.

Comrade Frank indiscriminately mixes the terms bourgeois democracy with Bonapartism, not explaining the specific traits of either. He interchangeably speaks of 'Bonapartism', 'elements of Bonapartism' and he contrasts democratic liberties with 'a regime which one can correctly define as democratic.' Yet the reader has to seek in vain for a definition of his ideal 'democratic regime' as distinguished from the very real bourgeois democracy. He denies the existence of democratic regimes in Europe today because 'there is literally no place for them.'

Economic Basis and Political Superstructure.

We will here repeat some elementary ideas of Marxism in order to arrive at the necessary clarity and understanding of the shifting processes and changes taking place in the regimes in Europe at the present time —at least in Western Europe. The Eastern half, dominated directly by the Stalinist bureaucracy, develops in a different direction and under different conditions.

The *political character of a regime* (Bonapartist, fascist, democratic) is basically determined by the relations between the classes in the nation, which vary at different stages. Its *fundamental* nature is determined, in the last analysis, by its *mode of production and property relations,* by its *class character.* Thus the regimes of Hitler* and

---

*Government leaders in Germany, America, Britain, Italy, Spain, France, Argentina, Portugal, Ireland and China in the period 1943-6 who presided over various types of regimes ranging from fascist to social democratic, but all based on capitalism.

Roosevelt, of Attlee and Mussolini, of Franco and Gouin, of Peron and Salazar, of de Valera and Chiang Kai Shek are all governments of the capitalist class, for they rest upon the economy of capitalist exploitation. However, the *class nature* of these regimes does not exhaust the problem. We have to classify the instrument — which differs in each case — by which the bourgeoisie ensures its dominance and rule. The character of this rule is decided not only by the *subjective* wishes and needs of the finance-capitalists, which remain but one factor in the process, but precisely by the objective-subjective inter-relations between the classes at a given stage, which has been predicated by the previous history and the development of the class struggle of the given country.

It is a vulgarisation of Marxism — vulgar materialism of the worst sort — to argue that the superstructure of a society is determined immediately by the development of its economy.

The disappearance of the economic basis on which the 'democracy' of the imperialists is based, does not immediately lead to the disappearance of the bourgeois democracy. It only prepares its collapse *in the long run*. Properly speaking, the development of capitalism into imperialism by the beginning of this century had already rendered outmoded the existence of bourgeois democracy. Yet we see that bourgeois democracy managed to maintain itself for decades after its economic base had disappeared.

That capitalism had outlived its historic functions was attested already by the first imperialist world war. But this did not, and could not by itself, lead to the overthrow of the capitalist system. The first world war led to favourable conditions for the overthrow of the bourgeoisie on a world scale. But the proletariat was prevented from carrying out its mission by the organisations of its own creation. The social democracy betrayed the revolution and saved the capitalist system from destruction. In the revolutionary epoch following world war one, the bourgeoisie was compelled to lean on the social democracy for support, the only reliable prop they had to maintain their rule. Where the bourgeoisie relied on such regimes based on social democracy, uniting repression against the revolutionary workers with reforms and half-reforms, these could only be characterised as regimes of 'bourgeois democracy.' Thus, Lenin and Trotsky characterised the counter-revolutionary regime in Germany in 1918, which was organised by social democracy, as a bourgeois democratic regime.

It is ABC that the democratic liberties were gained in the struggle against the bourgeoisie over a period of a century; the right to vote had to be fought for and wrested from the bourgeoisie at a period of *ascending capitalism*, at the time of the blossoming of bourgeois democracy. Even in its heyday there was never an idyllic democratic state without police intervention and without brute force.

Yet even at this stage when capitalism was still an ascending economy, there were not only democratic regimes but Bonapartist regimes as well. In the classic land of Bonapartism, both Louis Napoleon*, and Bonaparte himself came to power at a time when there was a veritable boom which lasted in the one case for two decades. According to Comrade Frank's conception there was no basis for Bonapartism; there should have only been bourgeois democracy. But we see the problem is not so simple.

And after Louis Napoleon, bourgeois democracy (with one or two threats of dictatorship −Boulangerism) lasted for decades in France. According to Frank's mysterious conceptions, after Bonapartism −which means that the economic basis for democracy is gone −it is no longer possible for the bourgeoisie to have democracy, but...only Bonapartism.

It is difficult to understand why Comrade Frank stops at 1934 to trace Bonapartist regimes in France. If we follow his method logically we have had Bonapartism since the coup d'etat of Louis Napoleon in 1851, or perhaps since the first Bonaparte!

If there is a grain of sense in his case that the economic basis for reforms has disappeared, all that it proves is not automatically and consequently a regime of Bonapartism is posed but that the democratic regime under such conditions will be of an extremely unstable character, afflicted with convulsions and crises, which must make way either for the revolutionary proletarian dictatorship or the open dictatorship of finance capital through Bonapartism or fascism.

Comrade Frank says the existence of democratic liberties does not suffice to make a democratic regime. A profound observation! What follows ? The existence of Bonapartist measures does not make a regime Bonapartist either, Comrade Frank! This argument is about as profound as those of the 'bureaucratic collectivists' who argued that we had the intervention of the state in the economy in Germany under Hitler, in France under Blum, in America under Roosevelt (National Industrial Recovery Act), in Russia under Stalin ... consequently all those regimes were the same. It is not the points of similarity only −all human societies have points of similarity, particularly different types of capitalist societies −it is the *decisive traits* which determine our definition of regimes.

---

*Napoleon Bonaparte (Napoleon I), came to power in a coup on 18 Brumaire (9-10 November 1799) and had himself proclaimed emperor in 1804. Louis Bonaparte (Napoleon III) won the presidential election in 1848. In a coup in 1851 he dissolved the legislative assembly and in 1852 declared himself emperor.

Counter-Revolution in a Democratic Form

The British RCP has characterised the regimes in Western Europe (France, Belgium, Holland, Italy) as regimes of counter-revolution in a democratic form. Comrade Pierre Frank claims that the idea of a 'democratic counter-revolution' is 'devoid of all content.' He would then be hard put to explain what the Weimar* Republic organised by the social democracy in Germany was. He would be compelled to argue that what took place in Germany in 1918, was *not* the proletarian revolution which was betrayed by the 'counter-revolution in a democratic form' (by the undemocratic and bloody suppression of the January 1919 uprisings), but was a democratic revolution which overthrew the Kaiser and replaced his regime by one of 'pure' bourgeois democracy! The fact that this regime was ushered in by martial law and the conspiracy of the social democratic leaders with the General Staff of the Reichswehr, the Junkers and the bourgeoisie, validates entirely the conclusion of Lenin and Trotsky that there was a 'democratic' counter-revolution, with the bourgeoisie using the social democrats as their agents.

In advance Trotsky foresaw and prepared theoretically for a similar situation with the collapse of fascism in Italy, when he wrote in a letter to the Italian comrades in 1930:

> Following the above comes the question of the 'transitional' period in Italy. At the very outset it is necessary to establish very clearly: transition from what to what? A period of transition from the bourgeois (or 'popular') revolution to the proletarian revolution is one thing. A period of transition from the fascist dictatorship to the proletarian dictatorship is another. If the first conception is envisaged, the question of the bourgeois revolution is posed in the first place and it is then a question of establishing the role of the proletariat in it. Only after that will the question of the transitional period toward a proletarian revolution be posed. If the second conception is envisaged, the question is then posed of a series of battles, disturbances, upsets in the situation, abrupt turns, constituting in their ensemble the different stages of the proletarian revolution. These stages may be many in number. But in no case can they contain within them a bourgeois revolution or its mysterious hybrid: the 'popular' revolution.
>
> Does this mean that Italy cannot for a certain time again become a parliamentary state or become a 'democratic republic'? I consider —in perfect agreement with you, I think —that this eventuality is not excluded. But then it will not be the fruit of a bourgeois revolution but

---

*Weimar was the city in Germany where the new constitution was formulated in 1919. The Reichswehr was the regular army of Weimar Germany. For a full account of the 1918 revolution and the January 1919 'Spartacist Rising' see *Germany – From Revolution To Counter-Revolution* by Rob Sewell (Fortress).

the abortion of an insufficiently matured and premature proletarian revolution. In case of a profound revolutionary crisis and of mass battles in the course of which the proletarian vanguard will not have been in a position to take power, it may be that the bourgeoisie will reconstruct its power on 'democratic' bases.

Can it be said, for example, that the present German republic constitutes a conquest of the bourgeois revolution? Such an assertion would be absurd. There was in Germany in 1918-19 a proletarian revolution which, deprived of leadership, was deceived, betrayed and crushed. But the bourgeois counter-revolution nevertheless found itself obliged to adapt itself to the circumstances resulting from this crushing of the proletarian revolution and to assume the form of a republic in the 'democratic' parliamentary form. Is the same —or about the same —eventuality excluded from Italy? No, it is not excluded. The enthronement of fascism was the result of the incompletion of the proletarian revolution in 1920. Only a new proletarian revolution can overturn fascism. If it should not be destined to triumph this time either (weakness of the Communist Party, manoeuvres and betrayals of the social democrats, the freemasons, the catholics), the 'transitional' state that the bourgeois counter- revolution would then be forced to set up in the ruins of its power in a fascist form, could be nothing else than a parliamentary and democratic state. (*Problems of the Italian Revolution,* 14 May, 1930)

Events in Italy have demonstrated the remarkable foresight of Trotsky. The bourgeoisie has been compelled to allow the jettisoning of the king* and the Stalinist-socialist traitors have headed off the developing proletarian revolution into the channels of a 'parliamentary and democratic state'. This of course, will not attain a stable base, but will be subject to crises and upheavals, movements on the part of the proletariat, and counter-movements of monarchists and fascists. Would Frank now deny the correctness of Trotsky's conceptions and assert that we have had a Bonapartist state since the fall of Mussolini?

It is incomprehensible that Frank, in his argumentation, should refer to this very article of Trotsky's which puts forward precisely the opposite point of view. After fascism what? asks the Old Man and answers that, as a means of preventing the revolution in face of mass upsurge, the bourgeoisie will turn towards the establishment of a bourgeois democratic republic. We note in this connection that the immediate introduction of Bonapartism (allegedly because democracy has no economic base) was not even considered by Trotsky.

From this can be seen that what is really 'devoid of content' is the mechanical conception that counter-revolution can only manifest itself in the form of fascism or Bonapartism, ie

*When the Allies liberated Rome in May 1944, they blocked any attempt, contrary to previous agreements they had, by the exiled King Victor Emmanuel, to return to the throne for fear of provoking a new uprising by the workers.

military-police dictatorships. The experience of history has shown, and events now unfolding in Europe demonstrate irrefutably, that the methods of the bourgeoisie in its struggle against the proletarian revolution vary widely and are not determined *a priori*. The bourgeoisie makes use of different methods, relies on different strata, depending on the class relation of forces in order to re-enforce or re-establish its rule.

Whether they can manoeuvre the Stalinists or manipulate their social democratic, Bonapartist, or fascist agencies, or as sometimes happens, *use all forces simultaneously*, does not depend only on the subjective intentions of the ruling class, or on this or that adventurer, but on the objective conditions and the inter-relations between all the classes in the nation —bourgeoisie, petty bourgeoisie and proletariat, at any given time. To repeat mechanically the conclusion that the existence of finance capital is incompatible with bourgeois democracy in the contemporary period (which is indubitably correct within certain limits), and thus that all regimes must be Bonapartist, is to substitute abstract categories formulated on the basis of partial and insufficient historical experience, or a narrow and incomplete view of the process as a whole, for a dialectical analysis of events.

To understand the nature of the regimes in Western Europe today, we must know the background on which they evolved. The revolutionary movement of the masses following World War One was paralysed and betrayed by the social democrats, *who alone were able to save capitalism from destruction under the banner of bourgeois democracy*. The bourgeoisie was compelled to rely on its social democratic agencies for mere survival.

The failure of the proletariat to take power could lead only to the further degeneration and decay of capitalism. The ruin of the petty bourgeoisie, which was shown no way out by the mass organisations of the proletariat, led to them becoming a tool of fascist reaction. Trapped by the intolerable crisis of their system in one country after another, through many transitions, the bourgeoisie turned in the direction of open and unbridled dictatorship.

The wave of revolution was followed by a wave of counter-revolution. In Italy, Germany and other countries, the bourgeoisie used the forces of the frenzied petty bourgeoisie to destroy the organisations of the proletariat. They were compelled at a later stage to turn on the petty bourgeoisie and transform themselves into Bonapartist regimes, ie *regimes resting directly on the support of the military-police apparatus rather than regimes with a mass basis*. This could not solve the contradictions of the capitalist system on a national or international scale but inevitably led to the second world war, in a frantic endeavour by the bourgeoisie to find a way out by a repartition of the world. But the second world war, even more than the first, put at stake the whole existence of capitalism as a system. The bourgeoisie realised, with dread, that the unleashing of the war would release tremendous revolutionary energy from the depths of the masses and recreate the conditions favourable to the overthrow of capitalism on a continental scale.

The victories of the nazis and the conquest of practically the whole of the continent of Europe had, as a by-product, the effect of *temporarily* destroying the mass basis of reaction throughout Europe. Reaction and the capitalist system rested directly on the bayonets of the nazi fascist armies. The hated Quislings played a purely auxiliary role. With the victories of the Red Army and the collapse of Hitler and Mussolini, the problem of the socialist revolution was posed on the order of the day throughout Europe. Reaction was without a strong base in the populations *and without a strong stable military-police apparatus.* The allied armies could not be a stable prop for reaction and open military dictatorship for long. In most of the European countries the bourgeoisie was faced with mass upsurge, *which they could not bridle with their own forces.*

Greece was the exception. Only after a civil war and a bloody war of intervention was it possible to install a semi-Bonapartist or Bonapartist regime, which is step-by-step attempting to impose a totalitarian regime in that country. The imperialists are aware of the impossibility of using such methods on a continental scale. In addition, in Greece the power of reaction had to be maintained at all costs for fear that this last outpost of British imperialism in the Balkan peninsula should, in common with the rest of the Balkans, fall under the sway of the Stalinist bureaucracy. But even here it was not possible to destroy completely the mass organisations of the proletariat.

Nothing saved the capitalist system in Western Europe except the betrayal of social democracy and Stalinism. When the bourgeoisie leans on its social democratic and Stalinist agencies *for the purpose of counter-revolution,* what is the 'content' of that counter-revolution? Bonapartist, fascist, authoritarian? Of course not! Its content is that of a 'counter revolution in a democratic form.'

Of course, the bourgeoisie cannot stabilise itself for any length of time on the basis of the democratic counter-revolution. Where the revolution is stemmed by the lackeys of the bourgeoisie, the class forces do not stay suspended. After a period, which can be more or less protracted according to the economic and political developments internationally and within the given country, the bourgeoisie shifts to Bonapartist or fascist counter-revolution.

That is how events manifested themselves in Italy within two years of the ebbing of the revolutionary tide provoked by world war one, and in Germany over a period of 15 years. The change in class relationships reflected itself in the change in regimes through democracy, preventative Bonapartism, to fascism, pure Bonapartist military dictatorship.

Despite the further degeneration of its economic and political base, the failure of the workers once again to take power, destroy capitalist relations and organise society anew, has resulted in the establishment of bourgeois democratic governments in Italy, France and other countries, based upon the manipulation of the Stalinists and social democrats. To argue that counter- revolution or the rule of the bourgeoisie in the present period can only manifest itself in Bonapartism, fascism or Franco-type governments, is to abandon the Marxist appreciation of the processes in modern society. Taking into account the many factors involved in the history of the period, including the weakness of the Marxist current, it could have been, and was, predicted in advance what the developments in Western Europe would be. But the process can only be understood if one takes into account the real nature of democracy, Bonapartism, fascism, and not merely their outward forms.

Differing Regimes in Capitalist Society

The classic Bonapartism of the first Napoleon rose out of the bourgeois democratic revolution in the period of the youth and vigour of capitalism. Bonapartism, *the rule of the sword over society*, represented a position where the state assumed a relative independence of the classes, balancing between the hostile classes and *arbitrating* between them. It remained, nevertheless, an instrument above all, of the big capitalists. Napoleon, by leaning on the support of the peasants, could maintain himself for a whole historical period because of the development of the productive forces in France at this period.

So with Napoleon the Little, who established his power in France in the coup d'état of 1851. Marx, in the *Eighteenth Brumaire*, described the position thus: 'the State has gone back to its earliest form, in which the sword rules without shame and club law prevails. (Hardly a mirror of the regime of de Gaulle in France after the liberation!). Thus is the *coup-de-main* of February 1848 answered by the *coup-de-tete* of December 1851.'

That is the essence of Bonapartism: naked, military-police dictatorship, the 'arbiter' with a sword. A regime which indicates that the antagonisms within society have become so great that the state machine, 'regulating' and 'ordering' these antagonisms, while remaining an instrument of the property owners, assumes a certain independence of all the classes. A 'national judge' concentrating power in his hands, personally 'arbitrates' the conflicts within the nation, playing off one class against another, nevertheless remaining a tool of the property owners. At the same time, we characterise as Bonapartist, a regime where the basic class forces of bourgeoisie and proletariat more or less balance one another, thus allowing the state power to manoeuvre and balance the contending camps and again giving the state power a certain independence in relation to society as a whole.

However, there is a big difference between the role of Bonapartism in the period of capitalism's ascending phase and the period of its decline. We give two quotations from Trotsky explaining this difference with the utmost clarity, in *Germany, The Only Road*.

In its time, we designated the Bruening* government as *Bonapartism* ('caricature of Bonapartism'), that is, as a regime of the military police dictatorship. As soon as the struggle of two social strata − the haves and the have-nots, the exploiter and the exploited − reaches its highest tension, the conditions are given for the domination of bureaucracy, police, soldiery. The government becomes 'independent' of society. Let us once more recall: if two forks are stuck symmetrically into a cork, the latter can stand even on the head of a pin. That is precisely the scheme of Bonapartism. To be sure, such a government does not cease being the clerk of the property-owners. Yet the clerk sits on the back of the boss, rubs his neck raw and does not hesitate at times to dig his boots into his face.

It might have been assumed that Bruening would hold on until the final solution. Yet, in the course of events, another link inserted itself: the Papen government. Were we to be exact, we should have to make a rectification of our old designation: the Bruening government was a pre-Bonapartist government. Bruening was only a precursor. In a perfected form, Bonapartism came upon the scene in the Papen-Schleicher government (September 1932).'

And further on:

However, in spite of the appearance of concentrated forces, the Papen government *as such* is weaker yet than its predecessor. The Bonapartist regime can attain a comparatively stable and durable character only in the event that it brings a revolutionary epoch to a close; when the

*Heinrich Bruening was German Chancellor 1930-32. At the end of 1931 he annulled virtually all union contracts and restricted the press. Kurt von Schleicher, a Reichswehr general, succeeded von Papen as Chancellor in December 1932. He was replaced by Hitler within two months.

relationship of forces has already been tested in battles; when the revolutionary classes are already spent; while the possessing classes have not yet freed themselves from the fear; will not the morrow bring new convulsions? Without this basic condition, that is, without a preceding exhaustion of the mass energies in battles, a Bonapartist regime is in no position to develop.

The Bonapartism at the stage of capitalism's rise, raising itself above society, suppressing and 'arbitrating' the open conflicts within it and regulating the class antagonisms, is strong and confident. Under the conditions of a powerful development of the productive forces, it attains a certain stability. But the Bonapartism of capitalism's decline is affected by senility. Rising out of the crisis of capitalist society, it cannot solve any of the problems with which it is faced. The main crisis of society, the conflict between the productive forces and private ownership and the national state, has become so great, the class antagonisms which it engenders, so tense, that this which alone allows the rise of senile Bonapartism, at the same time, as a consequence, makes it so weak and feeble that its whole structure is shaky and likely to be overthrown in the series of crises which confront it. It is this weakness of Bonapartism which leads to the bourgeoisie and military clique surrendering the power to fascism and unleashing the greedy bands of maddened petty bourgeoisie and lumpenproletariat against the proletariat and its class organisations.

The differing categories of regimes, though of vital importance for Marxist theory and practice, are not metaphysical abstractions, indicating a rigid, fixed and eternal differentiation between them.

There are so many factors involved, that it is necessary to examine each regime concretely before categorically defining its position.

It is only necessary to point out that even within each rough category, widely differing regimes can be comprised. England with her feudal remnants (House of Lords and monarchy) and barbarous oppression of colonial peoples, is a 'democracy'. The Federal Republic of Switzerland, and France with its laws based on the *Code Napoleon*, the United States, Weimar Germany and Eire —despite their wide differences, remain 'democracies'. What, then, is the dominating thread which places these regimes under one head?

Despite their diverse histories, which explains their different national peculiarities, *they all possess certain specific traits in common.* These are the traits which are decisive in determining the Marxist classification. All have independent workers' organisations: trade unions, parties, clubs, etc, with the rights which go with them. The right to strike, organise, the right to vote, free speech, press, etc., and the other rights which have been the by-product of the class struggle of the proletariat in the past. (Here we might add that the loss of this or that right would not, in itself, be decisive in our analysis of a regime. It is the totality of the relations which is the determining factor.) In one sense, the existence, *within capitalism*, of elements of the new society. Or, as explained by Trotsky in *Germany, What Next* in answering the Stalinist ultra-lefts, *under the regime of the bourgeoisie there already exists the embryo of the rule of the working class in the form of the workers' organisations.*

Where these organisations exist and play a powerful role (in France and Italy they are stronger than they have ever been) the bourgeoisie rules through the leaders and top layers of these organisations. It is not without interest, as Lenin pointed out, that at a certain stage, the bourgeoisie even ruled through the Soviets, or more correctly, the Menshevik leadership of the Soviets.

Fascism too, has its peculiarities. The regimes of Franco, Mussolini, Hitler and Pilsudsky*, all are comprised within this conception. Yet there are wide differences between them. What fundamentally unites the conception is the *complete destruction of all working-class organisations.* Yet even here we see that right up to the outbreak of the war, Polish fascism, far weaker than that of Germany and Italy, had not completely succeeded in destroying the workers' organisations and may have been overthrown before it finally succeeded in doing so.

Bonapartism too, shows a similar variety. Napoleon, Louis Napoleon, von Schleicher and Papen, Petain, and the fascist-regimes-become-Bonapartist —all   were   Bonapartist regimes. What is it that they have in common? The independence of the state, the concentration of power 'personally', resting directly and openly on the domination of the state machine *through the naked power of the military-police apparatus, 'Rule by the sword.'* Whatever differences there may be between the regimes, the existence of workers' organisations with attenuated or limited rights in certain cases, they all have the above mentioned features in common. The specific peculiarities in each case would again be determined by the history of the country, the development of the social contradictions which made the development of Bonapartism possible, etc., etc.

Thus the weak and sterile Bonapartism of Petain and von Schleicher in the epoch of capitalist decline resembled only as a caricature the vigorous and powerful regime established by

---

*Josef Pilsudsky led a coup in Poland in 1926, and became dictator until his death in 1935.

Napoleon in its period of ascent. In the change from democracy to fascism, there must be one, perhaps many, transitional phases. Thus the path for Bonapartism is prepared by the division of the nation into two hostile camps — that of the fascist petit bourgeoisie and that of the organised working class. Nominally, the state power assumes an independence of both and the military-police regime established prepares the way for the handing of power to fascism. (The bourgeoisie prefers to rule through democratic means. Under the impact of crisis, however, they utilise the fascist gangs as a terrorist agency for pressure on the proletariat so that they can push through Bonapartist dictatorial measures. Only as a last resort do they reluctantly surrender power to the fascists.) At least that was the process in Italy and Germany. Depending on many factors, including the policy of the revolutionary party of the proletariat, events in Europe and elsewhere may develop on somewhat different lines, should reaction succeed in temporarily stabilising itself.

However, it is important to note that the regimes of Schleicher and Papen, of Petain and General Sirovy in Czechoslovakia after Munich *all developed directly* (through intermediate stages perhaps) *out of the regimes of bourgeois democracy*. The pre-Bonapartist, or even Bonapartist regimes, of Doumergue*, Laval and Flandin prepared the way for the Popular Front in France which in turn paved the way again for a development towards Bonapartism. To call the Popular Front under Blum 'Bonapartism' as does Comrade Frank in the citation which follows, can only cause immeasurable confusion in the ranks of the Fourth International:

> . . . But the Bonapartism of declining capitalism can cloak itself in other costumes. In certain cases it is fairly difficult to recognise it, for example in the case of governments, of the left, even very much to the left, notably of the Popular Front type. There, Bonapartism is so outrageously varnished with a democratic sheen that many allow themselves to be taken in by it(!)

In those words of Comrade Frank is the key to the confusion in the characterisation of regimes. It is easy to slip into such errors because in the same way as the embryo of a new form of society exists in the workers' organisations, so the possibility of Bonapartism is rooted in the structure of society under bourgeois democracy. Within every state there is reflected the antagonisms

*Gaston Doumergue, a former president of France, became premier after the attempted coup of 6 February 1934, promising a 'strong' government. Pierre Laval, French premier 1935-6, and premier of the collaborationist Vichy regime in 1942. Pierre Flandin succeeded Doumergue as premier in 1934-35.

within society, even in the freest bourgeois democratic society. As Engels wrote in his book *The Origin of the Family, Private Property and the State:*

> The state is therefore by no means a power imposed on society from the ouside; just as little is it the reality of the moral idea, the image and reality of reason, as Hegel asserted. Rather it is a product of society at a certain stage of development; it is the admission that this society has become entangled in an insoluble contradiction within itself, that it is cleft into irreconcilable antagonisms which it is powerless to dispel. But in order that these antagonisms, classes with conflicting economic interests, may not consume themselves and society in sterile struggle, a power apparently standing above society becomes necessary, whose purpose is to moderate the conflict and keep it within the bounds of 'order'; and this power arising out of society, but placing itself above it, and increasingly separating itself from it, is the state. (Peking 1978 edition p.205.)

In the last analysis every state is based on naked force. The army officers, the general staff clique, the police and civil service bureaucracy, trained and selected to serve the interests of capitalism, provide the soil on which military plots and conspiracies thrive, given conditions of crisis and social ferment.

Pierre Frank confuses here the role of the state with Bonapartism. A democracy that was not based on force, that did not have an apparatus placing itself above society, has never existed and never will exist. But this does not make Bonapartism.

But because every state is based on armed bodies of men with its appendages in the form of prisons, courts, etc., and thus even under the fullest democratic regime we have the hidden dictatorship of capitalism, it does not follow that every repressive regime is necessarily Bonapartist. Repression and suppression of the rights of the workers under conditions of 'emergency' take place under every regime, including the democratic, when the basic interests of capital are threatened and till 'normal' conditions are restored — ie, till the masses accept without active rebellion, the yoke of capital. The bourgeoisie preserves an extreme flexibility, manipulating the regimes according to the resistance of the masses, the class forces, etc. Thanks to the betrayals of the workers' leaderships they are enabled to do this.

Prognosis in the Light of Events

Whatever their original desires or wishes to impose Bonapartist regimes in Europe, Anglo-American imperialism soon saw the impossibility of this (apart from Greece) in the incalculable dangers which it would bring and in Western Europe swung over to democratic regimes, based on a disarmed proletariat.

Events in France and Western Europe have confirmed the incorrectness of the method of Pierre Frank. Everywhere in Western Europe since the 'liberation', the tendency has been for a steady movement towards bourgeois democracy and not towards greater and greater dictatorial regimes; towards an increase in democratic rights, not towards their limitation. *At a later stage this tendency will be reversed,* but at present the motion in Western Europe is towards bourgeois democratic regimes. Thus in Italy we have the establishment of the bourgeois democratic republic, trade unions, etc; in France we have elections, parties, trade unions, etc; in Belgium and Holland we have democratic elections. The swing of the masses towards socialism-communism is reflected in the fact that these parties have secured a greater percentage of the votes than at any time in history. In order to mobilise the petty bourgeois reaction as a counterpoise against them, the bourgeoisie, *at this stage,* is leaning not on fascist reaction (that is still well in reserve) *but on the catholic and christian parties basing themselves on parliamentary democracy.* This gives the bourgeoisie a breathing space to prepare at a later stage and under the necessary favourable conditions for a transition through Bonapartist regimes to totalitarian dictatorship.

It is clear that the position today is entirely different from the position in Germany and Italy before the victory of fascism, where mass parties of fascism were organised and the possibility of the state manoeuvring between the two mortally hostile camps, was posed by the whole situation. Far from this, in Italy and France the Christian Democratic parties are collaborating with the workers' organisations in a typical coalition cabinet of bourgeois democracy. The bourgeoisie cannot do otherwise because of the danger of revolutionary disturbances on the part of the masses.

The situation is similar to that in Germany in the Weimar Republic. In order to stem the revolution the bourgeoisie organised a coalition government of social democracy and the Catholic Centre*.

Was this Bonapartism? Obviously not. But as a result of the policy of social democracy they were punished by the petty bourgeois swinging to reaction and a Bonapartist-monarchist attempt at a coup d'etat in the Kapp Putsch** in 1920. As is well known, this attempted Bonapartist coup was defeated by the masses, where the

---

*The Catholic Centre Party was a German Christian Democratic party.
**For a full account of the Kapp Putsch see *Germany − From Revolution to Counter Revolution* by Rob Sewell. (Fortress)

communists and socialists participated in a general strike. The indignation of the workers, *owing to the correct propaganda of the Communist Party* in warning of this danger and forming a united front to beat it off, led to the workers in the Ruhr attempting the seizure of power. The reaction then joined together with the social democrats to crush this movement of the masses. This in its turn, paved the way for an uneasy and unstable regime of bourgeois democracy.

The false position on the nature of the regimes in Europe flows from an incorrect perspective. The American comrades argued that only Franco-type military dictatorships were possible in Europe after the victory of the allied imperialists. Pierre Frank approvingly quotes a wrong position taken by the International Secretariat (IS) in 1940:

> If England should install de Gaulle in France tomorrow, his regime would not in the least be distinguished from that of the Bonapartist government of Petain.

A trifle different, Comrade Frank! For the workers a decisive difference! It is true that the capitalist class continued to rule under de Gaulle as they did under Petain. But to argue in 1946 that the regimes could not be distinguished is to fall into the sectarian stupidity of the Stalinists in Germany who couldn't distinguish between a capitalist regime leaning on the workers' organisations and the abolition of these organisations by fascism.

Pierre Frank's confusion is further exposed by his triumphant declaration that the Petain regime was Bonapartist. Trotsky said that the Petain regime was Bonapartist. But Frank just does not understand what Trotsky was driving at. In their period of decay and decline, Trotsky referred to the regimes of Hitler and Mussolini as Bonapartist regimes. The only difference between these regimes and that of Petain was that *Petain never had a mass base in the petty bourgeoisie,* like Hitler and Mussolini, and in that sense could not be called fascist, but Bonapartist. For this reason his regime was much weaker and could be more easily over-thrown by a movement of the masses. Petain had to lean on foreign bayonets for his rule. Otherwise there is no difference between the regimes of Franco, Mussolini and Hitler in their decaying phases and that of Petain.

Comrade Frank declares:

> ...our most responsible International body has predicted that a simple substitution of gangs following a victory of the Alllies would not signify a change in the nature of the political regime. We find ourselves in the

presence of an evaluation on the historical scale based on positions which were defended for many years by the Fourth International against all other theories and cheap labels spread by the other tendencies and formations of the labour movement. If an error was committed it would be truly a considerable one and we would be urgently obliged to seek the reasons for it and correct it. As for ourselves, we don't believe that our organisation was in error on this point...

The statement of the IS made in 1940 was incorrect. We made the same mistake. Under the circumstances it was excusable. But to repeat in 1946 a mistake that was already clear by 1943 is inexcusable. A British Trotskyist resolution, written in 1943, in which we corrected ourselves, analysed the coming situation in Europe as follows:

> In the absence of experienced Trotskyist parties with roots and traditions among the masses, the first stages of the revolutionary struggles in Europe will most likely result in a period of Kerenskyism or Popular Frontism. This is already presaged by the initial struggles of the Italian workers and the repeated betrayals of social democracy and Stalinism. (Main resolution at the National Conference of the Workers International League, October 1943).

Events have demonstrated the correctness of this analysis. Instead of frankly facing up to an error in perspective, Frank flies in the face of reality and attempts to convert an error into a virtue.

Frank takes France as the keystone of his thesis. He surely must be lamenting this by now. Because it is France, above all, which has mirrored the process very clearly. France is the key to Europe and any mistakes on the nature of the French regime could be fatal for the young cadres of Trotskyism.

Let us examine the situation. Pierre Frank visualises the development as follows: Bonapartism since 1934, because, you see, the bourgeoisie could not afford bourgeois democracy; Petain was Bonaparte: de Gaulle was Bonaparte; the Popular Front (Blum!) was Bonapartism; in fact, as the metaphysicians would say: 'in the twilight all cats are grey'. The thesis is that all were Bonaparte. It follows that Gouin is Bonaparte and the government which will follow also will be Bonapartist. If this madness should infect the French, our French Party will be in a sorry state. Happily, this danger apparently does not exist.

A Marxist appreciation would be somewhat different from that of Pierre Frank. What was the development of the regime −from what to what is it evolving? What is the position of the classes? What are the relations between the classes? A sober appreciation of the last two years will tell us that (a) here we have an unachieved proletarian revolution; result (b) unstable bourgeois democracy, assembly, elections, constituent, bourgeois-democratic constitution; (c) in this setting a candidate Bonaparte. The real power rests in the principal working class parties. A would-be Hitler striving for power and a Hitler in power are not one and the same thing. A would-be Bonaparte like de Gaulle and a real Bonaparte wielding real personal power with the sword, are two different things. De Gaulle may yet be a French Franco, but one does not declare the enemy victorious before the decisive battle has begun.

Bonapartism in the modern epoch, by its very nature, must be a regime of transition —transition to fascism, transition to democracy, or even to proletarian revolution: a period of manoeuvring between the classes. That there are *elements of Bonapartism in the situation in Europe, goes without saying.* These elements can be transformed into the dominant ones, but only under certain conditions. If one declares a regime Bonapartist, then the specific features of the regime must be brought out. In spite of Pierre Frank's zealous endeavours to elevate de Gaulle into a position to which he only aspired, the 'Bonaparte' de Gaulle, measuring the relation of forces, was forced to retire sadly from the scene to await a more propitious moment.

There precisely is the nub of the question: it is necessary to answer Stalinist and socialist propaganda by warning that their policies inevitably bring the dangers of counter-revolution and Bonapartism: to warn of the threat of military-police dictatorship which hangs over the proletariat if it does not disperse the Bonapartist nests, composed of the cadres of the general staff, police and civil bureaucracy, and take power into its own hands.

Comrades must not make the mistake of the German communists who declared every regime in turn 'fascist' till in the end, by their lulling and confusing the advance guard, the real Hitler arrived. Of course, if Pierre Frank continues to repeat it long enough, no doubt reality will, in the end, coincide with his definition and we will have a Bonapartist regime in France and other countries in Europe. But for Marxists this is not good enough. We must painstakingly analyse and explain every change in government. In that way we can prepare for the events to come.

Was the Kerensky Regime 'Bonapartist'?

Scattered through his article, Frank refers to 'Bonapartist *a-la*-Kerensky', the Bonapartism of Kerensky, thus assuming that Bonapartism had in fact been established under the Kerensky regime — entirely unwarranted by a knowledge of the period. Frank takes one or two conditional formulations of Lenin and Trotsky in relation to the Kerensky regime in Russia and tries to convert them into hard and fast definitions. In reality, the record speaks against him. It is significant to note that the chapter in the *History of the Russian Revolution* to which he refers, is headed, not 'Bonapartism', but *Kerensky and Kornilov —Elements of Bonapartism in the Russian Revolution.* Trotsky was always particularly careful on definitions and thus when he says 'elements', he does not mean the thing itself. And for very good reason. No doubt Kerensky would have *liked* to play the role of Bonaparte. The possibilities of Bonapartism were rooted in the situation. But Bonapartism was never achieved because the Bolshevik Party was strong and achieved. the proletarian revolution, leaving no avenue for adventurers to take control. Many citations could be given to show the conditional nature of the characterisation of the Kerensky regime as Bonapartist. In the very section quoted by Comrade Frank, from which he abstracts the single sentence characterising Kerensky as 'the mathematical centre of Russian Bonapartism', Trotsky wrote:

> The two hostile camps invoked Kerenksy, each seeing in him a part of itself, and both swearing fealty to him. Trotsky wrote while in prison: 'led by politicians who are afraid of their own shadow, the Soviet did not dare take the power. The Kadet Party, representing all the propertied cliques, could not yet seize the power. It remained to find a great conciliator, a mediator, a court of arbitration.'
>
> In a manifesto to the people issued by Kerensky in his own name, he declared: 'I, as head of the government . . . consider that I have no right to hesitate if the changes (in the structure of the government) . . . increase my responsibility in the matters of supreme administration.' *That is the unadulterated phraseology of Bonapartism. But nevertheless, although supported from both right and left it never got beyond phraseology.' (History of the Russian Revolution, Sphere, Vol lll p.155. Our emphasis)*

Trotsky wrote this as a historian, soberly evaluating and weighing every word. And if one studies the works of Lenin conscientiously, even though written in the heat of events, one cannot but see the falsity of Frank's position in confusing the germs with the disease. Lenin writes, for example, in his work *Towards the Seizure of Power*: 'Kerensky's cabinet is indubitably the first step towards Bonapartism. *(Collected works* Vol. 25 p. 224)

Here can be seen the *conditional* character of what Lenin and Trotsky were talking about. In the very section of *State and Revolution* quoted by Frank, in which Lenin refers to the Kerensky government as Bonapartist, the conditional character of this is shown by the paragraphs immediately following. In dealing with the state and all its forms in *an instrument for the*

exploitation of the Oppressed Class (that is what the chapter is headed
in which these references to Bonapartism occur, and that is what
Lenin is dealing with), he goes on to say:

> In a democratic republic, Engels continues, 'wealth wields its power
> indirectly, but all the more effectively', first, by means of 'direct
> corruption of officials' (America); second, by means of the 'alliance of
> the government with the stock exchange' (France and America).
> At the present time, imperialism and the domination of the banks
> have 'developed' to an unusually fine art both these methods of
> defending and asserting the omnipotence of wealth in democratic
> republics of all descriptions. Since, for instance, in the very first months
> of the Russian democratic republic, one might say during the
> honeymoon union of the 'Socialists' – Social-Revolutionaries and
> Mensheviks –joined in wedlock with the bourgeoisie. (*CW* Vol. 25,
> p.397)

To clinch the matter, in a later section of the same pamphlet
dealing with the same period, in contrasting a soviet to a
parliamentary body, Lenin goes on to say:

> 'A working, and not a parliamentary body' –this hits the vital spot of
> present-day parliamentarians and the parliamentary social-democratic
> 'lap-dogs'! Take any parliamentary country, from America to
> Switerland, from France to England, Norway and so forth –the actual
> work of the 'state' there is done behind the scenes and is carried out by
> the departments, the offices and the staffs. Parliament itself is given up
> to talk for the special purpose of the fooling the 'common people'. *This
> is so true that even in the Russian Republic, a bourgeois democratic republic, all
> these aims of parliamentarism were immediately revealed, even befor a real
> parliament was created...(Collected works.* Vol. 25, p. 428. Our
> emphasis).

We would have to reduce Lenin to a mass of stupid
contradictions if we used the method of Pierre Frank. For him
there is no real contradiction because he makes no real
contradiction between bourgeois democracy and Bonapartism. If
he carried this through he would have to argue that we had *both*
bourgeois democracy and Bonapartism in France and his objection
to the term 'bourgeois democratic regime' becomes entirely
incomprehensible.

Frank points to the fact that the British comrades have referred
to the Labour government in Britain as a Kerensky regime and
then proceeds to argue that this is incorrect because we have not a
Bonpartist regime in this country:

> Since we here speak of the resolution of our English comrades let us
> note that it defines the new Labour government as 'Kerenskyism'. The

Bonapartism, that they ignored, has found the means to insinuate itself into their document under a very special name. But we do not think the present Attlee government is Bonapartist *a-la*-Kerensky.

This merely serves to demonstrate that Frank has not understood the meaning of the Kerenskiad or of Bonapartism. The Kerenskiad is the last, or 'one before the last' left government before the proletarian revolution, or, we may add, the bourgeois counter-revolution. Under given conditions, the social tensions and sharp conflicts of the classes in such a period would tend to give rise to Bonapartist conspiracies and plots. That is precisely what happened in the Russian revolution, and that is why Lenin and Trotsky referred to the Bonapartist tendencies within the Kerensky regime. However, for Comrade Frank's benefit, this does not make a Kerensky regime a Bonapartist regime. Here perhaps we had better make haste to add, that in referring to the Labour government as a Kerensky government, this was not at all a finished evaluation, but an analogy which we invested with appropriate and necessary safeguards. To put the question beyond dispute, we quote from our resolution:

At a later stage the most resolute section of the bourgeoisie will begin to seek a solution in a Royalist or military dictatorship on the lines of the Spanish Primo de Rivera, or some similar solution. Royalist or fascist bands under the guise of ex-servicemen's or 'patrotic' association will begin to spring up.
Events may speed up or slow down the processes but what is certain is the heightening of social tension and class hatreds. *The period of triumphant reaction has drawn to a close, a new revolutionary epoch opens up in Britain. With many ebbs and flows, with a greater or lesser speed, the revolution is beginning.* The Labour government is a Kerensky government. That does not mean that the tempo of development will match that of the events in Russia after March 1917, on the contrary, the revolution will probably assume a long drawn out character but it provides the background against which the mass revolutionary party will be built.

Fortunately, to put the position in its proper perspective, Trotsky gave a definition of Kerenskyism —(he didn't call it Bonapartism!) when he dealt with the false positions of the Comintern in relation to the Spanish revolution of 1931:

. . .We see that fascism (we may add Bonapartism —EG) does not at all represent the only means of the bourgeoisie in its struggle against the revolutionary masses. The regime existing in Spain today (a coalition government of the bourgeois republicans and Socialist Party similar to that in Italy and France today. —EG.), corresponds best to the conception of the Kerenskiad, that is, the last, (or 'one before the last') 'left' government which the bourgeoisie can only set up in its struggle against the revolution. But this kind of government does not necessarily signify weakness and prostration. In the absence of a strong revolutionary party of the proletariat, a combination of semi-reforms, left phrases and gestures still more to the left and reprisals, can prove to be of much more effective service to the bourgeoisie than fascism. (We may add, naked military dictatorship −EG.) *(Germany, the Key to the International Situation,* Nov. 1931)

Frank's hazy notions of democracy and Bonapartism can be seen in his references scattered throughout his article. To take a few examples:

The use of democratic slogans −combined with transitional slogans is justified more precisely, *because the possibilities of a democratic regime are non-existent...*

Precisely because *we do not generally have in Europe at the present time democratic regimes, because there is literally no place for them...*

One must no more confuse the Bonapartism 'of the right' with fascism than the Bonapartism 'of the left' with democracy. We have seen that Bonapartism takes very different forms according to the conditions in which the two mortally opposed camps find themselves; *we maintain also that the existence of democratic liberties, even of very great democratic liberties, does not suffice to make a regime democratic.* The Bonapartists *a-la-*Kerensky, Popular Front... are even notorious for their flood of democratic liberty up to the point where capitalist society thereby even risks its balance and is in danger of capsizing. *Democratic liberties do not proceed, as in a regime which one can correctly define as democratic, from the existence of a margin for reform within capitalism, but on the contrary, from a situation of acute crisis,* the result of the absence of all margin or reforms.

...The regime of the Popular Front was not a democratic regime; it contained within itself numerous elements of Bonapartism as we shall see further on.

The conception of democracy which is put forward by comrade Frank never existed in heaven or earth. It exists only in the idealistic norms of liberalism. *Always, democracy, ie bourgeois democracy, has been built on the framework of repression.* Every bourgeois constitution or regime contains its Article 48 as in the Weimar Constitution. The very existence of class society presupposes a regime of oppression. But only one who has abandoned Marxist discipline of thought and operates on the basis of metaphysical categories can equate democracy with

Bonapartism, or for that matter with fascism. Though there are many points of similarity between these regimes, and elements of naked military rule in all these regimes in one degree or another. But quantity changes into quality. What dictates the nature of the regime is not this or that *element,* but its *basic features.* Democracy today can become Bonapartism tomorrow and be changed into fascism the next day. Fascism, as we have seen, can be transformed into democracy and the process repeated.

The Marxist method is not to lump all regimes indiscriminately together. That is the easy way, but it will lead to blunders and confusion. The Marxist method is to examine things in their process of change and evolution. To examine each government in turn, to establish its specific features and tendencies. To prepare for abrupt changes and transitions, which is the basic characteristic of our epoch, and thus to rectify and delimit, if necessary, our characterisations at each successive stage. The painful limitations of Pierre Frank's method (which he labels Marxism but is in reality impressionism) is summed up in his own words:

> The term 'Bonapartism' does not completely exhaust the characterisation of the regime, but it is indispensable to employ it in present day Europe, if one wishes to go forward with the least possible chance of error. Let us add finally that Marxism is not alone in the possession of such important general ideas: all the sciences do likewise. Thus chemists call bodies carbides which differ more widely from one another than the Bonapartism of Schliecher and that of Kerensky. And chemistry doesn't get along so badly either on that account. The contrary is true.

The Stalinists used the same method during the Third Period with lamentable results in Germany. Starting with a correct generalisation that all the parties from social democracy to fascism were agents of the captialist class...they ended up by saying that, therefore...there was no difference between them —all were fascists of different varieties. For the scientist as for the Marxist, the problem begins where, for Frank, it ends. A chemist can classify certain bodies under a general heading of carbides. But a chemist who stopped at this definition would not get along so well! If, for example, on the basis that a chemist had defined silicon carbide (carborundum) and calcium carbide, all under the same heading of 'carbides', one attempted to work an acetylene lamp on a bicycle with the former instead of the latter, some very sad results would occur. It would not be possible to light the path ahead. No more can Frank's method cast light on the nature of the regimes in Europe.

Ted Grant, Jimmy Deane and Jock Haston at the RCP headquarters in Neath during the 1945 by-election.

From... National Democratic Revolution or Proletarian Revolution: The Tasks in Germany.

January 1947.

THE COMRADES of the IKD (a section of the German Emigre Trotskyists) have replied to our criticism of their *Three Theses* in an article entitled *Two Balance Sheets* published in October 1946 *Workers' International News*.

While ostensibly correcting certain errors, viz: their claim that 'the national oppression has remained, only the uniforms of the oppressors have changed', they reinforce their fundamental revision which is contained in the assertion that what we are faced with in Europe was not, and apparently is not, the proletarian revolution, but wars of national liberation and a revolution *'basically equivalent to a democratic revolution'*. Ignoring the fundamental issue, the class character of the revolution, they jeeringly reiterate that the proletarian revolution, which had been confidently anticipated by the Fourth International, has not materialised.

True, it has not materialised. And an instructive discussion can and must be conducted as to the reasons for the failure of the proletariat to take power in the first revolutionary wave following World War II. But this does not invalidate the orthodox Marxist attitude towards the class struggle in Europe today any less than did the similar failure of the proletariat to conquer power anywhere in the world apart from Russia after World War I. Lenin and Trotsky explained this failure by the treachery of the Second International, of social democracy.

Today, the masses are deceived by two traitor 'internationals', the reformist and the Stalinist — with the latter being far more formidable owing to the authority usurped from the October revolution, having a base far stronger than that ever possessed by social democracy. This factor places exceptional difficulties in the path of the proletariat. The Stalinists have for the moment successfully switched the movement of the masses away from the proletarian revolution into the channels of the 'people's revolution', ie into the channels of bourgeois democracy, as did the social democrats after the last war.

Our German comrades of the IKD should remember the experience of Weimar. Had any sneering petit-bourgeois sceptic reproached Lenin and Trotsky, say in 1920, asking where was the promised revolution in Europe, they would have received a fitting but hardly polite reply. Our answer cannot be any different. The basic thesis of the IKD, which our comrades maintain without any real attempt at defence against criticism, is that capitalist 'retrogression' makes necessary in Europe a detour through what they define as *'basically equivalent to a democratic revolution'*.

For the basis of this, let us quote again the original *Three Theses*:

> The prisons, the new ghettos, the forced labour, the concentration and even war prisoners' camps are not only transitional political-military establishments, they are just as much forms of new economic exploitation which accompanies the development toward a modern slave state and is intended as the permanent fate of a considerable percentage of modern mankind.

This impressionistic evaluation, written at the height of the war, is being refuted by events.

This capitalist 'retrogression' theory is further developed on the basis of the temporary springing up of small factories during the war as evidence of a return to the 'slave state', the middle ages, and the dawn of capitalism. Temporary features caused by the needs of the war are transformed into permanent features of the present epoch. Thrown overboard is the Marxist theory of the concentration of big industry at the expense of small, of the replacement of handiwork by machinery, the development of the 'free' labourer as against the serf and slave labourer of the past.

The political wisdom of the comrades of the IKD is summed up thus:

> In contrast to the use of complicated machinery, and in contrast to the concentration and over-development of an industry fit only for war purposes, there is compulsory labour, that is the mass use of manual labour which is cheaper than machine labour, the founding and extension of small and middle-sized forms because of the shortage of consumer goods, the restoration of handwork, the dissipation and ruin

of the monetary system... The political situation in these systematically exploited countries (under nazi domination) is characterised above all by the destruction of workers' and non-fascist bourgeois parties.

Step by step unions, political and cultural societies of all kinds, religious organisations, etc., are wiped out according to the German pattern, changed or in some way put under direct fascist control. With certain exceptions, where this process has not yet been fully complete, there is no longer an independent traditional bourgeois or proletarian political or workers' movement, and in these countries (especially in Poland and Czechoslovakia) even the 'national' bourgeois is being more and more crushed by such means as 'aryanisation', compulsory sales and direct expulsion.

All that is left of the old organised 'movements' are today nothing but illegal circles which have little connection with each other and can in no way act as an entity... As it is pushed to that limit which is daily drawn closer by this enemy, it levels all and everything and takes a direction which can be described as nothing but a 'drive for national freedom'. In a few countries (Yugoslavia, Czechoslovakia, in part Poland, etc.) this drive has crossed the limit and has turned into a real people's movement. In it participate all classes and strata from workers, farm labourers, farmers, urban petit bourgeoisie (tradesmen and artisans, that is, together with the farmers, those classes, which in spite of their large numbers are remnants of pre-capitalistic modes of production) to officials, priests, intellectuals and generals.

If in the Europe dominated by Germany there is no longer an organised and active workers' movement and even the bourgeois organisations are out of the picture, there can also be no talk of the existence of real revolutionary organisations, in so far as they are understood as united structures which, even if illegal, would be willing and capable of influencing the development by means at least of correct agitation and propaganda...However one views it, the transition from fascism to socialism remains a utopia without an intermediate stage, which is *basically* equivalent to a democratic revolution. *(Three Theses)*.

With small changes, Dimitrov* and Stalin could have subscribed to such an analysis. So the workers' movement is still non-existent! On the contrary, the labour movement in Western Europe, far from having been destroyed, has come out of the war stronger than it entered it. True, the supporters of the *Three Theses* have tried to get round this little difficulty by decreeing that since the workers' movement is not led by Marxists, it is no workers' movement. But in that case there has not been a labour movement in Europe since 1923.

To tell the workers of France that their trade unions and political parties do not constitute a workers' movement would produce the

---

*Georgi Dimitrov (1882-1949) was a Bulgarian Communist Party leader. Living in Germany he was a defendant in the Reichstag fire trial staged by the Nazis in 1933. Acquitted, he moved to the USSR and became executive secretary of the Comintern 1934-43.

deserved reply! Of course, the IKD have only discovered this formulation recently. Before the re-emergence of the labour movement in Western Europe, they described the British Labour Party and trade-union movement as the only workers' movement left in Europe. The British Labour Party can hardly be described as 'Marxist' or conscious of the historic mission of the proletariat.

The re-emergence of the labour movement in all the countries of Europe reveals that the whole 'retrogression' theory of the *Three Theses* was fundamentally false. Under the totalitarian lid of fascism, the class struggle continued to boil. If the socialist revolution was to be achieved it could only have been led by the working class as a class, at the head of the mass of the people fighting against foreign oppression and its national agencies at home, ie, the national bourgeoisie and its appendages.

The proletariat could drag at the tail of the bourgeoisie through the 'all people's movement' (as was consistently carried through by Stalinism in Western Europe), or the mass of the petit bourgeoisie would be won to the programme of the proletarian revolution on the basis of a revolutionary proletarian policy. There was no middle way. Either with the bourgeoisie or with the proletariat. That is the sole alternative in the present epoch.

We ask the IKD comrades: Just reflect upon the development of Europe since the fall of the nazis! What has emerged? Not an all-class people's movement, but a division of political alignments in accordance with the basic class divisions in society; a polarisation with the working-class parties on the one side and the reaction on the other, with the petit-bourgeoisie uneasily balancing in the 'centre' Christian Democratic parties, a position which they cannot maintain indefinitely. Either they will go to the right in a neo-fascist reaction or will be won to the proletarian revolution under the leadership of the proletariat.

The Role of the EAM in Greece

The comrades of the IKD in their *Two Balance Sheets* say:

> Mistakes, if they are not investigated openly and corrected, must of necessity be repeated and become graver with repetition. Witness the British Section and the fighting in Greece. This broke out just after the RCP had drawn up a resolution on the national question, point 5 of which declares 'all national resistance movements to be agencies of one or the other group of imperialist powers'.
>
> This goes for the EAM as well, therefore the RCP would have had to make its stand against EAM with Churchill, if he was so blind as not to know his own agency. This was not done; the *Socialist Appeal* came out in **full support for the EAM and could hardly have done otherwise. But**

what about the resolution which had proved to clash with reality? Was it revised? No; it was reality that had to undergo revision. The revolt in Greece was promoted to the rank of the proletarian revolution. This valuable support, unfortunately, could not prevent the defeat of the revolt; upon which —again without any investigation —it was discovered that EAM after all was only a resistance movement, and Greece is paraded as an example of what devastating results followed from supporting a national movement.

If it is 'supported' as here, by ignoring it until the point of uprising is reached and then hailing it as the proletarian revolution, this is certainly correct.

The position of the RCP is somewhat distorted by the IKD comrades in the above quotation. To get a clear picture of the RCP's attitude towards the resistance movement, permit us to quote the relevant sections of the resolution on the national question in Europe:

1. The Revolutionary Communist Party condemns and fights against the national oppression of one nation by another; it supports the *right* of complete self-determination and political secession of every nationally oppressed people.
2. In the epoch of imperialism and its present phase of imperialist war, all the objective conditions demand that a genuine struggle for national freedom must be linked to the programme of the socialist revolution and the struggle for the United Socialist States of Europe.

While condemning the nazi oppression, the resolution condemns equally the national oppression which is carried on by the Allies, and defines the attitude of the revolutionaries to the resistance movements as follows:

4. The role of the European ruling classes is clear to see. They collaborated *as a class* with the foreign nazi oppressor and now seek to play the same role as agents of the military victors —Anglo-American imperialism and the Kremlin. Without the active support of Stalinism and social democracy the capitalists would long have lost all semblance of support among the workers and peasants. By subordinating the working class and its organisations to the leadership of the bourgeoisie and to the programme of Anglo-American imperialism and Stalinism, the social democratic and Stalinist parties play a counter-revolutionary role. It is the duty of revolutionaries, while striving at all stages of the struggle to win the rank and file to the banner of Trotskyism, to oppose and expose the role of these parties and their auxiliary organisations.
5. Despite their undoubted support from many thousands of the best proletarian fighters who see in the resistance movements not an instrument for the replacement of one master by another, but rather the instrument for the overthrow of capitalism and the emancipation of the working class, these national resistance movements in Europe today

are agencies of one or other group of imperialist powers. As movements they are incapable of genuinely struggling for national freedom.

That characterisation stands the test of events and requires no correction. It is clearly applicable to EAM as well. During the imperialist war EAM was on the side of Anglo-US imperialism against German imperialism. The RCP did not take an ultra-left position on the question of national liberation. It stood four-square for national liberation of the peoples of Europe from the shackles of German imperialism. But we never failed to warn that the leadership of EAM and other resistance movements were agents of imperialism.

Our warnings were confirmed by events. EAM did its best to come to a compromise with imperialism and tried to disarm the working class in the face of the royalist-fascist reaction and their imperialist backers. The fact that EAM came into collision with Churchill and the imperialists was due to the fear of the latter that EAM would not prove a reliable instrument in preventing the socialist revolution, and that through EAM Greece might come under the domination of Stalin, thus rounding off his hold on the Balkan peninsula.

The jibe about Churchill being 'so blind as not to know his own agency' befits the level of the rest of the arguments. They might as well have asked: Why did the Trotskyists support the Spanish republic against Franco, a republic which they designated as an agency of Anglo-French imperialism and Stalinism? Or do perchance the comrades now deny this and in retrospect discover that we had a 'people's movement' in Spain as well?

This characterisation did not prevent the Trotskyists from describing the Spanish events as an attempt at the proletarian revolution on the part of the masses, in spite of the content given it by the bourgeoisie and Stalinists. The movement in Spain was a proletarian revolution which was diverted into a 'people's bourgeois democratic movement' against fascism, in alliance with the 'shadow of the bourgeoisie', while the bourgeoisie itself was on the side of Franco.

So it was with EAM in Greece. The masses supported EAM. The bourgeoisie was with Churchill while the 'shadow of the bourgeoisie' united with the Stalinist leadership, and thus distorted the mass movement in a bourgeois direction. Despite the Stalinist attempt at 'national unity', the class struggle broke through the 'national people's movement'. This resulted in civil war between the proletarian-poor peasant wing and the bourgeois wing within the resistance movement, even while Greece was under the domination of the nazis.

After the so-called 'liberation', *de facto* power was in the hands of the working class, just as in Spain after the insurrection of the workers in Barcelona, Valencia and Madrid in the first days of the revolt. The EAM leadership frustrated the movement of the masses, gave up their arms and tried to arrive at an agreement with the imperialists. Despite their attempts at capitulation to the imperialists, civil war broke out because of the movement of the masses. If the IKD members deny that the revolt in Greece was an attempt at the seizure of power on the part of the proletariat, how do they characterise this movement? A 'people's movement'?

The revolt began as a spontaneous movement on the part of the masses, despite all attempts of EAM to prevent its breaking out. The incident which set the spark off was a classic one in the highly charged atmosphere to provoke a revolution. The firing on an unarmed demonstration on the part of the royalist-fascist Security Battalions was similar to the firing of the Czar's troops on the demonstration led by Father Gapon at the Winter Palace in St Petersburg in 1905. Should Lenin, instead of demanding the independence of the proletariat, have advocated the merging of the labour movement in the all-class people's movement? To pose the question is to answer it.

The firing in Constitution Square, Athens, as even the bourgeois *Times* understood, sowed the seeds of civil war. Civil war between which classes, and for what aims? For the 'people's revolution' or for the conquest of power by the proletariat? EAM was a classic example of a popular front betrayal of the proletarian revolution. Had EAM been successful, the regime that would have issued from the struggle could only have been a bourgeois regime. All talk of 'democratic revolution', 'national revolution', 'all class people's movement', etc., in the final analysis cannot but be a refurbished version of popular frontism.

There cannot be a 'democratic revolution' suspended in mid-air. The 'peoples' revolution' must have a class basis. And so we arrive back where we started. Define the class content of your revolution and then we will know where you stand!

What is the Aim of the 'Democratic Revolution'?

In dealing with the elusive 'democratic revolution' which is neither proletarian nor bourgeois, the IKD attempts to get out of the inextricable confusion by defining the content as follows:

(Grant is) fighting windmills. For instance the democratic revolution which we (IKD) are alleged to substitute for the proletarian revolution whereas, in reality, *we said that the democratic revolution in our epoch, 'can be realised only by the smashing of the framework of capitalism'. (Two Balance Sheets.* Our emphasis).

Confusion thrice confounded! We are gratified to learn from these comrades that the 'democratic people's revolution' which they state is necessary in our epoch cannot be accomplished by bourgeois democracy. They claim they are now *'alleged'* to substitute something for the proletarian revolution. What then *are* they substituting for the proletarian revolution? Do they seriously argue that all classes, including the oppressed bourgeoisie in the people's movement, are going to 'smash the framework of capitalism'?

Is there any other revolution, apart from the proletarian revolution, that can smash the framework of capitalism? When these comrades are pinned down to Marxian definitions, one can see how they slide back and forth, and their *Theses* become nothing short of nonsense. What then is the difference between the democratic revolution and the proletarian revolution? The real answer is that the comrades make it mean different things at different times, sometimes identifying it with proletarian revolution, sometimes a new stage, and sometimes one knows not what!

The Tasks in Germany

Just as they lumped the different classes in Europe under the rule of the nazis indiscriminately together, so now in relation to Germany, they lump together all classes oppressed by the Allies, to be united in an 'all-embracing national democratic revolution'. Germany, of course, has to wage a struggle for national freedom against her oppressors, just as the countries oppressed by Germany faced the same problem. But the whole crux of the problem lies in *how* the struggle for national liberation is to be waged.

The answer of the Fourth International is that national liberation can be accomplished only by the proletariat at the head of the movement. That will be the central idea put forward by German Marxists. Far from blurring over the class lines, these will be emphasised. Only a clear fighting class policy will win the petit bourgeoisie over to the programme of the socialist revolution, which is indissolubly bound up with the struggle against the Allied oppressors. Such a struggle can only be waged as a class struggle.

Yet the IKD comrades, again using intentionally vague

formulations, leave the door wide open to the most shameless opportunism, and even capitulation to reaction. They say:

> Unless the Fourth International makes the support of all movements for national liberation according to the *Three Theses* the main point in its programme for Germany, it will not be able to offer the masses anything beyond the programme of the reformists – nor even beyond the performance of the occupation authorities; for these have expropriated German capitalists (without compensation!) and clapped them into jail into the bargain – witness the action of the British military government against the coal owners of the Ruhr. *(Two Balance Sheets).*

The German workers, we can be sure, will weep no tears over the fate of the coal barons in the Ruhr, nor of the bourgeoisie as a whole in the territory occupied by the Russians. But the demand of the German Trotskyists in both sections of Germany will be *for the withdrawal of the occupation troops, and for the running and controlling of German industry by the working class.* To imagine that the problem of the German economy can be separated from the question: *which class* will control? is to turn one's back on Marxism. We can only penetrate the ranks of the social democrats and Stalinists by giving them a *class* alternative to the capitulation of their leaders to the Allies.

The struggle for freedom from national oppression in Germany can be waged on the lines of Schlageter*, the reactionary forerunner of the nazis, or it can be waged by the method of Lenin and Trotsky, on class lines. The petit bourgeoisie goes either with the bourgeois reaction or with the proletariat. In Russia the Bolsheviks waged a ruthless struggle against those who sought to surrender the class independence of the proletariat in the 'people's movement' against Czarism. In the East they denounced as the grossest treachery, the subordination of the communist movement to the bourgeois 'people's movement' for national liberation.

Only the proletariat, fighting on an independent class programme, could win the petit bourgeois masses to the struggle for national liberation, which could only be a struggle for power, ie, dictatorship of the proletariat. Transitional demands would be advanced – constituent assembly, expulsion of the occupation troops, but these would not be separated from the struggle for power. Events one after another, are revealing the petit bourgeois mode of thought, even the reactionary content of the ideas of the IKD comrades.

*Schlageter was a right wing nationalist Freikorps member who was executed by the French during their occupation of the Ruhr in 1923 for acts of sabotage. He became a nazi martyr.

The day before yesterday, as impressionists, they were driven off the class compass by the spectacle of the national oppression of Europe by the nazis. Then they floundered on the Allied conquest of Europe. Today, they have attempted to find their last hideout in Germany. But Germany again reveals pitilessly that the class structure of society results in a *political* division between the classes, and not at all their unification, even under the heel of a foreign conqueror, and even in a highly industrialised country like Germany whose industry has been partially destroyed.

In their practical activity in Germany, the protagonists of the IKD position looked towards university students and various strata of 'nationalist youth', without reference to class, to lead the 'national revolution' which supposedly united all classes in Germany! Naturally, with their conceptions of a destroyed working class and the incapacity of the proletariat, because of this, to give leadership to the nation, they turn their backs on the genuine forces of German national renaissance. They rejected the idea of the Fourth International concentrating on the working class organised anew under the banner of social democracy and Stalinism.

These, according to these sceptics, represented only the 'old' people with memories in the past. The 'nationalist youth' were the forces which would lead the struggle for the 'all embracing national-democratic revolution'. Now that the elections have been held in Germany, what has been revealed anew? The stubborn division of Germany *on class lines*. The middle class, as in the countries of Western Europe, have grouped round the reactionary banner of Christian Democracy, and thus become a counterweight of the bourgeoisie against the proletariat.

But the workers, despite all, despite the pessimists of the IKD, have clung tenaciously to their class traditions and voted for the workers' parties. The wonderful powers of recuperation of the working class, their aspirations to achieve the socialist revolution, their class instinct, is shown by the fact that despite the terrible betrayals, the workers' organisations received a greater percentage of the votes than before the coming to power of the nazis. There was no alternative revolutionary Marxist party, but the elections prove precisely the possibilities for a genuine Marxist current based on the class internationalist programme.

The struggle for national liberation does not and cannot prevent the inevitable differentiation of the population on class lines. And it could not be otherwise. National oppression does not abolish class exploitation, but merely aggravates it. A revolutionary criticism of the policy of Stalinism and social democracy, a class struggle waged on the traditional lines of Marxism-Leninism, offers the greatest possibilities for the Fourth International in Germany today. Even the Social Democrats go farther than the IKD.

In order to gain the support of the German proletariat, the Social Democratic leaders are making centrist pseudo-left speeches. They have as a consequence the support of the bulk of the youth, more particularly the working-class youth which is instinctively groping towards the socialist revolution as the only way out. The task of the German Trotskyists will be to demand that the Social Democratic leaders match their words with deeds. There are, of course, parties to the right of the Christian Democrats, playing with the ideology of nationalism. In every case they are either neo-fascist or represent some variety of extreme reaction.

It was not for nothing that Trotsky castigated the Stalinists for their flirtation with nationalist demagogy and slogans in competition with the demagogic denunciations by the nazis of the Versailles Treaty. Such a method cannot advance the struggle one single inch forward. It can only play into the hands of reaction. The struggle for national liberation must have a class axis, and cannot be separated from the socialist revolution. The petit bourgeoisie cannot be won to the socialist revolution by the adoption of a petit bourgeois 'national democratic' programme on the part of the proletariat. That would merely mean that the proletariat would drag at the tail of the petit bourgeoisie, and thus of the big bourgeoisie.

The petit bourgeoisie can only be won to the struggle against national oppression under the banner of the struggle against capitalism. Otherwise, they will once again become a tool of reaction, in a more frightful form. Germany will not go through the so-called 'necessary detour' of the national democratic revolution in any shape or form. We base ourselves on the traditions of 1918, not on the traditions of 1813. There can be no democratic revolution in Germany other than that achieved by the Allies!

In fact, the restoration of industry in Germany, even partially, which the Allies have been compelled to undertake will restore also the self-confidence of the German proletariat, whose temper has already been shown by the series of marvellous protest strikes directed against the 'nationalists' (who have thrown bombs against the American military government) and the protest strikes against the release of Papen, Schacht and other nazis. The demonstrations were undertaken to show that never again will the German proletariat allow German reaction to take power without a fierce struggle.

Whether speedy or protracted, whether conducted for economic and democratic transitional demands, for a united Germany and for a constituent assembly embracing all Germany free of Allied occupation, whatever demands will be put forward these can only be part of the struggle for the proletarian revolution during which soviets and workers' committees can be set up.

Other than this, there can only be the bourgeois counter-revolution in a democratic or fascist form, democratic counter-revolution which will be supported by the Stalinists and Social Democrats under conditions of mass upsurge, just as the Social Democrats supported it in 1918. If the position of the IKD were to be accepted by the German proletarian vanguard, it would result in a frightful trap for the German proletariat and new misfortunes and defeats of the working class.

General de Gaulle puts himself forward as the new leader of France (see France in Crisis).

From... Socialism and German Rearmament.

1953

THE GATHERING movement for the rearmament of West Germany has aroused a deep concern among the masses in this country. There is alarm and fear not only within the ranks of the working class but even the middle class and politically conservative elements have reacted in fear of the consequences.

Within the labour movement both those who oppose and those who support the rearmament of German imperialism all accept the same assumptions as the basis from which they draw their conclusions. The sole responsibility for the terrible slaughter and destruction of the two world wars is laid on the shoulders of German militarism. It is this propaganda and the fear of the third world war looming ahead in the future which has disorientated the mass of the labour movement.

The workers look with dismay at the terrible sacrifice in blood and suffering by which the defeat of German imperialism was accomplished in the second world war. Is all this to be in vain? Is there to be a new nightmare repetition of the bloody sacrifices and destruction? That is the question which is at the root of the outcry and opposition of the rank and file. Industrial workers, mothers of families, have been swayed into an outburst of anti-German feeling perhaps even more bitter than during the war itself, so far as the working-class movement is concerned.

The Labour Party National Executive Committee and the Parliamentary Labour Party have adopted a position of 'statesmanship' which echoes the propaganda of the government and the capitalist class, which they try to disguise as 'internationalism'. On the other hand the left wing, under the leadership of the Bevanites, hold up their hands in horror and, having started from false premises, land themselves in the position of nationalist self-righteousness and anti-German chauvinism. Neither of these approaches can serve the needs and interests of the workers of Britain, Germany, or of the world.

Without a class approach to the question, a fundamental

understanding of the absolutely irreconcilable antagonism between the interests of the working class against the capitalist class, nationally and internationally, a false attitude on the question is inevitable. It is not a question of nation against nation but of the working class against the capitalist class in a struggle in which the interests of the workers of Britain are the same as those of Germany, of Russia, of America and of the world. If these fundamentals are kept in mind then it is not so easy to be swayed towards the support of capitalism at home or abroad.

The history of the last fifty years, of the two world wars, is a history of the crisis of capitalism. The wars were not caused by the wickedness of the Kaiser or of Hitler but the insoluble contradictions of capitalism. Not only was German imperialism responsible but the imperialism of France, Britain, and America, and the criminal policy of the Stalinist bureaucracy in Russia as well. The fairy tale that Germany or German imperialism alone was responsible for the war is a pernicious falsehood intended to cloud a real understanding of the issue of war or peace.

An armed Germany is no more a menace to peace than an armed France, an armed Britain or an armed America. The policy of the capitalist class of all countries is not dictated by love of democracy, freedom or peace but purely by the needs and interests of the ruling class. Nor is the policy of the totalitarian Stalinist bureaucracy in Russia and her satellites dictated by love of socialism but by the needs and interests of the clique in control in Moscow and the other capitals. The defeat of Germany, Japan and Italy, contrary to the promises of the Allies, did not open up a new epoch of peace and prosperity to the peoples of the world but on the contrary, long before the question of German rearmament had arisen as a practical problem, inaugurated the worst arms race in the history of the world, dwarfing into insignificance the military preparation of Hitler before the second world war.

New submarine devices, rockets, ever-more deadly hydrogen bombs and other fiendish methods of destruction are being prepared every day. The arms programme of Russia, of Britain and America, represents a colossal expenditure of the substance of the peoples of these countries, thus exposing the hollowness of the claim that German capitalism alone was the cause of the first and second world wars. The idea sedulously disseminated during and after the war that the German people, and above all the German working class, are naturally militarist, does not bear examination. No more than the workers in Britain are the workers in Germany supporters of militarism and of war. The idea that the German workers were supporters of Hitler is a travesty of actual developments in Germany.

The responsibility for the victory of Hitler and all its tragic consequences for the workers of Germany and the world, was directly that of the leadership of the trade unions and Social Democratic Party, and of the so-called Communist Party in Germany. The German workers tried with all means in their power to overthrow German capitalism. But the labour and trade-union leaders on the one side, the Stalinists on the other, carried out policies of fratricidal struggle which reduced the working class to impotence in the face of the fascist threat.

However, despite the myth sedulously fostered in the movement by the Stalinists, Hitler never succeeded in gaining a majority of the German people. At the last free elections in 1932 the open capitalist parties received 4 million votes, the Social Democrats and Communists together over 13 million, the Catholic Centre Party over 4.5 million and the fascists 13.7 million votes. This was the apex of the nazi movement. A few months later while the vote of the working-class parties remained the same the nazi vote dropped by 2 million. It was in this situation with the threatened break-up of the nazi movement that the capitalist class handed power to Hitler in January, 1933. Even then the victory of the nazis was not assured.

Had the leadership of the Socialist and Communist Parties and the trade-union movement gathered together for resistance by a general strike, and had they been prepared to face the issue of civil war, Hitler would have been crushed by the working class. The workers were well armed and organised in the Republican Defence organisations, and in the fighting organisations of the Communist Party. They were better armed than the British Home Guard in the second world war.

The nazis had the declassed criminal element and the scattered middle class behind them. The overwhelming majority of the industrial working class was ready and willing to fight. The miners, dockers, railwaymen, engineers, chemical workers and the other sections of the industrial proletariat would have given a good account of themselves. They had as good a fighting tradition as the British or any other working class in the world. Today leaders of the labour movement attempt to shelve the responsibility for the betrayal of the Stalinist and socialist leaders onto the shoulders of the working class. But the responsibility for the tragedy in Germany which was to bring in its train the second world war once the main obstacle in its path, the organisations of the German workers, had been destroyed, rests not only with the leadership of the German labour movement. In other countries too, including Britain, the leadership of the labour movement and Communist Parties justified the policy of their respective counterparts in Germany.

The Communist Party in this country supported the crazy policy of the German Communists in directing the struggle against the 'immediate danger', the socialists. The labour and trade-union leaders in this country, Sir Walter Citrine at the Brighton Congress of the TUC in 1933, justified the betrayal of the German trade-union leaders by saying that it would have led to civil war and bloodshed had they called a general strike!

The Only Menace to Peace — an Armed Germany?

The fundamental question that is posed is 'Is an armed Germany a menace to peace?' We have endeavoured to explain already that what caused the first and second world wars was not alone the wickedness of German capitalism, but the policies of all the imperialist blocs and, in the case of the second, also the Russian bureaucracy. Long before Hitler had ever been heard of, and was but a corporal in the armies of the Kaiser, the great Marxist, Lenin had pointed out in a sober evaluation of the causes of the first world war, while the battles were still taking place, that unless the war was followed by a series of successful socialist revolutions then inevitably it would be followed by a second world war, a third world war — a tenth world war, till civilisation would be destroyed.

This analysis has been borne out by the facts. It is not Germany alone which threatens war, but American imperialism, British imperialism, and the policies of the Stalinist bureaucracy. Hardly had the echoes of the fighting in the second world war died out than already the victor nations, as after the first world war, were falling out among themselves. The Russian bureaucracy, incapable of a socialist foreign policy, continued with an enormous arms programme, imposing tremendous burdens on the then weakened structure of the Russian economy. On the other hand, after an initial period of demobilisation and the cutting down of arms by Britain and America (which was caused not by any love of peace, but by the pressure of mass opinion, sickened by six years of war and destruction) they embarked on an arms programme of staggering dimensions.

In the so-called cold war we have a period of strained relations far worse than any period short of war, in modern history. Here, as the result of the second world war, in which the real victors were Russia and America as continental powers, these two agglomerations of power face each other in Europe and Asia. Here again the cause of the conflict does not rest on the ill will or the good will of either of the two main protagonists in the cold war.

In the world today American capitalism-imperialism finds its

Ted, Jimmy Deane (centre) and Arthur Deane read Workers International Review in the 1950's.

It Need Not Happen
The Alternative to
German Rearmament

Aneurin Bevan

Barbara Castle

Richard Crossman

Tom Driberg

Ian Mikardo

Harold Wilson

THE DEAD OF 1939-45

THE DEAD OF 1914-18

vicky

Hands up all those in favour of a rearmed Germany !

Courtesy of the *Daily Mirror*.

Title page of the Tribune pamphlet It Need Not Happen with an uncritical reproduction of the Daily Mirror cartoon (see Socialism and German Unity).

path to world domination blocked by the mighty force of Russia on the one hand and the uprising of the colonial peoples in Asia for liberation on the other. The aims of America are no more than they were in the second world war guided by the defence of 'democracy, freedom and peace' but by the rapacious interests of Wall Street finance capital. That this is so is shown by the allies that America has succeeded in gathering behind her banner —Rhee*, Chiang Kai Shek and the 'great democrat', the butcher of the Spanish people, Franco.

These alliances demonstrate the falsity of the claim that American capitalism is opposed to the totalitarian dictatorship and the repressive system in Russia, China and Eastern Europe. This is the ideological cover behind which is hidden the real antagonism of American imperialism to state ownership of the means of production in Russia and the colonial movement for emancipation from capitalism and imperialism. The basic policy of British capitalism in reality is no better. The pacific policy of Britain in the Far East is not dictated by love of peace on the part of British imperialism but by the weakness of British capitalism as the result of the two world wars.

Her weakness has compelled her to lean upon America as the only counter-weight to the power of Russia. Her policy is dictated by the fact that she wants to preserve what is left of her shattered Empire, and wishes to avoid complications in Europe and Asia which, if they lead to a clash, whatever the result, could not but end in disaster for Britain, if not her total destruction. Churchill, like the class he represents, is neither a warmonger nor a peacemonger, but stands for war or peace according to the needs and interests of the capitalist class. And in their calculations also it is naked capitalist interests which dominate and not at all love of democracy, freedom, or peace.

On the other hand the aims of the clique in control in Russia are not much better. It is true that because of the elimination of capitalist private property they have no need of expansion in the same way as capitalist powers have expanded in the past. Therefore they are opposed to war which would be a risky proposition for them. Nevertheless they are not interested in socialism but purely the national aggrandisement of the officialdom in control in Russia. They are not interested in expanding the power of the working class but purely the power, income, privilege and prestige of the bureaucracy in Russia. It is true that in defence of these they stand guard over the state ownership of the means of production, from which these bounties

*The President of South Korea.

flow and in that sense play a relatively progressive historical role. Nevertheless, their whole policy is dictated not by socialist internationalism but by the needs and interests of the Kremlin clique.

If there were to be a resurgence of nationalism and militarism in Germany in the years which lie ahead the responsibility would be that of the Allied powers and above all of the Russian bureaucracy itself. The methods of conquest used by the victorious Red Army were hardly better than those of the nazis in the monstrous raping, pillaging, despoiling and annexations in Eastern Europe and the Ukraine. With the agreement of British and American 'democracy' East Prussia and part of German Silesia were arbitrarily annexed to Poland and Russia. A quarter of the area of Germany was forcibly cut from her living body.

Not only that but, aping the nazis, the German inhabitants of the area were compulsorily expelled into the truncated area of Germany. And in Czechoslovakia and other parts of Eastern Europe Germans who had lived in these countries for a millennium were ruthlessly driven out and also expelled to Germany. Ten million people, about a fifth of the population of the Federal Republic, were treated in this inhuman fashion and compelled to leave all but a few personal possessions behind.

The Two Germanies

Germany today is divided into two fundamentally hostile halves. In Eastern Germany the Stalinist bureaucracy with the aid of the bayonets of the Russian army has established a puppet regime on the model of the other regimes in Eastern Europe. Taking advantage of the position the Russian bureaucracy has bled Eastern Germany white for alleged reparations for the damage caused by the German army in Russia.

In nearly ten years it is estimated that they have taken the staggering total of £15 billion for reparations. Nevertheless in the early stages of the occupation, by introducing elements of workers' control in the factories and nationalising heavy industry and important parts of light industry, they succeeded in gaining a modicum of support from the working class. This has been rapidly dissipated by the totalitarian regime no different in its repression from the former Hitler dictatorship.

Despite nationalisation and planning, the lack of freedom, the arbitrary control, the mismanagement and bureaucratic despotism have repelled the East German workers and undoubtedly the regime exists at this stage only with the backing of the occupation forces of the Russian army.

After the second world war history, to a certain extent, has repeated itself. In the first period after the war the main concern of Western imperialism was to hold down the forces of German imperialism and to make sure that the possible socialist revolution would not be successful. The emphasis was to limit German industrial power as the basis of German military power. It was in this period that the programme of dismantling, of reparations and permanent disarmament of Germany was the official policy of the West. But with the end of the honeymoon period of relations with Russia and the beginning of the cold war, this reactionary and utopian policy was abandoned.

West Germany was included in the sphere of the Marshall Plan*. Far from extracting reparations from the Germans, in effect reparations were paid to West Germany. In this way, in the last few years, West German industry has been largely rebuilt in an even more modernised fashion than pre-war. Without the burden of an arms economy, with super-profits extracted from the workers and a higher rate of investment, West German industry has rapidly reached and exceeded the prewar development.

At the same time, as the Bevanites correctly point out, the forces which financed, backed, and benefited from Hitler are in power today. In steel, coal, chemicals, and big industry generally the same interests of finance and big business are in control. Behind the scenes the militarists and generals who controlled the army of the Kaiser and of Hitler are preparing to resume their accustomed role as a military caste, in a new West German army. Thus the question is anxiously asked by the sincere left-wing elements in the labour movement —'Isn't this where we came in?' High ex-nazi officials hold key positions in the government and civil service. Therefore, won't they prepare a new fascist coup in West Germany?

The posing of the question in this way is completely wrong. Fascism and military-police dictatorship does not arise merely from the will of capitalists and the generals. Fortunately it is impossible to impose fascism by decree. At this stage there are mighty trade-union and labour organisations in Germany. They learned a bitter lesson as a result of the experience of 1933. In the postwar period the attempt of the neo-nazis to organise was met by strikes on the part of the working class. Before the banning of the new fascist Socialist Reich Party the trade unions, under pressure of their members had threatened Adenauer** that they would take matters into their own hands if he did not act.

It was this that compelled the West German government to act

---

*Economic aid provided by the USA to Europe after the war, with the aim of preventing revolutionary movements by ensuring economic growth.
**Konrad Adenauer, a Christian Democrat, was the first chancellor (1949-63) of the Federal Republic of Germany (West Germany).

quickly, in addition to which capitalist forces are not sufficiently desperate to need fascism at this stage. The middle class, too, has become disillusioned in its experience of militarism and fascism. The boom West Germany is undergoing at the present time is similar to that experienced after the first world war. In the economic 'prosperity', with relatively full employment, and with the middle class in a reasonably comfortable position, there is no basis for reaction at this stage.

Thus at the elections in North Rhine Westphalia which includes the decisive Ruhr area, out of 10 million votes, the neo-fascists, or a thinly-disguised fascist front organisation, received less than 2000. This does not mean to say that as far as West Germany is concerned − a capitalist Germany − the problem of war and of fascism has been solved forever. The same causes that produced the eruption of Hitler and the attempt of German imperialism to conquer Europe are at work in West Germany today. This is not because the Germans as a people are any better or any worse than the other peoples of the world, but because of the specific problems of German capitalism.

A new slump, where the forces of the working class did not show a way out, would inevitably drive the middle class to despair, the West German capitalists seeking some form of fascist movement once again. Perhaps this time in some form of organisation like the one de Gaulle attempted to set up in France. German industry has again taken the road of attempting to conquer world markets. The productive forces of West Germany cannot be held within the narrow confines of Germany itself. In the long run they would endeavour to organise Europe and the world for the benefit of German capitalism.

In the early stages perhaps there might be propaganda for the recovery of the territories seized by the Russians and Poles, for the national unification of a divided Germany. Either way, before they could take to the road of war or fascism the forces of reaction in Germany would have to destroy the organisations of the working class, and the rights regained there in the last ten years. Fascists could only allow themselves the luxury of plunging into war, *because temporarily the home front, the most important front, was secure,* with the atomisation and powerlessness of the working class, and the psychological effects on the workers of the betrayal into Hitler's hands, without a struggle.

Such a repetition is extremely unlikely. Even from their own experience the leaders of social democracy and the trade unions would at least take to the road of their Austrian* and Spanish comrades − civil war rather than a craven submission to fascism.

*The Austrian workers rose in February 1934 in defence of a general strike against the reactionary government of Dollfuss, and the Spanish workers in July 1936 against the insurrection of Franco.

Bevan and NEC — Both Right and Both Wrong

On the lines of capitalism there can be no solution of the problem of Germany and Europe. Slumps, wars, and new crises are inevitable in the long run, if capitalism is allowed to continue. The Bevanites believe that German rearmament can be prevented in alliance with the forces of British, French and American capitalism together with that of the Russian bureaucracy. Let us examine this more closely.

The original Allied programme was that of draconic punishment of the Germans, of the limitation of Germany's industrial capacity, of a long term occupation by the four powers, and the visiting of the sins of Hitler and the SS on the German people. This programme was a programme of national oppression only one degree removed from the national oppression carried out by Hitler in the countries of Europe which he occupied. If it has been dropped by both East and West that is not out of tender concern for democracy or a change of heart and generosity on the part of the Americans and the Allies. It has been dropped firstly, because it was impossible to carry out for any length of time and secondly, because the Allies wish to redress the balance of forces which had arisen so disastrously for them on the continent of Europe as a consequence of the second world war.

The idea of the Bevanites of reverting back to the old policy is a reactionary dream. The question that the NEC put to the Bevanites, to which they have never given a clear answer is, 'how is this policy to be carried out?'. Any attempt to treat the Germans as a pariah nation would be doomed to failure. The attempt to enforce the non-fraternisation ban in the heated atmosphere engendered in the early months of the postwar period was impossible to apply.

The attempt to hold Germany down indefinitely with this policy would be precisely to fan the flames of nationalism and militarism in Germany. It would give a handle to their claims for equality and for national self-determination. British Tommies, French Poilus, and American GIs could not be used as SS for very long. Hitler could only use specially picked troops for his dirty work in occupied countries and not the ordinary German troops. Even then, the nazis could only succeed whilst provoking a tremendous resistance movement, because of a lack of democracy at home.

How long would public opinion in Britain, France, and America stand the national oppression of the Germans which this would mean? Apart from its non-socialist character such a policy is impracticable in the extreme. It is impossible, in the modern world, to hold down any great nation for any length of time. That is the lesson of history and something that the Bevanites with their glib phrases and easy attempts at popularity have still to learn.

The NEC is thus justified in their criticism of the Bevanites as being unrealistic on this question. On the other hand, what is the position put forward by the NEC? Previously, lumping together the interests of the capitalists and workers of America, France and Britain, and the other countries concerned, they have argued for support of the EDC (European Defence Community). Like the girl who justified her illegitimate child because it was only a small baby, so accepting the argument as to the original sin of German militarism and German militarists alone, they have argued for a 'controlled' and 'limited' or small German rearmament. Here the Bevanites have the laugh. For quite correctly, they point out that once German rearmament has taken place it is ludicrous to think that any paper limitations will have any effect. Once the generals and industrialists of Germany have the bit between their teeth, there will be no restraining their mad gallop except by the threat of force which, under those conditions, would mean provoking a new war. When the Bevanites say that it is quite likely that a rearmed West Germany will do a deal with the Soviet bureaucracy in the same way as they did in the Nazi-Soviet Pact of 1939*, which ushered in the second world war, they are quite correct.

That is quite likely. A rearmed Germany would be interested in the national interest of the capitalist class above all else. No more than the French, British or American capitalists have the German capitalists had a change of heart. It is the interests of German imperialism that they are concerned about. All agreements, as in all power political arrangements, will be unhesitatingly broken if they think they can derive an advantage from this. The rearmament of Germany will solve nothing, but will add a new element of instability into an already highly charged atmosphere.

The struggle on the European Defence Community has already shown what the process will be like. The positions of the different factions in France, apart from the Communist Party which, of course, is dictated by the foreign policy of the Russian bureaucracy, is devised to suit what they consider to be the interest of French capitalism. So too is the policy of British and American capitalism engendered by considerations of their interests.

If the French capitalists in their majority have apparently

*Having failed, despite the policy of popular frontism, to reach agreement with the 'democratic' imperialist powers, Stalin signed a 'non-agression' pact with nazi Germany in 1939. As Trotsky predicted, it turned out to be the opposite when Germany invaded the USSR in June 1941.

rejected EDC it is from fear of a too close embrace of a more developed and powerful economy, of their counterparts in Germany. The German capitalists, if they had the opportunity again, without too great a risk of failure, under the pressure of the contradiction between a highly productive economy and the limited German market would take to the road of dominating Europe without hesitation. *Thus German rearmament cannot solve the problems which beset Germany and Europe.*

The alleged safeguards suggested by the NEC would be as adequate as endeavouring to safeguard against a flood by digging a ditch in the middle of the affected ground. Like the savages who practise incantations, the NEC think that incantations can exorcise German militarism. Any new 'safeguard' limiting German rearmament would be about as practical a safeguard as the Treaty of Versailles. It could only be kept in being so long as it suited the interest of German capitalism. Not because Germany is different, but precisely because in the last analysis she is fundamentally the same as any other capitalist country.

The NEC states that in a state of emergency 'in case of a threat to their security *or an attempt to subvert the constitution of the German Federal Republic,* the three Western powers have the right, in consultation with the German Federal government, to declare a state of emergency'. This is a threat held in reserve against the danger of socialist revolution in Germany, and hardly a means of maintaining control of rearmament. In any event apparently the American imperialists are desperately searching for a strong and stable force on which they can rely in Europe to use against the danger of socialism and of the threat from the Russian bureaucracy. According to reports which are more likely than not to be correct, they already are secretly preparing for an army of at least 50 divisions in Germany, and not the 12 to which Germany was to be limited by EDC.

That is how much the alleged safeguards of the EDC or any other treaty that takes its place, are worth. It is a measure of the narrow and imperialist-saturated point of view of both the pamphlet *In Defence of Europe* and *It Need Not Happen* that both look at things from a viewpoint of German competition in world trade. And indeed on the assumption that capitalism will continue untrammelled in its present form, this is a formidable problem for the Western imperialists. It was the aggravation of this basic problem and the competition for world markets which was responsible for two world wars.

The economies of Germany and of Western Europe as a whole cannot be contained within the framework of the old national state.

That explains the anxiety of the capitalist forces in all the countries of the West. Private ownership of the means of production on the one side and the national state on the other, hamper and obstruct the full and free development of productive forces. It is this that has caused the chronic crisis of the last four or five decades, with its periodic bloodletting and destruction. If it were not so tragic the arguments used in this connection would be comical coming from socialists. The NEC for instance says that a neutralised Germany would be bad for Europe because it would mean a competition between West and East for the favour of Germany. 'In this auction the Soviet Union would be able to hold out the bait of markets for Germany's industrial goods to the East, and a possible return of the "lost territories«.'

It only remains to ask the NEC the gentle question: 'Once Germany is rearmed why shouldn't this problem be posed in the same way? What is to prevent this? The good intentions of the labour leadership, or their faith in the good intentions of the German generals and capitalists?' The Bevanite position on this is even more unrealistic. They say that there should be some delay on this question, because it 'can give statesmen the opportunity to think again and devise an entirely fresh policy'. Unfortunately, international politics is not a game of pat-a-cake, pat-a-cake, or postman's knock.

If for nine years the differences between West and East have got worse and worse and one conference after another has ended in failure or stalemate, it is not because Molotov* likes to say no, or because Mr Dulles is irritable and impatient, but because they are spokesmen of irreconcilable interests which are reflected precisely in the outbreak of the cold war. It is true that as the Bevanites say 'rearmament in Western Germany forms part of the strategy of the cold war, it would make well nigh impossible any negotiated settlement of the German problem. It would increase the likelihood of final catastrophe.'

But they do not see that in the last few years negotiations between West and East in Europe have been determined by the desire of both sides to place the responsibility for the division of Germany into two hostile states, onto the shoulder of their opponents. Both sides have used the negotiations as a means of propaganda to the German people, to place the responsibility in this way.

The reasons motivating this policy flow from the differences, which are fundamental. No more than it is possible to reconcile, except for a short period of time, the differences between the

---

*Vyacheslav Molotov was Soviet Foreign Minister, John Foster Dulles was the US Secretary of State who was influential in forming Cold War Policy.

workers and the capitalists in the single countries is it possible to get more than a temporary accommodation between two mutually exclusive and hostile social systems, such as that of Russia and the West. In fact if it is not possible to do so even in the case of countries with the same social system under capitalism, even more so is this the case where there is a class difference.

A so-called 'rational' policy of appeal to argument and reason is pitiably inadequate, and a cruel delusion and trap for the working class, when it is a question of struggle between mutually exclusive social systems, or classes. It is in this light that one must view the so-called Attlee conditions:

> German democracy must make sure that armed forces will be its servants and not its masters. I agree that there is always the danger of an emergence again of the same kind of forces that made Germany a menace, but you do not get rid of that by leaving a vacuum. The answer is that there should be democratic forces democratically controlled in Germany.

What possible guarantee can there be when the same officer caste will control the army as controlled it under the Kaiser, the Weimar Republic and Hitler? What kind of democratic control when the backbone of the civil service are the same elements again who faithfully served the Kaiser, cheerfully betrayed the Weimar Republic, obediently truckled to Hitler and, like the Vicar of Bray, have turned again and given lip service to democracy today? Here we might add that this problem is not peculiar to Germany.

In France there was a similar problem with the Vichy regime, with a similar result. And just to keep the record straight, in the island of Jersey the situation was nothing to boast of on the part of the British state forces there. If the conditions for the rise of fascism are repeated in Germany again, the consequences will be the same, unless the forces of the working class are organised and trained to meet it. Says the Bevanite pamphlet, 'There is still time to save Europe and the world from the dangers of rebuilding the military power of Germany. *It need not happen.*' Words, words, words! Hitler, amongst the few correct things he ever said, sneered at socialist politicians for becoming intoxicated with phrases.

Just how this pleasant consummation is to be achieved is not really explained. If only Eisenhower*, Malenkov, and Churchill would get together over a tea table, or a bottle of vodka, everything would be settled. Apparently the problem consists in reasoning with these gentlemen to see the horrors that would beset mankind otherwise. It is probably true that it wouldn't do any harm to have

*US President, Soviet Foreign Minister and British Prime Minister respectively in 1953.

the heads of all these gentlemen examined, but whether they are sane or insane, whether they are bad tempered or good tempered, whether they are humanitarians or warmongers, is beside the point. Either good or bad they are merely representatives of the policies of the capitalist class and imperialist countries, or the Stalinist bureaucracy in Russia.

Germany has been disarmed and helpless for nine years, and lo and behold, the calamities, the clash of national rivalries, have continued as merrily as before the war. And it is the clashing of capitalist interests which produces the conflict, and not the good or bad intentions of this or that politician, or even this or that party. At the annual Labour Party conference the NEC with their 'compromise' resolution outflanked the Bevanites and thus the latter's position on the question was rejected by a small majority. But supposing they had gained the victory, what would they have done with it?

Both the right and left wings are fond of talking 'practical politics'. What would have been the practical consequences of a Bevanite victory? One way or another, with the present relationship of forces in the world, and under present conditions, Germany is going to be rearmed and in the immediate future at that. She is going to be rearmed because that is the desire of the French, British and American capitalist forces, not to speak of the forces of German capitalism itself. Thus a victory for the Bevanites would not have presaged any action at all on their part.

The Bevanites claim to 'outline the constructive socialist policy'. In this regard, the Bevanites offer a prescription of agreement between all the big powers, for the benefit of the colonial peoples. This at a time when American capitalism is busy propping up every reactionary landlord capitalist feudal clique oppressing the colonial peoples in Asia. When American imperialism is still madly refusing to recognise the accomplished fact of the victory of the Chinese Revolution, maintaining Chiang Kai Shek in Formosa (Taiwan), and wistfully longing for the day when they can use Chiang Kai Shek against the mainland. This at the time when the Russian bureaucracy is oppressing the peoples of the national republics in Russia and satellite states of Eastern Europe. This at a time when British imperialism is busily holding down the peoples of Kenya and of Malaya. The facts of life are sad things. One could wish it otherwise but, like a maiden aunt wailing at the sinfulness of modern youth, the finger wagged didactically at imperialism and Stalinism to teach them their business, is about as sensible.

In a conflict of interest, there is no question of what is for the good of mankind, as the sentimentalists think. There is only one force in the world which is really opposed to war, which is through and through democratic, and whose interests are the interests of the future of man: *the force of the international working class.* And this, not for humanitarian or moral considerations. It is because the interests of the working class of Russia, Germany, Britain, France and America and China are actually one and the same. In fact, this is the basis of a real socialist policy. All manoeuvres and dreams, all diplomatic negotiations and shuffles can only, in the long run, be a jockeying for position in the shifting turns of foreign policy.

The Problem of German Unification

Germany is divided into two fundamental and hostile camps, and here again it is no accident that the Russian bureaucracy in their zone, whilst they have imposed a vicious dictatorship through their puppets, have nevertheless largely eliminated the forces of capitalism and organised a regime on the Stalinist model. Nor is it an accident that in their zones in the American, French, and British sectors it is forces of capitalism and reaction that have come to the fore, though reluctantly, room has had to be made at the same time for democracy on the Western capitalist model.

A major problem for Europe and the world in the years that lie ahead, is how Germany is to be unified. It is true that if free elections were to be held in the Eastern Zone, the Stalinists would be defeated. But that is something which the Stalinist forces cannot allow, with or without agreement from the West. Concessions would have to be of a fundamental far reaching character to compensate the Russians for the military, strategic and economic advantages which the domination of the Eastern zones give them. On the other hand for the Western capitalists, unification can only be accomplished on their terms, without these fundamental concessions. Thus, on this key question, in the capitalist way and the Stalinist way, there is no road out.

The laments of the Bevanites that it is a question of 'negotiation or fight' are beside the point. Negotiations can only take place for the solution of secondary questions and when both sides have concessions to make which mutually cancel out. That is the position as far as trade is concerned and in the immediate future trade between East and West will probably be increased. But the idea that one can 'settle the German problem by negotiations with Russia,' as the Bevanites suggest, does not bear any serious examination.

On the other hand, the Bevanites correctly say *that in the long run* this problem will be solved either by 'liberation' or 'negotiation'. This is correct, but all that it means is that in the long term future the problems will pile up and pile up till, if the forces of Stalinism and capitalism remain intact, in the long term perspective there will be an explosion! Isn't this a prognosis of gloom and horror, of destruction and misery? Not at all. It is true if the future of the peoples is to be decided by their present rulers, then the future of mankind is dark indeed.

Fortunately, there is another force which is being generated. The power of the working class of Germany and of the world. It is the only progressive force which really has no interests other than the advancement of mankind, because it means its own advancement. The German problem in the last resort can only be solved by the German working class, leading the German nation, in alliance and collaboration with the British and international working class.

The redevelopment of industry in Germany has strengthened its power enormously. To those with eyes to see, to those with an understanding of the fundamental ideas of socialism, this should have been proved by recent events. Despite 20 years of Hitlerite and then Stalinist tyranny in Eastern Germany, despite the war and all its consequences, despite the disorientation of the German working class, by the policies of the international labour movement and the so-called Communist Parties, we saw in Eastern Germany the mighty power of the working class, of their desire for democracy and socialism, in the inspiring June days of 1953*.

Against all odds, within a few days, the puppet regime in the Eastern zone was overthrown. Adenauer and the West German capitalists and militarists must have shivered in their shoes. This was not the kind of 'liberation' that they desired. The unification of Germany under these conditions would have meant the hegemony of the working class, and the speedy development of socialism through all Germany. Fortunately for them, the terrified Moscow bureaucracy intervened with the Russian army and restored the *status quo*.

But we have to look, not only to the East, but to the West to see the still developing power of the working class. In Western Germany the pressure of the workers in coal and steel has resulted in a relative measure of control by the trade unions, through the participation of their representatives on the board of management of these industries. The strikes in Bavaria have shown that the fighting spirit of the German working class has been reawakened. Theirs is the only force which, in alliance with the workers of other countries, can really ensure peace and plenty for the people.

*On 16 June 1953 a general strike movement began in East Berlin and rapidly spread throughout East Germany. At its peak it encompassed over 300,000 workers before it was suppressed with the aid of Russian tanks.

The problem for British labour on the German question is how best to help the German workers in their struggle against German capitalism, the Allied occupation, and the forces of Stalinist totalitarianism in the East. On the road of capitalism, on the road of diplomatic horse-deals and negotiations there is no way out, except an endless protracted stalemate, ending in catastrophe. A new slump, a new reaction, a new war! But this is the road that neither the Germans nor the workers of any other country wish to travel.

The first task of the allied working class, and of the British labour movement in particular,is to demand that all forces of occupation should be withdrawn, and that the fate of the German people must be decided by the Germans themselves. Any other policy is a shameful capitulation to the policies of nationalism, imperialism, and chauvinism. It is to repeat, in a different form, the racial lie of Hitler, that the Germans are different, only where he put a plus they put a minus. On this road there is no way forward. The only force really opposed to war through and through, to militarism and reaction, is the force of the working class.

In a progressive way, the only method of uniting Germany lies in action by the German workers themselves. The overthrow of German capitalism by the workers of Western Germany would undermine and paralyse the forces of Stalinism and of American imperialism. The only progressive way to a united Germany is a united, socialist-democratic Germany. That is why the main task of British Labour is not to collaborate with the British capitalists or the Stalinist bureaucracy but to support and assist by every means possible the forces of socialism in Germany. This can only be done by a struggle against the capitalist class at home.

As far as the labour movement is concerned, a thoroughgoing socialist programme at home, a militant policy to get rid of the Tories and force the resignation of the government, preparing the way for a new Labour government with a socialist policy at home and abroad, is the only real means of fighting against German rearmament in the interests of the working class here and abroad. *Home and foreign policy are inextricably bound together.*

A militant socialist government at home, which would nationalise all big industry on a democratic basis, could successfully appeal to both East and West. The American capitalists would be incapable of action in face of a real democratic socialist Britain. They could not point to the scarecrow of Russian or Chinese totalitarianism as an excuse for action; on the other hand, the Russian bureaucracy could not point to the very real danger of capitalist attack and the threat this represents to state ownership and planning in the

Eastern bloc. Not only that a real socialist Britain could offer the only practical alternative to the national and racial hatreds which besmirch the face of Europe.

The capitalist politicians in Europe and America themselves realise the hopeless mess to which national rivalries have reduced Europe in the last 50 years. But, whilst they recognise the problem, impotently, they can do nothing about it. They can occasionally dream of a United Europe as suggested by Churchill, Schumann*, Adenauer, Dulles and other capitalist politicians, but that is all they can do. And, incidentally, in this one fact is revealed the ineptness of all solutions such as that suggested by the Bevanites or the NEC of aid to the East in the interests of all!

From the viewpoint of capitalism as a whole, a united continental Europe would be as powerful a force, economically as well as militarily, as the United States of America. But *the individual* national capitalist interests clash to such an extent that a United Europe under capitalism is an idle dream!

However, British Labour occupies a strategic position in the world. If British Labour had on its banner the erection of a socialist Britain (as a preparation for a United Socialist States of Europe) in indissoluble alliance with the colonial peoples, the power of militarism and capitalism and of the Stalinist bureaucracy to which the NEC and Bevanites in different ways point, would be irredeemably broken. The way would be clear for an advance of democracy, socialism and peace. *The lesson of history is that there is no other practical way.*

*Robert Schumann, French Foreign Minister and former Prime Minister.

From: The Rise of De Gaulle and the Class Struggle.

May 29, 1958

THE 'LIBERATION' of France lifted the lid of the class struggle. It was achieved partly by the uprising of the Paris masses (August 1944). General de Gaulle's forces, indeed, were rushed frantically to Paris to forestall the possibility of a new Paris Commune. At the first general election in 1945 the shift in class relationships and the change in the psychology of the masses were reflected. Fascism and capitalism were completely discredited, and all the right-wing parties were overwhelmingly defeated. For the first time in history the Communist Party (CP) emerged as the strongest party, and socialists and communists together had a majority (51 per cent) of the votes: a higher proportion than the Labour Party obtained in Britain at about the same time (48 per cent).

The right wing, headed by clerical reaction, was forced, following the defeat of its open forces, to rally around the MRP (Mouvement Republicain Populaire), as in similar circumstances its Russian opposite numbers had grouped themselves around the Constitutional Democrats (Cadets) after February 1917. To retain the support of small peasants and backward Catholic workers, the right was forced to take on a 'left', 'socialist' coloration. The index to the revolutionary crisis was that the CP commanded the support of the overwhelming majority *of the workers*, obtaining five million votes. Big sections of the middle class swung over to the Socialist Party (SP).

The symptomatic significance of this is shown by the fact that even in the revolutionary crisis of 1936, the workers' parties were still in a minority. Further irrefutable proof that France in 1944-5 was rotten-ripe for revolution lies in the fact that for the first time *the majority* of the workers were organised in trade unions. This is something achieved in no other country at no other time under a capitalist regime: Lenin himself made the point that such a state of affairs was all but impossible under capitalism. In fact, such was the

mood of the workers that the CP took the leadership of the CGT
(the French TUC), and thus led both the official and the 'unofficial'
(factory committees, etc) movement of the French working class.
Capitalist reaction was helpless in face of the revolutionary wave. A
revolutionary policy on the part of the workers' parties would have
clinched a class victory, which in turn would have lit a conflagration
which could have swept Europe, including Britain. France would
have stood once more at the head of the revolutionary forces
throughout the world. Britain and America would have been
unable to intervene.

The American and British troops, weary of war and longing to be
home with their families, wanted 'out'; not only that —they
themselves would have been infected, as had the German soldiers
before them, by the agitation-propaganda of the revolution
(witness Russia 1917). This point is underwritten by the fact that
the USA was unable even to intervene directly against the Chinese
revolution at a later stage: if not in China, how much less in
France? The ruling class had to play for time. They were in a
similar position to that which they occupied in 1936, except that —
at least temporarily — they were far weaker. At such times, as
Lenin so often pointed out, the capitalists turn for comfort to a
coalition with the Labour and trade-union leaders. But this time
the most pernicious role was reserved for the leaders of the
so-called 'Communist' Party.

At that stage de Gaulle could not have carried even a majority of
the MRP for a programme of Bonapartist dictatorship. As a
consequence, he resigned and awaited events. The CP participated
in a 'government of national unity' in which, incidentally, there
were 11 capitalist ministers against ten from the workers' parties.
The masses still had tremendous faith in the Communist Party and
as late as 1947 hundreds of thousands of Parisians demonstrated in
the Party's favour. Yet, in the name of 'national unity', this CP
participated in the government which waged war against
Indo-China (Vietnam), was responsible for the slaughter of the
Algerian people, the Madagascar massacre and all the other
colonialist atrocities of French imperialism.

They acted as the worst strike-breakers, holding back the
movement in the factories. Later, they began to offer verbal
opposition, afraid of being 'outflanked from the left'. Then, having
fulfilled their scab role, the CP ministers were ignominiously cast
out of the government in 1947. But for the rest of that year they
functioned as a 'loyal opposition', until the new turn in the
Kremlin's line following the formation of the Cominform* in
October 1947.

*The Cominform drew together the Communist Parties of the East European
states, France and Italy. It was dissolved in 1956.

De Gaulle's First Bid For Power

Meanwhile de Gaulle tried to organise his own 'Society of December 10'* under the title of the Rally of the French People. The Rally managed to secure 40 per cent of the votes in the municipal election of 1947 and a fairly large percentage in the parliamentary elections of 1951. But the strength of the working class at that time was too great. The middle-class cadre of the Rally was not prepared to fight on the streets in support of its idol. The decisive section of the ruling class wanted peace in which to enjoy the profits brought by the mounting boom, and were not prepared to back a political adventurer, financially or otherwise; they were afraid of a civil war in which victory was by no means certain to be theirs.

The laws of revolution and counter-revolution are the same on this point. Twenty years of struggle against capitalism may be necessary to build up the exasperation and determination of the workers to destroy the system. But by its very nature a revolutionary situation cannot last. If the leadership of the working class does not avail itself of the opportunity to seize power —an opportunity which may last only a few days — the chance can be lost and many years may pass before a new occasion can arise. The working class becomes demoralised and, not understanding the reasons for the defeat, tends to blame the mass for the catastrophe and to bend anew to the yoke of capitalism.

The development of the counter-revolution follows a similar path. Failure to take advantage of the upsurge of the middle-class masses, disillusioned in the left and leaning towards the 'Great Man' as saviour, may mean the loss for the counter-revolution of the opportunity to seize power. De Gaulle's failure to seize control in 1951 meant the debacle of his hopes for a whole period —no thanks to pale-pink compromisers in the socialist and communist leaderships.

The instability of the Fourth Republic has continued. Despite the boom, the decay of French capitalism has continued apace. The attempt to 'modernise' France has been largely at the expense of the middle class and peasant masses. A symptom of this crisis has been the continued search by this class for its Messiah —first De Gaulle then (partly) Poujade**.

During a considerable part of this period (1948-52), the CP provoked all manner of adventurist strikes and demonstrations on

*The Society of December 10th was an organisation of the lumpenproletariat which supported Louis Bonaparte, in effect his private army.
**Poujade led a reactionary organisation of small business people and wealthy middle class, it was absorbed into the Gaullist movement.

an anti-American basis leading their men, like the 'grand old Duke of York', up the hill and down again, without ever posing a perspective which could justify the sacrifices so constantly demanded of the Party's supporters — the conquest of power. As a result the movement of the workers ebbed and ebbed. From the position when millions of workers could move into the streets at the CP's behest a time was reached when the Party was lucky if it could mobilise 10,000.

French imperialism emerged from the war weakened and debilitated. For 20 years the armies of France have suffered nothing but defeat. As a consequence of the anti-imperialist upsurge following the second world war France has lost Syria, the Lebanon and Indo-China, and direct control of Morocco and Tunisia. In every case the greedy and myopic ruling class was forced out only after tremendous struggles by the colonial peoples. In Indo-China alone, the cost of the war to France was more than she received in economic aid from the US. All this blood and treasure was spilled in vain, and French imperialism was compelled to retreat.

The Suez* adventure, under American pressure, turned into an inglorious fiasco. Yet all these losses pale into insignificance beside the potential loss of Algeria. French imperialism, after its experience in Vietnam, Tunisia and Morocco, would perhaps have preferred to make some sort of compromise with the Algerian nationalists. Yet ironically Algeria was the one place where such a compromise was least possible within a capitalist framework. The interests of the big landowners and capitalists in Algeria stood, breaker-fashion, in irreconcilable conflict with the surging wave of the Algerian independence movement.

Under pressure of the *colons*, a colonial war of classic pattern exceeding in violence, torture, murder, rape, all the past atrocities of imperialism, was launched against the Algerian people: a war that has stretched its shadow over the last three years, a war which is bleeding France to the extent of – 600million and more per year. Not the least tragic element in this situation has been the fact that the Algerian war could have been the basis of renewed struggle against the regime in France, in fraternity with the Algerian people.

Had such a struggle been waged, it could have split the settlers in Algeria, winning the lower middle class and small landowners to the demand for a socialist Algeria, linked fraternally and with full

*In 1956, after Egyptian president Nasser nationalised the Suez Canal, Britain and France conspired with Isreal to engineer a pretext to occupy the canal zone. They were forced to withdraw under international, especially American, pressure.

rights (including that of secession) with a socialist France. But the passivity of the Communist Party and the Socialist betrayal, whereby Mollet and his friends supported the war and even intensified it after gaining power on a programme of peace in Algeria, meant that the war became a ghastly conflict of extermination on both sides. The *colons* were welded into one reactionary mass, and the Algerian freedom fighters pushed back on to a purely nationalist programme. The first reaction of the reserves called back and the conscripts called upon to serve in Algeria was one of active opposition: demonstrations, the stopping of trains, strikes and agitation against the war. But there was no mass campaign against the war like that waged in 1925 against the war in Morocco — and this at a time when the CP was a hundred times as strong.

All that the CP did was to offer verbal opposition, not linked with the day to day work of the Party, in order to 'make the record'. Not only this, but the shameful treachery of Thorez* and Duclos was spotlighted when they voted for the war credits of the Mollet government.

It was with this vote — and not with their 'anti-colonialist' phrasemongering — that the leaders aligned the activities of their Party.

Conspiracy in Algiers

The pay-off for this crime is the recent events in Algeria. In Algeria, all workers' organisations have been long since illegalised. To carry on the war the French army and above all the paratroops have waged a war of terror in the areas they dominate. The paratroops have been revealed as a Praetorian Guard similar at best to Hitler's SA**, with Massu as their Roehm. They have become a hardened force of torturers, rapists, murderers, ready for anything.

In the meantime, with the workers' parties failing to give a solution to the problems of French society, the officer corps has begun more and more to express its discontent at the 'half-measures' of successive French administrations. General

*Guy Mollet was general secretary of the French Socialist Party, he entered de Gaulle's cabinet in 1958. Duclos and Thorez were Communist Party deputies and leaders.
**The SA, the Stormtroopers, were set up by Hitler as a para-military force for 'protecting' meetings. Ernst Roehm was the leader of the SA until 30 June 1934, the 'Night of the long Knives', when the leadership of the SA brownshirts were massacred by Hitler's SS. This was because the SA, with a mass membership, had become a threat to Hitler, with some of its members calling for a second 'social' revolution to follow the 'national' one.

Massu naively revealed the thinking of this corps in an interview in the *Evening Standard:* 'The army has suffered one defeat after another for the last 20 years. It is all the fault of the politicians, who would not give the generals a free hand.'

These people burn with the desire to destroy the workers' organisations and their rights, which frustrate them at every turn. These organisations, Massu and company believe, stand in the way of 'Greater France'. It was in this atmosphere that the basis was laid for a *coup*. Playing on the fears of the *colons* of a deal between the ruling class in France and the Algerian nationalist movement, the conspirators prepared their plans. In France the regime has been racked by continuous crisis: one prime minister has followed another, without any of the problems being solved.

Parliament has been deadlocked between the open representatives of capitalism and those deputies who, in a grossly distorted form, reflect the interests of the masses. In the last crisis, preparations were laid by the Algerian settlers for a *coup d'etat* – preparations directly involving the arch-conspirator de Gaulle himself. Using as their excuse the execution of three French soldiers by the FLN* – in reply to countless executions and tortures by the French – the settlers organised demonstrations in Algiers.

With no real opposition from the police, they marched on Government House. Then the paratroops, supposedly in Algiers to keep order, joined in helping to sack the building. Instantly General Massu appeared on the balcony of Government House and announced the formation of a 'Committee of Public Safety'. In this he was joined by Raoul Salan, commander of the French forces in Algeria.

Taking advantage of the fact that there was no government in France they demanded that Pflimlin (one of the MRP leaders) not be invested as prime minister, and that President Coty call General de Gaulle to power at the head of a 'Government of Public Safety'. It was intended that the movement should take place simultaneously in Paris and Algiers.

The right-wing rabble demonstrated on the Champs Elysees for a government headed by de Gaulle. As in 1934 they intended to intimidate the deputies into changing the government. But they were even weaker than the fascist razor-gangs of 1934. At this stage there is no basis for a mass fascist movement in France: all they could mobilise in all Paris was 6000 who ran in cowardly flight from the blows of the police.

*The National Liberation Front (FLN) waged a war of independence in Algeria from 1954 to 1962, when independence was won.

The movement in Algiers seemed on the point of isolation. The *coup* had failed. The 'brave' Massu and General Salan were explaining that they had been forced into this position and had only accepted 'the call' to preserve order. Admiral Auboyneau, who had already turned coat once, turned it again and vowed anew his loyalty to Paris. Two members of the general staff were arrested and the chief of the general staff resigned. It was at this point that General de Gaulle intervened, stating that he would take power 'if I am called'.

This declaration rallied the insurrectionists in Algiers —indeed, that was its purpose. It put fresh heart into the most reactionary elements in France. The three trade-union confederations, in response to the alarm of the workers, issued a call to general strike if there were any threat to constitutional government. In the meantime, Pflimlin had been hurriedly invested. One thing was clear: this was a crisis in which the whole fate of the regime was at stake. In this situation not only did the Socialists behave according to the classical social-democratic pattern, but the self-styled 'Leninists' of the CP succumbed to all the parliamentary illusions against which Lenin had so sternly warned. Saying that they were acting 'to bar the road to de Gaulle', they voted for the Pflimlin government and for the proclamation of a state of emergency forbidding meetings and demonstrations.

Yet the leaders of the French CP had been (correctly) among the most vociferous critics of the German Social Democracy for voting for Hindenburg* 'to stop Hitler' and supporting the decree laws of Bruening, leader of the Catholic Centre Party (the German equivalent to the MRP), as the 'lesser evil' to nazism at that time.

The *only* way to stop de Gaulle is the extra-parliamentary mobilisation of the working class, drawing behind it the plebeian masses. Truly the 'Little Plum' has proved 'worthy' of the support given it by the Socialist and Communist Parties. In the heat of the moment, Pflimlin had denounced the insurrection of the generals. But the basic class interests of French capitalism dictated a different course. The most barefaced high treason was meekly accepted and Pflimlin tried to placate the mutinous scum by adopting its programme: war to the death in Algeria, moves towards dictatorship by 'strengthening' the executive, castration of parliament, and so forth.

Then in the traditions of French bedroom farce we had the spectacle of the CP leaders appealing to Pflimlin, Pflimlin

*In the 1932 presidential election in Germany, the SPD, the largest workers' party, refused to stand a candidate, throwing their weight behind the reactionary militarist Hindenberg. On 30 January 1933 Hindenberg appointed Hitler as Chancellor.

appealing to Salan, Salan appealing to de Gaulle, and de Gaulle appealing for power.

If the Pflimlin government had been worth the least confidence, even from a 'democratic' point of view, it would have immediately cut off all supplies to Algeria, outlawed the generals, and appealed to the 350,000 conscripts in Algeria to arrest them and hand them to the authorities.

Gaullism Without de Gaulle

Instead, the government advanced a programme of 'Gaullism without de Gaulle'. In the words of *Evening Standard* reporter Randolph Churchill, who cannot be accused of a working-class or even an ultra-democratic bias, 'the most unprecedented thing in history has happened. Mutinous generals, instead of being denounced for their crimes, have actually been reinforced.' And these bewildered troops have been met on disembarkation by representatives of the Committee of Public Safety who have subjected them to a barrage of propaganda over the loudspeaker.

When General Franco organised his insurrection in Morocco against the elected Spanish government, Pflimlin's counterpart Azana had to negotiate secretly with the insurgents for fear of the masses' reaction. In this he was, from the standpoint of the Spanish bourgeoisie, justified, as was proven by the mass outbreak of the Spanish workers when news of the insurrection of the general reached them. How good for nothing then are the rotten leaderships of the French Socialist and Communist Parties when Pflimlin can allow himself the luxury of conducting similar negotiations *openly*!

Metaphorically slapping his tommy-gun on the table, Massu has put the issue squarely: 'Pflimlin has to support either us or the communists; and he prefers us.' Such is the record of the French 'communist' leadership.

The British CP newspapers *Daily Worker* and *World News* have had obvious difficulty in putting the sell-out across to their members. They have contented themselves with trying to fix all the blame for the betrayals on the Socialist Party:

> It is the result of the attempt to suppress the national liberation movement in Algeria which has been carried out by successive French governments with the full support of the leaders of the French Socialist Party... As on many occasions before, the Socialist Party leaders are in fact leaning on the right — and this means paving the way for the fascists'. (*World News*, 24 May, 1958).

We may ask these gentlemen: what the hell is the Communist

Party doing voting for Pflimlin and company? The full perfidy of the Stalinist leaders is revealed in a further passage. Correctly *World News* points out:

> The French events have once again underlined the nature of the state as in essence armed forces linked with the actual rulers of France — the big business interests, whose only concern is to keep their wealth and privileges. The immediate defection of the French generals has arisen over Algeria, but we must not forget that de Gaulle was seeking a fascist solution for French big business before Algeria became an acute issue.

This characterisation of the state is correct. Marx and Lenin have emphasised the fact that the state can in the last analysis be reduced to armed bodies of men. The officer caste is, then, the mainstay of the capitalist state. To proceed against them would be for capitalism to destroy the instrument of its own rule. The road to seizure of power by the workers would be opened. Yet in the very next paragraph *World News* proceeds on exactly the opposite assumption.

> Now the Pflimlin government is calling on the generals to serve it loyally and has removed some high officers from their positions; but it remains to be seen how far the military leaders are already committed to support de Gaulle. The police seem so far to be carrying out the government's orders, but it is well known that the heads of the police are fascists.

As if the generals are not in collusion with de Gaulle and as if Pflimlin would behave in any other way! So 'severe' has the Pflimlin government been with treason that the two generals removed, instead of being put under arrest and court-martialled preparatory to being shot for high treason as the mutinous *poilus** were in 1917, have been sent to different parts of France to live with friends — other high officers — where they can continue plotting to their hearts' content.

So 'loyal' have the police been that Soustelle** the Gaullist escaped from their 'protection' only to place himself at the political head of the rebel settlers.

This Pflimlin government, which is supposed to be barring the way to de Gaulle, has sent emissaries to him and to the revolting generals, as if they were the government and the government were some order of mendicant friars, supplicating favours.

Instead of arresting de Gaulle as the principal mutineer and

*A slang term for French soldiers.
**Jacques Soustelle, a Gaullist, became Governor General of Algeria in 1955. Robert Lacoste, a Socialist Party member, succeeded him from June 1957 until 1958.

arch-conspirator they beg him to mediate between the mutineers and themselves. Naturally, de Gaulle and the mutineers are emboldened to press all the more for 'adjustments' in their favour. How could it be otherwise? For it follows as the law of class society and....from the criminal policy of the Socialist and Stalinist leaderships.

The ruling class, of course, prefers if there is to be a *coup*, that it should take place in a 'cold' way, which will not threaten the destruction of property or risk the loss of power. But the policy of cowardly support for Pflimlin, this Alsatian hound cringing like a whipped cur before its master the General, can encourage the idea in ruling circles that a transition to a Bonapartist regime can occur in just such a 'cold' manner, without any unpleasantness on the streets.

It is the eighteenth Brumaire all over again with the Socialists and Stalinists in the roles of the democratic buffoons of 1848. Certain of the Socialists — Mollet and Lacoste, the latter a direct accessory to the crimes of the Algiers clique — are hoping to become the left wing of such a Bonapartism. Others, more responsive to the pressure of their rank and file, are prepared to 'struggle' to prevent the generals from coming to power. And the policy of the Communist leadership — flowing partly from dependence on the Kremlin, partly from sheer ineptitude, partly from its long history of betrayals over thirty years, partly because for all these reasons, a cadre capable of fighting has not been and could not have been assembled — plays into the hands precisely of the Bonapartist wing of the Socialists.

These traitors even abase themselves in the assembly and the senate to the extent of voting with the fascists to greet the army and its officers in their civilising mission in North Africa! This is hardly the way to explain the class nature of this army to the workers or to prepare them for a possible struggle to the death with its officer caste, the agents of the ruling class. It is, on the contrary, the way to demoralise and disorient the workers, and to pave the way for defeat. And yet apart from the top leadership the very lives of the members of the CP are at stake.

The top leaders can always flee to Moscow — it has happened before! But the ranks, and even the middle and lower strata of party officials must stay to suffer under the jackboot of a Bonapartist dictator. Let them be under no illusions as to the fate in store for them. If the leaders of the CP were even one per cent Leninists; if they even based themselves on the history of France; their whole policy would be the exact opposite of what they are advocating now.

The revolt of the generals is not some unlucky accident precipitated only by the problems of Algeria, but is rooted in the whole class structure and present position of French capitalism. Had Algeria not 'happily' chanced to be on hand as a pretext, the generals would have found some other excuse to move against the regime and to destroy what for them remains the real menace: the workers' organisations.

The State Laid Bare

Lenin pointed out how the whole class structure of capitalist society could be laid bare and the masses prepared, in the course of struggle in defence of their democratic rights and liberties, to pass over to the socialist revolution.

Surely now more than ever it is necessary in the tradition of Marxism-Leninism to warn the workers over and over again: rely only on your own unity, your own organisations, your own strength. No one can, no one will, help you if you cannot, if you will not help yourselves. Workers! there is no power on earth can stand against you once you are organised, once you are drawn up for action! But for this action the workers must be prepared ideologically no less than materially. The one is as important as the other. It is useless, worse than useless, for the workers to put their trust in some parliamentary clown, some tumbler who will perform nothing but crazy somersaults before the General, his ringmaster!

The struggle against Bonapartism is, in the main, an *extra*-parliamentary struggle: force must be met with force! If the CP leadership were communists they would be explaining that the workers and their allies among the middle class and the peasantry are the *only* force which stands for democracy — to the end.

Moch, Minister of the Interior, to frighten some air force brass who were threatening an uprising in metropolitan France, replied, according to the *Daily Express,* by telling them that he would arm 40,000 miners. If the CP leaders were worth their salt, they would have taken this as the starting point for their agitation. Arms to the workers! That is the only certain guarantee against any conspiracies on the part of the General or anybody else. Let workers' defence guards be formed!

The overwhelming majority of the rank and file, Catholic and Socialist as well as Communist workers, are against the victory of Bonapartism. The main problem is to arouse, organise and prepare the masses for direct action against any eventuality. If the Communist Party had come out for unity around a real programme of *action* on these lines even at the eleventh hour it would be possible to organise the united front on this basis. The Mollet wing of the Socialists would be isolated if they did not respond to the demand to arm the working class.

It is true that the monstrous Soviet intervention in Hungary in 1956 and the brutal crushing of the Hungarian workers has left the socialist and Catholic workers suspicious, especially as the French leaders, most particularly, defended to the hilt the foul crimes of Stalinism in Hungary. But the obeisance of the CP leaders to the icons of abstract democracy and republican virtue will cut no ice with the workers. It must be explained to the workers that what is involved is defence of democratic rights – free speech, freedom to organise, and so on.

These rights can at this stage only be defended arms in hand. And the only way to defend them finally is by dispossessing the millionaire owners of the press, radio, cinema and other means of moulding public opinion and the transfer of these organs to the workers' organisations in proportion to their strength and support among the working class.

The only road, not only to peace and plenty but to real freedom, lies through workers' democracy – expropriation of the means of production and their operation under a workers' plan with participation in management of the workers on the job at every level, and the running of the state by the masses themselves.

However, the Pflimlin government, to continue total war in Algeria against the Algerian people at the behest of the generals, has announced a programme of *increasing* service with the colours to 27 months (an increase of nine months), harsher taxes and two meatless days a week. Such a programme cannot enthuse the workers, nor the peasants and middle class. It is the way to demoralise the workers and prepare the painless victory of Gaullism.

The middle-class and peasant masses must be mobilised, alongside the workers against this programme of the Pflimlin government, against the war in Algeria, against the generals, against the trusts. In its place must be put a programme in the interests of these masses: cancellation of debts, cheap credits, cheap fertilisers, state tractors, assistance and loans to small businessmen, shopkeepers and professional people, and the like. Boldly and audaciously this programme, with the demands in relation to the workers already mentioned, must be advanced as the only road to salvation.

Historically, it is only yesterday that the Communist Party ridiculed the Social Democrats in Germany, who screamed: 'Act, state, act' – against Hitler. The state acted: Hindenburg kicked the

Social-Democratic ministers in Prussia into the street. The CP then had an ultra-left policy that was wrong but the only thing that was correct about it was their criticism of the passivity of the Social-Democratic leadership, with its reliance on the state authorities to bar the road to Hitler. But now their policy is a caricature of that of the social democracy and, if it depends on them, can only have the same results.

'Now,' said the political bureau of the French CP on May 25, 'is the time for anti-fascist action. It is time for the government which has all the necessary powers and which is supported by a strong Republican majority, to start such action'. (*Daily Worker*, May 26, 1958). The Pflimlin government also acted — by resigning to prepare the way for de Gaulle. The CP and the CGT, together with the CFTU (Christian trade unions), have threatened a general strike if a *coup* is attempted in France. But that, while correct in itself, is not enough.

The general strike is not a panacea that by itself will solve everything. A programme for power, on the lines sketched above, is a vital necessity as a *positive* aim for the masses. Not only that. Against the counter-revolution's committees of public safety, and even as a mass lever on parliament, which can capitulate to the generals, councils of action (which tomorrow can be organs of power), linked locally and nationally, must be set up. These councils of action must appeal for the formation of similar councils of action of the sailors, soldiers and airmen in France to watch over their officers and see that they do not attempt any counter-revolutionary acts.

The Communist Party should have conducted agitation among the dockers to refuse to load arms and supplies to Algeria, and appealed to the conscripts boarding the ships to form committees of action in conjunction with the workers in the ports, and to refuse to go to Algeria. It would be unbelievable if one did not know the class position of the SP leadership and the bureaucratic degeneracy of the CP leadership, that they should have learned nothing from the tragic pages of the past.

The only way to win the vacillating or apathetic ranks of the middle class and the peasantry would be by an audacious policy, striking blow after blow against the counter-revolution. Whatever one's view might be of the gang around the generals and Soustelle, they have understood this law of revolution and of counter-revolution: of moving continuously from one success to the next, of keeping the movement going by seizing the initiative and maintaining it throughout.

The capture of Corsica, in itself of no especial importance, was intended for this purpose. Yet the lack of a mass basis for the counter-revolution is the most striking aspect of the whole situation. That and the helplessness of the official organisations of the working class: for example, not a murmur was heard from the strong CP organisation in Corsica (where the party had an MP before the rigging of the electoral law).

When it is a question of struggle to the death against Bonapartist reaction, all that the CP can offer in the face of events is the proud boast: 'Until changes in the electoral constituencies took place, the island had some Communist MPs in the post-war years...The island's 300,000 people are in the main strongly pro-Republican, and the Communist Party has not inconsiderable support there' *(Daily Worker,* 26 May, 1958).

With all this support, it would have been possible to mobilise the workers and arm them against reaction. Instead of this, a meeting was held in Bastia, the largest town in Corsica, of the Municipal Council. Half the councillors were unable to attend, or prudently decided not to. Of the 16 present nine were members of the Communist Party and the *Daily Worker* proudly proclaims:

> This morning the Bastia Municipal Council holds a special session in the Town Hall, which Deputy Mayor de Casalta has refused to hand over. The Council sends a resolution to the government in Paris affirming its loyalty to the Republic and its support for the premier. *It calls on the population to remain calm and not carry out any demonstrations*(!) *(ibid).*

Thus it was in the early days of the Franco insurrection that the way was paved for Franco to seize towns on the mainland. In those towns where the masses took action with their own hands — Barcelona, Madrid, Valencia — while the Popular Front government were negotiating (secretly) with Franco, these masses were victorious. Even according to the capitalist press, they marched against the barracks with table legs, knives and sporting rifles taken from the shops.

Most of the rank and file soldiers, under the impact of this move, joined them; the police and the army disintegrated as a force. In those towns, however, where the masses listened to the advice of their Socialist and Communist 'leaders' — Oviedo, Cordoba, Huesca, Granada, Teruel and others — and after demonstrating for arms, dispersed peacefully to their homes, the fascists won.

The leaders of the CP and SP advised the workers to have confidence in the 'liberal' governors and mayors of the provinces and cities, and this prepared the generals' path for them. The officers of the garrisons rose during the night and, armed with lists prepared by the police, marched to the workers' quarters and massacred the leaders of the working-class organisations. A reign of terror followed against which the masses, politically beheaded, had no opportunity to mobilise.

As in Spain yesterday, so in Corsica and France today! As a direct result Bastia and all the Corsican towns have fallen to a handful of counter-revolutionary stormtroopers: 60 paratroops took one town! It is absolutely clear that the Pflimlin government has paved the way for de Gaulle, despite their highly 'revolutionary' act in depriving the insurgent deputy Arrighi (nominally a radical) of his seat. Only the shell of the republic remains. Unless there is an intervention in the immortal tradition of the workers of Barcelona, nothing can keep de Gaulle from power.

The responsibility for this rests fairly and squarely on the 'leaderships' of the Socialist and Communist Parties.

What of the future? It is the impasse of French capitalism that has led to this position. Even if de Gaulle takes power his dream will be rudely dissipated by the realities of the situation. Big Asparagus (as the cadets of St Cyr irreverently called him) will melt quickly enough in the maw of the wolf — the wolf at the door of French capitalism.

The wolf assumes the form of the unsolved problems of two decades: the lagging behind other nations of the capitalist West in technique; the running sore of Algeria; the developing movement for independence in French Africa, which no Bonapartist boot can permanently crush, against the background of the growing strength of the Afro-Asian peoples; above all, the developing slump, which will impose new burdens on the workers, ruin sections of the middle class and the peasantry and undermine the frail structure of French capitalism.

Fascism or Bonapartism?

It is vital, in this context, to grasp the difference between Bonapartism and fascism. Fascism is a *mass movement* of the middle class, the *lumpenproletariat*, the peasants and even backward sections of the working class, financed and organised by capitalism as a desperate last resort in the face of growing crisis and the threat of a possible socialist solution.

Unscrupulous demagogues, usually plebeian in origin, utilise anti-capitalist slogans to mobilise a mass force for destroying *all* organisations of the working class. Fascism means the complete destruction of any form — communist, socialist, christian, liberal — of independent working-class organisation: that is its job, and it is this which gives it its strength in the early stages. Using the middle class as a battering ram and with the support of the police and the army, fascism extinguishes every democratic right.

After the initial delirium, the middle class and plebeian masses discover their betrayal and become disillusioned (30 June 1934, in Germany): fascism is then transformed into an ordinary police-military dictatorship, able to retain power only on the basis of the apathy and inertia of the workers who feel themselves betrayed by their own organisations. Before it can be overthrown, new shocks – a new sweep of events – is necessary, to give back to the masses their perspective and to convince them anew of the hope of victory against the tyranny that oppresses them.

Bonapartism, as defined by Marx, is rule by the sword. It is *from the start*, a police-military dictatorship; but at the same time it is a condition wherein the state raises itself above the whole of society and, while remaining an instrument of the ruling class, arrogates to itself the role of 'arbiter' between the classes. 'I belong to everyone and everyone belongs to me' (Charles de Gaulle, the new candidate for the role of Bonaparte).

To play this role, the 'arbiter' has to balance between the classes and between the conflicting interests within the society. Thus de Gaulle's programme is not (immediately or even necessarily at all, dependent on events) the abolition of parties. But he will 'arbitrate' between left and right. For this purpose de Gaulle will need the support of at least a section of the Socialists and perhaps of the reformist unions. He needs a split in the working class to maintain the base of his rule.

It is quite possible that he will illegalise the Communist Party (perhaps by stages) and seek to smash the CGT in the interests of the Catholic and reformist unions. This will be his 'left' point of support. On the right he will lean on the 'Independents,' the existing neo-fascist organisations and right-wing ex-servicemen's movement and even on out and out fascist organisations which may arise with the development of the slump.

But the Bonapartism of Napoleon I and even of Napoleon III had a base in an expanding economy. The Bonapartism of de Gaulle has as little base as that of Petain: in fact it has less, for Petain could at least rely in the last resort on the German army for protection. Even Louis Napoleon had his victories in the early years; but what can de Gaulle offer by way of military triumphs?

De Gaulle will be faced with the problem of North Africa. The war may go on, and even if the French imperialist forces achieve a temporary victory, by letting loose the paratroops on the Algerian people, such a victory will not solve the Algerian question for imperialism. Even the occupation of Morocco and Tunisia would merely aggravate the North African problem for French imperialism besides involving the whole Arab world.

The burdens of this war and of the 'need to maintain France's position in the world' will mean a colossal drain on French resources and manpower. What little mass support has been rallied to de Gaulle during the last period will vanish. The temporary support he may gain through the intoxicant of nationalist phrases will soon evaporate. For the moment, the workers will be entirely disoriented and apathetic, arising from the deception of the official leaders.

The disgrace of Germany where Hitler took power without firing a shot has been repeated, and this in a country where the CP in number, organisation and support, was stronger than were the Bolsheviks in 1917 before the revolution.

However, no thanks to these leaders – the situation in France differs somewhat from the German situation of 1933. Hitler headed a real mass reactionary movement which swept away, in the first few weeks of his power, all the organisations of the working class. Through the Nazi Party he penetrated every sphere of social life, paralysed the working class, atomised and dispersed it. Apart from the disgust and disillusionment of the masses at the complete incapacity of their organisations to struggle against reaction, the secret-police apparatus – informers in every factory, spies in every neighbourhood block – was a powerful factor in the consolidation of the regime.

The Eighteenth Brumaire of Charles de Gaulle

Hitler and Mussolini, moreover, were lucky enough in each case to seize power on the eve of a boom. De Gaulle on the contrary assumes office on the eve of a slump. The paratroops, an elite of regular soldiers, are quite prepared to play the same role in France as in Algeria. But this small force, 50,000 to 60,000, strong enough in itself to seize power in the face of the apathy of the mass, is entirely insufficient to maintain it.

The ordinary sailor and soldier whom the nationalist intoxicant might temporarily affect, will not for long remain bemused. The social situation induced by slump must have its powerful effect. All history has shown that it is impossible indefinitely to rule through the army and the police alone. Any attempt to use the army against mass outbreaks will mean splitting it on class lines. A new mass upsurge in the coming period is inevitable. Events, national and international, will shake the senile regime in France. The twilight of the Franco dictatorship (shored up for the moment by de Gaulle's victory) will cast its lengthening shadows over France. The workers' struggles in Britain, Italy and West Germany will have their effect.

The Socialists, radicals and MRP have endeavoured to 'leave a good memory' by their vote for Pflimlin on the eve of the de Gaulle take-over. The CP is again pumping out the poison of people's frontism, claiming that had there been a popular front 'all this could have been averted' — notwithstanding the fact that it was precisely the People's Front which paved the way to defeat in Spain and that the People's Front in France prepared the groundwork for today's situation.

The mass demonstrations and strikes, convened at the twelfth hour, have shown that the masses would have responded to leadership in action rather than parliamentary manoeuvre 'at the top'. So much greater the disgrace of the CP-SP leaderships, which have put the working class in this peril at the behest of a handful of paratroop gangsters.

In striking contrast to Hitler in 1933 de Gaulle is coming to power, not only without the support of the middle-class mass, but in the face of its hostility. The coming to power of de Gaulle will be more akin to the situation in Spain in 1934 when Gil Robles, the leader of clerical fascism, was taken into the reactionary Lerroux government. Despite the defeat of the answering socialist insurrections, when the workers seized power in Asturias, the Gil Robles regime could not consolidate.

Fearing a new uprising on the part of the masses, Robles allowed a new election in 1936 and ceded to the Popular Front to demoralise the workers and prepare under its aegis for civil war against the masses. De Gaulle's take-over will be, therefore, premature from the capitalist standpoint. It was forced by the settlers and the officer caste in Algiers.

De Gaulle also will be unable to consolidate. The ruling class may prepare again for a retreat to a new popular front, counting on the confusion and demoralisation this would cause to prepare again for full-fledged civil war. When the de Gaulle dictatorship rots from within the capitalists can still turn, with the assistance (as ever) of the Communist and Socialist leaderships, to a new popular front as a way out for the regime. The advanced worker-militants must learn from the rich history of the French and international working-class movement. If the lesson is not assimilated in time, a new popular front bringing with it fresh defeat and disillusionment could prepare the way for a real fascist dictatorship on the lines of Hitler's monstrous regime.

We have confidence, however, that the best militants in the

French Communist and Socialist Parties and in the trade unions *will* learn from these events. The Communist Party will split and from its ranks the revolutionary elements will gather to them the best militants from the trade unions and the Socialist Party to create the Marxist mass party of the French working class.

This party, basing itself on the great tradition of the Commune, of the struggle against the Moroccan war, of the stay-in strikes of 1936, will lead its class in mortal combat against the class enemy. From this death-struggle the French workers and peasants will emerge victorious and proceed to the construction of the socialist order in France.

Many workers in the British labour movement regard the events in France with horror, but see them as of little direct consequence to themselves: 'It can't happen here!' 'England is different.' It is not well known that the strategists of British capitalism learned from the history of the continental class struggle in the prewar years and were making preparations for the fight against the British working class. In 1938 and 1939 army manoeuvres were based on the idea that civil war was raging in Britain.

A special strike-breaking force, composed of members of the ruling and upper-middle classes — to learn to man the basic posts in the economy, the running of locomotives, the operation of power stations, and so on — was created. The insurance companies were refusing to insure against the risk of civil war. And, as an interesting forerunner of present events, Duff Cooper, Tory MP and former First Lord of the Admiralty, was writing articles in the *Evening Standard* advocating the formation of Committees of Public Safety in Britain.

It is no accident that in the present crisis the leading organs of Tory opinion have rallied to de Gaulle. The *Daily Mail* and *Evening News*, flunkeys of Hitler and Mussolini before the war, have now been joined by the *Daily Telegraph*, the *Daily Express* and the *Evening Standard* in warm support for the Gaullist *coup d'etat*.

British workers will ignore this lesson at their own peril. Their fate is bound, as it has always been, to the international struggle of the working class against capitalism. In their hour of agony the French workers must know that they can draw, not alone on the passive sympathy, but upon the active class support of their British brothers and sisters. Side by side we shall rally against dictatorship and for a socialist France and a socialist Britain in a socialist Europe.

Stalin, Churchill and Truman meet at Potsdam to divide up the world between them.

Eastern Europe

Introduction

ONE OF the most important contributions made by Trotsky to the theoretical storehouse of Marxism was his analysis of the rise and development of Stalinism. He explained that the fundamental social gains of the October revolution remained intact, in the form of the state-ownership of the economy and the plan of production, but that the working class had been *politically* expropriated by a new ruling caste. Against those who saw this bureaucracy as a new ruling class, Trotsky argued that it was a parasitic growth resting on the economic base of a workers' state, and not a class.

But Trotsky also believed that the Second World War would decide the fate of the bureaucracy one way or the other. The end of hostilities, he suggested, would result in one of two possibilities: firstly, the overthrow of the gains of October, by a military defeat by nazi Germany or another imperialism, or secondly, an internal political revolution to establish workers' democracy. In either case, it would seal the fate of Stalinism.

Yet even the greatest political genius could not predict the exact outcome of the war, given the enormous multiplicity of factors that would come to bear. In 1943, the Workers International League, forerunner of the Revolutionary Communist Party, still reflected the pre-war thinking of Trotsky, arguing that Stalinism would not be likely to survive the war: 'The fate of the Soviet Union rests directly on the fate of the new wave of revolutions. Further defeats and a new epoch of reaction would inevitably usher in the bourgeois counter-revolution in Russia.' (*Workers International News*, September 1943).

But by 1945, it was becoming clear that rather than being weakened, the Soviet Union and Stalinism would emerge from the war stronger than before. Of all the Trotskyist organisations, it was only the British RCP which was able to come to terms and explain the new developments and the new balance of forces.

The Fourth International leadership, rather than use the method of Trotsky, hung on to the letter of his predictions. Reflecting this, for example, a document of the American Socialist Workers Party, of September 1944, stated that 'far from having increased its independent strength, under Stalin the Soviet Union has been debilitated and today is weaker than ever in relation to the capitalist world.'

Not to be outdone by concrete facts, such 'theoreticians' even went to the point of denying the world war had ended. Thus, SWP leader, James Cannon, speaking in November 1945: '...Trotsky predicted that the fate of the Soviet Union would be decided in the war. That remains our firm conviction. Only we disagree with some people who carelessly think that the war is over...'

This failure to face up to the new reality was characteristic of all the so-called theoreticians of Trotskyism: Ernest Mandel, Michael Pablo, Pierre Frank, James Cannon, Gerry Healy (then in a minority in the RCP) and others. Moreover, as Lenin often remarked, a mistake, if repeated and not corrected in time, becomes a tendency. The fundamental theoretical incapacities of the leadership of the Fourth International were to become a factor in the collapse of the RCP in Britain and the main cause of the degeneration of their international organisation to become a myriad of unimportant middle-class sects.

The RCP position, in contrast, was clear: '...by far the greatest event of world significance is the emergence of Russia, for the first time in history, as the greatest military power in Europe and Asia..' (see *The Changed Relationship of Forces* in the previous chapter).

A more complicated theoretical problem arose, however, over those countries occupied by the Red Army after 1945. The RCP at first put a tentative position, raising the possibility that Moscow could change the social relations in these states, albeit on a bureaucratic basis. Within three years, this tentative position was made firm and rounded out by the unfolding events. While the International Secretariat of the Fourth International once again clung to out-dated formulations — that Russia was a degenerated workers' state, but all those states occupied by the Red Army were still capitalist states — it was Ted Grant, as the leading theoretician of the RCP, who worked out a correct position.

The Marxist analysis of the Eastern European states was not arrived at lightly. Ted Grant has described how it was necessary to go back to basics, to the works of Marx, Engels, Lenin and Trotsky and for a whole period of months to read and re-read the relevant works, as a guide. The living experience of Eastern Europe was carefully examined in the light cast by the classics of Marxism and eventually, as Ted himself put it, 'we came to the conclusion that what we had here was a form of proletarian Bonapartism.'

The first article reproduced in this section, from the *Socialist Appeal* of June 1948, describes and explains the 'February events' in Czechoslovakia, the so-called 'Prague coup'. Here, the Stalinist-dominated government, leaning on the working class through 'action committees', overcame the resistance of the capitalist class and carried through the nationalisation of industry and the major part of the economy. The end result, as the article explained, provided 'the economic basis for a workers' state', but without the democratic control of the state by the workers, 'all the rights which the workers still possess will be strangled and an uncontrolled bureaucracy will ride roughshod over the masses, as in Russia.'

A more general and thoroughly developed treatment of Eastern Europe is contained in the second and major part of this chapter. In June 1948, Tony Cliff, an RCP member, published a lengthy document entitled *The Nature of Stalinist Russia*. This work has been extended over the years, and the arguments partly modified, but its essence has always been the idea that Russia, under Stalin, became 'state capitalist'. It followed from this that the other states of the Eastern bloc were also 'state capitalist'.

The reply by Ted Grant was published in two parts. The first, *Against the Theory of State Capitalism: In Answer to Cliff*, deals more particularly with economic arguments, thoroughly demolishing Cliff's confused and contradictory theories. It draws upon a wealth of material from the great teachers of Marxism and condenses from this a worked-out description of the character of the 'transitional' state between capitalism and socialism, when the working class holds the levers of political and economic power, but many of the vestiges of class society remain. The document explains how many of the 'capitalist' features of Russia, gleefully enumerated by Cliff, would exist in any workers' state, whether it was a 'healthy' state based on workers' democracy or a degenerated workers' state, as in Russia.

The second part, entitled *The Marxist Theory of the State, As Applied to the Stalinist States*, describes in more general terms the means by which the Moscow bureaucracy was able to extend its social and political system to the rest of Eastern Europe. It again throws an important light on the difficult theoretical questions of Bonapartism and the role of the state. While the alleged 'leadership' of the Fourth International found themselves in an increasingly untenable and unreal position, the analysis elaborated by Ted Grant has stood unchallenged for over forty years.

Taken as a whole, the reply is itself a modern 'classic', a major contribution to the theoretical arsenal of Marxism. It is to this day the most definitive defence, and a deepening, of the original arguments of Leon Trotsky, that Russia is a degenerated workers' state, and in that light, deserves not only to be read, but carefully and diligently studied.

The final piece in this chapter is a document giving a wide-ranging view of the nature of Stalinism after the war. The copy used for this collection was a poorly duplicated pamphlet*, dated 1951, but it is clear from the text that it was written earlier, some time in 1949. This is confirmed by other sources which quote large extracts from the same document and cite it as an internal discussion document of the RCP, of 1949**. It seems likely, therefore, that the original document, written at the time the RCP was disintegrating, lay for two years before it was published privately by the author.

This pamphlet, *Stalinism in the Post-War World*, once again describes the strengthening of Stalinism in Europe as a result of the war. Despite the temporary political stabilisation in Western Europe, it was not possible at that time to anticipate a prolonged economic upswing and for that reason, it was believed that the incipient social discontent in Spain, for example, would lead to a new outbreak of revolutionary struggle. It is only with the benefit of hindsight that it can be seen that the post-war boom unexpectedly underpinned the Franco regime for a whole period, although it was decidedly shaky in the first years after the war.

With the perspective for political upheaval in Western Europe, and given the mass support of the Communist Parties at that time, the document put forward the prognosis of growth in these parties, followed by left splits at a later stage. As it has turned out, the long post-war boom has led to such a degeneration of the Western European Communist Parties, in a liberal-reformist direction, that many of them have split into several different parts. A number of them are now unlikely to develop at all, especially alongside tendencies of genuine Marxism.

Another theme once again developed in this document is the method by which the Russian bureaucracy was able to transform social relations in Eastern Europe, establishing regimes of proletarian Bonapartism in the image of Moscow. But in a new

*The only available copy of the document is in a poor physical condition and is incomplete in one or two places. At these points a few words, indicated by squared brackets, have been added to maintain continuity.

**War and the International, A History of the Trotskyist Movement in Britain 1937-49 (Sam Bornstein and Al Richardson) gives quotes from a document called The World Situation and the Crisis of Stalinism, which correspond exactly to passages in Stalinism in the Post War World. The former is dated by the authors as 1949, but a copy of it has not been traceable.

departure, a significant part of it also provides a bridge to the issues dealt with in more detail in the next chapter: the Stalin-Tito split and the Chinese revolution.

In June 1948, the rivalry between the Moscow bureaucracy and the Yugoslavian state bureaucracy erupted into open conflict. The Yugoslav leader, Tito, was denounced by the Cominform and he in turn denounced the Kremlin. Yet again, the 'leadership' of the Fourth International were at sixes and sevens. Up to this point, they still held the view that Russia was a deformed workers' state, but Eastern Europe — Yugoslavia included — was still capitalist. Now, without any explanation, they ditched the view that Yugoslavia was capitalist and suddenly discovered instead that not only was it a workers' state, but a relatively healthy one at that! Because of his split with Stalin, the IS took the completely impressionistic view that Tito was some kind of 'unconscious Trotskyist' and gave their whole-hearted support to Belgrade in its struggle with Moscow. 'Long live the Yugoslav Socialist Revolution', crowed the IS, as they appealed for fraternal links between the Fourth International and the Yugoslav 'communist movement.'

Once again it was left to Ted Grant, alone among all the international theoreticians of Trotskyism, to explain these events. Using the analysis of Eastern Europe already worked out, it was now possible to describe in consistent Marxian terms, the nature and the origin of the split between Stalin and Tito. The document correctly described Tito as a 'Yugoslav Stalin' who was not prepared to be subjugated by Moscow, and, having a relatively independent base in the partisan movement which had brought him to power, was able to free himself from the political control of the Russian bureaucracy.

Furthermore, not only was Grant's analysis of the Eastern European states able to explain the Tito-Stalin split, it could also anticipate — and this is the test of the correctness of theory, in politics as in science — other splits, along national lines, within Eastern European monolith. 'To this day the national question remains a key question in the struggle against the bureaucracy...Stalin's tendency to convert Eastern Europe into a fief for the benefit of the Russian bureaucracy...was bound to awaken opposition among the masses, which had to arouse an echo even in the dominant Stalinist parties.'

More prophetically still, the document not only anticipated in advance the establishment of a Stalinist state in China after the revolution, but it predicted the inevitability of a split between the Chinese and the Russian bureaucracy, on the same basis, although on a far larger scale, as in the case of Yugoslavia. This issue is considered more fully in the next chapter.

Czechoslovakia: The Issues Involved

April 1948.

FOR WEEKS the capitalist class of the world has been whimpering about the measures taken against the capitalists in Czechoslovakia. The methods used by the Stalinists have been compared to the technique of Hitler. This propaganda is saturated through and through with capitalist hypocrisy. It is not the forcible methods of the Stalinists to which they object. They not only condone, but actively assist the terror of the Greek reaction which aims to establish a semi-fascist regime, as they condoned and assisted Hitler and Mussolini against the working class.

In reply to the capitalists, the Stalinists do not and cannot give a Marxist answer. They pretend that the changes were carried through 'in accordance with the Constitution.' This has further added to the confusion of Labour workers, who understand that these statements are not in accordance with the facts. The change was accomplished with the aid and the participation of the working class. The demonstrations of the armed workers on the streets convinced the capitalist elements of the uselessness of resistance. *It was this threat of force which ensured the peaceful change.*

The workers and peasants in Czechoslovakia undoubtedly gave wholehearted support to the change because of its progressive features.

The workers could not but support the measures: nationalisation of all important plants that remained in private hands since the mass movement in 1945; 70 per cent of the printing establishments, the whole of the chemical industry, all refrigerator plants and all building concerns employing more than 50 persons, all big hotels and the wholesale trade. No firm employing more than 50 people in any trade or industry is now allowed to be privately owned.

The monopoly of foreign trade has been formally instituted.

The peasants were solidly behind the reforms. Although the Stalinists did not do as the Russian Bolsheviks did, namely nationalise the land and then hand it to the peasants, they divided the land and gave it to the peasants as their own private property.

Trotsky On Occupied Territories

These are the progressive features supported by the Trotskyists despite the failure to nationalise the land. They are a necessary economic foundation for a workers' state. In order to carry through these measures the Stalinists were compelled to call on the initiative and pressure of the masses. As Trotsky pointed out in 1939, when dealing with the likely developments if Stalin invaded Poland:

> It is more likely, however, that in the territories scheduled to become a part of the USSR, the Moscow government will carry through the expropriation of the large land-owners and statification of the means of production. This variant is the most probable not because the bureaucracy remains true to the socialist programme but because it is neither desirous nor capable of sharing the power and the privileges the latter entails, with the old ruling classes in the occupied territories. Here an analogy literally offers itself: The first Bonaparte halted the revolution by means of a military dictatorship. However when the French troops invaded Poland, Napoleon signed a decree: 'Serfdom is abolished'. This measure was dictated not by Napoleon's sympathies for the peasants, nor by democratic principles, but rather by the fact that the Bonapartist dictatorship based itself not on feudal, but on bourgeois property relations. In as much as Stalin's Bonapartist dictatorship bases itself not on private property but state property, the invasion of Poland by the Red Army should in the nature of the case, result in the abolition of private capitalist property, so as thus to bring the regime of the occupied territories into accord with the regime of the USSR.
>
> This measure, revolutionary in character — 'the expropriation of the expropriators' — is in this case achieved in a military- bureaucratic fashion. The appeal to independent activity on the part of the masses in the new territories — and without such an appeal, even if worded with extreme caution it is impossible to constitute a new regime — will on the morrow undoubtedly be suppressed by ruthless police measures in order to assure the preponderance of the bureaucracy over the awakened revolutionary masses...' *(USSR in War,* September 1939)

Having used the pressure of the workers against the capitalist class, the Stalinists will despense with all the elements of workers' control. The speed with which this is accomplished will depend on the resistance of the Czech working class, whose level of culture, because of the industrialisation of the country, far exceeds that of the Russian workers. The Stalinists cannot afford to allow a workers' democracy in Czechoslovakia because of the inevitable repercussions on the Russian regime in the Soviet Union.

This was clearly brought out by Douglas Hyde, former news editor of the *Daily Worker*. In an interview with the *Daily Mail* he said:

> At the first meeting of the Cominform, held in a hunting-lodge in Silesia, Gottwald* was charged with 'petit-bourgeois Communism' because he had tried to work out a policy which took into account Czechoslovakia's traditions of Western culture and freedom.
>
> Gottwald's idea was to mould Communism to suit the needs of his country — so different from Russia. But with Russia at his back there was no point in arguing, and recent events in Prague revealed how thoroughly he was brought to heel.

Feeling the pressure of the workers, Gottwald is afraid of the future results of such a course.

Future of Action Committees

Shortly after the Czech events, the government officials issued statements about the limited role of the action committees. The *Telegraph* of 6 March reported: 'There are indications of some concern at HQ regarding the unhampered activities of local action committees. The Central Action Committee has ordered all other committees to refrain from interfering in the cleansing of the army. Henceforth all 'purge cases' will have to be referred directly to the Ministry of National Defence.'

Cepick, the Communist Minister of Justice in the new Gottwald government, declared: 'The action committees are not a second power. It is their task to facilitate the defence of the state by giving a popular base to government action.'

The Czech authorities have made a fundamental distinction between the action committees set up by the workers and peasants and those appointed by the political parties from above. Although they are called by the same name there is a vast difference between the two. The action committee of the National Front** appoints all the officials of the different parties, which is a caricature of democracy.

They have made it clear that the action committees will not play the role which the soviets, or workers' committees played in the Russian Revolution in 1917. The Russian Bolshevik government under Lenin was based on the soviets, which were the most flexible and democratic form of organisation. These had direct

*Klemens Gottwald was the CP Prime Minister from 1946.
**The National Front was the coalition government from 1945. After the 1946 elections the CP were the main influence, and after the 'Prague Coup' they had complete control.

representation of the workers and peasants on its bodies based on the localities. By this means Lenin pointed out there was no need for any separate state structure. The workers and peasants would administer the state. Because of the backwardness of Russia and the isolation of the revolution they did not succeed in carrying this out. In a highly cultured and industrialised country like Czechoslovakia, a genuine Communist regime could be introduced. The workers and peasants could begin immediately to administer the state themselves without a special state apparatus which will be utilised for the protection of privilege.

A parliament elected on a constituency basis is far less democratic than the system of direct representation on the basis of committees. The parliamentary form of representation is the most easily bureaucratised and far removed from the people.

The economic basis for a workers' state has been achieved. But for a state to act in the interests of the working class, the expropriation of the capitalists by itself is not enough. Democratic control of the state apparatus is an essential prerequisite for the march towards a communist society. All the great Marxists emphasised this.

Lenin reduced the essence of a workers' state to four fundamental principles. After the expropriation of the capitalists and the statification of the means of production, there would be:

1. The election of soviets with the right of recall of all officials.
2. No official to receive a wage higher than that earned by the average worker.
3. The abolition of the standing army and its replacement by the armed people.
4. No permanent bureaucracy. Each in turn would fulfil the functions of the state. When everyone was a bureaucrat, no-one could be a bureaucrat.

We organise large scale production, starting from what capitalism has already created; we workers *ourselves* relying on our own experiences as workers, establish a strict, an iron discipline, supported by the state power of the armed workers, shall reduce the role of the state officials to that of simply carrying out our instructions as responsible, moderately paid 'managers' (of course, with technical knowledge of all sorts, types and degrees). This is *our* proletarian task, with this we can and must begin when carrying through a proletarian revolution. Such a beginning on the basis of large-scale production, of itself leads to a gradual 'withering away' of all bureaucracy, to the gradual creation of a new order, an order without quotation marks, an order in which the more and more simplified functions of control and accounting will be performed by each in turn, will then become a habit, and will finally die out as *special* functions of a special stratum of the population. (Lenin *Collected Works*, vol. 25 p.431.)

The backwardness of Russia and the isolation of the revolution rendered this process impossible. But on the basis of the cultural level in Czechoslovakia the advantages of communist methods would be apparent to the whole world. Under real communist leadership they could be immediately implemented. But this is not what Stalinism desires. Stalin has stated that what is required is a stronger and stronger state in Russia. Czechoslovakia under Stalinist leadership will develop in the same direction. There will not be a process of the withering away of the state apparatus and the GPU*.

All the rights which the workers still possess will be strangled and an uncontrolled bureaucracy will ride roughshod over the masses as in Russia.

In the long run, the Czech workers will not tolerate a tyrannous officialdom. Experience will teach them that Stalinism is not communism. They will recognise the need to overthrow the bureaucracy with its police apparatus and establish their own direct control of industry and the state in a workers' democracy as outlined by Karl Marx. This on the model of the Paris Commune, and carried into effect in the regime established by the Russian revolution in 1917.

---

*Russian secret police, forerunner of the KGB.

Against the Theory of State Capitalism

1949

THE DOCUMENT of Comrade Cliff entitled *The Nature of Stalinist Russia* at first sight gives the impression of erudition and scientific analysis. However, upon careful examination, it will be observed that not one of the chapters contains a worked-out thesis. The method is a series of parallels based on quotations, and its basic weakness is shown by the fact that *conclusions are not rooted in the analysis*. From his thesis it is not possible to conclude whether Stalinist Russia remains a progressive system (despite its deformations), or whether for Cliff it has now assumed the same reactionary role as 'individual' capitalism or fascism. The weakness is sharply brought out by the fact that no practical conclusions emerge. Is Russia to be defended, or is the revolutionary party to be defeatist? Instead of the answer being rooted in and flowing from the analysis, it has to be worked out *a posteriori*.

Despite the fact that Comrade Cliff *asserts* that the Stalinist bureaucracy is a new class, nowhere in his thesis is a real analysis made or evidence adduced as to why and how such a class constitutes a capitalist class and is not a new type of class.

And this is not accidental. It flows from the method. Starting off with the preconceived idea of state capitalism, everything is artificially fitted in to that conception. Instead of applying the theoretical method of the Marxist teachers to Russian society in its process of motion and development, he has scoured the works to gather quotations and attempted to compress them into a theory.

Nowhere in the document does Cliff pose the main criterion for Marxists in analysing social systems: *Does the new formation lead to the development of the productive forces?* The theory of Marxism is based on the material development of the forces of production as the moving force of historical progress. The transition from one system to another is not decided subjectively, but is rooted in the needs of production itself. It is on this basis and this basis only that the superstructure is erected: of state, ideology, art, science. It is true that the superstructure has an important secondary effect on production and even within certain limits, as Engels explained, develops its own independent movement. But in the last analysis, the development of production is decisive.

Marx explained the historical justification for capitalism, depite the horrors of the industrial revolution, despite the slavery of the blacks in Africa, despite child labour in the factories, the wars of conquest throughout the globe — by the fact that it was a necessary stage in the development of the forces of production. Marx showed that without slavery, not only ancient slavery, but slavery in the epoch of the early development of capitalism, the modern development of production would have been impossible. Without that the material basis for communism could never have been prepared. In *Poverty of Philosophy* Marx wrote:

> Direct slavery is just as much the pivot of bourgeois industry as machinery, credits, etc. Without slavery you have no cotton; without cotton you have no modern industry. It is slavery that has given the colonies their value; it is the colonies that have created world trade, and it is world trade that is the pre-condition of large-scale industry. Thus slavery is an economic category of the greatest importance.
> Without slavery North America, the most progressive of countries, would be transformed into a patriarchal country. Wipe out North America from the map of the world, and you will have anarchy — the complete decay of modern commerce and civilisation.

Of course, the attitude of Marx towards the horrors of slavery and the industrial revolution is well known. It would be a gross distortion of Marx's position to argue that because he wrote the above, therefore he was in favour of slavery and child labour. No more can it be argued against the Marxists of today that because they support state ownership in the USSR that they therefore justify the slave camps and other crimes of the Stalin regime.

Marx's support of Bismarck* in the Franco-Prussian war was dictated by similar considerations. In spite of Bismarck's 'blood and iron' policy and the reactionary nature of his regime, because the development of the productive forces would be facilitated by the national unification of Germany, Marx gave critical support for the war of Prussia against France. The basic criterion was the

---

*Otto von Bismarck, chancellor of the Prussian government from 1862, introduced the Anti-Socialist Law of 1878. He carried through the unification of Germany under Prussia, by succesful wars against Denmark, Austria-Hungary and then France.

development of the productive forces. In the long run, all else flows from this.

Any analysis of Russian society must start from that basis. Once Cliff admits that while capitalism is declining and decaying on a world scale, yet preserving a progressive role in Russia in relation to the development of the productive forces, then logically he would have to say that state capitalism is the next stage forward for society, or at least for the backward countries. Contradictorily, he shows that the Russian bourgeoisie was not capable of carrying through the role which was fulfilled by the bourgeoisie in the West and consequently the proletarian revolution took place.

If we have state capitalism in Russia (ushered in by a proletarian revolution), then it is clear that the crisis of capitalism on which we have based ourselves for the past decades was not insoluble but purely the birth pangs of a new and higher stage of capitalism. The quotation he himself gives from Marx − that no society passes from the scene till all the possibilities in it have been exhausted − would indicate that if his argument is correct, a new epoch, the epoch of state capitalism, opens up before us. This would shatter the entire theoretical basis of the Leninist-Trotskyist movement. Cliff says, without explaining why, that if we hold on to the theory of the degenerated revolution, we must abandon the theory of the permanent revolution. Yet he fails to see that to accept the theory of state capitalism, the theory of the permanent revolution, which is based on the idea that capitalism has so exhausted itself on a world scale that it is incapable of even carrying out the tasks of the bourgeois democratic revolution in backward countries, would have to be abandoned. For in Eastern Europe, the 'state capitalists' would have carried out the tasks of the bourgeois revolution on the land etc. Cliff skirts around this question of the agrarian revolution, which in the backward countries, Trotsky argued, only the proletariat could carry through. If the 'state capitalist' parties of the Stalinists can perform this task, not only is the theory of the permanent revolution thrown out of the window, but the viability of the new state capitalism in a historical sense must be clear to all.

If Comrade Cliff's thesis is correct, that state capitalism exists in Russia today, then he cannot avoid the conclusion that state capitalism has been in existence since the Russian Revolution and the function of the revolution itself was to introduce this state capitalist system of society. For despite his tortuous efforts to draw a line between the economic basis of Russian society before the year 1928 and after, the economic basis of Russian society has in fact remained unchanged.

Incorrect Usage of Quotations

Comrade Cliff seeks to prove that Trotsky was moving to the position that the bureaucracy was a new ruling class. For this purpose he gives quotations from the book *Stalin,* and then from *Living Thoughts of Karl Marx.*

Cliff writes:

> A clear step in the direction of a new evaluation of the bureaucracy as a ruling class finds expression in Trotsky's last book, *Stalin.* He writes:
>
> 'The substance of Thermidor was, is and could not fail to be social in character. It stood for the crystallisation of a new privileged stratum, the creation of a new substratum for the economically dominant class. There were two pretenders to this role: the petty bourgeoisie and the bureaucracy itself. They fought shoulder to shoulder (in the battle to break) the resistance of the proletarian vanguard. When that task was accomplished a savage struggle broke out between them. The bureaucracy became frightened of its isolation, its divorce from the proletariat. Alone it could not crush the kulak* nor the petty bourgeoisie that had grown and continued to grow on the basis of the NEP; it had to have the aid of the proletariat. Hence its concerted effort to present its struggle against the petty bourgeoisie for the surplus products and for power as the struggle of the proletariat against attempts at capitalistic restoration'. *(The Nature of Stalinist Russia,* Tony Cliff. June 1948, page 10.)

And Comrade Cliff comments:

> The bureaucracy, Trotsky says, while pretending to fight against the capitalistic restoration, in reality used the proletariat only to crush the kulaks for 'the crystallisation of a new privileged stratum, the creation of a new substratum for the economically dominant class'. One of the pretenders to the role of the economically dominant class, he says, is the bureaucracy. Great emphasis is lent to this formulation when we connect this analysis with the fight between the bureaucracy and the kulaks with Trotsky's definition of the class struggle. He says: 'The class struggle is nothing else than the struggle for surplus produce. He who owns surplus-produce is master of the situation — owns wealth, owns the state, has the key to the Church, to the courts, to the sciences and to the arts'. (Cliff, page 10).

And Cliff concludes:

> The fight between the bureaucracy and the kulaks was, according to Trotsky's last conclusion, the 'struggle...for the surplus products'.

To illustrate the way in which Comrade Cliff has constructed his

---

*Russian term for rich peasant.

case, let us examine these quotations *in context* and we will see that the conclusion that flows is *precisely the opposite* to what he argues:

> The kulak, jointly with the petty industrialists, worked for the complete restoration of capitalism. *Thus opened the irreconcilable struggle over the surplus product of national labour.* Who will dispose of it in the nearest future — the new bourgeoisie or the Soviet bureaucracy? — that became the next issue. He who disposed of the surplus product has the power of the state at his disposal. It was all this that opened the struggle between the petty bourgeoisie, which had helped the bureaucracy to crush the resistance of the labouring masses and of their spokesmen the Left Opposition, and the Thermidorean bureaucracy itself, which had helped the petty bourgeoisie to lord it over the agrarian masses. It was a direct struggle for power and income.
>
> Obviously the bureaucracy did not rout the proletarian vanguard, pull from the complications of the international revolution, and legitimise the philosophy of inequality in order to capitulate before the bourgeoisie, become the latter's servant, and be eventually itself pulled away from the state feed-bag. (*Stalin* by L. Trotsky. Harper, London 1941, page 397, our emphasis).

Cliff makes Trotsky look foolish by appearing to contradict himself by juxtaposing the two quotations and adducing therefrom that Trotsky was changing his position on the class character of the bureaucracy. A few pages further on, Trotsky explains his idea. he shows the organic tendency of the decay of capitalism everywhere. It is only on this basis that the nationalised productive forces have been maintained in Russia. The whole tendency of the economy in the last 50 years on a world scale has been towards the statification of the productive forces. The capitalists themselves have in part been compelled to 'the recognition of the productive forces as social forces' (Engels). In fact, this is the key to the explanation of why Russia survived the war. The disorientation of the movement which is expressed in Cliff's document, is largely due to the failure to appreciate the implications of this tendency. In his book on Stalin, Trotsky raises the theoretical possibility of the bureaucracy continuing to rule for some decades.

A few pages after the quotations given by Cliff, Trotsky says:

> The counter-revolution sets in when the spool of progressive social conquests begins to unwind. There seems no end to this unwinding. Yet some portion of the conquests of the revolution is always preserved. Thus, in spite of monstrous bureaucratic distortions, the class basis of the USSR remains proletarian. But let us bear in mind that the unwinding process has not yet been completed, and the future of Europe and the world during the next few decades has not yet been decided. The Russian Thermidor would undoubtedly have opened a new era of bourgeois rule, if that rule had not proved obsolete

throughout the world. At any rate the struggle against equality and the establishment of very deep social differentiation has so far been unable to eliminate the socialist consciousness of the masses or the nationalisation of the means of production and the land, which were the basic socialist conquests of the revolution... (*Stalin*, p 405).

We believe this sufficiently demonstrates that Cliff has taken a quotation from Trotsky's *Stalin* out of context and read something into it which is not there. In his last work, as in all others on the Russian question, Trotsky had a consistent theme in his characterisation of the Soviet Union. It is not possible to draw the conclusion from any of his writings that he was altering his fundamental position.

Can there be a Struggle between Two Sections of the Same Class? French Revolution – Russian Revolution

To understand the Russian Revolution we can take the analogy of the French Revolution which is striking in its similarity and course although obviously on a different economic basis. As is known, the rule of the bourgeoisie was ushered in in France in the revolution of 1789. Marx explains the progressive rule of the revolutionary Jacobins: this revolutionary dictatorship of the *sans culottes* went further than the bourgeois regime. Because of that they made a clean sweep of all feudal rubbish, and did in months what the bourgeoisie would have required decades to achieve. This was followed by the Thermidorian reaction and the Bonapartist counter-revolution.

Anyone who compared the Bonapartist counter-revolution with the revolution – at least in its superstructure – would have found as great a difference as between the regime of Lenin and Trotsky in Russia and that of Stalin in latter years. To superficial observers the difference between the two regimes was fundamental. In fact, insofar as the superstructure was concerned, the difference was glaring. Napoleon had reintroduced many of the orders, decorations and ranks similar to those of feudalism; he had restored the Church; he even had himself crowned Emperor. Yet despite this counter-revolution, it is clear that it had nothing in common with the old regime. *It was counter-revolution on the basis of the new form of property introduced by the revolution itself.* Bourgeois forms of property or property relations remained the basis of the economy.

When we study the further history of France, we see the variety of forms of government and of the superstructure which developed in the course of the class struggle. The restoration of the monarchy after the defeat of Napoleon, the revolutions of 1830 and of 1848 — what was the *class* struggle there? There was a different division of the income, but after all these revolutions the economy remained *bourgeois*.

The subsequent history of France saw the dictatorship of Louis Bonaparte, the restoration of bourgeois democracy and the Republic and, in recent days, the regime of Petain. Under all these regimes there were differences in the division of the national income between the classes and between different strata of the ruling class itself. Yet we call all these regimes bourgeois. Why? It can only be because of the form of property.

Given the backwardness of the Soviet Union, which is very well explained by Cliff, and the isolation of the revolution, why should not a similar process take place? In fact it did. Let us return to Trotsky's book *Stalin*. The Old Man was clear. After the quotation where Trotsky shows that the substance of the Thermidor could not but be social in character and was the struggle for the surplus product, he went on to explain what was meant. Let us continue where Cliff stopped:

> Here the analogy with French Thermidor ceases. The new social basis of the Soviet Union became paramount. *To guard the nationalisation of the means of production and of the land, is the bureaucracy's law of life and death, for these are the social sources of its dominant position.* That was the reason for its struggle against the kulak. The bureaucracy could wage this struggle, and wage it to the end, only with the support of the proletariat. The best proof of the fact that it had mustered this support was the avalanche of capitulations by representatives of the new Opposition.
>
> The fight against the kulak, the fight against the right wing, the fight against opportunism — the official slogans of that period — seemed to the workers and to many representatives of the Left Opposition like a renaissance of the dictatorship of the proletariat and the socialist revolution. We warned them at the time: it is not only a question of *what* is being done, but also of *who* does it. Under conditions of Soviet democracy, ie, self-rule of the toilers, the struggle against the kulaks might not have assumed such a convulsive, panicky and bestial form and might have led to a general rise of the economic and cultural level of the masses on the basis of industrialisation. But the bureaucracy's fight against the kulak was single combat (fought) on the backs of the toilers; and since neither of the embattled gladiators trusted the masses, since both feared the masses, the struggle assumed an extremely convulsive and sanguinary character. Thanks to the support of the proletariat, it ended with victory for the bureaucracy. But it did not lead to a gain in the specific weight of the proletariat in the country's political life. (*Stalin* p 408, our emphasis)

When Trotsky speaks here of 'the creation of a new substratum for the economically dominant class' what is clearly meant is the proletariat, which dominates through the form of property. Cliff says: *'One of the pretenders to the role of the economically dominant class, he says, is the bureaucracy. Great emphasis is lent to this formulation...'* Here we see the dangers in the method of working on the basis of preconceived ideas and the attempt to select quotations to fit into these ideas.

In this same chapter, Trotsky shows the similarity and the differences with the French revolution and why the reaction took a different form in France to that which it took in Russia:

> The privileges of the bureaucacy have a different source of origin. The bureaucracy took for itself that part of the national income which it could secure either by the exercise of force or of its authority or by direct intervention in economic relations. In the matter of the national surplus product the bureaucracy and the petty bourgeoisie quickly changed from alliance to enmity. The control of the surplus product opened the bureaucracy's road to power.*(Stalin,* p 40)

The theme of Trotsky is sufficiently clear. The struggle for the surplus product can be waged not only between different classes, but between different strata and different groupings representing the same class.

Does the Law of Value Operate within the Russian Economy?

The whole of the section of Cliff's document on the law of value is unsound from a Marxist point of view. In the most involved and peculiar manner he argues that the law of value does not apply within the Russian economy, but only in its relations to world capitalism. He finds the basis of the law of value, not in Russian society, but in the world capitalist environment.

> Let us now find out what importance the internal relations in Russia has when abstracted from the influence of world economy.
> The abstraction has solved one fundamental question: that *the source of the activity of the law of value is not to be found in the internal relations of Russian economy itself.* In other words it has brought us so far nearer solving the problem of whether the Russian economy is subordinated to the law of value by showing us *where not to look* for its source. (Cliff, page 98. Emphasis in original).

According to the Marxist view, it is in *exchange* that the law of value manifests itself. And this holds true for all forms of society. For example, the way in which the break-up of primitive communism took place was through the exchange and barter between different primitive communities. This led to the development of private property. In slave society, in the same way, the products of the slave *became commodities* when they were exchanged. Through this development, the 'commodity of commodities' appeared: money. It was thus that the product enslaved the producer and in the end the contradiction caused by the money economy resulted in the destruction of the old slave society. Under feudalism, the exchange of the *surplus* produced by the self-sufficient lords and barons in their 'natural economy' became commodities, and in fact, was the starting point of capitalist development through the rise of *merchant capital.*

Therefore, if it was in exchange *only* between Russia and the outside world that the law of value manifested itself, all that this would mean is that the *Russian surplus* was exchanged on the basis of the law of value. What consequences that would have for the internal economy is a different question which would have to be worked out.

However, because of the small degree of participation of the Soviet Union on the world market, in comparison with the total production of Russia, Cliff unavoidably realises the weakness of this point. Thus, amazingly, Cliff finds the law of value manifesting itself not in *exchange,* but in *competition.* Even this would not be so bad if he argued that this was competition on the world market on classical capitalist lines for markets. But he cannot argue this because it is at variance with the facts. So he introduces a new conception. He finds his 'competition' and his 'law of value' in the production of armaments!

The pressure of world capitalism forces Russia to devote an enormous proportion of the national income on armaments production and defence on the one hand, and the greatest capital construction in history in proportion to the national income for the needs of defence, on the other. Here Cliff finds his law of value. The law of value manifests itself in the armaments competition between two social systems! This can only be described as a concession to Shachtman's theory of bureaucratic collectivism. If this theory is correct, the theory of an entirely new economy, never before seen in history or foreseen by the Marxists, would apply.

Here again we would point out the dangers of indiscriminate use of quotations and amalgamations of ideas to form a 'thesis'. In reality this document is not a state capitalist document; it is a hybrid in the union of bureaucratic collectivism and state capitalism. If this section of Cliff's document means anything at all, it leads straight to the road of Schachtman's bureaucratic collectivism.

This idea is partially borrowed from Hilferding* who

*Rudolf Hilferding was a German Social Democratic leader.

consistently argued that in Russia and in Nazi Germany the law of value did not apply and that these were entirely new social formations. It is also based on a misunderstanding of some passages in Bukharin's *Imperialism and the World Economy*, where he argued on the basis of 'state capitalism' — the organic union of trusts with finance capital — and in which he, together with Lenin, brilliantly prophesied a form of dictatorship which was later realised in Italian fascism and nazism. Not state ownership of the means of production, but the fusion of finance capital with the state. In fact Bukharin chose as one of his classic examples of such a state...America.

The argument on armaments partakes of a mystical and not an economic category. At best, even if we accepted it as correct, it would only explain *why* Russian produces armaments, but not *how* or on what economic basis the armaments are produced. Even if Russia were a healthy workers' state, in imperialist encirclement, there would be the absolute necessity to produce armaments and compete with the arms technique and production of the rival capitalist systems. But this argument about armaments is entirely false. The greater part of production in Russia is not armaments but means of production. Again, this would explain why the bureaucracy is attempting to accumulate the means of production at a frantic speed, but it explains nothing of the economic system of production itself. It is probably true that in a healthy workers' state accumulation of arms would be smaller for *social* reasons (internationalist and revolutionary policy towards workers in other lands), but it would nevertheless take place under the pressure of world imperialism.

A quicker or slower tempo in the development of the means of production does not necessarily tell us the method by which these are produced. Cliff says that the bureaucracy is developing the means of production under the pressure of world imperialism. Good. But all this tells us again is why the pace is fast. From the point of view of even classical bourgeois political economy, Cliff's argument is a pure evasion. It merely poses what has to be proved.

Not for nothing did Trotsky point out in *Revolution Betrayed* that the whole progressive content of the activity of the Stalinist bureaucracy and its preoccupation, was the raising of the productivity of labour and the defence of the country.

We have seen that if the law of value *only* applies because of the existence of capitalism in world economy, *then it would only apply to those products exchanged on the world market.* But Cliff argues two contradictory theses in relation to the Russian economy. On the one hand he says:

This does not mean that the price system in Russia is arbitrary, dependent on the whim of the bureaucracy. The basis of price here too is the costs of production. If price is to be used as a transmission belt through which the bureaucracy directs production as a whole, it must fit its purpose, *and as nearly as possible reflect the real costs, that is, the socially necessary labour absorbed in the different products...(Cliff,* p 94, our emphasis)

Two pages later, Cliff describes as the *central point* he intends to prove:

...that in the economic relations *within Russia itself,* one cannot find the autonomy of economic activity, the *source* of the law of value, acting. (Cliff, page 96. Emphasis in original).

In the first quotation, *Cliff shows precisely the way in which the law of value manifests itself internally in Russian society.* Even if one abstracts from the world market, leaving aside the interacting effect which it undoubtedly has — when Cliff says that 'the real costs, that is the socially necessary labour absorbed in the different products' must reflect the real prices, he is saying that the same law applies in Russian society as in capitalist society. The difference is that whereas in capitalist society it manifests itself blindly by the laws of the markets, in Russia conscious activity plays an important role. In this connection the second quotation crushingly refutes Cliff's argument that it is *capitalism* which exists in Russia under these given conditions because the law of value does not operate blindly, but is consciously harnessed. In capitalist society, the law of value, as he says, manifests itself through the 'autonomy of economic activity', ie, it is the market which dominates. The first quotation shows clearly that the market — and this is the point — is within given limits controlled consciously and therefore it is not capitalism as understood by Marxists.

Previously Cliff said that the law of value did not operate in Russia. Here he is showing precisely how it does operate: not on the lines of classical capitalism, but of a *transitional* society between capitalism and socialism.

We see therefore, that Cliff claims that Russia is a capitalist society — yet he finds the source of the basic law of capitalist production outside of Russia. Now, in any capitalist society in which the reserve fund is in the hands of the capitalist class, as Engels explained:

...if this production and reserve fund does in fact exist in the hands of the capitalist class, if it has in fact arisen through the accumulation of profit...then it necessarily consists of the accumulated surplus of the product of labour handed over to the capitalist class by the working class, over and above the sum of wages paid to the working class by the capitalist class. In this case, however, it is not wages that determine value, but the quantity of labour; in this case the working class hands over to the capitalist class in the product of labour a greater quantity of value than it receives from it in the shape of wages; and then the profit on capital like all other forms of appropriation without payment of the labour product of others, is explained as a simple component part of the surplus value discovered by Marx. (*Anti Duhring*, Progress Publishers, Moscow 1969, page 233).

This indicates that where there is wage labour, where there is the accumulation of capital, *the law of value must apply*, no matter in how complicated a form it may manifest itself. Further on Engels explains in answer to Duhring's* five kinds of value, and the 'natural costs of production', that in *Capital* Marx is dealing with the value of commodities and 'in the whole section of *Capital* which deals with value there is not even the slightest indication of whether or to what extent Marx considers the theory of value of commodities applicable to other forms of society'. In this sense it is clear that in the transitional society also: 'Value itself is nothing more than the expression of the socially necessary labour materialised in an object.' Here it is only necessary to ask: what determines the value of machines, consumer goods, etc, produced in Russia? Is it arbitrary? What determines the calculations of the bureaucracy? What is it that they measure in price? What determines wages? Are wages payments for labour power? What determines 'money'? What determines profits of enterprises? Is there capital? Is the division of labour abolished?

Cliff gives two contradictory answers to these questions. On the one hand he agrees that it is the law of value on which all calculations and the movement of Russian society develops. On the other, he finds the law of value only operating as the result of pressure from the outside world although how he does not explain in any serious way.

The Role of Money in Russia

The surprising thing is that Cliff himself points out that the bureaucracy does not and cannot determine prices arbitrarily. That it does not and cannot determine the amount of money in circulation arbitrarily either. And this has been so in every society where money (let us remember, the commodity of commodities) has played a role. Engels, dealing with this problem, pertinently asked Duhring:

If the sword (no matter who wields it − bureaucrat, capitalist, or

*Eugen Duhring was a prominent German social democrat. In 1874-5 he published works challenging the Marxist ideology of the German movement, to which Engels replied in *Anti-Duhring*.

government — EG) has the magic economic power ascribed to it by Herr Duhring, why is it that no government has been able to succeed in permanently compelling bad money to have the 'distribution value' of good money, or assignats the 'distribution value' of gold? (*Anti Duhring*, page 228).

In *Revolution Betrayed*, Trotsky explains this problem very clearly. He shows that the economic categories peculiar to capitalism still remain in the transitional society between capitalism and communism, the dictatorship of the proletariat. Here is the key: the laws remain, but are *modified*. Some of the laws of capitalism apply and some are abrogated. For example, Trotsky argues:

The role of money in Soviet economy is not only unfinished but, as we have said, still has a long growth ahead. The transitional epoch between capitalism and socialism taken as a whole does not mean a cutting down of trade but, on the contrary, its extraordinary extension. All branches of industry transform themselves and grow. New ones continually arise, and all are compelled to define their relations to one another both quantitatively and qualitatively. The liquidation of the consummatory peasant economy, and at the same time of the shut-in family life, means a transfer to the sphere of social interchange, and *ipso facto* money circulation, of all the labour energy which was formerly expended within the limits of the peasant's yard, or within the walls of his private dwelling. *All products and services begin for the first time in history to be exchanged for one another.* (*Revolution Betrayed*, NY, 1972, page 67, our emphasis.).

What is the key to this enigma? It can only be found in the fact that we have here a transitional society. *The state can now regulate, but not arbitrarily, only within the confines of the law of value.* Any attempt to violate and pass beyond the strict limits set by the development of the productive forces themselves, immediately results in the re-assertion of the domination of production over producer. This is what Stalin had to discover in relation to price and money when the Russian economy was inflicted with a crisis of inflation which completely distorted and disrupted the plan. The law of value is not abolished, but is *modified*. This is what Trotsky meant when he said:

The nationalisation of the means of production and credit, the co-operativising or state-ising of internal trade, the monopoly of foreign trade, the collectivisation of agriculture, the law of inheritance — set strict limits upon the personal accumulation of money and hinder its conversion into private capital (usurious, commercial and industrial). These functions of money, however, bound up as they are with exploitation, are not liquidated at the beginning of a proletarian revolution, but in a modified form are transferred to the state, the universal merchant, creditor and industrialist. At the same time the more elementary functions of money as *measure of value, means of exchange* and *medium of payment*, are not only preserved, but acquire a broader field of action than they had under capitalism. (*Revolution Betrayed*, page 66. Emphasis in original).

One has only to pose the problem in this way to see that an economic analysis must lead one to conclude that we have here a transitional society in which some of the laws peculiar to socialism apply and some peculiar to capitalism. That is after all, the meaning of *transition*.

Although Cliff does not recognise this, in fact he admits it, because when he says that the bureaucracy can consciously regulate (though within limits) the rate of investment, the proportions between means of production and means of consumption, the price of articles of consumption, etc, *he is proving that certain of the basic laws of capitalism do not apply.*

Is there a transformation of money into capital in Russia? In polemicising against Stalin, Trotsky answers this by showing that the investments are made on the basis of a plan, but nevertheless, what is *invested* is the surplus value produced by the workers. Here Trotsky shows the basic fallacy in Stalin's idea that the state could decide and regulate without reference to the economy. We might add that Stalin never denied that there was commodity production in Russia.

In spite of the fact that there is only one 'employer' in Russia, nevertheless, the state buys labour power. It is true that because of the full employment which would normally place the seller of the commodity labour power in a strong position, the state has imposed various restrictions on the free sale of labour power, just as in a period of full employment under fascism. Or even in Labour Britain, where the same situation exists, by means of regulations and devices the employers have the state intervene to offset the advantages which accrue from this situation for the sale of labour power. But only one who argued in abstractions, could argue that this negated labour power.

It is true that in the classical capitalist economy there was free sale of labour power. However, in Marx's *Capital* itself there was a whole section devoted to showing the ferocious laws which were introduced against the nascent proletariat after the Black Death in England had so reduced the population that the proletarians were in a favourable position to demand higher wages. Did this mean that the basic Marxian laws did not apply? On the contrary, Marx was dealing with a 'pure' capitalism which never did exist, from which he extracted the fundamental laws. The distortion of this or that element will not alter the basic laws. That is why in nazi

Germany, despite many perversions, it remained fundamentally a system of capitalist economy, because the economy was dominated by production on the basis of private property.

One has only to compare the slave labourer in Siberia with the proletariat in the Russian cities to see the difference. The one is a slave based on slave labour, the other is a wage slave. The one sells his labour power, the other is purely an instrument of labour himself. There is the fundamental distinction.

It is not at all accidental that the 'money' used by the state must *necessarily* have the same basis as money in capitalist society. Not accidentally, as Trotsky explained, *the only real money* in Russia (or in any transitional economy — even an ideal workers' state) *must be based on gold*. The recent rouble devaluation in Russia was in itself a striking confirmation of the fact that the law of money circulation, and thus of the circulation of commodities, maintains its validity in Russia. In a transitional economy the economic categories of money, value, surplus value, etc, must necessarily continue as elements of the old society within the new society.

Cliff argues that 'the most important source of state income is the turn-over tax, which is an indirect tax.' He introduced interesting material showing the tremendous burden which the turn-over tax imposes upon the masses.

However, the turn-over tax to which he refers in connection with the exploitation of the masses, in an indirect way, proves that the law of value applies in Russian society. Cliff shows how the turn-over tax *applies* in Russia. But he does not see that this tax must be *based* on something. No matter how much the state might add to the price by placing an additional tax, the price must be based on something: what else can this be but the value of the product, the socially necessary labour time contained in it?

Engels ridiculed Duhring's tax by the sword, out of which the surplus is developed, when he said:

> Or, on the other hand, the alleged tax surcharges represent a real sum of value, namely that produced by the labouring, value-producing class but appropriated by the monopolist class, and then this sum of value consists merely of unpaid labour; in this event, in spite of the man with the sword in his hand, *in spite of the alleged tax surcharges*, we come once again to the Marxian theory of *surplus value*. (*Anti-Duhring*, page 226).

The turn-over tax in Russia and the other manipulations of the bureaucracy do not in any way invalidate the law of value. What is the essence of the law of value? That the value of the product is determined by the average amount of socially necessary labour time. That must be the point of departure. *It necessarily manifests itself through exchange*. Marx devoted a great part of his first volume of *Capital* to explaining the historical development of the commodity form from accidental exchange among savages through its transitions, till we arrive at commodity production par excellence, capitalist production.

Even in a classical capitalist economy the law of value does not reveal itself directly. As is known, commodities are sold above or below their value. Only accidentally would a commodity be sold at its actual value. In the third volume of *Capital* Marx explains the price of production of commodities. That is to say, that the capitalist only gets the cost of production of his commodity plus the average rate of profit. Thus some capitalists will be paid below the actual rate, others above. Because of the different organic composition of different capitals, only in this complicated fashion does the law of value reveal itself. This is effected, of course, through competition. Monopoly is merely a more complicated development of the law of value in society. Because of the controlling position held by some monopolies, they can extort a price above the value of the commodities, but only by other commodities being sold below their value. The total values produced by society would still amount to the same.

Was there Surplus Value before 1928?
Cliff's Arbitrary Division

In this connection, Cliff is not at all consistent. Shachtman, in his endeavour to deny that Russia is a transitional society in which capitalist laws continue to operate, as well as the laws of the future society, at least argues consistently. He says that the law of value does not operate, therefore all the laws flowing from it do not operate. It is not surplus value which is produced, but surplus product; it is not labour power that the workers sell, since they are slaves, etc, etc. Cliff, however, admits that commodity production continues, labour power and surplus value remain. But once these Marxian categories are accepted as valid for Russian society, then clearly the law of value must operate internally, or the whole position becomes nonsensical.

The whole contradiction, a contradiction within the society itself and not imposed abitrarily − is in the very concept of the dictatorship of the proletariat. If one considers the problem in the abstract, one can see that this is a contradictory phenomenon: the abolition of capitalism yet the continuation of classes. The proletariat does not disappear. It raises itself to the position of ruling class and abolishes the capitalist class. But in the intervening period it remains the working class. Therefore, surplus product in the form of surplus value is produced. It is the case today as it was under Lenin and Trotsky. We have only to pose the problem: *what was the surplus value produced when Russia was still a workers' state* —though even then with bureaucratic deformations? What was the process by means of which surplus product *before* 1928 mysteriously became surplus value *after* 1928? What was this curious unexplained process? We would like to ask the question here: Did the existence of capitalism outside Russia before 1928 have a similar effect on Russia's economy? Of course it did. In fact a far greater effect because of the weakness of the Russian economy. Why was there not capitalism in Russia then?

Or further: leave aside the period from 1917 to 1923 — what was the situation from 1923 to 1928 when the Stalinist bureaucracy was consolidating itself? There were far more actual individual capitalist elements in the economy of the country then than there are today. The pressure of world capitalism from an economic point of view was indisputably far greater. Merely to pose the problem is to show the arbitrary method.

The abuse of power and the legal and illegal consumption of surplus value by the bureaucracy, necessarily took place even in the early stages of bureaucratic control. Comrade Cliff has to construct a lifeless scheme which bears no relation to reality in order to create a distinction between the two periods: the period when the bureaucracy represented a degenerated workers' state, and the period when the bureaucracy became a capitalist class. What, according to Cliff, is the difference? Incredible as it may seem, the bureaucracy really *earned* its income and only from 1928 onwards did they consume surplus value. Cliff writes:

> The statistics we have at our disposal conclusively show that although the bureaucracy had a privileged position in the period preceding the Five-Year Plan, it can on no account be said that it received surplus value from the labour of others. It can just as conclusively be said that with the introduction of the Five-Year Plans, the bureaucracy's income consisted to a large extent of surplus value. (page 45)

This is at variance with the analysis made not only by Trotsky but by the other Marxists of the time in relation to this problem. First of all, even in the most ideal workers' state, in the transitional period there will unavoidably be a certain consumption of the surplus value by the specialists and bureaucrats. Otherwise, we would have the immediate introduction of communism, without any inequalities or the continuance of the division between mental and manual labour. It is only necessary to refer here to the Left Opposition on this very problem. As early as 1927, the Left Opposition commented on the enormous part of the surplus value being consumed by the bureaucratic apparatus. They protested that the *'swollen and privileged administrative apparatus is devouring a very considerable part of the surplus value'*. (See *Revolution Betrayed,* page 141)

It is clear that from 1920 onwards, the bureaucracy consumed a great part of the surplus value, legitimately and illegitimately. As Marx explained in any case, in a workers' state in the transitional period, the surplus value will be used for the speedy building up of industry and so prepare the way for the quickest possible transition to equality and then complete communism.

What else was Lenin speaking of in 1920 and 1921 when he stressed the step backward the Bolsheviks had been forced to make, when they paid the specialists according to bourgeois standards and in the old 'bourgeois way'?

The Economics of the Transition from Capitalism to Socialism

The most significant thing about all tendencies who seek to revise Trotsky's position on the Russian question is that they always deal with the problem in the *abstract* and never concretely explain the laws of the transitional society between capitalism and socialism and how such a society would operate. This is not accidental. A concrete consideration would impel them to the conclusion that *the fundamental economy in Russia is the same as it was under Lenin and that it could not be otherwise.*

The germ of the capitalist mode of production, which began under feudalism through the development of commodity production, lies in the function of the independent craftsmen and merchants. When it reaches a certain stage we have *capitalist relations* with a feudal superstructure. These are burst asunder by the revolution and the possibilities latent in capitalist production then have the free possibility of fruition unhampered by feudal restrictions.

The whole essence of the revolution (capitalist and proletarian) consists of the fact that the old relationships and the old forms do not correspond with the new ripened method or mode of production. In order to free itself from these restrictions, the productive forces have to be organised on a different basis and the whole of human history and movement of history consists in the development of this antagonism at its various stages in different societies.

However, the bourgeois revolution does not immediately destroy feudalism at one blow. Powerful feudal elements still remain, and to this day the remnants of feudalism exist even in the most highly developed capitalist countries.

One can speak of the feudal mode of production in the sense of the superstructure, despite the capitalist basis which has developed beneath. Or one can even speak of the feudal mode of production at its inception where the germs of capitalism and the possibility of the development of capitalism could be faintly discerned.

The fundamental error of this 'state capitalist' theory and its abstractions relating to the transitional period, lies in the failure to distinguish between the mode of production and the mode of appropriation. In every class society there is exploitation and a surplus which is utilised by the exploiting class. But in itself this tells us nothing about the mode of production.

For example, the mode of production under capitalism is *social* in contradiction to the individual form of appropriation. As Engels explained:

> The separation between the means of production concentrated in the hands of the capitalists on the one side, and the producers now possessing nothing but their labour power, on the other, was made complete. The contradiction between social production and capitalist (read individual or private, as Engels had already explained – EG) appropriation became manifest as the antagonism between proletariat and bourgeoisie. (*Anti Duhring*, page 321)

The transitional economy which, as Lenin pointed out, can and will vary enormously in different countries at different times, and even in the same country at different times, also has a social mode of production, but with *state appropriation,* and not individual appropriation as under capitalism. This is a form which combines both socialist and capitalist features.

Under capitalism, the system of commodity production *par excellence,* the product completely dominates the producer. This flows from the form of appropriation, and the contradiction between the form of appropriation and the mode of production; both factors flow from *the private ownership of the means of production.* Once state ownership takes its place, whatever the resulting system may be, it cannot be capitalism because this basic contradiction will have been abolished. The anarchic character of social production with private appropriation disappears.

Under socialism also, there will be a social mode of production *but there will also be a social mode of distribution.* For the first time production and distribution will be in harmony.

Therefore, merely to point out the capitalist features in Russia today (wage labour, commodity production, that the bureaucracy consumes an enormous part of the surplus value) is not sufficient to tell us the nature of the social system. Here too, an all-sided view is necessary. One can only understand social relationships in the

Soviet Union by taking the *totality* of the relationships. From the very beginning of the revolution various sectarian schools have produced the most untenable ideas as a result of their failure to make such an analysis. Lenin summed up the problem thus:

> But what does the word 'transition' mean? Does it mean, as applied to economics, that the present order contains elements, particles, pieces of *both* capitalism and socialism? Everyone will admit that it does. But not all who admit this take the trouble to consider the precise nature of the elements that constitute the various social-economic forms which exist in Russia at the present time. And this is the crux of the question. (*Left wing childishness and the petty-bourgeois mentality.* Collected Works, Vol. 27, page 335)

To abstract one side must lead to error. What is puzzling about the Russian phenomenon is precisely the *contradictory character* of the economy. This has been further aggravated by the backwardness and isolation of the Soviet Union. This culminates in the totalitarian Stalinist regime and results in the worst features of capitalism coming to the fore — the relations between managers and men, piece-work, etc. Instead of analysing these contradictions Comrade Cliff endeavours as far as possible to try and fit them into the pattern of the 'normal' laws of capitalist production.

In addition, the tendency under capitalism for the productive forces not only to become centralised but even for measures of statification to be introduced can result in a wrong conclusion. To prove that 'state capitalism' in Russia is in the last analysis the same as individual capitalism with the same laws, Cliff cites the following passage from *Anti Duhring*:

> The more productive forces it (the state — TC) takes over, the more it becomes the real collective body of all the capitalists, the more citizens it exploits. The workers remain wage-earners, proletarians. The capitalist relationship is not abolished; it is rather pushed to an extreme. But at this extreme it changes into its opposte. State ownership of the productive forces is not the solution of the conflict, but it contains within itself the formal means, the key to the solution. (*Anti Duhring*, page 330)

In point of fact, Engels is arguing precisely the opposite. Let us re-examine the passages and see how we draw different conclusions:

> *If the crisis revealed the incapacity of the bourgeoisie any longer to control the modern productive forces,* the conversion of the great organisations forproduction and communication into joint-stock companies and state property shows that for this purpose the bourgeoisie can be dispensed with. All the social functions of the capitalists are now carried out by salaried employees. *The capitalist has no longer any social activity save the pocketing of revenues, the clipping of coupons and gambling on the stock exchange,*

where the different capitalists fleece each other of their capital. Just as at first the capitalist mode of production displaced the workers, so now it displaces the capitalists, relegating them, just as it did the workers, to the superfluous population, even if in the first instance not to the industrial reserve army.

But *neither the conversion into joint-stock companies nor into state property deprives the productive forces of their character as capital.* In the case of joint-stock companies this is obvious. And the modern state, too, is only the organisation with which bourgeois society provides itself in order to maintain the general external *conditions of the capitalist mode of production against encroachments either by the workers or by individual capitalists.* The modern state, whatever its form, is an essentially capitalist machine; it is the state of the capitalists, the ideal collective body of all capitalists. The more productive forces it takes over as its property, the more it becomes the real collective body of all the capitalists, the more citizens it exploits. *The workers remain wage earners, proletarians. The capitalist relationship is not abolished; it is rather pushed to an extreme. But at this extreme it is transformed into its opposite. State ownership of the productive forces is not the solution of the conflict, but it contains within itself the formal means, the key to the solution. (Anti Duhring,* page 330. Our emphasis)

Surely the idea in the foregoing is clear. Insofar as the forces of production have now developed beyond the framework of capitalist relations (that is, the germ of the contradiction has now grown into a malignant disease of the social system, reflecting itself through the crises) the capitalists are compelled to 'socialise' huge means of production — first, through joint-stock companies and then later, even to 'statify' sections of the productive forces. This particular idea was brought out sharply by Lenin in *Imperialism*, where he showed that the development of monopolies and socialisation of labour were in fact *elements of the new social system within the old.*

Once the productive forces had reached this stage, capitalism had already accomplished its historic mission, and because of this the bourgeoisie becomes more and more superfluous. From being a necessity for the development of the forces of production, they now become 'superfluous', 'parasites', 'coupon-clippers'. In this they are transformed into parasites in the same way and for the same reason as the feudal lords also became 'parasites' once their mission had been fulfilled.

This is merely an indication of the ripeness of capitalism for the social revolution. Writing in *Capital* Marx had shown that credit and joint-stock companies were already an indication that the productive forces had outgrown private ownership. Engels had shown that the *social productive forces* even compel the capitalists to recognise their character as *social* and not as *individual* productive forces.

Wherever the capitalist state is constrained to take over this or that sector of the economy, it is true the productive forces do not lose their character as capital. *But the whole essence of the problem is that where we have complete statification, quantity changes into quality, capitalism changes into its opposite.*

How otherwise explain the statement of Engels: '*But at this extreme it* (the capitalist relationship) *is transformed into its opposite.* State ownership of the productive forces is not the solution of the conflict, but it contains within itself the formal means, the key to the solution'?

If one takes into account the fact that this follows the previously quoted passage in the *same section* where Engels defines capitalist mode of production (as social production, individual appropriation), we must conclude that Engels hopelessly contradicts himself, if we accept Cliff's conclusions. But from the context, Engels' meaning is clear. He explains that the solution to the contradictions of capitalism lies in the recognition of the social nature of the modern productive forces: 'In bringing, therefore, the mode of production, appropriation and exchange into accord with the social character of the means of production.' But he shows that this 'recognition' precisely consists in asserting *conscious* organisation and planning, in place of the blind play of forces of the market on the basis of individual ownership. This, however, cannot be done at one stroke. Only 'gradually' can social control be fully asserted. *The transitional form to this is state ownership.* But complete state ownership does not abolish all the features of capitalism immediately, otherwise there would be social ownership, ie socialism would be introduced immediately.

But in the same way as we have the new within the old system in the development of society, so in the transitional society we still have *the old within the new*. Complete statification marks the extreme limit of capital. The capitalist relation is transformed into its opposite. The elements of the new society which were growing up within the old, *now become dominant*.

What causes the conflict within capitalism is the fact that the laws manifest themselves blindly. But once the whole of industry is nationalised, for the first time *control* and *planning* can be consciously asserted by the producers. Control and planning will, however, in the first stages, take place within given limits. These limits will be determined by the level of technique when the new social order takes over.

Society cannot step from the realm of necessity into the realm of freedom overnight. Only on the basis of a limitless development of the productive forces will freedom, in its fullest sense, become a reality. The stage will be reached which will witness the 'administration of things'.

Before such a stage is reached, society must pass through the transitional period. But in so far as immediately after private ownership has been abolished, control and planning become a possibility for the first time, then for the first time also the realm of necessity is left behind. But while it is now possible to speak of 'freedom', this is only so in the sense that necessity has become consciously recognised. At this stage (the transitional period), Engels pointed out:

> The social character of the means of production and of the products...is quite consciously asserted by the producers, and is transformed from a cause of disorder and periodic collapse into the most powerful level of production itself.
>
> The forces operating in society work exactly like the forces operating in nature; blindly, violently, destructively, so long as we do not understand them and fail to take them into account. But when once we have recognised them and understand how they work, their direction and their effects, *the gradual subjection of them to our will* and the use of them for the attainment of our aims depends entirely upon ourselves. And this is quite especially true of the mighty productive forces of the present day. (*Anti Duhring*, page 331, our emphasis)

Engels, quoting Hegel, further summed up the relationships between freedom, necessity and the transitional period, thus:

> Freedom is the realisation of necessity. 'Necessity is blind only insofar as it is not understood. (*Anti Duhring*, page 136)

Marx and Engels only touched on the contradictory character of the transitional period. They left its elaboration to succeeding generations, laying down only the general laws. But clearly they showed the need for *state ownership* as the necessary transitional state for the development of the productive forces. Engels explained the need for the state during this stage for two reasons:
1) To take measures against the old ruling class;
2) Because the transitional society cannot immediately guarantee enough for all.

The logic of Cliff's thesis is that in the transitional society there are no vestiges of capitalism in the internal economy. While comrade Cliff may argue vehemently that he agrees with the need for the state in the transitional period, it is evident that *he has not thought out the economic reasons which make the state necessary and what character the economy assumes in this period.* Before socialism can be introduced there must necessarily be a tremendous development of the forces of production, far beyond those reached under capitalism.

As Trotsky explained, even in America there is still not enough production to guarantee the immediate introduction of socialism. Therefore, there will still have to be an intervening period in which capitalist laws will operate in modified form. Of course, in America, this would be of short duration. But it will not be possible to skip this stage entirely. What are the capitalist laws which will remain? Comrade Cliff not only fails to answer this; he falls into the trap of bureaucratic collectivism by failing to recognise that money, labour power, the existence of the working class, surplus value, etc, *are all survivals of the old capitalist system* which were carried over even under the regime of Lenin. It is impossible to introduce immediately direct social production and distribution. Particularly was this the case in backward Russia.

Writing to Conrad Schmidt in 1890, Engels gave a magnificent example of the thoroughly materialist approach to the problem of the economics of the transition from capitalism to socialism. He wrote:

> There has been a discussion in the *Volkstribune* about the division of products in the future society, whether this will take place according to the amount of work done or otherwise. The question has been approached very 'materialistically', in opposition to certain idealistic forms of phraseology about justice. But strangely enough it has never struck anyone that, after all, the method of division essentially depends on *how much* there is to divide, and this must surely change with progress of production and social organisation, so that the method of division may also change. But to everyone who took part in the discussion 'socialist society' appeared not as involved in continuous change and progress but as a stable affair fixed once and for all which must, therefore, have its method of division fixed once and for all. All one can reasonably do, however, is (1) to try and discover the method of division to be used *at the beginning,* and (2) to try and find the *general tendency* in which the further development will proceed. But about this I do not find a single word in the whole debate. (*Marx, Engels, Selected Correspondence.* Progress, Moscow, 1975, page 393)

Writing in *Anti Duhring,* Engels pointed out:

> *Direct social production and direct distribution* exclude all exchange of commodities, therefore also the transformation of the product into commodities (at any rate within the community) and consequently also their transformation into values. (*Anti-Duhring,* page 366. Our emphasis)

But only socialism could realise this. In the transitional period, distribution still remains *indirect* – only gradually does society gain complete control over the product – and therefore the production of commodities and of exchange between the different sectors of production must necessarily take place. The law of value applies *and must apply until there is direct access to the product by the producers.* This can only take place on the basis of complete control of social production and thus direct social distribution, namely, each individual taking whatever he requires. Marx deals with this problem in passing in Volume III of *Capital* (Chapter 49), where he is discussing the problem of capitalist production as a whole:

> Accordingly a portion of the profit, of surplus value and of the surplus product, in which only newly added labour is represented, so far as its value is concerned, serves as an insurance fund... This is also the only portion of the surplus-value and surplus product and thus of surplus-labour, which would continue to exist, outside of that portion which serves for accumulation and for expansion of the process of reproduction, *even after the abolition of the capitalist system*...and the fact that all new capital arises out of profit, rent, or other forms of revenue, that is, out of surplus labour... (*Capital*, Vol. III. Progress, Moscow, 1971, pp 847-8. Our emphasis)

In this chapter Marx is dealing, in an analysis of the process of production, in his own words, with 'the value of the total annual product of labour (which) is under discussion, in other words, the value of the product of the total social capital.'

Repeating this in the same chapter, in answer to Storch, one of the bourgeois economists, he declared:

> In the first place, it is a false abstraction to regard a nation, whose mode of production is based upon value or otherwise *capitalistically organised,* as an aggregate body working merely for the satisfaction of the national wants.
>
> In the second place, after the abolition of the capitalist mode of production, but with social production still in vogue, the *determination of value* continues to prevail in such a way that the regulation of the labour time and the distribution of the social labour among the various groups of production also the *keeping of accounts* in connection with this, becomes *more essential than ever*. (*Capital,* Vol. III, page 851. Our emphasis)

This is in line with the scattered remarks of Marx and Engels at various times in dealing with the transitional period: where Engels explains that under capitalism joint-stock companies and state ownership are beyond the framework, properly speaking, of capitalist production; where Marx already pointed out that credit also extended production beyond its framework *even before the transition to the dictatorship of the proletariat.* After that, as shown in the above passages and also in the *Critique of the Gotha Programme,* Marx considered that bourgeois law, bourgeois distribution and in that sense a bourgeois state still remain.

Discussing the role of money and the state in the transitional period, Trotsky developed this idea even further:

> ...These two problems, *state and money*, have a number of traits in

common, for they both reduce themselves in the last analysis to the problem of problems: productivity of labour. State compulsion like money compulsion is an inheritance from the class society, which is incapable of defining the relations of man to man except in the form of fetishes, churchly or secular, after appointing to defend them the most alarming of all fetishes, the state, with a great knife between its teeth. In a communist society, the state and money will disappear. Their gradual dying away ought consequently to begin under socialism only at that historical moment when the state turns into a semi-state, and money begins to lose its magic power. This will mean that socialism, having freed itself from capitalist fetishes, is beginning to create a more lucid, free and worthy relation among men. Such characteristically anarchist demands as the 'abolition' of money, 'abolition' of wages, or 'liquidation' of the state and family possess interest merely as models of mechanical thinking. Money cannot be arbitrarily 'abolished', nor the state and the old family 'liquidated'. They have to exhaust their historic mission, evaporate, and fall away. The death-blow to money fetishism will be struck only upon that stage when the steady growth of social wealth has made us bipeds forget our miserly attitude toward every excess minute of labour, and our humiliating fear about the size of our ration. Having lost its ability to bring happiness or trample men in the dust, money will turn into mere book-keeping receipts for the conveniences of statisticians and for planning purposes. In the still more distant future, probably these receipts will not be needed. But we can leave this question entirely to posterity, who will be more intelligent than we are.

The nationalisation of the means of production and credit, the co-operativising or state-ising of internal trade, the monopoly of foreign trade, the collectivisation of agriculture, the law on inheritance − set strict limits upon the personal accumulation of money and hinder its conversion into private capital (usurious, commercial and industrial). These functions of money, however, bound up as they are with exploitation, are not liquidated at the beginning of a proletarian revolution, but in a modified form are transferred to the state, the universal merchant, creditor and industrialist. At the same time the more elementary functions of money, as *measure of value, means of exchange and medium payment*, are not only preserved, but acquire a broader field of action than they had under capitalism. (*Revolution Betrayed*, page 65-6, emphasis in original)

To sum up. Whereas before private ownership of the means of production is abolished, the market is dominant over man who is helpless before the laws of the economy he himself has created, after its abolition, he begins for the first time to consciously assert control. But consciousness here merely means the *recognition of law, not the abolition of law*. That is the peculiarity of the transitional period, that because man now understands the nature of the productive forces, to that extent he can exercise control over them. But he cannot transcend the limits of the given development of the productive forces. However, now that the productive forces have been released from the fetters of individual capitalist production, they can be developed at such a pace and with such expansion that very rapidly they can be transformed from state ownership as an intermediate form, into social ownership by society. Once this stage has been reached (socialism), there is real social production and distribution for the first time. Money withers away, the law of value withers away, the state withers away. In other words, all the forces of constraint which are a necessary reflection of the limits of technique and the development of production at any given stage, now disappear with the disappearance of the division of labour. Until such time, all the features referred to above, capitalist features carried over from the old capitalist society, will linger on in the transitional period.

The position of Comrade Cliff, as with Shachtman and all others who have revised Trotsky's position on Russia, remains, on the transitional period, a blank. And for a very good reason. If one considers the theory of the transitional stage in the light of the Russian experience, there are only one of two conclusions: either Russia today is still in a transitional stage, which has taken on horrible distortions, or Russia was never a workers' state from the very beginning. There are no other alternatives.

The Marxian Theory of the State
Two Classes One State — Cliff's Contradiction

In the first chapter of his work, Comrade Cliff endeavours to prove that Trotsky's analysis of the Russian state contradicts the theory of the state as developed by Marx and elaborated by Lenin.

The first chapter contains an elaborate scheme which sets out to prove that two classes cannot use one state machine. Here Cliff believes he has found a fundamental error in Trotsky. Taking the ideas developed by the Old Man at different times and in differing circumstances, he counterposes them to each other. He counterposes, for example, a quotation from Trotsky in the early stages of the degeneration of the bureaucracy and the expulsion of the Left Opposition, when he argued for the *reform* of the soviet state, and incidentally, also for the reform of the Bolshevik Party which controlled the state. (It was at this stage that Trotsky wrote the letter to the CC of the CPSU demanding that Stalin be removed.) Who can deny that had the international events developed differently it was theoretically possible that the

Bolshevik Party could have spewed forth the bureaucracy and re-established a healthy workers' state?

Cliff counterposes to this the quotation from *Revolution Betrayed*, in which Trotsky says that if the Russian workers come to power they will *purge* the state apparatus; and if the bourgeoisie come to power *'a purgation of the state apparatus would, of course, be necessary in this case too. But a bourgeois restoration would probably have to clean fewer people than a revolutionary party'*. Cliff's answer to this is:

> Whether we assume that the proletariat must smash the existing state machine on coming to power while the bourgeoisie can use it, or whether we assume that neither the proletariat nor the bourgeoisie can use the existing state apparatus (the 'purgation of the state apparatus' necessarily involving such a deep change as would transform quantity into quality) − on both assumptions we must come to the conclusion that Russia *is not* a workers' state. To assume that the proletariat and the bourgeoisie can use the same state machine as the instrument of their supremacy is tantamount to a vindication of the theoretical basis of social democracy and a repudiation of the revolutionary concept of the state expressed by Marx, Engels, Lenin and Trotsky. To assume that different layers, groups or parties of one and the same class cannot base themselves on the same state machine is equally a repudiation of the Marxist concept of the state. (Cliff, page 4)

This whole formalistic method is the fatal weakness of Cliff's case. It would have been impossible for Trotsky in the early stages to deal with the problem in the abstract. He had to deal with the concrete situation and give a concrete answer. But the further degeneration posed the problem in an entirely different way. Once it had been established that it was impossible to reform the Stalinist party, that it was impossible to reform the Soviet state (we assume that Cliff also believes this was the task since up to 1928 he says Russia *was* a degenerated workers' state), then the question had to be viewed in a somewhat different light. It is foreign to the Marxist method to search for isolated contradictions, real or apparent. What is required is an examination of a theory in its broad general development, in its movement, and its contradictions.

But let us examine Cliff's own thought processes on this subject. He too cannot avoid the very trap which he tries to lay for Trotsky. Chapter 1 (no less than eighteen pages) *is devoted to proving the impossibility of two classes using the one state*. But lo and behold, Chapter 4 accomplishes the miracle! The impossible gulf is bridged! *Both the capitalist class and the proletariat of Russia have used precisely the same state machine.* Why? Because more surplus value was produced! Realising this dilemma, Cliff is compelled to advance something truly new and unique in the movement: that the bureaucracy did not consume surplus value before 1928 but *by the introduction of the Five Year Plan, the state was changed from a workers' state into a capitalist state.* (Any enemy of the Fourth International could immediately retort that the state of Stalin on this basis is purely an extension and deepening of the state of Lenin. For in the economic sense nothing fundamentally was changed. We have dealt with this in preceding chapters. Significantly it is only on the *economic* argument — and this is astonishing — that Cliff advances his theory. Despite the title of his first Chapter 'An Examination of the Definition of Russia as a Degenerated Workers' State', he does not deal with the *political* question at all here or in any other chapter. Here is how Cliff sees the transformation from a workers' state into a capitalist state:

> The statistics we have at our disposal conclusively show that although the bureaucracy had a privileged position in the period preceding the Five-Year Plan, it can on no account be said that it received surplus value from the labour of others. It can just as conclusively be said that with the introduction of the Five-Year Plans, the bureaucracy's income consisted to a large extent of surplus value. (Cliff, page 45)

In other words, Cliff sees the transition from one system to the other not by smashing of the state machine. How does this fit into his scheme in Chapter 1?

Cliff's attempt to manufacture an artificial bridge between the workers' state and the capitalist state, because he has not been able to find the smashing of the workers' state machine, has led him to seek economic differences between the two periods — pre-1928 and post-1928. In this he falls into the most formalistic and abstract conceptions of the workers' state prior to 1928. As we have shown in the previous chapters, even in the healthiest of workers' states, according to Marx, surplus value must necessarily be produced in order to develop industry to the point where the state, money, and the proletariat itself and all the other survivals of capitalism will have disappeared. So long as the working class exists as a class, surplus value will be produced.

A statement of the Left Opposition in 1927 pointed out that the bureaucracy was *consuming an enormous part of the surplus value.* Cliff's method of introducing this subject is totally incorrect. Instead of setting himself the task of proving a thesis, he blandly makes assertions and takes them as proven. That Chapter 4 contradicts everything in Chapter 1 is another matter! Just examine the way in which Comrade Cliff sums up this Chapter 4, in which he openly claims that *a transition has been achieved without a revolution and without smashing the state machine.*

He begins:

> In this chapter we shall describe the transformation of the class character of the Russian state from a workers' to a capitalist state. We shall do this by dealing with the following points...(Cliff, page 33)

He thereupon proceeds to detail a number of *economic* changes which have nothing to do with the structure of or the transformation of *state power,* and ends up with the subsection: 'Why the Five Year Plan Signifies the Transformation of the Bureaucracy into a Ruling Class.' All the economic arguments in this chapter have nothing to do with the state or its overthrow.

Cliff deals at length with the differentiation in the army, the introduction of privileges for the officers, military discipline, etc. He here merely repeats what Trotsky said a thousand times on the transformation of the bureaucracy into an uncontrolled caste. But let us see his conclusions. He writes:

> Again the Five Year Plan marks the turning point. Then the organisation and the structure of the army began to change fundamentally. From a workers' army with bureaucratic deformations it became the armed body of the bureaucracy as the ruling class...(p 59)

Let us see now whether what excludes a gradual social revolution excludes a gradual counter-revolution.

> If the soldiers in an hierarchically built army strive for decisive control over the army, they immediately meet with the opposition of the officer caste. There is no way of removing such a caste except by revolutionary violence. As against this, if the officers of a people's militia become less and less dependent on the will of the soldiers, which they may do as they meet with no institutional bureaucracy, their transformation into an officers' caste independent of the soldiers can be accomplished gradually. The transition from a standing army to a militia cannot but be accompanied by a tremendous outbreak of revolutionary violence: on the other hand, the transition from a militia to a standing army, to the extent that it is the result of the tendencies inside the militia itself, can and must be gradual. The opposition of the soldiers to the rising bureaucracy may lead the latter to use violence against the soldiers. But this does not exclude the possibility of a gradual transition from a militia to a standing army. *What applies to the army applies equally to the state. A state without a bureaucracy, or with a weak bureaucracy dependent on the pressure of the masses may gradually be transformed into a state in which the bureaucracy is free of workers' control.* (Cliff, page 82. Our emphasis)

Cliff now sets out to prove that there *can* be a gradual transition from a workers' state to a capitalist state, and clinches his chapter by producing a quotation from none other than Trotsky...whom he has so sternly discredited as an authority on this subject in his Chapter 1.

Cliff writes:

The Moscow Trials* were the civil war of the bureaucracy against the masses, a war in which only one side was armed and organised. They witnessed the consummation of the bureaucracy's total liberation from popular control. Trotsky, who thought that the Moscow trials and the 'Constitution' were steps towards the restoration of individual capitalism by legal means, then withdrew the argument that a gradual change from a proletarian to a bourgeois state is 'running backwards the film of reformism'. He wrote:

'In reality, the *new constitution*...opens up for the bureaucracy "legal" roads for the economic counter-revolution, ie, the restoration of capitalism by means of a "Cold stroke".(*Fourth International and the Soviet Union,* Thesis adopted by the First International Conference for the Fourth International, Geneva, July 1936.) (Cliff, page 82)

Here we see the full light on Cliff's thesis and his bad method. Starting off with the thesis that Trotsky is no Marxist because he says two classes can use one state machine, Cliff ends up saying precisely the same thing and using as his authority the same Trotsky.

Nationalisation and the Workers' State

On page 2 of his work, Cliff gives a quotation from *Revolution Betrayed:*

The nationalisation of the land, the means of industrial production, transport and exchange, together with the monopoly of foreign trade, constitutes the basis of the Soviet social structure. Through these relations, established by the proletarian revolution, the nature of the Soviet Union as a proletarian state is for us basically defined. (*Revolution Betrayed,* page 248)

One of Cliff's conclusions is that, in this case, 'neither the Paris Commune nor the Bolshevik dictatorship were workers' states as the former did not statify the means of production at all, and the latter did not do so for some time.' Here we see that Cliff bases his case on whether or not the working class has control over the state machine. We will deal with the question of workers' control in a later chapter. But here let us examine Cliff's method of separating the economic basis of a workers' state from the question of workers' control of the state machine. For a temporary period, for shorter or longer duration, it would be possible for the proletariat to take power politically while not proceeding economically to transform society. This was the position in Russia where the proletariat took power in October 1917, but did not undertake major nationalisation until it was forced upon them in 1918. But if the proletariat did not proceed to carry through the economic

*The Moscow Trials of 1936 and 1938 were monstrous frame-ups resulting in a generation of revolutionaries and opponents of the bureaucracy being physically exterminated. In 1936 Stalin proposed a new constitution – it was abandoned on the outbreak of the Spanish Civil War in July 1936, as the bureaucracy was fearful of repercussions within the USSR.

transformation, then inevitably the proletarian regime would be doomed to collapse. The laws of the economy will always break through in the end. Either the proletariat would proceed to nationalise the entire economy, or inevitably the capitalist system would emerge predominant. *Cliff fails to show how the basic forms of Russian economy would differ under a healthy workers' state.* He has taken refuge in the surplus value consumed by the bureaucracy, but this evades the fundamental issue.

No better is Cliff's case based upon the experience of the Paris Commune and the first stage of the Russian Revolution. The same would apply to them as aforementioned. These regimes were a transition to the complete *economic* rule of the proletariat. Such transitions are more or less inevitable in the change over from one society to another. Both in the case of the Commune and in the case of the Russian Revolution, they could not be long lasting if the proletariat did not proceed to nationalise industry. Has Cliff forgotten that one of the main lessons taught by Marx and assiduously learned by the Bolsheviks, was the failure of the French proletariat to nationalise the Bank of France? So we see a state can be a proletarian state on the basis of political power, or it can be a proletarian state on the basis of the economy; or it can be a transition to *both* of these as we will show.

The same laws would apply to the counter-revolution on the part of the bourgeoisie. The Old Man correctly argued that in the event of a bourgeois counter-revolution in Russia, the bourgeoisie might, for a time, even retain state ownership before breaking it up and handing it to private ownership. To a scholar it would appear then that you can have a workers' state and a bourgeois state on the basis of state ownership, or you can have a workers' state or a bourgeois state on the basis of private ownership.

However, it is obvious that one could only arrive at this mode of reasoning if one failed to take into consideration *the movement of society* in one direction or another.

Not only that, but all sorts of unforeseen relationships can develop because of the class structure of society and the state. To take the example of Russia. In 1917 up to the capture of control of the soviets by the Bolsheviks, we had the situation as sketched by Trotsky in the *History of the Russian Revolution*, where, because of the Menshevik majority, in a certain sense the bourgeoisie ruled through the soviets − the organs of workers' rule *par excellence!* According to Cliff's schema, how could this possibly happen? Of course, had the Bolsheviks not taken power, the bourgeoisie, having used the Mensheviks and through them, the soviets in the transitional period, would have abolished the soviets as they did in Germany after 1918.

In the transition from one society to another, it is clear that there is not an unbridgeable gulf. It is not a dialectical method to think in finished categories; workers' state or capitalist state and the devil take any transition or motion between the two. It is clear that when Marx spoke of the smashing of the old state form in relation to the Commune, he took it for granted that the economy would be transformed at a greater or lesser pace and would come into consonance with the political forms. We will see later in relation to Eastern Europe that Cliff adopts the same formalistic method.

The Dialectical Conception of the State

It may be well to deal here with the nature of the state. According to Marxists, the state arises as the necessary instrument for the oppression of one class by another class. The state in the last analysis, as explained by Marx and Lenin, consists of armed bodies of men and their appendages. That is the essence of the Marxist definition. However, one must be careful in using their broad Marxist generalisations, which are undoubtedly correct, in an absolute sense. Truth is always concrete but if one does not analyse the particular ramifications and concrete circumstances, one must inevitably fall into abstractions and errors. Look at the cautious way in which Engels deals with the question, even when generalising. In *Origins of the Family*, Engels wrote:

> But in order that these antagonisms, classes with conflicting economic interests, shall not consume themselves and society in fruitless struggle, a power, apparently standing above society, has become necessary to moderate the conflict and keep it within the bounds of 'order', and this power, arisen out of society, but placing itself above it and increasingly alienating itself from it, is the state. (*The Origin of the Family*, Lawrence & Wishart, London, 1946, page 194)

On the next page he goes on to show that:

> ...it is enough to look at Europe today, where class struggle and rivalry in conquest have brought the public power to a pitch where it threatens to devour the whole of society and even the state itself.

Engels goes on to show that once having arisen, the state *within certain limits,* develops an independent movement of its own and must necessarily do so under given conditions: 'In possession of the public power and the right of taxation, the officials now present themselves as organs of society standing *above* society.' (Emphasis in original)

Contrary to Cliff's conception that the state plays a direct role, one can see the meticulous care with which Engels treats the question of the *independent* role of the state, relative of course, to society. In the whole of Cliff's material, the fact that the state under given conditions can and does play a relatively independent role in the struggle between the classes is forgotten. His is a 'logical' scheme: either it is a state of workers, directly controlled by the workers, or it must be a capitalist state. There is no room for the interplay of forces in Cliff's method. Again, contrast this with Engels:

> As the state arose from the need to keep class antagonisms in check, but also arose in the thick of the fight between the classes, *it is normally* the state of the most powerful, economically ruling class, which by its means becomes also the political ruling class, and so acquires new means of holding down and exploiting the oppressed class...Exceptional periods, however, occur when the warring classes are so nearly equal in forces that the state power, as apparent mediator, acquires for the moment a certain independence in relation to both...(page 196, our emphasis)

Again, on page 201, Engels wrote:

> The central link in civilised society is the state, which *in all typical periods* (our emphasis) is without exception the state of the ruling class, and in all cases continues to be essentially a machine for holding down the oppressed, exploited class...

Note the difference between Cliff's black and white formulae and Engels' careful formulations...'it is normally', in 'typical periods', etc.

Why is it that the proletariat cannot take over the ready made state machine? Not for mystical reasons but because of certain very concrete facts. In the modern state all the key positions are in the hands of those people who are under the control of the ruling class: they have been specially selected by education, outlook, and conditions of life, to serve the interests of the bourgeoisie. The army officers, particularly the higher ranks, the civil servants, and in the nationalised industries today the key technicians, are moulded in their ideas and outlook to serve the interests of the capitalist class. All the commanding positions in society are placed in the hands of people whom the bourgeoisie can trust. That is the reason the state machine is a tool in the hands of the bourgeoisie which cannot be used by the proletariat and must be smashed by them. Now, what does the smashing of the state machine mean? To say the least, Cliff's ideas on this question appear to be very nebulous.

It is possible that many, perhaps even the majority of the officials of the bourgeois state, will be used by the proletariat once they take power. But they will be subordinate to the workers' committees and organisations. For example in the Soviet Union, in the early days after the Czarist army had been dissolved, the Red Army was led by ex-Czarist officers. Likewise in the state apparatus where a proportion of the officials were the same ex-Czarist officials. Because of unfavourable historical factors this was later to play an important role in the degeneration of the Russian regime. Not for nothing did Lenin say that the Soviet state is 'a bourgeois Czarist machine...barely varnished with socialism'. (Incidentally this honest characterisation is very far from the idealised and false picture of the state under Lenin and Trotsky which is drawn by Cliff. How the process of degeneration could have taken place with the idyllic picture painted by Cliff would be difficult to understand. However, this will be dealt with in the later sections.)

The proletariat, according to the classical concept, smashes the old state machine and proceeds to create a *semi-state*. Nevertheless, it is forced to utilise the old technicians. But the state, even under the best conditions, say in an advanced country with an educated proletariat, remains a bourgeois instrument, and because of this the possibility of degeneration is implicit in it. For that reason Marxists insist on the control of the masses, to ensure that the state should not be allowed to develop into an independent force. As speedily as possible, it should be dissolved into society.

It is for the very reasons given above that, under certain conditions, the state gains a certain independence from the base which it originally represented. Engels explained that though the superstructure is dependent on the economic base, it nevertheless has an independent movement of its own. For quite a lengthy period, *there can be a conflict between the state and the class which that state represents.* That is why Engels speaks of the state 'normally' or in 'typical periods' directly representing the ruling class. The great Marxist teachers have analysed the phenomenon of Bonapartism to which Engels refers above. In the *Eighteenth Brumaire* Marx pointed out how the drunken soldiery of Louis Napoleon, in the name of 'the law, order and the family', *shot down the bourgeoisie whom they presumably represented.*

Thus, one can only understand class society if one takes into account the many-sided dialectical inter-dependence and antagonisms of all the factors within it. Formalists usually get lost in one or other side of the problem. For example, Cliff can write:

...It needs just as high a degree of mental acrobatics to think that

Mikolajcik* and his ilk who flee abroad or waste away in prisons are the rulers of Poland as to consider that the rulers of Russia are the slave labourers in Siberia. (Cliff, page 13)

Were the bourgeoisie under Louis Napoleon the ruling class? It needs no high degree of mental acrobatics to answer this.

When considering the development of society, *economics must be considered the dominant factor.* The super-structure which develops on this economic base separates itself from the base and becomes antagonistic to it. After all, the essence of the Marxist theory of revolution is that with the gradual changes in production under the embryo of the old form, ie, super-structure in both property and state, a contradiction develops which can only be resolved by abolishing the super-structure and re-organising society on the base of the new mode of production which has developed within the old.

Economy in the long run is decisive. Because of this, as all the Marxist teachers were at pains to explain, in the long run the superstructure must come into correspondence with it. Once having abandoned the criterion of the basic economic structure of society, all sorts of superficial and arbitrary constructions are possible. One would inevitably be lost in the maze of history, like Perseus in the mythology of ancient Greece who was lost in the Palace of mines, but without a thread to lead one out. The thread of history is the basic economic structure of society, or the property form, its legal reflection.

Let us take as a case extremely rich in examples the history of France. The bourgeois revolution took place in 1789. In 1793 the Jacobins** seized complete power. As Marx and Engels pointed out, they went beyond the framework of bourgeois relations and performed a salutory historical task because of that, accomplishing in a few months what would have taken the bourgeoisie decades or generations to accomplish; the complete cleansing from France of all traces of feudalism. Yet this regime remained rooted in the basis of bourgeois forms of property. It was followed by the French Thermidor and the rule of the Directory, to be followed by the classic dictatorship of Napoleon Bonaparte. Napoleon

---

*Stanislaw Mikolafjcik, leader of the Polish Peasants Party, was the head of the Polish 'government in exile' based in London, from 1943. On liberation in 1945 he became the deputy prime minister in Poland, but real power lay with the Stalinists, supported by the Red army. By the time elections were held in 1947 many of his supporters were imprisoned and the party was later suppressed.
*The Jacobins were the extreme radical wing of the French revolution. Their leader, Maximilien Robespierre (1758-94) wielded supreme power from 1793 until he was overthrown in 1794 and executed. The Directory was the government of the First French Republic from 1795-9.

re-introduced many feudal forms, had himself crowned Emperor and concentrated the supreme power in his hands. But we still call this regime bourgeois. With the restoration of Louis XVIII the regime still remained capitalist...and then we had not one but *two revolutions* — 1830 and 1848. These revolutions had important social consequences. They resulted in significant changes even in the personnel of the state itself. Yet we characterise them both as bourgeois revolutions in which there was no change in the class which held power.

Let us proceed further. After the Paris Commune of 1871 and the shake-up of the relations which this involved, we had the organisation of the Third Republic with bourgeois democracy which lasted for decades. This was followed by Petain, then the De Gaulle-Stalinist regime*, and now the Quielle Government. Examine for a moment the amazing diversity of these regimes. To a non-Marxist it would seem absurd to define in the same category, shall we say, the regime of Robespierre and that of Petain. Yet Marxists do define them as fundamentally the same —bourgeois regimes. What is the criterion? Only the one thing: the form of property, the private ownership of the means of production.

Take, similarly, the diversity of regimes in more modern times to see the extreme differences in super-structures which are on the same economic base. For instance, compare the regime of nazi Germany with that of British social democracy. They are so fundamentally different in super-structure that many theorists of the non-Marxist or ex-Marxist school have found new class structure and a new system of society entirely. Why do we say that they represent the same class and the same regime? Despite the difference in super-structure, *the economic base of the given societies remained the same.*

If we take the history of modern society, we get many examples where the bourgeoisie is *expropriated politically* and yet remains the ruling class. Trotsky describes the regime of Bonapartism, or as Marx calls it,'naked rule by the sword over society'.

Look what happened in China after Chiang Kai Shek had, with the dregs of the Shanghai gangs, crushed the Shanghai working class. The bankers wished to give him banquets and applaud him as the benefactor and saviour of civilisation.

But Chiang wanted something more material than the praise of his masters. Unceremoniously, he clapped all the rich industrialists

---

*From 1945-8 the French CP held various cabinet posts in the Government of National Union, headed by de Gaulle. The government of Henri Quielle, established in September 1948, was attacked by the CP for being 'directed against the workers'.

and bankers of Shanghai in jail and extracted a ransom of millions before he would release them. He had done the job for them and now demanded the price. He had not crushed the Shanghai workers for the benefit of the capitalists, but for what it meant in power and income for him and his gang of thugs. Yet who will presume to say that the bankers who were in jail were not still the ruling class though they did not hold political power? The Chinese bourgeoisie (no Marxists!) must have reflected sadly on the complexity of society where a good portion of the loot in the surplus value extracted from the workers had to go to their own watchdogs, and where many of their class were languishing in jail.

The bourgeoisie is politically expropriated under such conditions; naked force dominates society. An enormous part of the surplus value is consumed by the top militarists and bureaucrats. But it is in the interests of these bureaucrats that the capitalist exploitation of the workers should continue, and therefore while they squeeze as much as they can out of the bourgeoisie, nevertheless, they defend private property. That is why the bourgeoisie continues to be the ruling class.

Here lies the anwer to those who assert that it is sheer sophistry to claim that a working class can be a ruling class when a great proportion of them are in jail in Siberia. Unless we are guided by the basic property forms of society we will lose the Marxist road. Many examples could be given in history of the way in which one section of the ruling class has attacked other sections. For example, in the Wars of the Roses in Britain the two factions of the ruling barons virtually exterminated one another. At one time or another in history big sections of the ruling class were either in jails or were executed. One has only to consider Hitler's treatment of his bourgeois opponents. They lost not only their property but their lives as well.

In dealing with the role of the state, the most important question that must be answered and one which Cliff cannot answer is: the state must be an instrument of a class – which class does it represent in Russia and Eastern Europe? It cannot represent the capitalist class because they have been expropriated. It cannot be argued that it represents the interests of the peasant class, or the petty-owners in the cities. Under a fascist or Bonapartist regime, even though the gangsters might have the bourgeoisie by the throat, nevertheless there is a capitalist class in whose interests the economy operates as a whole, and on whom this parasitic excrescence clings. If they do not represent the proletariat, as Trotsky said, as a special form of Bonapartism in the sense that they defend the nationalisation of the means of production, planning and the monopoly of foreign trade, whom do the Stalinist bureaucrats represent? Cliff's answer is that the bureaucracy constitutes the new ruling class, the capitalist class of Russia. But serious consideration of this would show that this cannot be the case. What he is saying is that the *state is a class*. The bureaucracy owns the state, the state owns the means of production, therefore the bureaucracy is a class. This is dodging the issue, he is saying in effect that the state owns the state.

According to Lenin, the state:

....has always been a certain apparatus which separated out from society and consisted of a group of people engaged solely, or almost solely, or mainly, in ruling. People are divided into ruled and into specialists in ruling, those who rise above society and are called rulers, representatives of the state.

This apparatus, this group of people who rule others, always takes command of a certain apparatus of coercion, of physical force, irrespective of whether this coercion of people is expressed in the primitive club or — in the epoch of slavery — in more perfected types of weapons, or in the firearms which appeared in the middle ages or, finally, in modern weapons which, in the twentieth century, are marvels of technique and are entirely based on the latest achievements of modern technology.

The methods of coercion changed, but whenever there was a state there existed in every society a group of persons who ruled, who commanded, who dominated and who, in order to maintain their power, possessed an apparatus of physical coercion, an apparatus of violence, with those weapons which corresponded best to the technical level of the given epoch. And by examining these general phenomena, by asking ourselves why no state existed when there were no classes, when there were no exploiters and no exploited, and why it arose when classes arose — only in this way shall we find a definite answer to the question of the essence of the state and its significance.

The state is a machine for maintaining the rule of one class over another. (*The State, Collected Works*, Vol. 29, page 477)

The state by its very nature is composed of bureaucracy, officers, generals, heads of police etc. *But these do not constitute a class;* they are the instrument of a class even if they may be in antagonism to that class. They cannot themselves be a class.

We must ask Cliff: Which section of the bureaucracy owns the state? It cannot be all the bureaucrats, because they, the bureaucracy itself, are hierarchically divided. The little civil servant is part of the bureaucracy as much as the big bureaucrat. Is it then the commanding stratum in Soviet society? This is clearly unsound. In capitalist society, or in any class society, no matter how privileged the top, they wield the instrument to protect the ruling class which has a direct relationship to the means of production, ie, in the sense of their ownership. We know who Napoleon represented. We know who Louis Napoleon, Bismarck, Chiang Kai Shek, Hitler, Churchill and Attlee represented. But who do the bureaucrats represent: the bureaucrats? Clearly this is false. In another section we have shown that the relationship of the bureaucracy to the means of production is necessarily one of *parasitism* and partakes of the same parasitism as the nazi bureaucracy. They are not a necessary and inevitable category for the particular *mode of production*. At best they are entitled to wages of superintendance. If they take more, it is in the same way as the nazi bureaucracy consumed part of the surplus value produced by the workers. But they were not a class.

Innumerable references could be given to show that a capitalist state presupposes private property, individual ownership of the means of production. The state is the *apparatus of rule*: it cannot itself be the class which rules. The bureaucracy is merely part of the apparatus of the state. It may 'own' the state, in the sense that it lifts itself above society and becomes relatively independent of the economically dominant, ie, ruling class. That was the case in nazi Germany, where the bureaucracy dictated to the capitalists what they should produce, how they should produce it, etc, for the purposes of war. So in the war economy of Britain, USA and elsewhere, the state dictated to the capitalists what and how they should produce. This did not convert them into a ruling class. Why ? Because it was in defence of private property.

Cliff argues that the bureaucracy manages and plans industry. True enough. Whose industry do they manage and plan? In capitalist society, the managers plan and manage industry in the individual enterprises and trusts. But it does not make them the owners of those enterprises and trusts. The bureaucracy manages the entire industry. In that sense it is true that it has more independence from its economic base than any other bureaucracy or state machine in the whole of human history. But as Engels emphasised and we must re-emphasise, in the final analysis the economic basis is decisive. If Cliff is going to argue that it is in their function as managers that the bureaucrats are the ruling class, then clearly he is not giving a Marxist definition of a capitalist class. He is calling the Russian bureaucracy a class, but he must work out a theory as to what class this is.

The state is the *instrument* of class rule, of coercion, a glorified policeman. But the policeman is not the ruling class. The police can become unbridled, can become bandits, but that does not convert them into a capitalist, feudal or slave-owning class.

What Happened in Eastern Europe

Events in Eastern Europe and the nature of the states which have arisen can only be explained by the Marxist-Leninist theory of the state, and only Trotsky's conceptions can explain events in Eastern Europe from this point of view.

First it is necessary to understand what took place in Eastern Europe with the advance of the Red Army. No one can deny (leaving aside the question of Germany for a moment) that in all the Balkan and Eastern European countries the advance of the Red Army resulted in a revolutionary movement not only among the workers, but among the peasants as well. The reason for this lay in the whole background of these states, where, before the war, apart from Czechoslovakia, capitalism was very weak. We had here decaying feudal-military-capitalist dictatorships whose regimes were completely incapable of further developing the productive forces of the countries.

The general world crisis of capitalism was particularly exacerbated because of the backwardness and the artifical splitting up of the area which had followed the first world war. The very term *Balkanisation* comes from this part of Europe. Split up into small weak states, overwhelmingly agrarian in character, with a very shaky industry, these areas inevitably became almost semi-colonies of the great powers. France, Britain, and to a certain extent Italy, then Germany, became the dominant powers of this area. Through her trade relations, German industry dominated the backward economies of Eastern Europe in the Balkans. In all these countries foreign capital played an important role. In most of them, foreign investments were dominant in what little industry existed.

With the occupation of these countries by Hitler, not only was 'non-Aryan' capital expropriated, but also the native capitalists were to a large extent squeezed out and replaced by German banks and trusts. German capital seized the decisive place —all the key positions and sections of the economy. The capital that remained was owned by collaborators and Quislings largely, and remained subordinate to German capital.

The regime was made up of Quislings who relied on German bayonets for their support. What little popular support was possessed by the pre-war regimes — military police dictatorships — had, in the course of the war, disappeared. With the collapse of the power of German imperialism and the victory of the Red Army, an undoubted impulse was given to the socialist revolution. In Bulgaria, for example, in 1944, the moment the Red Army had crossed the frontier, there was an uprising in Sofia and other big towns. The masses began the organisation of soviets or workers' committees. Soldiers and peasants organised committees and workers seized the factories.

Similar movements took place in all the countries of Eastern Europe, apart from Germany. Let us examine what happened in Czechoslovakia. Here too, the advance of the Red Army was followed by insurrection in Prague, the seizure of factories by workers and land by peasants. Here too, there was fraternisation on the borders of Bohemia and Moravia between the Czech and Sudetan-German masses.

The elements of proletarian revolution were quickly followed by Stalinist counter-revolution. The trouble with Cliff is that he fails to separate out the elements of the proletarian revolution from the Stalinist counter-revolution which rapidly followed.

Let us take the two examples: Bulgaria and Czechoslovakia. In Bulgaria we had a situation which has developed over and over again throughout the tragic history of the working masses. The real power was in the hands of the working class. The bourgeois state was smashed. How? The Germans had gone; the officers no longer had control over the soldiers; the police had gone into hiding; the landlords and capitalists had no control. There was a vacuum; a classical period of dual power where the masses were not sufficiently conscious to organise their own power, and the bourgeoisie too weak to reassert their domination.

This is not a situation with which Marxists are unfamiliar: Germany 1918, Russia 1917, Spain 1936. Perhaps a comparison with Spain would be useful. Here too the masses seized the factories and the land in Catalonia and Aragon. The bourgeois 'government' was suspended in mid-air. The masses completely smashed the police and the army. There was only one armed force: the workers' militias. All that was necessary was for the masses to organise soviets or committees, brush aside the phantom government and take power.

It is well enough known what took place. The Stalinists proceeded to make a coalition not with the bourgeoisie —the factory owners and bourgeoisie had fled to the side of Franco as a consequence of the mass insurrection — but with the 'shadow of the bourgeoisie'. The Stalinists did this in Spain with the express purpose of destroying the socialist revolution for fear of repercussions in Russia and, of course, because of the existing international line-up and their desire to demonstrate to the British and French imperialists that they had nothing to fear. In Spain, therefore, gradually, they helped the shadow to acquire substance.

Gradually *they recreated a capitalist army and capitalist police force, under the control of the capitalist class.* Once this had been accomplished, the land was returned to the landlords and the factories to their owners. The consequence of this was seen towards the end of the civil war when the bourgeois state −the bourgeois military machine which they had helped to create, organised a *coup d'état* which established a military dictatorship in Republican territory and promptly illegalised the Communist Party itself.

In Bulgaria, as in all other countries of Eastern Europe, the Stalinists proceeded to make an agreement with the *shadow of the bourgeoisie.* The socialist revolution had commenced and there was a danger that it might be carried through to a conclusion. This, of course, the Stalinists feared. But on the other hand, *they also did not want the power to pass to the bourgeoisie.* They derailed the socialist revolution by organising the so-called Fatherland Front in Bulgaria and headed off the movement of the masses round slogans of chauvinism and anti-Germanism. Fraternisation in Bulgaria was swiftly made punishable, the soviets formed in the army were dissolved, the worker and peasant committees emasculated. They formed a front of 'National Unity', the union of the entire nation. But the difference with Spain was that here *the key positions in this so-called coalition,* where the shadow of the bourgeoisie possessed no power, *remained firmly in Stalinist hands.* They took over the police and the army. They selected the key and commanding personnel. All important positions in the civil service were placed in the hands of obedient tools. Clearly, behind the screen of national unity, they concentrated real state power in their hands. *They had created an instrument in their own image − a state machine on the model of Moscow.*

The process was crystal clear in the case of Czechoslovakia. When the Stalinists entered the country there was no government. The Germans with their Quislings and collaborators had fled. The committees formed by the masses had control of the industrial enterprises and the land. The Stalinists brought in the government of Benes* from Moscow. The real power, the key posts, were firmly in their hands; they retained the substance and gave the bourgeoisie the shadow.

Partly to destroy the socialist revolution, partly to arrive at a compromise with American imperialism, they allowed certain sectors of the economy to remain in the hands of private

---

*Edvard Benes, a member of the Social Nationalist Party, was President of Czechoslovakia 1935-38, and from 1941 head of the Czech provisional government in London. In 1945 he became president of the provisional government in Czechoslovakia. He resigned in June 1948 in the aftermath of the 'Prague Coup'.

enterprise. But the decisive power, ie, armed bodies of men, were organised by them and under their control. This was not the same state machine as previously. *It was an entirely new state machine of their own creation.*

In order to derail the revolution the Stalinists played on chauvinism and dealt the country a terrible blow with the expulsion of the Sudetan Germans. The original instinct of the masses was on internationalist lines. Reports from Czechoslovakia show that in the beginning there was fraternisation between the Czechs and Sudetan Germans. We see how Cliff does not see the element of the counter-revolution, the activities of the bureaucracy to destroy the revolution and the revolution itself.

Of course, the attempt of the Stalinists to maintain a compromise with the bourgeoisie — let it not be forgotten with their control and their state power — could not continue indefinitely. Shadows can acquire substance. The attempt of the American bourgeoisie to base themselves on their points of support in Eastern Europe in the shape of the remnants of the bourgeoisie and those sectors of the economy which they controlled, with Marshall Aid as the wedge, was the danger signal. With precipitous speed the bureaucracy acted and ordered all Eastern European states to reject Marshall Aid. All history has shown the impossibility of maintaining two antagonistic forms of property. Although the bourgeoisie were very weak, they had begun to gain a base due to the fact that they retained a good proportion of light industry under their control. The mounting antagonism of America, the impossibility of relying on the bourgeoisie, their incompatibility with a proletarian state with power in the hands of the bureaucracy, forced the latter to take measures to complete the process. Here we might add that Trotsky saw in the extension of nationalised property in the areas under Stalinist domination, proof of the fact that Russia was a workers' state. The February events on which world attention has been focused, highlighted in dramatic fashion, a process taking place in all Stalinist dominated areas. The factor which was decisive was that the Stalinists had the support of the workers and peasants in the nationalisations and the division of the land. All Cliff saw was that the state machine remained the same, presumably, as it was under the Germans. No doubt the bourgeoisie wished that it had!

According to all observers the Stalinists, because of their compromises and the disillusionment of the masses in the factories, would probably have lost votes in the forthcoming elections. The bourgeois elements were gathering strength, basing themselves on the petty bourgeoisie in the cities and among disillusioned workers and peasants. Gradually the bourgeoisie hoped to gain control ofthe state and organise a counter-revolution with the aid of

Anglo-American imperialism. Although the bureaucracy had control of the state machine, this was precarious by virtue of the way in which it had been obtained.

In order to complete the process, as Trotsky had foreseen, however cautiously, the bureaucracy was compelled *to call upon the masses*. They issued the call for Action Committees which were bureaucratically controlled at the top, but were nevertheless relatively democratic at the bottom. The Stalinists armed the workers, ie, organised a workers' militia. The enthusiasm of the masses under these conditions, naturally became apparent. Even the Social Democratic workers who hated and were distrustful of the Stalinists, enthusiastically participated in these measures against the bourgeoisie. Trotsky once said that as against a lion one used a gun, against a flea one's fingernail. Faced with a Stalinist state apparatus, with the mass movement as a threat, the bourgeoisie was impotent.

However, the formation of the Action Committees, the arming of the workers, meant necessarily that an embryo new soviet regime was in the making. Of course, the bureaucracy speedily proceeded to crush the independence of the masses and totalitarianise the regime. New elections were rapidly organised on Moscow lines, with *one* list and strict supervision.

In the face of these events, Cliff asks:

> What then is the future of the Fourth International; what is its historical justification? The Stalinist parties have all the advantages over the Fourth International — a state apparatus, mass organisations, money, etc, etc. The only advantage they lack is the internationalist class ideology...
>
> If a social revolution took place in the Eastern European countries without a revolutionary proletarian leadership, we must conclude that in future social revolutions, as in the past, the masses will do the fighting but not the leading. In all the struggles of the bourgeoisie, it was not the bourgeoisie itself who did the fighting, but the masses who believed it was in their interests. The *sans culottes* of the French revolution fought for liberty, equality, fraternity, while the real aim of the movement was the establishment of the rule of the bourgeoisie. This was the case at a time when the bourgeoisie was progressive. In reactionary imperialist wars, the less the masses who are the cannon fodder know about the war aims, the better soldiers they are. To assume that the 'new democracies' are workers' states, means to accept that in principle the proletarian revolution is, just as the bourgeois wars were, based on the deception of the people...
>
> If these countries are workers' states, then why Marxism, why the Fourth International? We could only be looked upon by the masses as adventurists, or at best impatient revolutionaries whose differences with the Stalinists are merely tactical. (Cliff, pages 14-15)

Cliff has addressed the questions to the wrong people. In reality, he should have posed these questions to himself and he should have given the answers. If his theory is correct, then the whole theory of Marx becomes a Utopia. Cliff thinks that if he sticks the label 'state capitalism' on to the phenomenon of Stalinism, he has salved his conscience and has restored the 'lost' role of the Fourth International to his own satisfaction. Here we see the fetishism of which Marx spoke and which even affects the revolutionary movement: change the name of a thing and you change its essence.

It is not possible to explain or trace the class historical threads of present day developments without the existence and degeneration of the workers' state in Russia. One can only trace the events in Eastern Europe to the October Revolution of 1917. It is useless for Cliff to argue that the bureaucracy used the masses in Czechoslovakia, without posing to himself the question as to who was used in 1917. Was not the October Revolution followed by the victory of Stalinism? The good intentions, or the subjective wishes of the Bolshevik leadership or the working class, is beside the point. According to the theory of Marx, no society passes from the scene till it has exhausted all the potentialities within it. If a new period of state capitalism looms ahead — and this necessarily follows from Cliff's theory because there can be no economic limit to the development of production under this so-called state capitalism — then to talk of this being a period of the disintegration of world capitalism reduces itself to mere phrasemongering. We have the absurdity of a new revolution — a proletarian revolution in 1917, organically changing the economy into...state capitalism. We also have the no less absurd postulation of a revolution in Eastern Europe, where the entire capitalist class has been expropriated...to install what? Capitalism! A moment's serious reflection would show that it is not possible for Cliff to maintain this position in relation to Eastern Europe without also transferring the same argument to Russia itself.

Cliff himself points to the fact that in the bourgeois revolution the masses did the fighting and the bourgeois got the fruits. The masses did not know what they were fighting for, but they fought in reality for the rule of the bourgeoisie. Take the French Revolution. It was prepared and had its ideology in the works of the philosophers of the enlightenment, Voltaire, Rousseau, etc. However, they really did believe in the idealisation of bourgeois society. They believed the codicils of liberty, equality and fraternity which they preached. As is well known, and as Cliff himself quotes Marx to prove, the French Revolution went beyond its social base. It resulted in the revolutionary dictatorship of the *sans culottes* which went beyond the bounds of bourgeois society. As Marx explained, this had the salutory effect of completing in a few months what would otherwise have taken the bourgeois decades to do. The leaders of the revolutionary wing of the petty bourgeoisie which wielded this dictatorship — Robespierre, Danton, etc, — sincerely believed in the doctrines of the philosophers and attempted to put them into practice. They could not do so because it was impossible to go beyond the economic base of the given society. They inevitably had to lose power and merely paved the way for bourgeois society. If Cliff's argument is correct, one could only conclude that the same thing happened with the Russian as with the French Revolution. Marx was the prophet of the new state capitalism. Lenin and Trotsky were the Robespierres and Carnots of the Russian Revolution. The fact that Lenin and Trotsky had good intentions is beside the point, as were the good intentions of the leaders of the bourgeois revolution. They merely paved the way for the rule of the new state capitalist class.

Thus, if the bureacracy used the masses of Czechoslovakia, and *this* constitutes the proof that it is state capitalism, no less did the Russian bureaucracy use the proletariat in the 1917 revolution. However, this theory can satisfy no one. The fact that the bureaucracy, because Russia is a workers' state, with all its degeneration, has assimilated Eastern Europe into the economy, and instantaneously strangled the developing socialist revolution, means that simultaneously with the socialist revolution, they have consciously carried through a process which extended over many years in Russia. They have telescoped developments in the image of Russia. This much should be clear: that without the existence of a strong degenerated workers' state, contiguous or near to these countries, these developments would have been impossible. Either the proletariat would have conquered with a healthy revolution on classical lines and spread the revolution, or imperialism would have crushed it.

Does this mean that the Stalinists have accomplished the revolution and therefore there is no need for the Fourth International? Many times in history we are confronted with a complicated situation. For instance, in the February revolution in Russia which overthrew Czarism, the masses then proceeded to come under the influence of the Mensheviks and Social Revolutionaries. This meant that the masses, having completed one task, the overthrow of Czarism — a political revolution — created new barriers in their path and had to pay for this by a second revolution — a social revolution in the form of October. The fact that the masses have accomplished the basic *social* revolution in Eastern Europe only to have this revolution immediately bureaucratised by the Thermidorian bureaucracy, means that they will now have to pay with a second revolution —a *political* revolution.

Cliff has only to pose the question: what are the tasks of the Fourth International in Russia? They are identical with those in Eastern Europe. In order to achieve socialism the masses must have control of administration and the state. This the Stalinists can never give. It can only be achieved by a new revolution. It can only be accomplished with the overthrow of the bureaucracy in Eastern Europe as in Russia. The tasks of the Fourth International are clear: *to struggle for a political revolution to establish workers' democracy* —a semi-state and the speedy transition to socialism on the basis of equality. *The form of property will not be changed.* The fact that Cliff calls it a social revolution alters nothing.

Where Trotsky found proof of a workers' state in the extension of the forms of property, Cliff finds proof of the reverse.

Cliff may argue, that unless the working class has direct control of the state, it cannot be a workers' state. In that case, he will have to reject the idea that there was a workers' state in Russia, except possibly in the first few months. Even here it is necessary to reiterate that the dictatorship of the proletariat is realised through the instrumentality of the vanguard of the class, ie the party, and in the party through the party leadership. Under the best conditions this will be effected with the utmost democracy within the state and within the party. But the very existence of the dictatorship, its necessity to achieve the change in the social system, is already proof of profound social contradictions which can, under unfavourable historical circumstances, find a reflection within the state and within the party. The party, no more than the state, can automatically and directly reflect the interests of the class. Not for nothing did Lenin think of the trade unions as a factor necessary for the defence of the workers *against their state,* as well as a bulwark for the defence of their state.

If it was possible for the party of the working class (the social democracy), especially through its leadership, to degenerate and fail directly to reflect the interests of the class before the overthrow of capitalism, why is it impossible for the state set up by the workers to follow a similar pattern? *Why cannot the state gain independence from the class,* and parasitically batten on it while at the same time (in its own interests) defend the new economic forms created by the revolution? As we have previously shown, Cliff tries to make a distinction by drawing a metaphysical line at 1928 between when he thinks surplus value was not consumed by the bureaucracy and when it was. Apart from being factually inaccurate, it is a singularly lifeless way of examining the phenomena.

In reality, the transition from one society to another was found to have been far more complex than could have been foreseen by the founders of scientific socialism. No more than any other class or social formation has the proletariat been given the privilege of inevitably having a smooth passage in the transition to its domination, and thence to its painless and tranquil disappearance in society, ie, to socialism. That was a possible variant. But the degeneration of both social democracy and the soviet state under the given conditions was not at all accidental. It represented in a sense the complex relations between a class and its representatives and state, which, more than once in history the ruling class, bourgeois, feudal and slave-owning, had cause to rue. It mirrors in other words, the multiplicity of historical factors which are the background to the decisive factor: the economic.

Contrast the broad view of Lenin with the mechanistic view of Cliff. Lenin emphasised over and over the need to study the transition periods of past epochs especially from feudalism to capitalism, in order to understand the laws of transition in Russia. He would have rejected the conception that the state which issued from October would have to follow a preconceived norm, or thereby cease to be a workers' state.

Lenin well knew that the proletariat and its party and leadership had no god-given power which would lead, without contradictions, smoothly to socialism once capitalism had been overthrown. That is necessarily the only conclusion which must follow from the Kantian norms categorically laid down by Cliff. That is why in advance Lenin emphasised that the dictatorship of the proletariat would vary tremendously in different countries and under different conditions.

However, Lenin hammered home the point that in the transition from feudalism to capitalism the dictatorship of the rising bourgeoisie was reflected in the dictatorship of *one man*. A class could rule through the personal rule of one man. *Ex post facto* Cliff is quite willing to accept this conception as it applies to the bourgeoisie. But one could only conclude from his arguments that such would be impossible in the case of the proletariat. For the rule of one man implies absolutism, arbitrary dictatorship vested in a single individual without political rights for the ruling class whose interests, in the last analysis, he represents. But Lenin only commented thus to show that *under certain conditions the dictatorship of the proletariat could also be realised through the dictatorship of one man.* Lenin did not develop this conception. But today in the light of the experience of Russia and Eastern Europe and with developments in China, we can deepen and understand not only the present but the past developments of society as well.

While the dictatorship of the proletariat can be realised through the dictatorship of one man, because this implies the separation of the state from the class it represents, it also means that the apparatus will almost inevitably tend to become independent of its base and thus acquire a vested interest of its own, even hostile and alien to the class it represents as in the case of Stalinist Russia. When we study the development of bourgeois society, we see that the autocracy of one individual, with the given social contradictions, served the needs of the development of that society. This is clearly shown by the rule of Cromwell and Napoleon. But although both stood on a bourgeois base, at a certain stage bourgeois autocracy becomes, from a favourable factor for the development of capitalist society, a hindrance to the full and free development of bourgeois production. However, the dictatorship of absolutism does not then painlessly wither away. In France and England it required *supplementary political revolutions* before bourgeois autocracy could be changed into bourgeois democracy. But without bourgeois democracy a free and full development of the productive forces to the limits under capitalism would have been impossible.

If this applies to the historical evolution of the bourgeoisie, how much more so to the proletariat in a backward and isolated country where the dictatorship of the proletariat has degenerated into the dictatorship of one man?

For the proletariat to take the path of socialism, a new revolution, a supplementary *political revolution* which will turn the Bonapartist proletarian state into a workers' democracy is necessary. Such a conception fits in with the experience of the past. Just as capitalism passed through many stormy contradictory phases (we are far from finished with them yet, as our epoch bears witness) so in the given historic conditions has the rule of the proletariat in Russia. So also by a mutual reaction, Eastern Europe and China are passing through this Bonapartist phase, resulting in the inevitability of new political revolutions in these countries in order to install workers' democracy as the prerequisite for a transition to socialism.

It is in the inter-relation between the class and its state under given historical conditions that we find the explanation of Stalinist degeneration, not in the mystical idea that a workers' state, under all conditions, must be a perfect workers' democracy or the transformation of the state into a class. In the long run, the economic factor, as in bourgeois society, with many upheavals and catastrophes, will emerge triumphant. The working class, having been enriched by the historical experience and profiting from its lessons, will victoriously overthrow Stalinist absolutism and organise a healthy workers' democracy on a higher level. Then the state will, more or less, correspond to the ideal norm worked out by Marx and Lenin.

Mr. Moneybags is in Florida this Christmas.

Where are you?   *In Korea!*

You risk your life, Big Business rakes in the dough.

Leaflet dropped by the North Koreans on American soldiers during the Korean war.

Stalinism in the Postwar World

June 1951

WORLD WAR Two ended in a complex and entirely unforeseen relationship of forces between the nations and between the classes. It ended in the victory of two continental powers on the world arena, US imperialism and the Russian bureaucracy. That became the dominant factor on a world scale: the division of the world between two competing blocs. For the first time in history the great powers of Europe were reduced to secondary positions; France, Germany, Italy, were defeated and England became a second rate power. Japan was reduced to the status of an occupied territory stripped of all her colonies and spheres of influence. The struggle between the classes can only be understood against a background of this decisive conflict of the era.

The decay of capitalism was reflected above all in the weakening of imperialism and the upsurge of the masses in Asia, with the revolutionary wave in Western and Eastern Europe. The upsurge of the masses in Asia in the struggle for national liberation was such as to compel the British to withdraw from India, Burma and Ceylon (Sri Lanka —Eds) and enter into a different relationship with the national bourgeoisie of these countries.

Dutch imperialism has been compelled to withdraw from Indonesia and arrive at a compromise with the native ruling class. In Indo-China French imperialism has been bogged down ever since the war in its desperate effort to hold down the national liberation struggle. In Malaya, British imperialism with all the resources at its disposal has not been enabled to defeat the Malayan peoples' fight for independence. In China American imperialism has sustained an unparalleled reverse. Despite the lavish pouring of munitions and supplies to the aid of the decrepit Chiang Kai Shek regime, the forces of Chinese landlordism-capitalism-imperialism, as represented by the corrupt Kuomintang* clique, have been pushed into the sea and retain but a shaky foot-hold on

*The Kuomintang (KMT) was a bourgeois nationalist party in China, founded by Sun Yat-sen in 1912. In 1927 the KMT, led by Chiang Kai Shek, bloodily suppressed the workers government of Shanghai and headed a weak and unstable military government, until its defeat in the revolution of 1946-9. After this the remnants of the KMT fled to Formosa (Taiwan), where they still hold power.

the island of Formosa (Taiwan —Eds), protected only by the sea and now the American navy.

Korea divided into Russian and American spheres of influence, reveals the weakness of imperialism in the whole of the Far East. Without the direct intervention of American imperialism the Korean Chiang Kai Shek would have collapsed as ignominiously as the Chiang regime itself. At best American imperialism will be enabled to retain a foothold after a lengthy struggle and American forces will be pinned down like those of the French in Indo-China and the British in Malaya, even in the event of a complete victory in the South. This is the measure of the decay of the old relations of capitalism and imperialism of the past. Capitalism rots at its weakest point.

In Europe, the victory of Russia in the war and the upsurge of the masses following the defeat of German-Italian fascism also developed a tremendous revolutionary wave which threatened to sweep capitalism away over the entire continent. However, the victory of Russia in the war had complex and contradictory consequences. Temporarily, but nevertheless for an entire historical period, Stalinism has been enormously strengthened. Despite the destruction and blood letting to which Russia had been subjected, which left her in an exhausted and weak state (while Anglo-American imperialism had hardly been touched during the war and suffered negligible losses in resources and manpower —America had reached the apex of her power militarily and economically), because of the mood of the peoples and the relationship of class forces on a world scale, the imperialists were impotent to intervene against Russia.

Intervention even on a scale following that of World War 1 was impossible. On the contrary, the allies were forced to swallow the Russian hegemony of Eastern Europe and parts of Asia which they would never have agreed to concede even to reactionary Czarism. The Russian bureaucracy had achieved the domination of the region beyond the wildest dreams of Russia under the Czars.

The process whereby capitalism was overthrown in Eastern Europe and Stalinism extended, took place in a peculiar way. The vacuum in the state power in Eastern Europe, following the defeat of the Nazis and their Quislings, was filled by the forces of the conquering Red Army. The weak bourgeoisie of these areas had been largely exterminated, absorbed as Quislings to German imperialism or reduced to minor partners of the Nazis during the years of the war. They had been relatively weak in Eastern Europe even before the war, as the states of this region were largely semi-colonies of the great powers on the lines of the South

American states. The pre-war regimes suffered from a chronic crisis due to the Balkanisation* of the area and the incapacity of the ruling class to solve the problems of even the bourgeois democratic revolution. They were nearly all military police dictatorships of a weak character without any real roots among the masses.

The victory of Russia during the war undoubtedly provoked an upsurge among the masses either rapidly or in some countries delayed for a time. The socialist revolution was on the order of the day. This was dangerous not only for the bourgeoisie but also the Stalinist bureaucracy. The bureaucracy achieved their aims by skilfully veering between and manipulating the classes in typical Bonapartist fashion. The trick was to form a 'popular front' between the classes and to organise a government of 'national concentration'. However this 'popular front' had a different base and different aims in view than the 'popular fronts' of the past.

In Spain the aim of the 'popular front' was to destroy the powers of the workers and the embryonic workers' state, by destroying the workers' revolution. This was achieved by making an alliance with the bourgeoisie, or rather the shadow of the bourgeoisie, strangling the control which the workers had established in the factories and the armed workers' militia and re-establishing the capitalist state under the control of the bourgeoisie. As a consequence of this policy towards the end of the war there was a military police dictatorship on both sides of the lines.

The aim of the coalition with the broken bourgeoisie or its shadow in Eastern Europe had different objectives than that of handing control back to the capitalist class. In previous 'popular fronts' the real power of a state − armed bodies of men, police and the state apparatus − was firmly in the hands of the bourgeoisie with the workers' parties as appendages. In Eastern Europe, with one important variation or another, *the real power ie control of the armed bodies of men and the state apparatus, was in the hands of the Stalinists.* The bourgeoisie occupied the position of appendage without the real power. Why then the coalition? It served as a cover under which a firm state machine on the model of that of Moscow could be constructed and consolidated.

The bourgeoisie was utilised by the bureaucracy in order to prevent the workers, awakened by the victory of the Red Army and the events of the war, from achieving the socialist revolution on the lines of October. The bureaucracy played off the bourgeoisie in the name of unity against the working class. They manipulated with Bonapartist manoeuvres the groping aspirations of the workers to establish control of the factories.

*From the Balkans, this refers to the division of an area into small states with conflicting national interests.

By introducing land reform and expropriating the landlord class, they secured for the time being the support or acquiescence of the peasants. Having consolidated and built up a *strong state under their control* they then proceeded to the next stage. Mobilising the workers, they turned on the bourgeoisie, whom they no longer required, to balance against the workers and peasants, and step by step they proceeded to their expropriation. The bourgeoisie without the support of outside imperialism was incapable of decisive resistance. A totalitarian regime approximating more and more to the Moscow model has been gradually introduced. After the elimination of the bourgeoisie, and the beginning of a large scale industrialisation the bureaucracy has turned against the peasants and started on the road of the collectivisation of agriculture.

The Case of Yugoslavia.

In Yugoslavia and China the pattern of events was somewhat different, although not fundamentally so, from developments in Eastern Europe. After the subjugating of Yugoslavia by the forces of German imperialism a struggle for national liberation against the foreign oppressor began to develop. This had a wide base due to the traditions of Yugoslavia and the struggles of its peoples against Turkish domination and that of Austria-Hungary before the First World War.

This resulted in a peasant war and a guerrilla struggle in the mountains. Under 'normal' conditions such a struggle could only have ended in the victory of the bourgeoisie and the possibility of land reform, even if carried to a successful conclusion. But the dominating factors of our epoch lie in the victory of 'October' and the distortion of the revolution by the bureaucracy. On the one hand the background of a strong 'workers' state' (even though in a degenerated form) and on the other the frightful decay of capitalism-imperialism on a world scale and the incapacity of the local bourgeoisie to solve a single one of the national or democratic problems facing the country, served to push the masses in the direction of the socialist revolution. Again, the distortion of the revolution results in a curious deformation of the struggle on the part of the local agencies of Stalinism.

The peasants cannot play an independent role. They must follow one or another of the basic classes in modern society. In contradistinction to the classical Marxist theory of the past, the struggle began with small sections of the workers and Stalinist leadership taking to the hills and organising the peasants in a war for national liberation. The overwhelming majority of the rank and file of the partisan army of liberation was composed of peasants. Its and file of the partisan army of liberation was composed of peasants. Its nature revealed itself in the civil war, which began even under the occupation, with Mihailovitch* representing the capitalist and upper middle class (or rather those remnants who had not sold out completely to German imperialism). The Bonapartist bureaucracy, basing itself on the peasants, led the struggle under the guise of a national 'popular front' similar to those later established in Eastern Europe. Apart from the big cities large areas were under the control of Tito towards the end of the war, though the assistance of the Red Army was necessary for the conquest of Belgrade.

However events in Yugoslavia developed on a different pattern to those in Eastern Europe. In the other countries of Eastern Europe the partisan struggles were in most cases either weak, almost non-existent or in an embryonic stage when the Red Army arrived. In those where a mass of resistance did occur, there were special circumstances which did not exist in Yugoslavia.

The important difference between Yugoslavia (as with China) and the rest of Eastern Europe lies in the fact that Tito and the Yugoslav Stalinists had established an independent state base before the arrival of the Red Army. They had the support of the big majority of the masses in the revolutionary struggle which they had undertaken. Thus the attempt of the Russian bureaucracy to establish firm control could be met with successful resistance on the part of the Yugoslavs. They were not so dependent on Moscow as were the other satellite parties.

In the Soviet Union itself conflicts inevitably arose between the national republics and the Stalinist bureaucracy because of the Great Russian tendencies of centralisation and bureaucratic oppression in the interests of the Moscow clique. In the Ukraine, Georgia, Azerbaijan, German-Volga Republic, opposition against the national oppression developed in all the republics of Russia against this stifling economic and cultural oppression. In the Ukraine, particularly, oppression developed to such an extent that Trotsky raised the slogan of an independent Socialist Soviet Ukraine. The opposition of the masses of the republic was such that the hand-picked Stalinist leadership had to be purged and killed in order to consolidate the rule of the bureaucracy.

To this day the national question remains a key question in the struggle against the bureaucracy. Thus Stalin's tendency to convert Eastern Europe into a fief for the benefit of the Russian bureaucracy through privileged and extortionate agreements and the subordination of the interests of the economy in these countries to the economic needs of the Moscow bureaucracy was bound to

---

*Draha Mihailovitch was the leader of the Chetnik guerillas who collaborated with the nazis in actions against Tito's partisans.

awaken opposition amongst the masses, which had to arouse an echo even in the dominant Stalinist parties. It was in this soil that the break between the Moscow Stalinist regime and the Yugoslav Stalinist regime had to take place. It was on this issue that the Yugoslav bureaucracy, because of its independent state base and its mass support, could successfully defy the Kremlin.

Even against the cruel Cominform blockade, paradoxically because of the tension between East and West, they could succeed in maintaining a precarious balance. It is the national question which explains the basis of the Yugoslav resistance. The Yugoslav bureaucracy wished to preserve the position of a smaller partner rather than be a puppet state of Moscow. Where the Ukrainian and Georgian bureaucrats could not succeed, they had the possibility.

In the other states of Eastern Europe the opposition was dealt with on similar lines to that of the opposition in the national states within the Soviet Union. The leading elements such as Gomulka*, Rajk, Kostov were executed or jailed and the state machine purged from top to bottom to bring it into line as an obedient tool of Moscow. The attempt in Yugoslavia, however, ended with the arrest and imprisonment of the Moscow Stalinist agents Zujobic and Hebrang.

Does the break of Tito with Stalin mean that the Yugoslav regime ceases to be Stalinist? The regime remains that of a Yugoslav variant of Russian Stalinism. Stalinism means a totalitarian regime with a privileged bureaucratic caste superimposed on the economic base of the workers' state. With this or that difference, with this or that modification, nevertheless the regime in Yugoslavia resembles that of Russia, just as the Dollfus regime in little Austria resembled that of Hitler and Mussolini.

In the same way as it is possible for there to be varying fascist regimes in different countries, so under given conditions there can be various Stalinist regimes, various democratic bourgeois states and various forms of workers' states conforming to the norm.

The decisive considerations in our characterisation of a regime are: firstly, the basic social characteristics...workers' state, capitalist state, feudal state, slave state, etc. Secondly, though still of vital importance, its political super-structure. In the case of capitalist states...fascist, democratic, imperialist, colonial etc in the case of a workers' state... bureaucratised or workers' democracy. On this basis Yugoslavia remains a deformed workers' state. [Marxists support the struggle of the Yugoslav masses against the] chauvinist national oppression of the

---

*Wladyslaw Gomulka was general secretary of the Polish Workers' Party from 1945-8. He was removed and jailed 1951-4. He was released in 1956 and became first secretary of the Party until the uprising in 1970. Traicho Kostov, a Hungarian CP member for 30 years, and acting Prime Minister in 1948, was executed in 1948 as a 'police agent'. Laslo Rajk, a lifelong Hungarian CP member, was executed in 1948 as a 'fascist spy'.

Russian bureaucracy, just as we as we support the struggle of the Ukraine or of Poland for freedom from the domination of Moscow.

In Yugoslavia itself the Fourth International must fight for the overthrow of the Yugoslav bureaucracy by means of a political revolution. The demands of this political revolution will be for the control to be placed in the hands of the masses through a regime of workers' democracy, with as a minimum, the right to participate freely in all political life for all working class tendencies, elimination of the privileges of the bureaucracy, restoration of the right to strike, etc.

The Yugoslav regime in its outlook and methods remains more on the path of Stalinism than that of revolutionary Marxism. The pressure from Stalinism compels the Yugoslav bureaucracy to borrow extensively from the Marxist criticism of Stalin. Verbal gestures to the left no more transform the regime to that of a healthy workers' state than the sometimes correct Stalinist criticism of reformism and capitalism turns it (the Stalinist bureaucracy) into a genuine Marxist current. In a similar sense to that in which Stalinism remains a centrist current so also does the Yugoslav bureaucracy.

This bureaucracy is fresher than that of Moscow. It probably has a greater mass support among the toilers. The Five Year Plan, like that of Russia in its early stages, has evoked the enthusiastic support of the masses who believe that they are building socialism. Nevertheless, already the differentiation is as great as it was in Russia in the early years of the Five Year Plan. The basic physiognomy of the ruling clique is indicated by the fact that they have remained wedded to the theory of socialism in one country —albeit on a lower level, on the basis of tiny Yugoslavia, in comparison with the tremendous resources of Russia.

The Utopian position of the Yugoslavs, hemmed in by the hatred of the bureaucracy in the East and capitalism-imperialism in the West; precariously blancing on this antagonism in order to maintain themselves, is shown by the first skirmishes in the struggle between the USA and the USSR. The pathetic capitulation to Western imperialism involved in the demand for the mediation of the United Nations in Korea, is the best indication of the non-Marxist character of the Yugoslav bureaucracy.

Not basing themselves on internationalism, like other small nations, they can only scurry backwards and forwards between the mighty powers of Russia and America, without the possibility of an independent role. Only an internationalist position would save them from the ignominous role which Yugoslavia plays in the United Nations (UN).

Zig-zags to the left, like the Stalinist zig-zags to the left —in words — cannot alter the fundamental relationships in Yugoslavia. The economic base of Yugoslavia — a backward country not much more developed than Russia before its industrialisation —brings forth the inexorable consequences of the bureaucratisation which developed in Moscow. With convulsive swings to the right and left, the economic tendency, given the same causes, would have the same effect. The Yugoslav regime will more and more approach that of Moscow.

Stalinism In China

The peculiar combination of forces which resulted in the victory of Stalinism in Eastern Europe, are working towards the same results in Asia. In China, we have an outstanding example of this result of the multiplicity of hisorical factors. The defeat of the revolution of 1925-7 (due to the mistakes of the Stalinists) which had had every promise of success, led the Stalinist leadership and the cadres they had managed to retain, to desert the cities and take to the mountains in order to base themselves on the peasant war —a war which had many precedents in China's long history.

The crumbling and decay of the capitalist-landlord military police regime was shown in its total incapacity to solve a single one of China's problems in the period 1924-45. Far more rotten than Czarist Russia, even at its worst, it succeeded in alienating almost the entire population apart from the tiny clique of Chiang Kai Shek at the top.

There were none really willing to strike a blow in defence at the hour of danger. In the same period the frightful decay of imperialism following the Second World War made the imperialists incapable of intervening. In 1925-7 British imperialism had replied to an 'insult to the Flag' by bombarding the main ports of China with their warships. This with the approval of the labour and trade union leaders. In 1949 such was the relationship of forces, the imperialists hailed with glee the sneaking away of the warship *Amethyst* from the waters of the Yangtze! So has the relationship of forces changed. The American imperialists intervened with huge supplies of arms, money and munitions, to aid the corrupt gang of Chiang Kai Shek, almost invariably the supplies falling into the hands of the Chinese Red Army.

These factors, together with the fact that they had mighty Russia as a neighbour, all had their impact on the development of the situation in China. Under 'normal' conditions the peasant war in China would have ended as all such wars have ended in the past, or the leadership of the Chinese peasants would have fused with the capitalist elements in the cities and the peasant masses would have found themselves betrayed. The revolution would have assumed a capitalist character.

However, all the factors enumerated above had to have a different result than could have been foreseen in advance. Without Russia as a neighbour, without the degeneration of the Russian regime as a further factor, without the complete breakdown of the regime in China, where the old ruling class had so pitifully outlived itself, without the degeneration of the international Stalinist movement, without the extreme weakness of the genuine Marxist current, without the weakness of imperialism on a world scale, events in China as in all Asia would have taken a different turn: either in the direction of a proletarian revolution according to the norm (with all its international implications in the spreading of the revolution in Europe and the world) or the victory of capitalist counter-revolution. Those would have been the alternatives.

History, however, is full of inexhaustible variants which cannot be foreseen in advance. Theory is grey, but the tree of life is green...All these complicated factors in combination have resulted in the revolution being accomplished in a different way than theory had previously indicated. Using the same technique as in Yugoslavia, with the mass movement of the peasants as their base, Mao* and the Chinese Red Army (with possibly an even more popular and greater mass base than Tito had) ...waged a revolutionary war for the land. The armies of the Kuomintang clique melted away. Here was a peasant war in the classical revolutionary tradition. The Bonapartist clique of Stalinism based itself firmly on the longing of the peasantry for the land. Leading the peasant war they gained the powerful support of the masses. Here we have a peculiar variation of the permanent revolution [where a victorious peasant army was led by] ex-Marxists.

Due to the crisis of the regime and the paralysis of the movements in the cities by Stalinism, Mao Tse Tung and the other Stalinist leaders established an independent base in the peasant army; the classical instrument of Bonapartism. But in line with the epoch and the various factors already exhaustively dealt with it could not end as normally a peasant war independent of the mass movement in the cities would end. Having conquered the cities, with at least the passive acquiescence of the working class and urban petty bourgeois masses,

*Mao Tse Tung (in the articles the old style transliteration is used, the modern is Mao Zedong) attended the founding conference of the CCP in 1921. After the defeat of 1927 Mao led the flight of the CCP to the countryside, organising the 'long March'. Became CCP chairman in 1935, and headed the People's Republic of China from 1949 until his death in 1976.

Mao Tse Tung and his group could succeed in Bonapartist fashion in balancing between the classes.

Starting with the gradual elimination of the landlords throughout the territory which they had conquered (after the initial stages of the movement the bureaucracy was concerned not to have any independent movement of either the peasants or the workers which could not be directly harnessed and controlled by themselves), and immediately confiscating what they termed 'bureaucratic capitalism' ie the key centres of whatever heavy industry and finance existed, the Bonapartist bureaucracy could manoeuvre between the classes. For a temporary period and in order to help consolidate the rise and control of the bureaucratic caste, they have tolerated merchant and industrial capitalism in a neo-NEP*.

Manoeuvring between the classes, they will establish a firm and strong state machine. Basing themselves now on the peasants, now on the workers, then on the bourgeoisie, to serve different ends they will balance between them as 'arbiter' and regulator of the relations between the classes. Inevitably they will move on to the confiscation of private ownership in industry and then at a later stage, to the expropriation of the peasantry as well, on the model of Russia and Eastern Europe. Because of the weakness and impotence of the bourgeoisie, with no historical perspective and no historical mission to perform, it will be eliminated with comparative ease. Mao will base himself on the workers in order to strike blows at the bourgeoisie, as Stalin did at the time of the elimination of the Kulaks and the 'nepmen'.

A Stalinist bureaucracy cannot tolerate the sharing of power with the bourgeoisie because this would weaken it and reduce it to a subordinate puppet role, with the corresponding diminution of income, power and privileges. The peasants, incapable of finding a different road, will be mercilessly repressed. Gradually a totalitarian state, more and more approximating to that of Moscow, will be established. Having based themselves on the workers for a time in order to eliminate the capitalists and consolidate their rule, they must turn on the working class and smash any elements of workers' democracy which may exist or be developed in the process.

Before Stalinism in China is a long perspective of power despite the social convulsions and crises of growth and consolidation. It is relatively progressive because of the development of industry and the unification of China for the first time and on this basis giving a

*The New Economic Policy (NEP) was introduced by the Bolshevik government in Russia in 1921 to replace War Communism. It was a temporary measure allowing limited concessions to small business in an effort to regenerate the economy which had been devastated by war followed by civil war. It was overtaken by the first Five Year Plan. Nepmen became a term for speculators.

tremendous impulse to the development of the productive forces. Purely on the basis of Chinese conditions they can maintain their rule for a long time. They will consolidate themselves more and more firmly in control in the next period. Factors making for this have been the endless war and civil war in which China hasbeen involved in the last two decades, the weariness of the people who demand peace, the relatively progressive role they play in China, and the lack of any alternative on the Chinese basis alone. All these factors strengthen powerfully the role of Chinese Stalinism.

Of course, events in China can be hastened or retarded by developments in Western Europe, America and Russia. These remain the decisive areas of the world. A successful proletarian revolution in the West producing a workers' state on the Marxist norm, would, of course, result in a revival of the revolution in China and open the road for a healthy development by hastening the political revolution. But taking Chinese forces as a basis it is clear that Mao, like Stalin, will develop the forces which will overthrow his machine in the future.

The relatively austere administration, without control from the masses, will become more and more corrupt. State power is a powerful source of infection and disease. Increasing their separation from the masses, the bureaucratic caste will raise themselves higher and higher above the people as a new aristocracy and will provoke the sharp hatred of the masses.

Because of the history of China, its traditions and its terrible backwardness, Chinese Stalinism with its own forces alone will inevitably develop an even more monstrous oppressive machine than that of Stalinism in Russia. The bureaucratic caste which is crystallising there will only be removed by force. The new political revolution will lead to the establishment of a healthy workers' democracy but on a higher industrial foundation. In the long run the fate of China, as of all the East will be determined by the fate of the revolution in Eastern Europe and America.

Having an independent base, the regime of Mao Tse Tung will most likely come into conflict with that of the Stalinist bureaucracy in Russia. Reluctantly, after the experience of Yugoslavia, the bureaucracy has been compelled to treat the People's Republic of China as a junior partner rather than an out and out satellite or a Moscow province. Despite the efforts to avoid this, at a later stage if favourable terms can be obtained from Britain and America, it is quite likely that Mao Tse Tung will break away and play an independent role. Thus, in that sense, once an independent basis is established, it is difficult if not impossible, for Moscow to maintain direct rule or domination.

Stalinism in Western Europe

The result of the war and the national liberation struggle, the general disgust of the masses, the rotting of the capitalist system which had provoked two world wars, the defeat of fascism, and the victory of Russia in the war...all led inevitably to a powerful revolutionary wave in all Western Europe. The tragic thing was that whereas the First World War had seen the revolutionary wave stemmed by reformism, after the Second World War it was Stalinism that saved Western European capitalism from destruction.

In France and Italy in particular, the Communist Parties became the dominant force within the working class and with their control of the unions and other mass organisations of the proletariat, with a powerful apparatus and machine, organisationally the Stalinist parties were far stronger than Bolshevism had ever been before the Russian revolution. The possibility of taking power peacefully, or almost peacefully, was rooted in the situation. But owing to the world diplomatic situation of Stalinism and its fear of the masses, they betrayed the first revolutionary wave in the coalition popular fronts which they formed. With this powerful aid from Stalinism and the usual role of social democracy, and thanks to the assistance of mighty American imperialism, decaying capitalism in Europe has managed to recover. With the assistance of Marshall Aid and the marvellous recuperative powers of modern production, ailing capitalism has managed to restore itself and the productive machine. In this situation, with the passing of the first revolutionary wave, the open struggle between American imperialism and the Stalinist bureaucracy, Stalinism, in the interests of the latter, has engaged in a series of irresponsible adventures without any real perspective except that of weakening Western Europe in the interests of the bureaucracy.

The wave of irresponsible strikes, without a clear perspective of a struggle for power, succeeded in exhausting and frustrating the proletariat. This policy assisted the bourgeoisie, after they had recovered from the first revolutionary shocks, in re-establishing their state machine, even though its firmness is only apparent rather than real. The crisis of the regimes in Western Europe is best shown in the situations in France and Italy.

In these countries the crisis of social democracy is the clearest reflection of this. Despite the failure of Stalinism to seize power the proletariat has produced a split in the Socialist Party in Italy* and a chronic crisis in the SFIO in France. There is a crumbling away of support from the workers and despite its crimes and losses in the last period with the despair of the workers, Stalinism remains the mass party of the working class. This is so precisely because of the lack of a mass revolutionary alternative.

However, while dents have been made in the armour of Stalinism with the experience of the workers, including the Tito movement, nevertheless, as yet, no decisive blow has been struck against the Stalinist forces. As elections have shown in France and Italy, they still retain the support of the basic strata of the working class. In the face of economic slump, Stalinism can recover and even gain support from further sections of the workers and petit bourgeoisie whom they have not affected in the past. The basic section of the workers in these countries still has many illusions in Stalinism as a revolutionary force; illusions which have been strengthened by the 'left' line of the Stalinists in the last few years. A long process of disillusionment will be necessary before the working class comes to understand the real nature of Stalinism.

It is theoretically possible under certain conditions that the Stalinists might even come to power in these countries. If they do so, they could not retain power for a lengthy period, and would be bound to come into conflict with the Moscow bureaucracy in any event. Whether they come into conflict with Moscow quickly or not, an immediate process of differentiation from top to bottom within the Communist Party would commence. Whatever the result of fissures in the CP which would be opened up, the Stalinists would be unlikely to maintain power for any protracted period.

Spain

The convulsive character of the present epoch and the impossibility of a lengthy stabilisation of capitalism is revealed not only by the weakness of imperialism and the national awakening of Asia but also by the shaky foundations of economic upswing and relative tranquillity in Western Europe. The Spanish problem once again is raising itself as a key question for Europe and the fate of the world labour movement.

It is twelve years since the Spanish workers were enmeshed in a terrible civil war, due to the mistakes and crimes of the labour movement, especially the Stalinists.

Now the decay and corruption of the regime have reached such a

*In 1947 the right wing minority of the Italian Socialist Party split to form the PSDI, in protest at the Socialist Party's close relations with the CP. The SFIO was the French socialist party

pitch that the awakening of the workers has already begun. The military-police fascist regime, far from solving any of the problems of the weak and backward Spanish economy, exacerbated them to an enormous degree. The regime in its inefficiency, futility and rottenness, basing itself on an alliance of Church, landowners, army and industrialists, bears more of a resemblance to the role of the Chiang clique than any European government. Like Czarism it has ceased to have any mass base within the population.

All strata of the population, *all the social classes*, feel the crisis of the regime and are beginning to search for a way out. Fascism, once established, can only maintain itself given the atomisation, inertia, despair, apathy and indifference of the masses. The recovery of working-class solidarity, initiative and action can spell the beginning of its doom. So the strikes in Barcelona and the Basque country, mark the beginning of the new Spanish revolution. The process of history of the revolution, interrupted in 1939 by the intervention of the brutal fascist heel, begins anew. The fascist regime is doomed. *The only question is that of the tempo of events in which its destruction will take place.*

The beginning of the end for Mussolini was marked by the strikes of the Italian workers − a few months later he fell. The events in Spain, like those of Italy, are an answer to the sceptics who saw only the monolithic strength of a totalitarian regime, and sagely preached the impossibility of its overthrow from the internal forces of the country itself. Italy was not a convincing example for them because of the defeats of the regime in wax, from which they deduced the causes of the collapse of the fascist system.

The peace-time crisis of the Franco regime provides a crushing refutation of this undialectical method of thinking. The same school of social 'philosophy' bows down in despair before the phenomenon of totalitarian Stalinism.

In the long run the intervention of the Russian workers will produce a paralysis of the Stalinist regime far more pitiful and helpless than the coming death agony of the Franco regime. The all powerful and almighty bureaucracy (which reveals its caste rule as one of permanent crisis in the never-ending purges and repressions of the regime) in its hour of trial will collapse into impotence under the hammer blows of the workers. Probably the hour of its collapse will begin with strikes on similar lines to those of Spain and Italy.

As has been determined by theory on the basis of historical experience, the conditions for revolution are now manifesting themselves under the blows of the awakening Spanish working class. The doomed ruling class is beginning to split at the top under the pressure of the rumblings of social discontent from below.

They wish some reforms and concessions to be granted to the workers and peasants, which will leave the basis of the social regime intact. So it was in the doomed Czarist regime. But any attempt to forestall the movement from below by restoration of the outlived monarchy or similar manoeuvres, will merely precipitate the movement which they so dread.

The unbearable social tension is reflected by this attempt on the part of its main beneficiaries, the landowners, Church, army and industrialists, to escape retribution, which they fear the overthrow of the regime will bring at the hands of the long suffering masses. But this plotting, percolating to the masses below, successful or not, can but add impetus to the gathering revolutionary [tide].

The ruling class is seeking a way of escape. The middle class, in most of its strata, from top to bottom, is vacillating or even manifesting open sympathy for the struggle of the workers. The regime cannot find a basis of support here.

Lastly, the magnificent strikes of the workers under such adverse conditions reveal once again the capacity for self-sacrifice, endurance and struggle which the heroic Spanish workers revealed in such large measure in the revolutionary struggles between 1931-7.

Yes! The conditions for revolution are present! In 1936, despite the sabotage of the workers' leadership, the Spanish workers revealed their aspirations for the socialist revolution by their deeds and activity. Without the unfavourable international environment and the intervention of Hitler and Mussolini, despite the criminal policies of their leaderships even in 1936, it would probably have been possible for the workers to defeat Franco. Without foreign aid, without the Moorish troops and the 'non-intervention' of Stalinist Russia and the capitalist 'democracies' in the early decisive stages it would have been difficult, if not impossible, for Franco to triumph.

Now the degeneration of the Spanish ruling class has gone further under the Franco regime. The desire of the masses for a socialist change has been intensified. They will not be fobbed off for long by merely superficial change and reforms. Especially as only fundamental social revolution can even begin to solve the problems of the Spanish nation.

In the meantime Spanish Morocco, far from being a reservoir for Franco's shock troops, will most likely be affected by rebellion once a mass movement begins on the mainland. The international bourgeoisie would find it impossible to interfere by direct intervention. If Britain finds it difficult to carry out armed intervention against Persia (Iran), it would be impossible for Spain.

The intervention of American dollars would most likely have no more auspicious results than the ill-omened aid for the doomed Chinese clique in the Pacific.

The continuity of the revolution, broken in 1939, bids fair to return to the situation of a *new 1936*, under even more favourable conditions nationally and internationally. *But 1936 means an upsurge towards power by the workers.* An upsurge in which the workers will learn rapidly under favourable conditions and in which the bitter experience of the past will have hardened and strengthened the will of the workers. Only the Stalinist counter-revolution saved the day for Spanish capitalism. But they only succeeded in this role (leaving aside the policies of the POUM, Anarchist, and Socialist left) due to the influence of Russia and the supply of arms and other vital materials by Russia. The Stalinist and bourgeois counter-revolution, succeeded (despite the absence of a Marxist revolutionary party) only because of the conditions sketched above.

Today the conditions are far more unfavourable for them. The bourgeoisie in a new 1931-6 upsurge would become as much a cypher and plaything of events as in 1936. The Stalinists most likely, in the revolution, despite their unpardonable crimes and betrayals, would become once again a powerful force, *but by no means a decisive one.* All the left parties and organisations would spring forward again as mass forces: the CNT, UGT*, the POUM and the Socialist Party.

Under these circumstances the possibility for the rapid creation of a mass revolutionary party would be present. But it is theoretically not excluded that the pressure of the Spanish workers, with the inevitably stormy initiative of the masses, might push *the CNT, the POUM, and the Socialist left in the direction of taking power into their own hands.* Under these conditions a new version of the Paris Commune might ensue in Spain.

A Spanish Commune in its turn would be of decisive world significance. It could be the beginning of the regroupment of the world labour movement. Already in Western Europe the splintering away of Cucchi** and Magnani in Italy, a split off in France, and the creation of a Titoist Communist Party in Germany, are symptoms of a positive crisis within Stalinism. At present, because of the impotence and practical non-existence of a revolutionary Marxist current, they have been in the main of mixed progressive and reactionary elements. In France and Italy it has been the cold war and the blatant revelation of the CPs as tools of the Kremlin's foreign policy which have produced this result.

*The Spanish syndicalist and socialist trade union federations respectively.
**Cucchi and Magnani were prominent CP members in Italy.

Because of the failure to draw clear internationalist and socialist conclusions – rather to stand on the position of the *union sacree* – they have been doomed to sterility and have left the Stalinist forces largely intact.

But a Commune in Spain would have entirely different results. It would split the CP's in Western Europe from top to bottom. It would produce a ferment and differentiation in social democracy in Western Germany and the Labour Party in Britain as well as other socialist parties in Western Europe.

It could mark a new chapter in the resurgence of the labour movement on new foundations. It would mark the beginning of the end of Stalinism in the Western labour movement. It would be the beginning of the end for Stalinism in Eastern Europe, Russia and Asia. It would begin the collapse of capitalism in the West. On this foundation, in a few years after initial confusion and muddle, it could result in the restoration of the world labour movement on Marxist foundations.

Britain and America

Both in Britain and America Stalinism remains as a weak force which has hardly penetrated the masses ... as yet. In the case of Britain this is to a large extent dictated both by historical and moral factors. The tremendous wealth of British capitalism, coupled with the skill of the ruling class in deceit on the one hand and its ability to retreat and compromise on the other in moments of danger, have established a firm position for British capitalism in the past. Even though the dominant position of British imperialism has now passed into history and Britain has been pushed back into the ranks of second-rate powers, nevertheless sufficient wealth (together with the assistance from America) has been accumulated to enable British capitalists, to a certain extent, to live on their fat. At the same time the crisis of capitalism on a world scale; the onrush of Stalinism in Asia and Europe; the loss of confidence of the ruling class; in the old age tradition of rule; the need for a bold programme if Britain is to renovate herself; the radicalisation of the working class: all these have resulted in a position where in the first term of power the Labour government has largely carried out a radical programme of reforms and the nationalisation of those industries ruined by British capitalism. All this has drawn the *decisive section* of the workers in the labour movement, above all the *organised working class,* solidly behind the Labour government. The latter has been compelled to introduce a period of counter reforms, due to the exigencies of the cold war and the increasing burdens of armaments, the brunt of which has been placed on the shoulders of the working and middle classes. While support of sections of the middle class and backward workers may have edged away, nevertheless, at this stage the core of the working class remains for the time being behind the Labour leadership.

In addition, the working class traditions in Britain nurtured over a long period, together with the even more profound tradition of democracy within the ranks of the labour movement, due to the prolonged struggle for political and trade union rights in the last century, have been additional factors repelling the workers away from Stalinism. More and more publicity as to Stalinist methods in Eastern Europe and Russia, the barbaric excesses of the Stalinists, in the conduct of affairs, the lack of democratic rights, slave labour, the concentration camps, and the whole totalitarian set-up of Stalinism cynically rediscovered by the capitalists and the social-democratic press, on the background sketched above, have further weakened the mass appeal of the Stalinists. The tactics of Stalinism in the cold war, skilfully utilised by the ruling class and the Labour leaders, have further alienated the mass of the working class from the CP.

However, despite all these obstacles, Stalinism has succeeded in maintaining a formidable apparatus, which, though weakened, has still managed to penetrate the trade unions and capture some of the key positions, owing to the militant and self-sacrificing work of the rank and file.

Whether Stalinism will succeed in attracting an important part of the British working class to its banner will depend on a series of factors. The sweep of Stalinism over Europe would inevitably assist them in gaining support in Britain. Big scale struggles in France and Italy could push the masses in the direction of Stalinism. While under conditions of crisis and slump which will follow the re-armament boom − if it does not end in war −an important segment of the workers will be impelled in a Stalinist direction. Nevertheless, whether they become dominant tendencies will depend on the effect repercussions will have inside the labour movement.

Events at home and abroad will push big sections of the workers in the labour and trade union movement to the left. The most conscious section will look for a revolutionary road which is different to the repulsive totalitarianism of Stalinism. It is not excluded that the mass of the Labour Party, including an important section of its leadership, will be pushed far in a revolutionary direction. New currents will grow up inside the

Labour Party; it is possible that the right wing will be isolated and a field for Marxist ideas to penetrate on a mass scale for the first time will be created by the wave of events.

In this situation the possibility will exist to win large sections, if not the dominant grouping within the Labour Party, to the banner of revolutionary socialist democracy. The democratic traditions in Britain constitute a precious heritage which can be utilised to prepare for the transformation from capitalist democracy to a soviet democracy, a transformation through revolutionary struggle. If revolutionary Marxism does not succeed in gaining the ear of the masses then a turn towards Stalinism would be virtually inevitable, *in lieu* of any other alternative. However, possibilities of the revolutionary awakening of the British masses are enormous. Events will teach important lessons.

Stalinism today has less attractive power than it previously possessed. Before they fall victim to the wiles of Stalinism the masses will try again and again to find some alternative means of expression within the labour movement. The lag of events and the long delay in the development of a revolutionary mass movement in Britain, act as a fortunate historical accident in the given condition.

In America, the working class has not broken politically from the old capitalist parties. This backwardness is due to a variety of historical factors: the richness of America, its freshness historically, the gigantic productive economy, the high standard of living of the workers, etc. This historical backwardness can be transformed by a leap ahead in the next epoch. The combativeness of American workers, as reflected on the trade union field and in the strike struggles, presages a similar militancy on the political field, once the bankruptcy of American capitalism has been clearly demonstrated. The 1929-33 economic debacle was but a dress rehearsal for the economic blizzard which will overtake America in the coming epoch. The greatest capitalist power of all will reveal the most pitiful helplessness in the face of the collapse of its system. Under those conditions, radicalisation and the awakening of the American workers would take place at great speed. Like the movement of industrial organisation which followed the world slump, so would the turn towards independent politics proceed. The weakness of Stalinism as a fifth column for Russian totalitarianism is apparent at the present time.

However, under the conditions of crisis even in America it is possible that they will grow. But the mass of American workers will move in the direction of independent politics first. Possibilities will be there of creating a mass revolutionary tendency fighting against **reformism, capitalist politics and Stalinism.**

The creation of a mass revolutionary party in any important country in the world, even without the capture of power, can be the beginning of the end for Stalinism on a world scale: first in the countries where they do not have complete power, then in the countries under the totalitarian heel.

Western Germany

Western Germany too is a decisive area where Stalinism is comparatively weak. The experience of the German masses of the barbarised Stalinist army and the experience of Eastern Germany, have pushed the masses back to social democracy for lack of an alternative. The revulsion against Stalinism has been such that in contradistinction to Italy, discredited social democracy has emerged as the overwhelmingly dominant tendency among the masses. However, this can only be during the period of economic upswing, occasioned by Marshall Aid and the building up of the ruined economy following the war. The social democracy has been forced to adopt a radical posture even now. The bitter experience of the German workers with monopoly capital, which financed the Nazis and destroyed their movements and rights, has left a profound impression on the minds of the German toilers.

This experience is reflected in the militancy in the trade union movement which won equal rights on the board of management in the coal and steel industry in the Ruhr. It was reflected earlier in strikes against the attemps at nazi revival.

The German workers have supported social democracy because of their violent revulsion against the Stalinist reaction. However, in the event of a slump and mass unemployment (on a scale similar to that which preceded Hitler) in Western Germany on the one side, while in Eastern Germany full employment continued, this would undoubtedly create a tremendous effect amongst the German masses. Possibilities would be there for Stalinism to regain influence. Far more important, however, would be the radicalising effect that such a situation would have on the social democracy and the trade union movement already tending in a semi-centrist direction. Revolutionary currents would spring up within the ranks of social-democracy.

One way or the other centrist and other left groupings would be created within its ranks. Either a revolutionary tendency would gain a majority within the ranks of social democracy or it would fall to pieces. Possibilities would exist for revolutionising the German masses, against capitalist democracy on the one side and Stalinist totalitarianism on the other: for a socialist soviet democracy as promised by the Russian Revolution. Only thus could the masses be prevented from falling into the hands of Stalinism through sheer despair.

The Situation in Russia

The most remarkable phenomenon in attempting to re-evaluate the economic, political and social realities in Russia lies in the fact that basically the analysis which was made by Trotsky needs no fundamental modification.

The tremendous advantages of state ownership (as the economic transitional form of the future society) have revealed themselves once again in the reconstruction following the Second World War. Despite the fact that Russia was the most devastated country, her speed of re-equipment relative to her productive capacity has far outstripped that of the West. Thanks to the achievements of the five-year plans her recovery has been far faster than in 1920-9. Once again, apparently, the speed of recovery has exceeded what was anticipated by the bureaucrats.

The idea that the collective farms would tend to break down and that on the basis of a weakened Soviet Union (in the war) this could be the starting point for the restoration of capitalism in Russia, has been revealed as false by the economic developments. It is true, that owing to the needs of the war for equipment such as tanks etc, the production of tractors and other agricultural machinery dropped catastrophically and thus, superficially at least, certain tendencies appeared which gave weight to this view. But as was predicted, on the basis of a more sober assessment, very rapidly this trend has been reversed. The wheels of progress cannot be so easily turned back. Agriculture following in the wake of the revival of industry, has seen new steps taken towards greater and greater centralisation and the further development from collectives to giant collectives. In a certain sense this marks the first beginnings of industrialisation of agriculture. As always with Stalinist measures, it has a contradictary content in that, on the one hand, it marks definite progress in the development of agriculture, eliminating as it does the scattered character of the peasantry, grouping them together in the 'agrotowns'; this measure having been carried out with typical bureaucratic brutality. On the other hand, the aim of the bureaucracy in carrying through this measure (aside from its economic aspect) lies in gaining better control and regimentation over the peasants by the familiar methods of the Stalinist apparatus.

The war and the post-war period revealed Russia as the major European industrial power with a dynamic economic base and through the four five-year plans technique has been vastly improved. The 20 years of industrial expansion in Russia would be equal in training and technique to a century of 'normal' capitalist development.

Thus Russian economy has been completely transformed. Even in the field of precision work, such as jet aeroplanes, the Russian products compare favourably with the best of Britain and America. During the war, Russian technique, as shown in the production of artillery and tanks, revealed itself as already equal to the West. With the completion of the new five-year plan, undoubtedly the Soviet Union appeared as the greatest industrial power that Europe has ever had, far exceeding the record of mighty industrial Germany. However it is not the enfeebled capitalism of Europe with which the Soviet Union is competing but the mighty colossus across the Atlantic; America dwarfs not only Russia but the combined economy of Europe.

The Russian economy, however, still develops in a contradictary way. The most modern technique still runs in harness with the most primitive forms of production(slave labour etc) This is reflected in the fact that on a *per capita* basis production in Russia is still extremely low, far lower than in Western Europe.

Thus even in the economic sphere Russian society evolves painfully and in contradictions.

In expanding their base into Eastern Europe the bureacracy proceeded blindly and empirically. *As far as the bureaucracy is concerned the destruction of capitalism and the extension of state ownership is not dictated in any way by the needs of socialism or the interests of the working class.* Like a ruling caste or class, the bureaucracy is only interested in the maintenance and extension of its own power, privileges, income and prestige. In the beginning, short-sightedly, they plundered and stripped Eastern Europe of machinery and raw materials for the immediate and pressing needs of the Russian economy. Now they are integrating Eastern Europe for the purpose of developing it in the interest of the Russian economy and the Russian bureaucracy. Thus the economic base has been extended beyond the bounds of the narrow horizon of the Russian state itself. This undoubtedly gives an impetus to the development of the Russian economy due to the division of labour and the industrial resources, manpower, etc, which Eastern Europe possesses. At the same time, it assists trade between Russia and her satellites and the Western world for the benefit of the bureaucracy.

Nevertheless, with all these added economic resources, Eastern Europe acts as an auxiliary – and not as a fundamental addition

— both economically and politically, to the Russian economy. It still remains subsidiary to the Russian economy itself.

The bureaucracy is preoccupied with the fear of a new world clash. After the experience of the Second World War they look with foreboding to an attack from the citadel of world capitalism, at the same time taking advantage of the extreme weakness and uncertainty of the capitalist world in the last few years by grabbing at its extremeties — Korea, Indo-China etc. The American resistance having hardened, the bureaucracy will tend to effect a compromise. Both sides under present conditions are afraid of resorting to arms because of the catastrophic consequences that would ensue; briefly, the danger to civilisation, the inevitability of an endless military conflict and the struggle which would become one between the Eurasian land mass and the American land mass; the danger of *political* revolution in Russia and Europe and the *social* revolution in America.

As the economic base has been extended the new aristocracy has raised itself in ever greater measure above the level of the masses. The gulf between the toilers and the bureaucracy has reached fantastic levels. At the same time, the needs of the industrialisation and the higher level of skill and technique, tend to force a gradual if slow increase in the standard of living. Undoubtedly, there has been an improvement in the standard of living over the terrible level to which it had fallen by the end of the war. Nevertheless, the bureaucracy, haunted by the disproportion between Russian and American industry, still places the main emphasis on the development of heavy industry. The consumer goods industries, in proportion, are lagging far behind. In housing, food, clothing, Russia as a whole still more approaches the level of Asia than the Western World.

The mounting contradictions in Russia force the bureaucracy to utilise the world situation in order to still the possibilities of opposition in Russia. The evils in Russian society are explained away under cover of the threat of attack from Western imperialism and the fear of restoration of capitalism by external intervention. The White Guard* puppets of American imperialism (Kerensky and Co) with their programme and policy of restoration of private ownership in the event of a victory of the West in the war, play into the hands of the bureaucracy, and this threat acts as a powerful means by which the masses can be held down.

Nevertheless, the contradictions, despite all repressions, continue to manifest themselves in Russian society. Symptomatic of these are

*The White Guards were counter revolutionary forces in Russia after the revolution.

the recurrent purges, especially in Eastern Europe and in the national republics. The latest is the removal of the entire Central Committee of Uzbekistan and Azerbaijain and the widespread purge in the Ukraine. The national question remains a permanent ulcer of discontent in Russian society. At the same time the increase in the proletariat due to the economic successes and the industrialisation of agriculture increases the mighty force of the working class. [The bureaucracy can] temporarily succeed, with the aid of the MVD* in maintaining the proletariat in a state of forced disunity, in face of the ever increasing power of the monster state. But Bonapartism remains, just the same, a regime of permanent crisis. The unstable relationship of forces, the stifling of all initiative and culture within the framework of the police state, the complete regimentation and the lack of democracy, will all come more and more into conflict with the needs of the economy itself. Despite the economic successes, the inefficiency and parisitism of the bureaucracy act as a relative fetter on the development of the Russian economy. Freed from this incubus, on a far more harmonious basis, even greater economic gains would be possible.

How long the bureaucracy will last, however, can be determined only by events both at home and abroad. Revolution in the West would cause repercussions in the East. However, developments in Russia itself, even without revolution in the West, could cause the overthrow of the bureaucracy. The never-ending purges show the possibilities of a shake-up in the bureaucracy under the pressure of the masses. Any incident, such as the death of Stalin, might precipitate a struggle between different cliques within the bureaucracy (though, this seems unlikely at the present stage) and this could open the way for the entry of the masses onto the political scene.

In the long run the movement of the masses from below will have its effect on the hierarchical structure of the bureaucracy. Discontent at the base, in due time, produces splits at the top. The example of Spain, not withstanding its different social structure, shows how a totalitarian regime can be suddenly shaken by the movement of the masses. Once it begins it could acquire a greater sweep in Russia than in Spain.

The time scale is indeterminate, years, perhaps decades. This will be decided historically by the conjunction of the multiple factors involved.

The totalitarian state will inevitably land in an impasse. The final

*Russian secret police.

hour of the bureaucracy will come. Inexorably, the political revolution will develop. There will be a return to workers' democracy, but on a higher level. However, the developments will take place with a different situation nationally and internationally. The fate of the Russian revolution is bound up now more than ever with the fate of the world revolution. Revolution in Russia would immediately provoke revolution in the West and vice-versa. The possibilities are manifold in the next historical epoch. On the background of the world decay of capitalism, the return to private ownership in Russia, by internal means, is extremely unlikely if not impossible. External American intervention might facilitate such a restoration.

Despite the encrustation of Stalinist reaction over the conquests of October, whereby only the basic economic structure remains, the viability of state ownership and planning provides the skeleton on which the flesh of socialism will be built. On this basis Stalinism is doomed as a parasitic growth which will be swept away and socialism will prevail in the long run.

General Conclusions and Perspectives.

Thus the possibilities on a world scale with a continuing decay and collapse of world capitalism-imperialism are manifold. The cold war between West and East is an expression in reality of the impasse of world capitalism and the impossibility of the bourgeoisie finding a way out. A long period opens out of struggle between Stalinism and capitalism and of the working class against both. The skirmishes in Korea and at other extremities of the world mark, on the one hand, the decline of imperialism, but on the other, the unlikelihood, for a long term of years ahead, of American and world imperialism attempting to solve their problems by force of arms. Despite the build-up against Stalinist 'aggression' and 'enslavement', as against the so-called 'free world', nevertheless the political prerequisites for war do not exist as yet.

The working class in Western Europe and the Anglo-Saxon world has not been defeated or regimented. War would almost inevitably mean the collapse of Western Europe and the seizure of possibly all Asia and all Europe unified under the domination of the Kremlin. An endless war between the continents would be in prospect a war which neither side could hope to win. A war which would mean the ruination of the entire world economy and the possible collapse of civilisation. It would mean a war of attrition which would have the possibility of continuing for decades from a purely military standpoint, a war in which there could be no winners and which would provoke revolutionary convulsions against the futile and senseless slaughter which it would involve. Only the defeat of the labour movement in Western Europe, Britain and America and the consolidation of reaction on its bones could prepare a firm foundation for imperialism to wage war. Far more likely, the re-armament boom will end in financial and economic catastrophe, though, of course, war is not excluded. The Western world still remains the decisive arena which will decide the fate of the planet.

For Marxism neither pessimism nor spurious optimism can play a role in determining the analysis of events. The first necessity is to understand the meaning of the conjuncture of historical forces leading to the present world situation.

The overthrow of Stalinism in the areas in which it holds sway will most likely be a long term process. It is true that Stalinism remains a regime of permanent crisis. In it, the element of socialism in the state economy is in permanent contradiction to the Bonapartist state apparatus and the privileged caste whose interests it serves. Thus, the regime of Stalinism in Russia itself bears a striking resemblance, even more than the Bonapartism of bourgeois origin, to the Caesarism of Ancient Rome in the epoch of the decay of the Empire. In that it bears a close resemblance to fascism. In the long run, the regime of Bonapartist autocracy is incompatible with the economic base set in being by the October Revolution. That is the source of the permanent convulsions, and the endless removal of officials by the insatiable moloch in the Kremlin. The victories of Stalinism can only be a preparation for its downfall. But this is only so from a long-term point of view. Undoubtedly, Stalinism has been strengthened for a temporary period.

History has shown nuances of development in the transition from one economy to another. Before our eyes we have another rich lesson in the fact that even the greatest historical geniuses cannot lay down a blueprint for the change from one society to another. Only the general laws can be worked out in advance. The transition from slavery to feudalism was preceded by a long epoch of Caesarism in Ancient Rome; the transition from feudalism to capitalism also saw the regime of absolute monarchy. In the early period of bourgeois dominance a long historical epoch of military-police dictatorship ensued. However, before the full potential of capitalist production could be realised, new revolutions for political democracy took place. These were an absolute necessity for a full flowering of the productive forces even on a capitalist basis. Without democracy the development of modern civilisation would have been hampered and restricted.

Owing to the rise of Stalinism the revolution in the West has been delayed. Due to the development of the revolution in a backward country and the failure of its extension to advanced countries in the West, a period of Bonapartism was historically inevitable. This in its turn unleashes new historical forces.

The bureaucracy, which grew out of the backwardness and the defeats of the proletariat, once having established its hegemony, is not prepared to give up its position, even once its temporary role has been fulfilled.

Thus in part of Asia, Eastern Europe and Russia, the transition from capitalism to socialism is taking place in the forms which could not be anticipated by either Marx or Lenin. However, the task of the emancipation of the working class can only be consciously completed by the working class itself. The bureaucracy has aims, intentions, and interests (in particular a vested interest in state dominance) of its own and like the Bonapartist cliques in the period of the bourgeois assent, cannot be removed except by force. At the same time, for the full development of the productive forces and for a transition to socialism, the abolition of the state and all forms of bureaucracy are essential. For a full flowering of productive forces, far more than capitalism (which is regulated to a certain extent through the medium of the market and thus automatically checked and developed), socialism, and just as much the transition to socialism, requires direct participation and democratic checking of planning in the process of production, by the masses themselves.

Without democracy, bureaucratic excesses clog and fetter the full harmonious development of the productive forces. Inevitably, as bureaucratic autocracy was overthrown and gave way to a higher political form of bourgeois domination, so *proletarian Bonapartism* − Stalinism − will have to give way to proletarian democracy. In those areas where Stalinism has extended itself in the form of proletarian Bonapartism, the proletariat will have to pay with the new political revolution, before the ascent to socialism can really be begun. Stalinism for a longer or shorter period can only remain a temporary check, in the evolution of the working class in the direction of socialism.

'All roads lead to Communism' is the confident battle cry of Stalinism at the present time. They are more right than they think. Either through a healthy proletarian revolution in a major country of the West, or if Stalinism extends its sway, inevitably political revolution against Stalinism, will prepare the way for the sounding of its death knell.

The Colonial Revolution and Proletarian Bonapartism

Introduction

ONCE THE capitalist class of Europe had ridden out the storms and stresses immediately after the second world war, the political basis had been laid for what turned out to be a long period of economic upswing. Underpinned by levels of economic growth that put all previous productive achievements in the shade, the advanced capitalist countries were thus able to enjoy decades of relative social peace, in marked contrast to the instability of the inter-war years.

But in the colonial and ex-colonial countries, the so-called third world, the post-war decades have been a period of unprecedented upheaval, characterised by famine, social unrest, wars, revolutions and counter-revolutions. There have been mass struggles encompassing tens and hundreds of millions in Africa, Asia and Latin America. In the course of these movements, in China, Cuba, Burma, Syria, Kampuchea (Cambodia), Vietnam, Angola, Mozambique, Ethiopia and elsewhere, regimes have been established, all of which, from the standpoint of pre-war developments, were new and peculiar. They were revolutionary formations that resembled neither the revolutionary capitalist regimes of the seventeenth and eighteenth centuries, nor the 'classic' workers' government of October 1917.

As was the case with so many post-war political developments, the colonial revolution was shrouded in mystery and confusion to the leadership of what remained of the so-called Fourth International, as well as to the theoreticians of Stalinism and reformism. Different 'Trotskyist' sects took turns to idealise Mao Tse Tung, Ho Chi Minh, Fidel Castro, Che Guevara and others, without a glimmer of understanding about what real political forces these leaders represented.

It was the Marxist tendency gathered around Ted Grant which was able to place all these leaders and movements in their correct context, explaining their origins and development. The extracts published in this chapter will demonstrate that these events can be explained, in Marxist terms, by the fundamental ideas worked out by Trotsky in his Theory of the Permanent Revolution, but showing how they find a completely novel and distorted application in the post-war period.

Before the Russian revolution, Trotsky had argued that the Russian capitalist class, because of its late entry onto the stage of history, was too weak economically and politically, too much tied to the old land relations and too subservient to its stronger international competitors, to lead the revolution in Russia. At the same time, the many-millioned peasantry was not able to play an independent political role. The leading role in the revolution, therefore, could fall only to the industrial working class, the proletariat, drawing the peasantry behind it.

But leading the revolution, carrying through the tasks of the capitalist (democratic) revolution, the proletariat would be bound by its social character and its methods of struggle, to progress immediately to the implementation of socialist tasks, and the establishment of a workers' state: the dictatorship of the proletariat. Trotsky accepted that Russia by itself was too backward economically to construct socialism, but he argued that on a world scale, capitalism was rotten-ripe for social change.

The Russian revolution, therefore, would begin what only the workers in the advanced countries could complete. Borrowing the expression from Marx, Trotsky characterised the coming revolution in Russia, because of the role of the working class and the necessity of an internationalist outlook, as a Permanent Revolution.

The correctness of Trotsky's prognosis, put forward years in advance, was shown by the process of the revolution in 1917. After the February revolution had overthrown the Czar, the capitalist class was utterly incapable of taking forward or consolidating even the most modest gains of the revolution. The 'democratic' tasks were in the end only achieveable by the coming to power of the working class, supported by the poorer peasants, through the October soviet revolution.

Trotsky's Theory of Permanent Revolution forms the starting point of a Marxist description of the revolutionary processes in the underdeveloped countries: the colonial revolution. But in the transitional period between capitalism and the establishment of workers' states the picture has been enormously complicated: given the delay in the revolution in the advanced countries, the degeneracy of the world-wide Stalinist movement and the subsequent absence of mass revolutionary parties in the third world, all kinds of new social formations unforeseen by Trotsky have been possible.

Under these conditions, with social and economic crisis reaching a pitch, it has been possible for the revolution to unfold, not on the lines of the 'classic' Russian pattern, but in the manner of a distortion of the Permanent Revolution. Based upon the already-present model of the totalitarian bureaucracy in Russia, regimes have been established on the same lines: with state ownership and planning of the economy, one-party government and the suppression of democratic rights. Moreover, these have been established on the basis of peasant- based wars, with a variety of petit-bourgeois or Stalinist leaderships, with the working class playing a relatively minor role.

The following documents show a continuity and development of the Marxist position on the colonial revolution, worked out by Ted Grant as the leading theoretician of the RCP, and further deepened and extended in the period after the RCP broke up. The first item is an article from the January 1949 issue of *Socialist Appeal*. The background to this was the civil war raging in China, between the Peoples' Liberation Army (or the 'Red Army'), led by Mao Tse Tung, and the 'Nationalist' forces of the Kuomintang, led by Chiang Kai Shek.

It was clear by this stage that the Red Army, on the basis of its revolutionary policy towards the land and the peasantry, was making huge gains. Yet there were still leaders in the Fourth International who believed that Mao Tse Tung would make a compromise with Chiang, or even capitulate to him. The failure of these 'theoreticians' to face the reality that stared them in the face led to a jibe, in one debate, that 'Mao may want to surrender to Chiang but the trouble is, he can't catch him!'

Building upon the theoretical work which had already been undertaken in relation to Russia, Eastern Europe and the Tito-Stalin split, the article by Ted Grant puts forward a perspective in relation to China that is lucid and consistent from a Marxian point of view, and moreover, brilliantly prophetic. With the world 'leaders of Trotskyism' still humming and hawing, the article goes straight to the point and applauds 'the destruction of feudalism and large-scale capitalism, in this important section of Asia, even though it is carried out under the leadership of Stalinism. In its long-term implications, it is as important as the October revolution itself.'

While hailing the social change as a huge step forward for the Chinese masses, the article also anticipates the setting up of another Moscow-like state: 'only a horrible caricature of the

Marxist conception of the revolution will result...Mao will look to Russia as his model.'

While all other theoreticians were hesitating to even accept the possibility of a deformed workers' state in China, Grant was already several steps ahead, predicting, years in advance, the inevitability of a break between the two mighty Stalinist states. Referring to the split that had already erupted beteen Yugoslavia and Russia, the article concludes: 'It is quite likely that Stalin will have a new Tito on his hands...Mao will have a powerful base in China with its 450-500 million population and its potential resources. The conflicts which will thus open out should be further means of assisting the world working class to understand the real nature of Stalinism.'

The clarity of the analysis and the perspective worked out in the above article did not mean that there was still not a great deal of confusion and questioning within the Trotskyist movement, not least in the ranks of the RCP. In a document that was in many respects typical of the doubts being raised, an RCP member, David James, wrote *Some Remarks on the Question of Stalinism* (dated February 1949). In this he questioned the conclusions arrived at in relation to China and Yugoslavia. This was published as a contribution to the internal discussion in the RCP, and precisely because it did reflect wider doubts about the leadership's (that is Ted Grant's) position it warranted a full reply.

This *Reply to David James*, forms the second part of this chapter. It deals once again with the Tito-Stalin split, in the same terms which it is dealt with in the previous chapter. 'The only difference between the regimes of Stalin and Tito', it says, 'is that the latter is still in its early stages. There is a remarkable similarity in the first upsurge of enthusiasm in Russia, when the bureaucracy introduced the first Five Year Plan, and the enthusiasm in Yugoslavia today.'

Using the method of Marxism to describe the regime of Tito, and hence explain the split with Stalin, the document takes the argument further and extends it to the example of China. It elaborates further the process by which Mao Tse Tung established his regime, explaining that it was, of necessity, 'deformed' from the very beginning: 'Basing itself upon the peasantry, it (the Chinese Stalinist leadership) enters the towns not with the aim and outlook of a genuine Communist Party, but with the aim of establishing its power by manoeuvring between the classes. It does so not by transferring its social basis to the proletariat – not as the direct representative of the proletariat as would a Bolshevik party –but in a Bonapartist manner.'

Just as Tito has been able to assert his independence of Moscow

—because he came to power largely through 'his own' Yugoslavian movement —so, therefore, Mao Tse Tung would also be able to assert his independence, by resting on the Peoples' Liberation Army and a nation of 500 million...'the danger of a new and really formidable Tito in China is a factor which is causing anxiety in Moscow'.

By the late 1950s, the predicted differences between Chinese and Russian Stalinism had begun to appear. Exchanges between the Russian leader Nikita Kruschev and Mao Tse Tung became increasingly bitter until, in mid 1960, there was a complete rupture, with the Soviet Union withdrawing all the scientists and technicians previously placed in China to aid its development. The public divisions between the Moscow and Peking bureaucracies had a profound effect on the Communist Parties throughout the capitalist world, with almost all of them suffering some split to form 'Maoist' parties.

As they had done previously with Tito, a section of the remnant of the 'Fourth International', now composed of small ultra-left sects, put Mao on a pedestal and hailed him as some sort of 'unconscious Trotskyist'. Encouraging the formation of Maoist Parties, one 'Trotskyist' sect even managed the brilliant feat of losing its members to the organisation, the first time in history that a 'Trotskyist' group participated in creating a Stalinist Party.

The third item in this chapter, *The Colonial Revolution and the Sino-Soviet Split*, is a document written in 1964, and first published by Sussex University Socialist Society. As the title implies, it once again explains the nature of the split between the Russian and the Chinese Stalinist bureaucracies, this time after the event, but it also extends the analysis of the Chinese revolution to encompass the broader processes of the colonial revolution.

At this time, at the height of the post-war boom, the ultra-left sects condemned the working class in the West as 'bourgeoisified', and turned their attention to the students and to the struggles for national liberation in the colonial world. For them, the centre of gravity of the world revolution was shifted from China to Cuba, from Cuba to Algeria, from Algeria to Vietnam, on each occasion slavishly and uncritically supporting the leadership of the liberation movements.

This document, therefore, was largely a polemic against these middle-class infatuations, providing a broad review of the colonial revolution. Building on the analysis first made in relation to China, it showed how similar processes could take place in smaller countries, like Burma, Vietnam and Cuba.

Referring to the war of liberation waged by the Vietnamese workers and peasants against US imperialism, the document pointed out that a victory for the Vietnamese people would be an historic step forward. But it correctly predicted that the regime that would be likely to be installed would be, like the government in North Vietnam, a deformed workers' state.

The general analysis gave a penetrating insight into the processes of the colonial revolution as they unfolded in a number of countries. It pointed to the tendency for the 'statification' of the economy, where there were radical regimes that faced grave economic crisis and the pressure of the masses, even though in some cases, like Egypt and Algeria, the process did not go all the way to the complete expropriation of landlordism and capitalism.

The fourth section of the chapter, *The Colonial Revolution and the Workers' States*, is yet a further development of the broad themes already worked out above. It was first published in the *Militant International Review*, in July 1978. In the fourteen years since the publication of the previous document, there had been a number of revolutionary movements in the third world which had resulted in the formation of proletarian Bonapartist states on the same lines as China and Russia.

These included Syria, Vietnam (unifying South and North), Laos, Kampuchea, Angola, Mozambique and Ethiopia. The formation of these states was consistent with the analysis of the colonial revolution already worked out in 1949, and elaborated since then. But in addition, in confirmation of the analysis of the origins of the Sino-Soviet split, some of the divisions between different bureaucracies had gone to the point of armed conflict. There had been armed clashes on the Russian-Chinese border, and on the Vietnamese borders with Kampuchea and China. There is no other explanation of the conflict between these alleged 'socialist' states, other than the basic position developed by Ted Grant at the time of the Tito-Stalin split, elaborated in relation to Chinese Stalinism and then further developed in his writing on the colonial revolution.

Particular attention is paid in this article to the position of Cuba and Ethiopia. In the case of the latter, a revolutionary movement overthrew the emperor, Haile Selassi, in 1974, and soon afterwards a military regime around Colonel Mengistu was consolidated by basing itself on the expropriation of landlordism and capitalism. This government, however, adopted the totalitarian methods characteristic of all the third world Stalinist states. In its policy towards its national minorities, it was no less repressive than the regime it replaced, and it became involved in wars against Eritrean guerrillas in the North and against Somali-backed secessionists in the Ogaden region.

It was at this point that the Russian Stalinists switched their support from Somalia (also a proletarian Bonapartist regime) to Ethiopia and began to give active assistance to the latter. The sectarian remnant of the old Fourth International now found itself in the impossible position of having to explain how a 'healthy workers' state' (Cuba) could be giving active support to a 'fascist state' (Ethiopia).

Once again, it was only possible to understand the events through the analysis previously worked out by Ted Grant, explaining how Stalinist states had come to be created in both Cuba and Ethiopia. This article, like the previous document, also illuminates the general processes taking place in the colonial revolution, referring, for example, to the coup in Afghanistan in 1978. This coup established the deformed workers' state which the Moscow bureaucracy set out to shore up by its invasion a year later, in December 1979.

No study by socialists of the colonial revolution today would be complete without the solid theoretical foundation —tested, re-tested and confirmed by events —laid down by Ted Grant in the form of the items in this chapter, as well as other related documents and articles by the same author, too numerous to be included.

A group of Chinese revolutionaries during the Long March.

From: The Chinese Revolution

January 1949

WITH THE spectacular advance of the Chinese Red Army, the diplomats of the State Department in America and the Foreign Office in Britain are seriously discussing the possibility of the complete collapse of the Chiang Kai Shek regime. The entire capitalist press writes gloomily of the prospect of North and Central China to the Yangtse coming under Stalinist sway.

Within three years of the collapse of Japanese imperialism, the Red Army has conquered Manchuria and most of North China. The Chinese capital Nanking, with the richest city of China, Shanghai, which has a population of five million, are rapidly coming within the grasp of the Red Army. The territory which the Stalinists already dominate has a population of more than 170 million.

The British capitalists, with investments in China amounting to £450 million, are dismayed at the prospect of the loss of this lucrative field of investment. American imperialism, within whose sphere of influence China fell with the weakening of the other imperialist powers during the war, has given the Kuomintang government aid to the extent of $3billion, in a fruitless attempt to save China for imperialist exploitation.

But the American imperialists now realise that further aid is merely throwing away good money after bad. With all the military and technical advantages in its favour in the early stages of the civil war that followed the world war, the Kuomintang has suffered defeat after defeat. The Kuomintang regime, under the dictatorial rule of Chiang Kai Shek, represents the feudal landlords and capitalists. It is controlled by an utterly corrupt military clique which oppresses the workers and peasants and battens on their masters.

Chiang Kai Shek came to power after the defeat of the Chinese revolution of 1925-7 in which he played the role of chief butcher of the working class. He succeeded in this because of the policy of Stalin and Bukharin and the leadership of the Chinese Communist Party. Their policy then was to form a bloc with the Chinese landlords, capitalists and feudal warlords, allegedly in the interests of the struggle against imperialism. In consequence, they sabotaged the attempts of the workers to take over the factories and the peasants to take the land. A 'communist' Minister of Labour sabotaged strikes and punished striking workers. A 'communist' Minister of Agriculture had peasants shot down when they attempted to seize the land.

The capitalist Kuomintang was taken into the Communist International as a sympathising section. In *The Third International After Lenin* by Trotsky, the Stalinists' role is shown in an explanatory note:

> The Kuomintang was admitted to the Comintern as a sympathising party early in 1926, approved by the Politbureau of the CPSU, with the sole dissenting vote of Trotsky. Hu Han-min, right-wing Kuomintang leader, participated in the Sixth Plenum of the ECCI, February, 1926, as a fraternal delegate from the Kuomintang. Shao Ki-tze a henchman of Chiang Kai Shek, was fraternal delegate to the Seventh Plenum, ECCI, November, 1926 (*Minutes* German edition pp. 403f.). (London edition, 1936).

On March 21 and 22, 1927, the workers of Shanghai captured the city. Chiang immediately began preparations to butcher them. He conspired with the imperialists to crush the workers.

Instead of preparing for the struggle the Stalinists gave full support to Chiang. The Comintern official journal *International Press Correspondence*, French edition, March 23, 1927, page 443, said: 'Far from dividing, as the imperialists say, the Kuomintang has only steeled its ranks.'

On March 30 they wrote:

> A split in the Kuomintang and hostilities between the Shanghai proletariat and the revolutionary soldiers are absolutely excluded for the moment....Chiang Kai Shek....himself declared that he would submit to the decisions of the party....A revolutionist like Chiang Kai Shek will not go over, as the imperialists would like to have it believed, to Chang Tao-lin (the Northern militarist) to fight against the emancipation movement....

Chiang proceeded to organise a coup, massacre the flower of the workers, illegalise the trade unions, the peasant organisations, the Communist Party, and deprive the masses of all rights.

The masses were utterly defeated and the remnants of the

Chinese leadership of the Communist Party fled to the peasant areas —and there tried to organise a peasant war.

Peasant Army

The guerrilla struggle threw up leaders of remarkable military genius. Mao Tse Tung, Chu Teh* and others succeeded in evading the poweful military forces which the Kuomintang had arrayed against them. Despite the false political line which led to successive disasters, in one of the most remarkable military feats in world history, Mao was driven from Central and South China in a 6,000-mile retreat to the mountain fastnesses around Yenan, where a 'soviet' republic was set up. There, despite all the efforts of the Chiang regime to dislodge them, they succeeded in holding out against one attack after another. The secret of their success was that the land had been divided among the peasants in this small area, comprising, according to some estimates, about 10 million population.

In the intervening period between the wars, the Chiang regime piled up ever increasing burdens on the workers and peasants. In some areas the taxes were collected from the peasants by the corrupt local officials *80 years in advance.*

There was an endless militaristic squandering of wealth, and the feeble Kuomintang regime showed itself incapable of waging a revolutionary struggle against the incursions of imperialistic Japan.

The Chiang regime resolved itself into one of bribery and police terror. In a period of two decades it became so completely degenerate from top to bottom that it had lost most of its support even among the middle class.

After the collapse of Japan, with a certain aid from the Red Army in Manchuria which helped the Stalinists to capture Japanese munitions, large parts of Manchuria and the North fell into the hands of the Stalinists. The Chinese Red Army had waged a guerrilla struggle against Japanese militarism throughout the war and were in a strategic position to seize certain areas with the Japanese collapse. Even throughout the war Chiang's main preoccupation was the social danger at home, to deal with the Stalinists and workers, and had it not been clear that Japan was going to be defeated in the later stages, it is quite likely that he would have capitulated and made a compromise with Japanese imperialism.

*Chu Teh joined the Chinese CP (CCP) in 1922. His military forces joined with those led by Mao Tse Tung in 1928. Chu became the principal military leader of the CCP on the long March and in the civil war against Japan.

A Dying Regime

American imperialism assisted Chiang by pouring in munitions and other supplies, and even direct military intervention in the transport of Kuomintang troops to Manchuria and North China by the US fleet and air force. Chiang had initial successes, but all in vain. He was leading a dying regime, more archaic than even the Czarist regime in Russia. So rotten was the regime that large parts of the supplies were *sold* by officials to the Stalinist armies for gold, and ministers and other officials in Chiang's government pocketed a great part of the dollars supplied for the war by America. Only the lesser part of the supplies and munitions actually reached the Nationalist troops at the front.

The military commanders ceaselessly intrigued against one another, as in all doomed regimes. Chiang, for example, starved General Fu Tso Yi, the only outstanding general who showed any real capacity on the Nationalist side, of supplies, for fear he might seek to replace him. The generals were outclassed by the superior strategy and tactics of the Red Army command.

Social Questions Involved

However, the main reason for the victories of the Chinese Stalinists has been readily pointed out by Mao Tse Tung: *the social questions involved.* 'Land to the peasants,' as in the Russian revolution, sounded the death knell of feudal landowners and their corrupt regime. In large part, the Chinese Stalinists have carried out the agrarian revolution. That is the significant difference between the struggle in 1927 and now. It is this which has been responsible for the melting away of the armies which Chiang tried to use to crush the agrarian rebellion. Chiang's armies are composed of peasants —the poorest peasants at that —who have not enough money to escape conscription by bribing the officials.

Even the *News Chronicle* (11 December 1948) admits:

> There is discontent among the rank and file of the Nationalist army. Chiang's privates get about five pence a month.
>
> In some villages conscripts are roped together on the way to barracks, and when they travel by train carriage doors and wagons are locked so that they cannot escape.

Naturally, they desert with their arms, even to the extent of whole divisions when confronted with the agrarian programme of the Stalinists.

The Stalinist Agrarian Programme

At the national agrarian conference of the Chinese Communist party held on September 13, 1947, it was proposed to carry through an agrarian law containing the following provisions:

> Article 1. The agrarian system of feudal and semi-feudal exploitation is abolished. The agrarian system of 'land to the tiller' is to be established.
> Article 2. The land ownership rights of all landlords are abolished.
> Article 3. The land ownership rights of all ancestral shrines, temples, monasteries, schools, institutions, and organisations, are abolished.
> Article 4. All debts incurred in the countryside prior to the reform of the agrarian system are cancelled.

Article 10, aimed directly at the soldiers and even the officers of the Kuomintang reads, in part:

> Section c. All personnel of the People's Liberation Armies, democratic governments, and all peoples' organisations whose home is in the countryside shall be given land and properties equivalent to that of peasants for themselves and their families.
> Section d. Landlords and their families shall be given land and properties equivalent to that of the peasants.
> Section e. Families of Kuomintang officers and soldiers, Kuomintang Party members and other enemy personnel whose homes are in rural areas, shall be given land and properties equivalent to that of the peasants.

One of the outstanding facts in the situation in China is the *relative passivity of the working class*. It is true that as a result of the collapse of the Chiang armies, there have been widespread strike struggles in the large cities, Shanghai, Canton, Hankow and Nanking, despite the repressive conditions. However, it is clear that as the Stalinists advance towards the big cities on the Yangtse, the workers, for lack of a mass alternative, can only rally to their banner. The workers never supported the Chiang Kai Shek regime.

Every socialist worker will wholeheartedly applaud the destruction of feudalism and of large-scale capitalism in this important section of Asia, even though it is carried out under the leadership of Stalinism. In its *long-term implications* it is as important as the October revolution itself. One could give no better Marxist analysis of the gloomy picture for the world capitalist class than that expressed in the editorial of *The Times*, 10 November 1948:

At the best this spells only a single check (Hsuchow held by the Nationalists at the time and since fallen) after months of gains which have swung the balance of power – military, industrial, ideological – to the communist side. Their widening hold on large areas of Northern and Central China has a much deeper meaning than the Japanese invasion of ten years ago, for the communists – decisively helped by Russia as they have been and Marxists as they remain – summon up and organise native revolutionary forces. In its vastness and in its all too likely consequences the present upheaval has rather to be compared with the Russian revolution of 1917 – from which it directly and obviously springs. Wider success for the Chinese communists would offer wider influence, and at the ripe moment wider success, for the power with which they ally themselves. Long-cherished Soviet plans for swinging the backward millions of Asia into the camp which already stretches from the Oder to Sakhalin would receive the greatest measure of reinforcement so far.

...They can draw upon the peasantry for their divisions, and they have been able to win over the support of the peasantry by expropriating most of the landlords and redistributing the land. So far the agricultural reforms of the communists have prospered the more obviously because they have not had to feed many large towns; the food has mainly been kept in the country areas.

In some regions a commander has ruthlessly shot or imprisoned those whom he has judged to be anti-communist; in others there has been a show of tolerance with few changes in the traditional way of life. Businessmen and others have even been given the choice of staying or leaving. This show of tolerance seems to be the policy of Mao Tse Tung, the highly astute communist leader. His writings and speeches show him to be an unshakeable Marxist, but one who recognises that Marx's analysis of the opportunities for revolution in the industrial Europe of last century cannot be applied strictly to the mainly agricultural and primitive state of much of China. He seems to have decided to reach his communist goal by two stages. First, there is to be a system of relatively free trading, similar to the New Economic Policy which Lenin introduced after the initial failure of militant communism in Russia. It is this stage which he proclaims at present, hoping, not without success – not only to win the peasants but to assuage the fears of many townspeople. Secondly when the first stage has been accomplished, he plans to make the further step to Marxist socialism.

The references to Marxism and the communist policy of Mao are of course false. The policy of Stalinism in Russia, in Eastern Europe and in China has been labelled Marxist by all present day capitalist journalists. It is a perversion of Marxism. Nevertheless *The Times* sees that the tactics of the Chinese Stalinists will be similar to those of the Stalinists in Eastern Europe.

Two Sides of The Coin

While supporting the destruction of feudalism in China, it must be emphasised that only a horrible caricature of the Marxist conception of the revolution will result because of the leadership of the Stalinists. Not a real democracy, but a totalitarian regime as brutal as that of Chiang Kai Shek will develop. Like the regimes in Eastern Europe, Mao will look to Russia as his model. Undoubtedly, tremendous economic progress will be achieved. But the masses, both workers and peasants, will find themselves enslaved by the bureaucracy.

The Stalinists are incorporating into their regime ex-feudal militarists, capitalist elements, and the bureaucratic officialdom in the towns who will occupy positions of privilege and power.

On the basis of such a backward economy, a large scale differentiation among the peasants (as after the Russian revolution during the period of the NEP) aided by the failure to nationalise the land: the capitalist elements in trade, and even in light industry, might provide a base for capitalist counter-revolution. It must be borne in mind that in China the proletariat is weaker in relation to the peasantry than was the case in Russia during the NEP owing to the more backward development of China. Even in Czechoslovakia and other Eastern European countries similarly, where the capitalist elements were relatively weaker, nevertheless the danger of a capitalist overturn existed for a time. The fact that the workers and peasants will not have any democratic control and that the totalitarian tyranny will have superimposed upon it the Asiatic barbarism and cruelties of the old regime, gives rise to this possibility. However, it seems likely that the capitalist elements will be defeated because of the historical tendency of the decay of capitalism on a world scale. The impotence of world imperialism is shown by the fact that whereas they intervened directly against the Chinese revolution in 1925-7, today they look on helplessly at the collapse of the Chiang regime.

However, it is quite likely that Stalin will have a new Tito on his hands. The shrewder capitalist commentators are already speculating on this although they derive cold comfort from it. Mao will have a powerful base in China with its 450-500 million population and its potential resources, and the undoubted mass support his regime will possess in the early stages. The conflicts which will thus open out should be further means of assisting the world working class to understand the real nature of Stalinism.

From....Reply to David James

Spring 1949

THE *BULLETIN* of comrade David James will serve a useful purpose if it assists us in facing squarely the new situation in the Stalinist controlled areas and making the necessary reorientation in perspective. However, there are certain dangers inherent in his *Bulletin* which, if not counteracted, could lead to a capitulation to neo-Stalinism. Its basic weakness lies in this: he abstracts and counterposes mechanically the state as a direct reflection of a class and sees all conflicts that arise within society as *immediately and directly reflecting antagonistic classes*. This leads him to the erroneous conclusion that struggles within the Stalinist bureaucracy must necessarily directly reflect antagonistic class interests.

The Marxist method starts with a class analysis of society and any of its phenomena or organs, but it does not end there. It is necessary from there to analyse all the cross-currents and interactions within the given class definition. In dealing with Yugoslavia and China, it is necessary first to have the essentials firmly in mind. Without the existence of Russia as a degenerate workers' state, without the weakening of world imperialism as a result of the war, Eastern Europe would have taken on an entirely different pattern. These events can only be explained on the basis of the survival of Russia with its nationalised property forms; the survival of Stalinism at the helm of a vastly strengthened Russia as the outcome of the war. It is this which led to the extension of the revolution in a deformed, Stalinist shape, to the other countries.

On the class nature of the states in Eastern Europe, there is agreement with comrade James. But precisely here the question is posed: once the class nature of the state has been defined, a whole series of intermediate, superstructural and other factors must be taken into account in determining one's policy towards the given state or party. The bare class analysis is not sufficient as a guide.

For example, there can be different varieties of bourgeois states —fascist, bourgeois democratic, Bonapartist dictatorship, etc —the differences between them being of great importance in determining our attitude. The attitude of the revolutionaries towards the workers' state under the leadership of Lenin, differed profoundly from their attitude towards the workers' state under the leadership of Stalin.

Comrade James writes:

> The Revolutionary Communist Party (RCP)....had come to the conclusion that the regimes in the USSR and the satellite states were basically identical, and we saw this (Tito-Stalin) clash as a crisis within Stalinism itself rather than between states of different social character.... There, however, we stopped....We failed ourselves to give a class characterisation of the Tito movement.... We say that it is a clash between two Stalinist bureaucracies or two sections of the bureaucracy. But when Trotsky spoke of the possibility of such an event, he was careful to describe the class lines on which it would break: he spoke of the 'fraction of Butenko'* (bourgeois fascist) and the 'fraction of Reiss' (proletarian internationalist). This was a necessary conclusion from his position that the bureaucracy is not a class but a caste, whose evolution is determined by the contending influences of the two decisive classes in society. We stand on the same ground, and we must ask: does Tito represent a workers' or a capitalist tendency? By failing to pose this question, we ourselves abandon the class criterion, abandon the Marxist method, and thereby ensure that we should not understand the events.

Where comrade James makes the mistake here, is in assuming that once the class basis has been decided, the problems are simple, and that all tendencies which are manifest must be a *direct reflection* of the *interests of opposing classes*. But he has only to ask himself the question: what class does Stalin represent in the struggle against Tito? And what class does Tito represent when he has already agreed by definition that the class basis of the regimes are 'basically identical'? Is there a struggle between the Yugoslav working class and the Russian working class? Clearly there is something wrong here.

First, we want to take up James's reference to Trotsky in this connection. It is true that Trotsky argued that different sections of the bureaucracy would tend to reflect class interests, one faction going with the proletariat and the other with the bourgeoisie. Butenko went over to the fascists in Italy. He did not represent any social grouping within Russia, but was merely an isolated case with no roots. Reiss represented the proletarian wing and as such found

---

*Fyodor Butenko was a Stalinist diplomat who defected to fascism in 1938. Ignace Reiss (Poretsky) was a GPU official who broke with Stalinism in summer 1937. He was murdered by the GPU in September 1937.

himself in the Fourth International. Trotsky did visualise the development of strong capitalist currents, as well as the strong proletarian currents at a time of crisis — that there would be a split in the bureaucracy under the pressure of class forces. But the differentiation which he expected, particularly during the war, did not take place. But Trotsky did produce arguments which were far more to the point in explaining clearly what forces are represented in the struggle within the bureaucracy, or as in the present discussion, between the two different workers' bureaucracies. We refer here to the Ukraine.

The Old Man pointed out that in the Ukraine after the purge of the Trotskyists and Bukharinites*, *nine-tenths of all Stalinist officials in the heads of the departments of government in the national republic were imprisoned, exiled and executed.* Did they represent a different class from Stalin? Of course not! They reflected the pressure and discontent of the Ukraine masses *against the national oppression of the great Russian bureaucracy.* The Ukrainian masses were oppressed not only as workers and peasants by the bureaucracy, but as Ukrainians. Hence the struggle for national liberation in the Ukraine. This was not confined to the Ukraine. The same process took place in all the national republics of Russia, oppressed by the Russian bureaucracy. The Stalinist officialdom in all these were, to one degree or another, affected by the prevailing mood of hatred against the bureaucratic centralising tendencies of Great Russian chauvinism centred in Moscow. According to Colonel Tokaev, writing in the *Sunday Express,* there were national uprisings during the war in the Crimea, the Caucasus and some of the other national republics. After the war, the great Russian bureaucracy punished this 'disloyalty' by banishing the entire populations of some of the national republics of the Crimea and others and dissolving the republics, in violation of even the paper constitution of Stalin. Clearly this was intended as a warning against disaffection in other republics.

This is the analogy with Yugoslavia. In the purge in the Ukraine, Trotsky showed that here it was not a case of different classes involved, but of different nations oppressed by the bureaucracy. *The Ukrainian Stalinists did not represent the fraction of Butenko, nor did they represent the fraction of Reiss.* What they wanted was more autonomy and more control for the Ukrainians (which meant themselves) over the national destinies of their republic. The fact that a national struggle of this character can take place after the proletarian revolution, is merely an indication of how far the

*Named after Old Bolshevik Nikolai Bukharin, they were the right opposition in the USSR. After the expulsion of the Left Opposition in 1927, Stalin turned on the Bukharinites.

revolution has been thrown back under Stalinist domination. (Here let us add that Lenin, with his far-sighted national policy, surprisingly raised in advance the possibility of clashes between different nationalities even after the abolition of capitalism. National cultures and aspirations will remain long after the proletarian revolution has taken place, even on a world scale and will constitute an important problem.)

One can say that in Yugoslavia and Eastern Europe, Stalin has attempted to carry through a similar bureaucratic policy as in the republics in Russia. The only difference in Yugoslavia is that the Russian bureaucracy did not have as firm control over the state machine as they had in the other satellite states. This was, of course, due to the fact that while in the other countries it was the entry of the Red Army which smashed the bourgeois state and precipitated the movement of the masses, in Yugoslavia, Tito had a mass base and built up a machine which he had under control, even under the Germans. The Red Army assisted in the liberation of Belgrade, but undoubtedly Tito had a far more popular base among the masses than in the other satellite states. In the eyes of the Yugoslavs, their liberation from German imperialism was achieved under the leadership of Tito and the Yugoslav CP. Thus, Stalin's attempt to completely subordinate Yugoslavia to the Moscow bureaucracy met with resistance from the local bureaucrats, who felt confident that they would have the backing of the masses. As distinct from this, the regimes in the other satellite states felt the need to *lean on the Moscow bureaucracy,* owing to a fear of the difficulties at home in the event of a conflict.

Stalin encountered difficulty in applying in Yugoslavia a Ukraine solution, or even a pseudo-independent solution as in Poland, where the joke circulates that Cyrankiewicz* phones the Kremlin to find out if he can take the night off to go to the cinema. Stalin's attempts to intervene in Yugoslavia resulted for the first time, in the arrest of *his* stooges instead of vice versa. It was as if the Ukrainian Stalinists had had their own state forces and backing of the masses, separate and powerful enough to oppose the Russian MVD, etc. On that basis, they could have resisted the demands of complete subordination to the Moscow bureaucracy.

This explained why Trotsky considered the *national question* to be of such importance that he put forward the demand for an *independent* socialist soviet Ukraine. At first sight this would appear to come into conflict with the strategy of the unification of all Europe in a socialist united states. From a purely pedantic point of

*Josef Cryankiewicz was secretary general of the Polish Socialist Party, became Prime Minister in 1947. In 1948 he forced through 'unification' of the PSP with the CP.

view it would appear that the enemy of the Ukrainian and Great Russian masses is the same and the task is a simple one of unifying their struggle for control in one unified state. Merely to find the class basis does not supply the answer. *The class basis of the Ukrainian bureaucrats is no different from that of the Russian bureaucrats.* Yet they come into conflict with one another and the victorious section savagely executes the other.

Similarly, it is clear that the mere fact that Tito is, for the time being, victorious, no more turns him into an unconscious Trotskyist than the Ukrainian bureaucrats.

Through the dictatorship of the Stalinist bureaucracy is expressed indirectly the rule of the proletariat. For the Soviet Union to return to a healthy basis, a new revolution, a political revolution, is necessary. The economic basis will remain the same, though of course the social consequences will result in profound changes in the overall plan, the division of income, the culture, etc. As in the case of France —where a regime of bourgeois autocracy required revolution before it could become bourgeois democracy, so in Russia, revolution will be required to transform the bureaucratic totalitarian regime into a really democratic one. The political revolution in France resulted in profound changes in its social consequences —different division of income, freer development of the productive forces, culture, etc. But the fundamental structure of the system remained the same. So in Russia, the class basis will remain: the superstructure will change. On this there is common agreement with James. But what of Yugoslavia?

What was an unconscious process in the early stages of Stalinist degeneration in Russia, is a semi-conscious or even conscious process in Yugoslavia. The regime of Tito is very similar to the regime of Stalin during the period of 1923-8. After the experience of Russia, it is clear that where there is no democracy, where no opposition is tolerated, where a totalitarian regime exists, then developments will proceed on the same pattern as in Russia. Here precisely it is not a question of the psychology of Tito or Stalin, but the relentless interests of the differing tendencies at work within society.

The state, as a special superstructural formation standing over society, of necessity tends to form a grouping with habits of thought, used to command, with privileges of education and culture. The tendency is to crystallise a caste with an outlook of its own, different from the class it represents. This is accentuated where the state takes over the means of production; the sole commanding stratum in society is the bureaucracy. Not for nothing did Marx and Lenin emphasise the need for the masses to retain control of the state or semi-state, because without this, new trends and tendencies are introduced which have a law of motion of their own.

If one would assume theoretically (abstracting the Stalin regimes for the moment from the world relationships and the internal social contradictions) that such a caste could maintain itself indefinitely (the modest estimate of a leading Siberian Stalinist was 1,000 years) *—it could not lead to an amelioration of the social contradictions or to the painless withering away of the state into society.* All the laws of social evolution, of the development of the classes and castes in society speak against this. Far from developing in the direction of communism, such a society, if it depended on the will of the bureaucracy, would inevitably develop into a slave state with a hierarchy of castes such as visualised by Jack London in his picture of the oligarchy under the *Iron Heel.*

Socialism does not arise automatically out of the development of the productive forces themselves. If it were purely a question of the automatic change in society once the productive forces are developed, revolution would not have been necessary in the changes from one society to another. As has been explained many times, the nationalisation of the productive forces alone does not abolish all social contradictions —otherwise there would be socialism in Russia. Once the bureaucracy gets a vested interest of its own, it will never voluntarily relinquish its privileged position. A further development of the productive forces will merely create new needs and open new vistas for the bureaucracy to dispose of the surplus in their interests. This is already shown by the development of the bureaucracy as a more and more rapacious and hereditary caste, instead of less and less with the development of the productive forces in Russia. (Here we are not dealing with inevitable movements of revolt on the part of the masses, the contradictions engendered by bureaucratic misrule which must lead to explosions, etc. This whole problem requires further elaboration).

The degeneration of Russia was not accidental. Where the proletariat has control, its position in society determines its consciousness and determines the evolution of that society in the direction of the liquidation of the state and the establishment of communism. Where the bureaucracy has control, its position in society determines its consciousness and determines the evolution of that society not towards its voluntary liquidation and communism, but to its own reinforcement. Conditions determine consciousness. And the methods, the organisation, the outlook and ideology of Tito and Mao are the same as those of the Russian Stalinists: not democratic centralism, but its opposite —totalitarian bureaucracy is what they base themselves on. The Cominform criticism of the 'Turkish terror' is well founded. All that Tito could reply in answer to the accusation that the discussion for the Party Congress was a farce, that no-one dared to oppose the resolution of the Central Committee, or even vote against it for fear of immediate arrest, that there was a dictatorship in the party and in the country —all that he could reply was to liken the criticism of the Cominform to that of the Left Opposition at the 1927 Congress of the CPSU.

Almost word for word the description of the situation was the same, except that *in Russia in 1927 there was more democracy as a lingering survival of the past than there is in Yugoslavia today.* At least before their expulsion, the Opposition was allowed to put forward its position at the Congress, and Stalin had not yet evolved the complete totalitarian technique of suppression. There was still the faction of Bukharin, etc, in the party. Stalin still had no idea of which way he was going. Tito has taken over *in toto,* the organisation, the ideology, the technique of Bonapartist rule.

The only difference between the regimes of Stalin and Tito is that the latter is still in its early stages. There is a remarkable similarity in the first upsurge of enthusiasm in Russia where the bureaucracy introduced the first Five Year Plan, and the enthusiasm in Yugoslavia today.

While Stalin can only rule through more and more unbridled terror, Tito, for the present, probably retains the support of the big majority of the population of Yugoslavia. But this is not a fundamental difference, it is a question of tempo and the experience of the masses.

If the difference between the living standards of the bureaucracy and of the masses in Yugoslavia (as in Poland, Czechoslovakia, Hungary, Rumania, etc —let us not forget this) is incomparably smaller than in Russia today, that is because after the upheavals which have involved the masses, it would be impossible to immediately introduce enormous inequalities.

As the bureaucracy would express it, 'socialism has not yet been realised', namely their complete and untrammelled domination has not yet crystallised out; their mode of existence has not yet reached a fairly stable position. And, moreover, on the basis of a backward economy (apart from Czechoslovakia) the productive forces are not yet sufficient to serve the needs of an expanding economy, together with an inflated standard of luxury for the commanding strata. It required in Russia a tremendous development of the economy before the basis was laid for the differentiation which has steadily increased with the development of the economy itself.

So in Yugoslavia, it can be predicted that only with the industrialisation of the country and raising the level of the productive forces from the pitifully low level, will the differentiation between the bureaucracy and the masses develop on similar lines. If Tito or any other individual tried to arrest this process, under the given conditions, they would be removed one way or another as the Old Bolsheviks were removed in Russia. Their fate was not accidental. The bureaucratic caste needed people who based themselves not on the proletariat, but on a new strata. The 'theories' of Tito are flesh of the flesh of the Bonapartist clique in the Kremlin, who educated and trained him. Even in his marshall's uniform, he slavishly reflects the ideology and methods of his tutors. The personal rule, the whole method of the Yugoslav bureaucracy, possibly more exactly than the other Eastern European states, reflects the same byzantine adulation and method as the Kremlin. As distinct from the Stalin of 1927, Tito has the ready-made pattern and it is therefore more likely that the differentiation and the excess which necessarily follow autocratic state dictatorship, will be far faster.

Between Tito and Stalin there is no difference in principle. Indeed, perhaps one of the most amusing and diverting episodes in this struggle was the spectacle of Tito raising aloft the banner of 'socialism in one country' and the Stalinists raising the banner of 'internationalism'. There is nothing in the perspective of Tito to show that only the victory of the proletariat in the advanced countries can solve the problems of the Russian and Yugoslavian masses through the international division of labour, interlinking the economies, nothing to show that Tito seeks to establish workers' democracy and control. Indeed, he has only praise for what Stalin is doing in Russia. All his actions and utterances reflect the interests of a Bonapartist bureaucracy. His 'love of gorgeous uniforms' is not just a 'drawback', it is symptomatic of his regime. Far more than Stalin of 1927, he reflects personal rule —the dictatorship of the bureaucracy reflected in a single individual.

Events in Yugoslavia amazingly recapitulate the phases which the Stalinist bureaucracies went through, even to the extent of the opportunism in relation to the peasants, followed by panic measures against the kulaks and the small proprietors in the towns. Already the first 'sabotage' trials have taken place where Tito puts responsibility for any deficiencies in the Plan on the shoulders of his opponents. Similarly we have the pattern of the Russian 'confession' trials on a smaller scale. The familiar outlines of the Stalinist police state are clear to see. The differences are superficial; the fundamental traits the same.

Tito's 'penchant' for murdering Trotskyists is not just a distressing by-product. Why does he murder Trotskyists? Because they bear the hated name of Leon Trotsky? Obviously because they represent the proletariat; because they fight for workers' democracy, for genuine elections, for internationalism, for all the basic tenets of the programme of international communism, as opposed to bureaucratic absolutism. Here it is not a question of having murdered his opponents and then adopting the programme of the people he has martyred. Trotsky replied to those who argued thus when the whole strata of Old Bolsheviks capitulated after Stalin introduced the Five Year Plan (originally put forward by the Left Opposition)* and conducted a drive against the kulaks and capitalist elements. The Left Opposition showed how Stalin annihilated the opposition and then borrowed their programme, which he carried through in a distorted way. They did not thereby conclude that Stalin was unconsciously a Leninist. They warned that it was not only a question of what was done, but who was doing it, how it was done, in whose interests and for what reasons. That was the decisive question!

Events demonstrated that it was not the capitulators to Stalin, but Trotsky who was right when he said that Stalinism, despite its introduction of the Five Year Plans, could not lead Russia to socialism. Kamenev, Zinoviev, Rakovsky, Bukharin *et al*, capitulated in vain. Finally they paid with their lives, because they could not reconcile themselves with the Bonapartist clique.

Stalin's turn in 1927 and his attack on the bourgeoisie in town and country, although it received the enthusiastic support of the proletariat, was dictated by the interests of self-preservation of the bureaucracy. As Trotsky expressed it, the Russian bureaucracy wanted the state feed-bag for itself and did not wish to share with the bourgeoisie, or have its position limited by the bourgeoisie in the disposal of the surplus produced by the proletariat. But their attack on the bourgeoisie did not lead to a freer and wider democracy for the proletariat; or to the diminishing of the differentiation between bureaucrats and the proletariat. Finally, it did not prevent the introduction of slavery in Russia.

Similarly, Tito has undoubtedly the support of the Yugoslav masses in his struggle against the Russian bureaucracy. In the struggle for the realisation of the Five Year Plan, the Bolshevik wing gave critical support to the bureaucracy against the

---

*The demand for a five year plan was first raised by the Left Opposition in 1923. As late as April 1927 Stalin mocked calls for electrification, then at the end of 1927 the bureaucracy conducted a sharp turn in face of the growth of the rich peasants and adopted many of the Opposition's plans, albeit in a distorted form.

bourgeoisie. In the same way, the Fourth International must give critical support to the Yugoslav bureaucracy because it represents in its struggle a progressive step forward, in that it helps to weaken the Russian bureaucracy and above all, because *we support the principle of the right of self-determination.* In the same way, we would have supported the struggle of the Ukrainian Stalinists in their struggle against the Russian bureaucracy. Once having achieved the right of self-determination, we would advocate the independent Ukraine be united in a federation with Russia.

However, we cannot and must not capitulate before these events, or have any illusions as to the motives, the aims and methods of the Yugoslav bureaucracy. Just as Stalin was not converted into a Trotskyist, conscious or unconscious, by his struggle against the bourgeoisie, so Tito does not become an unconscious Trotskyist because he has broken with the Kremlin and uses correct arguments on the national question and the right of self-determination.

For Tito, this period is not a stage towards socialism. It is a stage towards the consolidation of his rule. His aim is 'socialism' on the pattern of Russia. While the bureaucracy plays a relatively progressive role in developing the productive forces on the basis of nationalised property, they prepare the material base for the future. At the same time, the social contradictions will grow. From playing a relatively progressive role under the given conditions, the role of the bureaucracy will become completely reactionary. Far from the oppressive forces of the state withering away, they will be reinforced. The tasks of the proletariat are similar to those of the Russian proletariat, to the Bulgarian and the Czech proletariat.

Material for the Fourth International?

From the fact that the revolution —and undoubtedly it is a revolution taking place in China —springs from the 'innermost needs of the country' and is not merely a creation of Moscow, comrade James draws the conclusion that therefore Mao must be an unconscious Trotskyist:

> The RCP's position is vague, but at least we can say that it places Stalin and Tito on the same footing, and regards the overthrow of both as essential for socialist advance. Let us see how these will stand the test of a fresh event, the victory of Stalinism in China.
>
> The neo-Stalinist attitude will stand this test. As I remarked before, the Yugoslav revolution appears to have sprung from the innermost needs of the country, and not to have been imposed by Moscow, but no doubt is possible in the case of China. Clearly the revolution is primarily a native affair, consequently Mao, like Tito, is a genuine revolutionist

an 'unconscious Trotskyist', and fit material for recruitment to the
Fourth International. (Doubtless the IS is preparing a letter along
these lines). On the other hand if the IS insists on regarding the
Chinese Stalinist regime, like Yugoslavia, to be degenerate, we are
again faced with the question, 'what is the source of this early
degeneration?'
The RCP position on the other hand finally collapses. By no stretch
of the imagination can Red China be conceived as a Russian creation.
If we regard Mao, like Tito, as being equally as bad as Stalin, we must
acknowledge that the features which cause us to take this attitude are
inherent in the revolution. That is, it is not a degenerated workers'
state, but a bureaucratic class state, ie, we arrive at Shachtman's
position.

It is a truism in the Marxist movement that David James will no
doubt accept, that one must take a phenomenon not in isolation,
but in the context of its origin, laws of motion and perspective. But
it is one thing to accept this in words; it is another to apply it. James
says in effect, that a revolution is taking place in China, therefore it
is the same as the October revolution. Mao is leading this
revolution, therefore Mao is a Chinese Leninist or Trotskyist. The
Chinese Stalinists are leading the revolution, therefore why the
need for the Fourth International? One can explain the
development of the Stalinist degeneration in Russia by the
preceding world developments, the failure of the revolution in the
West, etc. Similarly, one can only explain the events in China, by
the existence of a strong but degenerate Russian workers' state; by
the weakness of world imperialism which found it impossible to
intervene in China effectively, as it did in 1925-7; by the internal
decay of Chinese society and by the history and developments of
the Chinese Stalinist movement.
It is unprecedented in the history of Marxism, that a revolution
which leads to the nationalisation of property and the division of
land, should begin among the peasantry and not the working class.
How is this to be explained?
Paradoxically, this peasant movement is an off-shoot of the
defeat of the revolution of 1925-7. With the defeat of the
proletariat, the Chinese Stalinists transferred their base from the
proletariat to the peasantry. It cut itself adrift from the cities and
led a peasant war. Its whole social basis, the psychology of its
leadership, which has been in the mountains and rural areas for
more than 20 years, became divorced from the working class and
its outlook. The psychology of this group was necessarily
determined by their conditions of life. The original nucleus that
formed the leadership and staff of this movement, was composed
of a small proportion of ex-worker militants, bandits, ex-peasants,

adventurers and intellectuals. In that sense, it was a classical Bonapartist grouping. It fused itself into an army.

Even at the dawn of the peasant war, at a time when the Stalinists were pursuing an ultra-left course and the links with the cities were not yet completely broken, the inevitable psychology of a Bonapartist army was being engendered by the whole environment. The Comintern and Chinese leadership — at that time not yet completely degenerate — regarded this process, even in the lower ranks, with a certain foreboding. For example, 'unions' were formed in the so-called 'soviet' districts in those days. Isaacs, in his *Tragedy of the Chinese Revolution* wrote:

> But the character of these unions, whatever their number, was so dubious that even the trade-union centre of the party at Shanghai had to complain. In its report for 1931 it spoke of the presence of 'shopkeepers and rich peasants' in the unions. The next year, it addressed a scorching letter to the trade-union officials in Kiangsi in which it accused them of admitting 'peasants, priests, shop-owners, foremen, rich peasants and landlords', while 'on the other hand, considerable sections of the agricultural labourers, coolies, employees and artisans are on various pretexts barred from membership'. The Party comrades engaged on this work were accused of being 'contemptuous of the workers and insolent toward them'. The letter described the unions as 'anti-proletarian in character, representing more the interests of the landlords, rich peasants and employees'.

Comrade James overlooks the relation of classes, groupings and castes in society. For example, in 1923 it is an undoubted fact that Trotsky, who was popular with the entire Red Army and popular among the masses, could have organised a coup through the army, arrested Stalin and the others and taken control of the state machine. Eastman*, never having understood the process, plaintively castigated Trotsky for being such a simpleton. Why didn't he? The reason was that the army, having come to power, would have exerted a specific weight of its own in society. Its officer caste would have been imbued with the idea that they were the masters. It would not have prevented the Bonapartist degeneration, it would merely have taken a different form. If Trotsky had tried to resist the process of degeneration, he would either have been a prisoner of the officer caste or would have been removed. Trotsky tried to base himself on the consciousness and control of the proletariat as the only force which could lead to a classless society. He knew that otherwise, the workers would have

*Max Eastman was the American translator of several of Trotsky's books. While sympathetic to the Left Opposition he never joined its ranks. He broke with Marxism in the late 1930's.

been onlookers, the army the decisive factor, with fatal consequences to the development of the revolution.

That is why comrade James's whole question as to whether the degeneration must be inherent in the revolution from the beginning is beside the mark. It is a question precisely of the psychology, the consciousness of the movement of the proletariat, which is necessary for the socialist revolution. Do we take it that David does not see the necessity for the conscious participation of the proletariat to make a healthy workers' state?

The revolution in China starts with a Bonapartist deformation, not because it is inherent in the needs of the revolution, but on the contrary because of the specific social circumstances nationally and internationally which we have dealt with.

There have been many peasant wars in China and what would have normally happened would be that the leadership would, when entering the cities, fuse with the bourgeoisie and there would be a classical capitalist development. The peasant movement, Marxism teaches, must find a leadership in the cities either in the bourgeoisie or in the proletariat. Where it is the bourgeoisie then, of course, we have a capitalist development. Where the proletariat takes the lead, then we have the socialist revolution. Here we have a peculiar variant of the latter, in that the peasant movement has a centralised leadership in the form of the Stalinist party, which had its roots in Moscow. Basing itself on the peasantry, it enters the towns not with the aim and outlook of a genuine communist party, but with the aim of establishing its power by *manoeuvring between the classes*. It does so by transferring its social basis to the proletariat —not as the direct representative of the proletariat as would a Bolshevik party —but in a Bonapartist manner.

In the past, Bonapartism has always represented a tendency which, while linked to the bourgeoisie, nevertheless raises itself above the classes, manoeuvres between the bourgeoisie and the petty-bourgeoisie and the proletariat, sometimes leaning on the latter and even striking blows at the ruling class. In Russia in the early days of the rule of the bureaucracy as a Bonapartist clique, nevertheless basing itself on the economy of a workers' state, it is well known that it balanced and manoeuvred between the kulaks, the Nepmen and the workers. In the capitalist state, in a certain sense, the social democracy, which leaned on the working class, tended to oscillate between the workers and the bourgeoisie, depending on the social pressures of the moment. If they did not play any really independent role, it was because in the last analysis they were dependent on the bourgeoisie. While bourgeois Bonapartism veers between the classes and plays one off against the other it represents in the last analysis the bourgeoisie, because its profits and privileges arise out of the institution of private property. This does not mean to say that it is not extremely burdensome to the bourgeoisie in its impositions and demands.

Stalinism is a form of Bonapartism that bases itself on the proletariat and the institution of state ownership, but it is as different from the norm of a workers' state as fascism or bourgeois Bonapartism differs from the norm of bourgeois democracy, which is the freest expression of the economic domination and rule of the bourgeoisie.

Stalinism, leaning on the proletariat can, under given conditions, balance between the opposing classes to strengthen itself for its own ends. We have seen how this was accomplished in Eastern Europe. We now have a similar development taking place before our eyes in China. Whereas it would be impossible for the revolutionary Marxist tendency to make a coalition with the bourgeoisie, precisely because of the need to ensure the independent self-mobilisation of the masses in the struggle to overthrow the bourgeoisie, Stalin has no need for such inhibitions. Stalinism makes a coalition under conditions *where the back of the bourgeoisie has been broken*, in order to play off the bourgeoisie against the danger of an insurgent proletariat. Thus the coalition which the Stalinists are proposing in China will not mean the victory or even the survival of the bourgeoisie. It will be used in order to gain a breathing space for the organisation of a Stalinist, Bonapartist state machine on the lines of Moscow. Not at all a state or a semi-state on the lines visualised by the Marxists — as the free and armed organisation of the masses, but a state machine separate and apart from the masses, entirely independent and towering over them as an instrument of oppression.

It is evident that the Chinese movement draws its viability from the 'innermost needs of the economy'. However, while a genuine revolutionary, Trotskyist leadership in a backward country would draw its strength from the proletariat, welding the peasant masses behind it, Mao rests on the peasantry and not only bases himself on the passivity of the proletariat at this stage, but ruthlessly suppresses any proletarians who dare to take measures against the bourgeoisie on the basis of independent class action. At a later stage, Mao will lean on the proletariat when he needs it against the bourgeoisie, only later to betray and ruthlessly suppress it. In this it would be far more correct to say that Mao, as Tito, is a *conscious* Stalinist, adopting consciously many of the Bonapartist manoeuvres which Stalin was forced to adopt empirically.

While the armies of the Kuomintang have melted away under the revolutionary agrarian programme and propaganda of the Stalinists —'land to the tiller' —one thing is clear: the programme of propaganda of Mao has not been directed to the revolutionary mobilisation of the proletariat and the organisation of soviets. Nor has it been directed to the overthrow of the Kuomintang regime in the towns through the conscious initiative and movement of the workers. On the contrary, it is his policy to ruthlessly crush any move in this direction. This refusal to mobilise the masses is not accidental. It expresses the fear of a mass movement in the cities at this stage. The difference between Trotskyism and Stalinism is no more strikingly illustrated than in this fact. There is an unbridgeable gulf between Marxism, which bases itself on the conscious movement of the masses, above all the proletariat, and Bonapartist Stalinism which manoeuvres between the classes and utilises the revolutionary instincts of the masses in the interests of this new caste.

Mao's regime will follow the pattern of the other Stalinist regimes. Having consolidated itself, it will become a military-police dictatorship with all the other malignant aspects of the Russian regime. The signs are already visible.

Comrade James asserts that we reduce it to a question of Mao's 'psychology devoid of any social basis' when we say that Mao will follow in the footsteps of Stalin and will if anything be far more barbarous. It is not a question of the individual inclinations of Mao. It is precisely a question of the psychology of the Chinese army and, later, civil bureaucracy. An uncontrolled totalitarianism has shown what it can do in Stalinist Russia. In China, far more backward than Russia, where life and liberty have always been regarded lightly, the social contradictions will lead to the same consequences as in Russia, with this difference: superimposed upon Stalinist barbarism will be the traditions of Asiatic barbarism. If Mao does not fulfil the function which the triumphant military and civil caste will demand, then he will be removed and some other Bonaparte will take his place.

The fact that in the mountains and rural areas the generals and officers have lived a simple and austere existence, is not relevant here. Napoleon in the revolutionary army in France passed through a similar phase. But once in power, the caste surrounded itself with pomp and privilege right down to the 'gorgeous uniforms'. Bourgeois observers, commenting on the difference between the corrupt and venal administration and officer caste of the Kuomintang, and the reasonably simple and honest administration and organisation of the army and the territories controlled by the Reds, pointed out that it was a question of waiting until the Reds had taken over the glittering prize of the cities of North and South China. On a low agrarian basis, no great social differentiation would take place. To repeat, it is not a question of 'psychology' of individuals devoid of social basis, but of the necessary outlook and psychology of a social grouping in society.

The fact that Mao has a genuine mass base independent of the Russian Red Army, will in all likelihood provide for the first time an independent base for Chinese Stalinism which will no longer rest directly on Moscow. As with Tito, so with Mao, despite the role of the Red Army in Manchuria, Chinese Stalinism is developing an independent base. Because of the national aspirations of the Chinese masses, the traditional struggle against foreign domination, the economic needs of the country and above all, the powerful base in an independent state apparatus, the danger of a new and really formidable Tito in China is a factor which is causing anxiety in Moscow. The Titoists have already predicted the likelihood of such a development, because of the similarity to the movement in Yugoslavia.

Already in Manchuria, where the Russians have control of the Chinese Eastern railway and bases at Port Arthur and Dairon, they have placed their puppet Li-Li San in control. A discredited Stalinist functionary, who carried through the ultra-left policy of Stalin in the Third Period in the early 1930s, and a traditional opponent of Mao, Li-Li San is placed as a reliable puppet in control of Manchuria. Significantly, he has spent years of exile in Russia. By control of Manchuria, which formerly contained the greater part of Chinese industry, the Kremlin hopes to maintain a base. In Sin-Kiang, Stalin has established a base of support by negotiating with the bourgeois government of the Kuomintang.

However, the subordination of the Chinese economy to the benefit of the Russian bureaucracy, with the attempts to place puppets in control who will be completely subordinate to Moscow – in other words, the national oppression of the Chinese – will create the basis for a clash with the Kremlin of great magnitude and significance. Mao, with an independent and powerful state apparatus, with the possibility of manoeuvring with the imperialists of the West (who will seek to negotiate with China for trade and try and drive a wedge between Peking and Moscow) and with the support of the Chinese masses as the victorious leader against the Kuomintang, will have powerful points of support against Moscow.

Stalin's very efforts to try and forestall this development will tend to accelerate and intensify the resentment and the conflict. However, if Mao breaks with Stalin, this will not turn him into a Trotskyist. We will give critical support to Mao against Stalin, as with Tito. But against both we will continue to put forward the internationalist Marxist position.

The last point, the most pertinent, is on the question of the role of the Fourth International. 'Meanwhile', says comrade James, 'the Stalinists are "establishing" a revolution in which the Trotskyists are playing no discernible role. Evidently Grant's references to the Stalinist perversion of Marxism, and to the coming role of the Trotskyists, have a purely ritual significance, derived from a prior conception of Stalinism which Grant himself has abandoned.'

And again, after quoting *World News and Views* in which Mao says: 'The revolution of the great mass of the people, led by the proletariat...' James comments: 'If this is true, we must support it, with criticism, but abandoning any ideas of an independent role for the Chinese Trotskyists.' If the revolution was led by the proletariat, why support it 'with criticism'? Without criticism comrade! We would join the ranks of Mao.

We think we have shown above the deformation of the Chinese revolution and its roots. We support the progressive measures that the Stalinists take in the same way as we supported them in Finland and Poland, but we warn against the inevitable corruption because of the social forces at work. Thus the role of the Chinese Trotskyists is clear. They support, yes hail, the progressive measures introduced; at the same time, they explain the need for soviets, for democratic control by the masses, etc, and they oppose any reactionary measures taken against the masses in the interests of the bureaucracy. Theirs is not an easy task. The Opposition has been virtually wiped out in Russia; does this mean to say that there is no role for the Trotskyists in Russia? We place our faith in Chinese Trotskyism, not as a mere ritual, but because we have faith in the future of socialism. Of its own volition, China will never be freed from bureaucratic strangulation.

From: The Colonial Revolution and the Sino-Soviet Split

August 1964

THE SECOND World War ended with a revolutionary wave in Western Europe which, thanks to the aid of Stalinism and social democracy, capitalism survived. Stalinism in the Soviet Union emerged strengthened for a whole historical period.

In the history of society there have been many methods of class rule. This is especially true of capitalist society, with many peculiar and variegated forms: republic, monarchy, fascism, democracy, Bonapartist, centralised and federal, to give some examples.

In a period where the revolution (apart from Czechoslovakia) has taken place in backward or undeveloped countries, distortions, even monstrous distortions in the nature of the state created by the revolution are inevitable, so long as the most vital industrialised areas of the world remain under the control of capital.

A decisive cause of the developments is Bonapartist counterrevolution in the Soviet Union. The malignant power of the state and the uncontrolled rule of the privileged layers in the Soviet Union have served as a model for 'socialism' in these countries. Bourgeois Bonapartism reflects a society in a state of crisis, where the state raises itself above society and the classes and obtains a relatively independent role, only in the last analysis directly reflecting the propertied classes, because of the defence of private property on which it is based.

The proletariat is not a 'sacred cow' to which analagous processes cannot take place. Proletarian Bonapartism represents a most peculiar form of workers' rule. Contradictions in a largely backward society in which the proletariat represents a small minority, as Lenin pointed out, can lead to the dictatorship manifesting itself through the rule of one person.

A proletarian form of Bonapartism by its very nature represents a caricature of workers' rule. In a society where private ownership has been abolished and there is no democracy, the powers of the state gain enormous extension. The state raises itself above society and becomes a tool of the bureaucracy in its various forms:

military, police, party, 'trade union' and managerial. These are the privileged strata within the society. They are the sole commanding stratum. In the transition from capitalist society to socialism the form of economy can only be state ownership of the means of production, with the organisation of production on the basis of a plan. Only the democratic control of the workers and peasants can guarantee such a transition. That is why political revolution in these countries is inevitable before workers' democracy is instituted as an indispensable necessity if the state is to 'wither away', but such 'transition regimes' can only be workers' states —deformed workers' states —because the economy of these states is based on nationalisation of the means of production, the operation of the economy on the basis of a plan.

Marx never considered the problem of revolution in backward countries as he considered the revolution would come in the advanced capitalist countries first. The Bonapartist regimes —regimes of crisis —reflect the unresolved economic and social problems, both on the narrow national plane and internationally —crises which can only be resolved by world revolution, especially in the advanced countries.

The development of the Chinese revolution, next to the Russian revolution the 'greatest event in human history' as the documents of the Revolutionary Communist Party proclaimed in advance, took place with a mighty deformed workers' state at its back, plus the frustration of the revolutionary tide in the West. Without the existence of the monstrously deformed workers' state in the East, and the paralysing of the hands of imperialism by the radicalisation of the workers in the West, the Chinese revolution could not have taken the form which it did.

Trotsky in the pre-war period had posed the problem of what would happen in the case of the Chinese 'Red' Armies emerging victorious in the civil war against Chiang Kai-Shek. He had tentatively forecast that the tops of the Red Army would betray their peasant base, and in the cities, with the passivity of the proletariat, would fuse with the bourgeoisie, leading to a classical capitalist development.

This did not take place because on the road of capitalist development there was no way forward for China. With the model of Russia, the Stalinist leadership of the peasant armies manoeuvred between the classes, at one time resting on the 'national' bourgeoisie, or the peasants, and at others on the working class and constructed a strong Stalinist leadership in the image of Moscow. At no time was there a period of workers' rule such as in Russia in 1917, when the workers through their Soviets controlled the state and society.

Just as bourgeois Bonapartism, manoeuvring between the classes,

in the last analysis, defends the basis of capitalist society, so in the same way proletarian Bonapartism rests in the last analysis on the base created by the revolution: the nationalised economy.

The Chinese revolution solved all those problems which bourgeois society was incapable of solving. The three decades of rule by Chiang Kai-Shek, the Bonapartist representative of finance capital, revealed the complete incapacity of the bourgeoisie to unify China, to carry through the agrarian revolution, to overthrow imperialism. It could only usher in a new period of decay for Chinese society. It was this which gave the impulse to the leadership of the peasant armies to overthrow the bourgeoisie and, thanks to the model of Russia at her back, construct a state on the Stalinist model.

The leadership was without international or Marxist perspectives. The conscious role and leadership of the proletariat, without which socialism is impossible, was absent. The Stalinist leadership, in the conquest of the cities, used the passivity of the proletariat, and where elements of proletarian action emerged spontaneously, met these with the execution of the leading participants.

However, the welding of the atomised and separate provinces into a single unified national state on modern lines, for the first time in the history of China; the agrarian revolution; the nationalisation of the means of production: all these gave a mighty impulse to the development of the productive forces. China advanced as no colonial economy has advanced for decades.

The Chinese bureaucracy, like all bureaucracies of a similar character, is interested mainly in advancing its own power, privileges, income and prestige. It defends the base of nationalised property on which it rests, because this is the basis of its income and power.

As predicted in advance, before the Chinese bureaucracy came to power, the possibility of a conflict between it and the Russian bureaucracy, was inherent in the situation. The attempt of the Russian bureaucracy to arrive at an agreement with American imperialism, without giving consideration to the needs and interests of the Chinese bureaucracy, precipitated the split between the two tendencies.

The rationalisation of the split by 'ideological' considerations was a means to try and gain support within the Communist Parties, on a world scale. The Chinese, for the moment, have used radical slogans as a means of mobilising support in the Stalinist world movement against the Russians, especially among the colonial peoples. Their open support of Stalin, repelling the workers in the

Soviet Union and the West, among other calculations, is intended to draw a line of blood and confusion between the Communist workers looking for a Marxist solution, and 'Trotskyism', ie genuine Marxism-Leninism.

Because of their radical slogans, at this time, the Chinese appeal to the cadre elements in the Stalinist parties looking for a revolutionary road. In that sense, every nuance, every cranny, must be utilised by the Marxist tendency for the purpose of finding a way to the sincere Stalinist workers.

The real face of Chinese Stalinism is revealed in the opportunism of the leadership in the colonial world, where they have given support to the rotting, feudal, bourgeois upper strata in many countries. The support of the Imam in the Yemen, the loans to Afghanistan, to Sri Lanka, to Pakistan, support of Sukarno in Indonesia, etc. Without being able to compete in resources, they have used the slender means of the Chinese economy in competition with the Russian bureaucracy and with imperialism. Their ideology, their conceptions, cannot rise above the narrow national interests of the Chinese bureaucracy.

Their 'internationalism' consists in trying to build an instrument of support similar to that possessed by the Russian Stalinist bureaucracy. Their ideology, methods and attitudes are a counterfeit of Marxism, as much as that of the Russian bureaucracy, at various stages of its development.

The idealisation of Stalinism in its crudest and most repressive form, is for the above-mentioned reason of the need to prevent any tendency of the militant workers to drift towards 'Trotskyism' and because of the nature of the Chinese economy. Like the Russian before it, such a regime, on the basis of the Chinese economy alone, may endure for decades, with its slender base in industry, in comparison with the hundreds of millions of peasants. Only the socialist revolution in the West, or the political revolution in the Soviet Union, could alter this perspective.

The viciousness with which the bureaucracy of the Soviet Union supported India in the conflict with China, withdrew their technicians and destroyed plans and blueprints in their endeavours to weaken China, is an indication of the real character of the bureaucracy in the Soviet Union. They have been ready to lavish loans and aid on the bourgeoisie and parasitic upper layers of the colonial countries, in order to prop up these regimes in competition with imperialism. But to the bureaucracy of another workers' state coming into conflict with them, they demonstrated their selfish national aims.

Similarly, China —as with the diplomatic agreement with

Pakistan and the tour of Prime Minister Chou En Lai, in Africa —apes the Russian bureaucracy in its endeavour to find friends. In Zanzibar they came to an agreement with the Sultan, before he was overthrown; they made no criticism of the governments of Tanganyika, Uganda and Kenya for calling British troops against their own mutinous troops.

The Chinese Stalinists, not accidentally, advised the Algerians to 'go slow' with their revolution. This was because of the forthcoming diplomatic agreement with French imperialism. The basic perspectives of Chinese Stalinism are determined by their national aims of obtaining a seat in the United Nations, and for strengthening the Chinese national state through whatever means possible, agreement with imperialism for trade etc. They have attempted to mobilise the Afro-Asian bloc with this in mind and not at all with the international perspectives of socialism and the social revolution.

The split between Russia and China, as with the split between Yugoslavia and Russia and now the development of new national Stalinism in the countries of Eastern Europe, Poland, Rumania, Czechoslovakia, Hungary, etc, is a symptom of Stalinist decay and, simultaneously, of the weakness of the revolutionary forces of Marxism on a world scale at the present time. Had there been in existence mighty Marxist revolutionary forces of the proletariat, consciously preparing the revolution in the industrially advanced countries of the world, such a phenomenon would have been impossible. As at the time of the Hungarian political revolution of 1956, before which the bureaucracies of these countries trembled and drew together for mutual protection and support, the Chinese bureaucracy would not have dared to launch the campaign against Russian 'revisionism'. All these bureaucracies would have been facing collapse and overthrow.

The split between the Stalinist bureaucracies on national lines adds further confusion among the broad masses throughout the world. Even among the advanced workers, while creating certain opportunities for the ideas of Marxism, it further complicates the task of revolutionary Marxism. However, in the long term, it undermines completely the former monolithism of Stalinism and its hold on the masses. The way is prepared for, on the basis of great events, tens and hundreds of thousands of workers to enter the revolutionary road. In the next great upheavals, both East and West, of social and political revolutions, Stalinism will crumble away.

Nevertheless, one of the basic tasks of the period is the education of the most conscious workers not to be infected by any of the variants of Stalinism. There is as great a gulf between Stalinism in its various forms, both of state and ideology and real workers' democracy and Marxism as there is between Bonapartism, fascism and bourgeois democratic state and ideology.

While defending the progressive aspects of the economy in Russia, China, Cuba and Eastern Europe, at the same time it is necessary to draw a fundamental distinction between the rotten nationalist bureaucratic ideology of Stalinism and its states, and the conscious control of the economy and of the movement towards socialism of the working class as explained in the methods and conceptions of international socialism.

Following the failure of the post-war revolutionary wave in the West, capitalism succeeded in stabilising itself for an entire epoch. Consequences became cause. A new period of capitalist growth was ushered in for all the metropolitan countries, of greater or lesser strength. The increasing power of the Soviet Union with its far faster tempo of industrial growth, together with the growth of the workers' states and the stabilisation of a mighty China, resulted in a new balance of forces on a world scale between the capitalist forces of the West and the workers' states of the East.

This is the background on which, in one country after the other, there has been the continual upheaval of national upsurge and revolution against imperialist domination and national oppression. At a time of rapid growth of productive forces in the metropolitan countries the gap between the industrially developed countries and the so-called 'undeveloped' areas of the world has become twice as great as before the second world war. The growth of industry on a modest scale in these latter countries has exacerbated the social contradictions.

In all these countries, the problems of the national revolution, the agrarian revolution, the liquidation of feudal and pre-feudal survivals, could not be solved on the old basis. This has been the period of national awakening of the oppressed peoples of Asia, Africa and Latin America.

Faced with this upsurge of the colonial masses, the imperialists have been compelled to retreat. A century ago, Marx explained that only the lack of national consciousness among the peasant masses allowed the imperialists to conquer and dominate the East and Africa. Once they were aroused, it was practically impossible to hold a whole nation in chains. Trotsky in the year prior to the second world war, had observed that the task of 'pacification' of the colonial revolts had become far more expensive than the fruits of the exploitation of the colonies. And this in a period when colonial uprisings were at an early stage.

Already in 1945, Britain had drawn the conclusion from the

revolt of the Indian people, of the necessity to arrive at some sort of compromise with the Indian bourgeoisie and landlords. Partly this was due to the impossibility, because of the radical mood of the soldiers of Allied imperialism and of the working class in Britain, of waging a large scale war of conquest or re-conquest of India and partly for fear of the upsurge of the Indian people.

French and Dutch imperialism had to learn the lessons after the squandering of blood and treasure in Indonesia, Indo-China, Algeria, etc. The Bourbons* of Portugal are in the process of learning the lesson at the present time.

Thus the lag of the revolution in Europe and other metropolitan countries has pushed the revolution to the extremities of the capitalist world, to the weakest links in the chain of capitalism. However, the development of Stalinism in Russia and its extension to China and Eastern Europe, the frustration of the revolution in the industrially decisive areas of the capitalist world, has meant that *the development of the permanent revolution in these underdeveloped countries has taken a distorted pattern.* The degeneration of the Russian revolution, the Bonapartist form of the Chinese revolution, in spite of its splendours, has meant in its turn that the revolution in the colonial countries *begins* with nationally limited perspectives and with fundamental deformations from the very beginning.

The revolution in Russia, which began as a bourgeois-democratic revolution, ended in a proletarian revolution of the most classic proportions, with the dominating role of the proletariat as the main decisive force of the revolution. It culminated in the October insurrection of the *working class,* which throughout was based on internationalist and Marxist perspectives. The Chinese peasant revolt, which culminated in the peasant war of 1944-9, was in a sense derived from the defeated revolution of 1925-7, but entirely different from it in the role of the working class. It was a *peasant war* carried out first as a guerrilla war, and culminating in the conquest of the cities by the armies of the peasants.

The socialist revolution, in contrast with all previous revolutions, requires the conscious participation and control of the working class. Without it, there can be no revolution leading to the dictatorship of the proletariat as understood by Marx and Lenin, nor can there be a transition in the direction of socialism.

A revolution in which the prime force is the peasantry cannot rise

---

*The Bourbons were the ruling dynasty in France until the revolution (1792). They were briefly restored from 1830-48. In Spain the Bourbons ruled almost continuously from 1700-1931. It is used here to describe leaders who learn little or nothing from history.

to the height of the tasks posed by history. The peasantry cannot play an independent role; either they support the bourgeoisie or the proletariat. Where the proletariat is not playing a leading part in the revolution, the peasant army, with the impasse of bourgeois society, can be used, especially with the existence of ready-made models, for the expropriation of bourgeois society in the Bonapartist manoeuvring between classes and the construction of a state on the model of Stalinist Russia.

The bourgeoisie of the colonial areas has come too late on the world arena to be enabled to play the progressive role which the Western bourgeoisie played in the development of capitalist society. They are too weak, their resources are too narrow to hope to compete with the industrial economies of the capitalist West. The disparity between the weak and underdeveloped economies of the colonial world and the metropolitan areas, far from being ameliorated, is gathering speed. It has been further emphasised during the last two decades by the upswing of capitalist economy in the metropolitan areas. Whereas in the capitalist economy in the West, the standard of living of the masses has increased in absolute terms, even though the rate of exploitation has increased, there has been an absolute decline in living standards in the East. By the peculiar dialectic of the revolution, the colonial revolution has actually helped the economies of the metropolitan countries by creating a market for capital goods.

The imperialists, except for the Portuguese, were forced to abandon the old method of direct military domination in Asia, Africa, and Latin America. Economic domination with nominally independent states became the norm.

The period since the second world war has seen unprecedented upheavals in the colonial areas. The period of national awakening of all oppressed peoples has been on a scale and in a measure that military means are doomed to failure, as evidenced by the British in even such as small island as Cyprus, the French in Algeria, and tomorrow the collapse of the attempt to pacify Angola.

All these revolutions and national awakenings have taken place with a lag and delay of the revolution in the West. However, the greatest force for change in society, which must always be regarded from an internationalist perspective, still lies in the decisive areas of Western Europe, Britain, Japan and the United States in the capitalist world, and Russia and Eastern Europe in the deformed workers' states. From the point of view of the change from one society to another, while of fundamental importance to revolutionaries involved in the actual struggle, a decade or two in the development of society is of secondary significance. The very growth of the   capitalist world, the very development of the economy in the underdeveloped areas of the world, are all drawing together the threads of change on a world scale. In the endeavour to compete with the advancing economies of the Stalinist countries, capitalism has been compelled to use up a great part of its social reserves. Direct domination and colonial tribute as a consequence of a military overlordship, have disappeared or are in the process of disappearing.

Economic domination and the crushing preponderance of the metropolitan economies over the frail economies of the colonial or ex-colonial states is even greater and further increasing than in the past. At the same time, in the metropolitan countries themselves, the very growth of monopoly, the growth of industry, the industrialisation of agriculture, have all led to the contraction of the peasantry and the petit-bourgeoisie and a further increase in the decisive weight in society of the proletariat.

From the point of view of Marxism, no more favourable situation could be envisaged. The potential power of the proletariat in both the deformed workers' states on the one side, and the capitalist countries on the other, has never reached a greater scope than in the present epoch. From this point of view, a tremendously optimistic perspective opens out for the future. The tremendous upsurge of productive forces will inevitably reach its end and result in a new period of paralysis and decay, such as the inter-war period, in the capitalist countries. In the Soviet Union and the East, the further development of productive forces will come increasingly into collision with the stranglehold of bureaucratic control. The bureaucracy will become more and more incompatible with the development of society. A new period of social revolution in the West and of political revolution in the East will be opened out.

It is on this background and with this perspective constantly in mind that the colonial revolution in Asia, Africa and Latin America must be regarded. Had Russia been a healthy workers' state, or even a state with the relatively mild deformations of the era of Lenin and Trotsky, then undoubtedly the revolution in all backward countries would most likely have taken a different form. As Lenin had optimistically declared with the first wave of revolutionary awakening in the backward countries of the world, it would have been possible for even tribal areas of Africa to 'go straight to communism' without any intervening period whatsoever. This could only have been, of course, on the basis of a genuine and fraternal federation, for the benefit of all. Of course, in any event, the problem would have been posed entirely differently; a healthy workers' state in Russia would have led to the victory of the revolution in Europe and the industrially advanced countries of the world, thus posing the problem for undeveloped areas in an entirely different way. That was the scheme of Marx, who had thought that with the accomplishment of the revolution in Britain, France and Germany, the rest of the world (with the crushing industrial preponderance of these areas at the time) would have been compelled to follow willy nilly.

The explanation for the way in which the revolution is developing in the colonial countries lies in the delay and over-ripeness of the revolution in the West, on the one side, and the deformation of the revolution in Russia and China on the other side. At the same time, it is impossible to continue on the old lines and old pattern of social relations. If, from an historical view, the bourgeoisie has exhausted its social role in the metropolitan capitalist countries, in the present stage of world society, it is even more incapable of rising to the tasks posed by history in the colonial areas of the world.

The rotten bourgeoisie of the East and the nascent bourgeoisie of Africa are quite incapable of rising to the tasks solved long ago by the bourgeoisie in the West. Meanwhile the bourgeois-democratic and national revolution in the colonial areas cannot be stayed. The rise in national consciousness in all these areas imperatively demands a solution to the tasks posed by the pressure of the more developed countries of the West.

The decay of world imperialism and the rise of two mighty Stalinist states, of Russia in Europe and China in Asia, has resulted in a peculiar balance of world forces. The bourgeoisie and to a certain extent the national petit-bourgeoisie and upper layers of colonial society, was allowed a role which would have been impossible without the world relationship of forces which emerged as a result of the second world war. Even the heightened role which the Afro-Asian bloc plays in the United Nations (albeit on secondary questions —they cannot play the same role when it comes to a fundamental issue) is an indication of this change. The competition between the West and Russia —and now China, Russia and the West —for the aid and support of the ruling circles in Africa and Latin America and Asia, is an indication of the result of this precarious balance of forces.

The degeneration of the Russian Revolution and the strengthening of Stalinism for a whole historical epoch was the main reason why the revolution in China began right from the start on Bonapartist lines. This in its turn has meant that *the revolution in other countries of Asia, Africa and Latin America had a ready-made*

Bonapartist model —which is associated in the minds of the leading circles of the intellectual strata as 'socialism'. Whilst the Chinese revolution was accomplished largely through a peasant war, and a peasant army as an instrument of proletarian Bonapartism, at least lip service was given in the later stages of the revolution, after the conquest of power, to the rule of the proletariat. This was the case in Cuba also, where the peasant army and the guerrilla war played the dominant role in the revolution, until the uprising of the proletariat in Havana. After the transformation of the bourgeois-democratic revolution under Castro's leadership into a state on the model of Yugoslavia, China and Russia, also a dominant role of the proletariat was conceded, but again in words.

All history has demonstrated that the peasantry by its very nature as a class, can never play the dominant role in society. It can support either the proletariat or the bourgeoisie. Under modern conditions, it can also support the proletarian Bonapartist leaders or ex-leaders of the proletariat. However, *in doing so, a distortion of the revolution is inevitable.* A distortion in one form or another on the lines of a military-police state.

Every Marxist who claims to base themselves on the scientific theory of Marx and Engels, with its deepening and extension in the ideas of Lenin and Trotsky, has explained the necessary role of the proletariat —and in the role of the proletariat of socialist consciousness —as the driving force of the changeover from capitalism into the new society. Without socialist consciousness, there can be no socialist revolution and no transition of society to socialism. Marxists like Lenin and Trotsky have not emphasised the role of socialist consciousness and the conscious participation of the proletariat in the course of the socialist revolution in the overthrow of the old society for idealist or sentimental reasons. They did so because without the participation of the proletariat in the socialist revolution (in the West, the success of such a revolution is impossible without the mobilisation of all the forces of the proletariat) and its conscious control and organisation of the transitional society, a development towards socialism is absolutely impossible.

There is no automatism of the productive forces without the control by the workers of the state —even in a highly industrialised state like Britain or America, the very existence of a state would be a capitalist survival from the past. Without conscious control on the part of the proletariat, whose dictatorship is intended to speedily dissolve all elements of state coercion into society, the state as evidenced in Russia and China, inevitably gains an impetus and a movement of its own.

If in China the bourgeoisie revealed its utter incapacity to solve a single one of the tasks of the bourgeois-democratic revolution, events will demonstrate the even greater incapacity of the Indian, still less of the other Asian and African, bourgeois elements to solve a single one of the problems posed in front of these countries by history.

It is the incapacity of the bourgeois, semi-bourgeois, upper middle class, landlords and petit-bourgeois to solve these tasks, that poses the problem of the permanent revolution in a distorted way. Had there been in existence strong Marxist parties and tendencies in the colonial areas of the world, the problem of power would have been posed somewhat differently. It would have been posed with an internationalist perspective. Even more than in the industrially developed countries of the West, socialism in one country, or, one might add, in a series of backward countries, is an impossible chimera. Nevertheless, the tasks of development in these countries are imperiously posed. With the world balance of forces, with the delay of the revolution in the West, with the lack of Marxist parties in these countries and with the social classes in these countries themselves, new and peculiar phenomena are inevitable.

For example, with a mighty Chinese revolution on its borders, developments in Burma have taken a peculiar form. Since the end of the war Burmese society has been disorganised. The national minorities have waged a constant struggle for self-determination and national autonomy in their own states (Kachins, Shans etc.) and at the same time, different factions of the Stalinist party have waged a terrific guerrilla war. One government has succeeded another, but each has been incapable of putting its stamp on society. Like the Chinese bourgeoisie before it, it has been incapable of unifying society, giving it social cohesion and satisfying the land hunger of the peasants, or breaking the economic power of imperialism. It is a striking symptom of the new developments in these backward countries that all the factions in Burma claim to be 'socialist'. Imperialism dominated the economy, by its ownership, largely, of whatever industry existed and of the main economic forces such as teak plantations, oil and transport.

With the example of China on the border, it became more and more apparent to the upper layers of the petit-bourgeois that on the road of bourgeois society there was no way forward for Burma. As in China, in the decades before the revolution, the bourgeois was incapable of bringing the guerrilla war to an end and ensuring the development of a stable society and the inauguration of industrialisation and the creation of a modern state.

Each succeeding government made only the feeblest attempts to try and develop the economy. The weakness of imperialism, the balance of forces nationally and internationally, led to a situation where the officer caste posed the problem before itself of finding some stability within society. In all these countries, the development of the bourgeois revolution, a bourgeois democratic state, and a development towards a modern bourgeois democracy, given the existing relationship of class and national forces and with the pressure of the world economy, for any lengthy period is impossible.

Consequently, some form of Bonapartism, some form of military-police state, was inevitable in Burma. The officer caste saw itself in the role of the only strata which could 'save' society from disintegration and collapse, as the feeble bourgeoisie obviously offered no solution. Consequently, the officer caste which had participated as one of the 'socialist' factions, decided that the only way forward was on the model of 'socialist' China, but called a 'Burmese model' of 'socialism'. They have moved rapidly on familiar lines —a one-party totalitarian state, and the nationalisation of foreign-owned interests, including oil, teak, transport etc. *They have begun the expropriation of the indigenous bourgeoisie.* They even threatened the nationalisation of the small shops. *They based themselves on the peasants and the working class. But they do not have a model of scientific socialism,* on the contrary, their programme is one of 'Burmese-Buddhist socialism'.

Thus we see the same process at one pace or another in all the colonial countries. At the moment the process is becoming marked in the Arab countries, which have been in a state of ferment for the last decade. In Egypt the revolution against the incompetent and corrupt Farouk* regime, agency of imperialism, was led by the officer caste. Over a period, Nasser adopted the policy of 'Arab socialism'.

The monotony with which such tendencies appear in all these countries is striking. The Great Aswan Dam, from the beginning, was owned by the state. Under the impact of economic crisis on a world scale, it can be predicted that the ruling caste, with the support of the workers and peasants, will nationalise the rest of the economy. The bourgeoisie is so weak and impotent that they are incapable of resistance. The officer caste which carried out the revolution, with the support and sympathy of the masses undeniably, did so because there was no perspective of modern development for the nation under the old system. There were no forces capable of resisting such change. Imperialism is too weak

*King Farouk I was overthrown in 1952. Gamal Nasser was prime minister 1954-56 and president 1956-70. In 1956 he nationalised the Suez canal.

and has learned the lesson in the failure of the wars against the national revolutions in the post-war period. With the model of Russia, China and now a whole series of states, with the example of developments in Algeria, there is no doubt that the ruling petit-bourgeois castes (as well as the basis that the Bonapartist regime of Nasser has among the workers and peasants) will support the complete nationalisation of the productive forces, stage by stage. Only thus can the Egyptian state enter into world developments.

It is easy for this caste to play this role because their own privileges and income, their social role, can be reinforced and increased. The bourgeois system in these areas is so effete and prematurely decayed that it can offer no perspective of development.

The most striking demonstration of the correctness of this thesis are the events in Iraq. The Communist Party, through its cowardly opportunism and the policy of Kruschev not to disturb the imperialists in this area, failed to take advantage of the revolutionary situation provoked by the fall of the old regime. The impulsion of the masses ended in disappointment and demoralisation. Nevertheless, the Kassem* regime, while waging war on the Kurds, at the same time was preparing measures of nationalisation.

The recent counter-revolutionary coup of the army took place to prevent these measures. But now to maintain themselves in power, and in view of the hopelessness of the situation, *this very caste* which is carrying on the reactionary war against the Kurdish people and which carried out the bloody counter-revolutionary coup against the temporising regime, has *itself* now announced measures of nationalisation, which embrace all important industry and banks. A great part of these were foreign owned, but nevertheless this coup has taken place. Like Algeria, for the present, the oil industry has been exempt from these measures, for fear of reprisals from the powerful international oil interests. But the tendency is there and will be further reinforced in the next period.

In Asia the remorseless peasant war of liberation in Vietnam, which has continued uninterrupted for 20 years, is nearing success. The American position in South Vietnam, tomorrow in South Korea, is becoming untenable. The attempt to prop up the old semi-feudal landlord capitalist state is doomed to failure, especially with the example of China in the near vicinity. The most

*Abdul Kassem became Iraq's prime minister in 1958 after leading an army coup. The Kurds are the major population group in Kurdistan, an area covering parts of Iraq, Turkey and Iran. In each country the Kurds are an oppressed national minority.

far-sighted representatives of capitalism are well aware of this process. De Gaulle, after his experience in Algeria, has understood this problem clearly and wishes to take advantage of it in the national interests of France. They understand that the American war of oppression is as hopeless as the French stand in Algeria. They see that landlordism and capitalism in this area are doomed. How to face up to this problem? There is no question with a peasant war under Stalinist leadership and with only limited nationalist perspectives of revolutionary contagion of the West. Why not then try and ensure the victory of a nationalist-Stalinist regime in Vietnam and the rest of Indo-China, independent of China, like Yugoslavia is independent of Russia?

They want a Vietnam —once the regrettable and inevitable end of capitalism in the area is accepted as the perspective —which would look to France and even America for aid and assistance, in order to prop it up as a force independent of Red China. The perspective of America in relation to Yugoslavia, Poland and Rumania is their perspective for South East Asia.   Their policy is that of the lesser evil. Why not make the best of a bad job and make the most of the contradictions of the national Stalinist regimes? After all, they pose no direct social threat to the metropolitan areas, no more than Algeria under nationalist leadership did to France.

In Africa, Nkrumah* in Ghana speaks of 'African socialism'. Under the impact of events it is not excluded that Ghana might take over all industry. This would be so in the event of economic crisis on a world scale.

A similar process is taking place in the Algerian revolution. Beginning as a national revolutionary war against colonial oppression, Algeria finds itself in an impasse. On the lines of capitalist society, there can be no solution. With the result, step by step, that Ben Bella and the FLN (National Liberation Front) are being pushed in the direction of a 'socialist solution'.

Algeria lacks an industrial proletariat at the present. The war was waged largely by the peasant-guerrilla army plus a large stiffening of rural proletarians and semi-proletarians. Had the leadership of the French proletariat conducted itself in a revolutionary way, it would have had its effect on the Algerian struggle but the betrayal of the French Socialist and Communist Parties in their turn pushed the struggle of the Algerian people through the FLN on to a purely nationalist basis.

---

*Kwame Nkrumah was Prime Minister of Ghana on independence (1957), became president in 1960 until 1966 when he was overthrown by a military coup. Ahmed Ben Bella was elected Prime Minister of Algeria on independence (1962) and became president in 1963 until he was overthrown in 1965.

This in turn led to the situation where the French workers, and technicians in Algeria, small *colons* and shopkeepers were pushed into the arms of the fascist OAS (Secret Army Organisation). The elements in Algeria supporting the Socialist and Communist Parties deserted to the OAS. This in its turn exacerbated the conflict. The victory of the revolution led to the fleeing of the French technicians, artisans and skilled workers to France, creating exceptional difficulties for the new Algerian state. Right from the start, the control of Algeria has been on the basis of Bonapartism. If in the early stages, the elements of a weak workers' control existed in the enterprises and partially in the estates expropriated from imperialism, these cannot be of decisive significance in the future. Without an industrial proletariat and without a conscious revolutionary party, with half the population unemployed, the regime will assume a more and more Bonapartist character.

History will demonstrate whether this will be a proletarian form of Bonapartism or a bourgeois variant of Bonapartism. The development of events should push the leadership of the FLN and the army in the direction of establishing the regime of nationalised property and of state ownership. It can only be, with the nationalist perspective of the leadership, with the social organisation of Algeria, with the lack of a conscious proletariat and in the world setting of the present time, a Stalinist dictatorship of the familiar model —a deformed workers' state.

Symptomatic of the process is the development of the ideology as put forward by Ben Bella —of Algerian 'Muslim' socialism. This Buddhist socialism, African socialism, Muslim socialism and various other aberrations of a similar character sum up themselves the process as it has taken place in the backward countries of the world. The difference between these revolutions and the proletarian revolutions as conceived by Marx and Lenin, is summed up in the difference between 'Buddhist-Muslim-socialism' and conscious 'scientific' socialism. Of course, every revolutionary worth their salt would hail enthusiastically the development of the colonial revolution even on bourgeois lines; every blow against imperialism, every lifting of the chains of national oppression, marks a step forward in the struggle for socialism and would even be welcomed by all enlightened elements of society.

Thus in the last 15 years the development of the colonial revolution in whatever form, is an enormous step forward for the world proletariat and for the mass of mankind as a whole. It marks the stepping onto the stage of history of peoples who have been kept at the level of animal existence by imperialism; an existence hardly worthy of being called human.

Thus if the revolutionary working class would hail as a step forward the victory of the colonial revolution and national independence, even in a bourgeois form, the defeat of capitalism and landlordism, the destruction of the elements of bourgeois and landlord society obviously marks an even greater step forward in the advance of these countries and the advance of mankind.

In the process of the permanent revolution, the failure of the bourgeoisie to solve the problems of the capitalist democratic revolution, under the conditions of capitalist society of modern times, is pushing towards revolutionary victory.

Even the victory of a Marxist party, with the knowledge and understanding of the process of deformation and degeneration of Russia, China and other countries, would not be sufficient to prevent the deformation of the revolution on Stalinist lines, given the present relationship of world forces.

Revolutionary victory in backward countries such as Algeria, under present conditions, whilst constituting a tremendous victory for the world revolution and the world proletariat, to be enthusiastically supported and aided by the vanguard as well as by the world proletariat, cannot but be on the lines of a totalitarian state.

Whilst constituting an enormous step forward from the point of view of ending the stagnation and restriction of productive forces imposed by imperialism, capitalism and landlordism and bringing these countries onto the road of a modern industrialised society, it cannot solve the problems posed in front of these societies. New contradictions on a higher level will inexorably be posed. The delay in the revolution in the West has, as a penalty for colonial peoples, meant that the revolution against imperialism and landlordism, moving forward to the proletarian revolution, takes place on the basis of Bonapartist deformation.

It is a striking indication of the weakness of 'Marxist' theorists and their lack of conscientiousness towards the problems of the socialist revolution, that nowhere are the problems of the different countries considered from the point of view of world revolution and world socialism. Even within the ranks of the so-called 'Fourth International', under the pressure of the great historical regression in theory and ideas, panaceas are put in the place of Marxist perspective.

Of all the historical tendencies, that of Bolshevism alone began with a clear internationalist perspective. The Russian revolution was carried through clearly and consciously as the beginning of revolution in Europe. The internationalist perspective, an indispensable necessary basis for socialist revolution, permeated not only the leading cadres but the masses of people led by the Bolsheviks. Internationalism was not conceived as a holiday or sentimental phrase, but as an organic part of the socialist revolution. Internationalism is a consequence of the unity of the world economy, which was capitalism's historical task to develop into a single economic whole. If Russia, with all her immense resources, and a most highly-conscious proletariat, with the finest Marxist leadership, could not solve its problems despite its continental basis and resources, it is ludicrous for Marxists even to think that in the present world conjuncture it would be possible in any of these backward countries, in isolation from any healthy *workers' states* to maintain anything but a Bonapartist state of a more or less repressive character.

Internationalism and conscious leadership —the two go together —are an organic part of Marxism. Without them, it is impossible to take the necessary steps in the direction of socialist society. Not one of these states is, in proportion to population, even as industrially developed as was Russia at the time of the revolution. Industrial development of a backward economy with the pressure of imperialism and Soviet and Chinese Bonapartism, the pressure of internal contradictions which a developing economy would mean, inevitably, in an economy of scarcity, would lead to the rise of privileged layers.

The independence of the state from its mass base, which all these countries possess in common (even where they have had or have the support of the mass of the population, either enthusiastically or passively), all indicate that on the basis of backwardness, it is impossible to start the process of dissolution of the state into society. The necessary dismantlement of the temporary structures of the state, which would be involved in a society with real democratic control and participation on the part of the population is in itself an indispensable pre-requisite of a healthy transition to socialism. Thus, the further development of these states is dependent on the development of the world revolution.

In these colonial or ex-colonial countries where the bourgeoisie has been enabled to maintain a precarious balance for a temporary period, such as India and Sri Lanka, they have maintained a semblance of bourgeois democracy. In many of the states in Asia and Latin America, bourgeois democracy in one form or another has been maintained on the basis of the economic upswing developed since the war. In India, which had perhaps the strongest bourgeoisie of all the ex-colonial countries, this regime has succeeded in maintaining itself but the bourgeoisie in the colonial world has no real perspective.

Thus, on the onset of the first economic crisis, if capitalism maintains itself in India, bourgeois democracy will be doomed. To maintain itself, the bourgeoisie will launch on the road of capitalist Bonapartism. The process was clearly demonstrated in Pakistan*. In the other countries of Asia and in practically all the countries of Africa, the upper layers of that society have only been able to maintain themselves on the basis of a one-party Bonapartist state – Ghana, Egypt etc.

On a bourgeois basis, such countries will be condemned to decay and degeneration. Economically, politically, socially, the bourgeoisie can only develop and aggravate the problems of society. In India, the bourgeoisie has not solved the problem of landlordism, the national problem or even the problem of caste. The standard of living, despite the industrial construction that has taken place, has actually declined relative to the increase in population. Of all these states, the Indian bourgeoisie had possibly the best opportunity of taking the road of the development of a modern economy and a modern state.

Imperialism with one hand has rendered assistance to India and with the other hand, through terms of trade and tribute extracted from investments, has undermined the position of the Indian bourgeoisie. If there has been a certain development in industry, the exports of such countries have been of light goods such as textiles, while the imports have been of heavy machinery. With the enormous development of trade through the division of labour between the metropolitan countries themselves, the imperialists could allow a certain latitude in the import of light goods from the colonial countries.

However, the last couple of decades have been the *best* economic circumstances under which these countries could function within the world market, to which they are bound like Prometheus to the rock, and from which there is no escape. Even in this most favourable period for capitalism as a whole, the colonial countries' economies, relative to those of the advanced countries, have suffered an even greater deterioration than in the period of colonial dependence in the years before the war. When it will be a question of the mighty imperialist states looking to find a way to save themselves from the crisis which the economic *downswing* will bring, the 'concessions' which they give to the colonial countries, because of fear of revolutions within them, will be terminated in an endeavour to prevent the mighty social explosions which impend

*The Pakistan constitutions of 1956 and 1962 were both replaced by martial law.

in their own metropolitan areas. Thus new convulsions and new storms will develop in the metropolitan areas and certainly in all the colonial countries.

No one, neither Marx nor Lenin nor Trotsky, could put forward a blueprint for the development of society. Only the basic and broad perspectives could be outlined. The failure of the revolution in the West, the degeneration of Stalinism, the failure of successive waves of the social revolution in Western Europe, the thwarting of the social revolution in the West and the expansion and consolidation of Stalinism, have been the world background on which the revolutionary awakening of the colonial peoples has been taking place.

In Asia, the Chinese revolution has imposed its imprint on the development of events. American imperialism's endeavours in Vietnam, in South Korea and other areas adjacent to China, has merely underwritten the rotting social formations of the past. They have endeavoured to step into the vacuum caused by the expulsion of Anglo-French and Japanese imperialism from these areas. The military police states in South Vietnam and South Korea and other areas in South East Asia can only be compared to the rotting regime of Chiang Kai-Shek in the period before the second world war.

The weak bourgeoisie in these countries cannot solve the problems of the bourgeois democratic revolution. Without the intervention of American troops and money in Vietnam and South Korea, these regimes would collapse overnight. Even with the support of American imperialism, the implacable peasant war in South Vietnam, which has continued uninterrupted since the end of the second world war, is undermining the regime and making the victory of the peasant armies, in the long run, certain. South Vietnam is as much a liability as was Chiang Kai-Shek. Only the resources of American imperialism permit the throwing of dollars down a bottomless sink.

In the immediate post-war period, only the treacherous policy of Stalinism, above all of the Russian bureaucracy, helped to maintain the precarious balance of forces in Asia especially in the South East. But the impossibility of finding a road to the development of modern society in these areas dooms these regimes to the dustbins of history. Consequently, at any stage, when the pressure of American imperialism will be relaxed, for whatever reasons, and even in spite of this, the collapse of these regimes is certain.

Developments in Burma, in Laos, in Cambodia (Kampuchea), are all indicative of the way in which the process will develop. On the road of capitalism there is no way forward, for all the countries of

Asia. *In one form or another, there will be an impulse in the direction of social revolution.* In India and Sri Lanka, particularly the former, with a developed proletariat, it is possible that the bourgeois democratic revolution could be transformed into the socialist revolution on the basis of the classical idea of the permanent revolution. The installation of a workers' democracy would be its crowning achievement, once the bourgeois democratic revolution has been accomplished, with the proletariat, directly through a revolutionary party, leading the struggle for power.

However, in these countries, even under the leadership of a Trotskyist party, such as that of the Lanka Sama Samaja Party* in Sri Lanka, the conquest of power by the proletariat and the firm establishment of a workers' democracy could only be an episode, to be followed by deformation or counter-revolution in the Stalinist form, if it were not followed, in a relatively short historical period, by the victory of the revolution in the advanced capitalist countries. It would, of course, even as an 'episode' be of enormous historical significance for the proletariat of the advanced capitalist countries as well as the peoples of the underdeveloped areas of the world. But even the greatest revolutionary theory cannot solve the problem without the necessary material base.

It is only the complete incapacity of outlived capitalism to solve the problems on its periphery which could allow the conquest of power in these countries. Of course, with a sub-continent such as India, the victory of the proletariat would have enormous consequences in Britain and other European countries as well, if it developed on the lines of China of 1925-7, with the proletariat playing the decisive part. On the other hand, any development of revolution on the lines of the Chinese revolution of 1944-9, with the peasantry playing the decisive role through guerrilla war, would unfold in the same way as the Chinese revolution of 1944-9.

However, the development of industry in India, the different traditions of the country, give the proletariat a preponderant weight in the social life of the country. Given that Indian Marxists should create a revolutionary party in time, then they could lead the working class to power, with the aim of creating a workers' democracy; with the aim of leading the peasantry to the overthrow of the landlord regime in the countryside; with the aim of unifying the country as a step towards the international socialist revolution.

Stalinist China, in its whole outlook, in its methods, in its

*The main workers' party of Sri Lanka in the late 1940's, 50's and 60's was the Lanka Sama Samaja Party. Originally a Trotskyist party, it degenerated, entered a coalition with the bourgeois SLFP, and by the mid-1970's had lost its mass support.

ideology, is not accidentally saturated with the narrow nationalism of a bureaucratic caste. *If, in the transition from feudalism to capitalism, a whole variety of regimes in all the kaleidoscopic colours have revealed themselves historically, it is because in this transition the development of productive forces themselves has assured a certain autonomism of progress; once the decisive bourgeois revolution had been accomplished in Britain, France and America.* Historically, due to the circumstances sketched out by Trotsky in a whole series of works, and by the British Marxists in the post-Trotsky period, *if the revolution is developing first in the backward and weakest countries, this factor* (the breakdown of capitalism at its weakest links) *has been decisive for a temporary period in unfolding the distortions and deformations in which the revolution in these countries is developing.*

The national limitations of the Chinese Stalinists, their insistence in the quarrel with the Russian Stalinists on mixing reactionary Stalinist ideas of the worst type with demagogic anti-imperialist demands, is an indication above all, of their incapacity really to understand the problems of the world revolution and of their real aims and interests. Even the solution of the national problems of the 'underdeveloped' areas of the world is only conceived as part of the diplomatic manoeuvres of the Chinese state.

Their idea of each country forming a national entity to build its own variety of socialism is reactionary through and through. But the idea of 'socialism in one country' did not drop from the skies; it reflected the interest of the narrow bureaucratic caste in Russia, and similarly also in Yugoslavia, Albania, Rumania and North Korea, these ideas reflect the same processes and the same contradictions.

More than a decade and a half ago the British Trotskyists, predicting in advance the victory of Chinese Stalinism, also foretold the probability, even the inevitability, of this narrow nationalist clique coming into collision and breaking away from their Moscow comrades. The revolution in China in that sense had a two-fold contradictory character. Enormously progressive in its solution of the problems of Chinese development, and giving an impetus to the national awakening of two-thirds of mankind doomed to hunger and misery in the so-called 'undeveloped' areas of the world, at the same time, it further reinforced the Stalinist dictatorship in Russia and strengthened Stalinism throughout the world.

In the metropolitan centres of capitalism the Stalinist parties could bask, not only in the usurped mantle of the Russian revolution, but in the aura of the great Chinese revolution. The history of Chinese Stalinism would show, since its advent to power, that it never rose, and by the nature of its ideology, methods and perspectives, never could rise above the narrow national horizon.

Its methods in Asia, even in the intervention in the Korean War, were dictated not by internationalist considerations, but purely by the strategic political and economic interests of the 'Chinese State' ie of the bureaucracy itself. Its opportunist agreement with the Indian government not to alter the social relations of the feudal theocratic state of Tibet, in return for an agreement with the Indian bourgeoisie, was upset by the attempted counter-revolution in Tibet. This compelled the bureaucracy to lean on the serfs and peasants and destroy the old Tibetan society.

Even in the war with India on the border and the strategic road between Sinkiang and Tibet, its conduct of the war was dictated only by nationalist considerations and not that of provoking internal class struggle in India itself. Its criticism of Moscow and of the opportunist policies of the French, Italian and other Communist Parties in the West, is more or less an afterthought and an attempt to gain support for the policies and methods and ideas of the Chinese state. *At no time has it raised the idea, elementary for Marxism, of a Federation of all Asia on a socialist basis.*

At no time has the problem of a *Russo-Chinese Federation* been put forward, which would automatically have been the issue in the event of a revolution on Leninist principles in China and had there been a Leninist regime in the Soviet Union. Thus, before the Chinese revolution and other revolutions in Asia could be placed on the road of transition to socialism, the proletariat and peasants, the people of these countries, would have to pay with a new revolution, this time not a social revolution, but a *political revolution*, to install workers' democracy.

It is the historic task, unconsciously perhaps, of these regimes to prepare the material and social forces (to a certain extent, the historical task which capitalism in these countries was incapable of developing to the same extent as in the West) of the proletariat and of industry to prepare the base for socialism. The victory in the backward countries of Asia of the social revolution in a bastardised form provokes social contradictions internally with the very growth of the productive forces themselves and at the same time, as far as the advanced workers of the West, and as the proletariat as a whole are concerned, a confusion of ideas in relation to socialism and its task.

The Russian revolution provoked an immense revolutionary awakening of the proletariat of the West and of the East. It raised the level of consciousness of the sleeping proletariat of Western Europe to a level never seen in history before. It raised the ideas of theory, of understanding, of Marxism, to a new and higher level. The idea of soviets, of workers' control, of workers' democracy, of a transitional society, were understood by broad layers of the advanced workers in the West.

This consciousness arose on the basis of the greatest democratic and social movement of the masses in the whole of human history. In its liberating effect, in the theoretical conclusions, even the Paris Commune and the lessons that the genius Marx drew from it, have paled into insignificance.

Had the revolution of 1925-7 in China succeeded, it could only have done so with a similar pattern to the events of 1917. That is why, at the time, Trotsky looked confidently to the effects that the Chinese revolution would have in Russia, leading to the overthrow of the Soviet bureaucracy, because it would rouse and mobilise in its revolutionary heat the Soviet proletariat. At the same time it would have aroused echoes within the proletariat of the capitalist countries of the West, thus tying the revolution together into one indissoluble knot. Trotsky looked to this development of 'permanent revolution' because he conceived the Chinese revolution with the background and perspective of world socialism.

The bureaucracy in Russia, while at best regarding the 1949 revolution with lukewarm favour (Stalin and the bureaucracy not believing in the possibility of revolutionary victory even in the caricatured form in which it was taking place) nevertheless did not and could not regard the victory of the bastardised Bonapartist form as a threat to the position, or, if one wishes, an immediate threat to the position of the bureaucracy in the Soviet Union.

It is an incontestable, historical fact, foreshadowed and explained by British Marxists, that ironically, the extension of the revolution to China, Eastern Europe and to the other countries of Asia where Bonapartist regimes had been established, added to the cohesion, the confidence and the power of the bureaucracy in the Soviet Union for a whole historical period.

One has only to compare the revolution in a backward country like Spain, which Trotsky likened to the relations of an Asiatic country rather than a modern European state, to see the difference that a revolution in which the proletariat plays the decisive and dominant role must have in its national and international effects. The 1931-7 revolution in Spain, had it succeeded, would have precipitated the revolution in France, in Germany and the other countries of Western Europe. The intervention on the scene of history of the heroic proletariat of Spain would have undermined the position of the Soviet bureaucracy also.

The desperate support of the bureaucracy for the bourgeois

counter-revolution in so-called Republican Spain was dictated by the frantic fear of the rising of the Russian proletariat. Victory in Spain on the basis of some form of workers' democracy would have led swiftly to the victory of the political revolution in the Soviet Union. In this international and national role of the proletariat in all these revolutions can be seen the difference between the hybrid form of the transition even where victorious in backward countries —and the proletarian revolution as conceived by Lenin and Trotsky.

Again it is not a question of sentiment or formalism but of the organic conception of socialism with a conscious participation and control of the working class.

One only has to compare the great Chinese revolution with the political revolution in Hungary*, to see the importance and difference between the revolution in its Bonapartist form and the political revolution. In Hungary we had the immediate participation and upsurge of the working class as the dominant force in the revolution, immediately organising its organs of self-expression, democracy and control.

After 20 years of fascist terror, after 10 years of Stalinist terror, the workers of Hungary revealed the tremendous tenacity of the ideas of socialism and workers' democracy, as the only means of assuring the development of future society. The workers, as if they had read the programme worked out by Trotsky, in every detail put forward the demands which Trotsky (reflecting the ideas, interests and aspirations of the proletariat) had worked out would be the demands of the workers in a political revolution in Russia.

Whereas the revolution in Eastern Europe and China had been regarded as a welcome adjunct and extension of the power, privilege and vested interests of the bureaucracy, *the revolution in Hungary struck terror in the hearts of the bureaucrats from Peking, through Moscow to Belgrade.* The fate of all the regimes of Eastern Europe hung in the balance. Not since the Spanish revolution had there been such a social earthquake, which stirred the proletariat of the Soviet Union and of the other workers' states. That is why, *on the frantic urging of Mao Tse-Tung and the other Stalinist leaders, the Soviet bureaucracy had to intervene in Hungary and drown the revolution in blood* before the proletariat could create in the fire of the revolution, as always in such circumstances, the necessary Marxist party and leadership. The hot flame of the revolution rendered the proletarian troops of the Russian army of occupation completely

---

*In 1956 the workers in Hungary rose up against the ruling bureaucracy. In six weeks they organised two general strikes and two insurrections. They were eventually defeated by the intervention of Russian tanks.

unreliable. They had to be withdrawn and only the most backward troops from Siberia, untouched at that stage by the revolutionary events, could be used to drown the revolution in blood.

As Marxist theory would expect, whereas the revolution in China appeared as a remote event, with perhaps the sympathy of the more advanced workers among the proletariat of Western Europe, it did not in the eyes of the proletariat of Western Europe affect them as an event directly connected with their interests and aspirations. The Hungarian revolution, like the Spanish before it, immediately awakened the interest of the mass of the working class in Western Europe. Apart from its repercussions in the Communist Parties of the West, among the advanced layers, it also aroused an echo among the broad masses in the factories, in the workshops and wherever the workers were gathered together in industry.

The difference between the effects of the revolution in colonial countries at present and the revolution in backward countries like that of China 1925-7, was because the latter was on the model of the Russian revolution as far as the participation of the social classes was concerned. Similarly for the Spanish revolution, also a revolution in a backward country. If these revolutions did not lead to victory over the bourgeoisie, it was directly because of the proletariat's leadership.

The proletariat strove, with all the efforts of which that class is capable, to carry through the revolutionary transformation of society *a la Russe*. In China and the other areas where the revolution had been victorious since the second world war, in the main all backward countries, the proletariat did not play the same role as it did in Spain, in China in 1925-7 and in the Hungarian revolution.

Those comrades who have newly discovered the peasantry and the semi-proletariat and even the village proletariat as the main revolutionary force in these colonial revolutions, have not understood the real significance of the role which these classes have played. Where the proletariat is led by a conscious revolutionary party, the petit-bourgeois in town and countryside, under the firm leadership of the proletariat, can support the victory of the working class and the installation of its revolutionary dictatorship, ie in the sense of the dictatorship of the proletariat, in Trotsky's expression, according to the norm. Even here, this can only be done where such a revolution organically, step by step, is linked to the prospect and the ideas of a socialist revolution on a world scale. In the *History of the Russian Revolution*, Trotsky quotes a peasant soldier influenced by the propaganda and agitation of

Bolshevism, who spoke of the world revolution as the only salvation for the revolution. Thus the Russian revolution in a backward country provoked the 'Ten Days that Shook the World'.

The idea of leaning on the peasant masses, of the 'revolutionary elements with nothing to lose' and of the lumpen proletariat as a revolutionary force, superior to the 'respectable industrial proletariat' which has a higher standard of living, as the decisive force in the revolution, is the idea of Bakunin* and not of Marx or Trotsky. True, these classes under the influence of the revolutionary leadership of the proletariat —again dependent on the revolutionary role of its leadership —can play an important role in the revolution, as the peasantry did in Russia and to a certain extent as the petit-bourgeoisie in the towns also rallied to the side of Bolshevism.

But by the very nature of these classes, where they played the dominant role in a transition, where they are 'used' in the Machiavellian sense by a Stalinist, an ex-Marxist or Bonapartist leadership, this places a decisive stamp on the revolution. Such a role for these classes is only possible because of the impasse of world capitalism and imperialism, on the one side, and the existence of the present balance of world forces on a world scale, the latent power of the proletariat in the industrially advanced countries and, most decisive of all, the existence of the mighty Bonapartist deformed workers' states. But where these classes play the dominating role in the destruction of capitalism in the backward countries, they lay their stamp on the development of events.

The revolutionary peasant armies of China could be likened to the armies of Cromwell, in the sense that the army and the party fused together in the fight. While using the phrases of socialism, they could not have the same collective consciousness of socialism, which almost instinctively develops in the proletariat in industry.

Thus these classes can play the key role of the reserve troops of the revolution of the *battering ram,* but the sharp point of the revolution can only be a revolutionary consciousness of the industrial working class. Religion and all the other prejudices and superstitions accumulated for centuries and even millennia still play an important and even decisive role in the ideology of these states.This is reflected in the ideology and public statements of the leaders of these movements, such as in Algeria, and is of decisive significance in characterising the type of state which has emerged and will emerge in the revolutions in these countries (without a victory of the proletariat in the industrial countries of the West).

*Mikhail Bakunin, the Russian founder of anarchism.

These traits are not accidental. To even suggest such abominations on the part of a Marxist leadership would be criminal. Only Stalinism and social democracy have debased the revolutionary consciousness for these purposes. Of course, with all the blemishes, warts and defects, the significance of the social change for Marxists is decisive. Whilst not throwing out the baby with the bathwater one must, at the same time, if one is to preserve the continuity of Marxist ideas and find the road to a correct policy, understand the inevitable result of the role and character of these revolutions.

These classes cannot play an independent role. Where they are organised by the leadership of ex-Marxists or by intellectual strata of the petit-bourgeoisie in one form or another —the army officers of Burma, Egypt, the ex-Marxists in China, the intellectual layers of the petit-bourgeois in Ghana and other countries —it is possible under the historical conditions sketched above, with a weak and rotting bourgeoisie, or even the absence of any real bourgeoisie, for a transitional regime of a *Bonapartist workers' state* to be set up.

When one considers the confusion that prevails throughout the labour movement and infects even the advanced layers of the Marxist cadres on these questions, one has only to think of the crystal clear ideas of Lenin and Trotsky on the role of the state.

Even under the most favourable of historical conditions, with a developed proletariat playing a dominant role in society, they have warned, echoing in this the elementary ideas of Marx, of the danger that lies in the very existence of the state. The state, or to be more accurate, the semi-state, even in the advanced countries, constitutes a source of danger and of infection, which only the highest revolutionary consciousness and vigilance on the part of the proletariat and its leadership can prevent from degeneration and deformation.

The rise of Stalinism in Russia was no accident, but was due to the isolation of the revolution from the advanced countries of the West. Even what is unthinkable in the present world relationship of forces, a proletarian victory in an advanced capitalist country that did not spread to other countries, would be in danger over a long and historical period of degeneration and collapse.

But the whole relationship of forces on a world scale, the whole development of the epoch, has been such that a single revolutionary victory in Western Europe, in Japan, in Britain or America will be sufficient to transform the world scene. It would spread like a bush fire, far faster and with far more profound effects than even the Russian revolution.

Let us go further and pose the problem that in a country like

Italy or France, where the proletariat plays an overwhelmingly decisive role and where its latent power has been further reinforced by the development of industry, that the Stalinists under the influence of the revolutionary wave should be pushed into power, which is not theoretically excluded. It is true that at the present time both the Italian and the French Stalinist parties are second-line defenders of the bourgeois state but, under the impact of a revolutionary wave, they would put forward their most left face.

If they were pushed in the direction of taking power, it could only be with a mobilisation of the full resources, revolutionary energy and capacity for organisation and struggle on the part of the proletariat. Such a proletariat would not allow the development of bureaucracy as in the backward countries, where the proletariat has not played the dominant role. Without the mobilisation of the proletariat to its uttermost extent, as in France in 1936, as in Germany in 1918, as in Spain in 1936 and 1937, victory over the bourgeoisie could not be assured.

But a revolutionary victory would transform the situation nationally and internationally. The Stalinist party would burst at the seams. On the other hand one can make the confident prognosis that the far more likely development would be that the great new revolutionary events would cause an immediate crisis within the ranks of the Stalinist parties in all the industrial countries, spreading to the countries of the Eastern bloc.

The events of the last two decades took place and were influenced by the Stalinist syphilis. At the moment the splits of world Stalinism, the development of nationalist deviations on the part of the deformed workers' states, the 'independent' nationalist role of the Communist parties in the capitalist countries, the ceding of the decisive role in social transformations in Cuba, Algeria, Ghana and other countries to petit-bourgeois layers of nationalist intellectuals, is an historical confirmation of the role which Trotsky predicted would mark the end of the Communist International as a revolutionary force.

The crisis within world Stalinism is of such a character that the fundamental unthinking adherence, the blind loyalty which was given by revolutionary workers, even by the advanced layers, has been ended. But even this takes a dialectical form. The old-style Stalinist was far more revolutionary than the present layers within the ranks of the Stalinist party, at least in the industrially advanced countries.

Two decades of 'peaceful' social relations, in comparison with the upheavals of the pre-war days, since the end of the revolutionary upheavals following the second world war, have dulled the consciousness of the advanced layers within the Stalinist movement. Two decades of theoretical and chauvinist poison systematically disseminated by the Stalinist party have lowered the theoretical level of the Stalinist movement. This, coinciding with the period of capitalist upsurge and growth, and interacting with it, has led to a lowering of the theoretical level of the rank and file of the movement.

Within the ranks of the Communist parties, however, the shocks and upheavals of the Stalinist world, the 20th Congress, Hungary, the new splits between Stalinist states, above all the split betweeen Russia and China, open the way at a later stage for the decisive transformation of the relations within these parties. Never again in the face of revolutionary events will the rank and file accept unquestioningly the counter-revolutionary role which the Stalinists played in the mass capitalist countries in the past epoch.

However, the development on these lines will be more complicated than could have been foreseen. In criticising the programme of the Communist International in the early stages, Trotsky had predicted that the theory of 'socialism in one country' would lead inevitably to the degeneration on nationalist lines of the parties of the Communist International. In a peculiar historical way this has been borne out by events in the countries where the Stalinists have come to power because of the peculiar development of history, as well as in the capitalist countries.

The brilliant prediction of Trotsky, perhaps in a way which could not have been foreseen, has nevertheless shown the power of Marxist foresight and analysis in dealing with the fundamental principles. These principles arise from the class relations within society. Any tendency in the labour movement which does not at each great historical turn review events from this fundamental standpoint, runs the risk, possibly the inevitability, of coming under the influence of hostile tendencies in the labour movement such as reformism or Stalinism.

The deformed character of the Chinese revolution, its inevitable reflection of the needs and interests of the elite bureaucracy, the shouldering aside of even the peasants, let alone the workers, in the ruling state inevitably stamps the outlook of the ruling Chinese clique. It has more in common with Mandarinism*, in the tradition of China, rather than that of a healthy workers' state, in the sense of the domination of the state by a ruling aristocratic, bureaucratic elite.

---

*Mandarins were Chinese civil service and state bureaucrats from early Han times until 1911. Speaking a special dialect and wearing distinctive robes, they occupied a privileged position in society.

Their entire criticism of other Stalinists is dominated by nationalist considerations, as is, of course, the rotting Stalinist bureaucracy of Russia. Their whole policy, both in world diplomacy and in their intervention in the workers' movement, is dictated by nationalist considerations. The most significant aspect of their struggle against the Russian bureaucracy is their nationalist orientation and perspective. They go even further than Stalin himself dared, to talk about 'centuries of building socialism in China.'

Their criticism of the opportunism of Togliatti, Thorez (Italian CP and French CP leaders, respectively) and the British and American communists, was linked to the idea that it was 'not their business' they did not want to 'interfere' in the internal affairs of these parties; only the criticism of the Chinese by these leaderships provoked the retaliation of the Chinese. It is obvious that the Chinese were not asleep for 15 years and suddenly rediscovered the works of Marx and Lenin.

Their criticism of the proposed Comecon agreement between the Eastern European states and Russia was of the worst type of narrow nationalism. It is true that the Russians proposed this to reinforce their control and domination over these states. But the solution lay in proposing a Balkan Federation of States, linked to federation with Russia. This in turn should be linked to a mighty federation with China. But that is what is impossible with the domination of the bureaucracy of all these countries.

What determines the policy of all of them is the narrow clique interests of the ruling elite. Consequently they all have to base themselves on the most reactionary nationalist prejudices and chauvinism. Only a party resting on the real interests of the proletariat can base itself on genuine internationalism through the inter-penetration of the economy of these countries, for the mutual benefit of all. The imperative need of the world economy to be joined in unity, as against the wastefulness and insanity of particularism, is recognised by the bourgeoisie themselves, as evidenced in the Common Market and other attempted agreements. The bourgeoisie cannot solve this problem, but can only take partial measures, which in the end will collapse into the opposite of 'internationalism' – virulent nationalism and tariff walls.

Trotsky many times emphasised that the twin evils of the modern epoch were private ownership, plus the hampering restrictions of the nation state. These were the main impediments to the development of the productive forces of the modern epoch and the reason why the capitalist system on a world scale was ripe and overripe for the social revolution.

In the backward countries, for a temporary historical period, the achievement of the national state by the expulsion of imperialism remains a powerful and relatively progressive force. But on the world scale, these states immediately come up against the hampering and overwhelming domination of the advanced countries.

But in the countries where the proletariat would come to power, whether in advanced or backward countries, it is the *international* perspective which is decisive. This alone would condemn the haughty nationalist bureaucracies of these countries. They simultaneously played a *progressive* role in relation to the defence of the foundations of the regime, ie nationalised property, but an enormously reactionary role in defence of their privileges, which is summed up in narrow nationalism.

It is not of importance here to go into the theoretical perspectives of modern development and the different variants gone into by Trotsky in his last articles, so misunderstood and distorted by Shachtman, Deutscher* and Cliff. But what is of interest is the emphasis which Trotsky gives to the fact that the historical task is not only the destruction of capitalism but the ending of the old national economies which are constricting and hampering the development of productive forces.

In fact, Trotsky gives decisive importance to the question of the reactionary role of the national state and shows that the mere destruction of private ownership, of enormous historical importance, would nevertheless only be an episode without the destruction of the former.

Had the Russian workers retained control of their state, the revolutions in China and Eastern Europe could not have assumed their reactionary nationalist character. The problems which the development of Siberia poses, would have been solved by the welcome emigration of tens of millions of Chinese peasants to Siberia, to be trained by Russian technicians and the joint use of resources of this fabulously rich area, for the benefit of both peoples and the cementing of federation between them.

Instead of this modestly practical scheme, neither the Russian bureaucracy nor the Chinese, limited by their caste interests, could pose the problem in this way. The Chinese, from their point of view, pose the problem of 'national' socialism, each country developing its own resources, while the Russians pose as 'internationalist' ie to use the power of their industrial position to dominate the weaker economies of the smaller Stalinist states in Eastern Europe. The national limitedness of Chinese Stalinism

*Isaac Deutscher joined the Polish CP in 1926, expelled in 1932 for his opposition to Stalinism. Biographer of Stalin and Trotsky.

screams from every page of their documents. In this respect, there is nothing to choose between the two powerful Stalinist states.

It is one of the ironical paradoxes of history that in the advanced economies of Western Europe, the degenerate Stalinist leaderships clothe themselves in the stinking rags of outmoded nationalism. They criticise from the nationalist standpoint the hopeless attempts of the bourgeoisie to overcome the impediment of the national state, a task which the modern bourgeoisie is incapable of carrying out, despite their ludicrous and feeble attempts.

For the Marxist wing in the labour movement any criticism of the warring Stalinist factions must begin with this standpoint. No concessions can be made to the degenerate nationalism of all wings of Stalinism. Trotsky explained the weakness of the Fourth International, among other reasons, by the power of nationalist ideas and traditions.

Now in the metropolitan countries of the West, the Stalinists have become partially a second reformist agency of the bourgeoisie rather than, as in the past, a faithful tool of the foreign policy of the Russian bureaucracy.

The struggle between Russia and China gives a certain independence to the bureaucracy of the Communist parties. Decades of poisonous and chauvinist propaganda have disorientated the upper layers of the Communist parties in the metropolitan countries and even affected the rank and file. But the big majority of the cadre elements, uneasily in opposition and looking to Peking for a revolutionary lead, will only be won to the banner Marxism if these aspects of internationalism and of theory are emphasised and stressed.

The entire cadres of the Stalinist parties have been miseducated on these questions for decades. It is our task in approaching these cadres to emphasise these problems. At the dawn of the struggle of the Left Opposition it was this problem that was emphasised, underlined and stressed by Trotsky. Not for nothing did Trotsky write a *Criticism of the Draft Programme of the Communist International* on these questions. Since the decades have passed — and what decades — every event has demonstrated the correctness of this approach. It was always central to the approach of Trotsky. Those comrades who dream of an 'easier' approach are deluding themselves. Nor is it feasible to imagine that an opportunist approach on 'current', 'modern' lines will succeed, while the revolutionary approach is left for the bedroom.

Why should any cadres in the Russian wing or the Chinese wing approach the Marxists unless they have something to offer? What have we to offer, at this stage, except the theories of the masters, reinforced and enriched by the experience of the last decades? Episodic criticisms will drive those cadres becoming critical to one side or the other. As far as the masses are concerned, we do not have their ears as yet.

In some senses, the crisis of Stalinism has sown further confusion within the ranks of the Communist parties. Their lack of education in the fundamentals of Marxism, the degeneration of Stalinism on nationalist lines, the apparent lustre of revolutionary victories in China and other countries, tomorrow the victory of the peasant war in Vietnam, have muddled and confused their ranks. But the quarrels of all the nationalist Stalinist factions, particularly that between China and Russia, have laid the seeds of terrific crises in the Stalinist parties, particularly in the metropolitan countries.

In a certain sense, the immediate effect of the Russo-Chinese conflict as far as the mass membership of the Communist Party is concerned, is to make the task of the Marxists more difficult. Many cadres, embittered by the opportunism of the Communist parties, have welcomed what they conceive as the 'revolutionary' turn of the Chinese. Instead of mighty Russia, they look to mighty Peking as the revolutionary centre. They will not be interested in incidental criticism.

Nevertheless, from a historical point of view, the crisis opens up a way for the complete transformation of the world scene. The labour bureaucracy in Western Europe have long lost the uncritical enthusiasm of their followers. The uncritical adherence of the ranks within the Communist Party is also now ended. There cannot be more than one Rome or one Pope.

On the basis of the great events which impend in the next decade or two, as Trotsky predicted, perhaps a little belatedly, not one stone will remain upon the other of the old 'Internationals' of the working class. The changed consciousness of the masses will be revealed in the mass Communist parties, especially in France and Italy. Never again will the ranks of the Communist parties tolerate without mighty movements of protest, the sell-outs and betrayals of 1936 in France and Spain and in 1944-7* in France and Italy. The Communist parties would be split from top to bottom.

*With the defeat of the German occupation forces in 1944, the workers in France and Italy moved in a revolutionary direction. The Communist Parties entered into 'national unity' governments which were used by the ruling class to diffuse the workers' movement. Once the immediate danger had passed, the CPs were jettisoned from the cabinets.

Above all, it is necessary for Marxists to make an implacable criticism of the nationalism of both the Russian and Chinese bureaucracies. For Marxists in the colonial countries, the problem is exceptionally difficult. It is not easy for peasant masses to see beyond the national horizon. Their outlook is strictly limited. They can be led in this direction only by the proletariat and by concrete linking up of their material interests with that of an international perspective.

The doctrine of Marx, Lenin and Trotsky, by its very nature, is suited to the outlook of the proletariat at certain stages in history. Of course the proletariat too is not impervious to the nationalist poison. That is why it is necessary in appealing to the advanced workers to *stress and emphasise* the problem of *an internationalist approach* not only in the advanced countries, but in the backward countries as well. Unless they understand this, the advanced workers will be lost. No concessions can be made on this question to any other tendencies in the movement.

Of course, from the point of view of world politics, the magnificent revolt of the colonial people is preparing an entirely new relationship of forces on a world scale. Once, however, the heavy battalions enter the scene of history in Western Europe, Japan or America, the whole relationship of forces on a world scale will be changed.

Trotsky once warned of the possibility of the disappearance of the Fourth International if it did not find a road to the masses. This can be reinforced with a further warning. Unless the basic ideas of Trotskyism, enriched and developed but in fundamentals the same, are not emphasised and drummed into the consciousness of the Marxists internationally, they too can degenerate impressionistically and tail behind the left reformists, Chinese Stalinists or Russian Stalinists. There must be no empirical bowing down to events, the basic issues must be brought forward again and again, especially in the theoretical works and journals of Marxism.

The problem has to be posed sharply: either the colonial revolutions have taken the particular form they have because of the delay in the revolution in the advanced countries...or there is no role for Marxist tendencies except as self-appointed and benevolent advisors to Castro, Mao and Ben Bella.

Here it should be made clear that from a Marxist point of view the arguments of Plekhanov and the theoreticians of Menshevism — that Russia was not ripe for socialism in 1917 — are and were perfectly correct...if Russia is taken in isolation from the world and the internationalist perspectives of Bolshevism. All other tendencies, cliques and groupings in the labour movement are doomed to sterility and collapse for lack of the internationalist perspective as the basis for their work. The colonial revolutions mark a gigantic step forward for all the ex-colonial countries. But the final solution of the problem can only be found in the international arena and in the victory of the working class in the advanced countries.

It was partly due to American intervention that Castro nationalised the Cuban economy. Castro is shown driving a tank during the Kennedy-backed Bay of Pigs invasion.

From: The Colonial Revolution and the Deformed Workers' States

July 1978

IN BOURGEOIS countries in the past, where the bourgeoisie has a role to play and looks forward confidently to the future — ie when it is genuinely progressive in developing the productive forces — it has decades and generations to perfect the state as an instrument of its own class rule. The army, police, civil service, middle layers and especially all key positions at the top; heads of civil service, heads of departments, police chiefs, the officer corps and especially the colonels and generals are carefully selected to serve the needs and interests of the ruling class. With a developing economy and a mission and a role they eagerly serve the 'national interest' ie the interest of the possessing class — the ruling class.

In Syria, as in all the ex-colonial countries, the imperialists, in this case the French, partly under the pressure of their rivals, especially American imperialism, were compelled to relinquish their *direct* military domination. The state which emerged is not fixed and static. The weakness and incapacity of the bourgeoisie gave a certain independence to the military caste. Hence the perpetual coups and counter-coups of the military. But in the last analysis they reflect the class interests of the ruling class. They cannot play an independent role.

The struggle between the cliques in the army reflects the instability and contradictions in the given society. The personal aims of the generals reflect the differing interests of social classes or fractions of classes of society, the petit-bourgeois in its various fractions, the bourgeoisie, or even under certain conditions the proletariat in so far as thay are successful in gaining power. The officer caste must reflect *the interest of some class or grouping* in society. They do not represent themselves though of course they can plunder the society and elevate their own ruling caste. Nevertheless they must have a class basis in a given society.

Bonapartist regimes do not rest on air but balance between the classes. In the final analysis they represent whichever is the dominant class in society. The economy of that class determines its class character. Some of these countries, as in Latin America, a semi-colonial continent which was under the domination of British then especially American imperialism for the last century, nevertheless, have been nominally independent for more than a century. In consequence, despite a period of turbulence the ruling class of landowners and capitalists has had sufficient period to perfect their state. Sometimes the armed forces of different fractions or factions of armed forces, can reflect different fractions of the ruling class and even the pressures of imperialism, primarily American imperialism.

But, up to now, they have always reflected the interest of the ruling class in the defence of private ownership.

In Burma, where the regime, newly emerged from British domination and where the ruling class was incapable of success-fully 'holding the country together', it faced a series of rebellions and wars. The army was formed from the the Anti-Fascist Peoples Freedom League, which described itself as 'socialist'.

With China as a model next door, the army leaders tired of the incapacity of the landowners and capitalists to solve the problems of Burma. Basing themselves on the support of the workers and peasants, they organised a coup, expropriated the landowners and capitalists and established Burma as a 'Burmese Buddhist Socialist State'.

China

Yet up to the Russian revolution even Lenin denied the possibility of the victory of the proletarian revolution in a backward country. The Chinese revolution of 1944-9 did not proceed on the model of the revolution of 1925-7. It was a *peasant war*, which took place because of the complete incapacity of the bourgeoisie to carry out the tasks of the bourgois-democratic revolution − the ending of landlordism, national unification and the expulsion of imperialism − it ended with victory to the Chinese Stalinists.

The programme of the Chinese Stalinists was not fundamentally different to that of Castro later in Cuba: 50 or 100 years of 'national capitalism' and an alliance with the 'national bourgeoisie'. Hence the belief of many American bourgeois that they were 'agrarian reformers'.

Only the Marxist tendency in Britain argued against the Stalinists and the alleged 'Trotskyist' sects and explained the inevabililiy of Mao's victory and the establishment of a deformed workers' state.

At a time when Mao and the Chinese CP had the programme of capitalism and 'national democracy' we could predict the *inevitability of proletarian Bonapartism* as the next stage in China. This had nothing in common with the methods of the proletarian revolution in Russia in 1917.

Power was gained through the peasant war by giving land to the soldiers in Chiang Kai Shek's army. Then, by balancing between the classes and playing them off against each other in Bonapartist fashion, once military victory was achieved, landlordism and capitalism were expropriated. Nearly all the so-called 'Trotskyist' sects now accept the accomplished fact. But never before in history has it even been theoretically posed that *a peasant war on classical lines could lead to a workers' state, however deformed.* The workers in China were passive throughout the civil war for reasons we will not enter here. But here was a perfect example of one class —the peasants in the form of the Red Army —carrying out the tasks of another.

It is amusing now to see the sects without turning a hair, swallowing the idea that a 'workers' state' was established in China by the peasant army, only because at the head of the army was the so-called 'Communist' Party. In classical Marxist theory this idea would be precisely considered hair-raising and fantastic. The peasants, *as a class*, are least capable of assuming a *socialist* consciousness.

It is an aberration of Marxism to think that such a process is 'normal'. It can only be explained by the *impasse* of capitalism in China, the paralysis of imperialism, the existence of a strong deformed Bonapartist state in Stalinist Russia, and most important of all, the delay in the victory in the industrially advance countries of the world. The colonial countries cannot wait. The problems are too crushing. *There is no way forward on the basis of capitalism.* Hence the peculiar aberrations in colonial countries. But the price for this, as in the Soviet Union, is a second *political* revolution to put the control of society, industry and the state in the hands of the proletariat. Only thus could the first genuine beginnings of the transition of socialism, or rather steps in that direction, commence.

The wide support for 'socialism' not only among the working class, but among the peasants and wide layers of the petit-bourgeoisie in the cities in colonial countries, is the expression of the complete blind alley of landlordism and capitalism in the colonial world in the modern epoch. It is also a result of the Russian and Chinese revolutions and their achievements in developing industry and the economy. It is this that lays the groundwork for the development of proletarian Bonapartism.

The state can be reduced to armed bodies of men, according to Engels. With the defeat and destruction of the police and army of Chiang Kai Shek, with the destruction of the army of Batista* in Cuba, power was in the hands respectively of Mao and Castro. The fact that nominally Mao was a 'Communist' and Castro a bourgeois democrat altered nothing.

Moscow's Image

So far was Mao from the model of the proletarian revolution that on entering Shanghai and other cities, workers who had seized their factories and met Mao with demonstrations of red flags were instantly shot in order to 'restore order'! The state created by Mao was in the image of Moscow, 1949, not Moscow 1917!

Mao, in typical Bonapartist fashion on the basis of the peasant army, always an instrument of (bourgeois) Bonapartism in the past, balanced between the classes. Having perfected a state in the image of Moscow, *leaning on the workers and peasants, he could snuff out the bourgeoisie painlessly.* As Trotsky put it, for a lion you need a gun, for a flea, a fingernail will do! Therefore, having balanced between the bourgeoisie and the workers and peasants in order to prevent the workers from taking power, Mao and his gang −after perfecting the state −could then crush the bourgeoisie before turning on the workers and peasants to crush whatever elements of workers' democracy had developed.

The bureaucracy then developed a totalitarian one-party dictatorship, centred round the Bonapartist dictatorship of one single individual − Mao. But, not for nothing has Marxist theory given the task of achieving the socialist revolution and the transition to socialism to the working class. This is not an arbitrary role but because of the specific role *in production* of the proletariat which gives it a *specific consciousness possessed by no other class.* Least of all can the petit-bourgeois peasant develop this consciousness. A revolution based on the latter class by its very nature would be doomed to degeneration and Bonapartism. It is precisely because a proletarian Bonapartist dictatorship protects the privileges of the elite of state, party, the army, industry and the intellectuals of art and science that it has succeeded in so many backward countries.

Marxism finds in the development of the productive forces the key to the development of society. *On a capitalist basis there is no longer a way forward, particularly for backward countries.* That is why army officers, intellectuals and others, affected by the decay of their societies can *under certain conditions* switch their allegiance. A

*Fulgencia Batista was the US backed Cuban dictator, from 1933 until his overthrow by the guerrilla army led by Castro in 1959.

change to proletarian Bonapartism actually enlarges their power, prestige, privileges and income. They become the sole commanding and directing stratum of the society, raising themselves even higher over the masses than in the past. Instead of being subservient to the weak, craven and ineffectual bourgeoisie they become the masters of society.

Transitional Economies

The tendency towards *statification* of the productive forces, which have grown beyond the limits of private ownership, is manifest in the most highly developed economies and even in the most reactionary colonial countries.

There is no possibility of a consistent, *uninterrupted* and continuous increase in productive forces in the countries of the so-called third world on a capitalist basis. Production stagnates or falls. In the world recessions, particularly in the smaller countries, living standards fall. There is no way out on the basis of the capitalist system. That explains the terror regimes of bourgeois Bonapartism like that of Pakistan, Indonesia, Argentina, Chile and Zaire. But with bayonets and bullets, on the basis of an out-dated and antiquated system, only very temporary respite is given. Discontent multiplies and is reflected in the officer caste of the armed forces and throughout the society. This in turn leads to conspiracies of individuals and groups of officers.

The army is a mirror of society and reflects its contradictions. That and not the mere whims of the officers concerned, is the cause of the upheavals as in Syria. It is an indication of the agonised crisis of society, which cannot be solved in the old way. These strata of society can espouse 'socialism' of the Stalinist variety —proletarian Bonapartism —all the more enthusiastically because of their contempt for the masses of workers and peasants.

The horrible caricature of workers' rule in Russia, China, and the other countries of deformed workers' states attracts them precisely because of the position of the 'intellectual' educated cadres of that society. What is repulsive to Marxism is what attracts the Stalinists.

All that these states have in common with healthy workers' states or with the Russia of 1917-23 is state ownership of the means of production. On that basis they can plan and develop the productive resources with forced marches at a pace absolutely impossible on their former landlord-capitalist basis. This is possible of course for only a *limited period* of time. At some point the Stalinist regimes become an absolute hindrance and a fetter to production. Russia and Eastern Europe are reaching these limits. In common with a healthy workers' state on the accepted Marxist norm is the fact that they are transitional economies between capitalism and socialism.

But Marxism teaches that a movement towards socialism requires the control, guidance and participation of the proletariat. With a privileged elite in uncontrolled dominance and not reconciled to the loss of its status in a 'withering away' of the state, this produces new contradictions. As the corruption, nepotism, waste, mismanagement and chaos which bureaucratic control necessarily involves comes more and more into contradiction with the needs of social development, this manifests itself in the heightened antagonism between the proletariat and the bureaucratic elite.

Trotsky long ago explained that in the case of Russia the bureaucracy developed the productive forces in a way in which the bourgeoisie was incapable of doing, but at three times the cost to the masses. The bureaucracy fulfills the function, a *relatively* progressive function, which the bourgeoisie had accomplished in the past. But Trotsky explained that this role also engenders its own contradictions. The bureaucracy is in some senses even less prepared than the bourgeoisie to reconcile itself to the loss of privilege and power. Instead it grows even more to become a monstrous cancer on society. It can only be removed by *political revolution*.

This will be triggered either by events at home or the successful gaining of power by the proletariat and the constitution of a workers' democracy in one of the advanced capitalist countries. It will be by social revolution in the West or by victorious political revolution in Russia and Eastern Europe that a healthy workers' state and a workers' democracy will be created. It must be emphasised that the only features these deformed workers' states have in common with the ideal workers' state is state ownership of the economy and a plan of production. Only one of the 'idealist' and 'eclectic' sects could discover a fundamental difference between the peasant war in which Mao came to power and the guerrilla war of Castro, based on peasants and semi-peasants and landless peasants as well as some ex-workers. There is not much difference, despite the bourgeois democratic ideas in Castro's head which in any event were not all that different from the programme on which Mao fought the civil war.

At least in the last stages of the struggle, the participation of the working class, with the general strike in Havana, turned the scales in Castro's favour. Nothing of this sort happened in the civil war in China of 1945-9. Nor was this kind of intervention desired by Mao; true, had it not been for the stupidity of American imperialism the outcome could have been different in Cuba. But with the impasse of Cuban capitalism like that of Chinese capitalism, just as Mao had used the strong proletarian Bonapartist state of Russia as a model, so *Castro used Eastern Europe and China as models in his conflict with American imperialism.*

In both cases this marked an enormous step forward historically. Landlordism and capitalism were eliminated. That meant the removal of the fetters of semi-feudal landlordism and of private ownership of industry. The monopoly of foreign trade, following the Russian model, is also a powerful progressive factor. These measures meant a gigantic release of the constraints on the productive forces. Hence *in advance* we could hail the Chinese revolution as the second greatest event in human history, the Russian revolution being the first. Nevertheless because of its Bonapartist character —and the inevitable vested interest of the bureaucracy in maintaining the rule of privilege, prestige, power and income for the ruling layers of the bureaucracy itself —the masses would have to pay with a second revolution before there could be a workers' democracy on the level of that in Russia of 1917-23.

Because of the incapacity of the sects to apply Marxism and 'Marxist philosophy' in a concrete manner they have landed themselves in ludicrous contradictions. Thus they declared Eastern Europe to be state capitalist in 1945-47 —while Russia, which occupied Eastern Europe with the Red Army, was a 'degenerated workers' state'.

When Tito broke with Stalin, overnight, from mysteriously being 'capitalist', Yugoslavia became a healthier workers' state than even Russia in 1917! This did not prevent these sects from simultaneously declaring Eastern Europe still to be capitalist. China remained 'state capitalist' according to them until 1951 or 1953. Then, 'Hey Presto', China, from being 'state capitalist', was mysteriously transformed into a 'healthy workers' state'!

All this muddle and theoretical confusion has never been explained by any one of these petit-bourgeois tendencies masquerading as Marxists. One sect claimed Cuba was a petit-bourgeois Bonapartist state while describing China as a relatively healthy workers' state in which political revolution was not necessary. Not a single one of these tendencies was capable of analysing the main forces and processes of the epoch, in which the colonial world saw *a caricature of permanent revolution* in which weird and deformed workers' states were being set up. Not a single one of them understood the meaning of the Chinese 'cultural revolution'. Some hailed this as a second version of the 'Paris Commune'! Only recently —some 30 years too late —some reluctantly concluded that the Chinese revolution was deformed from the start. *Our tendency explained the process in advance of Mao's victory.*

All the objective conditions for a socialist revolution are now maturing in Western Europe, Japan and the USA. The process, however, will be protracted because of the weakness of the forces of genuine Marxism. It is the delay of the revolution in the West, and now its protracted character, which gives room for these peculiar regimes in the neo-colonial countries. They are reaching unbearable tensions with semi-starvation of great masses without a roof or a crust. The insolent parasitism and luxury of the landlords and capitalists in contrast, leaning on imperialism, invests all the contradictions in these societies with an explosive force. It is on the basis of this weakness of imperialism, the glaring rottenness and decay of landlordism-capitalism — which makes possible the development of the curious process of proletarian Bonapartism. Taking advantage of the revolt of the masses of peasants, petit-bourgeoisie and even workers, the elite of officers, intellectuals etc, can emerge, as in Ethiopia, with firm power in their hands on the basis of the support of the workers and peasants. They can perfect a 'KGB' secret police of their own to silence anyone who would object to their privileges.

The peasantry, by its very nature a class of individuals not bound together by production, is therefore the perfect instrument for bourgeois or proletarian Bonapartism. It is a class that can inherently be manipulated and deceived; a class that looks towards the 'Tsar as a father of the people', or to the god-head, Mao. The urban petit-bourgeois too have these attributes; in Germany and Italy they looked to Hitler and Mussolini as 'leaders'. *Only the proletariat* stands firmly for genuine democracy — ie workers' democracy in a workers' state —which is the only system where its *direct rule* can be manifested.

Our tendency has explained and predicted these processes. There is no real possibility of moving forward in the colonial world on a capitalist basis. It is this, plus the lagging of the proletarian revolution in the advanced industrialised countries, which has led to these regimes taking ten steps forward and five steps back. They can — at least for a period in most cases — develop the productive forces with seven league boots, on the basis of proletarian Bonapartism. They carry out in backward countries the historic job which was carried out by the bourgeoisie in the capitalist countries in the past.

The whole essence of Trotsky's theory of the permanent revolution lies in the idea that *the colonial bourgeoisie and the bourgeoisie of the backward countries are incapable of carrying out the tasks of the bourgeois democratic revolution.* This is because of their links with the landlords and the imperialists. The banks have mortgages on the land, industrialists have landed estates in the country, the landlords invest in industry and the whole is entangled together and linked with imperialism in a web of vested interests opposed to change.

Under these circumstances the task of carrying out the bourgeois-democratic revolution fell on the shoulders of the proletariat. But the proletariat, having conquered power at the head of the peasantry and the majority of the nation, would not stop at the accomplishment of the bourgeois-democratic tasks of expropriating the landowners, unifying the nation, and expelling the imperialists. *It would then pass on to the socialist tasks,* the expropriation of the bourgeoisie and the setting up of a workers' state.

But the socialist tasks could not be encompassed in a single country, especially a backward colonial country. The revolution would have to spread to the more advanced countries. Hence the term for this process, *permanent revolution* beginning as a bourgeois revolution, becoming a socialist one, ending in international revolution.

It is true that, owing to the development of the Stalinist bureaucracy and the reformist degeneration of the Communist Parties, exceptional difficulties have been put in the path of the proletariat in both advanced and backward countries. But the impasse of landlordism and capitalism in the so-called third world has been aggravated during the course of the decades since the outbreak of the second world war. For a period, the industrialised capitalist countries passed through a relative development of productive forces, once the political pre-conditions had been established by the betrayal in the early post-war period of Stalinism and reformism.

But while living standards in the West increased at least in absolute terms, in the 'third world' with few exceptions there was a decline in already low living standards. The decay of antiquated land relations under the inexorable pressure of the world market continued apace. A large surplus population of paupers, beggars and lumpens is endemic in the colonial world. On the old relations there is no way out. *In Vietnam, Laos, Kampuchea, Burma, Syria, Angola, Mozambique, Aden, Benin, Ethiopia and as models, Cuba and China* (which in their turn had the model of Eastern Europe as a beacon showing the way) *there has been a transformation of social relations.*

This is because of the rotten ripeness of world capitalism for the socialist revolution. But all history shows that where, for one reason or another, the new progressive class is incapable of carrying out its functions of transforming society, this is often done (in a reactionary way, perhaps) by other classes or castes. Thus in Japan big sections of the feudal lords became capitalists and in Germany —as Marx, Engels, Lenin and Trotsky recognised —the landowning Junkers of East Prussia under Bismarck and the monarchy carried out the task of the national unification of Germany—a task of the bourgeois democratic revolution.

Attractive Power

As Marx long ago explained, there is no such thing as a supra-historical blue-print. It is necessary to take the material objective reality as it is and then explain it. That is the method of 'Marxist philosophy' and not the philosophical gibberish of the sects. But it is not only necessary to see objective reality as it is, but to explain the process that brought it into being, the contradictions encompassing it, the law of social movement which it represents and the future processes of contradictions and change which will envelop it. Its process of birth, development, decay and the changes which will destroy it.

Under the conditions of the decay of capitalism-landlordism in the colonial countries, all the social contradictions are aggravated to an extreme. Social tensions reach an unbearable level. Hence in one country after another in Asia, Africa and Latin America, bourgeois democracy is replaced by bourgeois Bonapartist dictatorships or proletarian Bonapartist dictatorships.

In the above-named ex-colonial countries not one proceeded on the model of the norm of the socialist revolution. Neither did the countries of Eastern Europe before them in the aftermath of the second world war.

The great Marxist teachers in the past have often explained that once the norm of the socialist revolution has been established in the main capitalist countries, it would have an irresistible appeal to the rest of the world and result in a painless transformation without conflict. Even the bourgeoisie would recognise the superiority of workers' democracy, apart from the effect this would have on the world working class. Marx himself believed that in this way the backward areas of the world, and even the backward countries of Europe, would be brought forward by the advanced industrialised countries acting as a magnet and a model of socialism. Lenin and Trotsky conceived of the socialist revolution taking place in some backward countries first *only* with the leading role and participation of the proletariat. The proletariat would lead the petit-bourgeois masses, especially the peasantry, to the overthrow of landlordism and capitalism and then link the workers to the international working class and the tasks of the world revolution.

The Bonapartist totalitarian dictatorship in Russia, a completely deformed workers' state, repels workers in advanced capitalist countries. This is because nothing remains of October except the abolition of landlordism and capitalism, a plan of production, plus the monopoly of foreign trade, albeit bureaucratically twisted and distorted.

But nevertheless the mighty achievements of the revolution, the productive advances, the abolition of backwardness bringing Russia to the position of the second industrial power of the world, have an enormous attractive power for the colonial masses. (This is further reinforced by the example of the Chinese revolution which in the space of less than a quarter of a century has transformed China into a mighty power.) In most of the colonial countries where it still exists, bourgeois democracy is a hollow and empty shell backed up at various times by 'states of siege', states of emergency and even martial law.

Consequently the lack of workers' democracy in these proletarian Bonapartist states is not such a drawback in attracting the masses. It is a positive attractive feature as far as the professional and lower army officers are concerned. The solution of their most pressing problems of food, clothing and shelter loom large in the minds of the colonial masses.

Ethiopia

This in its turn has an enormous effect in the countries of Asia, Africa and Latin America. The bourgeois-Bonapartist regimes in the colonial countries are charged with terrible contradictions. Their problems are insoluble. They spend large sums on armaments, further exacerbating the poverty of the masses. They are inherently unstable. They provoke the hatred of the workers, the petit-bourgeoisie, the students and peasants. Even the weak bourgeoisie they represent comes into collision with them.

It is in this social soil that plots, counter-plots and conspiracies in the army flourish. The army (or armed forces) is always moulded in the image of society and is not independent of it. Where the army dominates that indicates a crisis in society and a regime of crisis.

Different cliques, groups or even individuals at the top in the army come to reflect groupings, sections of classes or classes in society. They do not represent themselves but precisely reflect the antagonistic interests of different classes in society.

Under conditions of social crisis people change. This applies to classes and even individuals. Thus Marx explained that with the decay of feudalism a section of the feudal lords, bigger or smaller as the case may be, goes over to the side of the bourgeoisie in the bourgeois revolution. A section of the bourgeoisie, particularly the intellectual bourgeoisie, can also put themselves on the standpoint of the proletariat.

No more barren, formalistic, anti-dialectical, philosophically idealist, anti-'Marxist philosophy' idea in the history of the movement has been put forward than by those who argue that because *Castro began his revolutionary struggle as a bourgeois democrat with bourgeois democratic ideas and goals* that therefore he must remain a bourgeois democrat for all eternity. They forget that Marx and Engels themselves began as *bourgeois democrats* who broke decisively with the bourgeoisie and became leaders of the proletariat.

Under conditions of the crisis of capitalism in Portugal*, a semi-colonial country, a majority of the officer caste, sickened by the decades of dictatorship and the seemingly unending wars in Africa which they realised they could not win, moved in the direction of revolution and 'socialism'. Only our tendency explained this process.

This gave an impetus to the movement of the working class, which then reacted in its turn on the army. This affected not only the rank and file, and the lower ranks of the officers, but even some admirals and generals who were sincerely desirous of solving the problems of Portuguese society and the Portuguese people.

This was something that would have been impossible in previous revolutions. Thus, 99 per cent of the officer caste supported Franco in the Spanish civil war.

True enough, because of the reformist and Stalinist betrayal of the Portuguese revolution which prevented it from being carried through to completion, there has been a reaction. The army has been purged and purged again to become a more reliable instrument of the bourgeoisie.

But how far this has succeeded remains to be tested in the events of the revolution in the coming months and years.

But what it has demonstrated is the need for a genuine dialectical understanding and interpretation of the events of the present epoch. If such a transformation was possible, in a semi-colonial but imperialist capitalist Portugal, how much more could similar processes take place in the newly independent countries of Africa and of Asia?

*On 25 April 1974, a movement of armed forces officers overthrew the Caetano dictatorship in Portugal, ushering in a revolutionary crisis.

Events in Ethiopia have crushingly confirmed the theses we have worked out. There, the famine brought about by Haile Selassie and the landlord nobility, was the last catastrophe even the officer caste was prepared to tolerate. The callous indifference of the Emperor and the landlord class to the famine and the death from starvation of hundreds of thousands and possibly even millions, plus the accumulated social contradictions in a backward country under the pressure of imperialism, pushed the middle layers of the officer caste to organise a coup.

This in its turn awakened the movement of the small working class in Addis Abbaba and the students and petit-bourgeois layers in the capital and in the towns. It awakened the peasantry also into a cataclysmic movement to gain control of land. Thus the 1000 year old 'empire' and its class structure crumbled to dust.

The crisis in the army and the attempts at counter-revolution, the further impetus this gave to the guerrilla war in Eritrea, the guerrilla war in the Ogaden, aided by the direct intervention of Somalia, the uprisings of the Galla and other tribes, all acted as a spur to the revolution.

The movement of the classes in turn had its effect on the new ruling junta in the army. It produced splits and individual and group conspiracies of officers. These reflected the classes in battle in Ethiopia and the developing civil war in the whole country. *Whatever the individual whims of the officers, they reflected (as in Syria) — and had to reflect — the class struggle taking place.* Hardly any wished for a return to the old regime.

The model of the Emperor's landlord semi-feudal regime was rejected by the bulk of the officer caste. But there were differences as to how far to go, which ended in armed conflicts and executions. This, in a distorted way perhaps, reflected the struggle of the classes in Ethiopia.

It ended in the victory of Lieutenant Colonel Mengistu. Already the land had been divided among the peasants and industry nationalised without compensation to the imperialists and the native capitalists (though of course compensation is not necessarily the decisive factor).

In the struggles Lieutenant Colonel Mengistu emerged victorious as a Bonapartist dictator under the influence of the wars and civil wars. In order to *obtain mass support* Mengistu, formerly a high-up officer of the Emperor, has been forced to go all the way. He has declared himself a 'Marxist-Leninist' (probably without reading a single word of Marx or Lenin) and set about creating a one party 'Marxist-Leninist' totalitarian dictatorship. This is in the image of Moscow or Peking. The landlords and capitalists are expropriated and the imperialist countries are without real influence on the processes taking place in Ethiopia.

In this case the process is clear. It is even clearer than in Mozambique, Angola or the former Aden, and this without a direct struggle against imperialist occupation.

The imperialists are too weak and debilitated to intervene directly by military means and can only grind their teeth in impotence.

But undoubtedly only the *Militant* foresaw these possibilities in advance for many countries in Asia, Africa and Latin America. The revolution, or rather the primary tasks of the revolution, in backward countries have been accomplished in the regimes mentioned above. Landlordism has been eliminated. Capitalism has been destroyed, the influence of imperialism dispelled.

Thus the bourgeois origin of the leadership of the guerrilla movement in Cuba was of third or fifth rate importance. What was important was the attempt to take action to bring Cuba back to neo-colonial status which precipitated the break of Castro with American imperialism.

It is the social and economic similarities which are decisive for a Marxist in the social overturns in these countries.

To carry through a revolution like that of Russia in October 1917 requires the consciousness, the action, the understanding and the active participation and movement of the proletariat itself in the overthrow of capitalism and landlordism. It requires organs and organisations through which the proletariat can move, such as soviets, shop stewards committees, trade unions and so on. After the victory of the rule of the workers, the checking and control can be effected by such organs of workers' rule.

In a revolution according *to the norm* such ad hoc committees and traditional organisations are indispensable. They are a training ground for the workers in the art of running the state, of developing the solidarity and understanding of the workers. After a victorious overthrow of capital they become vehicles for workers' rule, the organs of the new state and of workers' democracy.

But where — as in Eastern Europe, China, Cuba, Syria, Ethiopia — the overthrow takes place with the *support* of the workers and peasants certainly but *without their active control,* clearly the result must be different. The petit-bourgeois intellectuals, army officers, leaders of guerrilla bands use the workers and peasants as cannon fodder, merely as points of support, as a gun rest, so to speak.

Their aim, conscious or unconscious, is not power for the workers and peasants, but power for their elite. They had and have their model in Stalinist Russia. The revolution — change in property relations —begins where the Russian revolution ended, Stalinist Russia of 1945-9, or if you prefer, Stalinist Russia of 1978. They are fundamentally the same; a one party totalitarian state where the proletariat is helpless and atomised, with an apparatus of control of the state by the officials. The guerrilla army chiefs, who with an iron hand imposed discipline, take control undoubtedly with the support of the masses but with no organs of workers' rule independent of the state. Also, none of the rights and powers of the workers and peasants, which the existence of soviets as organs of workers' power would mean, exist.

For a transition to a Bonapartist workers' state such organs of workers' democracy, indispensible for a healthy workers' state, would be an enormous hindrance. They constituted a tremendous obstacle to the Stalinist bureaucracy in Russia, which had to wage a Herculean struggle and even a one-sided civil war to erase the last remnants of workers' democracy, which stood in the way of their untrammelled and dictatorial rule. This was reflected through the one man dictatorship of Stalin and his successors.

What is important is that this was the model of 'socialism' for Mao, for Castro, for Mengistu, for the Burmese generals and for the Baathist 'Muslim' generals in Syria.

Army and Intellectuals

It is important to see that what all these variegated forces have in common is not the secondary personal differences but the social forces and class forces they represent.

Mengistu, Castro, the Burmese generals broke with their class background and the advantages or disadvantages of their bourgeois and university education and outlook. It is true that they did not put themselves on the standpoint of the proletariat —as Marx and Lenin did —but they accepted the much easier 'socialism' which entailed the individual rule of *them and of their elite* on the backs of the working class and peasants.

All individual differences are stamped out by the decisive class and economic changes which they have presided over in their countries and their societies.

All the self-styled 'Marxist-Leninist' sects have not even understood the ABC of Marxism as taught by its founder and echoed by Lenin and Trotsky. This is something to marvel at. The emancipation of the working class is the task of the workers themselves. This is not because it is some kind of penance which the workers must do or because they are 'nice people'. It is because without this there is the inevitability of a small minority having a monopoly of culture they will then use —and inevitably abuse

—against the interests of the workers and peasants and in their own interests. Also, mobilisation of the proletariat, its conscious struggle for power, and fight for workers' democracy, transforms the proletariat and fits it for the task of workers' rule. This then partially rubs off onto the peasants and petit-bourgeoisie which follow the proletariat in both the advanced and the backward countries. This process does not take place with the struggle of the petit-bourgeois guerrilla bands or where radical army officer cliques take power.

Thus, the intellectual and army elite in all the *social* revolutions and overturns in the countries mentioned took state countrol firmly into their own hands. They had the passive —or more or less active support —of the masses. But there was not the *conscious organised* movement of the proletariat. The peasants and petit-bourgeoisie are not a viable substitute for the 'self-movement' of the proletariat.

It is a striking fact that in the case of every sect, they accept Mao and the Chinese revolution *ex-post-facto* and find in the 'Communist' badge of Mao the excuse for this. In reality Mao was an ex-Communist who had broken with the proletariat and put himself at the head of a peasant war.

The fact that he later balanced between the classes and in typical Bonapartist fashion, leaned on the workers for a time, alters nothing. The fact that the Peking gangsters called their hideous caricature 'socialism' or sometimes the dictatorship of the 'proletariat' also alters nothing. There is no fundamental difference economically or socially between any of these regimes. This means that the secondary differences in comparison with the fundamentals are only of trifling importance.

Lenin's Mistake

It is no accident also that all the sects base themselves on the mistake of Lenin in *What is to be Done* — that the proletariat *on its own* is capable only of 'trade union consciousness' and not 'socialist consciousness'. In reality this is not Lenin's idea but appropriately Kautsky's. Lenin discovered his mistake, and Lenin's works, as those of Marx and Engels and Trotsky, not to add Luxemburg and Mehring, are the living refutation of this idea. In all 55 volumes of Lenin's works there is never again the repetition of this error. In fact, without idealising the proletariat, as with all the great Marxists —*all* his works, down to the smallest article, are saturated with confidence and trust in the *mighty power* of the proletariat as the *only vehicle* which would lead mankind to socialism. This, of course, comes from the dialectical materialism of Marx.

In reality all these gentlemen of the sects have a haughty if secret
—and sometimes not completely secret at that —contempt for the
working class. Dialectically, while embracing enthusiastically this
false idea about trade union consciousness, at the same time, they
worship at the shrine of Ho Chi Minh or Mao or Castro or Tito or
some other proletarian Bonapartist dictator. They are incapable of
understanding the process of history and the temporary
conjuncture of the economic upswing which led to a long lull in the
class struggle in the West and the continuing crisis of society in the
underdeveloped world. This was one of the corollary factors of the
West's boom and inevitably led to the rise and development of
proletarian Bonapartism in the colonial world, which the
dominance of Stalinism in Russia and the predominance of
Stalinism and reformism in the workers' movement in the world
contributed to. Only genuine Marxism has been able from the
beginning to explain all these 'outlandish' phenomena from the
viewpoint of the working class and the class nature of society and
the organic crisis of *world capitalism* which is manifested first of all at
its weaker and more backward extremities.

All these proletarian Bonapartist regimes are temporary
aberrations on the road of the world revolution. The excrescence
which Stalinism represents will be eliminated almost in passing
when the mighty proletariat of one of the advanced countries takes
power in the West or the regimes of Russia and Eastern Europe are
regenerated by the overthrow of bureaucracies.

In a number of works we have traced the contradictions and
inconsistencies which the sects show on the question of what is a
healthy workers' state with 'bureaucratic deformations', or what is a
deformed workers' state. Though both are based on state
ownership, *they are fundamentally different in their super-structure.* For
that reason a *political revolution* is necessary in the case of a
deformed workers' state before a 'workers' democracy' or 'the
dictatorship of the proletariat' in its political as well as economic
sense, can be established. On the other hand, a workers' state with
'bureaucratic deformations' is a workers' state under conditions of
backwardness and isolation which can still be *reformed* through the
restoration of party, trade union and state democracy, ie a return
to the control of the workers and peasants and where, if only in
vestigial form, these organisations still exist under the pressure of
the workers.

Some sects have bowed down before Castro as the leader and
organiser of a 'healthy workers' state'. They went even further and
compared his 'struggle against bureaucracy' with that of Trotsky
against Stalinism. They actually committed the indecency of

publishing the photographs of Trotsky and Castro together as fighters against bureaucracy and for democratic socialism. They thus showed that they understood neither the role of Trotsky as an immortal fighter against the Stalinist bureaucracy nor Castro's role as the incarnation of the Cuban Stalinist bureaucracy.

Words are cheap. 'Castro's struggle' against the Cuban bureaucracy was no different in essence to that of Stalin on occasions against the Russian bureaucracy. Stalin as a Bonapartist dictator sometimes attacked the 'bureaucracy' *in words*. He went further on occasions and leaned on the workers and peasants. This happened when the greedy bureaucrats went too far in their swindling, speculation and plundering of the state and threatened to devour the foundations of the state.

Stalin took action even against high-up bureaucrats and certainly against wide sections of the lower ranks of the bureaucracy. This was to preserve the Stalinist system by making scapegoats of some bureaucrats, especially the lower ranks.

Fundamentally, Castro's role in Cuba is the same. True, he played the leading personal role in the guerrilla war, the overthrow of Batista, the movement towards expelling imperialism, and overthrowing landlordism and capitalism.

Stalin had lived through a proletarian revolution together with the existence of a workers' democracy, yet he carried out a counter-revolution against it. But right *from the first day, the Cuban revolution was deformed and distorted*. The proletariat never held political power directly as in Russia. The fact that even today probably the decisive bulk of the Cuban people, as the Chinese people too, support the regime at this stage, alters nothing as to its character. Castro's strictures against bureaucracy, like Stalin's, are necessary if he is to preserve the role of 'Bonapartist arbiter' and 'father of the people'.

Now, when dealing with Ethiopia, some of those who bow the knee before Castro, declare Mengistu — whose regime is basically a copy of that of Russia, China and Cuba — to be 'fascist'. This particular example of contortions and eclectic acrobatics can only be greeted with gales of laughter by genuine Marxism.

State Capitalism?

Why is Mengistu's regime 'state capitalist' and different to the others? There is no explanation. They merely echo the arguments of the student, Maoist ultra-lefts in Ethiopia. At least the Ethiopian Maoists have the consistency to declare — as the Maoists have done everywhere —that Russia too is 'state capitalist'.

The proof of the 'fascist' character of the Mengistu regime, they claim, is the vicious repression, the executions, the repression of national rights and the national revolutions of a similar character to that of Ethiopia – of Eritrea and the Ogaden – and the suppression of other national minorities. The crushing and dissolution of independent trade unions and all the nascent democratic organs of self-expression of the workers and peasants is certainly to be condemned. So also is the concentration of power into the hands of the Army junta clique and the dictatorship of Mengistu.

But one rubs one's eyes in disbelief at the shallowness of the 'Marxism' of these self-styled Trotskyists'. For every crime committed by Mengistu in this regard, Stalin committed a hundred times more! The repression of independent organs of the workers must have reached a state of perfection by the bueaucracy in Russia. Puppet unions' exist which resemble the *Arbeitfront* of the Nazis in Germany. The Russian 'Communist' Party is the arm of the bureaucracy itself and has long ago ceased to be a workers' party. Concentration camps, or 'labour camps' as they are called, and psychiatric 'hospitals' have been established for all dissidents –right or left.

The national oppression of the minorities, and especially of worker dissidents, reached levels never reached even under Tsarism. A one-party totalitarian machine has been established without allowing any opposition anywhere among workers, peasants and intellegentsia. The regimentation of art, science and government into a Stalinist strait-jacket, without any independent initiative or thought, has been unequalled in history except, possibly, in Hitler's Germany. More or less, that is the picture common to all the proletarian Bonapartist states, including China and Cuba.

Some of the sects pick up the characterisation of the Mengistu regime from the Maoists. They also support the heroic guerrilla peasant war in the Ogaden and in Eritrea, which, if victorious, would probably end in a carbon copy of Cuba or of Mengistu's Ethiopia. That would be inevitable with a backward economy and with the limited nationalist leadership looking to their own resources alone and not seeing the necessity of linking up with the workers of the advanced capitalist countries. If there is a struggle for national rights of these peoples –so long as there is not the direct intervention of imperialism –we would give critical support to the struggle as we would for example to the struggle of the Ukranian people for independence from Stalinist Russia. An independent socialist soviet Ukraine would prepare the way for a genuine and voluntary socialist soviet federation of all the peoples of the USSR. This could only be achieved by the overthrow of the Russian Stalinist bureaucracy by the Russian working class.

Support for Revolution

Unfortunately in Eritrea and the Ogaden, as in Ethiopia for the next period, democracy will receive short shrift. This is inevitable on the bases of a peasant war, as well as the Stalinist ideology of their leaders.

But as we did in the case of Vietnam, Laos and Cambodia (Kampuchea) and for that matter China also —we would give support without closing our eyes to the inevitability of Stalinist totalitarian regimes whatever the result of the conflict.

Because of its character as a *national struggle* (though on the basis of state ownership and the elimination of landlordism and capitalism) and the limited outlook of its leadership, neither the Somalis nor the Eritreans have a means of influencing or winning over the peasant soldiers of Ethiopia. They too have carried through a revolution and are influenced by the national idea of a united Ethiopia.

The proletarian and far sighted policy of Lenin —in standing firmly for the bourgeois-democratic right of self-determination —has no place unfortunately in the policy of the Ethiopians. But neither is there present, on any side in the conflict, the other policies of Marxism —democratic-centralism in the Party, democracy in the soviets, trade unions and so on.

Our policy is dictated first by the international socialist proletarian revolution and its interests. The defeat of imperialism and the overthrow of landlordism and capitalism in the Horn of Africa are big steps forward.

This is despite the conflict between 'socialist states' which sows confusion among the advanced workers and the proletariat generally. The complexity of the problem and the need to keep our ideas clear is shown by the way imperialism and the Russian and Cuban bureaucracy have changed sides.

Yesterday the imperialists supported Haile Selassie and the landlord-capitalist regime in Ethiopia against Somalia and the guerrilla movement in Eritrea. Russia and Cuba financed, armed and organised the Somali state and supported the guerrillas in Eritrea with arms, finance and technical assistance. Ethiopia assumed more importance in their eyes, with the collapse of the Emperor, followed by the overthrow of the semi-feudal landlord-capitalist regime. Ethiopia has 35 million people against approximately 2 or 3 million each in Eritrea and Somalia.

Opportunistically taking advantage of the civil war in Ethiopia, organised by the landlord-capitalist counter-revolution, President Barre of Somalia sent troops into the Ogaden. He hoped for the disintegration and collapse of the Ethiopian revolution. He was nationally limited and short-sighted, interested only in a 'greater Somalia'. Undoubtedly the imperialists, surrepitiously through the semi-feudal reactionary Arab states like Saudi-Arabia, gave support to the Somalis, as they now give support to the Eritreans despite the social character of the movement in Eritrea. They wish to weaken Ethiopia and strike a blow against the Russian bureaucracy.

The Russian bureaucracy and Castro have changed horses in mid-stream after vainly attempting to persuade the Somali rulers to make a compromise and establish a federation of Eritrea, Somalia and Ethiopia. This would undoubtedly have been the best solution, given the character of all these regimes either as Bonapartist deformed workers' states, or such states in the process of formation.

When the Somalis rejected this proposal the bureaucracy switched sides. It is not certain that the Ethiopians were in agreement with this proposal either. Now they are trying to negotiate some form of agreement between Eritrea and Ethiopea. If the Eritreans do not accept some form of limited 'autonomy' Cuba and Russia seem certain to support the crushing in blood of the Eritrean attempt at self-determination. The imperialists, unable to intervene directly, will weep crocodile tears about the national and democratic rights of the Eritrean people. (Yesterday they brutally tried to suppress the rights of the Vietnamese people.)

But what is really entertaining about these dramatic conflicts is the position of some of the sects. They solemnly declaim that Russia (correctly) is a deformed workers' state and Cuba (incorrectly) a relatively 'healthy' workers' state. But in no way do they explain how and why the relatively 'healthy' workers' state of Cuba or the deformed workers' state of Russia actively helps the 'fascist' state of Ethiopia to establish itself and suppress the national rights of the people of Eritrea who are attempting to establish a 'Marxist' regime and the Somalis of the Ogaden and the other minorities.

Undoubtedly, on the basis of land distribution, the overwhelming majority of the Ethiopian peasants support the Ethiopian regime for want of an alternative.

It is theoretically possible of course that for the purpose of 'defence' against other capitalist states, a deformed workers' state or even a healthy workers' state could ally itself with a reactionary or fascist state. Stalin's Russia did this in 1939 with the 'non-aggression' pact with Hitler's Germany.

But what strategic necessity was there for Brezhnev and Castro to switch from supporting Somalia and Eritrea to their 'fascist' rivals? The rulers of the deformed workers' states would look with trepidation at the rise of a healthy workers' state in the industrialised countries because of the social reverberations it would provoke in their own countries. But they would welcome the establishment of social regimes on the pattern of their own regimes in the backward and neo-colonial countries.

This strengthens them internationally against their capitalist imperialist rivals. The basic world antagonism between the social structures of these countries and capitalist countries remains.

Stalinism and Fascism

Ethiopia is a country far more backward than Russian Czarism or even pre-revolutionary China, and is under conditons of civil war on every front. With a leadership which takes Cuba and China as its model, without revolutionary training, this officer leadership has moved towards Stalinist conceptions in the course of the revolution. But we cannot throw out the baby with the bathwater. We must separate out the enormously *progressive* kernel from the *reactionary* wrappings. Landlordism and capitalism have been eliminated and this decisive fact will have far-flung effects on the whole of the African revolution in the coming epoch.

Not for nothing did Trotsky explain to the American Socialist Workers Party that, *separated from state ownership of industry and the land,* the political regime in Russia was fascist! There was nothing to distinguish the political regime of Stalin from that of Hitler except the decisive fact that one defended and had its privileges based on state ownership while the other had its privileges, power, income and prestige based on the defence of private property. That was a fundamental and decisive difference! There is no difference in the fundamentals of economic and political structure of Ethiopia from China, Syria, Russia or any of the deformed workers' states.

The latest events in Indo-China have served again to show the ridiculous contortions of the policies of all the sects. Our tendency gave whole-hearted support to the struggle of the Vietnamese 'Communist' Party of Ho Chi Minh and its Laotian and Cambodian off-shoots *in their peasant guerrilla war against American and world imperialism* and their native puppets.

We supported the struggle unconditionally and whole-heartedly.

We supported it because it was a colonial war for liberation. We would have supported such a war even under bourgeois or petit-bourgois leadership which had fought merely for the right of national self-determination alone. But it inevitably became a war for *social liberation* as well as *national liberation* −in the sense of fighting for the elimination also of landlordism and capitalism. Without this, the struggle could not have been carried on for decades against overwhelming military odds.

How far the sects have strayed from the Marxist or Trotskyist method was shown by the polemics between two different sects of the same international tendency about how far the Vietnamese were 'unconscious' Trotskyists operating on the basis of the permanent revolution.

None of these worthies have understood the peculiar character of the epoch as far as the colonial or ex-colonial areas of the world are concerned. Nor have they understood the inevitable perversion of the revolution under either open Stalinist −or pseudo-communist leadership −or that of radical sections of the officer caste. They have not understood the inevitable consequences when a colonial revolution is led to its progressive and 'final' conclusion of eliminating capitalism and landlordism but when the main force is not that of the working class with a Marxist leadership.

When the main force is a peasant army using classic peasant tactics of guerrilla war, then it must result in a 'deformed workers' state' *even if that were not the aim of the leaders*. In the event of an army coup of the younger officers, allied to 'intellectuals' and students, the consequences would − inevitably − be the same.

This is particularly the case given the world environment of strong Bonapartist workers' states, in the form of Stalinist Russia and other countries. Taken together with the existence of the imperialist powers there could be no other outcome.

Of course if there were in existence healthy workers' states −for instance in Russia, or one of the big industrialised states of Europe, or Japan −then the results and the possibilities would be entirely different. The proletariat and people of the advanced workers' states would give aid and assistance to a workers' state in a backward country, linking the economies together, and sending tens of thousands of technicians to small countries and hundreds of thousands to one with a big population. That would mean rapid industrialisation plus workers' democracy. That is what Lenin meant when he said Africa could move straight from tribalism to communism.

But given the present relationship of class forces in international affairs, with classical reformism and Stalinist reformism dominant in the workers' movement of the advanced countries, such a conclusion in Vietnam, Cambodia and Laos was ruled out.

Indo-China Clashes

That is why our tendency, while wholeheartedly supporting the Vietnamese and Indo-Chinese revolutions, *warned the workers and peasants* of these countries that while they should actively support the struggle and fight for social and national liberation, at the same time the dominance of the struggle by the Stalinist leadership would mean that while an enormous social step forward would be taken by the victory of the national liberation movement, it would be succeeded by a new enslavement by the totalitarian Stalinist bureaucracy. Without a Marxist party and without Marxist leadership the goal of the 'Communist Party' leadership would be a state in the image of the so-called 'socialism' of Russia or China.

We appealed to the advanced workers of Britain, America, France and the world, to support the social and national liberation struggle of the Indo-Chinese peoples, because it weakened imperialism and world capitalism. The liberation of the productive forces of these countries, by the overthrow of the rule of capital, would be of immense long-term benefit to the people of these countries and also to the world proletariat.

But *we never deceived ourselves* or the workers and peasants of the world as to the inevitable nature (the class relationship of forces) of the regimes which would be set up in these countries.

We warned of, and predicted, the inevitable setting up of *nationalist totalitarian Stalinist regimes in these countries* but even we had not expected just how far they would go in their distortions.

The armed clashes between Cambodia and Vietnam are a crushing condemnation of all those 'Trotskyist' sects in Britain and internationally who did not understand the class nature of these regimes and their *Stalinist* character. There was no surprise in these events for our tendency. The clashes on the borders between Russia and China when tens of thousands were killed had shown what nationalist bureaucrats are capable of.

These bureaucracies cannot look beyond the boundaries of the national state. Behind these clashes in former Indo-China are the aspirations of the Vietnamese to set up an Indo-China federation of 'socialist states'. Obviously this would have been of immense benefit to the economies of all these countries. But the reason that the Cambodians are against the setting up of such a federation is that under conditions of Bonapartist totalitarianism they would inevitably come under the nationalist domination and national oppression of the Vietnamese bureaucracy. Leaving aside the virulent national chauvinism of the Cambodian Stalinists, this would be as inevitable as it was in Stalinist China and in Russia.

For the same reason, the Vietnamese Stalinists, in their turn, would refuse to federate with Stalinist China. They know, as the minorities in China have seen, that they would come under the national oppression of the Chinese bureaucracy. Even though economically it would be of immense benefit, they would not agree to this, no more than would the Chinese bureaucracy agree to a federation with Russia, though economically and even in terms of world power politics, it would be colossally beneficial to the peoples and the economies of both these countries. What stands in the way are the national vested interests of the bureaucracies of all these countries.

Only workers' democracy, without any hint of national superiority or advantage as in the days of Lenin and Trotsky, can have such a programme. But a Bonapartist regime, basing itself on privilege and inequality, is incapable of such a policy: the chauvinistic excesses of Stalinist Russia and China are proof of this. Bonapartist totalitarian regimes by their very nature, can never look beyond the narrow horizon of the national state. By the very nature of bureaucracy and its privileges they are nationally limited.

Basing themselves on peasants, students and intellectuals, and without the decisive domination and participation of the working class, they are inevitably nationally limited.

Afghanistan

The working class can secure its emancipation and the domination of society only by overcoming all the prejudices of the past —national, racial, caste, sex or any other. But only the working class and no other —and only under Marxist leadership at that —is capable of this feat. But the emancipation of the workers means the emancipation also of the petit-bourgeois strata in society who, under the leadership of the working class, and only under these conditions, would be capable of rising to these heights.

The petit-bourgeois and the intellectuals can adopt the standpoint of the proletariat only by breaking completely with their origins and the outlook of their class. Under modern conditions that is extremely difficult where genuine Marxists, as in the early days of Marx and Engels, have been reduced to a handful.

This is particularly the case today when the struggle is not merely in the ideological sphere but where the immediate issue in country after country is the transformation of society. In this situation it is easy for the intellectuals to come under the domination of the muddled ideas of Stalinism in its various forms.

Only a strong workers' movement dominated by Marxism could make the metamorphosis of such intellectuals possible.

This is especially difficult in colonial or neo-colonial countries where the problems are immediate, where the masses live an almost animal existence, where also there are insuperable obstacles to modernisation and the development of society on the basis of the semi-feudal landlord capitalist regimes.

It is easier for the intellectuals, the radical officers, even civil servants and upper layers of professional people, doctors, dentists, lawyers and so on to make the transition to Stalinist Bonapartism than to support genuine but tiny Marxist tendencies. Especially this is so in most of these countries where 'Marxism' does not exist as an organised tendency.

The 'Marxist-Leninism' of Russia, China or Ethiopia suits them perfectly. It fits all their prejudices. A 'socialism' where the elites of state, party, industry, army and the professions have a standard of living way above that of the masses seems perfectly normal and natural to them. A society where these strata become the dominant and governing caste, has an enormous attraction for them, especially as they see the enormous strides which backward countries make with a forced march of 'socialism'.

Thus it is easy for them to rationalise their class position. They have a hatred of the corrupt landlords and capitalists under whose control their societies and countries are either decaying or only inching ahead. They have a contempt for the downtrodden masses of peasants and even for the weak working class.

These stratas, apart from their economic position, are imbued with an overwhelming conceit and concern for their own importance in society. They are concerned with perks, status, standing, power, privileges, income and prestige. Thus, it is easy in the modern world to see how they can embrace 'socialism' on the pattern of Cuba, for example.

In the past period the fresh example of Afghanistan underlines the analysis we have made of the colonial revolution. The 'Communist' Party of this terribly backward country was only formed in the last decade or so. Like the Baath Party in Syria, it had no difficulty in swallowing the doctrine of 'Islam' as well as 'communism'. It has done so because religious superstition has deep roots among the overwhelmingly backward peasant majority, 90 per cent of whom are illiterate.

Complete Transformation

Now, as with the Baath Party in Syria, the CP leaders in Afghanistan have allied themselves with the radical lower and middle ranks of the officer caste in the army.

The immediate issue which precipitated the coup was famine —as in Ethiopia —and the impossibility of the corrupt, semi-feudal Asiatic ruler, to cope with it. Afghanistan has had many coups in the past decades leading to different tribal leaders and groups gaining power. They merely changed the tops, leaving the social structure intact. The same corruption inevitably developed, leading, when the imposition had become unbearable on the masses, to a famine, or through foreign intrigue, to a new coup. Thus, social relations were contained in the same vicious circle. This new coup opens up the possibility of striking in a new direction. 'Communists' have become Prime Minister and President and also have a dominant role in the government. This indicates in which direction the officers wish to go. One of the first acts of the new regime has been to seize the lands of the monarchy, which, though overthrown by the former Daud* regime, still possessed 20 per cent of the land in Afghanistan! This is a new departure and may be the beginning of a complete transformation of social relations.

As in Poland, where the Polish Stalinist bureaucracy came to an agreement with the Catholic church, so in Afghanistan the Communist Party leadership, together with the officers, can arrive at an agreement with the mullahs of Islam. The fact that Taraki, the new Prime Minister, is the leader of a so-called Communist Party alters nothing. He pursues the same policy as that of the Syrian leaders of the Baath.

In the case of Afghanistan, only two roads are possible at this stage. The working class is miniscule. Sections of the intelligentsia, and apparently the majority of the officers and a great part of the professionals, want to construct a modern civilised state. The peasants want the land.

On the road of capitalism and landlordism, there is no way forward. The army officers wish to take the road traversed by Outer Mongolia. In fact these peculiar changes are only possible because of the international context. The crisis of imperialism and capitalism, the impasse of the backward countries of the third world and the existence of the proletarian revolutions in the West, are powerful factors in the case of Afghanistan.

*Mohammed Daud came to power, overthrowing the monarchy in 1973. He was overthrown by the Armed Forces Revolutionary Council on 27 April 1978, which brought the Taraki regime to power.

The barbarous regimes also of Pakistan, Iran and nearby India have no attractive force. The army officers, many, if not most, trained in Russia, are attracted when they see the consequences of the Stalinist regime. It has a big effect on the tribesmen, of similar peoples and even the same tribes, in areas bordering Russia when they see the modernisation of areas of Russia which formerly had as low a standard of living, and just as great illiteracy and ignorance as themselves.

Marxist Approach

The industrialisation, complete literacy and high standards in comparison to Afghanistan, are bound to impress these strata. In contrast, the backwardness and barbarism on which the nobility thrived in Afghanistan cannot but appal all the best elements —the intelligentsia, the professionals and even the officer caste. They wish to break out from poverty, ignorance and dirt from which their country suffers. The capitalists of the West, with unemployment and industrial stagnation, offer them nothing. They wish to break away from the vicious circle of tribal rulers and different military regimes which change nothing fundamental.

The world crisis of capitalism hits the backward regions of the world even harder, and impels them to draw the conclusion that capitalism offers no way forward.

The 'republican' regime of Daud —incidentally, backed and propped up by Moscow in the past —alters nothing. The upheavals and coups, leading to mere changes of dynasties by different clans of the nobility during the last fifty years have been completely sterile. The nobility and the relations on the land on which they were based, was the main obstacle to modernisation.

Under these circumstances, if the new regime leans on the support of the peasants and transforms society, then the way will be cleared for the development of a regime in Afghanistan, like that of Cuba, Syria or Russia. This, for the first time for centuries, will bring Afghanistan society sorward to the modern world. If the socialist transformation is completed, it could comprise a new blow at capitalism and landlordism in the rest of capitalist-landlord Asia, especially in the area of South Asia. It will have incalculable effects on the Pathans and Baluchis of Pakistan and will have a similar effect on the peoples on the borders of Iran. The rotting regime of Pakistan in coming years will face complete disintegration. A revamping of social relations in Afghanistan can further contribute to the decay of this regime.

The tribesmen will be influenced by the process taking place among their brothers across the borders. On the North West frontiers of Pakistan and among the Baluchis there is already endemic and simmering revolt, with these peoples looking towards a unity with their brothers in Afghanistan. The effect would be in widening circles, the repercussions of which could be felt in Iran and further afield, also in India.

This is the road which the 'Communist Party', which holds power together with the radical officers, will take. The opposition of the old forces in Afghanistan, as in Ethiopia, will in all probability impel them in this direction.

If they temporise, possibly under the influence of the Russian ambassador and the Russian regime, they will prepare the way for a ferocious counter-revolution based on the threatened nobility and the mullahs. If successful, counter-revolution would restore the old regime on the bones of hundreds of thousands of peasants, the massacres of the radical officers and the near extermination of the educated elite. For the moment —until there is a movement of the only advanced class which can bring a transition moving in the direction of socialism in the industrially developed countries —the most progressive development in Afghanistan seems at the present time to be the installation of proletarian Bonapartism.

While not closing our eyes to the new contradictions this will involve, on the basis of a transitional economy of a workers' state, without workers' democracy, Marxists, in a sober fashion, will support the emergence of such a state and the further weakening not only of imperialism and capitalism but also of regimes basing themselves on the remnants of feudalism in the most backward countries.

The Post War Boom: Origins, Effects and Decline

Introduction

THE MOST important feature of the entire post-war epoch, overshadowing and influencing all other factors, was the long, 25-year economic upswing. This represented the greatest explosion in investment, production, trade, science and technique in the whole of human history and it put its stamp on political developments in all the different parts of the world. In the advanced capitalist countries, as prosperity reached and then easily surpassed pre-war levels, it rekindled illusions in capitalism as a viable and 'natural' economic system. These illusions were transmitted to and articulated in the labour movement by the theoreticians of the right, who were indistinguishable from the spokespersons of capitalism.

But in the immediate post-war period, the longevity of the post-war boom could not have been anticipated. What was an issue within the Trotskyist movement was whether or not there would be any economic recovery at all. The material of the British Revolutionary Communist Party, and particularly the writings of Ted Grant, argued that there was a temporary political stabilisation in Western Europe, because of the influence of the social democratic and Stalinist leaderships, acting as a brake on the workers' movement. The political recovery of capitalism provided the political basis for, and was itself further underpinned by, economic recovery. (See the parts in Chapter Two, dealing with 'counter-revolution in a democratic form').

As on all the other main political issues dealt with, the international leadership of the Fourth International were incapable of facing up to new conditions. The European Executive of the International, based in Paris, argued in January 1945 that 'the revolutionary action of the masses' had removed the 'last possibilities for the bourgeoisie to restore the economy which has been ruined and dilapidated by the war.' In a further report in December, the same body argued that the countries of Europe 'would remain on a level approaching stagnation and slump.'

Because Trotsky had argued before the war that capitalism could not further develop the productive forces, the leadership of the Fourth International, the International Secretariat, were loath to say otherwise. Rather than using the Marxist *method* that Trotsky had applied, they stuck rigidly to the *letter* of his writings, despite the increasing weight of evidence that an economic recovery was underway in the capitalist countries.

The draft resolution put forward by the IS for the International Pre-Conference of April 1946 stated: 'The most probable perspectives of the evolution of the world economy may be outlined as follows: The revival of economic activity in capitalist countries weakened by the war, and in particular continental European countries, will be characterised by an especially slow tempo which will keep their economies at levels bordering on stagnation and slump.'

Members of the IS, including supposed economic 'experts', doggedly argued that the 1938 production levels of the European countries would not be exceeded. Ernest Mandel, for example, wrote in 1947 that 'the situation in the British economy is not that of a boom if one wishes to give this term the significance that Marxists have always given to it...it is necessary to abandon right now any juggling with a boom that has not existed and that British capitalism will never experience again.'

The draft theses put forward in 1947 by the IS for the forthcoming world congress, still refused to acknowledge the new conditions that were staring them in the face. They harped on the same theme as the year before: that there would be 'increased disequilibrium', and that capitalism was 'incapable of restoring the world market and a balanced development of world trade.'

It was the RCP, as on other questions, that argued the theoretical line which was proved correct. Basing themselves on the figures for production, investment and growth, particularly but not exclusively for Britain, the RCP leaders demonstrated the irrefutable fact that a rapid economic boom was developing. The first item in this chapter is a statement on *Economic Perspectives*, put forward as an amendment to the IS resolution at the April 1946 International Pre-Conference. It was published in *Workers' International News*, November-December 1946. In contrast to the IS position, it argues that:

> ...the laws of capitalism...ensure the upswing of economy and make a new 'boom' inevitable. Particularly in view of the fact that this crisis is

not a crisis of over-production...It is not excluded that particularly for Western Europe (with the exception of Germany and Austria) the production figures can even reach and surpass the pre-war level in the next period...All the factors on a European and world scale indicate that the economic activity in the next period is not one of 'stagnation and slump' but one of revival and boom.

It is important to note that no-one in the Trotskyist movement internationally, including the RCP, believed that the post-war boom would last more than a few years, before it gave way to an inevitable downturn. The amendment (which, incidentally, was defeated at the conference) agreed with the IS statement in emphasising 'the epoch of the decline and collapse of world capitalist economy...there is not the least ground for the hope or fear that the economic revival, which in and of itself is inevitable, will be able to overcome the general decay in world economy and in European economy in particular.' In the early stages of the post-war boom, therefore, it was Ted Grant and the RCP leadership who were insisting, against the economic 'theoreticians' of the IS, that there was indeed a revival. But ironically, once the revival took hold, and unexpectedly developed into a fully-fledged upswing, the nature of the debate turned to its opposite.

It was in this period of upswing that the right wing of the labour movement — who always base themselves on the capitalist system, as opposed to socialist ideas — were given a new lease of confidence. The theoreticians of the right wing, in the Fabian Society, for example, fell over themselves to announce that class struggle was at an end and that the very concept of 'class' was losing its meaning. Slumps and mass unemployment were the horrors of the past that would never be repeated, society had learnt to overcome past conflicts and from now on, they argued, there would be a gradual and unbroken increase in living standards. The leadership of the Labour Party, around Hugh Gaitskell, even tried (unsuccessfully, because of the resistance of the rank and file and the trade unions) to remove the socialist Clause 4 from the Labour Party constitution.

The second part of this chapter consists of an article in the *International Socialist* (edited by Ted Grant), November- December 1952, commenting on the *New Fabian Essays*. In the *Essays*, writers like Richard Crossman, Anthony Crosland and Roy Jenkins, put forward the idea that the 'welfare state' or 'welfareism' had superseded class society. 'By 1951', Crosland argued, 'Britain had in all essentials ceased to be a capitalist country'.

Cutting through the superficiality of the Fabian theories, Grant defends the basic Marxist position, that as long as the market dominated the economy, then there would inevitably be cycles of boom and slump. Explaining the causes for the longevity of the boom, he also points out its limitation and the inevitability, at a later stage, of new recessions and slumps. This article, although directed particularly towards the British economy, was no less relevant to the other main capitalist countries, where similar conditions prevailed and similar arguments raged.

Nearly forty years later, the arguments in the article have lost none of their relevancy, because in all their essentials, the so-called 'modern' policies put forward by the right wing in the Labour Party in the late 1980s are the same as the discredited notions of their 1950s' predecessors.

The third article in the chapter is a development on the same theme as above. Written as a discussion document in 1960, at the height of the boom, and published by Sussex University Socialist Society in 1967, *Will There Be a Slump?* was a major contribution to the debate on economic perspectives. The right wing and the Fabians, arguing from the basis of the economic theories of John Maynard (later Lord) Keynes, alleged that the capitalist state – by limited nationalisations, economic intervention and state expenditure such as on social welfare – could smooth out the natural economic cycle and thus overcome crises.

They were also echoed on the left, by alleged 'Marxists' who effectively adopted similar Keynesian theories. Influenced by what seemed to be an endless expansion, the same economic gurus who had originally denied the possibility of recovery now went to the opposite extreme. After having belatedly acknowledged the upswing, they also came forward with wonderful new theories describing how capitalism had been fundamentally changed so as to be able to avoid crises and slumps. It was argued, for example, (by Tony Cliff, and others) that arms expenditure represented a means by which the capitalist state could stimulate the economy so as to avoid slump: thus a 'permanent arms economy' was coming into being.

In the pamphlet *Will There Be a Slump?*, all these arguments are debunked. State intervention, it is explained, can increase the scope and scale of an upswing, but only if the fundamental conditions for capitalist upswing are present. In conditions of crisis, state expenditure (including spending on arms), rather than a benefit, becomes a monstrous incubus that tends to drag the economy even further down.

Once again, the fundamental perspective of an inevitable slump was put forward: 'Whatever the exact date, it is absolutely certain that the unprecedented post-war boom must be followed by a catastrophic downswing, which cannot but have a profound effect on the political thinking of the enormously strengthened ranks of the labour movement.'

The validity of these arguments have been well demonstrated by the onset of economic crisis in all the advanced capitalist countries since the mid-1970s. At the same time, it is now clear that the level of state expenditure of the boom period, rather than acting as a means of avoiding slump, has become a source of unbridled inflation, a destabilising factor that the capitalists of all countries have tried to avoid by slashing government spending on welfare, education, health and so on.

As postscripts to the above documents, the fourth and fifth parts of the chapter are relatively brief extracts from discussion documents, dealing with world perspectives in the post-boom period. The Marxists had not been able to predict the long duration of the post-war boom, but what was clear was that the first recession to affect all the advanced capitalist economies simultaneously, in 1974-5, marked the end of one epoch and the beginning of another. Later than may have been anticipated, events nevertheless vindicated the correct stand that had been made by Ted Grant on the fundamentals of capitalist economics.

As these two extracts argue, and as subsequent events have demonstrated, the outlook for world capitalism has changed fundamentally since the mid-1970s. The present epoch is one of stagnation and slump, interspersed with periods of recovery that are weak and anaemic compared to the boom period of the 1950s and 1960s. In all capitalist countries there has been a return to mass unemployment, economic instability and social crisis.

Moreover, the crisis facing the advanced capitalist countries is paralleled by crisis in the under-developed countries and in the Stalinist states, especially Eastern Europe. For the first time, because of the interpenetration of economic and political crises in all the main parts of the globe, there is the perspective, in the full meaning of the term, of world revolution.

Economic Perspectives 1946

April 1946

THE PRESENT epoch is the epoch of definite capitalist decline. The general crisis of capitalism is reflected in the contradiction between the development of the productive forces and the private ownership of the means of production and the national state. Capitalism fulfilled its historic function, the development of the national state and the creation of the world market in the decades prior to the First World War. Capitalism can no longer serve for the development of the forces of production. Despite the immense increase in the productivity of labour and the continued development of technique, production on a world scale finds itself hampered and restricted by the fetters of private ownership of the means of production, transport and exchange, and the national state.

Already by 1850-70, the basic historical role of capitalism had been fulfilled. It had, even at that stage, become a fetter on the development of the productive forces. That is the explanation for the error in perspective of Marx and Engels in believing that the victory of the proletarian revolution was imminent. However, through the development of the world market, which gave it new resources, capitalism revealed itself not yet as an *absolute*, but as a *relative*, fetter on the development of the forces of production at this stage. Marx pointed out that no society would give way to a new society until all the productive possibilities within it had been completely exhausted. Between 1870 and 1914 capitalism revealed itself as an ascending economy. Of course, had the proletariat come to power (the productive forces had already been sufficiently developed for this) the expansion of the productive forces would have been immeasurably greater. Nevertheless, capitalism could succeed in maintaining itself because it still remained a relatively progressive factor.

Between 1879 and 1914, the figures of production of the most important commodities in Germany, France, United States and Britain showed a general tendency to rapid increase.

The first world war marked a definitive change in the role of capitalism. The world had been divided into spheres of influence, markets, sources of raw materials and could only be re-divided by bloody imperialist war. The epoch of capitalist decay and of capitalism's death agony was ushered in. This it was that presaged the period of wars, revolutions, uprisings and convulsions, which was clear evidence of the insoluble impasse into which the capitalist system had landed humanity.

The general crisis of capitalism was reflected in the fact that the productive forces had ceased to grow with the same rhythm as in the past. The inevitable cycle of capitalist production now took a somewhat different curve. No longer short slumps and long booms, with each succeeding boom at a higher level than the last, but now an epoch in which short booms were followed by long slumps and depressions. The productive forces oscillated round the level of 1914, taking into account increases of population and resources.

Nevertheless, the first post-war crisis of capitalism, in which the proletariat failed to take power, led inevitably to a new economic boom. The partial collapse immediately after 1921 did not last long or have major effects. In most countries of the world, the figures of production in 1929 were higher than those of 1914, only to prepare for a complete collapse of the productive forces in a way never witnessed by capitalism in the past. The slump was one of unexampled severity, afflicting all the main capitalist countries simultaneously, and causing frightful devastation and chronic decline in the utilization of the productive potential. (Japan was an exception for reasons which it is not necessary to deal with here.)

But again, even this slump could not continue indefinitely. Where the proletariat was paralyzed by its parties, and failed to utilize the crisis to overthrow capitalism and take power into its own hands, a new economic upswing commenced. In many countries of Europe this crisis was not finally resolved until the preparations for the new slaughter of the peoples (itself a reflection of the impasse of capitalism) was in full swing. But on the basis of armaments preparations and the war measures generally, economic activity even exceeded the figures of 1929 in the main capitalist countries apart from France.

Thus, in the downswing of capitalism it can be seen that production tends to oscillate around the level of 1919-37 (owing to exceptional conditions produced by the war, German production virtually collapsed and American production soared to record heights), without being enabled to gain the steady rhythm of increase in the decades prior to World War I, when each crisis was succeeded by an enormous upswing on a higher level of the productive forces.

World War II, a further proof of the death agony of capitalism, resulted in the frightful destruction of men, of the productive forces, in the disorganisation and disintegration of production in Europe and Asia, such as has never been exampled in history. Imperialism and capitalism have thus shown the barbarism into which their continued existence will plunge mankind. In opposition to the reformists and Stalinists, who seek to lull the masses with a perspective of a new renaissance of capitalism and a great future for democracy, the resolution of the International Pre-Conference is one hundred per cent correct in emphasizing the epoch of decline and collapse of the world capitalist economy. But in a resolution that seeks to orientate our own cadres on *immediate economic perspectives* — from which the next stage of the class struggle will largely flow, and thus our immediate propaganda and tactics — the perspective is clearly false.

The present crisis and low level of production, is *not* the economic crisis as understood by Marxists in the classic sense. It is a crisis of 'underproduction' arising from imperialist concentration of productive forces for war and on war destruction itself. It reflects itself in the lack of capital goods, lack of consumers' goods, lack of agricultural goods. Just the opposite of an economic crisis of capitalist over-production as understood by Marxists.

The frightful famines which have stricken the peoples of the entire world, the disorganisation and decay of Europe, are indications of the disruption of the capitalist system. These could easily have led to the destruction of capitalism and the organisation of socialist production on an all European and all Asiatic scale, were it not for the weakness of the revolutionary party and the capitulation of the mass organisations of the working class. For the second time in a generation capitalism has been enabled to gain a new breathing space.

The theory of spontaneous collapse of capitalism is entirely alien to the concepts of Bolshevism. Lenin and Trotsky emphasized again and again that capitalism will always find a way out if it is not destroyed by the conscious intervention of the revolutionary party which, at the head of the masses, takes advantage of the difficulties and crises of capitalism to overthrow it. The experience of World War II emphasizes the profound correctness of these ideas of Lenin and Trotsky.

The prostration of the proletariat through the betrayal of its mass organisations, the cyclical upswing of the productive forces, the wearing out of machinery, the slashing of wages, all lead to an absorption of surplus stocks and the restoration, or partial restoration of the rate of profit. Thus, the way is prepared for a new cyclical upswing which in its turn lays the basis for an even greater slump. Thus Trotsky wrote of the world slump:

> The ruling classes of all countries expect miracles from the industrial upswing, the speculation in stocks which has already broken out is a proof of this. If capitalism were really to enter upon the phase of a new prosperity or even of a gradual but persistent rise, this would naturally involve the stabilization of capitalism and at the same time a strengthening of reformism. But there is not the least ground for the hope or fear that the economic revival, which in and of itself is inevitable, will be able to overcome the general tendencies of decay in world economy and in European economy in particular. If pre-war capitalism developed under the formula of expanded production of goods, present day capitalism, with all its cyclical fluctuations, represents an expanded production of misery and of catastrophe. The new economic cycle will execute the inevitable readjustment of forces within the individual countries as well as within the capitalist camp as a whole, predominantly towards America and away from Europe. But within a very short time it will place the capitalist world before insoluble contradictions and condemn it to new and still more frightful convulsions. (*Germany, The Only Road,* September 1932)

No matter how devastating the slump, if the workers fail, capitalism will always find a way out of its economic impasse at the cost of the toilers and the preparation of new contradictions. The world crisis of the capitalist system does not end the economic cycle but gives it a different character. The theory of the Stalinists put forward in the last world crisis that this was *the last* crisis of capitalism from which it would never recover, has been entirely un-Marxian. There is a grave danger that this theory will be revived in our own ranks today.

After World War I the capitalists were faced with large if inexperienced revolutionary parties striving to take advantage of the capitalist crisis in production in order to overthrow capitalism. This further aggravated the chaos, and rendered difficult the capitalist recovery. Despite this, however, production was largely restored.

If the Stalinist parties had been genuine revolutionary parties, the capitalist class would now be faced with an entirely different perspective in economy as well as politically. The proletariat in France would have paralyzed the attempt of the capitalists to restore production at the expense of further sacrifices and burdens on the part of the masses. But the two traitor organisations of the proletariat are straining every nerve to prevent, frustrate and sabotage any struggle, economic and political on the part of the proletariat.

Meanwhile, with the weakness of the parties of the Fourth International, which remain small sects at this stage, the capitalists have been enabled to find a way out of the collapse and decline of economy. This has prepared the way in Western Europe for a steady and fairly rapid recovery.

If a conflict develops between Stalin and Western European capitalism and the Stalinist organisations are used to disrupt and force concessions by means of mass strikes, the situation can deteriorate for the capitalists overnight. Even the assistance of American finance would not and could not prevent the crisis that would follow. The specific position taken by the International Pre-Conference and supported by the Minority of the British Party, that the Western European countries —France, Holland, Belgium and others —will remain on a level approaching *stagnation and slump,* and cannot reach the level of production attained pre-war, is entirely false. The Pre-Conference resolution says:

> This restoration of economic activity in the capitalist countries hit by the war, and in particular in the countries on the European continent, will be characterised by its particularly slow rhythm and these countries will thus remain on a level approaching stagnation and slump.

Eastern Europe in particular, under the control of the Stalinist bureaucracy, will undoubtedly recover and even increase its productive resources more rapidly than after 1914-18. It is impossible for Anglo-American imperialism and the bourgeoisie of Western Europe to allow complete stagnation and decline on one half of the continent, while economic activity will develop in the other half under the domination of the Stalinist bureaucracy.

However, apart from these political considerations, there are the laws of capitalism which themselves ensure the upswing of economy and make a new 'boom' inevitable. Particularly in view of the fact that this crisis is not a crisis of over-production and that the capitalists are not being attacked in Western Europe by the mass organisations, but receive the direct assistance and support of social democracy and Stalinism, *a cyclical upswing is inevitable.* It is not excluded that particularly for Western Europe (with the exception of Germany and Austria) the productive figures can even reach and surpass the pre-war level in the next period.

Even in Germany, depending upon the relationship between the imperialists and Russia, a greater or lesser revival will take place, though here because of the conflict between the powers and the division and occupation of Germany, it is impossible that pre-war figures will be reached in the next period.

All the factors on a European and world scale indicate that the economic activity in Western Europe in the next period is not one of 'stagnation and slump' but one of revival and boom.

The main feature of capitalist crisis 'stagnation and slump' as revealed for example by the classic crisis of 1929-33 which assumed unexampled scope and severity on a world scale, was over-production of capital goods, consumer goods and agricultural produce. The industrial crisis was thus supplemented with a simultaneous agrarian crisis. The economic revival which followed the last world slump, as always, was achieved by the destruction and deterioration of capital goods, the deterioration and destruction of consumers' stocks, the cutting down of the areas sown with crops, etc. Though this involved immeasurable misery and suffering for the toilers, nevertheless, particularly with war preparations, by 1937-8 the production figures exceeded even the record years of 1928-9 in most countries of the world. The destruction wrought by the war has achieved similar results to those which the capitalists achieve when they consciously set out to destroy wealth in a period of crises of over-production.

The classic conditions for boom are present in Europe today: a shortage of capital goods; shortage of agricultural produce; shortage of consumer goods. The shortages impose new miseries for the masses and new strains on the system. These conditions engendered by wilful destruction and the normal processes of decay of capitalist slump are here produced by the devastation and havoc of totalitarian war. This devastation did not lead to the overthrow of the system through the victory of the proletariat. In the same way as recovery follows a slump which does not lead to the overthrow of the system, so the restoration of the productive forces will follow the present chaos, even on a capitalist basis.

However, such a recovery, as already stated in the citation from Trotsky, cannot lead to a blossoming of the economy of capitalism. A new recovery can only prepare the way for an even greater slump and economic crisis than in the past.

The Stalinists and social democrats have largely persuaded the working class to accept the burden of reconstruction with the cries of 'Production! Production!' With this they have undoubtedly had a certain success among the broad masses. The Fourth International will only discredit itself if it refuses to recognise the inevitable recovery, and it will disorientate its own cadres as well as the broad masses by predicting a permanent slump and slow rhythm of recovery in Western Europe, when events are taking a different shape.

The argument of the comrades of the American SWP, which has been echoed by the Minority of the British Party, that only after the proletariat has been decisively defeated would American imperialism give loans to assist the recovery of Western European capitalism, has already been demonstrated to be a false one. The proletariat has not been defeated, *but loans have already been given.* Equally false is the argument that only if the proletariat is decisively defeated can economic recovery and revival take place. Such an argument lumps together political-economic problems visualising an immediate reflection of one upon the other. Undoubtedly, a decisive defeat of the proletariat gives the bourgeoisie stability and confidence. But unless the *economic pre-conditions* for a boom are present, a boom would not necessarily follow even in that event. It is not a law of the development of capitalism that only the defeat of the proletariat in a revolutionary situation can lead to a boom, any more than a slump automatically leads to a revolution. History teaches us that capitalism, even in its death agony, recovers after a slump, despite the revolutionary possibilities, if the proletariat is paralyzed or deadened by its organisations and rendered incapable of taking advantage of its opportunities.

After the revolutionary wave of World War I had been stemmed by social democracy, capitalism was enabled to revive at the expense of the intensified exploitation of the working class. The first post-war revolutionary wave of World War II has been stemmed and paralyzed by social democracy and Stalinism. Economic revival is taking place before our eyes in most countries of Western Europe and Britain. Not only this, the bourgeois state machine in the Western countries, which had been disrupted and shattered after the fall of Hitler, has gradually been rebuilt on the basis of bourgeois democracy. A precarious 'stabilization' of the bourgeois state and the restoration of the economy from the position of almost complete disruption and chaos has taken place. The rhythm of recovery is proceeding at a fairly rapid pace in all of Western Europe, apart from Germany.

The paralysis of the proletariat, through its organisations, has allowed the bourgeoisie the opportunity to recover control of its economy. It does not follow from this that the proletariat is defeated.

In reality, ebbs and flows of the workers' movement, together with ebbs and flows in the economy will take place, and not necessarily in direct dependence one upon the other.

Economic revival is not necessarily a debit for the revolution. On the contrary, with the paralysis of the proletariat, the harnessing and knitting together of the masses in industry will strengthen their confidence and fighting capacity. It can prepare the way for big struggles (America 1936) which can pose again the political questions in a clear and sharp fashion. The economic revival, in any event, can last only a few years and the new slump again pose before the workers the treachery of the Stalinist and social democratic leaders who shouted 'Production'...and produced unemployment and want because of 'over-production.'

While the proletariat can be lulled and reconciled by its organisations in a period of universal shortage, to accept the yoke of increased slavery and the burdens of increasing production, they will find it intolerable when they see the impasse into which these sacrifices have led them. But only if the Fourth Internationalists have carefully explained the process in a theoretical fashion, can we reap the benefits from the advanced section of the working class. Only on that basis will it be possible to talk of leadership of the masses.

The new slump will reveal once again, as did the wars and the previous slumps, the degeneration and chronic crisis of world capitalism. Great class battles, revolution and civil war will be on the order of the day.

The definitive decline of Europe, already begun in 1914, has been aggravated in the succeeding decades, and World War II has put its seal on this decline. While cyclical upturns will take place and are taking place at the present time, there can be no real growth of the productive forces as in the past. The chronic crisis and death agony of capitalism will once again be revealed in its full scope when the catastrophe of the peace will be added to that of the war; the paradox of poverty and plenty, of idle factories and idle workers, of starving populations while food is rotting, of the burdens of the new rearmament programme, will pose insistently the need for the reorganisation of society in the consciousness of the proletariat. The programme of the Fourth International will become the banner of the European and world proletariat.

Marxism Versus New Fabianism
Part One

November 1952

A Political and Philosophical Basis for the Left Wing

THE PUBLICATION of the *New Fabian Essays* with an introduction by Attlee marks a stage in the development of the labour movement in Britain. In it is supposed to be summed up the experience of the last 50 years both nationally and internationally, by the intellectual elite of the Labour Party including Crossman, Crosland, Strachey, Mikardo, Denis Healey, Austen Albu, Jenkins and others.

The old programme of the Fabians, having been largely carried out by the Labour government between 1945-50, is recognised as being inadequate or outmoded to solve the problems of creating a socialist society. At the same time there is ferment within the ranks of the labour movement; the rank and file are looking for a theoretical and practical explanation of the inadequacies of the government of 1945-50 in order to implement policies which will clear the way for socialism.

The publication of Bevan's book*, the new Socialist Union publication, and the *New Fabian Essays* are all symptomatic of the awakening and the searching for a fresh policy. The Bevan controversy which has shaken the movement from top to bottom is the best indication of this search for a policy and programme which will serve the needs of socialism.

To analyse adequately and criticise all the arguments in *New Fabian Essays* would require another book as lengthy or lengthier than the *Essays* themselves, especially as the *Essays* contradict each other in many fundamentals and do not constitute a harmonious philosophical, theoretical or political whole. Despite the varying views and some healthy criticisms of the bureaucratised nationalised industries (from the point of view of pressing for

In Place of Fear by Aneurin Bevan, was published in 1952 in the aftermath of the 1951 election defeat.

greater democracy and greater participation of the workers in the
control of these industries), there are some basic threads of
thought underlying all the *Essays:* the idea that the structure of
British society has been fundamentally changed by the
nationalisation of some of the basic industries and the creation of
the 'Welfare State', the rejection of Marxism which is equated with
the doctrine of totalitarian Stalinism, and the theory that this is the
epoch of the so-called 'managerial revolution'.

One striking feature of the *Essays* is the rejection at least in words
of the narrow and provincial view of old Fabians who confined
themselves to Britain and British problems and ignored world
developments. At a time when even capitalist politicians have been
forced by the realities of economic evolution to recognise the
interdependence of the world, and when events have brought
home crushingly the urgency of international problems even from
the point of view of day to day policies, it is no longer possible to
maintain such a provincial outlook. At the same time, on home
problems too, Fabian pace, snail's pace, has been discredited as a
method of obtaining the socialist objective. Without a drastic
overhaul of social relations reaction is bound to set in.

Leadership Holds Back

Richard Crossman perhaps unwittingly gives the key to the
solution of the dilemma facing the workers in the labour
movement when he says 'At that time (first months of Labour rule)
the British people were ready to accept the peaceful socialist
revolution; and if what it got was merely welfare capitalism, the
fault lay with the politicians and not with the public.' Thus a golden
opportunity of transforming Britain into a workers' democracy
and shaking the world by her example was lost by the cowardice
and shortsightedness of the leadership. A bold and radical
nationalisation of all industry with, perhaps, compensation on the
basis of a means test, an appeal to the workers of Europe and Asia
to join and set up a United Socialist States of Europe and Asia
would have changed world history and begun the transition to
socialism for the people and states of the whole world.

The people of Britain, and of the world, will have to pay in agony
and suffering for the failure to accomplish the overthrow of
capitalism which lay within the grasp of the Labour government in
Britain. The rearmament race, and the undermining of the
reforms of the Labour government, even in the latter period of
Labour's rule, indicate that 'welfare capitalism' cannot maintain
itself for any extended period of time. In the situation of British

and world capitalism reforms are inevitably undermined by the impasse of the system itself. Only a fundamental change, economically and politically, can stabilise reforms and steadily prepare the way for a new socialist society.

The new Fabians are haunted by the experience of Stalinism in Russia, China and Eastern Europe. This leads them to stress the dangers of the 'concentration of power in the hands of *either* industrial management *or* the state bureaucracy'. Says Crossman:

> This task was not even begun by the Labour government. On the contrary, in the nationalised industries old managements were preserved almost untouched, and appointments to the national, regional and consultative boards were made as if with the express intention of reaffirming that no change was intended. The government's attitude to central planning was simple. Up to 1947, no serious attempt was made to construct even a central mechanism for assessing resources and requirements of wealth and labour, and allocating them to the various needs....Nor was an effort made to encourage popular participation in the new Welfare State....the impression was given that socialism was an affair for the Cabinet, acting through the existing Civil Service.

Crossman and the other Fabians might have added that the power of the capitalists remained largely as it was. Over the period of Labour's rule the profits of the capitalists actually increased, while the state machine: army, police, civil bureaucracy, in its topmost strata remained the preserve of faithful members and supporters of the ruling class. In the structure of rule the power of the ruling class thus remained virtually intact. It is this, at least in part, which the new Fabians are compelled to recognise and to call for the *active and direct participation of the masses in industry* and, we might add, in the direct administration of the state from top to bottom, if enthusiasm and activity are to be engendered.

Has Capitalism Been Transformed?

Nevertheless, as a result of full employment in Britain consequent on the post-war boom, the mirage appears of a change in capitalist economy which has transformed it into a post-capitalist 'managerial', 'controlled' economy, *in which the laws of capitalist economy no longer operate, thus eliminating slumps and booms.* This receives its finished expression in the essay of Anthony Crosland.

He starts with a complete distortion of the Marxist analysis mainly because, to put it mildly, of his ignorance of the economic and philosophical doctrines of Marx. It is a pity he did not take Engels's advice '....a man who undertakes to discuss scientific questions should learn above all to read the works of the author whom he wishes to study, just as they have been written, and especially not to find anything in them which they do not contain'. For example, the idea theat 'capitalism would collapse of its own accord'. An idea more foreign to the method of Marxism would be more difficult to conceive. And a few paragraphs after the assertion that the Marxist prognosis is false (how explain the revolutions in China, Russia and Eastern Europe on this basis?) he asserts 'The resistance to change, moreover, has been weakened by the fact that the capitalist bourgeoisie is no longer as self-confident as in its hey-day.' And again 'Savage taxation of income and property and the nationalisation of private industries have aroused scarcely more opposition than measures to limit child labour a hundred years ago.'

It never occurs to him that it is the twilight of capitalism nationally and internationally which has undermined the confidence of the capitalists; the development of capitalism beyond the framework of private ownership which forces the capitalist class to swallow limited measures of statification to keep the economy going. It is the industries *ruined by capitalism,* too expensive to regenerate by old methods, in which the capitalists swallow nationalisation as a necessary evil. But, as soon as a favourable opportunity occurs, *profitable* industries like steel and road transport are handed back, at a handsome discount, to big business.

This it is which makes so dangerous the complacency of Crosland and others in the Labour Party who think as he does that the capitalists will inevitably swallow other reforms as tamely as in the last period of office of Labour. Shortsightedness could not go further in analysing the reaction to reforms by the capitalists. You can trim the claws of a tiger but its dangerous strength remains, especially when its teeth are untouched. Woe betide the unwary who place their bodies at the mercy of the wild animals of big finance.

After the first world war capitalism in Western Europe, especially in Germany, accepted many reforms to ride the revolutionary tide and save the system from complete overthrow. It did not prevent them later, in desperation, from financing and supporting Hitler. In 1936 the French capitalists acquiesced in many reforms for fear of the masses, following the stay-in strikes. This did not prevent them from returning to the attack and whittling away the reforms as soon as the mass upsurge was spent. After 1918 in Britain many reforms were achieved which did not prevent Baldwin later from launching an all out attack which precipitated the general strike of 1926.

Under Crosland's nose and as he wrote, the Conservative government of Churchill is cautiously whittling away the gains made by the workers in 1945-9. And this while 'full employment' remains!

In what would undoubtedly have been written in humorous vein if Crosland had even a nodding acquaintance with Marxist doctrine, he says 'The propertied class has lost its traditional capitalist function —the exploitation with its own capital of the technique of production —and as the function disappears so the power slips away.' Leaving aside the error in the last few words, Marx had already observed the process and predicted the result a century or so ago. The 'modern' Crosland is a little behind! And as if the necessity of change from one social system to another is not signalised by the loss of function in production (as Marx explained a thousand times) of the old ruling class! Thus the loss of function of the feudal lords who became parasites before the Cromwellian and especially the French revolutions, as even Carlyle observed. And as if the socialisation of labour under capitalism, the centralisation of capital, the creation of joint stock companies —had not been analysed by both Marx and Engels. Also the consequent transformation of the entrepreneurs from a necessary function in production to complete parasites and drones has been shown as an inevitable result of the process of capitalist production:

> Stock companies in general, developed with the credit system, have a tendency to separate this labour of management as a function more and more from the ownership of capital, whether it be self-owned or borrowed. In the same way the development of bourgeois society separates the functions of judges and administrators from feudal property, whose prerogatives they were in feudal times. Since the mere owner of capital, the money-capitalist, has to face the investing capitalist, whilst the money capital itself assumes a social character with the advance of credit, being concentrated in banks and loaned by them instead of by its original owners, and since, on the other hand, the mere manager, who has no title whatever to the capital, whether by borrowing or otherwise, performs all real functions pertaining to the investment capitalist as such, only the functionary remains and the capitalist disappears from the process of production as a superfluous person. *(Capital,* Vol. 3, p.387)

Ironically enough it is precisely Crosland and his colleagues who believe that capitalism collapses automatically by transforming itself into something else once the function of the entrepreneurs has disappeared! Marx, on the contrary, pointed out the necessity under these conditions for the proletariat, organised in the labour movement, consciously to overthrow the dying system of capitalism. The reaction to these conditions would produce the party and leadership, despite many errors and lost opportunities, which would ultimately destroy capitalism. The existence of such conditions, to a Marxist, would merely prove the extreme decay of capitalism and the ripeness of the social system for the socialist revolution.

Crisis Ended?

Crosland, however, excels himself in his analysis of the economic plight of capitalism. Airily dismissing the Marxist thesis on the contradictions of capitalism he observes that 'The 1931 depression, although unusually severe, was not the first depression of such severity —the famous slump of 1873-7 was at least as bad.' This is to compare the effects of a cold in youth to pneumonia in old age. The slump of 1873-7 marked a great economic convulsion of capitalism. It succeeded in escaping its effects by the intensive expansion of the Californian gold fields, the opening-up of Africa and Asia, the development of imperialism. These were some of the reasons why, after the slump of 1873 there was a relative ascent of capitalism. Says Schumpeter*:

> The broad fact of great steadiness in long term increase....remains, both in the sense of rough constancy of the gradient of the trend and in the sense of what, merely by way of formulating a visual impression, we may term the general dominance of trend over fluctuations....*In no country does 1873 look very catastrophic*. In America 1844 produced almost no fall at all. The crises of the early nineties shows, for Germany, only a considerable dent. In the long English series it happens only twice that absolute fall outlasts two years. In the case of Germany, this occurred only in 1868, 1869 and 1870; in America also but once. (*Business Cycles*. McGraw-Hill Vol. 2, p.494, our emphasis)

But every authoritative capitalist economist and observer was profoundly dismayed at the spectacle of the slump of 1931-3. The period of rising capitalism came to an end in 1914. After 1873-7 there were depressions but not such as to shake the economy from top to bottom. After the 1929-33 collapse had been painfully overcome only the rearmament boom and the war prevented an even more shattering recurrence of the slump. It was this in economic terms which precipitated the second world war of 1939-45. This is hardly a symptom of the health of the economic system. Periodic wars of destruction which threaten to annihilate

---

*Joseph Schumpeter was a member of the 'Austrian School' of economists, who put forward an alternative theory of business cycles to that of Marx, emphasising the innovative role of small businesses.

the cities man has built and technical conquests achieved, are hardly an inspiring alternative for capitalism to offer to periodic crises of over-production. But here Crosland, Strachey and others deny or half deny that over-production or slump will occur. They think the full employment which obtained in Britain under the Labour government (and to a slightly less extent obtains also under Churchill's government) was a consequence of the policies of the Labour government.

This was so only to a secondary extent. Full employment obtains in America, the last stronghold of capitalism, also since 1945. In both cases this is due to the boom which usually follows every war. War has the same effect as a slump, where the ruin, destruction and wearing out of capital and consumer goods paves the way for recovery, but in an enormously intensified form.   The capitalist crisis is overcome in war by the destruction of consumer and capital goods, by the production of fictitious capital in the shape of arms and arms production, which has, after the war, to be made good by economy. But despite measures of 'regulation' and 'control', despite the enormously increased role of state and of militarism (incidentally forecast by Marx and Engels) *the problems of capitalism are not overcome,* neither is the elimination of capitalism achieved thereby. Where, as in Britain, 80 per cent of the economy is privately owned, the laws of capitalism basically continue as before. The capitalists *continue to operate for profit* not for the sake of keeping the economy on a high level. Any spending by the state by so-called 'Keynesian techniques' can only aggravate economic crisis *once the crisis of over-production begins.*

A simple point which even the orthodox capitalist economists can understand is that 'money' or 'credit' is not created in the void. It has to be obtained by taxes ie *by cutting into the profits of the capitalists,* or the subsistence standards of the workers, or by 'deficit financing' which in a roundabout way comes to the same thing. This is because by artificially increasing the note issues, it decreases the purchasing power of money by inflation and thus in the long run has the same effect as the above. Either way a fall in the rate of profit is inevitable. Purchasing power is cut and endeavours of this sort can only aggravate the outbreak of mass unemployment and crisis.

Effect of Rearmament

In a certain sense rearmament on a world scale is having this effect in the capitalist countries. The expenditure on arms creates an enormous amount of fictitious capital which gets its share of the total wealth, of the surplus created by the working class. It has as a consequence a rise in prices, and usually a decrease in the standard of living of the workers. While injecting a further element of disease in the already decaying organism of capitalism, it cannot prevent but only *delay* the outbreak of crisis.

It is true that many in the Labour Party, particularly some of the Bevanites, think that rearmament can be replaced and slump avoided by an extended 'point 4' programme. But even a 'plan' (if it were to be agreed upon by the European powers and the USA) greater in scope than point 4 would, despite the ballyhoo, be microscopic in relation to the needs of Asia and Africa. It would be even less able to absorb the production and potential over-production in the capitalist world and would not succeed in preventing crisis.

In particular Crosland and others of like mind are living in a fool's paradise when the problems of the world market are taken into account. *A minor economic recession* or fall in production of a few per cent, which would hardly provoke a ripple in America, will mean major economic convulsions in Britain and Western Europe. It can be imagined then what would be the effect of a big fall in production. This is recognised fearfully even by such journals as the *Observer* and *The Economist*.

Nationally and internationally the market economy still dominates in Britain. In his muddled way even Crosland has glimmerings of the problem. He says 'Under the post-war Labour administration the tempo of change was enormously accelerated and by 1951 *Britain had in all essentials ceased to be a capitalist country*' (my emphasis). And on the very next page he unconsciously contradicts himself. 'It ('Welfare State', 'Mixed Economy') is capitalist to the extent that private ownership of industry predominates, that most production is for the market, and that many of the old class divisions persist.' *To what extent?* Where 80 per cent of the economy is privately owned, capitalism, its economy and its laws are predominant. The public sectors, like the post office in the past, will *operate for the benefit of the private sector*. No amount of financial juggling can overcome that decisive fact. Until the dominating heights and the dominating proportion of industry is nationalised the laws of capitalist economy will dictate to the government, whether Labour or Conservative.

It is from this fundamental error that flow the mistakes and dreams of Crosland and other Fabians. No more Jarrows and Ebbw Vales. 'Both the area, and the bitterness, of social conflict are much reduced....no uniquely delineated ruling class, nor clearly defined class struggle.'

Class Antagonisms Intensified

In reality, however, the rumblings of the coming storm are faintly foreshadowed in the strike of steel workers and miners in America and the wage demands of the engineers, miners and other workers in Britain, in the face of the steadily increasing cost of living. The capitalists are cautiously preparing for the struggle. If in the post-war period in Britain and America (not on the Continent be it noted) a relative period of quiet has ensued, that has been because of international relations, the class relations within the countries themselves, the mighty strength of organised labour, the fear of the ruling class, but above all *because the ruling class could afford crumbs of concessions from the feast of profits in the post-war boom.*

But this period is now drawing to a close. Far from the fond dream of class reconciliation, a period of bitter, more implacable class conflict looms ahead in all its stark horror. The 'new' Fabians may think their themes are really 'modern', 'realistic' and 'new'. In fact in one form or another every boom has seen the dissemination of these panaceas and utopias, of a change in capitalism, of a new stage, of sedate, kind and tolerant amelioration of class antagonisms, of a rosy period of gradual change for the better, of great reforms which all ended in disaster. On the basis of the new Fabians' themes the labour movement could only find catastrophe.

Will There Be A Slump?

1960

THE PROLONGED upswing of British and world capitalism since the second world war, in the areas where the capitalist system has been maintained, calls for an examination of the basic ideas of Marxism on the question of economic development. If there is a fundamental change in the working of the system then it is necessary for Marxists to make a suitable reappraisal. Marxism represents the concentrated analysis of the laws governing the development of society. In the field of economics, the laws underlying the development of capitalist society have been worked out and explained by Marx. Despite extension and deepening in the works of Lenin and Trotsky, these basic laws have remained fundamentally the same for more than a century.

Undoubtedly the economy, since the second world war, has developed on somewhat different lines to those following the first world war. But every decade of capitalist development has tended to be different to every other decade. The basic laws underlying the development of capitalist economy have, however, remained intact.

The immediate perspective in the economy is of a rise in production, this year, of probably 6 per cent. This in its turn will mean a strengthening of the demand of the working class for a bigger share of production. Hence the concessions of capitalism in the field of wages and hours in the last few months. The victory of the railway workers has been predicated by this fact.

The world economy is beginning to move towards slump (or recession —a small slump that does not deepen into long-lasting depression —according to the definition of the capitalist economists). Until recently, there has been quite a high rate of development of the economy in all the major capitalist countries, in fact largely throughout the capitalist world. This development in Western Europe and in many of the 'undeveloped' areas of the world is beginning to slow down. There are already signs in the fall of prices of shares on Wall Street —always a sensitive, if not always correct, barometer —that the economy of the United States may have its downswing in a deeper 'recession' or 'slump' soon.

The huge investments in industry, the turn to mechanisation and automation, increase, at the same time, the amount of constant capital in proportion to variable capital, ie the capital invested in machinery, buildings, plant etc, rises in proportion to the amount invested in wages. This must lead to a fall in the rate of profit. The present decline of investment is a reflection of the capitalists' realisation of this tendency, even though they do not understand the reason for it.

However, these swings, up and down, are normal to the development of the trade cycle, at every phase of the development of capitalism. What has to be established is not the episodic differences, but whether there is a new element, such as the intervention of the state, which changes fundamentally the movement of the trade cycle from anything experienced by capitalism in the past.

The basic Marxist postulates, on this question, are that the exploitation of the working class by the capitalists means that the surplus value, created by the workers, is accumulated by the capitalists and then reinvested in industry. The explanation of the development of the economy under these conditions is the division of the economy into 'department 1' (production of the means of production) and 'department 2' (production of the means of consumption). The surplus produced by the working class, over and above its own subsistence is, apart from a small part consumed by the capitalists, ploughed back into production. The whole historic role of capitalism has been the development of the productive powers of society by the use of the surplus in capital construction. Hence the growth of production.

Competition between different capitals produced the need for ever greater productive equipment. This, in its turn, meant the gradual accumulation and concentration of capital in fewer and fewer hands. The continuous expansion of expenditure on constant capital (C) or means of production, in relation to the amount spent on variable capital or wages (V), in its turn produced the *tendency* of the rate of profit to fall. This is confirmed in different language by all serious economists including Keynes. Even the university professors, on studying the data, are compelled to admit the truth of this proposition for the modern epoch, even more than in the past.

The fundamental cause of crisis in capitalist society, *a phenomenon peculiar to capitalist society alone*, lies in the *inevitable over-production* of both consumer and capital goods for the purposes of capitalist production. There can be all sorts of secondary causes of crisis, particularly in a period of capitalist development – partial over-production in only some industries; financial juggling on the stock exchange; inflationary swindles; disproportions in production; and a whole host of others – but the fundamental cause of crisis lies in *over-production*. This in turn, is caused by the *market economy*, and the division of society into mutually conflicting classes.

None of this has been changed by the developments of the period since the second world war. This can be demonstrated by a comparison of the inter-war period, pre-1914, and the post-second world war period.

Since the second world war, because of the pressure of competition from America, the rise of Soviet and Eastern European and Chinese production as a formidable threat to capitalism projecting into the future, the economy of formerly relatively backward economies such as those of Japan, Britain, France and Italy has had to be rationalised. The development of world production has meant that *competition between national capitalisms* has forced further modernisation and further division of labour and specialisation even between the major capitalist nations. (This is one of the reasons why the Common Market, on however shaky a basis, has been formed, provoking in its turn the Outer 7* countries grouped round Britain as a reply). The 'national' economies thus work more and more together with the state and using the state as a lever. Monopoly capitalism and the state intertwine and fuse.

In his book *Trends and Cycles in Economic Activity* William Fellner demonstrates that the trade cycle in the post-war period has not been fundamentally different to the trade cycle of the past:

> While averaging for decades smooths out much of the cyclical instability, the decade-averages remain noticeably influenced by the somewhat depressed character of the decade of the 1890s as a whole, and by the war and post-war prosperity of the entire decade of the 1940s...a basic tendency towards a proportionate rate of increase of between 30 per cent and 40 per cent per decade...when two decades are 'abnormal', in opposite directions as the 1930s and the 1940s, the tendency asserts itself for a 20-year period.

Dealing with the United States, JA Schumpeter in *Business Cycles* declares: 'The number of minor interruptions between the major downturns seem to have been greater in the United States

*The European Economic Community (EEC or Common Market) was formed in 1957. The 'Outer 7' was the European Free Trade Association (EFTA) founded in response to the EEC in 1960. The UK was a member of EFTA until it joined the EEC.

than in most European countries, even though the secular trend
has been particularly steep in the United States.' Dealing with the
difference in the trade cycle between Britain and America, to
explain the present tendency Fellner points out:

> It may be that the British cycle is still somewhat lengthier than that in
> the USA. Earnest students record that in the 19th century the length of
> the British cycle was between seven and ten years; American
> investigators found a cycle of somewhat shorter duration...The
> difference may be due to the structure of the economy, or even to a
> difference in national temperament. One might say that the Americans
> are quicker off the mark, in reacting to a change in circumstances, or
> one might say that they are more volatile.
>
> For a number of years the British cycle, and that in continental
> Europe also, has been out of phase with the American cycle...The
> primary cause of this divergence was the larger scale of the American
> defence effort, even in proportion to the size of her economy, after the
> Korean episode*.

It is true that the rate of growth in the period 1870-1914 was at a
higher tempo than in the period between the wars, but that
reflected the fact that the relatively progressive nature of
capitalism had changed. The world war of 1914-18 marked a
definite stage in the development of capitalism. This was reflected
in the impasse in which the private ownership of the means of
production and the national state had landed society.

The economic upswing, following the second world war, is due to
a whole series of factors. There is nothing 'unique' in such an
upswing. The possibility of such an economic upturn of capitalist
society was foreseen by Trotsky in his criticism of the blind
mechanical conceptions of the Stalinists:

> Will the bourgeoisie be able to secure for itself a new epoch of capitalist
> growth and power? Merely to deny such a possibility, counting on the
> 'hopeless position' in which capitalism finds itself would be mere
> revolutionary verbiage. There are no absolutely hopeless situations
> (Lenin). The present unstable class equilibrium in the European
> countries cannot continue indefinitely precisely because of its
> instability...
>
> There will be no new boom of world capitalism (of course, with the
> prospect of a new epoch of great upheavals) only in the event that the
> proletariat will be able to find a way out of the present unstable
> equilibrium on the revolutionary road. (*The Third International After
> Lenin* page 64-5)

*At the end of the Second World War Korea was divided. A Stalinist regime was
established in the North and a capitalist regime under US domination in the South.
The Korean War between the two regimes lasted between 1950-53. Sixteen
capitalist powers, under UN auspices, sent forces under US general MacArthur to
the South, while China backed the North. During the war about 5 million died.

And again:

> From Marx on, we have been constantly repeating that capitalism cannot cope with the spirit of new technology to which it has given rise and which tears asunder not only the integument of bourgeois private property rights but, as the war of 1914 has shown, also the national hoops of the bourgeois state, (*ibid* page 52)
>
> Politics, considered as a mass historical force, always lags behind economics...the international capitalist system has already spent itself and is no longer capable of progress as a whole...
>
> Theoretically, to be sure, even a new chapter of a general capitalist progress in the most powerful, ruling, and leading countries is not excluded. (*ibid* page 81)

Dealing with the trade cycle, The American National Bureau of Economic Research has prepared a table, dating back about a century. This table shows the peaks and troughs of economic activity in the United States in this period. (See Table2, p412).

To these could be added the peak of 1953, the trough of 1954, the peak of 1957, the trough of 1958, the peak of 1959-60 and the subsequent decline.

What then are the basic reasons for the developments of the post-second world war economy?

1) The political failure of the Stalinists and the social democrats, in Britain and Western Europe, created the *political* climate for a recovery of capitalism.

2) The effects of the war, in the destruction of consumer and capital goods, created a big market (war has effects similar to, but deeper than, a slump in the destruction of capital). These effects, according to United Nations' statisticians, only disappeared in 1958.

3) The Marshall Plan and other economic aid assisted the recovery of Western Europe.

4) The enormously increased investment in industry.

5) The growth of new industry —plastics, aluminium, rockets, electronics, atomic energy and by-products.

6) The increasing output of the newer industries —chemicals, artificial fibres, synthetic rubber, plastics, rapid rise in light metals, aluminium, magnesium, electric household equipment, natural gas, electric energy, building activity.

7) The enormous amounts of fictitious capital, created by the armaments expenditure, which amount to 10 per cent of the national income in Britain and America.

8) The new market for capital and engineering products, created by the weakening of imperialism in the undeveloped countries, which has given the local bourgeoisie the increased opportunity to develop industry on a greater scale than ever before.

9) All these factors interact on one another. The increased demand for raw materials, through the development of industry in the metropolitan countries in its turn, reacts on the undeveloped countries and vice-versa.

10) The increasing trade, especially in capital goods and engineering products, between the capitalist countries, consequent on the increased economic investment, in its turn acts as a spur.

11) The role of state intervention in stimulating economic activity.

All these factors explain the increase in production since the war. But the decisive factor has been the increased scope for capital investment, which is the main engine of capitalist development.

The relatively progressive role of capitalism between 1870 and 1914 consisted in the development of the productive forces, at a fairly rapid rate. It is true that sufficient productive forces had been developed for the working class to take power, ie the material conditions for workers' power had been created by the previous expansion of the productive forces under private ownership. Under workers' power the productive forces would then have developed faster. But nevertheless, so long as capitalism can develop the productive forces at a fast pace, it serves the need of progress and can maintain itself so long as it serves this purpose.

Since the second world war, capitalism, in an uneven, contradictory fashion, has suffered such a period of 'rebirth'. It is true that it is a temporary uplift of a rotten and diseased economy, reflecting the old age of capitalism rather than its resilient youth, that it shows all the feebleness of a decayed system. But even within the general decline of capitalism such periods are inevitable so long as the working class, through faulty leadership, fails to end the system. There is no such thing as a 'last crisis', a 'last economic slump' of capitalism, a 'ceiling on production' or any of the other primitive ideas put forward by the Stalinists during the great depression of 1929-1933. Nevertheless the enfeeblement of capitalism is reflected in the revolutionary events following the second world war.

From the viewpoint of Marxism, this economic revival of capitalism is not a negative phenomenon only. It enormously strengthens the numbers and cohesion of the working class, and of the position of the working class within the nation. The next break in the economic conjuncture will pose even greater problems in front of capitalism than in the past.

It is this *economic revival*, and not the role of government spending, or the increased role of the state, which is the main factor explaining the *recessions* or little slumps which have followed the second world war. Of course the increased role of the state with the end of *laissez faire* had already been pointed out by Marx and Engels. The tendency of the productive forces to outgrow the envelope of private ownership, forces the state to intervene more and more in the 'regulation' of the economy.

Lenin, Bukharin and Trotsky had shown the enormously increased role of the state, during and after the first world war. In his last writings Trotsky had reinforced the arguments on the increased economic role of the state. The greatly increased role of the state was explained by the growth of productive forces, the concentration of capital, the growth of trusts and the development of monopoly capital. All these developments had been summarised in Lenin's *Imperialism*. There was a fusion of monopoly capital with the state which acted as the direct agent of big business. This did not mean 'regulation' or a 'plan' of production in the sense of the economy of a workers' state. Neither did it mean an abolition of the domination of the market. Within the limits, especially of arms production, it increased the contradictions within capitalism. The 'regulation' was principally at the expense of middle-sized and small business, as in the recent credit squeeze and the increase in the rates of interest, which affect big business very little but are burdensome to the minor capitalists.

The subsidies to big business, the de-nationalisation of profitable sectors of nationalised industry are an indication of the real role of the state as the tool of the banks and trusts. The state has taken over those sections of industry rendered unprofitable by the development of new industries and techniques, and by the need for huge capital expenditure and modernisation, which were not economic or profitable for capitalism.

In the case of Britain there was the need to transform the basic industries: coal, gas, electricity, transport and steel, for purpose of rendering engineering, shipbuilding, chemicals and other industries, competitive on world markets. Thus the measures of state capitalism, which constitute an important argument for statification, do not in themselves alter the basic laws of capitalism.

But the factors which have assisted in maintaining full or relatively full employment in the main capitalist countries, that is expenditure on armaments, have led in their turn to the persistent and steady inflation. In West Germany, which did not have such a burden, taking advantage of the difficulties of her rivals in this connection, and with a large reserve of labour from the former German territories, Czechoslovakia, and East Germany, the price level up to the recent period was relatively stable. In addition, the amount ploughed back in capital investment was correspondingly higher. Now, with full employment, they are beginning to face the same problems as their rivals:

> In West Germany the non-recurrent elements in the process of expansion were particularly striking; large scale unemployment early in the 1950s and the high rate of immigration of labour from East Germany; gaps left in the stock of physical resources by the destruction of the war, by the post-war dismantling of plant, and by the partitioning of the country. These factors in combination yielded high rates of profit in a process of expansion distinguished by a rapid growth of employment and by a high rate of investment, in extending the capital structure. (*The Economic Bulletin for Europe*. Volume 3, 1959).

The economic experts of the United Nations, regarding with dismay the last few slumps, have come to understand that the bourgeoisie has by no means been enabled to solve the economic problems facing their system. The *Annual World Survey* of the United Nations published in 1959 contained the following wry estimate:

> No special factors of major significance can help to explain the downturn in United States economic activity in 1957-8 or the virtual standstill in total West European production in the course of 1958...Regardless of the extent to which the recession may have been inherent in the build-up of excess capacity or might have been accelerated by government restriction, it is evident that the world has not yet learned how to avoid the costs of recurrent industrial slumps.

And again commenting on the sharp character of the fall in 1958...'Nor would it be wise to assume, on the basis of the post-war experience, that in the future all recessions are bound to be short and mild.'

Incidentally, the United Nations' economists estimate that the last 'recession' cost the United States billions of dollars in both real income and capacity to import. Reflecting the illusions of the 'under-consumptionists' who believe that all will be well if the capacity to consume is maintained, the United Nations' economists speak of 'an array of automatic stabilisers, including progressive tax systems, social security, and farm support programmes...' But even they make the point:

> It is important to bear in mind, however, that stabilisers can only slow down a rate of decline; they cannot in themselves initiate an upturn...While depressions of the order of magnitude of the nineteen thirties have become unthinkable both on social and on · political

grounds, recessions of greater duration and depth that those heretofore experienced in the post-war years cannot be prevented by exclusive reliance on any automatic stabilisers. (*World Survey* page 4)

The development of the economies in Western Europe, Japan, the United States and Britain – with this or that national difference – all demonstrate the same phenomenon: the increase in capital investment, as the key to the economic upswing in the decade and a half following the second world war.

Apart from the subsidies to private industry, which amounted to £385 million in Britain in 1958, and the enormous expenditure on armaments, which constitutes unproductive expenditure, in many of the countries of Western Europe –but particularly in Britain –the ruined basic industries were nationalised, in order to modernise them so as to serve as useful instruments in increasing profits of private enterprise, especially in the more modern industries.

Those sections which showed profitable possibilities, such as steel and road transport, were denationalised by the Tories and now the suggestion has been made of hotels and catering, and non-railway properties and activities of the railways. Thus the nationalised sector which constitutes 20 per cent of the economy in Britain serves as the handmaiden of private industry.

Even if these industries had remained in the hands of private enterprise it would have meant large expenditure, as in America, in order to modernise them. But the investment in these fields is still only *half* that of the industries which have not been nationalised. As the total of capital investment in 1957 was 14.7 per cent, the *highest* level of investment in Britain since the war, it can be seen that the nationalised industries would have invested roughly five per cent as against 10 per cent invested by private industry. At the same time the output of the industries under private enterprise is six or seven times the output of the industries under the control of the state. This means that it is the private sector of the economy which dominates over industry in the economy as a whole, and not vice-versa. This can easily be demonstrated by the statistics given by the Census of Production published in 1958 (see Table 2 on p412):

What do these statistics show? On two fundamental problems they provide an unanswerable reply to the theories of the revisionists. The argument of Strachey, Crosland, Gaitskell and others is that the relative share of the working class in the increased production has increased. These figures demonstrate irrefutably that the share of the working class, relative to the total production, has fallen. Statistics from America, Italy, Japan and West Germany would undoubtedly demonstrate the same thing.

It is true that the absolute standard of living has increased (overtime, women working, increased productivity of labour, bonus schemes, full employment etc would be the explanation) but the relative share of the working class has dropped. So the 'under consumptionist' idea that the capitalist crisis has been overcome by the increased share of the consumers is demonstrated to be palpably false. The share of the 'consumers', including the capitalists, has dropped from approximately 67 per cent in 1938 to a little over 54 per cent in 1957 of the total 'cake' of national production.

The increase in productive capacity in Britain has been 3 per cent a year since the war —twice as high a rate of increase as that achieved in the inter-war period and probably faster than for many years before 1914. After the war until 1951 one fifth of output was offset by increases in the price of imports. Output rose between 1946 and 1951 by 14.5 per cent...Real national income by 11.5 per cent. Between 1951 and 1955 real national income rose by 15.5 per cent as against a rise in gross domestic product of 12.5 per cent. Between 1955 and 1958 gross national product rose by 5 per cent as against a rise in production of only 3 per cent. Between 1951 and 1958 gross national investment, savings and depreciation increased from 15 per cent to nearly 20 per cent. Net national income rose from under 7 per cent to over 11.5 per cent.

From the point of view of Marxism, in any case, a continuing rise in the share of national production by the working class, in itself at a certain stage would *cause crisis* and slump by cutting into the share of the national income going to the capitalists, thus over a period causing a fall in the rate of profit. This is so because it is only out of the surplus created by the workers, that the capitalists find the wherewithal to invest. Meanwhile the continuing technological progress means that the capitalists are compelled to invest (in real terms leaving aside the fall in the value of money) more and more in production for the purpose of competing on the national and international markets. Thus the explanation of the post-war period of ascent cannot be explained by the increase in the standard of living —*a la* Crosland and Jay.

On the other hand the statistics of national production, which, allowing for marginal errors, are an accurate description of the national economy from a capitalist point of view, demonstrate the shallowness of the theories of Maurice Dobb and of various Stalinists that it is the increased role of the state which has prevented another 1929. It is true that the role of the state has increased. But the statistics demonstrate the limits of this phenomenon. From 1938 to 1957, including the expenditure of the national and local authorities on building, social services and armaments, the total proportion of the increased national income spent by the state amounted to 14.7 per cent of the national income in 1957. If one includes also the figures of expenditure of the nationalised industries it would amount to about 20 per cent of the national income, or one fifth, in itself a gigantic figure but not sufficient to determine the basic movement of the economy. It is not state industry which dictates the movement of private industry, fundamentally, but private industry which dictates the movement of state industry.

In an epoch such as this it is necessary for Marxists to have an answer to any tendencies, bourgeois, social-democratic and revisionist (this is particularly necessary in the political climate created by the temporary upswing of capitalism).

A restatement of the fundamental Marxist doctrine on this question puts the whole problem in its proper perspective. There can *never* be a slump in an economy which is state-owned, as far as 'the commanding heights of the economy' are concerned, because it is then possible to plan production on the same lines as an individual factory. If mistakes are made, as in the plan of the Soviet bureaucracy, it is easy to overcome this by simple administrative decree.

The only limits to production, apart from the mistakes of the bureaucrats, their swindling, inefficiency, red tape, etc, is the level of production and the productive forces themselves. They can *plan* to produce consumer goods, capital goods, rockets or cannon, or what-have-you, but so long as the level of the productive forces is taken into consideration, and due limits of proportion observed, with this or that error, nevertheless the entire capacity of production (leaving out discrepancies in raw materials etc) can be used to its utmost limits! That is the fundamental distinction between an economy based on state ownership and an economy of partial ownership by the state, an economy of state capitalism.

Why cannot expenditure by the capitalist state solve the problems of the economy in a capitalist society? In an economy where private ownership is the dominant form of production, production remains for the market. All taxes must come from the economy itself, either they must come from the profits of the capitalists, or they must cut into the income of the working class. In either case it cannot over a period prevent crisis. To cut into the income of the capitalist would cut into the rate of profit; money spent by the state, taken from the pockets of the capitalists, cannot be spent by the capitalists. Similarly, money extracted from the workers in taxes for the benefit of the capitalists and their state, cuts into the market for consumer goods. Thus, either way, the state eats into the vitals of the economy. The state in the modern period has become a monstrous incubus and parasitic burden on production. What the state gains on the swings, the capitalists lose on the roundabouts. The worst thing from a capitalist point of view is for the state to cut into the profits of the capitalists. For that aggravates the crisis while 80 per cent of the economy remains in the hands of private 'enterprise'. That is why as speedily as possible the capitalists get their state to lessen the taxes on profits and especially the allowances for new investments. The Tory government (and the Labour government after them) systematically lessened the taxes in this way.

On the other hand the various Keynesian 'solutions' of this problem are basically unsound. If the state, by 'deficit financing', as advocated by Gaitskell, spends in effect money it does not possess, it means that there will be an inflation of the currency, and over a period it would amount to the above propositions on the distribution of the national income. The only difference being that crisis would be aggravated by the ruin of the currency. The reason for this would be the inevitable rise of prices, other things being equal, to the same proportion as the increase of the money in circulation not backed by goods or money.

As stupid is the suggestion by Gaitskell, and echoed by others, of an increase in the expenditure of the nationalised industries. The nationalised industries cater as basic industries for the capitalist economy as a whole. The money for these industries, in so far as it is not provided on 'normal' lines to be financed by the market, must be gained by deficit financing or taxes, and thus cuts into the amount that can be spent by industry as a whole. The economic unreality of the suggestion that increased expenditure by nationalised industry could solve a crisis of production is indicated by the present crisis in the coal industry. The railways, electricity, gas and other nationalised industries are dependent (apart from individual consumption) on the orders of private enterprise, of the engineering, chemical, food and other industries. A fall in production in these industries means inevitably a fall in production in the nationalised industries. The crisis in the coal industry demonstrates the truth of this proposition even during the current boom. It is only because of the boom that the government can afford an accumulation of tens of millions of tons of coal at the pit-heads.

Expenditure on armaments is expenditure on ficticious

(unproductive) capital. Expenditure on public works, roads, hospitals, schools is necessary if marginal expenditure (not directly linked to production, but necessary to it) but can only be an amelioration of the problem, for the reasons sketched above. Incidentally the Radcliffe Commission demonstrated conclusively the fallacy that the economy was controlled by monetary measures. In fact, as Marxists have always argued, the reverse is the case. The development of the economy in the direction of inflation or deflation compels the raising or lowering of the bank rate. The general conclusion of the Committee was that:

> Monetary measures cannot alone be relied on to keep in nice balance an economy subject to major strains from both within and without. Monetary measures can help, but that is all...We suspect that extravagant hopes would not have been placed in monetary policy in recent years had it not been for the desire above all to avoid increases in taxation and reduction in government expenditure. *The gradual diminution of the burden of taxation should make it easier for more realistic views to prevail in the future.*

In other words, far from regarding the expenditure of the state as a saving grace and a blessing, the bourgeoisie is constantly groaning at the burden of the state (a necessary Old Man of the Sea it bears on its back). An increase in state expenditure on police and army to defend the loot of the bourgeoisie, and social services necessary to keep the social demands of the masses in check, education etc, etc, means *less* in the pockets of the capitalists themselves. In fact, since the war, in proportion to total income and the increase in wealth, while armaments' expenditure has enormously increased, there has been a neglect of the services, in real terms, which indirectly cater to the needs of the economy. *The Times Review of Industry* in December 1959 comments: 'The cumulative effect of under-investment in "non-industrial" public assets — is likely to give rise to economic and social problems of a major order.'

In the United Nations' *World Survey* there is an explanation of the slump of 1957-8 which fits in with the theoretical conceptions of Marxism: 'There is now virtually unanimous agreement that a substantial building up of *excess capacity* (in Britain and America) throughout the economy in 1955-7 was a major factor in bringing on the recession in 1957-8.' Meanwhile, the first flush of capitalist expansion since the war is coming to an end:

> Contrary to widespread illusion about the magnitude of the 1955-7 boom — fed in part by the self-same fear of inflation — *the true dimensions of the expansion were modest indeed.* In the US, even in the peak quarter of 1957, the volume of industrial production did not exceed the pre-recession peak level of 1953 by more than six per cent and at the low point of the 1957-8 recession the volume was

only three or four per cent above that of the corresponding period of 1951 —fully seven years earlier...Although the rate of growth has been higher on the average in other industrial countries, most notably France, Italy, the Federal Republic of Germany and Japan, it has been quite modest, *especially in the United Kingdom.(ibid*, page 6)

The 'excess capacity' in industry in Britain is a symptom of over-production of capital and the limits of the market. There have been a series of partial crises, affecting different sections of the economy in the past period, 'excess-capacity' of capital, industry, consumer over-production, over-production of raw materials, food, etc, etc at various stages and at different times. It was only the *simultaneous* concatenation of all factors of crisis which led to the devastating depression of 1929-33. Gradually the proportion that pertained in the 1920s in a whole series of economic sectors are assuming similar proportions at the present economic tide. At each successive stage the assumptions of the economic experts of the United Nations and of the bourgeoisie as a whole have been falsified. The industrial upswing in the Western countries produced in its turn a demand for raw materials and foodstuffs (primary products). This led to an increase in production in the 'undeveloped areas'. The boom in production of minerals etc, led to an increase in the price of these products (the market still dominates nationally and internationally) and an improvement in the terms of trade. But this in its turn, according to the strict logic of capitalism, led to 'over-production' and a fall in prices. The fall in the prices of primary products in the recession of 1957-8 alone amounted to between seven and eight per cent —equivalent to six years' lending to the undeveloped areas by the International Bank for Reconstruction and Development at 1956-7 rates.

According to the United Nations' survey 'the terms of trade in the late 1950s appear to be about the same as in the late 1920s'. The idea has been sedulously disseminated that a solution to the problems of capitalism can be found in the development of the undeveloped areas. It is true that a big increase in capital expenditure will ameliorate the problem for a short period of time but it can only render it worse at a later stage. However, on a capitalist basis, the limits of this development must be seen. The United Nations admits:

> It cannot be said that the present level of international aid is a negligible contribution to the development of the poorer countries; in the aggregate it *fully offsets the decline in the share of private foreign capital* in relation to the exports of primary producers since the nineteen twenties (only offsets! —EG). Yet it needs only to be realised that on a per capita basis the total assistance amounts to only $5 *per annum* for the

great) but mostly *lower than in the depressed 1930s and the tax structure had become very much stiffer.*

A similar process can be seen in the recession of 1957-8. It was *not* government expenditure but the development of the economy itself which pulled the economy in Western Europe, Britain, the United States and other countries out of the recession, ie the 'automatic' workings of the economy itself. In fact the bourgeoisie, the economists of the United Nations, and serious economists in Britain and America, were pleasantly surprised by the brief character of the recession in 1958-9. Succeeding it there was a typical capitalist boom, in which production leaped ahead in Britain, Western Europe, Japan and the United States.

Commenting on present claims to have solved the problem of consistent growth Oscar Hobson writes in the February issue of the *Banker*: 'Shades of 1929, when the problem of perpetual boom-cum-stable price level was almost everywhere proclaimed to have been solved.'

The economists of the bourgeoisie understand very well that investment is the key to the rise of the economy. On page 179 of the *World Economic Survey* (1959) the expert of the United Nations writes:

The economic upswing had been based primarily on large scale investment in fixed assets and a rapid growth of private expenditure on automobiles and other durable goods. Unlike the Korean boom, *no part was played in the process by rising government expenditure.* On the contrary it was the levelling-off of or decline in government expenditure as the Korean conflict ended that released resources for use in the private sector. In some countries, however, exports rather than domestic expenditure provided much of the impetus to higher activity.

Writing in the *Financial Times*, the 'orthodox' former Financial Secretary to the Treasury, Enoch Powell MP, says:

This (increase of production in 1959 in Britain) domestic increase was part and parcel of a general trade recovery, just as the lull which had preceded it belonged to a widespread trade recession: both were participated in by countries whose governments were purporting to behave quite differently...the government have *taken out* of the economy by taxation and borrowing from the public as much extra as they have put into it by increased expenditure.

This, in turn makes it unlikely that the government has in fact, as opposed to intention, done anything to 'stimulate the economy'. the recovery, like the recession, has taken place in response to other forces of a wider and different character; or, if you like, in the immortal words of the steward to the sea-sick lady: Madam, you don't have to do anything, it does itself.

This is perhaps on theoretical grounds —though hardly on any others —to be regretted. Once again we have been denied the privilege of observing at first hand a British government coping with a recession on orthodox Keynesian lines. We still *do not know* approximately what would be the result if, in the face of a persistent fall in propensity to spend, a British government equally persistently increased its expenditure and financed it by the creation of money through floating debt. At any rate that was not the history of the 1958-60 recovery. (*Financial Times*, 7 January 1960).

Here Powell is arguing on the lines of a market economy, that the attempt of the state at pump-priming will no more solve the problem than the Rooseveltian pump-priming of before the war. Powell understands some of the limitations of a capitalist economy; that what the government 'puts in' is determined by what it can take out in the form of taxes etc., so long as it is a market economy based on private enterprise.

In the *Financial Times*, an American economist, writing on the prospects for the American economy, is, of course, filled with optimism. But even he is cautious. Dealing with the factors leading to the rise in the American economy, he comments:

In all probability the next decade will not be marred by a serious depression...There will be changes of pace, and we should count on a brief dip or two; but worse than this we do not expect. Since the depression decades of the 1930s, Americans have learned a good deal about the functioning of their economy... The resurgence of faith in what a market economy can do has been important in maintaining consumer spending in recessions; unemployment compensation and improved asset positions and credit facilities have also contributed...

The last factors mentioned can only be a sop to a declining economy and cannot maintain the economy on a stable foundation for any length of time. These factors have been in existence in Britain since after the first world war, without affecting the economy fundamentally. However, there are certain factors which have kept the economy on an even keel. The amount spent on research and development of new techniques and products in the United States last year amounted to $12,500 million and out of this $9,000 million was contributed by private industry in the United States. The real explanation of the protracted boom in the United States the above economist gave in the following terms:

The dependence of firms on new products, materials, methods for survival and growth in a competitive economy forces their introduction as quickly as feasible, lest the temporary differential profits which pay for research are lost. Since technology does not pause for economic recovery, new investment now can operate to shorten recessions and lessen their severity.

But such a process cannot continue indefinitely. No firm is going to invest in new techniques and products if the sale of these will be *lower* than the previous sales of the product. If their returns will not cover their margins, plus at least the same profit as formerly, there would not be any point in continuing to plough in good money, in order to recover what has already been invested. Moreover, the rate of profit must decline over a period with continually new investments, to such an extent as not to be compensated by the increased surplus value, even though there was an increased rate of exploitation with an increased productivity of labour.

The *Financial Times* of 26 January 1960 reports the activities of the Eisenhower administration: 'It seems clear that a major revolution in thinking has taken place in high circles in the US. It adds up to no less than the rejection of the Keynesian doctrine — at least where periodic deficit financing is involved.' 'The Budget', again to quote *The Economist's* Washington correspondent, reporting the Administration's viewpoint 'should not merely be balanced over the business cycle...it should also show a substantial surplus.' Already in face of the recession of 1958 the Republican government had insisted on the need to balance the Budget. 'They did this because of the fear of inflation, which threatened to get out of hand'.

The new recession bids to be far more serious and long-lasting than the last. The New York Stock Exchange is a harbinger of the coming collapse. The *Financial Times* of 30 January, 1960 in its editorial was already sounding the alarm:

> The disturbing feature in Wall Street's behaviour is the talk of a new business recession...It is little more than a year since the USA was suffering from the effects of the last recession and another downturn in 1960 would be intolerable...On this side of the Atlantic the odds still appear against an early business downturn.

The same tale of woe is told by *The Times Review of Industry*:

> It is entirely possible that the prospective 1960 boom will be strong enough to carry through most or all of 1961 as well. Even if it does, however, its unnatural birth as the aftermath of the steel strike may make the eventual recession something more than the mild readjustment to which the USA has become accustomed since the war. (February, 1960)

Thus the ink had hardly dried on the prophesies of a new upswing before the first tremors of a new collapse were being reflected in the press. The capitalists themselves have too much at stake to share the optimism of the Croslands and the Jays as to the stability of capitalism. Whatever the exact date, it is absolutely certain that the unprecedented post-war boom must be followed by a period of catastrophic downswing, which cannot but have a profound effect on the political thinking of the enormously strengthened ranks of the labour movement.

Table 1: Economic activity in the United States 1857 – 1949

Peak Jun 1857		Oct 60	Apr 65	June 69
Trough	Dec 58	Jun 61	Dec 67	Dec 70
Peak Oct 73	Mar 82		Mar 87	Jul 90
Trough	Mon 79	May 85	Apr 88	May 91
Peak Jan 93	Dec 95		Jun 99	Sep 02
Trough	Jun 94	Jun 97	Dec 1900	Aug 04
Peak May 07	Jan 10		Jan 13	Aug 18
Trough	Jun 08	Jan 12	Dec 14	Apr 19
Peak Jan 20	May 23		Oct 26	Jun 29
Trough	Jul 21	Jul 24	Nov 27	Mar 33
Peak May 37	Feb 45		Nov 48	
Trough	Jun 38	Oct 45	Oct 49	

Table 2; Distribution of Final Demand For Britain

	1938	1948	49-51	52-54	55-57	1957
Consumers	67.2%	61.2%	57.7%	55.6%	54.7%	54.2%
Public Authorities	12.8	12.7	13.2	15	13.9	13.7
Capital Formation	10	11.8	11.6	12.1	14.1	14.7
Exports	11	14.4	17.5	17.3	17.3	17.3

World Perspectives

June 1977

THE LAST 30 years marked a period where the imperialist industrialised states built up industry on a scale, and at a pace probably greater than any time since the inception of capitalism. They retreated from *direct* military domination of the colonies, because of the revolt of the colonial peoples; but in the former colonial areas where capitalism and landlordism have been maintained they exercise an even greater domination, economically. Thus *collectively* the ex-colonial powers of the EEC, the USA and Japan exact super-tribute from the exploitation of the colonial peoples. They do this through the disparities in the terms of trade, where the price of industrial goods, consumer and capital goods have increased in price far more than the food and raw materials mainly exported by the under-developed countries. This is so even in the case of oil, where the price has gone up more than four times. This increase in price followed the oil embargo of 1973 due to the Arab-Israeli war. Despite the screams of anguish by the imperialists, and further increases in oil prices since that period, these increases do not completely compensate for the increase in price of capital and manufactured goods since the war.

The disparity is even more marked for the non-oil producing under-developed countries, because the oil costs, plus more, are added to the cost of capital and consumer manufactured goods.

Thus the economic basis was laid in the colonial world for a period of upheaval; of revolutions, counter-revolutions and coups unexampled in history. It must be the most disturbed period for the colonial world in the history of capitalism in all its main areas: Asia, Africa and Latin America.

This will seem peaceful in comparison with the titanic conflicts and upheavals of the next two decades.

In the countries where capitalism has been overthrown, especially China and Russia, the last 30 years have seen a temporary consolidation of the power of the Stalinist bureaucracies in a totalitarian proletarian Bonapartist system.

In all the three main economic and social areas of the world, a new epoch is opening up. From the point of view of Marxist theory this development of the economy was a preparation for the coming period of social convulsions. This is so in the industrialised capitalist world, the ex-colonial world and the Stalinist states. The world economic upswing of capitalism, with its apparently endless industrial growth, with only incidental interruptions of production in the form of minor recessions in one country or another, is now at an end. This period has been explained in a series of documents only by the Marxist tendency, and there is no need to repeat that analysis here.

But as argued in the material, *all the factors making for an unprecedented boom were the same factors preparing the way for economic and social catastrophes and upheavals.* The accumulation of fictitious capital resulted in a world-wide explosion of inflation. The inter-penetration of trade intensified the world division of labour. The gap increased between the under-developed and the developed world.

The further disparity between the relatively 'weak' countries of Italy, Britain and France and the relatively 'strong' countries of West Germany, Japan and the United States, increased the instability of the workings of the world-wide capitalist system.

The leap forward in the increase of world trade by a rate of 12.5 per cent per annum in its turn led to a partial dismantling of tariffs and other impediments to a free exchange of goods and this gave impetus to world trade and to the world division of labour. This has now slowed down. World trade in 1976 and in 1977 (projected according to the calculations of the OECD*, UN, and the capitalist powers) will increase only at the rate of 5 per cent per annum. That is an enormous drop. Together with the other factors, it marks the end of the epoch of economic upswing. Now a new period of booms and slumps is ushered in.

But because of the growth of productive forces, together with the growth of the social and economic contradictions in the intervening period, the rhythm of the booms and slumps will no longer be that of the classical period of capitalism of a decade or so ago. They will be of a much shorter duration, between two and six years. This is already shown in *the first simultaneous slump (1974-5) since the second world war.* This has resulted in the re-appearance of a permanent army of unemployed in the capitalist countries, which will further

---

*The Organisation for Economic Cooperation and Development (OECD), founded in 1961, incorporated the main capitalist powers aiming to expand trade and coordinate aid.

aggravate the hopelessness of the position of the tens and hundreds of millions of unemployed and under-employed in the under-developed countries.

The recession or small slump of 1974-5 has been succeeded by the boomlet (in most capitalist countries) of 1975-6. But in all of these countries the 'boom' has not been anything in the nature of the upswing of the post-war period. Supplementing the unemployment of labour has been the underemployment of resources. Only 80 per cent of industrial capacity has been used in most of the industrialised capitalist countries. Inflation, even in the economically 'strong' countries still remains an ever-present threat. In Britain and Italy it is between 20 per cent and 30 per cent, in France 15 per cent, Japan and the United States 8 per cent to 10 per cent and even West Germany 4 per cent to 6 per cent (at the time of writing in June 1977).

Investment under these circumstances has been at a far lower rate than in previous booms. The 'entrepreneurs', ie the monopolies, are not interested in an extensive increase in capacity when they cannot see a future market, and when they cannot make use of already existing capacity. Consequently the rate of increase of production too is smaller than after previous recessions or small slumps.

With the complete discrediting of the theories of the 'witch doctor' Keynes, there is a reluctance to increase state expenditure by 'priming the pump', for fear of inflation getting out of hand. This explains the 'deflationary' measures of Britain, France and Italy and also why, despite pleas from the 'weaker powers', the governments of West Germany, Japan and the USA have refused to entertain the idea of 'reflating'. They prefer to trample their capitalist rivals and weaker brethren in the bog, lest they too be sucked into the mire. Thus Fukuda, the Prime Minister of Japan, observed brutally: 'What would be the point of making the strong weak, by reducing them to the level of the weaker powers?'

Thus the summit of the seven powers in May solved not a single one of the burning problems facing the capitalist world. It brought no cheer to the weaker powers, and nothing to the under-developed regions of the world. Nor did it strengthen the 'stronger' powers. They were all looking to their own resources and flailing round like drowning men who could just keep afloat. They pushed under their stricken companions afflicted with cramp, in their frantic efforts to get a lift back to safety.

The large economically dominant powers, West Germany and Japan, with a substantial surplus in their balance of payments, and the United States with its crushingly dominant continental economy, were not prepared to increase state expenditure and thus budget deficits in order to lessen the balance of payments deficits of the weaker economies of Italy, Britain and France. This would mean sucking in imports and thus lessening their surpluses, but would give a twist to the spiral of inflation nationally and internationally.

At the same time the 'strong' powers were demanding cuts in state expenditure and deflation, in the weaker states. This with the reluctant agreement of their weaker rivals. The latter were fearful of uncontrolled inflation and thus were slashing the reforms of the past, described as the 'social wage'. State expenditure was formerly regarded by the bourgeoisie as a painless way of increasing the market. Now they wish to curb inflation by cutting down state expenditure and at the same time hold down the wages of the workers in order to increase the mass and rate of profit of the capitalist class.

In all capitalist countries the tendency of the rate of profit to fall has manifested itself in a steep decline. Hence the pre-occupation of the ruling classes to increase the rate of profit. In West Germany between the 1960's and 1970's the rate decreased sharply. That decline is continuing according to *The Economist* (26 February, 1977): 'In the early 1960s, German industry earned on average a net return after tax of just over 6 per cent on sales. In 1967-71 the average return came down to 5.3 per cent and in 1972-5 it was only 4.1 per cent....In 1970, German employers had to pay about DM 42 billion for social security contributions. By 1975, this total has almost doubled.'

The decline in the markets, simultaneously with a decline in the rate of profit led in West Germany, as in the other main capitalist countries, to a decline in manufacturing investment. In 1970 gross fixed investment in industry was DM 35.5 billion. This was an increase of 17 per cent on the previous year. Investment as a percentage of sales was 6.9 per cent, and investment per employee was DM 4,280. In 1976, which was recovery year after the recession 1974-5, gross fixed investment had dropped to DM 26.5 billion, only slightly higher than the recession year of 1975. Investment in 1976 was 1 per cent higher than in 1975. Investment as a percentage of sales actually dropped slightly to 4.6 per cent. Investment per employee was DM 3,685.

Similar figures could be quoted for all industrialised capitalist countries. The contradictions pile up. Yesterday the capitalists were intent on expanding the market through measures such as reducing tariff barriers and state restrictions on a freer flow of foods and trade between the capitalist countries (through the General Agreement Tariffs and Trade). Internally they used state expenditure to boost the home market. Now they are faced with the major problem of limited markets both at home and abroad, while saddled with surplus capacity. Industrial investment, which for a period creates its own market in an economic spiral, has fallen. The whole spur to increased production has sagged. The production of machinery and buildings creates a market for materials, steel, building materials and so on. Extra workers employed mean increased purchasing power, which means more sales for consumer goods, a further possible market for new machinery. The extra workers in steel and building (or increased earnings etc), create a further market and so on.

The measures of the British Labour government, and those of the French and Italian governments, have restricted the market and consequently, despite lavish inducements, investment has not reached the *real* level of 1970 in Britain, Italy and France. It is lagging far behind previous figures under world boom conditions. The economic miracles of Japan and West Germany have ended with investment little above the recession figures of 1974-5. The USA is in an even worse predicament, considering its enormous capacity.

The slump of 1974/5 was the first serious world check to the development of productive forces since the early post-war period, although the fall in production was not high in comparison with the inter-war period. Painfully the bourgeoisie has recovered economically in the boom of 1976-7. But the boom has nothing of the character of the world rhythm of production in the post-war period. *One* of the economic witch-doctors of capitalism writing in *The Economist* of 30 April 1977 says:

> The best guess is that the world is not set for slump. If the trade cycle has changed from seesaw to sluggardliness, by the same token (?) output is unlikely to plunge into the same kind of sharp downturn that followed real booms. (!?)
> More likely is a steady climb off the plateau in the second half of 1977. At an annual rate (for OECD countries) of perhaps 3-4 per cent, sustained into 1978.

In other words the boom has been sluggish. The bourgeoisie has foresworn another dose of economic opium, increasing state expenditure, because it means inflation under both boom and slump conditions. They have painfully learned that to increase state expenditure might give them an economic 'high' for a year or two (or even possibly only months), only to bring more inflation on Latin American lines, more unemployment and all the nightmare reality of 'stagflation', stagnation and inflation, or even worse 'slumpflation'.

But cutting state expenditure and cutting real wages would lead
to the distressing 'withdrawal symptoms' of deflation, once the
opium is withdrawn from the sick economy of world capitalism. So
The Economist hopefully argues that by missing the boom, they can
also miss the inevitable aftermath of slump, and permanently
maintain a slow plateau of growth. The superstitious
representatives and idealogues of the bourgeois have these utopian
fancies. If the production does not increase then the market will
continue to stagnate. Investment will fall even if the measures to
hold down real wages succeed, and because they succeed!

Marx divided production into *department 1*, production of means
of production (capital goods, machinery, buildings etc.), and
department 2, production of means of consumption (consumer
goods). The two sections are inter-dependent. A fall in one means
ultimately a fall in the other.

The whole system of capitalism, where every factor interacts on
every other factor, requires rising production, investment and an
increased market in a spiral. In the end through credits this would
exceed the limits of the capitalist system and lead to bust. But
without a real boom the limits would be reached even sooner!
Greater overproduction of capital and consumer goods would be
the consequence and hence slump would take place even sooner.

Serious commentators of capitalism expect a world slump,
beginning (as could be expected) in the United States, towards the
end of this year or during the course of next year, 1978. All the
economic factors point towards this with all the political and social
consequences. However, at the first signs of a break in the
economy, with more bankruptcies and rising unemployment, in a
panic the capitalist governments would again reach for the dope
syringe as a 'solution'. President Carter and Denis Healey have
both hinted at reflation towards the end of the year if necessary to
restore production. In other words the very measures that have
meant a crisis of inflation will once again be resorted to by the
capitalists. This over a period would exacerbate the problems of
inflation, which by raising prices causes dissatisfaction among both
workers and the middle class, by cutting the purchasing power of
the masses. In the end it has the same consequences. In addition
faith in the currency is undermined. Inflation delays slump for a
relatively short period only to make it worse when production
collapses.

Either way there would be resistance, even if delayed, by the
working class at still further cuts in real standards of living. Even if
the slump is delayed for a short period, that would open up a
period of bitter battles between the classes. Even more bitter will be

the reaction to empty factories side by side with enforced idleness of the workers.

The new epoch which began in 1974 of short booms followed by slumps is an epoch of storm and stress. *The relative development of the productive forces by the bourgeoisie for a period of a quarter of a century or so, also gave relative stability to the main capitalist countries* in the period since the post-war years. Marxism has always explained that a period of social revolution opens up when the ruling class and their economic system become a drag and a fetter on the development of the productive powers of society. This also applies to the development of society under a ruling caste, as in the Soviet Union, which hampers the development of productive forces. Then opens up a period of political revolution. Trotsky had assumed in 1938 that this was exactly the period which the world bourgeoisie and also the Stalinist bureaucracy had entered.

Owing to the peculiar development of events, and the treacherous role of Stalinism and reformism, the bourgeoisie gained a breathing space, and for reasons explained in other material the development of productive forces (relatively and to a certain extent absolutely) gained an impetus. Now, generally, the productive forces cannot be contained within the confines of the national state and private ownership.

Hence during the next decade on a world scale a new period of upheavals and titanic class clashes is on the order of the day. A period of social and political convulsions in all three spheres —the capitalist West, the former colonial world, and the Stalinist bloc —is inevitable. It was for such a period in 1917-21 that Lenin and Trotsky tried to prepare the forces of the Communist International. Trotsky prepared for a similar period which would follow the outcome of World War II. He predicted the inevitability of this cataclysm in 1938.

These political upsurges did take place, but for lack of Marxist leadership and Marxist mass organisations, the bourgeoisie succeeded every time in avoiding complete overthrow. Capitalism was restabilised albeit on a more shaky basis. Stalinism, as a governmental system in Russia with extensions in the Communist parties of other countries, also recovered from its crises and even expanded its power and influence.

But the old dialectics of world development have been burrowing beneath the apparent stability of Stalinism and capitalism. Five to six decades of economic progress in the industrialised world, in the Stalinist states, and even to a limited extent in the ex-colonial world, have ploughed the field for the revolutionary crop which will follow. Marxism sees in the development of productive forces the key to the development of society and of history. While productive forces are being developed it gives a relative stability to any class society. In the last twenty-five years there has been phenomenal development of productive forces, especially the most important productive force, the working class.

The new organic crisis which is maturing marks a new stage in the development of post-war capitalism. *It opens up a new period of struggle between the classes over the next five, ten or twenty years which poses the problem of the entire fate of mankind.* In its train, the upswing brought an immense accumulation of fictitious capital in the shape of so-called Euro-dollars. More than $150 billion of worthless currency were foisted on Europe by the United States during the period of her overwhelming economic supremacy in the early post-war period. Supplying the necessary 'liquidity' in the period of upswing, the paper money served to fructify industry, but it was also one of the factors leading to world inflation.

In a period of economic storms it acts like unbattened-down lumber on a ship, which causes holes in the hull and sides as it moves from one side to another with the waves. So the Euro-dollars are moved from one country to another in order for the monopolies to profit from the successes or the difficulties of the economies of the capitalist industrialised nations. So also the enormous waste of resources in unproductive arms expenditure, which also acts as fictitious capital, while imposing crippling burdens on the peoples of the world. This has reached the fantastic level now of £1,000,000,000,000 ie a million million pounds every six and a half years.

There is the stark contrast between poverty, hunger and starvation in the colonial world, and the profligate waste of resources in research and production of ever more devilish means for the extermination of mankind. This ominous threat suspended over the head of mankind makes ever-more imperative the need for the masses to take the fate of society and the world into their own hands.

The twilight of capitalism, through its incapacity to serve the needs of the masses, not only in the colonial world but now also the developed world, makes this a period of inevitable disillusionment with capitalism and of class awakening on the part of the proletariat.

World Perspectives

August 1979

A NEW world recession is developing at the present time. This marks the definitive end of the world economic upswing. It expresses the twilight of world capitalism and shows that the economic system internationally has reached an impasse. The mightiest power, American capitalism, finds itself in serious economic difficulties. As a consequence of a large balance of payments deficit and the deficit financing in the budget, she is faced with 12 per cent to 15 per cent inflation. This has caused the collapse of the dollar. Gold, from being $34 an ounce −which American imperialism artifically kept as the exchange rate for a whole historical period −is now over $300 an ounce. American imperialism finds itself with the two evils of capitalism in the present epoch −inflation and stagnation −at one and the same time.

The recession in the biggest market in the world, that of American capitalism, will in its turn have a chain reaction on the EEC and on the smaller powers. But the recession will be of a peculiar character, it will be 'a small recession'. It is projected by bourgeois statisticians and economists that there will be an actual fall in industrial production only in Britain and the United States. In Japan and the EEC countries there will be a fall in the rate of growth of production. 'Small' recessions of this character, following upon 'small' booms, will have more explosive political consequences than even a deep recession.

This recession has followed the shaky boom which in its turn followed the recession of 1975. In that recovery, what marked a new crisis for capitalism was that there was hardly a single capitalist country using more than 80 per cent of productive capacity. This in its turn meant a fall in the rate of investment. With this very shaky recovery from the first simultaneous world slump since the second world war, the capitalists are already faced with a new recession.

As we predicted, the new recession has come swiftly on the heels of the last one. It is roughly three to four years since the last slump or small recession and we are now back to what will possibly be a somewhat deeper recession than that of 1975.

However, we must view cautiously the economic processes. The slump in 1975 only meant, so far as the OECD countries together were concerned, a fall in production of 0.5 per cent. But it also meant unemployment of 16-20 millions.

Unemployment will now increase in all the main capitalist countries of the world. It no longer merely forms a reserve army of labour but indicates an organic sickness of capitalism as it did in the inter-war period.

This new recession, which might last anything from 9 months to 18 months —possibly more possibly less —will in its turn be followed by a new shaky boom. This in turn will be followed at a faster or slower rate, by a new recession. We are in a cycle of booms and slumps moving far faster than at any other time in the history of capitalism.

It means that we are now in the epoch of the death agony of capitalism. *There will be a tendency for living standards to fall in all the countries of capitalism, including the industrial countries, with only temporary exceptions.*

This rapid succession of booms and slumps is precisely a period in which revolutionary conclusions can be drawn by the masses. In a sense, small changes leading to minor booms and then to minor slumps mean the worst of all possible outcomes for capitalism.

As Trotsky explained, the constant change from one economic situation to another produces uncertainty which in its turn has a political effect on the masses. Thus, a period of political explosions opens up —in Spain, Italy and France, West Germany, Japan, the USA and even Scandinavia —as the case of Denmark shows. This formerly placid country has had a whole series of general strikes in the past half decade or so. Now in certain 'backwaters' of capitalism, such as formerly prosperous Australia, Canada and New Zealand, we see a whole series of struggles on the part of the working class leading to a situation of virtual general strike.

This instability of capitalism in its turn has an effect on the outlook of the bourgeoisie in all countries of the world. There has been an outbreak of pessimism, gloom and fear as to the economic future. The decay of capitalism is reflected in its representatives becoming totally perplexed.

Meanwhile, in the traditional organisations of the working class, the Stalinists and reformists are reflecting the previous period of capitalism in its economic upswing. They are utterly incapable of evaluating the new stage in the development of world history. The objective conditions for socialist revolution exist in all the countries of capitalism at the present time.

The impasse of capitalism is reflected in the aggravation of the contradictions between social production on the one hand and national states and private ownership on the other. The latter becomes an enormous drain and fetter on the development of the productive forces (in which Marxists find the key to history). Capitalism is no longer capable of fulfilling this task as it succeeded in doing for a period of two to three decades after the war.

The capitalist countries partially overcame the contradictions for a time by the development of world trade and the lowering of tariff and other barriers between the capitalist nations. The domination of American imperialism was sufficient to dictate this policy to her rivals, and that was a means of partially overcoming the limits of capitalism – the nation state and private ownership. World trade increased about six times in the period from 1947-75.

Through GATT (General Agreements on Tariff and Trade) and other measures we had the internationalisation of markets. There was a deepening of the world division of labour and an extension of the integration of the world economy into one indivisible whole.

The internationalisation of capital took place through the multi-nationals. Perhaps for the last time an impetus was given to the development of productive forces in the industrialised countries and partly even in the undeveloped countries of the world as well.

But in the partial overcoming of these contradictions greater contradictions have been created by capitalism. The economy, in reality, has developed beyond the limits provided by the capitalist system. That is why we are in the twilight of world capitalism – an epoch of revolutions and of minor 'secondary wars'. ('Secondary' is in quotation marks because even in the Arab-Israeli war enormous resources were squandered.)

However, the death throes of capitalism will not appear in one simultaneous sweep. In the period of the economic upswing capitalism has created *enormous resources which can, and will, be used for the purpose of propping up capitalism when its life is in danger.* At a time of mass upsurge the capitalists will give concessions in order to gain a breathing space. They will take them back as soon as the situation has changed and the mass movement of the working class has ebbed. This, of course, is inevitable, given the conditions under which the masses live in capitalist society.

That is why under modern conditions the *subjective factor* is perhaps the most important factor of all. Time and again, the role of the leadership of the workers' organisations has been to save capitalism from destruction at the hands of the working class. However, there will be not just one revolutionary crisis but a whole series of revolutionary crises in one country after another in the period that lies ahead. Again, capitalism has changed from being a *relative* fetter holding up the development of productive forces into being an *absolute* fetter. As Marxism teaches us, this is the epoch of social revolution.

If we take even the strongest capitalist power, America, we can see the perplexity of the ruling class. With this goes a corresponding perplexity of the masses of the people. There is an unprecedented disgust with both political parties −with the Democrats, to which the trade union leaders have attached the trade unions merely as a tail, and with the Republicans as virtually open representatives of big business.

The reason for this is that during the course of the past 12 years there has not been an actual increase in workers' real incomes before tax. After tax there has even been a fall in the living standards of the American working class. In the last seven years there has actually been a decline in real incomes before tax.

That explains the attitude of the masses towards the bourgeois parties −the repulsion, the scepticism and the cynicism towards the Democrats, towards President Carter and towards the Republicans.

In the blind alley of American capitalism the government threshes about from one economic policy to the opposite one. This in turn adds to the instability of the economy.

Very rapidly the American workers can come to the conclusion that they need to organise an independent party of Labour. If the Democrats win the election through adopting Edward Kennedy as their candidate (as seems most likely) a big blow will be dealt to any illusions which remain in that party*. The working class blacks and other oppressed layers would be pushed into industrial and political action.

The organised workers would exert pressure for an independent proletarian organisation of labour and the exploited masses. With the sluggish nature of the boom in America, and following it, the effects of stagflation, political conclusions can be rapidly drawn by the American workers. The tempo of American life is different from that in Europe. The American workers can achieve in seven years what has taken the British workers 70 years to achieve −the creation of a mass party of labour.

*In the event, Jimmy Carter was the Democratic Party candidate for the presidential election in 1980, supported by Walter Mondale. The Republican Party candidate, Ronald Reagan, won an overwhelming victory.

The economic upswing had the effect of powerfully reinforcing support for capitalism. Skilled sections of the workers gained high standards of living. They would have two cars, a boat, a shotgun, good holidays and so on, and quite a comfortable level of existence.

Now that has ended. Even when the recession is followed by a further period of anaemic boom, it will require enormous efforts on the part of the American workers to win back what they have lost through the inflation of the last few years. It will require strenuous battles and strike struggles, probably on a considerably higher level than the impressive strikes of the past two years. The fact that a minimum of 10 million workers in the USA are unemployed, and 16 to 20 million in the OECD countries as a whole, shows that economically, world capitalism cannot repeat the balmy experience of 1950-75.

There will be periods of upsurge, periods of revolution, periods of struggles, by workers in every capitalist country. They will be succeeded by new periods of bafflement, despair and indifference, stemming from the frustration of the movement of the workers by the policies of the socialist and communist parties. But over a period of 10 to 15 years, the masses will rapidly come to the conclusion that there is no other road than that of the socialist revolution.

It is significant in this respect that both in Holland and in Australia the workers in the more dynamic unions are coming to the conclusion that there has to be a root-and-branch transformation of society. Tinkering with capitalism, they recognise, cannot solve the problems of the working people. And this objective process as far as the unions are concerned indicates the possibilities that lie ahead for a Marxist tendency.

Even on the basis of the situation that exists at the present time, such a tendency can grow by leaps and bounds. *Workers will continue as they have done over a period of decades to turn to the traditional organisations of the working class.* But as we already see in relation to the Labour Party, a differentiation will begin within the framework of the social democracy and also within the Communist parties (where they are a mass force, and even in countries where they are weak).

More and more, the active layers of the working class will be demanding policies in the interests of the workers. They will see that these interests can only be served by a transformation of society. In this atmosphere, it is entirely possible for the ideas of Marxism to secure a powerful hold within the traditional organisations of the class at a time when the crisis of capitalism is deepening.

This mood will not be changed by shaky booms of a few years' duration which do not fundamentally enhance the working class's standard of living as it was enhanced during the course of the '50s, '60s, and '70s. As a consequence, the climate will be there for the ideas of Marxism and Leninism to gather enormous support in the mass organisations of the working class.

The growth of contradictions in the capitalist world is matched by the contradictions developing in the Soviet bloc and China. In Eastern Europe and Russia, from being a *relative* fetter the bureaucracy is becoming an *absolute* fetter on the development of the forces of production.

For a whole historical period most of the countries of Eastern Europe and especially Russia have had a *lower* rate of the development of the productive forces than capitalist Japan. This is because the productive forces are snared in a mesh of bureaucratic mismanagement, chaos, waste and corruption which partially cancel out the advantages of state ownership and a plan of production. Where there is no workers' democracy and no check on production it leads to a chaotic situation. The working masses are used merely as another factor in production. New contradictions have developed.

The bureaucracy has raised itself as a privileged caste, separate and above the mass of the population. Productive forces are going ahead at a snails pace for a state-owned, planned economy —slower than capitalist development in Western Europe during the boom.

The bureaucracy tends to try to find a way out of the contradictions in the economy which it has itself produced by an increased participation on the world market. The illusions of building socialism in one country are at an end in China where Mao's ideas of autarky have been overthrown.

Also in the Soviet Union, autarky is now seen as an entirely impractical policy. It restricted productive forces and prevented the development of the economy to the maximum extent. That wing of the bureaucracy which wanted to continue Stalinist policies in this respect has been utterly defeated. In the new Russian constitution, which Brezhnev for his own reasons has had adopted, 'participation in the world market' is put as one of the fundamental aims of the state. That is intended as a warning to those sections of the bureaucracy who still hanker for an autarkic policy.

This is confirmation of Trotsky's brilliant prediction that, with the growth of productive forces in Russia, she would be compelled more and more to move into the world market. The persistence of the idea of autarky in such a situation is an indication of the reactionary and nationalist character of the bureaucracies of all the Stalinist states. Even with the expansion of world trade links they cannot regain the growth rates of the past. That constitutes a death sentence for these bureaucracies. China remains probably one of the few deformed workers' states which is still *relatively* progressive in her development of productive forces.

The crisis in Vietnam, which caused anyone of Chinese ethnic origin to flee, is just one indication of the horrors of Stalinist totalitarian rule. The unfortunate plight of the so-called 'boat people' has given a magnificent opportunity to capitalism for propaganda against the ideas of 'Communism'. The limited war between China and Vietnam served to smear the ideas of communism. The crimes of the Vietnamese Stalinists as well as of the Chinese Stalinists stink to high heaven, perpetrated as they are in the name of Marxism.

In Vietnam and China, in Ethiopia and the other deformed workers' states that have been set up in the former colonial world, there is a relatively progressive role for the bureaucracies. They can develop the productive forces faster than capitalism. Consequently there will be relative stability for these Stalinist regimes in the coming period.

In Eastern Europe and Russia, on the other hand, beneath the official mask, enormous discontent has been gathering. The decay of official 'Marxism' is expressed in Poland in the gigantic demonstration in favour of the Pope's visit. The masses are opposed to bureaucratic misrule. However, there is not the slightest ripple of a movement by the masses in the direction of accepting capitalism as an alternative. In Eastern Europe, new Hungarian revolutions are inevitable.

In Russia too, all the elements of discontent have been gathering up for decades. The oppression of the nationalities, the oppression of the peasants, the differentiation of standards between the workers and the bureaucrats have produced explosive contradictions. Over a period of two generations an hereditary bureaucracy has been created to which access on the part of the talented workers has gradually been closed. That is an indication of the ossification of the regime.

In every layer of the population, hatred for the bureaucracy is accumulating. The masses are well aware of the inefficiencies, the waste, and the inability of the bureaucracy to develop the productive forces. According to the capitalist press and the economists, it is expected that this year the growth of industry in Russia will only be about 3 per cent, which again is lower than the extremely low figures to which Japan's growth has dropped in the last few years, and way below the previous rates of 12-14 per cent per annum achieved by capitalist Japan. It means the bureaucracy is no longer capable of fulfilling the role of developing the productive forces.

Like the bourgeoisie of the West they have become a drag on society. They were always parasites on the masses, but had a relatively progressive role to play —now they are only parasites. This means that at any time there could be an explosion in Russia like that of Hungary in 1956.

It is still a race as to which will come first, a social revolution in the West, or the political revolution in the East. Either would have a tremendous social effect on the other. A victory for the workers in any important country of the West would sound the death knell of the bureaucracy in the whole of Eastern Europe and in Russia. This in turn would lead very rapidly to a collapse of the bureaucracy in China and the other countries of proletarian Bonapartism.

On the other hand, political revolutions in the East would restore the methods and ideas of the revolution —of workers' democracy —as in the days of Lenin and Trotsky. All that would flow as a consequence both in social and political terms would have a cataclysmic effect on the countries of the West. A political revolution in Russia or in Eastern Europe would rapidly spread.

That is one of the reasons for the *detente* between American imperialism and the Russian bureaucracy. The military situation is one where there is a virtual stalemate in nuclear arms. As far as conventional weapons are concerned, the Russian bureaucracy has an overwhelming superiority.

In these circumstances, the fears shared by the bureaucracy and the bourgeoisie for their continued existence in the face of political revolution in the East and social revolution in the West, create a common basis for agreement and *detente* between the powers.

In Eastern Europe and in Russia the bureaucracy has succeeded to a certain extent in erasing the traditions and the social achievements of the revolution of the first period of 1917-23 with an overlay of bureaucratic excrescence. Because of the weakness of Marxism in the West, and because of the purges and the massacre of an entire generation of revolutionaries in Russia and the long period of five or six decades of bureaucratic, totalitarian misrule, it will require events themselves to re-educate the masses. Explosions are inevitable in Russia and in Eastern Europe in the period that lies ahead. What we saw in Hungary in 1956 will be repeated in Russia and the other countries of Eastern Europe.

Capitalism and Stalinism have before them a period of prolonged death agony, the accumulation of contradictions within Eastern Europe and Russia will result in outbursts and explosions. There will be a quantative change into qualitatively different movements of the masses.

The very weakness of capitalism has meant it has not been possible to maintain authoritarian or totalitarian regimes anywhere in Western Europe. This is not because the bourgeoisie has been converted to democracy. As events have demonstrated they can switch from totalitarian regime and back again to 'democracy', so long as their rule is preserved. The decay of capitalism and the difficulty of holding down the masses in any other way except through deceit and parliamentary methods of deception, lies and distortion indicates their weakness. However we must not be caught by surprise by events in the East or in the West. 1968 in France was not at all accidental, but was an indication of the processes that will take place.

In one country after another, the masses will take the road of struggle: in Britain, France, Germany, Italy, Sweden, or any of the smaller countries of capitalism. The United States and Japan also cannot escape from the new period which is opening up. This is the outlook for the developed countries of the capitalist West and also the developed Stalinist totalitarian states. But the upheavals and social explosions that have taken place even in the last three decades, in particular in the underdeveloped countries, are a pale foreshadowing of the future movements in these countries.

One of the reasons for the rise of productive forces in the West and the increases in the standards of living has been the exploitation of the colonial people in the post-war period. The EEC, Japan, the United States and the other industrialised capitalist powers have organised the collective exploitation of the colonial peoples. This is not directly by military domination but by economic domination. Due to the unfavourable terms of trade for the underdeveloped countries, the prices of food and raw materials have not increased to the same extent as the price of industrial goods and capital goods.

There has been a super-exploitation of the colonial peoples. Whereas up to the recession of 1975, the standards of living in the West had generally increased, the two-thirds living in the under-developed world have experienced an absolute fall in living standards, apart from a few exceptions. There has been a very partial development of industry, uneven at that, in certain countries such as Brazil, Argentina, Taiwan, South Korea, Nigeria, India and other countries of Africa, Asia and Latin America. But the very partial development of industry in its turn has increased the strength of the working class. This increase in industry creates new problems for the hundreds of millions of under-employed, unemployed and pauperised peasants of Africa, Asia and Latin America. There has been a gigantic increase in landless, jobless and shelterless peasants streaming to the slums around the cities. This in turn has increased the contradictions in each country. All are entirely dependent on world markets and dependent economically on the big imperialist powers.

The whole of the post-war period has been rent with explosion and upheaval in Asia, in Africa and Latin America. The economic basis for this is the impossiblity of developing productive forces harmoniously and at a high rhythm when imperialism dominates these areas. The economic upswing between 1950 and 1975, provided the most favourable conditions that could be expected under capitalism in the underdeveloped countries. Because this led to stunted and limited growth of productive forces and low living standards in these countries we have had the biggest period of upheaval in the history of mankind in Asia, Africa and Latin America.

Now that the economic upswing is at an end and capitalism will move in a cycle of small booms and of small slumps following each other, imperialism will attempt to load the burdens of capitalist crisis on the underdeveloped world. Then the conditions of the colonial masses will become much worse. At their expense, the big powers will attempt to solve the contradictions of their system. The increase in the price of oil has been passed on to the non-oil or underdeveloped countries. In addition, they will have to pay more for the products of industry and capital goods. That means that the development of productive forces, even to the extent of 1947-75 in a number of countries, cannot take place, at least at the same pace. Already in the post-1975 period there has been a fall in the rate of increase of industrial development and production in the underdeveloped world mirroring the process taking place in the industrialised countries. Industrial development looks to export markets in the West because of the weak home markets and the poverty of the masses. Meanwhile the ruin and impoverishment of the peasant masses is intensified.

The crisis of capitalism bears down more harshly on the underdeveloped world than on the capitalist countries. This in its turn is preparing greater explosions and new movements in the 'Third World'. In the front line will be Brazil, Argentina, Indonesia, Nigeria, Ghana. What we have seen in the Central American republic of Nicaragua can tomorrow be repeated not only in Central America, but especially in the countries where bourgeois military police Bonapartist regimes have been established. These dictatorships were engineered when the ruling class found itself in a cul-de-sac, and yet this was the most favourable period economically that could be expected as long as market forces dominate.

Now with the crisis that is developing in the industrialised world, the problems will bear even more harshly on the peoples of the underdeveloped world. This sets the stage for revolution in all the three continents concerned.

In Latin America and in some parts of Asia such as Pakistan we have seen swings by the ruling class from one regime to another, from democracy to dictatorship and back again in the endeavour to escape from the contradictions with which they are faced. In every case — either of dictatorship or uneasy 'democracy' they have failed to stabilise the social and economic situation.

In India we saw the collapse of the semi-Bonapartist government of Mrs Gandhi. Now the Janata Party — a rag-bag coalition of differing elements — has fallen to pieces as a consequence of the instability of the situation that exists. India will take its place with Brazil, Argentina, Indonesia, Nigeria and the other main countries of the underdeveloped world as being an unstable country. This will prepare the way for big social explosions.

In the case of such countries as India, unless there is a socialist revolution, then it is possible that there will be a break-up and 'Balkanisation'. (This can come after a period of military-police dictatorship. Pakistan was an earlier example of such a process).

Africa is Balkanised. Latin America is Balkanised. Even the Indian sub-continent can find itself in the same position unless Marxism finds the road to the working class. On the road of capitalism there is no way out. As a consequence of the impasse of the system there will be movements of tens and hundreds of millions of peasants and of the working class.

In the underdeveloped countries, as in the developed world, events will not proceed in a straight line. There will be ups and downs of the economy which will be followed by movements of the masses, not necessarily in consonance. In the underdeveloped countries, more than any other area the capitalists are absolutely incapable of developing productive forces except to a very limited extent. As in the Western capitalist countries, the improvements in the economy which will take place from time to time can only encourage the masses and the demands of the working class in particular.

Private ownership and landlordism and capitalism are utterly incapable of playing a consistently progressive role under the modern conditions of imperialism in the underdeveloped world. The psychology of the masses, particularly in the underdeveloped world, is changing. The perplexity of the bourgeoisie and the failure of the ruling class to show a way forward for society, has revolutionary consequences in colonial countries. There the bourgeoisie is utterly incapable of playing the role which was played by the bourgeoisie in the West in the past. The paralysis of the bourgeoisie will be reflected in the anger of the masses.

The blind alley that imperialism and semi-feudal, semi-landlord capitalist states find themselves in has been responsible for the revolution in Iran and the revolution in Ethiopia. A new period is opening up, when there will be one convulsion after another in the economically backward continents of the world.

Marxism must find a way of reaching the masses, particularly in countries that have a developed labour and trade union movement. Only on this road can there be a healthy development of the revolution. Such a possibility existed in the Chinese revolution of 1925-7 when the working class was the spearhead and the dominant force in the revolution.

In India, Argentina, Brazil, Nigeria and, in fact, in most of the countries of Asia, Africa and Latin America there is now a numerically important proletariat which is even more decisive in its social weight in society. It could play the role of rallying the mass of the nation if it had the necessary leadership and gained the necessary understanding. *The subjective factor is decisive.*

It is only the impasse of capitalism in the colonial countries that has resulted in the development of proletarian Bonapartist, totalitarian states such as in China, Ethiopia, and other countries. They partially solved the problems, in the sense that landlordism and capitalism are eliminated. But they pave the way for a new revolution —a political revolution —without which the masses could not even begin the construction of socialism or establish a healthy workers' democracy. A political revolution is necessary in these states for the control of industry, the state and the whole of society to pass into the hands of the workers and peasants.

The Special Crisis of British Capitalism

Introduction

PREVIOUS CHAPTERS have dealt with post-war developments in the advanced capitalist countries as a whole. The material in Chapter Two illuminated the role played by the leaderships of the social democratic and Stalinist parties in Western Europe, ensuring that capitalism was able to survive the critical early years after the war. This provided the political foundation for the long post-war upswing, dealt with in Chapter Five.

In the debates about likely international developments – whether the post-war economy was heading for slump or boom, how long the post-war boom would last, whether or not capitalism had learnt to 'overcome' cyclical crises, and so on – Ted Grant often drew on the immediate experience and the statistical data of political and economic developments in Britain, for obvious reasons. In these cases, the intention was, nevertheless, to illustrate those processes that affected the advanced capitalist countries as a whole.

But in addressing activists in the British labour movement it is also essential to point to those features and characteristics which, among the advanced countries, are peculiar to British capitalism. Within the *general* crisis of world capitalism, in other words, consideration has to be given to the *special* crisis of British capitalism.

In the years after the first world war, the writings of Leon Trotsky, and especially his masterpiece, *Where is Britain Going?*, had already laid bare the contradictions of British development. From having been the first and easily the most powerful of the industrial nations, by 1914, Britain's primacy was threatened by American and German imperialism. The first world war effectively ended Britain's pre-eminent position, placing her in hock to the fast-expanding imperialism across the Atlantic. This relative decline continued unabated during the inter-war years.

After 1945, although once again emerging from war as a nominal 'victor', the British economy continued its slide compared to America, later to Japan and West Germany, and later still to almost every other major capitalist economy. It was only the strength of the post-war boom − affecting all the capitalist countries − that increased the British economy (and living standards) in *absolute* terms, and thus for a whole period disguised a catastrophic *relative* decline. This collapse of British industrial competitiveness, on the world and even the home market, will mean titanic political convulsions in a period of world economic stagnation. If such events have been delayed, it has only been because of the very temporary boost given to the economy by North Sea Oil.

The extracts in this chapter are only a tiny sample of Ted Grant's writings that deal specifically with political and economic developments in Britain. They are an indispensible study-guide to any Labour Party or trade union members seriously examining the course of events since the war, and especially during the Labour governments of 1945-51, 1964-70 and 1974-79. The first item is an extract from a resolution presented on behalf of the leadership to the RCP conference in 1946. Like the other documents dealing with Western Europe as a whole, it corrected the previous perspective of the RCP, of an immediate economic crisis after the war. 'We anticipated that British imperialism would be faced with a crisis as soon as the war ended. However, the concatenation of circumstances has served to screen the disastrous results of the war for Britain...'

The resolution went on to outline a perspective for British capitalism of 'relative stability', which, at a later stage, would give way to 'a catastrophe greater than she has experienced in the whole of her history.' As we have already pointed out, the RCP leadership around Ted Grant were involved in an intense debate just to demonstrate to alleged Marxist 'theoreticians' that there was a boom of any kind in the immediate post-war years. But what was not apparent at that time was that the recovery would extend to become a prolonged upswing, beginning in the late 1940s and lasting two and a half decades. It is for that reason that the resolution draws a clear distinction between the short-term perspective of growth and the long- term perspective of decline and crisis, due to the chronic weakness of British capitalism.

The analysis of the 1945 Labour government is also very penetrating, showing the pressure of the labour movement, in forcing through reforms and nationalisations, but also showing the limitations of a government still essentially based on the framework of capitalism...'no fundamental measures against capitalism are being taken by the Labour government. We are in a classic period reformist illusions — a reformist government coming to power at a period of economic boom.'

Pointing to the massive compensation, the bureaucratic control and the fact that only run-down industries were being taken over, it describes the nationalisations as:

> a compromise with the bourgeoisie as a whole...as the best method of bringing about the necessary measures of rationalisation and placing the burdens on the shoulders of the masses. By means of state rationalisation they hope to gain efficient and cheap coal, electricity, steel, fuel and transport, in order more effectively to compete on the world market.

The RCP perspective of a collapse of the British economy, after the initial post-war recovery, was also linked to the question of the revival of fascism.

This was particularly true because there were already signs, by 1948, of a certain degree of disillusionment with the Labour government, especially among sections of the middle class. In by-elections throughout that year, the percentage vote for the Labour Party was down and the Tories' vote was increased, largely due to abstentions by former Labour supporters.

In a pamphlet entitled, *The Menace of Fascism, What it is and How to Fight it*, written by Ted Grant, the RCP explained the social basis of fascism, as a mass movement based on the middle-class and set in motion by the capitalist class to smash the labour movement. Faced with the danger of social revolution and the loss of power, the British capitalists, no less than their European counterparts, would be prepared to mobilised and finance fascist gangs to atomise the workers organisations.

The pamphlet describes how the British capitalists were sympathetic to Hitler and Mussolini before the war, and how they supported the nascent fascist movement in Britain around Oswald Mosley. Mosley himself, with the recent history of the war and his association with nazism, may not have corresponded to the specific needs of the ruling class in a crisis. But the form is secondary to the content. Even if Mosley was not to be the model, then some other vehicle, more in keeping with 'British' tradition, would be found to develop a movement of reaction.

The warnings of the Marxists in 1948 about the dangers of fascism contrasted to the lullabies sung by the workers' leaders and the 'liberality' of the Labour ministers who allowed Mosley's new 'Union Movement' to meet and organise. The attitude of the right wing then is not much different to their ostrich-like behaviour forty years on: faced with virulent fascist thuggery, a common response is, 'ignore them and they'll go away'.

The extracts of the RCP pamphlet published here are those that concentrate on the role of British capitalism in giving political support to German nazism and Italian fascism before the war, and on the possible development of reaction in Britain. Large sections of the original, dealing with the rise of these counter-revolutionary movements in detail and drawing extensively on Trotsky's writings, are unfortunately left out for reasons of space.

The third item is a discussion paper on *Perspectives for Britain*, written in 1977. There are literally scores of articles, speeches, documents and notes written by Ted Grant on political and economic developments in Britain throughout this period, but the 1977 document adequately sums up the general position of British capitalism in its long and debilitating decline. With a mass of statistical evidence in relation to productivity, investment, manufacturing exports, expenditure of health, education, welfare, etc etc, it catalogues Britain's decline relative to the other major capitalist powers.

After the election of the 1974 Labour government, the Labour leader, Harold Wilson, (followed later by James Callaghan) persuaded the trade union leaders to accept a form of wage restraint, the so-called Social Contract. In the interests of 'improving the economy', the rank and file of the trade unions accepted this, if reluctantly, even though it would result in a 'temporary' decrease in living standards. But after three years of wage erosion, in addition to cuts in public expenditure, there was no significant improvement in the economy and workers were not prepared to tighten their belts any further. The document anticipated the explosion of anger building up within the ranks of the trades unions:

> It will be impossible for any length of time for trade union leaders to hold back their members...if the union leaders will not lead official national strikes, over a period there will be a rash of unofficial strikes in many areas...what happened after similar periods of 'restraint' will be repeated on a higher scale...

The disillusionment in the Labour government and the frustrations of organised workers did in fact burst into the open, as predicted, in the 'winter of discontent' in 1978-79, prior to Labour's defeat in the general election.

All the main features of the Tories' government since 1979 were forecast in this discussion document: the assault on the trade unions, the drive to slash public expenditure, the emphasis given to finance capital at the expense of industrial capital, and even the growing splits within the Tory Party. As a consequence of the Thatcher policies, there have been titanic clashes with the unions in mining, steel, printing, and so on. These have been the most bitter struggles since the war, the miners' strike, for example evoking what the capitalist press described as an 'insurrectionary' mood in parts of Yorkshire.

The furious reaction of the working class to the onslaught of the Tories has not led, as was originally expected, to an early collapse of their government. Other, unpredictable factors have intervened, like the Falklands war in 1982, the longevity of the world boom since 1982 (upon which the British economy has been able to ride) and the abject weakness of the trade union leaders in the face of attacks on workers' rights. These temporary postponements notwithstanding, the fundamental theme outlined in the document, that Britain is entering the stormiest period of her history, will be well demonstrated in the coming years.

It should also be noted that the 1977 document modifies some of the fundamental perspectives worked out at an earlier period. In the 1946 resolution already mentioned, the Communist Party was still considered to be a serious force in British politics. 'In spite of set-backs for the CP', it argued, 'at a time of crisis for the Labour government the swing of large sections of workers to the Communist Party, as a temporary phase, is inevitable.'

But as the later document makes clear, this original prognosis has had to be considerably modified because of the complete degeneracy of the CP, to become little more than a middle-class sect. Even the dwindling support for the CP among trade union activists, worth a mention in the mid-70s, is hardly a factor a decade later.

Similarly, the perspective for the development of fascism has been qualified. At the time the RCP produced its pamphlet on the question, it was thought that there was the possibility of a fascist movement being sponsored and supported by the ruling class as a counter-weight to the labour movement.

But the post-war experience of Italy, Greece and Chile shows that the social basis for fascism has been historically weakened by the decreased social weight of the middle classes, not least in the advanced capitalist states. Parallel to this, the power, strength and cohesion of the working class have been enhanced, and a mass movement of fascism could only develop after a whole series of major defeats for the workers' organisations.

In addition to this, the ruling class itself is less inclined than before to hand power over to unpredictable and uncontrolled movements of the 'enraged petit-bourgeois', after the experience of Hitler and Mussolini. Where there has been a turn to reaction in the modern epoch, there has been a tendency for the capitalist class to lean on the tops of the armed forces — for them a more reliable prop — to effect a military coup against the labour movement. In these circumstances, the noisy but largely impotent fascist movements are cast in the 'chorus', rather than in the leading role. Even then, the capitalist class would only turn to military-police regimes as a last resort.

Ted Grant with comrades, including Muriel Browning (right), at the South Wales Camp, 1960s.

From: **Perspectives in Britain**

July 1946

A YEAR of peace has clearly revealed the changed relationship of forces between the great powers on a world scale. British imperialism is now definitely reduced to a subordinate position between the two giants, American imperialism and the Soviet Union. While attempting to maintain an independent position in relation to the USA, Britain has entered upon the epoch of definitive decline. She no longer even aspires to a position of world domination and unchallenged superiority possessed by her in the nineteenth century. Desperately, Britain attempts to maintain the Empire, and at least a secondary status in the world. But she is compelled to play a vassal role to American imperialism.

American imperialism now has unchallenged domination of the seas. As a result, she holds the lifelines of Britain —the channels of sea trade —at her mercy. In Eastern Asia, China tends to come under the sway of America, with Britain crowded out. An independent or pseudo-independent Egypt and India will tend also to gravitate towards the almighty dollar. Britain's dominions come more and more within the American orbit. On her own, Britain cannot hope to match her puny forces against the industrial and military might of the USA.

Britain emerged 'victorious' from the first world war. She strengthened temporarily her position on the continent of Europe, increased her control of the gateways to her Empire through the Middle East and expanded the territory controlled by her central government and armed forces by one million square miles. Despite this, the first world war marked the decline of Britain in relation to American imperialism.

The result of the second world war was a veritable disaster for the British imperialists. In Europe, having defeated the Frankenstein which they helped to create in the shape of nazi imperialism, the British capitalists are faced with an even greater

menace in the domination of half of Europe by the Soviet Union.
The immediate cause of Britain's declaration of war on Germany
was to prevent the domination of the Balkans and Eastern Europe
—which could only be a stepping stone to the Empire. Now, not
only in this region, but in the Middle East and Asia, Britain is faced
with a refurbished version of her nineteenth century nightmare
—a Balkans dominated by Russia with control of the Middle East
and India at her mercy. She is today faced with a power not only
stronger than Czarism, but a greater threat than either the Kaiser's
Germany or Hitler's Third Reich. A power which, because of its
revolutionary traditions and an economy based on state ownership
of the means of production, has a social appeal to the Asiatic
peoples oppressed by British imperialism.

Britain is compelled for this reason alone to try and arrive at a
compromise with sections of the colonial bourgeoisie. That is the
significance of the treaties Britain is attempting to negotiate in
Egypt and in India. She is faced, however, with a development of
national consciousness and a ferment on the part of the masses far
greater and more profound in its implications than after the first
world war. This is the principal reason why she must make
concessions to the colonies.

In addition, the masses of Britain have lost all zest for the glories
of the Empire and could not be relied on to put down, by force of
arms, a long and protracted struggle against the uprisings of the
colonial peoples as soldiers and occupation forces.

Another factor is the pressure of American imperialism which
seeks to break the bonds of Empire in order to gain a freer channel
of trade and to make Britain absolutely dependent upon her.
Britain's economy is not strong enough to maintain her hold on the
Empire by the old methods of economic control, nor has she the
military force to guarantee and maintain her old colonial military
oppression. Thus, while preserving the formal framework of the
Empire, in reality the liquidation of the Empire is taking place.

The tame acceptance by the Tories of the policy of the Labour
government is dictated by their recognition of the real changes in
world relations. Thus, by concessions, the bourgeoisie hope to
disguise the process of the disintegration of the Empire and by
some miracle, to delay it. The sun is setting on the British Empire.
It can look forward only to further disturbances and decline. In so
far as it continues to exist, it will do so largely by the gracious
consent of Wall Street.

Long Term Economic Perspective

The economic basis of this process was long ago analysed and foreseen by Marxism. Britain's accession of wealth and power and her domination of half the world was gained at a period of the rise of capitalism and at a time when there were no other challengers in the race for world supremacy. Her advantages, as Trotsky has shown in his book *Where is Britain Going?*, have become her disadvantages. Her technique fell behind that of Germany and the United States. Because of their incapacity to compete, the British capitalist class —above all the monopolists —deliberately sabotaged the development of technique hoping to entrench themselves, like the empire of France, on their huge resources and their own backwardness. Basing themselves on a semi closed-in system of the sterling bloc, with assured markets, British capitalism had no incentive to begin large scale rationalisation of industry, which could only lead to increased production, without the possibility of finding increased markets.

This privileged position has been lost forever by the war. The vampire economy of Britain which, through her investments abroad, extracted tribute from her empire and semi-colonies and spheres of influence, has been undermined through the loss of foreign investments through the war. The unfavourable balance of trade, which was formerly a weapon in the hands of British imperialism, now becomes a dreaded threat to the standard of living of the masses and the very existence of British capitalism. What was the greatest stability in the system has now become the source of the greatest instability. Britain is more than ever dependent on the markets of the world, with the result that her economy will be even more affected by economic slumps than in the past. Britain is compelled to launch the struggle for markets with a greater ferocity and intensity than German imperialism launched the struggle for exports under the nazis. The character of British world trade has changed. Her privileged economic position which cushioned the full impact of world slump, as in the crisis of 1931, now changes into its opposite. The export of coal, which was her staple export, has dropped to almost nothing. The weakness of her economy is expressed in the fact that today she has not sufficient coal for her own needs. Meanwhile, because of the industrialisation of formerly backward areas of the world —above all of the Dominions and the Empire —Britain is no longer exporting the same type of goods. There has been a transformation of Britain's exports, which in turn has resulted in a change in the industrial structure of the country. In the long run this makes Britain more vulnerable than ever in the fluctuations of the world market.

Exposed to the vagaries of the world market, no longer able to protect herself on the basis of a closed-in Empire from competition, above all from America, Britain is compelled to abandon the policy of maintaining antiquated equipment in order to ensure profits, and to modernise her equipment to enter into competition against American production.

However, all these measures of British capitalism will be in vain. It is too late to catch up with the colossus across the Atlantic. Senile British capitalism cannot rejuvenate itself and capture new positions in a world market −which is shrinking in relation to world productivity. The long-term outlook for British imperialism is one of certain catastrophe.

Short-term Economic Perspective

This long-term perspective of British imperialism is indisputable and has been long foreseen. However, a mistake in conjuncture which was made was the telescoping of the inevitable long-term crisis with the immediate perspective for Britain.

We anticipated that British imperialism would be faced with a crisis as soon as the war was ended. However, the concatenation of circumstances has served to screen the disastrous results of the war for Britain. The huge markets created by the destruction of the war can be utilised because of the temporary quiescence of the proletariat. What was an unfavourable relationship of forces has been turned into a temporarily favourable one. Germany has, for the time being, collapsed as a competitor; America has been faced with a series of unprecedented strike struggles in basic industry; Europe and the world needs tremendous quantities of capital goods, above all machinery.

At home, six years of war have created a huge market for consumer goods. The desperation of British imperialism compels the introduction of new capital equipment into the coal mines and steel industry. Rationalisation and streamlining of cotton and other industries are being pressed as a measure of survival. The housing shortage and the destruction in the blitz create a boom in the building industry. The fusion of finance capital and the state inevitably results in increasing measures of regulation and of 'planning'. The tendency towards state capitalism and state control is shown by the projected nationalisation of the mines, steel, transport and fuel, and by the blocking of export of capital and partial control of investment. These measures will undoubtedly temporarily aid the economy as a whole in the economic upswing. The lavish subsidies of the state, directly and indirectly, rebates of excess profits tax, subsidies to the cotton barons, subsidies to the food and chemical trusts, etc, help to prop up the structure. All these burdens, of course, are basically at the expense of the British masses.

In addition US imperialism, anxious to use Britain as a future base against the USSR, has granted a huge loan. This will tide Britain over the next few years. Even without it, her export-import position has improved with amazing rapidity. The export rate now exceeds pre-war levels and is reaching record figures. The loan, however, will be swallowed up by the needs of capitalist economy. Despite the increase in exports, it is impossible to bridge the unfavourable balance of trade.

All these factors, however, lead to the situation where British capitalism temporarily attains a relative stability, only later, we repeat, to be faced with a catastrophe greater than she has ever experienced in the whole of her history.

The inevitable crisis, however, will not be immediate. It will be delayed for a time. The orientation and strategy of the Revolutionary Communist Party is firmly based on the long-term perspective of crisis and decline; but its eyes are also wide open to the immediate conjunctural upswing and its meaning. *For it is on the basis of the economic upswing and the political and industrial moods it will engender, that the immediate evolution of the proletariat will depend.* Before a new radicalisation takes place which will lift the workers onto new and higher levels of struggle, deep economic and political transformations will come into being. The growth and building of the revolutionary party, the strengthening of its ties with the advanced sections of the working class, will depend to a considerable extent on a correct prognosis of this period.

Politics of the Capitalist Class

The perplexity of the capitalist class and lack of confidence in the future, was reflected in their policy during the war and during the general election. While *The Times*, organ of the basic section of the British bourgeoisie, regarded the election with an air of impartiality, the Tory Party tried desperately to make use of the Churchill mascot and to frighten the petit bourgeoisie with the spectre of a Gestapo-like dictatorship under the Labour Party. But the change in the psychology of the workers was too deep-seated for the success of such tricks.

However, the result of the election indicates that capitalism still has many heavy reserves in the backward sections of the population, who still live in the past. The Tories and Liberals together received a vote equal to that of the combined working-class parties. It was the peculiar electoral system of Britain which gave the tremendous majority at the polls to the Labour Party. Nevertheless, 12 million votes for the Labour Party is a sign of the tremendous radicalisation that has taken place.

The Tories are seeking to gain agreement for the defeat of the Labour government. But such an agreement and such a defeat is not a perspective which is likely to mature without a crisis. At present, the ruling class, through the Tory Party, prepares to bide its time and, while utilising every opportunity to discredit the Labour leaders, it relies upon them to carry on the burdens of imperialism. Both at home and abroad, in the present relationship of forces, it is more suitable to have Labour leaders do the dirty work of capitalism. At this stage they have no intention of disturbing the present relationship of forces and thereby rousing the anger of the masses, who tolerate the present standards under a Labour government, but would not accept these under the Tories.

At this stage the bourgeoisie has no need for the fascist bands, even as an auxiliary weapon to discipline the proletariat. Nor, it must be added, could they immediately succeed in forming such bands. But moods within the Tory reformers and the right wing of the Tory Party indicate the possibilities, at a later stage, of a swing towards the formation of royalist-dictatorial or fascist movements.

The Liberal section of the capitalist class tends, at this stage, to lean towards the Labour government and to support the reforms or semi-reforms which it is introducing. But the Liberals, already a dwindling and vanishing force, have only a perspective of further decline.

Of course, in the event of a serious crisis, all the forces of the bourgeoisie will gather together, with a big section of the Labour MPs −a majority of whom are petit bourgeois, even bourgeois in origins and outlook− to try and refurbish a new version of the National government.

However, such a development is not an immediate perspective. The Labour government of 1929-31 was a government of crisis right from the start, having come to power at a time of the world slump. On this basis the bourgeoisie was enabled to manipulate the situation, because of the incapacity of the Labour government to cope with the crisis, to precipitate its downfall and prepare the victory of the National government in the panic election of 1931.

The economic situation today is entirely different to that of 1929-31. The bourgeoisie does not wish to disturb the present relationship of class forces, and by rousing the proletariat to action, precipitate an anti-capitalist movement among the masses which would have serious consequences for the economy.

The bourgeoisie is waiting for the slump, when they will use the crisis against the Labour Party and the working class. However, they dread the possibilities latent in such a situation. A collapse of the Labour government −even though a section of the petty bourgeoisie and backward workers might be temporarily stampeded to the right −would prepare the advanced workers for a sharp swing left, and thus polarise the two camps, bourgeoisie and proletariat. In addition to which, such a background of a temporary upswing of British capitalism, led to a comparative tranquillity of class relations up to the period just prior to the war. Far from tranquillising the class relations, such a victory for the Tories would precipitate the working class on the road of open class battles. Those sections of the population, temporarily stampeded in the direction of the Tories, would swiftly react even more violently both to the left and to the right.

The collapse of the traditional capitalist parties would be accelerated and the Conservatives suffer the fate of the Liberals. But this is the perspective of the future.

The Labour Government

Despite the difficulties at home and abroad, the Labour Party has attained power at a favourable period from the standpoint of short-term perspective. We anticipated that the coming to power of the Labour government would precipitate tremendous struggles on the part of the working class. We also anticipated large scale battles on the industrial field, with tremendous pressure on the Labour government. Had Labour come to power under conditions of industrial crisis and slump, undoubtedly the pressure of the workers for measures in their interests would have been insistent and immediate. Political developments would have been speeded up inside and outside the Labour Party.

It is necessary to make a correction in this short-term prognosis. As in the economic field, where long-term perspectives were telescoped with the short-term, so this was reflected in our political prognosis. We anticipated that the coming to power of the Labour government would almost immediately open up a situation of political crisis in the country. On the international and national arena, the class struggle has developed at a slower tempo and the decisive clashes have not yet taken place. Consequently political trends have developed in a somewhat different fashion. Because of the circumstances outlined above, the crisis will, in fact, have a more drawn out and delayed character.

The long-term perspectives remain that of crisis and collapse for the Labour government. But unless we correct our analysis, the Party will be disoriented in the coming period. While a series of minor and even important crises are inevitable, these political crises will not be of such a fundamental character as to shake the Labour Party from top to bottom, or pose the question of its downfall because of the movement of the masses in a revolutionary direction in the immediate period. Consequently there cannot and will not be a speedy polarisation within the Labour Party.

That the masses are critical of the Labour government is undoubted. But they are tolerant and are prepared to extend a large credit of time to the Labour government. The British masses are traditionally slow to change. Only big events will cause them to break with reformism. The masses feel keenly the burdens of food shortages and rationing, the vagaries of the black market, etc, and they are well aware that the bourgeoisie are still doing quite well under the Labour government. But they largely accept the argument of the Labour leaders that these conditions cannot immediately be alleviated because of the inheritance of the war and its aftermath.

Despite new restrictions which cause grumblings and a certain exasperation with the Labour government, these are not sufficient to provoke a real movement of revolt against the Labour leadership. Meanwhile, the acute shortages can only be temporary. Conditions will undoubtedly improve over what they have been in the war years. Already clothing, household utensils and other consumer goods are appearing on the market in increasing quantities. This process will be accelerated in the next few years. Notwithstanding the decrease of wartime earnings, the conditions of the British working class remain on a bearable level.

The undoubted economic boom masks the fact that no fundamental measures against capitalism are being taken by the Labour government. We are in a classic period of reformist illusions — a reformist government coming to power at a period of economic boom. Small reforms and semi-reforms tend to lull the masses with the perspective of a slow but steady improvement in their conditions.

In 1929, the Labour government operated in a period of slump and could not carry out anything of its declared programme, but on the contrary was forced to initiate counter-reforms on the pretext that it was not in a majority. Today, the Labour government rides in power at the crest of a tremendous wave of radicalisation seldom seen in British history, when the bourgeoisie lack confidence in their own future. The Labour government, with the agreement of sections of the capitalist class, is proceeding to nationalise coal and other industries for the purpose of modernising and preserving the structure of British capitalism. It is actually carrying out, in part, its declared election programme. In the eyes of the masses, this reconciles them to sacrifices because they have illusions in the 'theory' of a gradual and painless transition to socialism.

The fact that the illusion of 'full employment' can be maintained in the present period of boom; that, apart from the nationalisation measures, other reforms and semi-reforms have been introduced by the Labour government – National Health Bill, old age pensions, the housing plan, abolition of the Trade Disputes Act – these have served to assure the masses that the government is making a serious effort to do the job for which it was elected.

The policy in Greece and Indonesia aroused trepidation and misgivings among the workers. But the weakness of British imperialism, which dictates concessions to the colonial bourgeoisie in Egypt and India, enables the Labour leaders to cover their reactionary policy as though it was a genuine liberation of these peoples and a blow against imperialism. This is especially the case since the Tories have in words greeted with criticisms and dismay this 'liquidation of the Empire'.

Because mass unemployment will only begin towards the end of Labour's term in office, and because of all the other factors referred to above, it is quite likely that not only will the Labour government see through its term of office, but that we may see a second Labour government.

The most likely course of events, therefore, would appear to be a slow tempo of development. But this is partly dependent upon events abroad. The development of the class struggle in France to the point of civil war, or the outbreak of revolution in India, could speed the process in Britain.

Swing to the Right in the Labour Party

The conjunction of circumstances has resulted in a deep political lull among the masses. This is reflected in the Labour Party as a political *swing to the right*.

The Labour organisations which tended to revive after the election are largely quiescent or dormant. The left-wing leadership has fused with the right wing, the most prominent leaders taken into the cabinet and given government posts. Even the incipient left wing has been dispersed at this stage. The 'Victory for Socialism' group has collapsed. The circulation of left Labour publications such as *Tribune* and *Forward* has sharply declined.

There is much less political life in the Labour Parties than before the war. This is the general tendency while there are exceptions mainly in the rural areas. *Until the economic situation changes and a left wing with prominent Labour figures develops inside the Labour Party, the general tendency will be for political life in the Labour Party not to increase but to remain at a low level.*

This is the honeymoon period for the Labour bureaucracy. A symptom of the processes within the Labour Party was the overwhelming defeat of the Stalinist application for affiliation, largely on the grounds that it stood for 'red revolution and communism'. Undoubtedly the anti-Russian campaign had a certain effect which was helped by Stalin's policy in the occupied areas. It was not mainly because of the reactionary features of Stalinism that the swing against CP affiliation took place, although this undoubtedly assisted the Labour leaders; it was because of the reactionary campaign of the Labour leaders against communism and the renewed illusions in reformism. Only a handful of Labour Party branches throughout the whole country supported affiliation resolutions.

In our last conference document we stated:

> It is quite likely that the leaders of the left wing such as Aneurin Bevan will go over directly to the side of the right wing, accepting posts in the government. Thus the left wing, completely scattered and disorganised, will get even less of a national expression in the immediate period ahead. However, events will lead to the crystallisation of a new left wing in which sections of the newer and younger MPs in parliament will play a leading role. (RCP conference resolutions, August, 1945)

Such a crystallisation is inevitable and will most likely take place at a time of political crisis of the whole regime which will come with the development of the economic slump.

Class Struggle in the Industrial Field

Meanwhile, the struggle between the workers and the employers will largely take place in the industrial field. These struggles will, in the long run, reflect themselves in the political field, inside the Labour Party. But not immediately; not as a direct and automatic process. The most important industrial struggles for many years —the dock strike, the movement of the London building trades workers, the engineers, and more recently, the tin-plate strike in South Wales —all of these movements passed by without affecting the *internal* life of the Labour Parties on a local or national scale.

While tolerating the Labour government in the hope of benefits to come, and satisfied that nearly all have work, the economic boom will invest the workers with confidence. They will attempt to improve their hours and conditions by a direct struggle against the employers. The epidemic of little strikes, even in those industries where no strike struggles have taken place for a generation (tin-plate workers), and among the most exploited sections (dairy workers), is an indication that hitherto unaffected strata of the workers will be brought into the struggle. The strikes in cotton, engineering, shipbuilding and other basic industries against victimisations of trade-union militants, is an instinctive preparation in which the workers are defending their organisations for the battles to come. (At the present stage, large numbers of these strikes revolve around the issue of workers' control of hiring and firing, in which the workers express what will later be the tendency to workers' control of production.)

Strikes of a scope such as have never been seen before in Britain will take place. At this stage, the ruling class will be forced to give small concessions to the masses in wages and conditions. The miners are expecting great results and benefits from the nationalisation of the pits. They are demanding concessions: many will be given to them. Without concessions, the ruling class and the Labour government would be faced with a series of gigantic battles in the coalfields, once the miners realise the fraud of the reformist nationalisation measures.

However, the slump will take away all the secondary reforms and improvements and entirely transform the character of the struggle.

In the industrial struggles which will take place in the interim, the Labour government will support the employers against the militant elements of the working class. This will inevitably arouse a deep hostility from the left to the Labour government, *and even to the Labour Party*. While in the past the Labour Party was the mass alternative to the existing government in power, it was inevitable that the workers should turn to the Labour Party as an organised mass political force directed against the Tories, against the government of the day. But it is not easy to conceive of the growth of a new mass orientation towards the Labour Party, or growing confidence in the Labour Party, in a period when the Labour government is supporting the capitalists against the workers in strike struggles.

Meanwhile, the trade-union apparatus will become further integrated into the state apparatus and organisations of joint production and class collaboration. This tendency will be accompanied by a growing hostility to the policy of class collaboration and the crystallisation of an organised movement of opposition.

The Militant Workers' Federation* failed to strike roots and grow as a centre for trade-union opposition during the war and immediately following its conclusion, and it is now clear that the industrial opposition will find a different organisational expression.

The experience of the great dock strike and of the building trades movement indicates that the workers will throw up unofficial co-ordinating organisations for the purpose of directing their struggle against the employers and overcoming the sabotage of the union leaderships. The Party must constantly seek to integrate itself with these co-ordinating bodies and to link them up on a regional and national scale. At the same time, the Party must seek, as it did in the past, to find the maximum expression, support and organisation for these unofficial movements through the trade-union organisation as a whole.

It is from the industrial field and the trade unions that the militant and growing class opposition will find its first important expression in opposition to the Labour government. The task of our Party is to seek that opposition wherever it arises, and to try to give it a correct industrial and political orientation. It is in the industrial field, therefore, from industrial militants (among them Labour and CP members and sympathisers) that the Revolutionary Communist Party will make its most important gains in the period that opens up.

Nationalisation

Under the influence of the impasse of British imperialism, and the powerful pressure of the working class, the Labour leaders have gone further on the road of carrying through their election programme than we anticipated. Nationalisation of the mines is already accomplished. Steel, electricity, transport and fuel, sections of the basic industries on which the economic structure of the country rests, are apparently to be nationalised. However, the method and form in which statification is being accomplished — with compensation and without workers' control — is a compromise with the bourgeoisie as a whole, and is carried out in agreement with important sections of the bourgeoisie. The nationalisation of the Bank of England merely made *de jure* what was already *de facto*. These are measures of state capitalism and not of socialism.

*The MWF was established by the WIL in 1943 to organise rank and file activists, especially in the engineering and mining industries, at a time when the Stalinist apparatus in the Trade Unions was using all its resources to hold workers back from struggle.

All these steps show the increasing tendency towards the fusion of finance capital with the state. It is not an accident that the most serious representatives of the capitalist class, reflected in *The Times* and *The Economist,* are supporting the nationalisation of those industries that have become a drag on the British economy as a whole.

These serious representatives of the ruling class are willing to accept the taking over of these industries by the state —even with Labour in power —as the best method of bringing about the necessary measures of rationalisation and placing the burdens on the shoulders of the masses. By means of state rationalisation they hope to gain efficient and cheap coal, electricity, steel, fuel and transport, in order more effectively to compete on the world market. The capitalists are becoming reconciled to the terms of compensation and the manner in which the change is being accomplished. Their acceptance of these measures is a reflection of the decay of British capitalism; the lack of confidence of the capitalist class in its future; its weakness in face of the working class; its desperation to seek a solution. Ten years ago, when the bourgeoisie were endowed with more confidence in the future of their system, suggestions of such measures would have been greeted with savage opposition.

From the standpoint of economic development, state capitalism is a step forward from *laissez-faire* or monopoly capitalism. But it is not socialism. *The state remains a capitalist state.* Nationalised industry will be run for the benefit of the ruling class as a whole, not in the interests of the working class. The shareholders are to be richly rewarded with lavish compensation, although they brought the country to the edge of economic ruin. The industries are to be run as state capitalist corporations, largely staffed with their former capitalist owners and managers. The workers will have no control in the running of these industries, and will thus find themselves in the same position as the Post Office workers have been for the past generations.

The Leninist demand : 'Nationalisation without compensation under workers' control' assumes the character of a basic demand in the coming period. The workers in nationalised industry must demand that from top to bottom they should be managed and controlled by committees elected by the workers, to which technical experts would be attached.

While consistently exposing the partial and reformist character of the policy of the Labour government, and advocating the revolutionary programme, we defend even those partial measures against any attempt of the Tories to return to individual capitalist ownership. But it would be a crime to create illusions among the workers as to the meaning of these state capitalist measures. Our propaganda must stress that half-and-half measures are inadequate to meet the needs of the working class, and illusions created by the Labour leaders will lead the workers to disaster.

It is impossible to plan and take advantage of the enormous potentialities of modern production in the interests of the masses, without destroying capitalism and taking over finance and all big industry without compensation, and without the active and conscious intervention and democratic participation of the proletariat in the running of industry and the country.

The measures taken by the Labour government will temporarily assist in the alleviation of the capitalist crisis, but it cannot solve it. In the inevitable economic crisis which the continued existence of capitalism will bring, and which the nationalisation measures will not avert, the very conception of nationalisation will be discredited in the eyes of the masses. Large sections of the middle class and the more desperate section of the capitalist class, will be pushed onto the road of fascism. This debacle of reformism will, however, inevitably prepare the way for the revolutionisation of the masses, as in the days of their Chartist forefathers.

The Decline of the Independent Labour Party

The failure of the ILP to gain affiliation to the Labour Party resulted not so much from the fear that the ILP would form an independent left wing within the Labour Party, as from the unholy fear of the affiliation of the Communist Party. The Labour leaders had no desire to accept ILP affiliation, which would thus have assisted the CP to that end. This has resulted in the degeneration of the ILP to the point where its very future existence, even as a sect, is imperilled.

A continuous process of splintering has occurred which has decimated the organisation. Leaders and members alike lack a principled political base and a clear historical perspective. It is this, primarily, that has led to the present disintegration.

The ILP could only have survived or played an important historical role if it had worked out a revolutionary policy, or if it had entered the Labour Party, where it would have become the organisational-political base for the growth of a left wing in the mass party. But it had already lost any revolutionary possibilities before the end of the war.

The collapse of the ILP has strikingly confirmed the prognosis of our last Party conference that:

As a current separate and apart from the reformists and

revolutionaries, the ILP will not be able to maintain itself. Like its brother parties on the continent of Europe it will disappear ignominiously from the scene. (RCP conference resolutions, August 1945)

True, the ILP has not yet disappeared, although *for all practical purposes it has ceased to play the slightest role in British political life.* The defection of Fenner Brockway* will speed up the process of disintegration. It will be a few short months before the remnants of its parliamentary wing will break and openly enter the Labour Party.

The rump of the ILP can still vegetate for a few years to come. But a much more likely perspective is that it will fuse with the rump of Common Wealth. Even in this event there is no future for the ILP as an important factor in the ranks of the working class.

Stalinism in the Coming Period

Unlike its brother parties on the continent of Europe, the British Stalinist Party failed to secure the leadership of the majority or even a considerable proportion of the working class. The workers clung to their traditional mass organisation, the Labour Party. Nevertheless, it did secure the leadership of *the most courageous and influential industrial and political militants* in the years before the war and in the period of anti-war activity. The result was an influential penetration of some of the most important trade unions in the country. This was an important capital, an accumulation from years of self-sacrificing activity by these militants, gained despite the false political line of the leadership.

The incredible switches of party policy which took place overnight and without discussion, the strike-breaking activity of the party during the latter part of the war, and especially since its end, have served to disillusion the best and most critical elements of the party. For the first time a bridge exists from the Trotskyist party to these militants.

Our theoretical criticism of Stalinism in the plane of international politics had not succeeded in gaining a hearing among these workers in the past. It was in the course of their own experiences —the effects of the strike-breaking activities of their own party —that these worker Stalinists began to comprehend the fruits of 'socialism in one country'.

For the first time, serious fissures opened up within the British Communist Party. A continuation of the open class-collaborationist line would have led to splits and significant resignations. Only the

*Fenner Brockway was chairman or secretary of the ILP throughout the 1930s.

lack of a mass base in our own party rendered it possible for the leadership of the CP to prevent a serious split.

A new turn on the part of the Communist Party, however, a turn which appears to be definitely to the left, but which depends upon the agreements between Molotov and Bevin for its further evolution, will halt that process for the time being and cement these critical elements to the Communist Party again.

The Communist Party was shaken from top to bottom as a result of the general election. The worker elements, already in opposition to the pro-Churchill line, were disgusted by the general election policy which argued the impossibility of a Labour victory without the support of the 'progressive Tories and Liberals'. The results of the election demoralised them. Many of the petit bourgeois and most backward sections who approved of the line of class collaboration, tended to drift towards the Labour Party or to inactivity. Many of the best elements lapsed into apathy and left the party. Nevertheless, the Stalinists recovered from the effects of this crisis because of their tremendous machine, their basis in the factories and unions, and the substantial section of militants who still clung to the party.

A further setback for the Stalinists was the overwhelming defeat they suffered, not only in the factories but in the unions, on the question of affiliation to the Labour Party. Even where the executive supported affiliation (AEU, Mineworkers) when the issue was carried to the rank and file, it was overwhelmingly defeated. The AEU conference endorsed the decision of the Labour Party conference on this issue.

Because of the general political stagnation and the tendencies among the masses, unless Stalinist policy swings left, the decline of the CP will continue. The defeat on affiliation has left the Stalinist leadership with no alternative but to manoeuvre to give their policy as 'left' a coloration as possible, while its content has remained the same.

Nevertheless, this turn to the left and participation in a militant struggle will bring about certain difficulties for the leadership of the Communist Party. It will not be possible to separate their militants from the Trotskyists in the course of common action in the industrial field. The Trotskyists, moreover, have a *consistent policy*. Only they will seek to draw the necessary class lessons from individual struggles, and push these struggles to their logical conclusions. Common action in the industrial field will fuse the Trotskyists in comradeship with the rank and file of the Communist Party, and create the necessary conditions to enable us to counterpose our policy to that of the Stalinists.

Disillusionment with the policy of the Labour government will inevitably lead to a turn toward communist sentiments among the working class. To prevent that revolutionary sentiment being dissipated by Stalinism, and to turn it into a real struggle for communism, is the task of the RCP.

In spite of the setbacks which the Communist Party may experience in the immediate period ahead, at a time of crisis for the Labour government, the swing of large sections of the workers to the Communist Party as a temporary phase is inevitable. This could only be avoided by a swift and powerful growth of the revolutionary party which could offer an alternative.

Trotsky explained that the processes on the continent of Europe reflect themselves in Britain, though with some delay. In the same way as the finest strata of the European working class (even in the traditionally reformist countries) have swung to the Communist Parties, so we will see a like process in Britain. Mass unemployment in Britain, while a swift growth of the productive forces in the Soviet Union will be taking place simultaneously, cannot but influence the workers and precipitate an enormous swing towards the CP. This is especially the case as we will have a Labour Party with an overwhelming majority in parliament. Illusions in reformism, which still remained after the last world slump, will be dissipated among wide sections of the workers in the coming slump.

This process will undoubtedly be assisted by the fact that the Stalinists pursue a quasi-oppositional role to the Labour government. To the extent that discontent with the Labour government increases among the industrial workers, they will undoubtedly manipulate their policy and begin the preparation of the development of a mass base.

It is a fact of great significance that all the outstanding representatives of finance capital evaluate the coming developments in this direction. Eden, Churchill, Quintin Hogg and others foresee with dread that this will be one of the results of the coming disillusionment in the Labour government.

From: The Menace of Fascism —
What it is and how to fight it

1948

ONLY TWO years after the war allegedly fought to destroy fascism, the British fascists have commenced to regroup their forces. Throughout the country, cautiously and unobtrusively at first, but more and more boldly, the fascists have come into the open.

At first they emerged as local and separate organisations and adopted a host of names for reasons of expediency. The aim was clearly to prepare for unification at a later stage. Among the most important of these organisations were the British League of Ex-Servicemen and women; Mosley's Book Club and Discussion Group; the Union of British Freedom; the Sons of St George (Derby); the Imperial Defence League (Manchester); the British Workers' Party of National Unity (Bristol); the Corporate Club (a student group at Oxford University).

These organisations are not short of money. Before the war the British Union of Fascists (BUF) had extensive funds at its disposal. The fascists had intimate links with big business. Mosley boasted that he had spent £96,000 of his own personal fortune 'in support of my beliefs during my political life'. On two occasions Mosley himself married into millionaire families. In 1920 he married Lady Cynthia Curzon, a daughter of the late Marquis Curzon of Kedleston and a granddaughter of Levi Zeigler Leiter, a Jewish Chicago millionaire. Lady Cynthia inherited £28,000 a year from her own family (there are two children of this marriage). After the death of his first wife a few years prior to the war, Mosley married again, this time, into the Guinness millions. His wife is the sister of the notorious Unity Mitford, friend of Hitler.

In the early days of the fascist movement, Mosley was enthusiastically backed by a number of prominent capitalist and military figures. True, later when Mosley became discredited and it was clear that the movement was not timely, many of them dropped away or fell into the background. Apart from the open members of the Fascist Party, a powerful club composed of members of the ruling class was formed to back the blackshirts. In a pamphlet entitled *Who Backs Mosley* published by Labour Research, some enlightening facts were revealed:

> On New Year's day 1934 was formed the January Club, whose object is to form a solid blackshirt front. The chairman Sir John Squire, editor of the *London Mercury*, said that it was not a fascist organisation but admitted that 'the members who belonged to all political parties, were for the most part in sympathy with the fascist movement'. (*The Times*, 22 March, 1934). The January Club held its dinners at the Savoy and the Hotel Splendide. *The Tatler* shows pictures of the club assemblies, distinguished by evening dress, wines, flowers and a general air of luxury. The leader is enjoying himself among his own class...

The members of this club were:

COLONEL LORD MIDDLETON, a director of the Yorkshire Insurance Co, Malton Investment Trust, British Coal Refining Processes Ltd, and three other companies. He owns about 15,000 acres of land and minerals in Nottinghamshire.
GENERAL SIR HUBERT DE LA POER GOUGH, GCMG, KCB, KCVO, Commander of the Fifth Army 1916-18 and Chief of the Allied Mission to the Baltic, 1919 (Russian intervention), now director of Siemens Bros, Caxton Electric Development Ltd, Enfield Rolling Mills, and two other companies.
AIR COMMODORE CHAMIER, CB, CMG, OBE, DSO, late Indian Army. Now aviation consultant and agent to, and lately director of, Vickers Aviation Ltd.
VINCENT C VICKERS, director of the London Assurance Corporation and a large shareholder in Vickers Ltd.
LORD LLOYD, former Governor of Bombay....
THE EARL OF GLASGOW, Privy Councillor, brother-in-law to Sir Thomas Inskip, the Attorney General, who was responsible for the Sedition Bill in the House of Commons. The Earl owns Kelburn Castle, Ayrshire, and about 2500 acres.
MAJOR NATHAN, Liberal MP for NE Bethnal Green....a member of the Jewish Agency under the mandate for Palestine....Chairman of the Anglo-Chinese Finance and Trade Corporation...
WARD PRICE, special correspondent to the *Daily Mail* and director of Associated Newspapers and *British Movietone News*.
WING COMMANDER SIR LOUIS GRIEG, KBE, CBO, RAF, partner in J and H Scrimageour, stockbrokers, director of Handley Page Ltd, and an insurance company and Gentleman Usher in Ordinary to the King.

LADY RAVENDALE, Baroness, sister-in-law to Mosley and granddaughter to Levi Leiter.
COUNT and COUNTESS PAUL MUNSTER.
MAJOR METCALFE, MVO, MC, brother-in-law of Lady Cynthia Mosley and Lady Ravendale, late aide-de-camp to the Prince of Wales and the Commander in Chief in India.
SIR PHILIP MAGNUS, Bart, a leading Conservative.
SIR CHARLES PETRIE....
HON. J F RENNEL RODD, heir to Baron Rennell, and a partner in Morgan, Grenfell & Co.
RALPH D. BLUMENFELD, Chairman of the *Daily Express*, formerly editor. He was once editor of the *Daily Mail*. He is the founder of the Anti-Socialist Union and a member of its Executive Committee.

It is significant that among the early supporters of Mosley are named a number of wealthy Jews. This was before Mosley adopted anti-semitism as an indispensable means of rallying ignorant and backward supporters.

Mosley had the financial backing of fascists abroad. He received a subsidy of £60,000 a year from Mussolini. This has been confirmed by the discovery of documents in the archives in Rome dated 1935, and was revealed by Chuter Ede, the Home Secretary, in the House of Commons. Mosley paid visits to Hitler and Mussolini and was in close touch with the nazi leaders.

With the outbreak of the war, the Mosley movement declined. Like other fascist movements in Europe the BUF became an agent of German imperialism on whose victory they banked to assure their future. The British capitalists at war with German imperialism had no use for the fascists and were compelled to illegalise them as part of the ideological war against fascism. But Mosley was well protected in prison and pampered with many of the comforts to which he was accustomed, including the best foods, furniture and servants. As one of their class who had perhaps ventured too early, the British capitalists treated him solicitously with an eye to the future.

Are the British Capitalists Anti-Fascist?

The British capitalist class fought the war, not because they opposed fascism and what it represents, but in a desperate struggle against rival imperialisms for world markets, for sources of raw materials —for profit. Their victory has not brought and will not bring the end of fascism.

Throughout the world, the British ruling class has supported fascism and reaction against the progressive movements of the working class. Let us take but a few examples.

When Mussolini was subjecting the Italian working class to his castor oil 'treatments' and other bestial tortures, Churchill became deeply impressed with his 'gentle and simple bearing'. Speaking in Rome on 20 January, 1927, Churchill found only praise for the fascists:

> I could not help being charmed, like so many other people have been, by Signor Mussolini's gentle and simple bearing and by his calm, detached poise in spite of so many burdens and dangers. Secondly, anyone could see that he thought of nothing but the lasting good, as he understood it, of the Italian people, and that no lesser interest was of the slightest consequence to him. If I had been an Italian I am sure that I should have been whole-heartedly with you from the start to finish in your triumphant struggle against the bestial appetites and passions of Leninism. I will, however, say a word on an international aspect of fascism. Externally, your movement has rendered service to the whole world. The great fear which has always beset every democratic leader or a working class leader has been that of being undermined by someone more extreme than he. Italy has shown that there is a way of fighting the subversive forces which can rally the masses of the people, properly led, to value and wish to defend the honour and stability of civilised society. She has provided the necessary antidote to the Russian poison. Hereafter no great nation will be unprovided with an ultimate means of protection against the cancerous growth of Bolshevism.

Here the outspoken mouthpiece of British capitalism clearly indicates that in the last resort, faced with the revolutionary working class, the 'nation' (the capitalists) will not be 'unprovided'; it will always be able to imitate Mussolini and adopt the fascist method of rule over the workers.

In the struggle of China against Japanese imperialism, the British backed Japan because they saw in her victory a bulwark against the rising struggles of the masses in Asia. Mr LS Amery, then Secretary of State for India, a position which he held right up till 1945, said on 27 February, 1933 in the House of Commons:

> I confess that I see no reason whatever why, either in act or in word, or in sympathy, we should go individually or intentionally against Japan in this matter. Japan has got a very powerful case based upon fundamental realities.... Who is there among us to cast the first stone and to say that Japan ought not to have acted with the object of creating peace and order in Manchuria and defending herself against the continual aggression of vigorous Chinese nationalism? Our whole policy in India, our whole policy in Egypt, stand condemned if we condemn Japan.

The nazis were aided and financed by the British ruling class. Hitler received the unqualified approval and support of British big business. Lloyd George, the 'Liberal', described Hitler as a 'bulwark' against Bolshevism. As early as February 1934, the British government published a memorandum which allowed for an immediate increase in all German arms. 'The German claim to equality of rights in the matter of arms cannot be resisted and ought not to be resisted. You will have to face rearmament of Germany,' declared the British Foreign Secretary, Sir John Simon, on 6 February, 1934. Export to Germany of unwrought nickel, cotton waste, the basis for gun cotton, aircraft and tanks rose tremendously. When asked in March, 1934 if Vickers Ltd were engaged in rearming Hitler Germany, its chairman replied:

> I cannot give you an assurance in definite terms, but I can tell you that nothing is being done without complete sanction and approval of our own government. *(War is Terribly Profitable,* Henry Owen.)

The big financiers and bankers openly advocated a policy of support and assistance for Hitler. A short time after he came to power, the Governor of the Bank of England declared that loans to Hitler were justified as 'an investment against Bolshevism'.

Large loans were given to Hitler. His occupation of the Rhineland, the rearmament of Germany, the *anschluss* with Austria, the seizure of Czecholslovakia —all were supported by British capitalism. The reason: they feared a nazi collapse and what might replace it. Just before the war, the British, through RS Hudson, then Secretary of the Department of Overseas Trade, made an offer of a loan of a thousand million pounds to conciliate the nazis and prevent them from expanding at the expense of British imperialism while remaining a bastion against the German workers and against the working class throughout Europe.

Churchill looked upon the nazis with unbounded approval. In the 1939 edition of *Great Contemporaries,* Winston Churchill wrote about Hitler's rise to power:

> The story of that struggle cannot be read without admiration for the courage, the perseverance, the vital force which enabled him to challenge, defy, conciliate, or overcome, all authorities or resistance which barred his path....I have always said that if Great Britain were defeated in war, I hoped we should find a Hitler to lead us back to our rightful position among the nations. (The same book by Churchill contains a venomous attack on Trotsky, who earns his bitter hatred as builder of the Red Army and one of the leaders of the October revolution.—EG).

Lord Beaverbrook, writing in the *Daily Express* on 31 October, 1938 said:

> We certainly credit Hitler with honesty and sincerity. We believe in his purpose stated over and over again, to seek an accommodation with us, and we accept to the full the implications of the Munich document.

This, of course, did not prevent him from holding ministerial office in the Coalition government in the 'war against fascism'.

In the Spanish civil war, the British capitalists were in sympathy with Franco. Under the cover of so-called 'non-intervention' they assisted him to crush the Republic.

No reactionary anti-working class movement went unsupported and unaided by British capitalism. Only when the nazis encroached on their preserves did they declare war in the name of 'anti-fascism'. But when the needs of their class are such that fascism becomes necessary, they will as readily turn to Mosley or some other fascist adventurer, just as the German capitalists turned to Hitler and the Italian to Mussolini. Today, the fascists are not necessary for the defence of their profits. But tomorrow....

What is Fascism and How Does it Arise?

Most important for anti-fascists and working people is an understanding of fascism and why it arises. Without such an understanding of fascism it is not possible to effectively combat and destroy it. And unless it is viewed from the angle of the class structure of capitalist society and the class forces at work, the workers cannot prepare themselves for the future struggle against any rising fascist movement.

Capitalism as a system of society developed out of the decay of feudalism. In the period of its rise, up to the outbreak of the first world war, it was a progressive system because it resulted in the development of the forces of production, ie the power of man over nature, and consequently raised the level of culture of mankind.

Despite crises, wealth increased and in the main capitalist countries, the standards and the culture of the masses rose. With the development of technique the increased productivity of labour resulted in a further expansion of industry at the expense of the older methods of production and with this a numerical increase of the working class.

During the past 100 years, in their fight against capitalism, the working class organised their own class organisations, the trade unions and labour parties. It must always be remembered that the rights of today —the right to withhold labour —to strike, to organise, the right of free speech and press and even the right to vote, were not handed down benevolently by the capitalist class: *these were won only after a bitter and ceaseless class struggle on the part of the workers.* Before the first world war, the capitalists could still afford to give concessions from the enormous profits which the expansion of capitalism and imperialism brought them.

But capitalism inevitably brings in its train the concentration of capital and the growth of monopoly and of the combines. Because of the development of the world market, which is the historical function of the capitalist system, at a certain stage the capitalist nations inevitably and necessarily come into conflict with each other in the frantic endeavour to find and extend markets. The development of the productive forces expands more rapidly than the markets, outstrips the boundaries of the national state and private ownership of the means of production. It is this contradiction that led to the first world war, as it led to the second.

Capitalism in its last stages not only reduces the working class, which it cannot provide with any security in either employment or sustenance, to the state of pauperism; it ruins also the middle class —small shopkeepers and businessmen, professional people, white collar workers, small traders and all those strata of the population whose social position is lodged between the industrial working class and the capitalist class.

To combat the working class it is not possible for the capitalists to rely only on the old forces of repression embodied in the state machine. In modern conditions no state can last very long which does not, at least in its initial stages, possess a *mass* basis. A military police dictatorship does not serve the purpose. The capitalists find a way out in fascism which finds its mass support in the middle class on the basis of anti-capitalist demagogy. It is important to understand that fascism represents a mass movement: that of the disillusioned middle class.

The working class, in times of crisis, seek to express their aspirations and struggle through their existing organisations. Joined together by production, organised as a class in large factories and plants, the workers think in terms of a socialist solution to their problems. Their social position gives rise to a social consciousness.

The middle class, because of their position in society, wedged half-way between the capitalists and the workers, sway between these classes. If the working class cannot show a revolutionary way out for the middle class, the latter turns to the capitalist class and becomes the main pillar of support for the fascist movement.

With the increasing rivalry on the world market, unable to secure their position while the organisations of the working class exist, the capitalists seek a way out of the crisis by the destruction of these organisations, thereby depriving the workers of the weapons through which they defend their rights and conditions. As the crisis affects one country after another, the capitalists look to fascist movements to smash the working-class organisations and parties. Herein lies the function of fascism.

The difference between capitalist democracy and fascism is explained thus by Leon Trotsky:

> After fascism is victorious, finance capital gathers into its hands, as in a vice of steel, directly and immediately, all the organs and institutions of sovereignty, the executive, administrative and educational powers of the state: the entire state apparatus together with the army, the municipalities, the universities, the schools, the press, the trade unions and the co-operatives. When a state turns fascist it does not only mean that the forms and methods of government are changed in accordance with the patterns set by Mussolini —the changes in this sphere ultimately play a minor role —but it means, first of all for the most part, that the workers' organisations are annihilated; that the proletariat is reduced to an amorphous state; and that a system of administration is created which penetrates deeply into the masses and which serves to frustrate the independent crystallisation of the proletariat. Therein precisely is the gist of fascism. (*What Next? The Key Question for Germany.* 1932).

Mosley Before the War and the Anti-fascist Struggles of the Workers

The laws of the decline of the capitalist system are the same in Britain as in other capitalist countries. The legend, assiduously cultivated, in particular by the leaders of the labour movement, that Britain is 'different', has no basis in fact. This has been demonstrated on many occasions in the history of capitalist Britain. Fascism, as an expression of the decline of capitalist society, can become under certain conditions, as real a menace in Britain as it became in capitalist Germany and Italy.

The world slump of 1929-33 saw the emergence of the Mosley-fascist movement as a serious force for the first time in this country. The capitalist class of Britain recognised in the Mosley movement a militant and extra-parliamentary weapon which they could utilise against the working class in a period of social upheaval, in times of crisis and slump. Only the fact that the British capitalists succeeded in emerging from those critical years without the need for direct action against the workers determined their limited use of fascists at that time. Nevertheless, they kept the fascist movement in being as an 'insurance' against the future.

The myth, propagated by the capitalist class, that all issues can and will be settled through parliament is exploded by the very preparations undertaken by the capitalists themselves when it seemed possible that the working class would take to the road of struggle. With the threat of an economic slump looming before the war, the British capitalists were preparing extra-parliamentary steps against the working class.

In the few years before the war of 1939-45, army manoeuvres in Britain were conducted on the basis of civil war tactics. Strategic government buildings were prepared for defence. The civil guard was created as a special strike-breaking force, composed of recruits from the ranks of the ruling and upper middle class and trained in the use of machine-guns, rifles and tanks. They were taught to drive locomotives, heavy transport lorries and to do ground staff work at aerodromes. The civil guard was to constitute the backbone of any strike-breaking force in the event of serious troubles with the workers.

A significant portent was the fact that the big insurance companies which, together with the big banks, are the decisive rulers of Britain, refused to insure against the risk of civil disturbances and civil war. The capitalists understood that Britain, no more than Italy, France, Germany or Spain, could escape the social upheavals of the sick and decaying capitalist system. If the second world war had not intervened, the impending economic slump would have struck the country with far greater effect than even in 1929.

At this time the fascists were receiving support from numerous influential British industrialists. Towards the end of 1936 Mosley boasted in an interview with the Italian fascist paper *Giornale d'Italia*, that he was 'receiving support from British industrialists'. And that 'a number of industrialists in the north who hitherto had given his movement secret support, fearing commercial boycott, are now stating openly that they are on the fascist side'. (*News Chronicle*, 19 October, 1936). Mosley received the backing of the powerful newspapers, the *Daily Mail, Evening News* and the *Sunday Dispatch*.

Then as now, the blackshirt movement carried out its anti-working-class and anti-semitic provocations under the protection of the state. The British fascists were soon to prove that in brutality and method there was little to choose between them and Hitler's stormtroops or Mussolini's *squadri*. At a mass rally of British fascists at Olympia on 7 June 1934, the British working class were given an idea of what to expect if fascism triumphed. The savage and calculated brutalities inflicted by the specially trained fascist thugs upon any of the audience who dared to voice even the mildest opposition to Mosley's speech by interjections, outraged all sections of the population. Organised bands of fascists set upon hecklers, men and women alike, beating them unconscious, kicking them while on the ground.

Nurtured and aided by the authorities and the police, the fascists insolently organised provocative marches in working-class and Jewish districts, imitating the tactics of the nazis at the dawn of their movement in Germany. The British working class gave the blackshirts their answer. Every demonstration called by the fascists was answered by a great counter-demonstration of workers and anti-fascists. At Trafalgar Square, Hyde Park, in Liverpool, Merthyr, Newcastle —all over the country —the workers rallied against the fascists. In red Glasgow, the fascists were unable to hold meetings. In the working-class district of Bermondsey, London, barricades put up and manned by tens of thousands of workers successfully prevented the Mosley-fascists from marching through Long Lane.

Outstanding in these struggles of the workers against the fascists was the defeat of Mosley's projected march through the East End of London in 1936. Despite appeals from all sections of the working-class movement, including even the labour leaders, the then Home Secretary, Sir John Simon, refused to ban the march. On the contrary, he sought to facilitate it in every way. Ten thousand foot and mounted police drawn from all over London and the provinces were mobilised to protect Mosley and his 2500 fascists to ensure their march through the East End. This police protection was thoroughly organised even to the extent of wireless equipment and an autogiro hovering overhead. The weight of the state was brought to bear to protect the blackshirts in the teeth of the opposition of the London working class. The police authorities planned for Mosley's protection as though it were a military project.

Despite these measures of the state, the fascist march was defeated. Half a million workers turned out on the streets. Rallying around the slogan, 'They Shall Not Pass', the workers formed a wall of bodies on the route through which Mosley was to march. From early morning, baton charges were made by the mounted police against the workers to clear a path for the fascists. But the determined opposition of the workers made it impossible. The police tried to create a diversion by clearing Cable Street. But here again, the workers of London threw up fresh barricades of furniture, timber, railings, doors torn from houses nearby, and anything that would help to bar the path of the hated fascists. This magnificent mass action, including and representing all shades of working-class opinion and organisations, Labour, Communist Party, ILP, Trotskyist, League of Youth and Youth Communist League (YCL) —forced the then Commissioner of Police, Sir Philip Game, to order Mosley and his thugs to abandon the route. United action of the workers had defeated Mosley!

The defeat at Cable Street in 1936 dealt a severe blow to Mosley. Afraid of the organised might of the working class so militantly demonstrated, the East End fascist movement declined. The spectacle of the workers in action gave the fascists reason to pause. It induced widespread despondency and demoralisation in their ranks; their victory over the fascists imbued the working class with confidence. This united action of the workers at Cable Street demonstrated anew the lesson: only vigorous counter-action hinders the growth of the menace of fascism.

At that time the Communist Party was mainly responsible for calling militant workers to counter-demonstrations against the fascists. The YCL played a magnificent role. But after 1936 this militant policy of the Communist Party changed and they now avoided any counter-action against the fascists on the wide and militant scale witnessed before. With the coming of Hitler to power the Communist Parties throughout the world had degenerated into nothing but instruments of Russian foreign policy, and their activities reflected this. When Stalin found it impossible to arrive at an agreement with Hitler at that time there was a right about-turn on the part of the then Communist International.

From a refusal to offer a united front with the social democratic workers against fascism, the Communist International embarked on a policy of popular frontism. In line with Stalin's efforts to make agreements and gain alliances with the 'democratic' capitalist classes, they advocated class-collaboration between the workers and the 'good' capitalists. This foreign policy of the Stalinists was reflected in the British Communist Party which even went to the extent of advocating a 'National government' of Churchill, Attlee and Sinclair*. Having branded the united front of workers' parties against fascism as 'counter-revolutionary', the Stalinists now rejected the Marxist class analysis of capitalist society and advocated a united front with Tories and Liberals.

*Leaders of the Conservative, Labour and Liberal parties respectively.

In their efforts to placate those Tories and Liberals who favoured an alliance with Stalin, the Communist Party made every endeavour to paint itself as just another party of respectable and law-abiding citizens. To that end the hammer and sickle emblem of working-class unity was withdrawn from the masthead of the *Daily Worker*; the language of Marxism was replaced by that of middle-class suburbia. More importantly, the policy of militant class struggle went by the board and this was reflected in the new 'ostrich' attitude towards the fascist movement. To take militant action against the fascists would offend the new-found Tory and Liberal 'friends' of the Stalinist party. The activities and provocations of the fascists now went unheeded; counter-demonstrations and actions of the workers against fascism were no longer organised. The former policy of militant action was replaced by appeals and pleadings to the state to take measures against the fascists. From a reliance upon the working class to deal with fascism, the Stalinists turned towards a policy of relying on the very state apparatus which had in the so-recent past demonstrated its partiality towards the blackshirts!

How this new policy of the Stalinist leaders worked in practice was indicated by one instance of many similar examples that could be given. Just prior to the war, a monster rally of blackshirts, imported from all over the country into London for the purpose, gathered at Earl's Court to hear Mosley. On that day the Young Communist League of London organised a ramble in the countryside!

Demonstrating against the blackshirt rally outside Earl's Court were only the Trotskyists and a small number of anti-fascist militants. Of the Communist Party there was no sign. This new policy of the Stalinist party served to foster apathy in the ranks of the working class in the struggle against the fascists and emboldened and encouraged the blackshirts. It seemed that the fascist movement would gain new strength in face of the lack of organised and militant action on the part of the workers' organisations. But the war cut across these developments and gave them a new direction.

Mosley's 'Programme'

Today, in Britain, the signs of a fascist revival are unmistakable. Having tested the reaction of public opinion to the emergence of the various fascist groups, aided and encouraged by police protection, Mosley has launched his new party, the 'Union Movement'. The new party is no different from the former BUF, the same Jew-baiting, the same promises of the destruction of the trade unions and labour organisations, the same demagogy to attract the disillusioned and despairing middle classes and backward elements.

All Mosley's publications uphold the principle of private enterprise. In one of the recent Mosley 'News Letters', he demagogically champions the 'small' man, not against the capitalist monopolies, but against the nationalisation measures of the Labour government. Mosley boasts that his 'opinions remain unchanged'. In his *Greater Britain* (published before the war) he wrote that : 'the making of profit will not only be permitted but encouraged'. In an *Open Letter to Business Men* published in the *Fascist Week*, in 1934, Mosley reassured the industrialists that: 'In the corporate state you will be left in possession of your businesses.' To the coupon-clipping parasites who live on their dividends, Mosley promised: 'Hitherto, the holder of ordinary shares, who is the true risk-bearer in industrial enterprise, has been treated for taxation purposes as the holder of "unearned income".... the whole procedure is illogical, and calculated to discourage the enterprise upon which our industrial future depends.'

Whereas before, Mosley emphasised the idea that Britain and the Empire must isolate itself for economic 'autarky', today he advocates the 'union of Western Europe'. Recognising the weakness of British capitalism and the danger of economic collapse on the continent of Europe, Mosley proposes the idea of a union of capitalist Europe based upon the enslavement and exploitation of the African peoples. In the Mosley 'plan' 'there will be no nonsense about "trusteeship for the natives",' and 'negroes are to have no parity with their white superiors'.

One of Mosley's main planks is for war on Russia. If he were in power he would 'send Russia an ultimatum that she must accept the American offer to scrap atomic weapons and submit to inspection', which, if unaccepted, would be followed by a 'preventive' war.

In the press interview which Mosley gave on 28 November, 1947, to announce the imminent launching of his new party, he further elaborated on his 'programme'. The present parliament would be replaced by the corporate state modelled on Mussolini's two chambers. Instead of elections there would be plebiscites where the voters would have the privilege of recording 'yes' or 'no' to whatever Mosley's government did. His government would 'resign' if defeated, but this, of course, 'was most unlikely'. Mosley promises to suppress communism.

By this Mosley means that his government would suppress *all* working-class parties and organisations. The trade unions would be 'obsolete' if they did not 'cooperate' with the fascists.

The new party of Mosley is thus openly modelled on the fascist totalitarian regimes of Hitler and Mussolini. Mosley has clearly revealed his calculations. He anticipates being called to power at a time of crisis in the same way as Mussolini was called to power by the Italian monarchy and the Italian capitalists. In his *Greater Britain,* Mosley wrote:

> If the situation develops rapidly, then the public mind develops slowly, something like collapse may come before any new movement has captured parliamentary power.
>
> In that case, other and sterner measures must be adopted for the saving of the state in a situation approaching anarchy. Such a situation will be none of our seeking. In no case shall we resort to violence against the Crown; but only against the forces of anarchy if, and when, the machinery of state has been allowed to drift into powerlessness....
>
> Anyone who argues that in such a situation the normal instruments of government, such as police and army, can be used effectively, has studied neither the European history of his own time nor the realities of the present situation. In the highly technical struggle for the modern state in crisis, only the technical organisations of fascism and communism have ever prevailed, or in the nature of the case, can prevail. Governments and parties which have relied on the normal instruments of government (which are not constituted for such purposes) have fallen easy and ignoble victims to the force of anarchy. If, therefore, such a situation arises in Britain, we shall prepare to meet the anarchy of communism with the organised force of fascism; but we do not seek that struggle, and for the sake of the nation, we desire to avert it. Only when we see the feeble surrender to menacing problems, the fatuous optimism which again and again has been disproved, the spineless drift towards disaster, do we feel it necessary to organise for such a contingency....

Thus, the fascists viewed the coming struggle with the forces of 'anarchy', ie the working class, as an extra-parliamentary one. In the second edition of *Greater Britain,* Mosley deleted the chapters dealing with this problem, for they were too outspoken. Nevertheless, this remains the basis of Mosley's ideas today. Not accidentally did he declare at the meeting launching the new party on 7 February, 1948 that he and his followers were 'prepared to meet force with force'.

The anti-semitic and anti-working class activities of the fascists are on the increase and although small at present they constitute a challenge to the working class. Fascism must be defeated in its beginnings. The death camps of the nazis, in which hundreds of thousands of German workers were tortured and murdered, should act as a permanent reminder to the working class never to allow themselves to be lulled into a false sense of security. The British fascist movement will not differ from the German or Italian fascists either in social composition, objectives or methods.

The Labour Government and the Fascist Revival

The re-emergence of Mosley and his new 'Union Movement' in Britain today is regarded with complacency on the part of the labour leaders. The bitter lessons of Germany and Italy have passed these labour leaders by. They translate into English the same false words and ideas of the German and Italian social-democratic leaders: 'It can't happen here.' The British, they claim, are 'different', a 'tolerant' people with a democratic tradition. Fascism is 'alien' to the British and so on. *Famous last words!* The crime of the labour leaders is not that they lull themselves with the pretence that 'it can't happen here' but they disarm the working class by sowing illusions and objectively aid the growth of the reviving fascist movement by affording them police protection.

The working class who voted Labour into power may well stand bewildered and indignant as they witness Mosley and the fascists holding provocative meetings under the protection of large numbers of police specially detailed for the job, when they witness the Labour-controlled London County Council affording facilities for Mosley and his movement to meet in schools and halls under their control. This at a time when the fascists have the utmost difficulty in booking public halls because of the pressure of public opinion. Arising out of protests Home Secretary Chuter Ede replied that he is 'considering' the banning of loudspeaker equipment at public meetings. But this would apply to 'all' parties who use loudspeakers at meetings. This, instead of striking a blow at the fascist movement, in practice would be a blow against working-class organisations who use such equipment for propaganda. This is the result of the 'impartiality' of the reformists. Their 'impartiality' consists in hamstringing the anti-fascists and allowing the fascists to carry on.

Despite the past six years of terrible war, allegedly to destroy fascism, at the present time, as if nothing had taken place the fascists have taken up from where they left off at the outbreak of the war. The familiar picture of police and courts taking strong action against anti-fascists while the fascists are treated lightly and even protected is once again presented.

All this, in the name of the liberal idea of 'democracy', of 'impartiality' and 'freedom for all'. In reality, this is the opposite of freedom as taught by the great socialist teachers. Under this guise of 'freedom' and 'impartiality' of the state the labour leaders used the police to baton pickets striking for their elementary democratic rights of trade-union organisation. No socialist worker who is not a

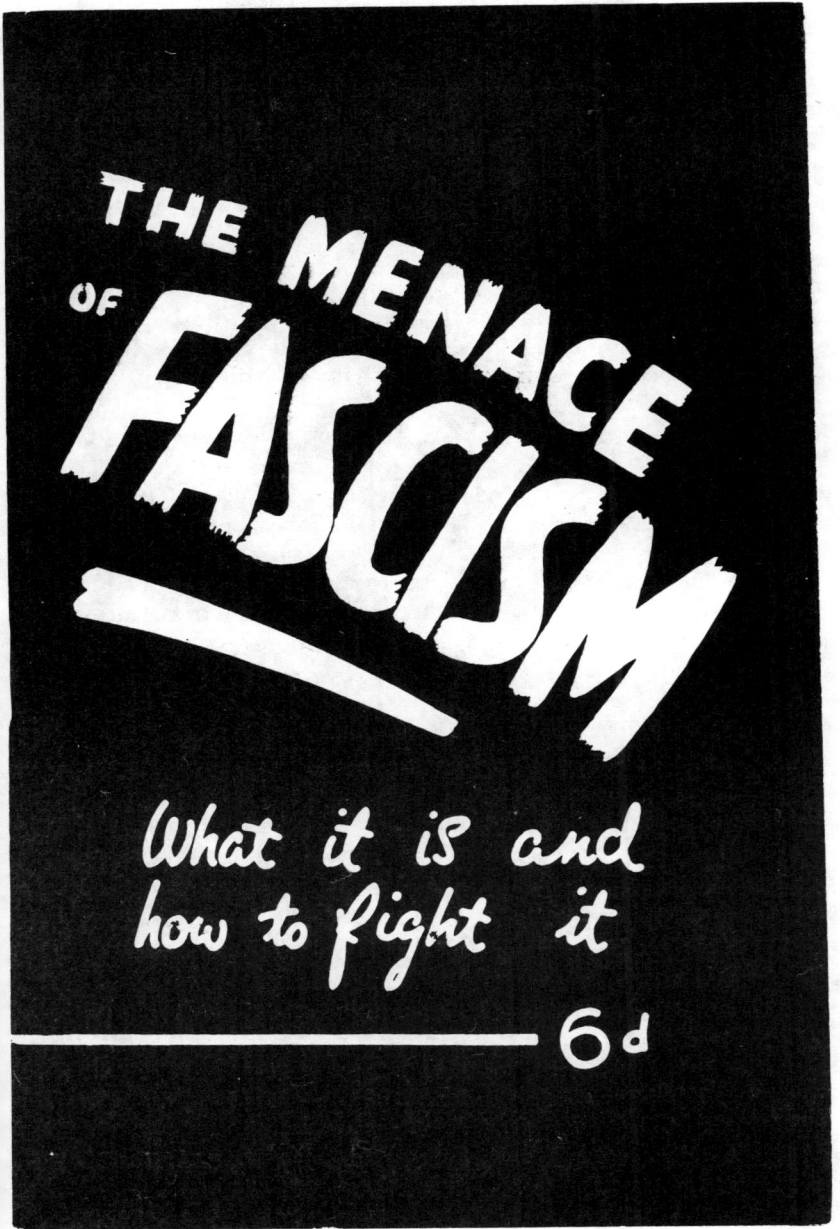

THE MENACE
OF FASCISM

What it is and
how to fight it

6d

Front cover of the RCP pamphlet The Menace of Fascism, *written by Ted Grant.*

Oswald Mosley, leader of Britain's fascists, in two typical poses; as the new Feuhrer on parade, and practising nazi-style salutes.

traitor to his class will put on the same plane the freedom of a scab to break a strike and the freedom of the strikers to prevent him doing so. Yet this force of most despicable scabs, the fascist movement, is given every facility to flourish and prepare to destroy the very right to strike and every other freedom dearly won by the working class. This is neither freedom nor democracy. It is a violation of workers' democracy and the very negation of freedom.

As a crowning piece of folly the labour leaders have given facilities to Mosley to publish his propaganda.

Instead of welcoming the instinctive protests on the part of the workers against any attempted revival of fascist activity, the Labour government organises the police force to protect the fascists against the workers. Labour leaders worthy of the name would welcome workers' action against the reaction and would back it by legislative enactments. This would be a warning to the capitalists that any attempt to establish a fascist dictatorship would be ruthlessly acted on by the labour movement as a whole. In the name of 'free speech' the fascists are given every facility to put forward their propaganda, this to the very people who stand for the destruction of free speech and every vestige of democracy won by the working class. In time of war —and the class struggle is a war between the classes —the enemy is not given points of vantage by means of which he can better attack and massacre your own ranks at a later stage.

The election of the majority Labour government after the second world war expressed the aspirations of the British workers to establish a new social system. The masses swung left and in this swing drew behind them large sections of the middle class, whose position had been undermined during the war. The war had placed heavy burdens upon the backs of sections of the middle class, the rise in the cost of living having affected those with fixed incomes most severely. Large numbers of small shopkeepers have been driven out of business by the competition of the big capitalist combines and the measures of concentration encouraged by the state in the interests of 'more efficient' big business. Of a total number of 10,000 firms in certain trades in London alone during the war, including furriers, dry cleaners, repairers etc, there was a cut of about 40 per cent. As a consequence, the middle class looked to the Labour Party for a solution.

A Gallup Poll revealed that, in the first months of the rule of the Labour government, their popularity increased enormously as a result of the social reforms they introduced. Had the labour leaders introduced wide measures aimed at destroying the privileges and vested interests of the capitalist class, had they taken over all large scale industrial and financial enterprises without compensation and operated the economic life of Britain on the basis of an overall economic plan under the democratic control of the working class, there could have been little effective resistance from the capitalist class. This would have been the socialist solution to the ills which capitalism inflicts not only upon the working class but the middle class as well.

But what is the reality today? Under the Labour government capitalism remains intact. Lavish compensation is given to the previous owners of nationalised industries, which continue to be run on purely 'business lines' and largely by the same capitalist managers who were in control before. The overwhelming sector of the economy remains under the control of private enterprise and the nationalised sectors are geared to and serve the interests of private ownership.

Even in the nationalised industries there is not a trace of genuine democratic control by the workers. While the labour leaders talk a great deal about the sacredness of democracy, there is no democratic control extended to the miners or the workers in the industries which are supposedly owned by 'the people'.

In Britain elements of workers' democracy exist in the form of the trade unions, the workers' parties, factory organisations and the rights which they have won. But the effective control is in the hands of the capitalist class. They control the economic life of the country through their ownership of the means of production; they have the decisive means of influencing public opinion through the control of the press, radio, cinema, schools and church and all other instruments necessary for the purpose. This is the reality of capitalist democracy. Bourgeois democracy, said Trotsky, means that everyone has the right to say what he likes as long as finance capital decides what is done. But once the workers reach out to take real democratic control, then the capitalists decide that the time has come to abolish democracy altogether.

If the labour leaders' chief concern was democracy, they would have introduced real workers' control and democracy. The elements of democracy which are already there would have been brought to full fruition.

Real democracy for the majority and not for the capitalist few, that is, workers' democracy, would mean not only the complete destruction of the economic stranglehold of big business, but the ending of their control of the means of influencing public opinion through their economic control. The Labour government should have immediately taken the press, cinema and radio out of the hands of monopoly capital and placed them at the disposal of the people. Every workers' tendency would be given the fullest free access to the means of propaganda to advocate their point of view. All political parties, including even the Tories and Liberals, who are willing to accept the democratic will of the majority, would have freedom of speech and press. But the fascists would be suppressed outright.

Having organised soviets or workers' committees in the plants and districts and established for the first time a democratic participation of all strata of the population in governing and running the country, the superiority of such a workers' state would be so obvious that any counter-revolution on the part of the capitalist class would be rendered impotent.

Instead of a revolutionary socialist solution, Labour leaders are tinkering with capitalism. The half-and-half measures of the Labour government have resulted in a swing away from Labour, particularly among the middle class and more backward sections of the workers. In the municipal elections of 1947 and in the parliamentary elections of the same year, there was a marked increase in the Tory vote.

And as a symptom of the rightward trend, the fascists re-entered the political arena.

This has taken place in a period of *full employment* and capitalist boom. British capitalism has lost the advantages she possessed in the past. Despite the efforts of the working class which have resulted in a 20 per cent increase in production over pre-war, there has not been a proportionate increase in the standard of living. Britain is far more dependent on the world market than in the past. With increasing competition the standards of life will not be raised but, on the contrary, the capitalist class will be forced to cut wages.

Already, the Labour government is waging an offensive to persuade the workers to accept a freezing of wages as the exhaustion of the sellers' market looms in sight. With the vociferous applause of the capitalist class and its press, the Labour leaders are exhorting the workers to make more sacrifices in the frenzied drive to increase production and accept a wage freeze and speed-up in the interests of reducing costs in the competitive struggle for world trade.

Cripps explains to the workers that if they do not *voluntarily* accept the yoke of capital, the British workers will be faced with the iron yoke of totalitarian dictatorship. In his own words:

> It is, therefore, essential that we should get a general agreement amongst our people to act upon sound economic lines: the alternative is likely to prove to be some form of totalitarian government.

The proposals on 'sound economic' lines advocated by the labour leaders are, of course, sound capitalist lines.

Here are the symptoms of decline, of impending economic slump, of over-production. Even if the labour leaders should succeed in their objective of increasing production to further record heights, this cannot solve the problem. On the contrary, it can only prepare catastrophe for the Labour government and the British working class.

Under the impact of the radicalisation in 1945, the capitalists were compelled to retreat. But they have not been overthrown by the Labour government. Today they are biding their time. But they are systematically whipping up the discontent of the middle class and backward sections of the workers in preparation for an offensive in the future.

Under the capitalist system, with the crisis of over-production, slump will follow boom as night follows day. And if already the middle class are discontented, how will they react when the slump comes? The workers will be impelled in a revolutionary direction but unless they show the Marxist road, the middle class will be drawn into the orbit of the fascist movement. The capitalists will declare the 'Marxists' and the labour movement responsible for the crisis of their system and gain the support of the middle class for action against the workers.

In the grip of economic crisis, the capitalist class will be forced to launch savage attacks on the standards of the workers. They will find the pressure of the workers' organisations irksome, especially the trade unions. Mosley's programme of annihilation of the trade unions and workers' organisations, his defence of private property, are designed to appeal to big business precisely in such a crisis. To eliminate the unions and terrorise the workers into submission, the capitalists will need fascist bands and will look towards a totalitarian state as the means of their salvation. Then they will really commence to subsidise Mosley or some other fascist less discredited among the population.

There could be no greater danger today than to sit back and content ourselves with the idea that the fascists have little political weight in Britain. While capitalist society exists, the weapon of fascism also exists as a potential menace to the working class. Events may prove that Mosley's 'Union Movement' will not be the leading fascist movement in this country. Mosley and his followers were greatly discredited during the war. Nevertheless, some new form of fascist organisation can well arise, an organisation not overtly fascist but of a character similar to de Gaulle's 'Rally of the French People' movement which, while it disavows fascism, is, in fundamental policy and aims, designed to serve the same purpose.

As a germ of the disease already present even today in Britain, WJ Brown, Independent MP for Rugby, formerly a leader of Mosley's 'New Party' in 1931, has tentatively advocated a 'Rally of the British People'. Even more indicative is the fact that the *Statist*, in an article *Can Our System be Modified?*, on 29 November, 1947, writes approvingly on General de Gaulle and says:

> General de Gaulle, naturally alarmed by the chaotic state of politics and economics as exemplified in France at present, has asked the people to give him power to form what he calls a national rally. At the same time he warns us that our system is so unstable that it may lead us at a date not indefinitely remote to serious trouble. It would not be wise to ignore such a warning.

Unless the working class can offer some alternative in the form of a bold programme and above all, daring action, the misguided middle-class youth who today support Toryism will be drawn into a fascist movement, whether it be a 'Union Movement' or some sort of 'Rally of the British People', or 'British Royalist Empire Saviours Society'.

How to Fight Fascism — the Policy of the RCP

With the re-emergence of the fascists, the main task of the labour movement is to educate and explain to the workers the *class* nature of fascism and its function as a combat force against the working-class organisations. But to explain the class roots and function of fascism is not enough. The working class must participate in actively combatting the fascists wherever they raise their heads. For this it is necessary that the organisations of the working class rally the militants around a militant programme of struggle against the anti-semitic, anti-labour propaganda meetings, against the press and other menacing activities of the fascists.

Trade unionists must refuse to print, handle or transport fascist propaganda of any description and demand that their executives make this a rule. All who violate such a rule must be blacklisted.

The first step in mobilising the workers is to unite all sections of the movement — Labour, trade union, Communist Party, Trotskyist, Cooperatives— in a common working-class united front. This is the key to a successful struggle against the menace of fascism. Fundamental differences separate these organisations from each other, but on this question of fascism it is, it must be, possible to have common agreement in forms of struggle. Retaining the right to criticise each other, it is a necessary task to organise joint counter-demonstrations, joint meetings, and joint anti-fascist propaganda campaigns. Fascism is no respecter of working-class opinions and democracy. It seeks to destroy all opposition workers' parties whether they be Labour, Communist, or Revolutionary Communist. To defend and protect working-class meetings and premises, Jewish and other minorities against fascist provocations and attacks, a Workers' Defence Corps must be established based on the trade-union, cultural and political organisations of the working class.

Mosley once boasted that he had a detachment which is joined by 'nearly every man who is physically strong...They are highly disciplined in a semi-militaristic manner.' Organised detachments of blackshirts can only be combatted by organised detachments of militant proletarians.

In campaigning for the Labour government to 'ban the fascists' the workers must bear in mind that history has taught that the enforcement of laws by a capitalist state inevitably acts to the disadvantage of the working class. The state rests upon the army, the police and the courts. And these are riddled from top to bottom with elements sympathetic to the aims of fascism, *especially at the top*. Even if the pressure of the workers succeeded in enforcing the passage of anti-fascist legislation, clearly it could only be put into effect by the enforcement of the workers. This means that the demand on the Labour government can only be effective when backed by the activities of the organised workers.

This does not mean that we do not strive to bring pressure on the Labour government to take action against the fascists. But it does mean that our demands can only be effective if backed by determined and organised activity on the part of the workers.

We must demand of the Labour government that it immediately:

Publish the names of all the known pro-fascists contained in the *Red Book* of Captain Ramsay.

Publish all evidence and information in the hands of the British Intelligence which reveals the connections between the nazis and the British fascists and representatives of the British ruling class.

Introduces legislation illegalising the propagation of anti-semitism and race hatred of any form.

Introduces legislation to make fascist propaganda and organisation illegal and at the same time to protect any section of the population which enforces this law, or is engaged in any activity against the fascists.

Today it is true that the fascist movement is only a small factor in British political life. But from a scratch comes the danger of gangrene! We must not repeat the same mistakes as the German working class.

Historical experience has shown that it is not possible to legislate fascism out of existence. The very nature of the capitalist state precludes that, for fascism in the nature of things is the naked weapon of capitalist class rule. Only the mass of the organised working class, understanding the nature of fascism and with a militant policy of struggle against it, will be capable of dealing effectively with the menace of fascism. In the final analysis the destruction of the capitalist system, which needs and breeds fascism with all its attendant horrors and repressions against the working class and racial and religious minorities, is the only means of ensuring the decisive defeat of fascism.

Britain in Crisis

September 1977

WITHIN THE web of the general crisis of world capitalism exists the special crisis of British capitalism. In reality, for the whole of the twentieth century there has been a decline in the power and position of British capitalism. This has been disguised because of the difficulties, upheavals and revolutionary crises which have faced her rivals, especially between the two world wars.

But even more important has been the relative social stability given to British capitalism by the policies of the leaders of the mass organisations of the working class —the Labour Party and trade unions —in periods of both Tory and Labour governments. In the period since the second world war, there has been a collapse of British power, unprecedented in scope and depth. The only thing that has cushioned the frightful social consequences of this steep decline has been the growth of world trade and of the world market during the world economic upswing.

British capitalism has fallen further and further behind her main rivals. In 1960 Britain's share of world trade in manufactured goods was 16.5 per cent. In 1973 it had fallen to 9.5 per cent.

While her rivals increased their industrial production at a record pace, during the world economic upswing British capitalism increased much more slowly. Consequently, her position relative to her rivals declined.

The *National Westminister Bank Review* of November 1975 points out that from 1969 to 1974 Britain's National Product increased by 11.4 per cent in real terms. But industrial production only increased by 6.7 per cent in real terms. 'Thus industrial production fell by 5 per cent in relation to the National Product.'

Again, industrial production in the ten years from the first quarter of 1955 to the first quarter of 1965 increased by 35 per cent. But in the next ten years it increased by only 15 per cent.

'Thus the annual growth of industrial production has actually fallen by one half since 1965.'

Productive capacity increased by 35 per cent or 3 per cent per annum between 1955 and 1965, by 22 per cent or 2.5 per cent per annum between 1965 and 1973. Since 1973 the growth rate has been only 1.5 per cent.

The ratio of net investment to value added was 8.6 per cent in 1965. It was only 3 per cent to 5 per cent in 1971-73. Inclusive of investment in petrol and gas it rose in 1974 to 6.3 per cent. But without petrol, for the rest of industry, it was only 4.9 per cent. The ratio of gross investment in industry fell from 17 per cent in 1965 to 14 per cent in 1972 and 1973.

However, as the *National Westminster Review* says: 'Government statisticians believe that something like 10 per cent of industrial production must be invested in industry each year to maintain the industrial capital stock and make good wear and tear, technical obsolescence...' According to estimates they quote, industrial capital stock increased by 8.6 per cent of industrial production in 1965, only 3.4 per cent in 1972 and 4.1 per cent in 1973. This has worsened since the recession and the following squeeze. The rate of growth of productive potential is now only 2 per cent per annum.

The rate of net investment fell by one-half during 1965-74 and employment fell by 12.5 per cent in manufacturing in the same period. The 'de-industrialisation' of Britain, of which Tony Benn has spoken, is shown by the fact that *industrial profits* have not been ploughed back but invested in more profitable fields *outside* industry. 19.1 per cent of industrial production was invested outside industry in 1965. This had risen to 26.5 per cent in 1973.

An OECD report points out that Britain 'has lost ground not only in productivity but in quality, design, punctuality of delivery, and after-sales delivery, and after-sales service....'

The *Midland Bank Review* of May 1977 says: 'Economic miracles seem at a discount, and the prospect is for no more than a minor upturn in a long recession.'

Manufacturing in Britain accounted for 37 per cent of employment in 1961, and only 30 per cent in 1976, such has been the fall in the rate of industrial investment. With shipbuilding, for example, Britain's share of world production in 1955 was 26.6 per cent; in 1976 it was 4 per cent.

In 1960 Britain's share of world manufactured goods exported was 15.3 per cent, according to statistics compiled by the OECD. In 1975 this had dropped to 8.9 per cent. France and Germany's share remained about the same. France's share of world exports fell only by 0.1 per cent to 9 per cent. But now it slightly exceeds the British share.

Germany's industrial exports, which were about 20 per cent higher in 1960 at 18.2 per cent of world exports of manufactured goods, are now more than double those of Britain.

Italy, the other sick man of Europe, has increased her share of world manufactured exports by nearly half from 4.5 per cent to 6.7 per cent. This is a little over 2 per cent less than Britain, whereas in 1960 Britain's share was three times as great.

The one economy of world capitalism that really developed in the last two decades was that of Japan. In the period of capitalism's impasse, that will guarantee future convulsions. For the moment Japan has outstripped her rivals in development of exports. From less than half that of Britain, at 6.5 per cent in 1960, she has increased her share nearly 2.5 times to 15 per cent —more than 50 per cent higher than the share of Britain.

The USA still remains the world's biggest industrial exporter, though her share of world trade has declined somewhat. It has fallen from 22.8 per cent in 1960 to 19.0 per cent in 1975. But West Germany and Japan are treading on her toes (Japan even in the American market) to anguished shrieks from the industries affected.

The absolutely astounding collapse and enfeeblement of British captialism can be seen in these figures. In the past, the British ruling class looked down on the 'lesser breeds'. Through the virtually exclusive domination of the empire, they could afford to concede a higher standard of living in the upper layers of the working class and even the working class a whole. Now, Denis Healey, the Chancellor, boasts to industrialists that they have the cheapest labour of all the industrialised countries, big and small. This was true already in 1975 *before* the 'Social Contract' and the deep cuts in the living standards of the working class.

The United States Bureau of Labour Statistics for 1975 gives the average hourly remuneration in industry, according to preliminary estimates in the leading industrial countries. For the UK it was $3.37. Japan had increased her wage rates by practically three times since 1970 reaching $3.32 —a negligible difference from Britain. Now she has outstripped Britain in this field as well!

In France the hourly pay in industry was $5.47. West Germany was $6.21 and the disparity has increased yet further since 1975.Even the pay of workers in formerly backward Italy considerably exceeded that of British workers reaching $5.51 per hour in 1975. The United States rate was $7.26, second highest in the world to Sweden. These wage rates do not take into account the level of prices, which is far higher in all these countries than in Britain. Nevertheless, it is a rough index of how the British workers, from being among the highest paid, have now fallen to the status of the 'coolies' of Western Europe.

One of the peculiar problems of British capitalism is the domination of the City of London and thus of finance-capital. Between 1975 and 1976, 'invisible exports' ie shipping, insurance, banking, dividends from investments abroad and tourism rose by 25 per cent to £13,000 million *—more than half* the total value of exports. With 9.9 per cent of the worlds' invisible earnings, British capitalism was second only to Wall Street.

The division of interests in Britain between the City (finance-capital) and industrial capital is one of the causes of the steep decline in industrial strength of British capitalism. Concerned only with financial return rather than the production of real wealth in the form of factories, machinery and consumer goods, the City has sapped and undermined the economy of the country. It is these contradications which have undermined completely the role of British capitalism on a world scale.

The partial turning of Britain into a parasitic *rentier* state, similar to that of France in the past, has been the result of the export of capital and services such as banking and insurance. A Treasury Report of June 1977, confirms: 'Gross invisible receipts were £13,700 million per annum and that *invisible earnings now exceed the value of the export of finished manufactures* and, last year, were equal to over half the earnings from all exports of goods.'

'In the recession years of 1971, 1972 and 1975, about one million manufacturing jobs disappeared', according to the *Economic Progress Report* of the information division of the Treasury of June 1977.

As late as 1970 there were 8.2 million people employed in manufacturing, but in 1977 the total was only 7.2 million. Average production per head in 1977 was only equal of that in 1973. But 1973 manufacturing output-per-person-employed was 15 per cent lower than in 1970! This indicated a critical fall.

The reason for this is the failure of big business to invest the surplus extracted from the labour of the working class. *Management Today* in its issue of July 1977 admits: 'Investment in British manufacturing industry remains low. Since (1965) total capitalisation per worker has fallen well behind that of Britain's

EEC partners and other industrial nations. It is not uncommon to find capital available per worker in West Germany, say, amounting to 2-3 times the British level – particularly in such industries as motor manufacturing.'

In 1972, Japan's investment ratio to Gross Domestic Product (GDP) was 34.4 per cent; West Germany 26.3 per cent; France 26.34 per cent; Sweden 22 per cent; and the UK 18.2 per cent.

Thus Britain has fallen further and further behind in the booms and recessions of the post-war period. In 1965 capital expenditure per employee in manufacturing industry was £142. In 1970 this had reached £191 and then fell back in succeeding years to £158 in 1975.

All the measures taken by the government in the post-war period to 'control the economy' have only made the situation worse. However, in the main, the same ills affecting British capitalism have affected her rivals as well. Such is the case with the tendency for the rate of profit to decline. The fall in West Germany and other countries has been as steep. But the surplus in Britain has flowed into property speculations, service industries, investment abroad etc., and not back into manufacturing.

In the Bank of England *Quarterly Report* of March 1976, it was estimated that the 'real' (ie after interest and other charges), return on capital employed by industrial companies fell from about 11 per cent in the early 1960s to around 4 per cent within the decade, and was down to 2 per cent in 1974.

The OECD confirmed this by pointing to the fall in rates of return on capital employed by industrial companies from about 12 per cent in the first half of the sixties to 4 per cent – 'among the lowest in the OECD area'.

In their blind greed for profit, each monopoly, combine, bank, trust or individual capitalist is only concerned to maximise its returns, without worrying about the resulting effect on the economy as a whole. Thus the enormous speculation in property, until the bubble burst recently. Now there is as much speculation in agricultural land as there was formerly in building property. The money pouring into agriculture matches that still pouring into buildings.

Despite a heavy premium on money invested abroad, it remains at a very high level, reaching £1500 million in 1976. Lavish inducements have been given to industry and a 'bonanza' of nearly £2000 million a year extra profit made out of the limitation of wages by the Labour government's 'Social Contract'. In spite of this, investment is still very sluggish in 1977, and according to projected figures, may reach an increase of only 3 per cent over the low levels of recent years.

This means a further falling behind for Britain. The 100 monopolies which control 80 per cent of British exports use currency fluctuations to increase their profits rather than to increase the share of Britain on world markets. Consequently the situation for British capitalism is actually worsened. Prices of imported manufactured goods rise, but British capitalism does not gain even the advantage of a breathing space for new investment. The monopolies will not increase investment to increase capacity because their market abroad is not increased and inflation further limits their market at home.

As *The Director* of June 1977 cynically observes '....in a world of complex products, multi-national corporations, oligopolistic competition, price leadership and price discrimination....short term exchange rate changes are likely to be regarded as a windfall addition to profits.'

During the course of the post-war period, the 'Welfare State' was the theme of the speeches and articles of the right wing and left wing reformists. The 'difference' between Britain and other countries was emphasised by the right wing theorists like John Strachey, Douglas Jay, Anthony Crosland, Roy Jenkins, and others. In this, they merely echoed the propaganda of the spokesmen of big business.

Now nothing is left of the 'Welfare State' except the shell. In comparison with most of the main capitalist countries, the British workers are worse off in welfare expenditure. More of the GNP of many of these countries goes on transport, health, education, social services and unemployment pay, than in Britain. This was so even before the drastic cuts of 1976 and 1977.

The expenditure by the state and its share of GDP was not much different in Britain to that of her main European rivals, contrary to the poisonous propaganda in the media. The massive cuts of the last three years, in fact, must have brought state expenditure's share of GDP below that of her major competitors.

These cuts have been mainly in public sector investment, because the local and state authorities have found it difficult, especially with an inflation rate of 17 per cent, to cut actual expenditure. It has been estimated by government statisticians that, on present levels, by 1978-9 public sector investment will be back to the level of 1965, in real terms, 13 per cent below the average since 1966.

This will mean a further fall in the 'social wage' in coming years. As an article in *Management Today* of July 1977 cynically comments: 'Perhaps because of the fanfare with which this was introduced, the cost of the British welfare state has ever since been the main target of those who reject the phenomenon altogether...'

John Strachey, who wrote *Contemporary Capitalism* as an apology
for the policies of right wing reformism, must be turning in his
grave. If the contemporary right wingers are not writhing it is
because those in the Cabinet and government have, as predicted,
abandoned all the false shibboleths of reformism and adopted
instead a programme of 'extremist' Tory measures to try and save
capitalism. Of course they will be impaled on the contradictions this
engenders in the struggle between the classes for the division of the
national product produced by the labour of the working class.

So far as health expenditure is concerned, despite the former
fame of the National Health Service, Britain is falling behind in her
percentage of GNP devoted to health. In the field of medicine and
health care the UK spends 4 per cent of the GNP. Her main rivals
spend far more: Holland 5 per cent; West Germany and France 6
per cent; Sweden 7 per cent; and the USA 6.5 per cent.

In fact in practically every field of social services Britain is behind
most of her rivals. This should give her an advantage in the field of
competitivity. Her industrialists have the lowest wages to pay and
the highest subsidies; yet they are falling further and further
behind.

The continuation of sluggish production is due partly to the
measures of the government in the alleged fight against inflation.
These were, in reality, measures to cut the share of the working
class in the national product in order to increase the share of the
capitalists, in a vain endeavour to give a push to investment.

Writing for the literate members of their class, the journals of
capitalism are sometimes brutally frank. Thus *Management Today* of
July 1977, says on the so-called Social Contract, 'the
unions....accepted what was, in everything save the name, an
enforced retraint of wages.'

The Economist, right wing Tory journal, points out that the 'stage 2
agreement....cut real earnings by a remarkable 7 per cent. This is a
signal achievement. No previous post-war income policy, statutory
or voluntary has achieved such a gap between pay and prices.' (23
July, 1977).

The real secret of the world economic upswing was the
dovetailing of a whole series of factors, all interacting on each
other. One of them was increased division of labour with the
greatest increase of world trade for a whole historical period. This
led to a dismantling of tarriff barriers and many other obstructions
to trade. Another factor was the development of new industries on
the basis of the expansion of the world market.

This in turn led to increased standards of living in the
industrialised countries. Increased super-profits were wrung by

the industrialised countries from the colonial world, and a whole series of other factors led to the expansion of the market. This in turn led to an explosion of investment in the capitalist world. Investment of a great part of the surplus extracted from the labour of the workers is the vital essential for the development of an economy. Most of the OECD countries were re-investing 25 per cent of total output each year. In the inter-war period the average had been less than half that, at 12 per cent. It was usually less than 10 per cent per annum in the nineteenth century. Since the war, Britain's investment has been lower than that of her rivals.

British capitalism for the whole of the twentieth century has been sluggish in investment. Previously she relied on her entrenched position and her accumulated wealth and industrial power.

All these advantages have disappeared. Even in banking, the French and German banks are now bigger than the British banks. The *Banker* of June 1977, laments: 'Our list of top 300 banks in the world....reveals sharp declines in the rankings of the major British banks. No British bank is amongst the ten largest banks. Barclays has slipped to twelfth place, National Westminster to twentieth, Midland to fortieth and Lloyds to forty-second place. At the other end some merchant banks have dropped out of the list altogether. Japanese, French and German banks have taken up the running.'

Thus even the City has not been exempt from the general decline of British capitalism.

With the change in the world economic outlook the situation has changed for the worse for British capitalism. From a haughty dispenser of favours she has become a supplicant. Despite the favourable factors of coal and now *oil* resources, the capitalists, afflicted by the general crisis, have not taken advantage of the measures of the Labour government which restricted the share of the working class in the wealth they produce. The capitalists, fearful of a new slump, have not been prepared to invest in manufacturing when only 80 per cent of productive capacity can be used because of the restriction of the market by wage restraint and cuts in state expenditure.

The reformists have been endeavouring to increase the profits of the capitalists by cutting the share of the workers and to cure inflation by cutting budget deficits. But they are caught on the other horn of the dilemma of capitalism —without big profits the capitalists will not invest. The result has been that in 1976, despite the practical standstill in production, the volume of imports (excluding oil) rose by 8 per cent.

Manufacturing output in 1976 was 6 per cent below the level of the crisis year of 1974. This was the year of the 'confrontation' politics of Heath leading to the three-day week and an enormous loss in production. Last year, too, the output of the building industry fell by 17 per cent compared to that of 1973. Personal income, according to official figures, fell by 0.5 per cent. 'Consumer spending' in 1977 fell a further 1.5 per cent in April to June 1977. This downturn depressed the market.

All the sacrifices and falling living standards, all the state cuts in the social wage have not moved the hard-faced and hard-fisted capitalists. They failed in their objective. The programme of counter-reforms has left British capitalism in an even worse state than formerly.

The crisis of capitalism has produced different wings among the politicians and among the economic witch-doctors. Some are willing to risk a further bout of inflation by increasing state expenditure to try and increase the markets. *Others, the majority, are in favour of even more drastic cuts in state expenditure.* All are for holding down the wages of workers.

The windfall of North Sea oil (only rendered economic by the quadrupled price of Middle East oil) *will not solve the problems of British capitalism.* If the price of oil on the world market were to drop in the next recession it would cut some of the advantages of British oil production. The oil is extracted at fifteen times the cost of extraction of the oil of the Arab states.

But even if the oil price remains steady, or continues to rise slowly, the main advantage will be to remove one element of instability in the British economy. It could result in a favourable balance of payments in world trade and increase the revenue of the state by some few per cent. But it will not change this fundamentally.

The Economist of 23 April 1977, points out:

> Britain's pessimists like Mr Wynne Godley of Cambridge believe that private industry is more likely to slide from recession to extinction —a slow death obscured by an oil-buoyant balance of payments; that the government is likely to float sterling too high too long on that buoyancy, eroding export profit margins and pushing Britain's share of less than exuberant world trade down even more sharply; and that a strong boost to the economy is needed to raise growth from Mr Healey's forecast 1.5 per cent for 1977-8 to 5 per cent a year, if Britain is not to emerge from its oil years with 3 million unemployed and a skeletal industrial base.

The reformists, like the bourgeois, would like a high growth rate, but are constrained by the inevitable increase in inflation that further deficit-financing would engender. That is why they have capitulated to the treasury 'experts', who really decide policy, and to the pressure of big business.

Thus the spokesmen of capital vacillate between the 'orthodox' monetarists and the neo-Keynesians. Both sets of 'remedies' are worse than the disease.

The Conservative Party

An inevitable future split in the Conservative Party between the right wing 'ultras' and the so-called 'moderates' is foreshadowed by the differences between Keith Joseph and the shadow Labour Minister, James Prior, over the Grunwick strike.

The right wing Bourbons, using the 'philosopher' Joseph as a front (though his views are of the blackest reaction) want an out-and-out struggle against the trade unions, bringing down the full force of the state and the 'law' against the organised workers. They represent one wing of the ruling class, which comprises those sections of big business who are financing the National Association For Freedom (NAFF)* – 'freedom not to belong to a union' ie the 'divine right' of employers to tyrannise and doubly exploit unorganised workers in getting them to meekly accept low wages, their 'right' to decide everything in the workshop and to destroy the 'closed shop' – the solid defence of the well organised workers.

This split in the ruling class party of big business –which will be patched up and papered over for the moment –is an indication of the beginning of a revolutionary crisis in Britain. It is only at moments of great social tension and stress that the ruling class openly reveals their differences in strategy and tactics. That is especially so in the case of the Tory Party in Britain.

This party has based itself not only on the interests of the capitalist class and landowners. It has also rested on the active support of the different layers of the middle class –especially its professional and upper layers –and on the passive support of an important minority of the politically backward workers –including even a third of the workers organised in the trade unions.

The support of these sections is due only to the bankruptcy of the policies of reformism. Labour governments have solidified and hardened the prejudices of these layers by their failure to carry out their promises and programme when in power. Without this support the Tory Party would long ago have collapsed. The failure of the last Tory government with their policy of confrontation with the unions and the working class reduced them to a suburban and mainly South East England party.

*The National Association for Freedom, an extreme right wing, anti-trade union organisation, which gave advice and support to the Grunwick company in a bitter and long running dispute over trade union recognition. Forerunner of the Freedom Association.

The counter-reforms of the right wing Labour government have allowed the Tories to make an *electoral* recovery. The disillusionment with increased inflation, greater unemployment and lower living standards has meant a comeback.

But the background to this comeback is the sickness of British capitalism sketched in these perspectives. For a time the Tories tried to paint themselves as a second party of reform — Tweedledum to Labour's Tweedledee. In fact, after the *deflationary* policies of the 1964-70 Labour government, it seemed for a moment that the parties had changed roles. With the failure of the policies of the first two years of the Heath government, the Tories became a party of heavy state expenditure as against Labour's 'orthodox' financial policies of the last period of office.

In reality this merely reflected the desperate crisis of British capitalism and the frenzied policies of the representatives of big business to find a way out. Now, in place of the Labour government's policy of savage cuts and measures to reduce living standards, *the Tories stand for a policy of even more draconian cuts in state expenditure* and even deeper cuts in living standards.

On this theme the ravings of the former 'sober' journal — the voice of Toryism and of big business — *The Times*, is an indication of the cul-de-sac in which British capitalism finds itself. Some Tory MPs, reflecting the views and interests of 'the City', (ie finance-capital) even rationalise the bankruptcy of British capitalism. They seriously suggest the 'service' sector (ie insurance, banking, and investment abroad, tourism, catering etc.,) should replace manufacturing industry as the basis of British capitalism.

By the enormous investment of the surplus produced by the workers overseas and the services of the City, they wish to undertake a caricature of the role French capitalism played pre-World War One and partially between wars. But the world situation has changed. Upheavals abroad would be reflected in Britain.

This same wing of the Tories, like the rest, is also constantly raving about the need for more expenditure on arms and *more* arms. With a shrinking industrial base that would impose even greater burdens on the workers. This parasitic clique has long forgotten that the only real wealth is manufacturing wealth and that investing abroad, especially in the 'under-developed' world, is to give hostages to fortune.

Rather than the 3 million unemployed which Keith Joseph complacently contemplates, a shrinking industrial base would mean 5 or even 7 million unemployed with one third of the population redundant to requirements. Britain is a manufacturing nation or it is nothing.

But the threshing about of the Tories like a wounded ox (an appropriate analogy for the castrated capitalism they would see) is itself a symptom of the deep crisis of British capitalism. The switch from Keynesianism to 'monetarist' ravings is an empirical expression of the blind alley of world and British capitalism.

The ruling class tried to crush and tame and render impotent the organised working class, using the Conservative government as its instrument. In this first dress rehearsal they were defeated, without a real mobilisation of the working class by the trade union leaders, or even a clear explanation of the issues and what lay behind the battle. This was not even a real show-down because of the weakness of British capitalism's forces and the mighty potential and actual strength of the organised working class.

But the desperate situation of British capitalism forces the ruling class to try and undermine their moral enemy whom they regard with fury and hatred — the organised working class. *If they come to power, driven forward by the pressures of their class needs, the Tories will try again to undermine, subvert and tame the unions.*

The stark reactionism of Thatcher, Keith Joseph and Heseltine shows that this is an undercurrent within the Tory Party. The cannibalistic ravings against the closed shop, from the Secretary General of the Institute of Directors, Jan Hildreth, in *The Director*, shows the feelings of his class. He claims the support of the overwhelming majority of directors in industry and commerce.

They work empirically from day to day without thinking or really understanding the relation of forces and what tomorrow will bring. Yesterday they leaned heavily on the Labour government 'to do the dirty work', as Tory MPs explained in the lobby of Parliament and in the privacy of their clubs. No-one but a right wing Labour government could impose big cuts in standards of living and reduce the welfare state to a decrepit shadow of what it had been.

'The Moor having done his duty...' the ruling class is preparing to abandon him. When the labour and trade union leaders can no longer hold back the movement of the workers to regain what they have lost in living standards during the last three years, the capitalists will turn towards an open reactionary government either of the Tories or a National government.

In spite of the lessons of 1970-4 the representatives of capital are preparing to embark on a new conflict with the unions. Politics is not a question of rationality but the movement of class forces, dictated in the last analysis by class economic interests. The crisis of the system is such that they must attempt again a showdown with the unions.

This is a recipe for class conflict which dwarfs anything in British history. Gone is the boast about the British 'genius for compromise' which was the theme *ad nauseam* of the media in the whole of the post-war period. It is certainly true that British capitalism in the past could work on the principle of agreement and bargaining with the working class, owing to her privileged position, stemming from her industrial ascendancy and the centuries of pillage of the colonial and other peoples.

That was the historical basis of 'enlightened Toryism'. The fat years are now ended and an epoch of lean years begins. There is no room for compromise, except very temporarily, between the classes. Consequently Toryism will be forced more and more to reveal its real policy —the defence of the interests of big business.

If only the labour and trade union 'lefts' had one per cent of the determination and will of the strategists of capital, the social overturn would be smooth and peaceful. In addition, in a primitive way —a groping and empirical way —these strategists work on the basis of perspectives. The labour and trade union leaders, right and left, prepare nothing and foresee nothing; they act only when they get burned by the fire of events.

The Tories have been emboldened by the recovery of their support. But the support they have regained is from the disillusioned middle class, many traditional supporters of the Labour Party, typified by the now reactionary playwrights John Braine and John Osborne, and the journalist Paul Johnson. They reflect the frenzy of the middle class, faced with high taxes and declining living standards.

In addition sections of the lumpen-proletariat and the politically backward workers have swung back to the Tories. But the basic core of organised labour has remained faithful to its traditional organisations.

This means that an election victory either for the Tory Party under its own banner or under the disguise of a National government would be a Pyrrhic one. Their electoral recovery in the industrial areas of England and in some areas of Wales and Scotland will be very temporary. Even in the middle class suburbs they will lose ground as the crisis of capitalism in Britain and the world develops. Their complete incapacity to solve the problems of the workers or of the middle class will become clear to the masses.

In elections and 'on the knocker' the Tories conduct a campaign of demagogy and of lies to deceive the people. But the real programme of the dominant leadership of Thatcher, Heseltine and Joseph is the absolutely utopian one of a return to the untrammelled exploitative society of Victorian times which 'built

Britain's greatness'. The idea of 'back to Adam Smith' or 'back to laissez faire' is an impotent dream of the long gone past.

The reality is the interest of the monopolies which dominate the British economy. The reality will also be the 3 million unemployed to be used as a whip against the employed and against the unions. Any attempt to 'confront the unions' would soon be abandoned because of the conflict it will provoke and the impotence of parliamentary laws to make a decisive difference.

What is written with workers' organisation and mobilisation cannot be changed by lawyers' tricks. That is why *The Times*, reflecting the impotence of the ruling class, is ultimately threatening·—in effect —physical confrontation with the workers. That is why supplies of CS gas, riot shields and other paraphernalia are already being stockpiled and why shields were used at Lewisham* as a test.

Before the 1970 election the manoeuvres of the Tories were similar. There was the Heathian 'Selsdon Man' and the bloodcurdling threats to 'deal with the unions' and 'cut them down to size'. The reality was different; the fantasies of reaction and their actions provoked a counter-attack by the organisations of the working class. The Tories were shattered by trade union resistance, which included the miners' strike.

Now an even more hopeless period is opening up. The projection of the production of 35 to 40 million tons of steel by 1985 has been abandoned and a minuscule target of 25 to 27 million tons set instead. The latter figure is only as high as that reached by British capitalism in 1973. This means a further deterioration in living standards, far lower than the last three years, and a continuation of the ruin and decay of Britain. Consequently the support for a Tory government would melt away faster even than in 1970-4.

But the ruling class prefers to rule through their direct instrument, the Tory Party, where possible, both in times of calm and in times of social turbulence. They concede to Labour governments only when they perceive there is no other way of 'disciplining' the workers at a time of crisis.

Now the large number of small strikes in every area —affecting engineering and other industries —indicates that the usefulness of the Labour government as a brake on the movement of the workers is very limited.

In a period of turmoil, under pressure, a Labour government

---

*In July 1977 the fascist National Front attempted to march through an area with a large black population. They were blocked on the streets by a counter demonstration in which the Labour Party Young Socialists played a prominent role. The police used riot shields in defence of the NF's 'right' to march.

would concede far more than a Conservative government. If possible the strategists of capital would, therefore, prefer a Tory or possibly a 'National government'.

If the next election is fought with the main parties intact and under their own banner, it seems likely that the Conservative Party will gain a majority, probably of 30 to 50 seats. The size of the majority will be small because of the image of Thatcher-Joseph-Heseltine, and because a decisive section of organised workers will rally round their party, the party of the trade unions. But this is just an estimate of the situation at the present time. It is always difficult to predict the result of elections. This is especially true in a period of volatility in class relations, with the sharp changes of opinion in the working class and especially the erratic swings of opinion in the middle class. *An epoch of reformism is at an end. Reform and concessions can still be gained through pressure and struggle, but can only be temporary.* At this time the bourgeoisie prefers to try and install a reliable government which will be prepared to serve its interests without looking over its shoulder at the union leaders and the Labour Party.

Big business ruled and got measures in their interests due to the acquiescence and acceptance of the trade union leaders and the Labour government during the last three years, although the interests of capital have always been decked up as the 'national interest'. The right wing trade union leaders, and sections of the left, through lack of alternative policies (which would have meant a policy for the overthrow of the rule of capital), persuaded the rank and file to accept lower wages and the whittling down of the welfare state. They leaned on the workers' loyalty and trust in their leaders and their organisations. The faith of the workers was put at the service of capital.

But the advanced workers have decided 'enough is enough'. They see such policies resulting only in an electoral weakening of the Labour government. They see the sacrifices as having been useless, the numbers of unemployed getting worse and inflation still continuing at a high rate. The ruling class too has decided that that particular 'ballgame' is over. They must look to different methods of rule, not the conveyor belt but rather more open 'confrontation' and bludgeoning of the workers.

In the inter-war period and particularly during the Tory government of 1951-64 there was a tacit acceptance by the right wing trade union leaders and by the right wing leaders of the Labour Party, of the 'divine right to rule' of the capitalists and their representatives, the Tory Party.

The Labour Party was a tame and 'loyal' opposition only

suggesting meekly the amelioration of some of the worst sores of capitalism. The trade union leaders were ensnared and entwined with the capitalist state; there had not been any national official strikes for decades. The unions were regarded almost as a department of the state machine.

But the developing crisis of decaying British capitalism resulted in the election of a Labour government in 1964. By 1967-8 already there were symptoms of the breakdown of this relationship by the pressures of the rank and file. Even under a Labour government there were official national strikes such as those of the seamen.

The strategists of capital evolved policies to put the unions in a straitjacket through enforced collaboration of the unions with the state in lowering living standards. This was the meaning of 'In Place of Strife', Labour's proposed anti-union bill which was smashed by the resistance of the unions and the rank and file of the Labour Party.

The attempt of capital, through the Labour leaders, to force this collaboration with the state was unsuccessful, however. The pressure of the workers, the move to radicalism and the active participation of the advanced layers led to a partial transformation of the unions. Left leaders more sensitive to the pressures of the rank and file were elected. They broke away from the embraces of the state machine.

In a sense the same process is taking place at the present time though the union leaders are terrified of the possible consequences. Cautiously the 'Social Contract' wage restraint policies have been repudiated at conferences and at the TUC, though the leadership has succeeded in formal votes reaffirming the rule that there should only be one wage claim every twelve months. Whether they can make this hold remains to be seen.

Protest against actual cuts in living standards has been muted. The trade union leaders have been terrified of the consequences of an avalanche of strikes and social conflict. In 1968 to 1970 they were prepared to show the way in defence of the workers' living standards. Paradoxically, the repetition of the same process has been muted by fear of a clash with the forces of the state, opening up incalculable consequences.

The secret discussions between the Tory Shadow Labour Minister, Prior, and leading members of the TUC (including former left wingers like Scanlon and Jones) were intended to find a way of compromising with the Tories if they come to power.

The TUC is trying to avoid a clash with the state similar to 1970-4, which had been provoked by the Industrial Relations Act. But the clash was not caused simply by the wish or the stupidity of the ruling class. It was caused by the frightful decay of British capitalism. *It was the expression of the irreconcilable clash of class interests in the division of 'the national cake'.*

The TUC would like to return to the relationship they had with the Tories and the state of 1951-64. They are terrified of the implications of a renewed battle on the lines of 1970-4, not because the unions are weak but because they are *stronger!* Despite mass unemployment, more workers are organised than in the whole of British history −11.5 million −more than half of the working population. A much higher proportion of the industrial working class is now organised than ever before in Britain.

Lenin conceived that it would be very difficult under capitalism for more than one-third of the workers to become organised in unions. Yet, in most of the industrialised world, the unions now comprise the majority of the working class. That is the expression of the immense power accumulated by the working class during the last three decades.

The TUC leaders and the 'sober and moderate' Tory representatives of capital (terrified by their own weakness as revealed in the events of 1970-4) may wish to come to an agreement. But such an agreement will be built on sand. The rabid bayings of the directors against the closed shop indicate the real attitude of capital.

On the other hand, the sweet cooings of Margaret Thatcher are a deception (her ideas are in reality those of Keith Joseph). She merely intends to paper over the cracks in the unity of the Tory Party before a general election. As a representative of capital she does not wish to rouse the trade union movement to mobilise the workers in advance. The serious strategists of capital wish to avoid a conflict. It is a different situation to that of 1926 or 1937-9. The ruling class prepared to provoke the General Strike on the one hand and confidently prepared in the latter period, for a bloody repression of the workers through civil war.

Now, because of social weakness, the ruling classes wish for some sort of *modus vivendi* with the trade union leaders, some sort of arrangement like that of 1951-64. The union leaders, fearful of the forces awakened and aroused in the mass movement of 1970-4, are only too willing to reciprocate and as Len Murray the General Secretary of the TUC said: 'Talk business with any government.'

But the decline of Britain, in the long term, makes this impossible. The social forces of workers and bosses cannot be reconciled. Conflict will open up, opening up in turn, not differences but great rifts in the Tory Party as to how to 'deal with the organised workers'. Nor can the trade union leaders hope to hold their members when they see further cuts in living standards while the rotten bourgeoisie is further pampered and cosseted with massive subsidies by the state.

The press, radio and TV —the entire mass media —have conducted a poisonous campaign of vilification and denigration for ten to fifteen years against the trade union movement. The difficulty for them has been that practically every section of organised workers in the different trade unions has been involved in battle and suffered from the lies, distortions and demagogy of the press since 1966.

In the meantime an element of control or, at least, checking of arbitrary sackings, has developed in the organised factories, workshops and even in organised offices and amongst white-collar workers. Solidarity action for fellow workers on strike has been developed in a whole series of disputes. This is the first heat-lightning of even bigger actions in the future.

Not seeing any mass alternative however, and regarding the Labour government as their 'own' government for a period of years, the rank and file of the trade union movement has accepted increased unemployment, inflation and cuts in living standards without mass protest.

The experience of the last three years has resulted in the accumulation of an enormous pent-up anger, resentment, frustration and bewilderment among the workers. The changed votes at union conferences, and the refusal of the TUC leaders openly to commit themselves to the 10 per cent limit on wage increases of the 'third phase' of wage restraint, was a reflection of this.   The Tories might succeed in mobilising the middle class, former Liberal voters and sections of the politically backward workers in electoral terms, because of the counter-reforms and counter-revolutionary policy of the right wing government. But in terms of social forces, this will not be decisive.

The mood of the workers is changing. They will not tolerate from a Tory government, their class enemy, what they would accept —for a time —from 'their' government. The world economic situation, as well as the shaky national situation would undermine the position of the Tory Party from its very first days.

The social peace of 1951-64 cannot be repeated. The crisis of capitalism has reached a chronic phase which threatens to engulf the workers in poverty, want and penury. Consequently, the battle of the workers will be more bitter.

Marx once wrote that a whole series of titanic battles were necessary to educate the working class —a period of wars and class struggles. The period of the last 70 years has been such a period. If capitalism has only lost a third of the world — and that mainly in the peripheral, backward areas — that has been because of the role of Stalinism and reformism.

But in Britain the policy of 'enlightened' reforms is now at an end. The ruling class is caught in the toils of the contradictions of capitalism and its own incapacity to fulfil the mighty role that it played in the past, a role that was relatively progressive for a period.

It is not a question of 'rationality', as the pragmatists in the leadership of the Labour Party and trade unions have imagined in the past. It is the lack of resources on a capitalist basis which demand the 'irrational' holding down of the wages of the workers under a Labour goverment, cutting consumption and therefore the market. If that is so under a Labour government, caught in the toils and the contradictions of capitalism, how much more so under the Tories?

The capitalists, in the last resort, do not dictate policies. The *policies are dictated to them by the crisis of their system,* for which there is no way out —except possibly for a period, at the expense of the working class. Workers are in no mood to accept tamely more sacrifices and insecurity for the benefit of big business. This is because of the impossibility of reconciling this fundamental contradiction, which the reformist and Stalinist leaders can never understand. Class conflict is inevitable.

The clash of forces will decide. The crisis — the battle over the division of the surplus produced by the workers — will therefore be very basic. There is not room for much horse-trading and bargaining as there was during the period of super-profits. Consequently, *despite the desires of the representatives of both antagonists —union leaders and Tory leaders —their relations will become even more stormy than under the Heath government of 1970-4.* Under the pressure of their impotence in the face of mass action a further differentiation would take place in the Tory Party. A gulf would open up with the backwoodsmen right wingers impatient at the failure to come to grips with the trade unions and their leadership. The right wing would be financed by the most impatient and the most stupid and reactionary wing of big business. Fissures and even an open split would develop in the Conservative Party.

At present both sides, capitalists and the leaders of the trade unions, dread a general strike —the capitalists because of their weakness, the trade union leaders because of the massed strength of the forces behind them. Nevertheless, there looms the possibility of a general strike as the culminating point of a series of clashes in various industries —local, regional and national —possibly within one or two years of a Tory government coming to power.

If Mrs Thatcher is not prepared to support her mentor, Joseph, in the question of legislation outlawing the closed shop under the next Tory government, it is because such legislation has been shown to be useless and had the opposite effect on the organised workers. It was counter-productive and merely imbued the workers with contempt for capitalist law which was clearly operating in the interests of big business. It demonstrated to the working class the immense latent power of their organisations.

The events of 1970-4 taught the strategists of capital a painful lesson. It was not possible to act on the level of 1917-20 or 1926, dangerous as these actions were to the capitalists. Even then a threat was posed to the existence of capitalist society.

But they could secure the capitulation of the trade union leaders without much difficulty. They could win a victory in 1926, although at some cost, because the generals of the enemy like JH Thomas, the railwaymen's leader, were bent on capitulation from the first hour − indeed even before the strike started.

As the great Marxists, Lenin and Trotsky explained, an all-out general strike always poses the problem of power. It is a question of either / or. Under modern conditions, the problem would be even more starkly posed. With a Marxist leadership, the trade unions could assume power peacefully, as was possible in France in 1968*. With the weakness of Marxism within the labour movement and within the working class at the present time, however, the problem will not present itself in the same way in a possible future general strike. The results could be very different to those of 1926. Before the general strike Trotsky posed the possibility that it could push the labour and trade union leaders into power. With the present relationship of forces, a general strike could mean the collapse of a Tory government and its resignation. It could force a general election. Under such circumstances, with a roused working class, Labour would win. A left Labour government would be propelled into power with all the pressures that that would set into motion.

The question is only posed here because it is necessary for Marxists to understand and prepare for the possibility of events which seem remote at the present time. *This is a period of sudden turns and breackneck changes more that at any other time in history.* The events in France of 1968 are a warning that we must keep a sensitive finger on the pulse of the changing mood of the working class.

The possible collapse of a future Tory government would see the coming to power of a left Labour government. Because of the acceleration and deepening of the processes taking place within the working class and the absolute impossibility of solving the problems

*See Clare Doyle's *Month of Revolution* (Fortress) for a full account of the revolutionary general strike which gripped France in May-June 1968.

of the crisis of capitalism (except precariously for very short periods), such a government might be forced, under the pressure of an aroused movement of millions, to go much further than its leaders would think possible at the present time.

The events in Chile in 1973 however, constitute a warning of the lengths to which the ruling class will go in defence of their profits and privileges, if they are able. It was no accident that *The Times* and *The Economist* showed approval of the coup in their editorials. The major world industrial capitalist powers have re-adopted a democratic posture, including the hypocritical espousal of 'human rights', only because there is no viable alternative for the next period.

The example of Italy has highlighted their dilemma. They have almost stepped over the point of no return in preparing to organise a military police takeover and dictatorship. Fear of the consequences, not love of democracy, has stayed their hand —fear of a counter attack by the working class on the lines of the Spanish workers' reply to the Franco coup of July 1936. But this will not permanently hold them from taking action, given the organic crisis of capitalism.

The position of the British workers is much more powerful than their Italian brothers and sisters. Their organisations are potentially much stronger. They constitute the overwhelming majority of the population. It is this power which causes the strategists of capital, like *The Times* editorial writers, to gnash their teeth in impotent rage.

The ruling class would like to emasculate the power of the trade union and labour movement and turn it into a harmless eunuch, completely obedient to the whims and dictates of capital. But they cannot do this easily. It would require a surgical operation ie civil war. Like the Italian ruling class, they are not at all certain of victory under such circumstances. They toyed with and swiftly rejected the idea of a military coup in 1974; they were faced with the revolt of the miners, backed by the labour and trade union organisations —at the bottom, and even to a large extent at the top. They had to drop the idea and were defeated in the subsequent general election.

For a whole historical period of years, stretching to possibly even a decade or more, British capitalism will stagger from crisis to crisis. The ruling class will swing desperately from one government to another.

There will be further radicalisation of the workers. Millions will be involved in political and trade union activity. The middle class will swing feverishly from one side to the other. The lumpen proletariat will be stirred from its usual passivity into political action. They too will swing from one extreme to the opposite.

What we will have in Britain, given the deep organic crisis, is the Italianisation of British politics.

There may even be the lunatic terrorist activities of a home grown English variety of ultra-lefts. The fascists have already begun such activities from the right. Like a stagnant pond under the influence of social storms the scum rises to the surface first.

But however long such a period will last, because of the weakness of the subjective factor to take advantage of this, in the ultimate, it will have to end in a solution. The militarists will risk all and take to arms to crush the labour movement even if it means civil war. *The social crisis of Britain will be protracted.* It will end either in the greatest victory of the working class achieving power and the overthrow of the rule of capital, with the installation of workers' democracy, or a military police dictatorship which will destroy the labour movement and kill millions of advanced workers, shop stewards, ward secretaries, Labour youth, trade union branch secretaries, and even individual members of the labour movement. The workers have an ominous warning —the example of Chile.

These are *long-term perspectives* over the coming period of 10 to 15 years. Events in Britain will be affected by events on the Continent, such as developments in Spain, Italy and France.

Liberals

The Liberals are a secondary party of big business in the eyes of the strategists of capital. Their function since the war was to prevent a complete and open polarisation of society between the Labour Party, as representatives of the workers, and the Tory Party, as the party of big business.

In periods of Tory government with economic difficulties and class conflict, the mass media, including the press, TV and radio, skilfully built up the Liberals. The calculation was to create a safety net to prevent disillusioned elements, particularly among the middle class and among politically backward workers, from swinging to a changing Labour Party —one which was no longer a bulwark of stability for the social system. Thus they would prevent the Labour Party from gaining an absolute majority of the votes.

It is true that they were helped in this by the timid and false policies of the Labour leaders. But leaving this aside, the ruling class have always been fearful of the effect on the workers of an absolute majority of votes for Labour, particularly if the only other party was the Tories.

In periods of Labour government the need for a safety net is not so pressing. The decisive section of big business, and their obedient tools in the media, wish for a swing to the Tories and a Tory majority. Thus the Liberals receive mainly bad publicity when they are given any prominence at all.

While desiring the continuation of the Liberal Party, for future use, the main goal of big business is a systematic smearing of the Labour Party, to the benefit of the Tories. Once right wing Labour has done sufficient to discredit the ideas of 'socialism' the way must be cleared for a strong reactionary Conservative government.

Consequently the ruling class does not worry too much if the support for the Liberals shrinks and they become a mere handful in Parliament. In any case, polarisation of the classes tends to take place under such conditions. The professional people and those sections of the middle class inclined to vote Liberal tend to swing over to the Tories. Trying to paint themselves as the 'middle way' between Labour and Tory, the Liberals are almost obliterated by the class poles of attraction.

The Liberals were 'converted' to proportional representation when their support had dwindled to a small minority of voters. They want that system because they hope to hold the balance, like the Free Democrats in Germany, between the two big parties.

Alarmed by the developing swing to the left of the workers in the trade unions and the Labour Party, the media started a campaign for proportional representation. This has been dropped —for the present —because of the opposition of the main group of Tory polititians led by Mrs Thatcher. They are afraid that *they* will not gain an absolute majority of votes at the next election. The possibility would exist then of an open Lib-Lab coalition, or more likely, as in 1924 and in 1929-31, a Labour government dependent on Liberal votes. This would be a more decisive version of the present situation.

In addition, the Tories with their utilitarian and empirical approach, thinking in fixed terms, see the Liberals as permanent arbiters deciding whether there will be Tory or Labour governments. (They see social processes very dimly and only through the spectacles of their class interest, as well as the narrow interest of their own political party and personal ambitions). They have scented the possibility of a Tory majority in the next elections. That determines their immediate policies on this question.

Of course, with a Marxist policy and leaders, the labour and trade union movement could gain a crushing majority of votes in the polls. Even without it, the intensification of the class struggles, which is inevitable in the next stage, will see millions actively involved and discussing politics.

A Tory government would mean further instability of class relations. The formula of Thatcher-Joseph-Heseltine, giving further lavish concessions to big business and taking away concessions to the workers (even if the formula was diluted), would exacerbate relations between two classes. Consequently, mass action, demonstrations and strikes could then result in a sizeable majority of votes for Labour at the polls in the future.

The Liberals have been squeezed because the capitalists and their representatives the Tories are playing for safety and the 'assurance' of rule by the Tories gaining a victory at the next election.

The Liberal leaders have been the chief propagandists for a 'National government'. This would mean a much bigger contingent of Liberals in Parliament on the 'National ticket' —a 'government comprising all parties' ie Tory, Liberal and right wing Labour. The latter are not far removed from the Liberals in outlook anyway, as Prentice, Taverne, Mayhew and George Brown* have shown. There are others of the same ilk still in the Parliamentary Labour Party.

Ironically, by the dialectic of the class struggle, the polarisation of classes that this would involve would mean, over a period, not the enhancement of the role of the Liberals, but their massive destruction as a serious political force.

The Labour Government

Disillusionment among the advanced workers at the result of the policies of the Labour government is widespread. Among the backward workers there has been a revulsion against Labour politics.

The Social Contract was accepted grudgingly by the workers because they believed the pleas of the Labour leaders who argued that through the acceptance of sacrifices and lowered standards of living they would secure the end of inflation and mass unemployment. The promises of massive industrial revival through greatly increased investment which would lead to greater increases in living standards had their effect. In addition, the appeals for patriotism and the 'Give a year for Britain' slogan undoubtedly evoked a response.

But the main reason for this support was the lack of a viable *mass alternative* that the workers could see offering a way out. With the left trade union leaders committed to acceptance of government policies, with only faintly expressed criticism from the Tribunite MPs, the workers could see no practical way out.

*Prominent right wing Labour MPs who all left the Labour Party and ended up supporting the Conservative, Social Democrat or Liberal Parties.

Even most of those militant layers of the shop stewards' committees who were sceptical of the government's promises and the attitude of their own union leaders could not convince the rank and file on the shop floor that it was a practicable proposition to take on the combined weight of the employers, the government and their own union leaders at the same time.   The mood of the workers was to accept and hope for better times in the short term future. After two years of falling living standards, increased unemployment (which shows no sign of abating) and with inflation still at a high level, the mood has begun to change.

A 10 per cent limit on wage increases (the official target) would not even allow compensation for the inflation of 17 per cent let alone taking into account the level of taxes which would reduce the increases for the higher levels of earning by at least 30 per cent to 50 per cent.   The excuse used for increasing prices was 'extraneous influences', like devaluation. This is one of the main causes of the present inflation and represents a further cut in real wages as its effects work through the economy.

The myth of wage increases being responsible for price increases and for the rise in unemployment has largely been exploded in the minds of the big majority of workers. The attempts to maintain a third year of wage restraint, with the support of the union leaders, has met resistance and has been rejected by delegate conferences representing a majority of workers and even at the TUC itself.

However, the limit of 12 months between wage settlements was accepted by the TUC conference. There is enormous pressure on the individual union leaders to make it stick. Reluctantly, large sections of workers have accepted it. But it just requires one important union to break through for it to collapse. Even if there were a national strike on the issue by one union the psychological barriers would be broken.

To maintain the 10 per cent limit on wage increases will be virtually impossible. The hyena press would once again be perfidiously howling that wage increases cause inflation.

The slight fall in the inflation rate from 17 per cent to 16.5 per cent announced in September 1977 (on the July figures) has been caused by the difficulties of the world market and the fall in the price of raw materials and foodstuffs imported from abroad. This trend may continue if the *decline in the rate of increase* of world capitalist industry continues and the capitalist world moves into recession and slump.

But as in 1974-5 that will not mean a fall in prices, merely a *fall in the rate of increase in prices* and much bigger unemployment. Under present day capitalism the workers are trapped between the devil of high inflation and the deep sea of recession, suffering both at once in what has been termed 'recession-flation' or 'slump-flation'.

After all the sacrifices, Britain will simply have moved from slump to slump. The media, after the TUC conference, changed tactics. They had been careful, slanting the news to undermine the Labour government and even attacking the Prime Minister, who ceased to be 'Sunny Jim' Callaghan and became a 'shifty politician' not to be trusted. Now they changed to present the situation of 'the country' as rosy —a balance of payments surplus, inflation overcome, share prices booming, good prospects for industry —'Britain' is ready to leap ahead again. The reason for this is that the organised workers want to regain the standards of living lost over the last three years. They are thoroughly angered by the results of enforced wage restraint.

The ruling class is still hoping that the 12 month rule can be maintained and that they can limit wage increases by the fear of renewed inflation. Hence the propaganda that there will be a 'solution' of British capitalism's problems in the coming period. They gloss over and hide the fact that the *increase in investment is miniscule and that there is an actual fall in production.*

The ruling class have —temporarily —reversed their attitude to the Labour government in the faint hope that it can still 'deliver the goods', through the aid of the trade union leaders, and at least partially maintain wage restraint. The City and the industrialists must hardly believe their luck in succeeding to cut standards of living by the biggest amount in over 40 years —and this without any mass upheaval.

One reason why the Labour government maintained itself in power for a much longer period than the Marxists anticipated was because the ruling class had no immediate alternative. As long as the government was increasing their profits and succeeding in holding back the workers, why risk a change and stir up the opposition of the organised workers?

The acceptance by the workers of the measures of the Labour government (because the organised workers saw no other way out) had, as a further consequence, created the political and industrial 'lull' which lasted for about 12 months. It was not only a period of lull but even of mild reaction. The right wing in the trade unions and the Labour Party had a temporary resurgence. Amongst the advanced workers there was a feeling of frustration and dismay, in many cases verging on demoralisation.

A mood of pessimism and confusion swept the advanced trade unionists and active Labour Party workers. This mood, and the apathy and inertia of the mass, yet further emboldened the worst reactionary elements in the factories, even to the extent of the more demoralised elements supporting, half-surreptitiously, the National Front.

One main reason for this development was the lack of understanding on the part of the advanced layers of shop stewards and active workers in the trade unions and labour movement of perspectives and theory —ie the fundamental ideas of Marxism. Historically of course, this is understandable, given the policies of the left reformist trade union and labour leaders and the degeneration of the Communist Party leadership.

What it meant was that, in the eyes of the masses, the workshop union representatives and the leading elements in the Party branches had no explanation and no answer to the problems of inflation and unemployment.

In fact many millions even half accepted the propaganda of the Labour and TUC leaders. Most were bewildered and confused. This reacted on the mass of more inert and politically indifferent trade unionists on the shop floor —even on those closest to the rank and file workers, the shop stewards. It was a case of one factor reacting on the other and back again.

Many of the most militant shop stewards, councillors and Labour Party activists, failing to understand the temporary mood of the workers, and instinctively recognising that they were being duped, succumbed to moods of despair themselves. The mood of the ranks infected the attitude of their leaders. This in turn was relayed back, further reinforcing the mild reaction.

Even within the most revolutionary periods there will be interludes of reaction, despair, frustration, indifference and apathy. There will be irrational actions and reactionary attitudes by broad sections of the working class. Even advanced layers, not understanding the reasons for this, can lapse into reactionary moods of despising and blaming the workers for their apparent quiescence or particular mood, regarding themselves as separate and apart from the workers. In a sense that is the basis for Stalinism and reformism among some layers of the advanced workers.

Experience will teach the workers en masse as they move into activity, which will be forced on them by the struggle against unemployment, for shorter hours, better conditions etc, in defence of living standards and for their improvement. They will come up against the granite barrier of the world crisis of capitalism. More and more broad sections will begin to understand that capitalism is responsible for their daily problems and anxieties.

The real difficulty has been that the most active and advanced workers in the trade union and labour movement, though feeling this themselves, have not been able to convey it to the working class as a whole, even to the rank and file workers in the factories where they work. This problem arises from the mis-education of militants by the Communist Party and from the narrow, merely trade union 'education' of shop stewards by the unions themselves.

The lull, in terms of the passivity of the workers, is now at an end. There have been no big defeats of the working class during the last three years.

In a sense the workers have been resting after the Herculean struggles of 1970-4. They have waited on events, hoping for some miraculous changes from the Labour government which they brought to power.

Disappointed in their hopes, they have begun to turn to the industrial struggle. Far more than in 1968-70 there has been an epidemic of small strikes in most important industries and in practically every sizeable town in every region.

The media has deliberately refrained from giving publicity to these strikes, as they have covered up reports of strikes in other countries. They are afraid that, with the present mood, the contagion may spread.

Only strikes such as the bakers', or ones involving tens of thousands of workers in lay-offs or actions like the strike in the car industry, have been given any real publicity. The small strikes taking place are on a whole host of different issues —victimisation, conditions, bonuses, holidays, sick pay, pensions and wages among many others.

An important development is the large number of small factories and workshops, previously unorganised or with small union membership, fighting against sweatshop conditions and for union organisation and recognition. Contrary to what the sectarians would have us believe, this indicates the enormously attractive power of the organised trade union and labour movenent, inherited from the past.

It is no longer possible for the employers to concede a comfortable and bearable standard of living —that is why Callaghan and Healey have openly warned against attempts to regain lost living standards, because British capitalism cannot afford this. It will be impossible for any length of time for trade union leaders to hold back their members. Pressure of the members, particularly the active layers, will force them to change attitudes as is the case with the miners, the railwaymen and, partly, the TGWU leaders. With a conflict of interests of massive proportions, the employers in the strong sectors of engineering who employ large numbers of workers —on the docks, in the car industry etc, will have to concede increases higher than 10 per cent or face bitter strikes.

If the union leaders will not lead official national strikes, over a period there will be a rash of unofficial strikes in many areas. Learning that isolated action would not be sufficient, there would then be the tendency to link up through the shop stewards on a national scale to take joint action.

Such mounting pressure is more likely to have the result that union leaders would act on a national scale; national strikes would be on the order of the day. The struggles already involve skilled and unskilled, white collar as well as industrial workers. Some of the mass production industries, like Leyland and Fords, have seen big, unofficial strikes and demonstrations.

What happened after similar periods of 'restraint' (ie after disguised cuts in real wages) will be repeated on a higher scale, this time not during a period of Tory government, but of Labour government. The Labour government can maintain itself in power over the next months, and possibly into the New Year, so long as it can maintain even a partial incomes policy.

From the viewpoint of the capitalists this is 'the best government we have got' while it acts so favourably. It is not accidental that, for the first time in history, the possibility of the coming to power of a Tory government resulted in a fall in shares on the Stock Exchange. £1400 million was wiped out in 24 hours in March of this year (1977), when the vote of no confidence in the Labour government was being moved.

That expressed a lack of confidence that the Thatcher leadership could prevent a titanic confrontation between the classes. For the same reason, after the TUC's reassurance on the 12 month rule, shares rose recently.

The inevitable exasperation of the working class, expressing itself in mass action, will result in pressure on the government, the TUC, the left Labour MPs and the union leaders. This will be particularly so in the industrial unions like the TGWU, the AUEW and even the GMWU.

Under such conditions, with a further fall in production, any small reflationary measures from Healey, like the suggested £1000 million or even £2000 million, will evaporate like a drop of water on a hot stove.

Mounting unemployment of up to 2 million this winter will get the government into serious difficulties. There will be irresistible pressure for further action to be taken, though it goes against the wishes of the TUC leaders who want to do nothing but wait for a better situation next year.

The recession which is developing on a world scale may be temporarily halted by panic measures on the part of the powerful states of capitalism — West Germany, Japan and the United States — and following them, the others. But marginal measures of deficit spending etc., will be merely cosmetic without affecting the situation fundamentally. If they are not then successful, the decline in world trade of the last few months will increase even further. That will have a catastrophic effect on all the major capitalist countries, particularly the weaker ones like Britain.

The big employers have had a profits binge during the last few years of wage restraint. If the TUC and the union leaders can succeed in compromising and preventing big strikes in such industries as engineering and mining, there is still the possibility of the minority Labour government staggering on well into next year.

The strategists of capital are still hoping that they can manoeuvre the trade union and labour leaders to restore right wing control of the Labour Party, by new reforms which would re-institute control by the right-wing over the NEC and the constituencies. This would give them the old game of Peter and Paul once again. They build their hopes on such fantasies.

The objective situation which is developing however — the collisions between the classes — would make this a repulsive anachronism. The eggs have been broken, and cannot be put back in the shell again. Any attempt on these lines would provoke a violent reaction from the rank and file of the trade unions and the Labour Party.

Such schemes are hatched in the editorial offices of *The Times* and the Tory clubs where the right wing Labour leaders and some right wing trade union leaders are quite at home, completely remote from the rank and file of the wards and union branches. The right wing of the Labour Party still fantasises that it can restore complete and untrammelled domination of the Labour Party and the trade unions as in the 'fifties' and early 'sixties'. They delude their cronies in big business that this is still possible.

The serious elements like Roy Jenkins* have accepted the impossibility of regaining complete control of the Labour Party or of organising an intermediate 'social democratic' (in reality pseudo-Liberal) Party through agreement, fusion or alliance with the Liberals. He has departed to the lush pastures of the EEC Commission. Brian Walden has followed to a highly paid job in TV. Dick Taverne, Christopher Mayhew, Woodrow Wyatt and Reg Prentice, being more obtuse, have tried the 'middle way' and will

---

*Roy Jenkins, a former deputy leader of the Labour Party, was a driving force in the split by a number of Labour MPs in 1980-1 to form the Social Democratic Party.

sink into obscurity. The parlous plight of the Liberals at the present time is sufficient testimony to this dead-end.

If there were a new 'golden age' of capitalism internationally and nationally —a new period of capitalist expansion —then a middle way would be a viable proposition. The ruling class could make some concessions to the workers giving them some crumbs from a greatly increased cake. But that is not the perspective. More and more right wing ideas will seem as if they come from an antediluvian past. The right wing MPs are Neanderthal fossils.

The strategists of capital have inconsistent and contradictory aims. On the one hand they try to paint a picture of Callaghan and Healey having 'solved' the problems of the economy, in order to reconcile the workers with the 12 month rule, salvaging as much of the Social Contract incomes policy as possible. On the other hand they wish to rub the noses of the masses in the mess, to convince them of the errors and consequences of 'socialism'.

The strategists of capital will switch to an out and out reactionary government, more right wing than the Tories have been for generations, with its leaders even more reactionary than Baldwin in the 1920s. But before they do that, they will try and demoralise the working class by further attacks on living standards, discrediting the union leaders by making them accomplices of the Labour government in these measures.

Nineteen seventy-eight will be the fourth year of the Labour government. This is the usual 'normal term' of a government in Britain. Dialectically, one of the reasons for the lasting in office of what is now a minorty Labour government, is the extreme enfeeblement of British capitalism. The government is delaying an election like Mr Micawber in Dickens' novel, *David Copperfield* —in the hope that 'something will turn up'.

But the realities of the world market, the grim fall in industrial production, in the output of real wealth, a possible increase in the number of unemployed to close to 2 million during the winter all makes the outlook for what might 'turn up' quite grim.

The figures of profits and stock exchange shares, the balance of payments figures, a small fall in inflation, cannot provoke more than a passing euphoria, despite the propaganda of the media. The workers will contrast them with the continuing fall in their real wages, the lack of spending money for a few 'extras', and the stark poverty of the lower paid just above or, in many cases, below social security levels. This will alienate them even more. The flaunting of the frivolous waste of resources by the rich, while many more youngsters are plunged into the insecurity and despair of life on the dole will further anger the workers. More redundancies and more insecurity, the lack of real investment in manufacturing industry will infuriate the workers as the facts percolate through to them.

The expectation of Denis Healey or, in reality, the Treasury officials, of an increase in world trade giving succour to the British economy was a gambler's throw against all the odds. World trade is already beginning to fall and that will create new difficulties for British capitalism.

The Labour Party

It now seems unlikely that the Labour Party can win an election next year.

Organisationally the Party has suffered a further decline. As its 1977 conference report shows, the membership of the wards and constituencies has declined. In many areas the wards and General Management Committees (GMCs) are composed largely of old people. Many wards and GMCs have shrunk to a handful of Neanderthal councillors, with a small clique of supporters.

The right wing policies of the Labour government are hardly a means of stimulating the active rank and file with enthusiasm. Nor are they calculated to induce active trade union workers and shop stewards to join. Most of those who join, at present, are more likely to do so to oppose the present policies of the government.

This steady decline in the active membership has extended over more than a quarter of a century with many minor ups and downs. But the decline in the passive dues-paying membership has been even more marked.

Despite this there has been an even greater decline in the power and influence of the Neanderthal MPs and councillors. They retain a semblance of influence only in the worst rotten boroughs, wards and GMCs that have a 'dead' membership and a virtually complete lack of outside activity. These are almost the only parties where the right wing has succeeded in maintaining their influence.

Even there, the influx of some active people, in many cases putting forward some sort of alternative policies, can rapidly change the position. That is an anticipation and a harbinger of the coming processes of change.

The experiences of the Labour government of 1964-70 and of the present Labour government are preparing explosive changes of consciousness of the active workers in the Labour Party and trade unions.

Also, within the broad masses —usually apathetic or even luke-warm, politically —changes of consciousness are forcing themselves to the surface under the whip of necessity. As in the past, there remains a core of organised workers supporting the Labour movement.

As events develop, particularly with a reactionary government, with Labour in opposition and the trade unions and the Labour Party swinging to the left, new layers will become active. They will turn inevitably to the mass trade unions and to their political expression, the Labour Party.

What the sectarians on a world and national scale are incapable of understanding is the practically inexhaustible reservoir of support retained by the traditional organisations of the working class, especially the Labour Party in Britain.

Millions of workers, not awakened to active political life, are being shaken up by the results of capitalism's inability to maintain employment or to give reasonable conditions of existence. They will turn to the trade unions first and then, drawing political conclusions, will swing to the Labour Party.

With the convulsions that capitalism is suffering, a Thatcher-led Tory government would provoke countless thousands of workers to mobilise against them. It was in this sense that Marx spoke of the revolution sometimes needing the whip of the counter-revolution. Of course Toryism is not counter-revolution as such, but it will be a government of counter-reforms in relation to the living standards and the social wage and one of capitalist attack. It will correspondingly rouse the active workers into opposition.

This will be because of an enormous wave of criticism in the Labour Party and the trade unions as a consequence of a new defeat for Labour, following the counter-reformist policies taken by the Callaghan government. The Labour Party, under a left, Tribunite leadership, will move further towards radical policies than at any time in its history. The groundswell of criticism will have this effect. In addition, the influence of Marxism in the Labour Party will be increased. It has already under difficult conditions, had a perceptible effect in raising the level of consciousness wherever Marxist ideas have been influential.

There will be an enormous ferment of ideas among the workers, and hundreds of thousands will become active, as the crisis deepens and the battle between the classes develops. The clear ideas of Marxism must be expounded with a patient, friendly approach. The platform of Marxism will gain a greater support *as events demonstrate its correctness*. The ideas of Marx, Engels, Lenin and Trotsky will become a powerful influence throughout the labour movement.

Neverthless, initially the ideas of the left Tribunite MPs and the left leaders will become the dominant ones in the movement —both in the trade unions and the Labour Party. In the decisive areas they will become almost completely dominant and practically take control of the organisation of the Labour Party and the unions. In a sense *they would constitute the labour movement.* Processes that have been accumulating for more than a decade would have meant a quantitative leading to a qualitative change.

The Youth

Mass unemployment will now be a permanent feature of capitalism throughout the now shortened trade cycle, both under 'boom' and 'slump' conditions. It bears particularly harshly upon the youth and upon women workers.

More than half the unemployed are aged 25 or under. Hundreds of thousands are going straight onto the dole from university, colleges and schools. A great part of the unemployed youth are black, without hope of a job.

The youth on the dole will be looking for an explanation of their misfortune and a solution to their problems. Hatred of the capitalist system will grow. Tens of thousands could be won to the programme of Marxism. Even more important are the new layers of youth entering employment in industry, the factories and also the offices. They too will be looking for a political lead. Tens and even hundreds of thousands of young people in the schools and universities are worried about their future.

New moods begin to affect the youth even before they affect the working class as a whole, and before it moves into action. In that sense they are like the students —a barometer of moods in society as a whole.

In particular, the middle class fluctuates and moves in a very violent and volatile way in periods of social crisis. Electorally, for example, sections of the middle class in Britain have swung 180 degrees to the Tories after swinging completely against them in 1974.

The middle class, and particularly students, do not have a stable social basis in society as do the bourgeoisie and the proletariat. They are squeezed between the mighty antagonists in class society and swing between the opposite class poles.

In the rarified atmosphere of the universities all sorts of sects can get a hearing. The students they influence usually drop out of politics soon after leaving the isolated cloisters of the universities, when the huge gap between the ideas they have accepted and the reality of life become apparent.

But many layers of worthwhile students, school students and, in particular, students in the colleges of further education from working class origin, can be won to the standpoint and ideology of the working class.

Throughout history, in all countries, the youth have been the backbone of the revolutionary movement in its early stages of development. This is just as true in relation to the movement in Britain. When convinced of ideas, young people will apply enormous energy, enthusiasm and sacrifice for the cause.

The Communist Party

After 50 years of existence the Communist Party of Britain (CP) is once again in crisis. Lacking the advantage of the mass membership and support that the Communist Parties of Italy and France have, it finds itself in difficulties, similar to those being experienced by the small Communist Parties of Western Europe.

Where the masses can discern no fundamental difference between a mass party and a very much smaller one, they will tend to support the bigger one. That is a social law of politics.

In the past the association with the October revolution was a powerful magnet and a source of strength for the Communist Party in Britain. That has changed into its opposite. The abandonment of 'Marxist-Leninist' pretences by the leadership has reinforced this process. There is not room for two mass reformist parties in Britain; therefore the reformist degeneration of the British CP has contributed massively to the decline of its organisation.

They have the worst of both worlds. They have the odium of totalitarian policies linked to Moscow and have lost the dynamism of the past and the revolutionary policies that constitute the real attraction for the militant minority. As a consequence there has been a staggering decline in the mass support of the CP.

At elections, under conditions of mass upsurge, their vote has fallen below that of nearly half a century ago. In this parliament they have not dared to put a single candidate forward in by-elections because they probably would have obtained an even more derisory vote than the sects.

At a time of disillusionment with the policies of the Labour government, a genuine revolutionary Communist Party might have made at least limited gains in mass support and big gains in the support of the active conscious layer of workers seeking an alternative to the counter-reformist policies of the Labour government. But far from this, they have declined in support not only among the masses, but among the trade union and Labour Party activists.

Only among the students, ironically the former stamping ground of the ultra-left sects, has the Communist Party made any sizeable gains. Even in Scotland they have declined, where for a period they seemed to be holding their ground in the traditionally red areas of Clydeside and other industrial areas.   Their appeal to youth –the key in the long term –is negligible. It was not for nothing that Lenin declared that 'he who has the youth has the future'. The Young Communist League is an organisation of a few hundred mainly 'paper members'. Without education, without real cadres, with its leaders as much soaked in the cynicism and contempt for the working class as their elders, this organisation has no future as a mass organisation. It is largely a fictitious organisation propped up by the CP in a desperate attempt to build a counter-weight to the Labour youth who have rejected Stalinism.

Among the unions, however –particularly the key ones of the miners, TGWU, AUEW and other industrial workers' unions –they have retained powerful positions inherited from the past. They also have strategic and influential positions in some engineering factories among the shop stewards.

The organic scepticism and lack of perspectives of members of the CP is reflected in its degeneration in many areas into an old peoples' club. It has no attraction for people looking for a revolutionary way out of their problems. Harold Wilson's sneer at the lack of social danger to capitalism from the palsied and sclerotic Communist Party is not very wide of the mark.

The Stalinists retain all the worst vices of bureaucratic centralism inherited from the past. The have lost the former revolutionary faith of their predecessors. At least the old leadership such as Gallacher, Pollitt and Campbell, had some real connection with the revolutionary movements of the workers in the past. The new leaders reek of middle class respectability. The degeneration of the CP into largely a petit-bourgeois sect –in outlook and now, to some extent in membership –is faithfully reflected in the leadership.

The CP leadership has never intended to institute a real Marxist criticism of the way the Moscow bureaucracy grew up and carried through a *political counter-revolution* against the state set up by Lenin and Trotsky, or of the fact that, while state ownership and a plan remain without workers' democracy and control, the state will continue to be used for the purpose of defending and increasing the power, privileges, incomes and prestige of the bureaucratic caste who control the USSR. *They will not explain that Russia remains a grotesque caricature of the ideal of Marx, Lenin and Trotsky and that it is a monstrously deformed, bureaucratic Bonapartist workers' state.*

While they assert their 'independence' from Moscow in their own mild way, the CP leadership has become dependent on another pole of attraction −the pole of reformism which, in the last analysis, reflects the pressures of the interests of capitalism in a class society.

The reason for the muffled discontent of industrial workers in the Communist Party with the policies of their leaders, is that they have become indistinguishable from the policies of the left union leaders and the left Tribunite MPs. They wish to ingratiate themselves with 'respectable society' by showing that they are as 'realistic' and 'down to earth' as the reformists. This arises from an underlying contempt for the workers and a disbelief in revolutionary perspectives.

The modern leaders of the CP have never really studied the works of the great teachers of Marxism, as a fundamental guide to action, strategy and tactics. They have busied themselves with little horse-deals and manoeuvres with the ruling class parties and the reformists. They have miseducated their members for decades. This has taken its toll on them.

The CP can out-match the reformist leaders in every way as far as 'putting it across on their own members' is concerned, but now the chickens are coming home to roost. If their policy is hardly distinguishable from that of the left reformists, why should the mass of workers support them, especially since, in spite of cautious and careful efforts at presenting themselves as 'independent', their party is tarred with the same brush as 'totalitarian Russia'.

The lack of a decisive break with Moscow on Marxist lines condemns the 'liberal' wing of the Communist Party to sterility. Their organic contempt for theory as a guide (not as some abstract mysticism) condemns them to oscillate between left-reformism in their own country and muted critcisms of Russian Stalinism and a break with their own past and with Stalinism in Russia.

They have edged away from from nationalist Russian Stalinism, not back to the internationalism of Lenin but to a vulgar petit-bourgeois nationalism. If they have not yet reached the depth of reformism reached by the Spanish and Italian Communist Parties, it is because of their own weakness.

The active sections of the official CP, in the leadership as well as in many branches, are now dominated by trendy middle class types. The students and professional people tend to elbow out the workers and to set the tone in the attitudes of the Communist Party. Like the sects they take up as major issues all sorts of incidental by-products of the class system.

The CP remains a sect. If somewhat smaller than it was, it is still by far the biggest of the sects.

Fascism

The decay of capitalism brings in its train misery and want for large sections of the population. To the working and middle class it brings anxieties, worries, unemployment and privation for many. The inner areas of the big cities have been left to decay and rot, as has happened in the strongest capitalist country in the world, the United States.

All the utopias of the reformists, left and right, of unemployment being a thing of the past, of an enlightened state looking after the unfortunate victims of a competitive society, of cities booming, are now shown up for what they are — mere fictions. The Macmillanite and Churchillite Tories also disseminated the illusion of a 'never had it so good' society. Now a Labour government presides over a real slashing of living standards. So far this year (1977), according to official figures (which are dolled up with averages), earnings including overtime etc, have risen by 8.8 per cent while prices (to September) have risen by 17.8 per cent, which is more than double the rise in earnings not allowing for taxation.

The social wage has also been slashed. Health, housing, transport and social services have been cut to the bone, while in many cities some Labour, as well as Tory councillors, have grown fat on graft and corruption. In decaying inner city areas, vandalism among the youth is rife. Football hooliganism is a symptom of despair amongst the youth who vent their frustrations by emotional involvement with a certain team.

Petty crime among black and white youth has leaped to unheard of figures. Youth without jobs and without amenities are searching for answers to their problems.

For a period, the trade unions supplied no answer because of the Social Contract.

The black population has tended to be concentrated in the worst areas of housing and congestion in the slums of the big cities. They came at a time of great opportunities for employment etc. Now these are past and there is competition for even the most menial of jobs.

Many youth, adults and old people are not at work, where they would become subject to the disciplines of a job and come under pressure to adopt a trade union outlook involving solidarity and organisation.

The poorer strata of the population are now virtual paupers, worse off than pre-war. Labour councils, in power for decades, have merely uprooted many communites and replaced them with the abomination of high rise flats. The Labour government seems to have forgotten them. All these factors, and many more have resulted in the demoralisation of some of the lower strata of the population.

The middle class too has received short shrift from both Labour and Tory governments. That is why in Scotland and to a certain extent in Wales also there has been a resurgence of long dead nationalism. Scotland and the Strathclyde area in particular have the worst slums in Europe. This is the climate of despair in which small shopkeepers, professional people, small businessmen and farmers react against the remote and 'uncaring' English bureaucrats and officials in London, pulling behind them also politically backward layers of white collar workers and even industrial workers.

There have been Labour governments in Britain for 16 years, but in every direction people can see only a worsening of the situation. Nationalism was the penalty the labour movement paid for the policies of reformism which have collapsed in ruins.

In England, for similar reasons though on a smaller scale there has been resurgence of reaction. Rising prices, lack of jobs, no solution to the housing problems — the whole gangrenous sickness of capitalism in decay leads to frustration and anger. For the moment the middle class have swung back to the Tories.

Many prejudices among the backward layers of the working class have been inherited from the imperialist past. Many of the old people have been shaken by the influx of 'aliens' or black 'foreigners' into their areas. There is an acute shortage of any sort of accommodation. Unemployment affects the inner areas of the big cities nearly as much as the 'depressed regions' of the North East, Wales, Scotland and Merseyside. There all the problems of capitalism come together in an acute and aggravated form.

There is frustration too at the apparent passivity and acceptance of cuts in living standards by the labour and trade union movement, at the failures of the 'socialism' of the Labour government and the incapacity and feebleness of the Communist Party.

The large scale immigration of an earlier period was used in the poisonous slanting of news in the mass media, planting the idea that immigrants were taking jobs and housing from the native population, or were living in luxury on social security payments etc.

All this had its effect on the backward layers of the population. The black immigrant population was an ideal target as a scapegoat. It is in this atmosphere that various virulent groups have sprung up.

As we predicted, the 'high-falutin' fascist reaction of Mosley was a non-starter. He based himself on the grandiose dream of being the 'leader of one European nation' (impossible to create because of the discordant imperialist-capitalist antagonisms) with the whole of Africa turned into a slave satellite.

Mosley ingloriously faded away. Fascism requires not a world utopia but a reactionary *nationalist* standpoint, appealing to the prejudices of the backward layers of the population.

The National Front, stemming partly from the defunct 'League of Empire Loyalists', bases itself on the gut prejudices of the criminal lumpen proletariat that infest the inner areas of big cities like London and Birmingham.

Since the split with Kingsley Reed forming the National Party, it has taken on many of the attributes of the open fascist and nazi groupings from which its main leaders, John Tyndall and Martin Webster came. This association with fascism will, in the long run, be the kiss of death for the Front.

The lurid campaigns in the press about the tens of thousands of Ugandan Asians descending after their expulsion by Amin*, came as a tonic to the National Front at a time when they were in the doldrums. The stoking up of prejudice by the press prevented the disintegration of the Front at that time.

But it is significant that most of their gains have come from the demoralised lumpen section of the population in the inner areas of some of the big towns and cities. These are areas of high concentration of immigrant populations.

In the East End of London, they have gained support in the former areas where Mosley was strong —in some parts of Hackney, Shoreditch, Limehouse and Bethnal Green.

The same types of hawkers, small businessman and small shopkeepers looking for some explanation for their difficulties have fallen for the poison of racialism expressed in an even viler form since the split: Webster and Tyndall have adopted the Nazi and Klu Klux Klan definition of an Indian and a Negro as anyone with a single grandparent of this origin. All are to be forcibly deported without exception! This repugnant racialism delights the criminal lumpens who compensate themselves for their lowly position by regarding themselves as belonging to a 'superior' race. These are the overtones of open nazism —not disguised but open racialism.

*Idi Amin, the Ugandan dictator presided over mass murders and expulsions of Ugandans of Asian origin. Some fled to Britain, leading to racist propaganda by the press.

There is a sprinkling of middle class elements and even some politically backward workers within their ranks. But from the point of view of a would-be fascist organisation, the tactics of the Front have been suicidal for the long-term.

They have attempted to get a basis among the working class, trying to penetrate areas and constituencies where the Labour Party and the labour movement are strongest. This will be a fatal turn for the Front because a fascist movement must gain its *main* support from the middle class. With such a basis it can *then* draw behind it certain crazed sections of embittered and backward workers.

Fascism by its very nature must draw its main forces from the 'frenzied petit-bourgeois, ruined by capitalism'. This is only possible where the labour movement is paralysed by its leaders, and fails to show an alternative to the people as a whole.

In any event the situation has changed completely since the pre-war years. The ruling class has learned a sharp lesson in the dangers of losing political control and handing over the reins of the state to mad demagogues such as Hitler and Mussolini. They are not predisposed to cede power to their slavish and lunatic imitators in Britain or any other country for that matter.

In countries where there has been a counter-revolution in the post-war period such as Greece and Chile it is the *army and police apparatus* which has been used to establish a military-police Bonapartist dictatorship. It is true that these have acted in the same way as the fascists, using them as a model in order to establish a totalitarian state. They have attempted the complete destruction of the organisations of the working class and all the democratic rights which go with them. But they have been far weaker and without a mass basis. The Greek Colonels' regime* collapsed after seven years —a relatively short period. Probably the Chilean regime will not last much longer, despite ferocious repression.

The Chilean ruling class used the fascist 'Fatherland and Freedom' party as an *auxiliary* to the generals. Their role was one of provocations, bombings, assassinations and the creation of chaos in the country. *They could never hope to take power on their own.* They have played no significant or any independent role since the assumption of power by the Generals' junta.

In Italy the neo-fascists have tried to play the same role. They did not dare to aspire to seize power for themselves. The working class, through its organisations —trade unions and workers' parties —was too strong for them to be able to do so.

They have played the role of *jackal* to the military, trying to

---

*The regime collapsed after supporting an abotive coup in Cyprus in 1974.

provoke the army to take power by creating an atmosphere of lawlessness and chaos with bombings and assassinations. They have attacked trade unions and workers' political demonstrations and headquarters with bombs, blown up banks and business premises etc, all to give the impression of an anarchic breakdown of society.

All these activites over a period of years (over a decade or so) were carried out in collusion with the Christian Democratic Ministers of Interior and Justice, and with the heads of police, Military Intelligence and the Special Branch.

The neo-fascists were merely an auxiliary of the state to carry out the dirty work for capitalism in a society undergoing crisis.

This is entirely different to the position with Mussolini and his fascists. He burned, assassinated and butchered his way to gain support for fascism from among the petit-bourgeois and prepare his own coup with a mass force behind him. This was also the position with Hitler. The forces of the state were placed at his disposal once he had won the big majority of the maddened middle class.

In Italy, at the prompting of the CIA, the bourgeoisie and the state machine braced themselves for a seizure of power by the military, with the fascist thugs as an auxiliary. At the last moment they hesitated and abandoned the project.

The reason was their fear of the inevitable reaction from the powerful proletariat. *It would lead to a civil war,* which they were not certain they would win. A coup of the military would have provoked a situation like that of July 1936 in Spain.

So the capitalist rulers are not prepared to risk this kind of action until there is absolutely no other way out and they are forced to put their whole existence at stake. Consequently they have largely dispensed with the service of the neo-fascists — at least for the time being. The latter have anyway split in two and are now completely ineffective.

Thus we see that *it is wrong to draw lessons from the past in the way the sects do — expecting every detail to be repeated in exactly the same way.* The only time they use the writings of Lenin and Trotsky they misuse them because of their lack of understanding of Marxist method.

This method takes all social processes in the interaction on the classes in society, the strength and the relation of forces, the international environment, balance of classes and so on. The enormous preponderance of the working class as a social force, the fact that it is the overwhelming majority in all the main countries of industrialised capitalism must be weighed against the shrinking numbers, strength and cohesion of the various strata of the middle class. Their combative power is shrinking when opposed to that of the working class.

Of course, it is possible for individuals and even small politically backward groups infected with racialist ideas to support the National Front. Some will even join. But they can only be attracted in any numbers by a dynamic mass movement of fascism −even then they will be mainly unemployed and absolutely demoralised workers. This kind of development can only come after *some decisive defeats* of the workers. Not only one, but under modern conditions there would have to be a few. Yet there has been no great defeat for the proletariat in decades.

Despite unemployment, the trade unions are growing in numbers and strength! The position of the proletariat is one of unprecedented power, despite the recent paralysis caused by the Social Contract and the disillusionment with the measures of the Labour government.

The Marxists must publicise the dangers of fascist reaction and attacks on Labour Party premises and meetings. The attempts to burn down various left wing bookshops and premises underline the danger these scum represent to the labour movement even at the present time.

The movement and the working class must be educated to the danger these organisations, however small, represent to the rights of workers.

Supporters of Marxism will never tire of pointing out that the real aim of these organisations is to atomise *the working class* and render it helpless in the face of the ravages of the capitalists.

Their programme is the complete destruction of the trade unions and the Labour Party, to take away from the workers all their democratic rights − the right to organise, the right to strike, the right of assembly, free speech and a free press and even the democratic rights of elections and the right to vote freely for candidates of their own choice. That is, the fascists aim to destroy the elements of a new society that exist in the labour and trade union movement. They would stop at nothing to prevent the possibility of an overthrow of capitalism, using the savage methods of concentration camps, police and military terror etc.

Marxist supporters must expose these views but they must have a sense of proportion as Marxists did in the post-war struggle against the Mosleyites. As we predicted, the latter have largely disappeared as an organised force. The esoteric doctrines of their leader had no appeal to plain reactionary petit-bourgeoisie.

The real menace of fascism, perhaps in the not too distant future, will probably come from the reactionary wing of the Tory Party. The howls over the closed shop and the bayings for action embodied in resolutions from the Tory constituency parties, are indications of upper middle class and middle class reaction.

Under conditions of a protracted economic decline, with the social storms which would face a Tory or National government, the right wing Tories, plus so-called 'liberal' Tories in groupings like the Tory Reform Group, plus a section of ex-Labour Party right wing reformists, would reveal increasing discontent. They would demand drastic action against the unions, 'those Bolsheviks and extremists' with their 'unreasonable' and 'intolerable pressures', 'throwing their weight about' etc.

The elements that form the Monday Club are the types that would hive off to the right and form the core of a new organisation. Besides union-bashing, they would also engage in social demagogy. Like the Monday Club, such an organisation's racialism would be overt —'stop all coloured immigration', 'send back all illegal immigrants and black criminals and muggers'. The poison would be there without the crude nazi-like ravings and outpourings of the National Front.

If there were a *big majority* National or Tory government the right wing would move increasingly into opposition over the lack of measures against the workers' organisations. Under heated conditions, an early split would be possible. More likely a split from the Tories would take place under a new Labour government, particularly if it were a left wing one, and the Tory Party were incapable of effective opposition.

Such a right wing party would try to organise the small shopkeepers, the small business people, professionals, technicians, managers, staff, white-collar workers and politically backward workers, lumpens and criminals into some sort of force.

But we have to emphasise that it would only be the failure of the labour movement to transform society which would bring about this punishment. It would be the penalty to be paid for temporising over drastic measures against capitalism which could result in a further recoil of the middle class from the 'crime' of reformism, just as nationalism in Scotland, and partly in Wales is the consequence of local and national incompetence by the reformists.

But with the rise of a mass movement, as workers, the Labour Party and trade unions move into action with demonstrations and strikes and other means of struggle, the advanced workers will draw behind them the big majority of the more politically backward layers. The National Front has only gained because of the passivity and inaction of the labour movement during the last two or three years.

Once the movement goes into action the Front will be left stranded. Feuding amongst the fuehrers and ego-maniacs who compose its leaders will break out again as support ebbs. The National Front will have new splits as they will be incapable of explaining or understanding what will be happening with the movement of the working class.

Like the sects they live in the past without understanding the specific conditions which led to the victory of fascists in Italy, Germany and Spain. They will be like a poisonous insect which irritates a giant who moves to crush it because it stings. Recently, when the North West TUC moved −threatening to bring 20,000 workers into action, distributing 2 million leaflets etc., the authorities were compelled reluctantly to take action and ban the National Front march in Tameside.

Nevertheless the opportunity should be taken by Marxists to explain the deadly effects of racialism, the evils of capitalism and the loathsome, evil and malignant cancer of fascism and of the National Front itself.

The dialectics of class relations are like a book sealed with seven seals to the 'gentlemen' of the sects. The 'old cart horse' of the TUC, under the flick of the whip of reaction, would flex its muscles and the working class would show its strength.

By involving the mighty Labour Party and trade unions in the struggles against fascism and racialism, typified by the activities of the National Front, Marxists can raise the level of understanding of the working class as a whole to the need to change society.

The Method of Marxism

Introduction

AS HAS already been mentioned in the introduction, there are many more articles and documents written by Ted Grant than could ever be contained in a single volume. Moreover, a section on the 'Marxist method' could, with justification, have included any or all of these contributions to socialist theory. Whatever the selection made, there would always be some glaring omissions. The three items included do not easily fit into any of the previous chapters, but the editors feel that each one is worthy of inclusion in its own right.

The first item is reprinted from the *International Socialist* of May-June 1953, and it defends the Marxist view on the question of morality. At that time, with the post-war boom beginning to accelerate, the capitalist class and their ideological representatives in the labour movement discovered a new-found confidence in their system. Right-wingers, writing for example in the *New Fabian Essays*, sought to demonstrate that the ideas of 'class struggle' and 'capitalist crisis' were no longer applicable to the modern 'welfareist' state. Grant's defence of socialist theory in the field of economics has already been dealt with in Chapter Five.

But the right wing also regurgitated the pompous middle-class philosophy of the earlier, Victorian Fabians, dismissing the alleged 'crude materialism' of the Marxists and basing themselves instead on a more lofty Christian morality. In the golden age that capitalism seemed to promise in the 1950s, it was the middle class, and not least the careerists and place-seekers in the labour movement, who were guaranteed their place in the sun before all others. Many of the latter became senior Labour ministers, before betraying the Party as it moved left.

Having been granted their personal 'socialism', therefore, the philosophers of the right wing were uneasy living with the radicalism of the post-war years and still less comfortable with the memory of the bitter class struggles of the inter-war period. The political 'morality' they advocated, as Ted Grant explains, was in reality no more than a reflection of their own middle class prejudice; it was shallow, and vague, lacking either consistency or method. Today, unfortunately, the same muddle-headedness characterises much of the political 'theory' of sections of the labour movement. Grant's critique of Richard Crossman's essay, therefore, although written thirty-five years ago, is still one of the most modern articles in defence of the Marxist method and the morality of the socialist movement.

The second item is a document, dictated in 1966, in defence of the basic tenets of Trotskyism. It was a reply to an Irish socialist, Brendan Clifford, who put the classic Stalinist position, using garbled and one-sided quotations from Lenin to show how Trotskyism was a 'counter-revolutionary trend' opposed to the ideas and methods of 'Leninism'.

Clifford circulated his views inside a small left wing group, the Irish Communist Group. His document was of more than historical interest because the position he adopted was an attempt to justify a Stalinist 'stages' theory of social revolution in Ireland. That would mean that the first task for the labour movement would be to participate —with middle class groups and the 'nationalist' elements within the capitalist class —in a struggle for the unification of Ireland, with socialism relegated to some distant future.

The position adopted by the Trotskyists was that there was no barrier between the struggle to unify Ireland and the fight to transform society, that they were indissolubly linked. The unification of Ireland on a capitalist basis was ruled out, and conversely, the socialist transformation of society would be the basis upon which the unification of Ireland would become a reality.

But the starting point of the Trotskyist position on Ireland was a defence of the general theories of Trotsky and Trotskyism. The reply to Clifford, therefore, was a broad statement, outlining the early, pre-revolutionary differences between Lenin and Trotsky, and showing how their theoretical concepts compared to the living experience of the October revolution. Trotsky's formulations proved more precise than Lenin's 'algebraic' formula, but in reality both were vindicated by events: arriving at exactly the same position in 1917 after having travelled different paths. After the Revolution, both Bolshevik leaders considered their previous differences to be redundant and they were only dredged up after Lenin's death, by the Stalinists eager to peddle the myth of 'Trotskyism'.

The reply also described the rise of the Stalinist bureaucracy in Russia and drew a sharp contrast beween the 'four conditions' for workers' democracy laid down by Lenin and the real situation as it became in the Stalinist USSR. As a matter of interest, some of the comments made about the attempts by the Russian bureaucracy to introduce reforms in the 1960s have a very modern ring to them. Like Gorbachev twenty years afterwards, Nikita Kruschev tried to move the sluggish Soviet economy forward by giving 'incentives' to managers and by 'de-centralisation' of economic planning —to little effect in the long run.

The final item is the speech made by Grant at Labour Party annual conference in 1983, appealing against his expulsion by the National Executive Committee in February of the same year. The NEC had begun an 'enquiry' into the newspaper *Militant*, on the urging of the capitalist press and Tory ministers, who goaded Michael Foot, the Labour leader, with having 'extremists' in his party.

The NEC eventually decided to expel the five members of the *Militant* editorial board the day before a parliamentary by-election in Bermondsey, in South London. As a result of the pre-occupation of the Party leadership with attacks on its own left-wing, and the campaign of the media to highlight the divisions in the Party, Labour lost what up to then had been a safe seat. This was an anticipation of the equally disastrous general election result later in the year.

All five members of the editorial board, Ted Grant, Peter Taaffe, Lynn Walsh, Keith Dickinson and Clare Doyle, were given leave to appeal to the annual Party conference in October. When their appeal speeches were made, contrary to normal practice, the press and TV were excluded. As the transcript shows, there was considerable sympathy among the delegates, easily a majority, against the expulsion. But the big block union votes, controlled by a handful of trade union officials, carried the day for the right wing.

As the *Militant* argued at the time, the expulsion of the five became the prelude for a wide-ranging witch-hunt in the Party, and a large-scale shift of policies towards the right. Increasingly, the apparatus of officials has become tied down in keeping dossiers, organising enquiries, closing down Party branches and constituencies and expelling Marxists. Party rules have been modified several times, and even then, bent somewhat, to engineer expulsions.

But it is equally true, as Ted Grant said in his contribution, that those expelled will be back. Whatever may be the subjective wishes of this or that MP, union leader or Party official, there is no power on earth that can stop the growth of Marxist ideas inside the Labour Party.

In the development of a mass Marxist current, embracing thousands and hundreds of thousands of workers, an invaluable role will be played by discussion, education and the study of theory. The best and most class conscious activists must be armed with an understanding of the richness, the breadth and the development of socialist thought. This publication will play a central part in that because it is due to the work of Ted Grant, more than anyone else in the post-war period, that Marxist theory has been defended at the same time as being significantly deepened and extended.

Campaigning for Jock Haston during the Neath election.

Marxism Versus New Fabianism
Part Two

May 1953

Two Moralities Counterposed

THE SECOND main thread in all the *New Fabian Essays* is a criticism of the totalitarian regimes in Russia, China and Eastern Europe, and the identification of Marxism with Stalinism. Here it is necessary to steer between two fatal mistakes. The one typified by the mixed group of fellow travellers and miscellaneous pro-Stalinists who are active in the Labour Party and who maintained long and discreet silences about the crimes of Stalinism, with only the faintest trace of 'criticism' (criticism which sounds like an apology); and those who fail to make a distinction between the political regimes of Stalinism and the basic economic revolution on which the Stalinist bureaucracy and its satellites base themselves. Either mistake can be fatal for the developing left wing in the Labour Party.

The attitude of the new Fabians is expressed in its sharpest form by the essay of Crossman. Events have forced him (and the new Fabians) to reject the cosy optimism of the Victorian Fabians, with their illusion of gradual development, of an inevitable progression slowly towards a better and better world. A 50-years epoch of wars, crises, upheavals, fascism and Stalinism has brutally crushed this dream of peaceful development. (Marx, by the way, forecast precisely such an epoch of turbulence for capitalism). The possibilities of frightful reaction and even a plunge into barbarism through atomic war, have forced their way into the consciousness of everyone who tries to think out the future course of the evolution of society.

Crossman and the other new Fabians recognise that the lack of theory within the movement has driven it into its present impasse and crisis. But, while rejecting the former empiricism of the old Fabians and of those who are the present leaders of our movement, they do not replace it by any coherent and worked out philosophy. The prejudice against Marxism after all is only a prejudice of ignorance and lack of study. Theory is the summing up of the experience of society and the labour movement past and present, in order to uncover the laws of its development and so provide a guide for the policies of the movement; as far as possible avoiding the mistakes of the past, and preparing an easier transition to the future society.

The philosophy of the new Fabians, summed up by Crossman, is in no way superior to that of the old and present day leaders of the labour movement in Britain. Bits and pieces of ideas borrowed from everywhere, a pious adaptation of Christian morality mixed up with some socialist ideas, a borrowing from the shades of Liberalism and to cap it all the pessimism of the philosophers of decadent capitalism. This is the half-cooked stew of ideas which is presented as an alternative to 'outmoded' Marxism.

Mechanism Confused with Materialism

Instead of thinking things out, Crossman takes a step backwards even in comparison with the Victorian Fabians when he says:

> This materialist conception of progress was based on assumptions about human behaviour which psychological research has shown to have no basis in reality, and on a theory of democratic politics which has been confused by the facts of the last thirty years. There is neither a natural identity of interests nor yet an inherent contradiction in the economic system. The growth of science and popular education does not automatically produce an 'upward' evolution in society, if by 'upward' is meant from servile to democratic forms; and the apocalyptic assumption that, after a period of dictatorship, a proletarian revolution must achieve a free and equal society is equally invalid. *The evolutionary and revolutionary philosophies of progress have both proved false.* Judging by the facts, there is far more to be said for the Christian doctrine of original sin than for Rousseau's fantasy of the noble savage, or Marx's vision of classless society. (emphasis in original).

He tries to find consolation in a supra-historical morality, beyond time, class or space, for the cruel and savage world of conflict which faces us. But this explains nothing and solves nothing. Marx was, to put it gently, a little too familiar with the differing currents of social relations, to put forward the naive views attributed to him by the new Fabians. First, as far as capitalist reaction is concerned, Marx had already analysed Bonapartism, the forerunner of fascism, in many works. (A pity Crossman and other denigrators do not take the trouble to read Marx in order to refute him). In them, he showed the power vested in the state machine used even against the class which it represents under given conditions.

Then again Marx did not at all believe that the *overthrow of capitalism in one country* would automatically solve all problems for the working class. On the contrary he explicitly repudiated the theory of 'Socialism in One Country' which was later to be developed by Stalin. The developments of the Russian revolution are not at all to be explained by the 'morality' or lack of 'morality' of the Stalinist bureaucratic rulers of Russia. On the contrary the opposite is the case, *the morality of the bureaucracy can only be explained by the developments in Russia.* And this is precisely in accordance with Marxist doctrine. Says Crossman:

> The Soviet Union is the most extreme example of managerialism because its Stalinist rulers consciously repudiate the primacy of morality over expedience, and so destroy the possibility of an active social conscience, which could save them from the corruption of power. The capitalist class never did that, and this is why capitalist development did not fulfil the prophecies of Marx. No capitalist country was ever so theoretically and methodically capitalist as Russia is Stalinite today. This is also the reason why, judged by European standards, the USA is a better form of society than the USSR. In America, a liberal and Christian morality and a constitution and political tradition derived from it, have frustrated the full development of capitalism and still put up strong resistance against totalitarian tendencies. To reject America as a capitalist country and to treat the Soviet Empire as an example of socialist planning is to make a nonsense of every one of our ideals. In reality they are two great examples of the modern managerial state, the one consciously and systematically managerial, the other moving towards the same end under the pressure of the Cold War.

In every line of this paragraph there is an error, sometimes two or three. However, let us try and disentangle the main threads. The Russian revolution led by Lenin and Trotsky was begun with Marx's ideas and Marx's methods. The idea behind it was to establish the 'dictatorship of the proletariat' (another name for the democracy of the working class). It should be noted incidentally that even the freest capitalist democracy remains *a veiled dictatorship of the capitalist class,* because the capitalists, apart from the ownership of the means of production, in Crossman's words, 'control the media of mass communication and the means of destruction (propaganda and the armed forces)'. According to the Marxist ideas of the leaders of the Russian revolution, Russia was to begin, Germany, France and England were to finish the job. However, for many reasons which cannot be entered into here, the

Russian revolution remained isolated. But Russia being one of the most backward countries in Europe, *the material basis for socialism* had not been prepared within its borders. The revolution can only be understood as part of the international revolution. The isolation and gross *material factors* it embraced, not the subjective wickedness and the amorality of Stalin and his parasitic caste (however revolting this may be) *explain the development of the Stalinist bureaucracy, including its vile morality.*

But such is in accordance with the Marxist theory and not with that of theology. Engels explains the rise of classes in society by the low development of the productive forces and the needs of the division of labour.

Marxists insist on democracy −*real democracy* −in the transition to socialism and the full participation of the masses in industry and the state, precisely because 'conditions determine consciousness', because when art, science and government remain in the hands of the few, they will inevitably use and abuse their position (and incidentally create a morality and psychology to justify it) to further their own interests against those of the class they are supposed to represent.

In a cloudy way Crossman and the other essayists recognise this in drawing the balance of the experience of the nationalised industries −in their criticism of bureaucracy and the demand for participation in management and control by the workers.

But this does not clear up the puzzle. Crossman criticises those who maintain that Russia remains a workers' state. He looks only to the 'primacy of morality over expediency'. Poor fellow! Churchill and the capitalists of Britain (together with the churchmen −conscience and all) yesterday supported Franco, Mussolini and Hitler as saviours from Bolshevism and looked the other way from the concentration camps, where their opponents were being 're-educated'. The day after that they sighed (at least in public) in an ecstasy of admiration for the 'Great Warrior Stalin' and overlooked such trifles as slave camps and other horrors. The American capitalists and government despite 'liberal and Christian morality' did the same thing under the liberal Roosevelt. Christian morality did not prevent Hiroshima, or the vile treatment of the negroes in the South.

Definition of Morals

Crossman expatiates: 'The socialist measures this progress of social morality by the degree of equality and respect for individual personality expressed in the distribution of power and in the institutions of law and property within a state. This standard indeed, is what we mean by the socialist ideal.' He does not see that all these ideas are the reflection of the development of society, in its turn the result of the development of the productive forces in the past. The 'Christian morality' to which Crossman appeals, as against the amorality of Stalinism, did not at all find itself in conflict with but on the contrary justified the institution of slavery under the Roman empire. Under the feudal regime it found nothing immoral in the centuries of serfdom of the peasantry. It justified and continues to justify the veiled slavery of capitalism. Doctor Malan* finds it not at all in conflict with his Christian conscience to support the 'God-ordained' oppression of the South African blacks by the whites. The Christian Franco with the blessing of the Pope, finds it not at all incompatible with the doctrines of the Church to maintain his totalitarian regime in Spain.

Christian ethics therefore cannot provide a reliable standard of morality for the socialist movement. Nor does Crossman's particular 'definition' fare any better.

From the point of view of Marxism, whatever conduces to the material, social and intellectual development of the masses is moral; whatever assists this process in the direction of socialism is moral; whatever assists towards the organised and conscious activity of the masses for the overthrow of capitalism is moral. Contrarily whatever hinders or hampers this process is bad and immoral. These are the rules of conduct for those striving for socialism. But in and of itself such a definition must have a material basis. The class position and the interests of the proletariat within capitalist society and in the transition to a classless society are the material base for such a morality. This will disappear with the dissolution of class society into socialism. *Capitalist morality or amorality in its various grades and manifestations is also a reflection of the class interest of the capitalist class in a class society. Stalinist morality or amorality reflects the interest of a particular caste within the given society.*

Although Crossman is not aware of this the morality which he puts forward also has its class roots. It is the morality not at all of eternal verities, but of a variant of *middle-class morality* and a reflection of the position of the intellectual and professional elite within the labour movement.

Marxist socialists, beginning with Marx and Engels have always supported democracy as against any form of despotism. Thus they have supported republicanism against monarchism, capitalist democracy against capitalist dictatorship. *But they always recognise the*

*Daniel F Malan was leader of the right wing Afrikaaner Nationalist Party. On becoming Prime Minister in 1948, he began the systematic introduction of apartheid as the basis of the South African state.

limitations of the above. Crossman contradicts himself when he points out that the very democracy which he extols so much is the fruit of revolution in Britain and of the civil war in America in the past. He says, 'Even in Western Europe, the destruction of feudalism did not take place under the forms of representative government.'

However, it is true that all the forces of capitalism-imperialism in all its stark reaction never achieved full fruition except perhaps in nazi Germany. But that is in the tradition of Marxism, not at all against it. The crude mechanical materialism or economic determinism which Crossman and the others assail have not the slightest resemblance to the real doctrines of Marx.

The reason why capitalism in America has taken the particular form it has, lies in the history of the country —its richness and resources, its origins and beginnings, its traditions, the War of Independence, the Civil War and the way it developed, the rise of the trade-union movement —and all the conflicting forces struggling against each other in the given society.

Crossman thinks nothing through to the end. Some correct ideas are mixed with utter balderdash but never linked with a clear conception of the historic process or the role of the conscious socialist within it. He can say correctly, 'Living in an age not of steady progress towards a world welfare capitalism but of world revolution...' He wishes to fight the forces of Stalinism on the one side and the forces of American imperialism on the other, mightily armed like a modern Don Quixote with...a socialist ethic!

Possibilities of capitalist totalitarianism or of socialist democracy are vested in the forces at present latent in American capitalism. In the conflict which looms ahead, the liberal Christian mask will be dropped by its masters as it was in Germany, in an endeavour to save the capitalist system. Christian morality will not prevent the massacre of the negroes, as it did not that of the Jews by nazis in Europe, if the forces of reaction gain the ascendancy in America. The Constitution and the political tradition deriving from it, no more than that of Weimar Germany, are obstacles in themselves to such a development. In America, as in Britain and the world, *only the working class is the guardian of democracy and freedom*, because these are the vital conditions for its development —for the achievement of economic and political emancipation. *In this gross material fact is rooted proletarian morality.*

Social Morality

According to Crossman, 'Social morality, freedom and equality do not grow by any law of economics or politics, but only with the most careful cultivation. So far, therefore, from viewing history as a steady advance towards freedom, we should regard exploitation and slavery as the normal state of man and view the brief epochs of liberty as tremendous achievements.' From whence do they spring then? Do they drop from the skies or from the magnanimity of intellectuals such as Crossman, who apparently have a mission as the keepers of the public conscience? Are these eternal laws of morality which curiously enough are found to obtain different meanings in different epochs by different classes at different times? Religious people at least maintain that their morality is given by divine providence beyond time and space. Crossman tells us that his 'morality', 'freedom' and 'equality', like that of Christians, does not grow by any law of economics or politics, but only by the most careful cultivation. The only question is, who cultivates and how? And what do they cultivate? Any farmer will tell him that seed cast on stony ground will not sprout. The conditions must be there before these ideas can receive powerful support. But *unless the economic and political conditions have been developed, ie the material conditions prepared, the most careful cultivation will produce no result.*

There is nothing mysterious about the fact that slavery and exploitation of man have been the 'normal' condition and the epochs of 'liberty' been brief. It arises neither out of the absence nor the need for a supra-morality but out of the *class structure* of society. This despite the fact that at certain periods an equilibrium could be maintained between the classes (without open oppression and force) because of temporary sufficiency and the relationship of class forces at a given time.

This constant harping on an amorphous social conscience which seems to exist in the stratosphere, leads Crossman precisely into the error for which he condemns Stalinism. After strong moral condemnation of Stalinist elite society he finds the cultivators of his morality...only in an 'elite'!

Society, Crossman says, must be '...*policed* (our emphasis) by the social morality which can only reside in a minority of citizens'. Here we have confusion of mind developed to an extreme. Crossman makes this worse by declaring that 'The school, the press, the radio, the party machine, the army, the factory, are all instruments through which man (what kind of man?), unless checked by social conscience armed with sanctions, will exert power over the minds of his fellow men.' What sanction and what man? What morality and how and by whom is it determined?

Amorality is not something new in history. It takes shape usually in a period of breakdown of the old social system, and the transition to a new social system. With the loss of function of the old ruling class, the moral codes pertaining to its rule also break down. And similarly in a period of transition, the new morality based on new relations of production also takes time to emerge.

Thus abominations similar to that of Hitler and Stalin took place in the period of decline of the Roman slave system and the transition to feudalism. Who has not heard of Nero and his court? Again in the transition from feudalism to capitalism, despite the glories of the Renaissance we have the spectacle of the Borgias*. Thus we have no need of mystical theories to explain these events but can only explain them on a *materialist* basis.

But understanding them does not justify either the Borgias or the modern Borgias in the court of the Kremlin. It does not mean that they are not to be condemned. History, said Marx, is a cruel goddess to whose chariot are tied hecatombs of human skulls. Stalin, the modern Genghis Khan, has surpassed all his predecessors. Notwithstanding all this and in spite of Stalinism, there has been an unprecedented development of the productive forces in Russia. This in its turn, due to the contradictions it develops, prepares inevitably for the time when this excrescence will be cast off in a mighty movement of the Russian proletariat and all the ugly and repulsive features which disfigure the regime will disappear with the regime itself and be replaced by a regime of workers' democracy, this time on firm economic foundations due to the material progress that has been made.

Similarly despite all the wars, massacres, conspiracies, blood and cruelties, the Renaissance was a period of preparation of advance in all fields of human endeavour —in industry, art, science, technique and....in morals!. After all, the nineteenth century advance of which Crossman speaks, and its attitudes towards democracy and freedom, were predicated on the tremendous upsurge of the productive forces in capitalism's period of ascent. This it was that gave the illusion of illimitable progress under the regime of private enterprise.

Despite Crossman's lumping of America and Russia together he says 'We can co-operate with the Americans as allies, influencing their policies despite their superior strength. It would be folly to expect such a relationship with the Soviet Union. Co-existence, yes. Mutually beneficial agreements, yes. But never co-operation.' Where does Crossman find the reason for this? In his socialist morality or in the Christian ethic of America? He forgets that both Britain and America did not find it impossible to co-operate with Stalinist Russia during the war —when it suited the interests of those countries. Nazi Germany and Stalinist Russia co-operated

---

*A powerful Italian noble family from which several popes were elected during the 15th and 16th centuries. Their involvement in Italian and papal politics has become a by-word for intrigue and ruthlessness in the struggle for power.

also for a while in the Nazi-Soviet Pact, when it suited the bureaucracy in Russia and the nazi imperialists in Germany. In reality none of the agreements had anything to do with 'morality' or 'freedom', but everything to do with the interests, at various stages, of the classes and castes involved. No different is the co-operation between capitalist Britain and capitalist America at the present time. It is the interests of Wall Street, not Christian morality, which are paramount in the deciding of American imperialist policy.

The interesting question arises as to who Crossman has in mind when he refers to 'we'. Who is this 'we'? Is it the capitalist class or the working class? Is it some mythical national interest separate and apart from these classes? It is precisely this lack of precision which is typical of all this mish-mash (Christian ethic and all) which Crossman wants to palm off in place of the clear ideas of Marxism.

He says that the managerial society (he includes in this both America and Russia) *can* be civilised into democratic socialism. How? By the might of his 'socialist ethic' perhaps? Like his ethic the question is left hanging in mid air without a material base.

America —a Contrast

In America, despite the freedoms, in reality the productive forces have stagnated since 1929 in the contradictions of private ownership. Temporarily, only on the basis of war, war production and preparation for war, has there been an important development of the productive forces.

But sooner or later crisis will intervene and we will see the Christian morality (of the capitalists) cast off as a thin veneer and the ugly inner essence of imperialism reveal itself. Then either the workers will recognise the problem and take power, nationalising the means of production, or face a new slavery, and a new barbarism, on the part of capitalism.

In returning to the problem of Russia we recognise the case as somewhat different. Notwithstanding the waste, chaos and inefficiency of bureaucratic dictatorship, nevertheless, on the basis of state ownership and planning of the means of production, we have a continuous development of the means of production. This despite the setbacks occasioned by war, and the mistakes and crimes of the leadership, such as forced collectivisation and the great purges. Notwithstanding the existence of slave labour (also a feature of transition of society in the past) and the other depraved features of Stalinist society, we have a steady rhythm and development of the productive forces. The contradictions are the opposite of those under capitalism. The bureaucracy is compelled to maintain a totalitarian terror, with its amorality etc, not by accident but because its privileges can only be maintained thereby.

Under capitalism, the capitalists were necessary and had a necessary function, with the private ownership of the means of production, acting as the repositories of the means of production, or in the words of Marx as 'the trustees of bourgeois society'.

In Russia the state acts as the repository of the means of production, and like managers and technicians under capitalism, from the viewpoint of their economic function in production and the state, all the bureaucracy is entitled to, is the wages of superintendence and management. But they consume far more than this and in order to do so act as *economic parasites* on production. It is this which explains their role and their morality.

The cynicism, hypocrisy and lies with which the bureaucracy rules on the one hand, while maintaining a totalitarian terror on the other, are an expression of its role in society. If under 'democratic' capitalism while the hypocrisy, cynicism and lies are just as evident, *the methods are different* because of the checks and balances provided by the forces contending within it. Remove the organisations and the rights won by generations of struggle by the working class and the result is seen in nazi Germany. The morality of the capitalists under Weimar, the nazi regime and today, were not really fundamentally different, only the conditions under which the regime functioned. Repression and lies are merely different sides of the need to maintain exploitation and domination over the masses. They are symptoms of a society shot through and through with contradictions. This explains the inconsistency and hypocrisy of Christian morality in a society based on class antagonism. Similarly, the morality of Stalinism is based on the contradictions within Russian society, which have not been solved merely by the destruction of capitalism. Its bestial morality is conditioned by the uneasy hold which they have in Russian and satellite society and the fear which springs from their insecure and artificially maintained vested interests —in their privileged hold on Russian society.

The mistake of Crossman and the other Fabians is not to recognise this contradiction and all that flows from it. A new revolution will be necessary in Russia, but a *political not a social revolution*, before there can be any steps taken anew in the direction of socialism.

From the Marxist view of the development of world history this should not at all disconcert us. Marx never declared that to one system of production only one form of superstructure or state pertained. The most superficial acquaintance with history would show that this was incorrect. To every system, a large number of *political forms* is possible, depending on a whole series of fundamental and secondary factors.

In modern times (with all the extremely important if secondary results) differing forms of dictatorship and democracy, but all on a capitalist basis, have revealed themselves. Fascism, military dictatorship, democracy, monarchy, republic and other variants. They were all the same type of society from the viewpoint of the economic foundations despite the extreme, sharp and striking differences, 'morally' and in every other way.

A real workers' democracy would have the same relationship to Stalinist Russia as Hitler's Germany to the Weimar Republic or to democratic capitalist Britain. Thus under all conditions the socialist workers should defend the state ownership of the means of production and the planned economy in Russia, while conducting an implacable struggle against the clique which has usurped control and transformed a workers' democracy (despite its limitations and shortcomings) into a totalitarian Stalinist state.

The Far East

The attitude towards the colonial revolution of the East is also somewhat different. Recognising the progressive character of the undermining of imperialism in the East, the new Fabians extend half-hearted support to this movement.

Undoubtedly in its potential for the future, the Chinese Revolution is the greatest event in history since the October 1917 transformation in Russia. It will result in the modernisation and industrialisation of China, which was stagnating under the capitalist-landlord regime of Chiang Kai Shek. However Mao Tse Tung and the Chinese Stalinists have taken the regime of Stalin, not that of Lenin, as their model. Given the backwardness of China, a similar regime in the long run will be installed.

If the democracy and freedom of the West are to be maintained, heightened and extended it can only be accomplished by the social revolution at home and internationalism abroad.

In the past internationalism seemed a utopian ideal. Now for the workers of Britain, Europe and the colonial world it is a vital economic necessity. Especially is this so in the case of Britain. With the loss of her imperialist overlordship of the world only decay and decline of her standards and rights open up before the working class on a capitalist and nationalist basis. Only a socialist United States of Europe and the world can guarantee culture, democracy, freedom and a rising standard of living, preparing the way for socialism.

Crossman says correctly that the Cold War is the dominating factor in world relations at the present time. But socialism, revolutionary democratic socialism, can only find a way out in supporting the extension of the revolution and state ownership, while opposing the deformation of Stalinism.

Neither Washington nor Moscow has a way out for the working class. Only a militant socialist programme and policy can provide an answer to both. Not by rejecting Marxism but by basing itself on its fundamental tenets can the labour movement in Britain solve the problems of our time.

The permanency of capitalist 'democracy' was shattered by the Greek colonel's coup. Ted Grant speaks at a meeting of the Aid Greek Workers' Committee in the 1960s.

From: A Reply to Comrade Clifford

1966

COMRADE CLIFFORD has raised the question of Trotskyism in a most peculiar way. We have to ask: What is Trotskyism? How did it arise? What theories does it represent? What class interest does it express? Why has the question been raised today? Because in raising these problems and in raising what the Trotskyists have said we have the opportunity to understand the real issues —though not at all, of course, in the way in which they are posed by Comrade Clifford. Clifford has thrown down the gage to us. He says that the difference between Stalin and Mao Tse-Tung, on the one hand, and Trotskyism, is that one is revolutionary and the other is counter-revolutionary (and it is obvious that of these two incompatible theories, only one can be correct in the sense of representing the historical interests of the working class on a national and international scale). The question is: which?

In reality, the simple way, the garbled way in which Clifford tries to dismiss this problem cannot result in educating anyone as to the real issues themselves. Clifford repeats in a garbled fashion the fairy tales and lies of Stalin and of the Stalinists as to the real issues. The problem is in reality much more complex than simply 'revolutionary' and 'counter-revolutionary', because both stem, in the last analysis, *from the Russian revolution and the fate of the revolution.*

And if we are to understand the fate of the revolution, the first thing that is necessary is that when we use terms used by Marxists, we use them in the sense in which they were meant by both Marx and Lenin. Otherwise we are not Marxists at all. We are simply being dishonest.

Comrade Clifford has touched on the question of the dictatorship of the proletariat in the Soviet Union, and in doing so has shown that he *does not understand the ABC of what the dictatorship of the proletariat means.* The quotations he gives from Lenin deal only with one aspect of the dictatorship of the proletariat, that is

—and in that Lenin was 100 per cent correct —that the dictatorship of proletariat *in Russia at that stage* rested on an alliance between the workers and the peasants and in particular between the workers and poor peasants.

But that does not tell us *at all* what the dictatorship of the proletariat *is!* What then *is* the dictatorship of the proletariat? If we understand this question, all that stems from it will be understood too: whose interest Trotsky really represented, whose interest Stalin represented, what are the *real issues* in the debates that have taken place between Stalinism and Trotskyism over the past 40 years. And in reality, once one gets down to fundamentals, the question is not so difficult to understand. First of all, as Marxists, we base ourselves *on the ideas of Marx.* Marx did not suck the idea of the dictatorship of the proletariat out of his thumb. Marx did not come forward with the idea of the dictatorship ready made. All that happened is that Marx generalised the experience of the working class in relation to the Paris Commune of 1871.

What were the ideas that were put forward by Marx in his book on the Paris Commune? The first point that he made was one that in the past would have been accepted by those who claim to stand for communism. Today it is not accepted by the Moscow communists; it is allegedly accepted by the Peking communists, but in practice, and as we can see from the way in which they carry through their diplomatic manoeuvres in the colonial countries, it is not accepted by them at all. Marx explained that it is impossible for the proletariat to take over the old bourgeois machine; that it is necessary, therefore, to have revolution and to smash the old state machine. And what then was to replace the bourgeois state machine? *That* is what Marx explained is the dictatorship of the proletariat. And when he spoke of the 'dictatorship' he meant a far more democratic system, a far wider measure of democracy among the mass of the people than could ever be realised under bourgeois democracy, which is the *disguised dictatorship* of the bourgeois ruling class.

Lenin, taking up and faithfully reflecting the ideas of Marx in his book *State and Revolution,* restates all the principles on which Marx based his work in the past. And in order that there should be a dictatorship of the proletariat he explains —as Marx explained —the conditions for the rule of the working class; adding perhaps to the ideas of Marx the question of the soviets (which, in its turn, was not whistled out of the mind of Lenin, Trotsky, Marx or anyone else, but came out of the initiative and direct experience of the working class itself in Russia in the revolutions of 1905 and 1917.)

In place of the bourgeois parliament, Lenin said, once the bourgeois system had been overthrown and the proletariat had taken power, we would have a system of soviets, of committees elected by the workers, housewives and even small shopkeepers, professional people etc, together with the peasants (which is the impression which Comrade Clifford's 'thesis' would impart to the unwary —again displaying the continuing capacity of Stalinism to distort Leninism, to dishonestly misrepresent Marxism). In 1917 whereas for the workers there was one soviet representative for every 10,000 votes, for the peasants there was one for every 100,000.

In other words, the peasants did not have the same representation in the soviets, once the revolution had taken place, as the working class; thereby making a distinction between workers and the peasants; making a clear distinction in the plebian mass, in the people as a whole, between the workers who were uncompromisingly devoted to socialism, and the peasants who would always have tendency to veer, to sway, and to be hesitant in their support of the dictatorship of the proletariat itself.

The first condition, then, for the rule of the working class, according to Lenin, is the existence of soviets, these committees with the right of election and recall. The second condition that Lenin laid down for the rule of the working class was that no official was to receive a wage higher than that of a skilled worker. The third condition was that there was to be no standing army, but an armed people. The fourth condition was that there be no permanent bureaucracy: in the words of Lenin himself, 'every cook should be able to be Prime Minister.'

These are the conditions under which the dictatorship of the proletariat *begins*, not where the dictatorship of the proletariat *ends*. And here we get the arguments on the question of the difference between Stalinism and Trotskyism.

We shall return again to the conditions for the dictatorship of the proletariat at a later stage in the discussion.

Stalinism and Trotskyism

The difference between Stalinism and Trotskyism originally arose *not* on the question of the peasantry. That was thrown in merely as a disguise, a trick —as Comrade Clifford is using it as a trick —to confuse the mass of the people in Russia as to the difference between the Trotskyists and the Stalinists. The original difference between Stalinism and Trotskyism had nothing to do with the theory of the Permanent Revolution, even. The original difference arose over the demands of the Left Opposition, as they were called and —in which demands the Left Opposition had the full support of Lenin —for a restoration of workers' democracy in the Soviet Union on the lines of the points of the dictatorship of the proletariat that have just been sketched out.

Unfortunately, because of the civil war, the famine, and because of the retreat that the Bolsheviks had had to make with the New Economic Policy, which allowed the development of bourgeois elements in the towns, through the so-called Nepmen, and in the countryside through the so-called Kulaks —gradually, more and more the power which the working class had established in the Soviet Union began to be taken away from them. The same process as had developed in the past, which Lenin had so carefully and meticulously analysed in relation to social democracy, was now taking place *after* the capture of power by the proletariat. Lenin had explained the role which social democracy and the trade union bureaucracy played, not purely from the point of view of ideas but from the *material interests* of the bureaucracy of this movement. This bureaucracy had separated itself from the working class, only indirectly reflected the interests of the working class and tried to act as an arbiter between the working class and the bourgeoisie. *That* is how Lenin explained the betrayal of social democracy and of the trade union bureaucracy in the first world war, when in each country they came out in full support of their own ruling class. Let us note that fact, that crude material fact! That the *conditions of existence* of the bureaucrats, of the labour and trade union bureaucrats before the first world war, were the reason for the change in the consciousness of these bureaucrats and for their betrayal of the working class.

In Russia, after the victory of the revolution, the original intention of the Bolsheviks had not been to suppress *even a single party*, except of course for the forerunners of the fascists, the Black Hundreds*. In the early stages of the revolution even the liberals, the Constitutional Democrats, were not suppressed; nor was their press suppressed. Later, the Bolsheviks were forced to suppress them; then the right-wing social democrats; then the Left Social Revolutionaries (and, by the way, it should be remembered that the first government of the soviets was a coalition government of Bolsheviks and of Left Social Revolutionaries). But at each stage, it was because of the weakness of the revolution, because of the

*The Black Hundreds were a proto-fascist league of monarchists and nationalists who carried out terrorist attacks on workers' organisations and were the chief instagators of pogroms. The Constitutional Democrats (Cadets) were a bourgeois liberal party in pre-revolutionary Russia, which became openly counter-revolutionary after the October Revolution.

taking up of arms against the revolution, because of the failure of the international revolution on which Lenin and Trotsky —as we will later explain —had based their whole perspective of the future of the Russian revolution, that these suppressions were made necessary. Every peasant, every peasant soldier, as John Reed shows in his *Ten Days that Shook the World*, understood the *international perspective of the revolution* because of the propaganda of the Bolsheviks.

The differences between Stalinism and Trotskyism were not differences as to whether the revolution should be extended into Europe or elsewhere in the early stage of the Russian revolution. The Russian revolution was prepared, and began, with the perspective that it was only the beginning of the revolution in Europe and of the international revolution.

Again, before dealing with this aspect of the thing, let us examine the arguments that are put forward by Clifford on the question of the proletarian dictatorship and on the question of the permanent revolution and the so-called underestimation of the peasantry —a series of most peculiarly assembled quotations, taken out of context from Lenin, and which do not deal with the subject under discussion at all.

What were the conceptions with which the Russian revolution was prepared? Within the Marxist movement, within the social democratic movement —because let us remember that up to 1912 even Bolshevism was not an independent party, as one would imagine from the statements of Clifford; only in 1912 did the Bolsheviks* become an independent party —there were certain theoretical conceptions of how the revolution in Russia was going to develop. These conceptions were necessary to guide the work of preparing the victory of the revolution. To take just one aspect of these conceptions for the moment: Lenin, far from being the self-centred Russian nationalist which Clifford and the Stalinists have tried to make him out to be, raised the question at various stages in the revolution, that if it was necessary for the German revolution to succeed, which was far more important than the Russian revolution, then *they would even be prepared to sacrifice the Russian revolution for the victory of the revolution in Germany.* The whole conception of Bolshevism, and of Leninism, was imbued through and through with ideas of international socialism. And right through the whole period of the Russian revolution, this

*While the Bolsheviks and Mensheviks appeared as separate factions within the Russian Social Democratic Labour Party after the 1903 Congress, until 1912 both regarded themselves as groups within the same party. The issues raised here are dealt with fully in *Lenin and Trotsky — What they really stood for*, by Ted Grant and Alan Woods (*Militant*).

conception was held by Lenin. We can give not one, but a hundred, a thousand quotations to show that this was so!

We need mention only one: where Lenin said that we are bound to the world market, we are bound to world developments, we cannot solve the problem of the Soviet Union on our own, *we have to hold out* —that was the conception of Lenin! —we have to hold out till the development of the socialist revolution in the more developed countries of the West.

We might also point out that when, during the Eighth Congress of the Communist Party of Russia, Podbelsky inferred that some formulations of the programme had reference only to the revolution in Russia, Lenin replied as follows in his concluding speech on the question of the party programme (March 19, 1919):

> Podbelsky has raised objection to a paragraph which speaks of the pending social revolution...His argument is obviously unfounded because our programme deals with the social revolution on a world scale.(*CW* Vol. 29, p187.)

It will not be out of place here, either, to point out that at about the same time Lenin suggested that the party should change its name from the Communist Party of Russia, so as to emphasise still further that it was a party of international revolution. Trotsky was the only one voting for Lenin's motion in the Central Committee.

What then gave rise to the differences between Stalin and Trotsky? What then gave rise to the victory of Stalin? Was it because Stalin understood the problems better? Was it because Trotsky underestimated the peasantry, or any other nonsense of that character?

On the contrary, again if we use the Marxist method, we have to see the different material interests which came to be expressed by these two different tendencies. The isolation of the revolution (in a backward country at that), the famine, the civil war etc., led to seizure of control by the bureaucracy in the Soviet Union; by millions of officials in the party, in the trade unions, in the army and in industry. These were the ones who now gradually began to concentrate power in their hands, as a direct consequence of the exhaustion of the masses. And the key year when these things came to a head was 1923.

In 1923, that revolution which the Bolsheviks had expected did have the possibility of taking place in Germany. Those people who have no faith in the working class, who sneer, have only to consider how, in one country after another in the past 40 years, the working class has taken to the road of revolution; how the workers organised the struggle, how the workers tried to take power, in Germany, in Hungary, in China, in Britain, in France, in Italy, in Spain and in other countries —struggles which, at the moment, we cannot deal with. But at any rate in 1923 in Germany again an opportunity was given to the working class to take power into their own hands.

Lenin was ill, Trotsky was ill, and unfortunately, when the delegation of the German Central Committee, which was preparing for the revolution in Germany, arrived in Moscow, the people they met were Stalin and Zinoviev. And unfortunately, the advice which Stalin gave them was *not to try and take power*. In that sense we have the same sort of crisis which led Trotsky to write his book *The Lessons of October,* the same crisis in the leadership as existed in 1917 with Stalin, Zinoviev, Kamenev, and other leaders of the Bolsheviks who hesitated at the time when the insurrection was being prepared —in the case of Zinoviev and Kamenev, directly opposing the insurrection.

It is interesting to note in this regard that following the February revolution, from February to April 1917, while Lenin was in Zurich, Stalin and Kamenev (who had returned to Petersburg) were running *Pravda*. Lenin daily sent articles to Petersburg in which he called for no conciliation with the capitalists. He sent covering letters demanding that these be published. Stalin and Kamenev refused to publish them. Instead, during those vital months, they published Stalin's own miserable bits and pieces of journalism in which Stalin called for and worked for conciliation with the Mensheviks, who in turn were calling for conciliation with the bourgeoisie. Stalin in the pages of *Pravda* actually described the differences between Lenin and the Mensheviks as 'a storm in a tea-cup'!

Stalin, not having understood the experience of 1917, gave the advice to the German comrades not to try and take power, and as a consequence the revolutionary opportunity in Germany was lost.

As Engels has explained, sometimes twenty years of history can be summed up in few days; if the revolutionary leadership of the proletariat does not take advantage of these days it might be twenty years before a new opportunity would return. The opportunity was lost for the proletariat to take power in Germany in 1923, with all the fatal consequences that that has had for the Russian revolution and the revolutionary movement on a world scale.

It was the failure of the German revolution that gave the opportunity to Stalin, who more and more began to reflect the ideas and interests of the millions of officials and bureaucrats within the Soviet Union.

What, then, was the programme on which the Left Opposition was constructed in 1923 and 1924? It was to return to the ideas of Marxism, of Leninism; to return to the conditions that Lenin had laid down for the rule of the working class; to reintroduce workers' democracy in the Bolshevik Party and in the Soviet state. That was the main plank in the platform of the Left Opposition.

The second plank, as important as the first, was the need for the Soviet Union to industrialise, the need for five-year plans in the Soviet Union. And it is significant, in relation to the understanding of the problems of Stalinism and Trotskyism, that the tendency which was against 'socialism in one country', that tendency which was for international socialism — that was the tendency which came out for the industrialisation of the Soviet Union and for five-year plans.

As far as the question of 'socialism in one country' is concerned, one would pose the question to Comrade Clifford: If the Bolshevik programme before coming to power was not based on an international socialist perspective, how did it happen that in his book *Problems of Leninism*, published in January 1924, Stalin said, echoing the Bolshevik programme adopted after the seizure of power (this idea of international revolution naturally appears in the Bolshevik programme), that socialism is impossible in a single country and that six months later Stalin published a new edition of this book in which he argues for the exact opposite, that socialism can and must be built in a single country?

It is here we see the complete lack of foresight, the complete narrow-mindedness of this bureaucracy and of Stalin himself. When it was suggested that the five-year plans should be put into force on the basis of increasing production by 20 per cent a year, it was Stalin, and at that time his ally Bukharin, who laughed at this 'sheer adventurism' on the part of the Opposition.

How could a peasant country like Russia hope to develop industry faster than the countries of the West, he asked? In Bukharin's phrase, they would 'reach socialism at a snail's pace'. And when it was suggested, for example, that the Dnieperstroy power works — now one of the most famous hydro-electric schemes in the Soviet Union — should be constructed, and on which the first five-year plan was based, Stalin said that to talk about such a project was like suggesting that a peasant should buy a gramophone instead of a cow. The whole thing, he said, was beyond the resources of the Soviet Union at that time.

We can see very clearly from reference to Trotsky's *Revolution Betrayed* what was at stake and what actually happened in the Soviet Union in those vital years: why the bureaucracy pursued its course toward the kulak, scoffed at the 'super industrialisers', and rejected any attempt at democratisation and a change of policy. Then, suddenly, panic ensues. The 'impossible' becomes not only possible but 'exceedable'. Those who stood for industrialisation, and gradual collectivisation on the basis of a growing industry (not on the basis of a wooden plough and thousand year old methods) while awaiting the maturing of the revolutionary possibilities in Western Europe, were locked up, exiled and deported (what policies the victorious bureaucracy later imposed on the workers through the Comintern when that revolutionary situation did mature, we shall see later). The forced collectivisation was then proceeded with — not as we said on a bases of tractors, but of wooden ploughs, a few thousand bureaucratic collectivisers and a large army of police.

The results are well known. The wholesale destruction of livestock by the peasants, the situation of virtual civil war with Moscow and other centres surrounded by armour, millions dead of famine. Today in the Soviet Union 40 per cent of the total food produced comes from six per cent of the cultivated land, from the private plots.

So we can see that the argument between Stalinism and Trotskyism was not whether the Soviet Union should be developed or not, because the people who were in favour of developing the Soviet Union were the Left Opposition. The argument was between those who stood for a thorough *democratisation or re-democratisation* of the Soviet Union and those who stood for a *further bureaucratisation* of the Soviet Union.

Lenin, in 1924, was already becoming alarmed at the processes that were taking place in the Soviet Union. And Lenin, in contradistinction to Stalin and all the acolytes of Stalin, was always honest and ready to face the facts. And in his last articles and his last speeches he referred to the fact that if one took away the 'thin varnish of socialism' (his own words) which existed in the Soviet Union, there was the same old *Tsarist* state machine, the same old *Tsarist* bureaucracy in control.

It was precisely because the revolution had taken place in a country where the working class was only 10 per cent of the population, precisely because of the backwardness even of the working class (we must remember the large amount of illiteracy that existed in the Soviet Union) that the Bolsheviks were forced to rely largely on the same old *Tsarist* officials in the ministries, etc., in order to carry through the administration of the country. What happened was that the newer elements in this bureaucracy began to raise themselves above the level of the working class. These elements moved away from the conceptions of Marxism, away from the conceptions of Bolshevism.

In the international arena, the developments that gave Stalin the opportunity to come to power were the defeat of the working class in Germany in 1923, in 1925-7 in China and the defeat of the British working class in the general strike of 1926. These were the factors that allowed the bureaucracy in the Soviet Union to consolidate its power.

Socialism in One Country — an Anti-Marxist Concept.

Marxists are not internationalists for abstract, sentimental reasons, just because they think that the workers of one country must love the workers of another country.

We are internationalists, as Marx explained, because the whole essence and function of capitalism, apart from developing the productive forces in each country, are summed up in the fact that the whole world was drawn into one single inter-dependent unit by the capitalist system, where every country is dependent on every other country. The whole world is drawn by capitalism into one single inter-related economic unit. It is this which gives us the essence of the internationalism of the working class. Events that occur in one country affect the workers of other countries. That is why Lenin, Trotsky, Marx, Engels and all the great teachers of the working class movement, always based themselves on internationalism — not from abstract sentimentalism, but from the actual organic needs of the development of world economy, from the organic needs of the working class itself.

How, then, did the idea of 'socialism in one country', entirely foreign to the ideas of Marxism, appear within the Soviet Union? The answer, as always given by Marxists, is that no theory, once it gets mass support or the support of a large section of people, can be a theory in the abstract; it must reflect the material interests of classes or of strata within classes. Whose interest, then, did 'socialism in one country' reflect? Did it reflect the interests of the Russian workers? Or did it reflect the interests of the bureaucrats, of the officialdom within the Soviet Union? Had the same process which Lenin sketched in relation to the labour bureaucracy in the industrially advanced Western countries taken place once the workers in Russia had taken power?

The answer we can give as to whose interests the idea of socialism in one country represents, has been given by history itself. *There*, Comrade Clifford, is the explanation of why Trotsky and the Left Opposition were defeated, and why Stalin won! *Whose interests* were reflected in the struggle is shown by the development of the Soviet Union itself. What happened to the Soviet state under Stalin? In the early stages, nominally, all the conditions that we've spoken about continued to exist, though the bureaucracy remained corrupt. The bureaucracy illegitimately *stole and had a greater share* than they were allowed according to the laws of the Soviet state.

But what has happened to the soviets of which Lenin speaks? There are *no soviets* in the Soviet Union! The name remains, but in place of the living, acting democracy of the soviets, we have a so-called parliament −a caricature of a bourgeois parliament, because at least in a bourgeois parliament different organisations, different tendencies can put up. But in the so-called Soviet parliament we have what amounts to a Reichstag −one totalitarian organisation, where only a single candidate is put up, or as Marx would explain, a plebiscital regime and not at all a workers' democracy as existed with the soviets in the early days of the Soviet Union.

Far from the right of recall which Lenin spoke of, the system had degenerated to the extent that when Stalin carried through his purge in 1936-9, about one-fifth to two-fifths of the members of the parliament were arrested, exiled to Siberia and shot, and mysteriously, without any new elections or bye-elections, new MPs appeared to take their place. Under the rule of Stalin, in the last election in which Stalin took part, in his own constituency, he received the magnificent total of 105 per cent of the votes. And that in itself is sufficient indication of the kind of system we are dealing with as far as democracy of any kind is concerned.

All this was no accident. Again, whose interest is reflected? The law that no official should receive a higher wage than a skilled worker was abolished by Stalin as long ago as 1931 and today the difference in wages between a parliamentary representative or the President of the Soviet Union, and an ordinary worker in the Soviet Union, is far far greater than the difference in wages between the parliamentarians at Westminster and the working class in Britain. Lenin had made a concession in the early days of the revolution because they had no other alternative; he had made the concession of allowing a difference in wage of a maximum in the Soviet state of four to one. A specialist, a technician, could receive four times the wage of a skilled worker. That was the absolute maximum. That long ago has been abolished and in the Soviet Union today the difference between the top strata of the managers and the workers, is as great and in many cases, even much greater, than in America, Germany, Britain and other capitalist countries.

Whereas Lenin had openly proclaimed even the difference of

four to one as a *capitalist differential,* now the bureaucracy which seized control reigns untramelled and uses the Soviet state not in the interests of the working people, but in the interests of the bureaucracy itself.

What has happened to the demand of Lenin for the dissolution of the army into the armed people? It is now nearly 50 years since the revolution. As late as 1931, an army general was court-martialled because a peasant, seeing that his *felinki* or big top boots were dirty and having a liking for this general, had polished his boots. This was considered degrading in a workers' army. Under Stalin, as the economy went forward, so the differences appeared and grew. Whereas in the early days of the Soviet state and even in the early years of the Stalinist regime the soldiers and officers mingled as equals after work (when off duty), now the officers have special clubs, special barbers, special batmen, special everything, in addition to the fact that the difference in wages between a private and an officer, is greater than in the armies of the capitalist countries.

Whereas Lenin had spoken of the armed people, now we have the position of an armed elite that has been created and conditioned *apart* from the people. The reason why an army separate and apart from the people has to exist under capitalism has been explained many times by Marx and by Lenin as being for the defence of privilege and inequality and not at all for the defence of the rights of people. So that condition laid down by Lenin for a workers' state, of the ending of the monopoly of arms in the hands of an elite and having instead an armed people, has disappeared.

What has happened to the last point that was raised by Lenin —that is, of not having any permanent bureaucracy? Lenin had conceived that as the workers' state gradually moved forward, more and more of the tasks of administration, more and more of the tasks of the state, would be carried out by the working class themselves. As they moved toward socialism, and toward communism, the state would dissolve into the people. On the contrary, under the rule of Stalin, we have had a constant re-inforcement of the state machine and more bureaucratisation, oppressing the working class in the Soviet Union.

What then is left of the revolution? Why, then, do the Trotskyists still maintain that the Soviet Union remains a workers' state, albeit a Bonapartist workers' state or a deformed workers' state?

The answer is that so long as the nationalised economy, and the plan, continue to exist, then the Soviet Union is a workers' state, entirely distinct from the states (of greater or lesser democracy, as the case may be) where private property and the unplanned domination of the market continue to exist.

In the Soviet Union the planned nationalised economy is the last, and only, conquest of the revolution that remains.

Why, then, did these developments take place? Why was Stalin victorious? The answer is that socialism cannot be built in a single country, more particularly in a single backward country. The reason for the victory of the bureaucracy in the Soviet Union lies in the *material conditions* in the Soviet Union itself at the time. Marx almost a hundred years before had explained that in order to have communism, the material conditions must exist, and these do not exist in the Soviet Union.

Let us examine Lenin's writings. We will see for example how in 1919, at the time of the seizure of power by the workers in Germany, in the provinces of Bavaria and Saxony, in his letter to the German workers dealing with this problem, Lenin said the first act of the government must be to introduce the seven-hour day. This was not so much because it was a reform −of course Lenin and ourselves would be in favour of such reforms −but because the extra hour a day which would be given to the working class would give them time to take part in the administration of the state industry, because that was how Lenin saw the question of workers' power and socialism.

But that was not possible, at the stage with which we are dealing, in an isolated, backward, peasant and largely illiterate Soviet Union.

It is true that the Soviet Union has made enormous strides, on the basis of state ownership and a plan, in spite of the mistakes and the crimes of this monstrous bureaucracy.

The Soviet Union has become the second most powerful industrial state in the world. But dialectically, the fact that industry has developed to a stage where the working class, from being a tiny minority, is now by far and away the majority of the people in the Soviet Union, where the working class is perhaps the most highly cultured and educated in the world, means that the bureaucracy, having taken power, is not prepared to give it up. This bureaucracy will have to be overthrown before we can have a restoration, not of socialism −and here, may we say Comrade Clifford is apparently under the illusion that socialism was mysteriously established in the Soviet Union at a time when the material level in the Soviet Union was not one third of that of the United States and of the capitalist countries −but of workers' democracy on the level that existed in the days of Lenin and Trotsky.

Trotsky has spoken of the 'betrayal' of the revolution and these facts that we have here adduced are an indication of this betrayal. Stalin was compelled, in order to make certain of the victory of his bureaucracy, to carry through the counter-revolution to the end; to purge the Soviet state of nearly all those who had created the state —to murder two-thirds of the Central Committee, not only those who had supported Trotsky, but also those who had supported Stalin; to murder the heads of the Red Army*. The leading marshalls of the Soviet Union; Yakir, Gamarnik, Tukhachevsky (the latter developed the idea of mobile or lightning war later used by Hitler) were all wiped out. A whole generation of marshalls, generals, officers, and cadres —in fact, 70 per cent of all officers —were liquidated. The disastrous results of this we will deal with later.

Stalin was forced to destroy all the elements who still rested on the October revolution of 1917. At the time that he took power, he unfortunately probably did not understand the role that he was later to play. Stalin really believed that he represented the interests of the revolution in the Soviet Union and in the other countries. At the time of Lenin's funeral he declared how the party and the leadership were going to remain faithful to the ideals of the Communist International and international socialism.

Stalin did not understand that in developing the policy he did develop, more and more he would become a prisoner, a tool and an agent of the bureaucracy itself. He foresaw nothing, and understood nothing. As Trotsky expressed it: if one could have taken a picture in 1923 and shown Stalin what would happen as a consequence of his policy, even Stalin would not have taken control. He would have refused to operate along the lines he did. And to see how the fate of the Soviet Union as it is today, as it was in 1917, as it will be in the coming years and decades, is bound up with the fate of the international working class, as the fate of all sectors of the revolution are bound together, we can see how the policies of this criminal and irresponsible bureaucracy led to the victory of Hitler in 1933.

In 1925-7, in China, and in 1924-6 Britain, Stalin had the aim —because he had lost confidence in the international revolution —of trying to placate the bourgeoisie in China, and the petty bourgeois democrats of the Labour Party and of the trade union bureaucracy in England. As a consequence, he burned his fingers on this policy, and reversed policy completely. Whereas in the

---

*In 1937-8, Stalin purged the Red Army, arresting 25,000 officers —over a quarter of the total number. Many thousands were shot, including almost the entire leadership of the General Staff, many of whom, like those mentioned, had participated in the building of the Red Army during the civil war.

Soviet Union the bureaucracy had based themselves on the kulaks and the Nepmen growing into socialism, after the repulsion of the revolution in 1927, Stalin was in a panic, because of fear of the restoration of capitalism. Because of fear of counter-revolution, the bureaucracy was compelled in a caricatured form to adopt the policy of Trotsky, in relation at least to the industrialisation of the Soviet Union and the collectivisation of agriculture. But as always with the bureaucracy, from one extreme they went to the other; from denying the need for collectivisation in the villages, they now passed to the insane policy of forced collectivisation. Similarly in relation to industry: having declared that they could go ahead at six per cent to nine per cent a year, they now declared that anything was possible.

And then, along with the ultra-left turn in the Soviet Union we had an ultra-left turn in the capitalist countries. So far as the 'social-fascist' period of Stalin and Stalinism is concerned: in Britain there was the ludicrous position of the Communist Party not only not uniting with the petit bourgeoisie — as Clifford now suggests must be done in Ireland — but refusing to unite with the working class leaders of the labour movement, with those in whom the working class unfortunately had confidence at that time.

We had the infamous Stalinist formula that 'social democracy and fascism are not antipodes but twins'! To which Trotsky made the famous reply that 'twins are born at the same time' — that social democracy is at its strongest when the rate of profit is high, when capitalism is booming and the labour and trade union bureaucracy can get concessions for the workers from the capitalist class. He stressed that fascism, far from being the 'twin' of social democracy as the 'genius' Stalin declared it to be, arises as a defence of the bourgeoisie when crisis sets in, when there are no profits and when no concessions can be made. Then the capitalist Black Hundreds, or brownshirts or what you like to call them, go to work to split and terrorise the workers, who are in process of turning from the reformism of the social-democratic bureaucracy and of taking the revolutionary road.

In Britain the result of this criminal policy dictated by the Stalinist bureaucracy, was that the tiny British Communist Party was breaking up Labour Party meetings, trying to beat up Labour leaders — Pollitt, Campbell and other hacks and mouthpieces announced in the *Worker* that the Labour Party *was not to be allowed to hold any meetings in the open anywhere in the country.* And, of course, as a consequence of this, the Communist Party became isolated from the workers who were completely indignant at the ultra-left and insane tactics of that party.

But in Britain it was merely comedy. In Germany on the other hand, *the policy of Stalin was absolutely tragic — a monstrous betrayal of the working class.* The failure of the working class to give a lead to the petit bourgeoisie — and that, Comrade Clifford, is where the problem of the petit bourgeoisie comes in; where the working class fails to give a lead, then the petit bourgeoisie goes over to the side of reaction — the failure of the revolution of 1918, the failure of the revolutionary opportunity of 1923, this led to the petit bourgeoisie moving in the direction of the counter-revolution, of fascism. In 1930 for the first time Hitler secured six million votes at the polls, and instead of the Communist Party immediately offering a united front to the Social Democrats and preparing for a struggle to the death against Hitler and the Nazi gangsters, the Communist Party refused. They even attempted to compete in the most base fashion with the nationalist propaganda of the Nazis. They split the German workers in the most insane fashion possible. For example, in the period 1930-3 they even came out with the slogan 'Beat the little *Zoergebiels* in the playgrounds!', — inciting the children of Communist workers against the children of Social Democratic workers (Zoergebiel being the Prussian chief of police, who was a Social Democrat).

In this criminal way Stalinism paralysed the German working class. In 1931 in Prussia, the state in which the Social Democrats held power, the Communist Party even united and voted with the Nazis in the so-called Red Referendum, for the purpose of turning out the Social Democratic government.

The Communist Party at that time was putting forward the demagogic nonsense that because capitalism ruled under fascism and because capitalism ruled under democracy, therefore fascism and democracy were one and the same thing. What did it matter, ran the propaganda of Thaelmann, whether one gets bullets from the fascists or bullets from the so-called democrats? Whether one starves under the Social Democrats or whether one starves under Hitler? In this way they paralysed the working class. They refused to unite the working class. They refused to organise the working class on a programme that could have won also the mass of the middle class who had gone mad and in their agony, due to the slump of 1929-33, had turned to the fascists for a solution.

For the first time in the history of the working class in the period of a century, monstrous totalitarian reaction was allowed to take power, and to crush the working class, as Hitler boasted, 'without a window-pane being broken'.

We should remember in this connection that whereas Stalin was preaching the insane theory of 'social-fascism' — that the Social Democrats were the worst form of fascists — Trotsky wrote four books warning that the victory of Hitler would be a blow not only against the German working class but against the international working class, warning that the victory of Hitler *would mean war on the Soviet Union.* At that time the so-called 'communists' were attacking Trotsky as a 'counter-revolutionary' for putting forward the conception of the united front of the working class, a united front of struggle on the basis of the working class.

Trotsky appealed to the German workers and more especially to the communist workers, not to go down without a fight. A defeat of the German workers, he said, at the hands of Hitler, would be worse than a hundred other defeats. Comrade Clifford says there was no Communist Party to speak of in Germany; that there was no possibility of any effective armed resistance. Yet we know there were over one million armed communist workers, Comrade Clifford, and two million armed workers in the Republican Guard. There were even some tanks from the Spartacist uprising. Of course, we realise that for Comrade Clifford to recognise these facts would mean that he might have to look more closely and in a Marxist manner at the 'theory' of 'social-fascism'.

In Britain —as we could give scores of quotations to indicate —in Germany, everywhere, Trotsky revealed himself as a 'counter-revolutionary' according to the Communist Party, because he was proposing and demanding a united front between the social democracy and the Communist Party in order to prevent the coming to power of the fascists.

This was one of Stalin's greatest crimes and greatest betrayals. In the current (August 1965) issue of *Marxism Today,* in a most dishonest and ignorant way, the issue is not dealt with at all as it was in reality. It was not a question of a defence of bourgeois democracy, but of a defence of the rights of the working class, of the elements of a new workers' state that exist within democracy —of the rights of the trade unions, the rights of workers' parties, which are concessions that had been wrested from capitalism over a perod of a hundred years.

It was this 'great teacher' of the workers, Joseph Stalin, who was entirely responsible for the victory of Hitler; no Stalin —no Hitler! That should be ingrained on the working class.

Here we might point out that up to 1933 the supporters of Trotsky considered themselves as part of the Communist International, and stood for reform within the Soviet Union and within the Communist Parties. But after 1933, the Communist Parties showed that they had learned nothing from this greatest defeat in the history of the working class, and continued with the same policy as in the past. In France, as late as 1934 when an attempt was being organised at a fascist coup (we would refer you here to *France in Crisis**) the Communist Party, having learned nothing from the terrible experience of the German workers, united with the fascists for the overthrow of the bourgeois parliament in February 1934. It was only the instinct of the working class, who had seen what had happened in Germany, that led them to come out in a general strike, and prevent the move to power of the fascists.

It was the continuing reactionary policies dictated by the bureaucracy, which saw a mortal danger to its position in the revolutionary coming to power of the workers anywhere in Europe, that forced Trotsky and the Left Opposition to break and establish the Fourth International.

Stalin attempted to arrive at an agreement with Hitler at that time. For him, the victory of Hitler was only an episode, not a terrible defeat. He was busy building so-called 'socialism in one country'; in reality, building the interests of his bureaucratic clique. It was only in 1935, again by the dictate of Stalin, that the Communist Party once again changed its line, and instead of the united front which they had rejected in the past, turned 180 degrees, and came forward with the people's front or popular front. And the idea of a popular front was again dictated purely by the foreign diplomatic needs and interests, not of the Soviet Union, or the Russian or the international working class, but of this gangster caste which had seized control in the Soviet Union.

Stalin was prepared to sacrifice —and this meant in the end the sacrifice of the interests of the Soviet Union —the French workers, the workers of Spain, the working class of Britain and of other countries (including Ireland, for we have not forgotten what happened to the Irish Communist Party) —when it became clear that Hitler intended war on the Soviet Union. In order to try to come to some kind of military agreement with the so-called democratic capitalists of France and Britain, against Hitler, Stalin followed a policy of popular frontism.

Yet we know that the so-called democratic powers backed Hitler to the hilt; they supported Hitler because they wanted to see the crushing of the German working class. The British imperialists in particular supported the taking over of the Rhineland in order to break the power of France, and above all in order to prepare Hitler as a weapon of intervention against the Soviet Union. And if the war and the developments that took place later were not in the interest of British imperialism, it was no thanks to the criminal policy of Stalin and the Stalinists, as we will show later.

*included in this volume under the title *The Rise of De Gaulle*.

But now that this bureaucratic caste had seized complete control in the Soviet Union and had purged the working class, the whole rosy perspective was spoiled by the outbreak of the revolution in Spain. And now for two reasons the bureaucracy was scared out of its wits by the revolution in Spain. First of all, from the so-called diplomatic point of view, that it might frighten its would-be allies into the arms of the reaction. Secondly, a victory for the working class, an installation of workers' democracy anywhere in the world, would mean the end of this bureaucratic caste itself in the Soviet Union. The victory of the workers and the establishment of a state on the lines outlined by Marx and Lenin would immediately have led to the Russian workers, seeing they were no longer isolated, settling accounts with this monstrous tumour which had grown on the Soviet state — they would have lanced it with the weapon of political revolution.

As reports indicate, even from bourgeois observers, it was the revolution in Spain which shook the basis of Stalin's rule and which now led to the consummation of the bureaucratic counter-revolution in the Soviet Union. It was then that Stalin organised his purge trials. It was then that Stalin massacred hundreds of thousands of worker-Bolsheviks. It was then that Stalin exiled to Siberia and into slave labour camps, between ten and fifteen million people. All this because of the fear of revolution on the part of the proletariat.

The crimes of Stalin were not an accident, as Khruschev and others made out, although to Comrade Clifford this counter-revolutionary bureaucratic ruthlessness was 'necessary' to the maintenance of the 'dictatorship of the proletariat'. Another particular favourite of Comrade Clifford, apart from the monster Stalin, is Mao Tse Tung. The latter also, strangely enough for a 'Marxist', thinks the crimes of Stalin were accidental, and that the so-called 'cult of the personality' was only a question of a mistake. It is absolutely an insult to the intelligence even of non-Marxists to speak as if one man could dominate a whole country, and embark on a programme of crimes of that sort, without being the representative of the material interests of some powerful stratum or strata of society; in this case, the bureaucracy.

The cult of personality was launched, the terror was launched, against the working class in the Soviet Union, against the October revolution, out of fear of the throwing aside of the usurpers of the revolution and the restoration of democracy on the lines of the October revolution. That is the explanation of the crimes of Stalin. And in the lunatic lengths to which this insane bureaucracy proceeded we had at various stages whole nations being uprooted

and exiled to Siberia, as Khruschev was later to reveal —the
Chechen Ingushes, the Crimean Tartars, the German Volga
Republic, all these entire peoples, men, women, and children
exiled into Siberia. What did all this have to do with socialism,
Comrade Clifford? What did it have to do with the dictatorship of
the proletariat, never mind socialism?

It was not for nothing that Lenin in the period of 1923-4, as the
new documents have now revealed, was already beginning to take
action against Stalin for his Great Russian chauvinism and his
attitude to the backward and minority peoples (including the
Georgian people) of the Soviet Union. Lenin explained that Stalin
did not understand the ABC of the problem of nationalities —and
incidentally, we might mention just in passing that the book on
nationalities published by Stalin was merely a paraphrase of the
ideas of Lenin, which Lenin went over many times before it was
published.

As with all his other policies, Stalin's crimes in regard to the
nationalities had nothing in common either with the programme of
Bolshevism, or the means with which they won the peoples in the
Soviet Union in the period of the war of intervention and the civil
war.

The Hitler-Stalin Pact

The Stalinists came out for the 'popular front'. In the most cynical
fashion which it is possible to imagine —having betrayed the
revolution in Germany, the revolution in France (the French
workers also had the opportunity of seizing power), the revolution
in Spain —Stalin made the second world war inevitable. For five
years, having put forward the programme of popular frontism, of
agreement with democracy —using the Communist International
as a tool of the foreign policy of the Russian bureaucracy —Stalin
then cynically turned around and signed the Hitler-Stalin Pact, a
pact that Trotsky predicted would result in war on the Soviet
Union. This pact was a preparation for the intervention of Hitler.

Trotskyism, while all during this period and at each stage making
a relentless criticism of the crimes and betrayals of Stalinism,
nevertheless always stood for the defence of what was left of the
October revolution.

Stalin, by operating this policy of popular frontism, prepared the
way for Hitler's victory. The French working class was
demoralised; and as a consequence we had the victory of Hitler in
the West, which in turn prepared the way for war on the East.
Many people have believed, (and Comrade Clifford still does) that

it was Stalin's 'clever policy' which led to the situation where the ruling class of Britain and of America were prepared to make an alliance with the Soviet Union against Germany. This is absolute nonsense.

Even in 1917 at the time of the seizure of power by the Bolsheviks the imperialists of Britain and France were quite prepared to support the Soviet Union —temporarily of course —against Germany, their main enemy and main danger to their interests at that time. And in the same way, 'supporting the Soviet Union' —in Lenin's phrase, 'like the rope supports a hanged man '— they were quite prepared to come to an alliance with the Soviet Union at a later stage again because of Hitler's conquest of the greater part of Europe.

In the second world war, we get an entirely different way of operating on the part of the Stalinists than that which we had seen on the part of Lenin and Trotsky in the period of the intervention against the Soviet Union following the first world war.

At the time of the most desperate peril for the Soviet Union, when the German army stood at the gates of Moscow, Leningrad and Stalingrad, when Stalin asked for a second front, he was told that it was militarily impossible, that the resources, tanks, landing craft and men were not available. A million troops were in the Middle East (in Persia, Iraq etc.) and by sheer 'coincidence' were facing toward the richest part of the Soviet Union (the Urals, Baku, Batum and the Soviet oilfields). Again by sheer 'coincidence' there were a million Russian troops facing the British troops. When Stalin in desperation asked that these British troops should fight with the Russians on the Eastern Front, Churchill replied that Stalin should withdraw the million Russian troops from these frontiers and send them to fight on the Eastern Front. He (Churchill) was perfectly willing that the million British troops should garrison Baku, the Caucasus, the Urals and the richest parts of the Soviet Union. Even Stalin knew what that meant. He turned down the generous offer of the great democratic gentleman.

What all this revealed was the calculations of the ruling class —that at some stage the Soviet Union would be destroyed and they would collect the lot.

Khruschev has revealed something of the crimes of Stalin in regard to the conduct of the war. First of all they were caught completely unprepared by Hitler's attack. In spite of the fact that many warnings were given by the imperialists and by workers and peasants on the frontiers who saw pontoons, etc, being prepared, Stalin clung to his agreement with Hitler.

What is not generally realised is that at the time of the attack by the German forces the fire power of the Russian army was greater than the firepower of the German army; and other things being equal, the Soviet Union should have defeated the Germans within the first six months of the war. The reason for the terrible victories of Hitler which cost the Russian people so many millions of dead, and the Soviet Union such terrible sacrifices, was the crime of Stalin in destroying over 70 per cent of the effective officers and cadres of the Russian army in order to maintain his totalitarian rule; and in putting in their place such nonentities as Voroshilov, Budyenny and Timoshenko.

The Russian armies were decapitated, and in desperation Stalin had to release Zhukov and Russokovsky from the jail for the purpose of conducting the war!

Instead of Lenin's internationalist policy, as would be natural with a workers' state —relying on the working class of other countries and above all on the German soldiers and working class, to win them over to the revolution (as the Russians had succeeded in doing in 1917-18) —Stalin waged the struggle as a *nationalist* struggle, even as a *racial* struggle.

If one reads the poison disseminated by the Communist Party, in Britain, France and other countries, following the lead of Stalin, one will see and be shocked by this. In Russia itself such slogans as 'Death to the Germans', 'The only good German is a dead German', 'To each a German', and so on, were raised by the bureaucratic conductors of the so-called 'Great Patriotic War'. This policy offering nothing but retribution —not, mind you to the German fascists, the German capitalists, the SA or the SS —but to the *German people as a whole,* led to the war lasting much longer than it need have done, and led to the imposition of immeasurably greater sacrifices on the Russian people than would otherwise have been necessary.

Just to point to what we have said, we would add that Hitler *actually distributed and redistributed Russian propaganda material to the German army,* because it aided discipline in that it left no way out for the German soldiers except nazi discipline. *Can anyone imagine the German High Command helping with the circulation of Bolshevik propaganda in the period 1917-18?!! That* was the difference between Stalinist propaganda and Bolshevik propaganda.

Outside Moscow there were one million German soldiers, not clad for the winter, without sufficient food, or sometimes any at all —they died frozen in heaps. Not one international call, not one call to them *as workers* was made —not a single offer of a bowl of soup even. The bureaucracy could only offer anti-Boche, anti-Hun racialism and hate.

We should remember that the second world war, in the European arena at least, was a Russo-German war. British and US imperialism *remained onlookers*. The only reason they made the second front in 1944 was, not because they were dear allies of the great warrior Stalin, but because of their fear that if they did not intervene at that stage, when the Russian army was marching on Berlin, they would find the Russians on the English Channel. Their only reason for intervening was to save capitalism in Europe, to prevent the occupation of the whole of Europe by the Russian armies.

And here we can say in regard to the second world war that it was not only the gigantic sacrifices and mighty struggles of the Russian people themselves that saved the Soviet Union from destruction after that war. Russia was at her weakest, she had been bled white. She produced at that time eight million tons of steel, all of which went into the production of armaments. (Only a bare three or four per cent of Russian equipment was Western aid, and this mainly in the form of food, clothing, boots etc.) The armaments themselves were Russian-produced, and here let us say that in the field of armaments, the Russians outproduced Nazi Germany with the whole of Europe at her disposal.

America alone was producing 120 million tons of steel —that is, apart from Britain and the other capitalist countries of the West. The American and the British troops who were engaged in Europe were fresh, the overwhelming majority of them had engaged in hardly any real fighting at all. Had it not been for the revolutionary wave which swept Europe after the war —the radicalisation of the British workers and the American people who wanted the troops brought home once the war was over — it would not have been possible for the Soviet Union to be saved. America had the atomic bomb, the dropping of which, incidentally, was approved and supported by Stalin and by his lackeys in Britain and other other countries. America was at her strongest, Russia at her weakest, and still America was paralysed because it was impossible to swing the American workers behind a war against the Soviet Union. That is the reason why the Soviet Union was victorious.

In this regard it can be said that the salvation of the Soviet Union was not so much a result of the reactionary policies of Stalin and alliances with imperialism. On the contrary, the Soviet Union was saved *in spite of these alliances and this policy.*

The Bureaucracy Today

We have said that Stalin represented the bureaucracy —not the working class, but the millions of officialdom in the Soviet Union. From a Marxist point of view this can easily be explained. Engels, in *Anti-Duhring*, has shown that the division into classes in society, in the last analysis, is due to the division of labour.

Engels explained that so long as art, science and government remain the preserve of a small group of people and not the masses, this small group of people would use and abuse their position in their own interest and not in the interest of the people as a whole. He went on to explain that this was inevitable as long as the masses of the people had to work seven, eight, nine or ten hours a day for the barest necessities of existence.

In Russia, at the time of the revolution, the per capita income and standard of living were less than in Britain three centuries ago. On the basis of weak industry, backward agriculture, ignorance and illiteracy —where the working class had to work long hours merely, as Engels said, to get the barest necessities of existence —it was not possible for the working class to maintain itself in power. That is the explanation for the victory of the Stalinist bureaucracy.

By the dialectic of history the very victories of the Soviet Union in the last ten to fifteen years have gradually been underminig the power of the bureaucracy within the Soviet Union. The bureaucracy has ceased to function even as a relatively progressive force. In the period between the wars, given the failure of the international revolution (the reasons for which have been mentioned) the bureaucracy played a relatively progressive role in the industrialisation of the Soviet Union.

But already by 1953, the bureaucracy, in Marxist terms, had become an impediment, a fetter on the development of the productive forces. Marx explained the role which capitalism played in the past —the development of the material conditions for socialism. We can say that developments like those in the Soviet Union are possible in backward countries, where capitalism might be destroyed by various means (which we don't want to go into at this moment). Where, on the other hand, the proletariat would take power in a country like Britain, America, France or Japan, there is already a sufficiency of the material development of production. But even so, as Marx explained when he foreshadowed the revolution, it would require the efforts of the Germans, the French and the English —of the most advanced countries at that time —for the building of socialism. So also in America, we can *begin* the dictatorship of the proletariat. We cannot construct socialism even in America on its own.

But today one cannot imagine the revolution in America, Britain, France, or Germany without it spreading to other countries of Europe and of the world.

In the period 1950-3 the bureaucracy, as with the capitalist class in the last four or five decades, has become more and more an impediment on the planning and development of production. It is impossible to operate a so-called socialist plan without the direct participation and control of the working class, the peasants and the people as a whole. In the Soviet Union the rule of the bureaucracy is increasingly hampering development. According to Russian economists themselves, one-third of the entire national effort is wasted because of the corruption, mismanagement and nepotism of the bureaucracy.

In 1953, as in 1936, Stalin, feeling the ground once again moving under his feet, was preparing another purge. That is the explanation of the so-called 'Doctors' Plot'* of that time. But the bureaucracy decided that Russia could not afford a new purge — the terrible purge of 1936-40 had terribly weakened the Soviet Union. We have already dealt, albeit briefly, with the terrible effect of that purge on the armed forces, and the consequences of this in the war. The whole of the country was paralysed by the purge which was waged by Stalin at that time. It was a virtual civil war.

Stalin prepared a new purge in 1953, which would also have meant the purge of the top bureaucrats —Khruschev, Voroshilov**, Zhukov, Beria and others. They decided to strangle Stalin. And Stalin probably got his just deserts, strangled by his own bureaucrats and policemen, in 1953.

In the intervening period, since 1953, the Stalinist bureaucracy, headed by Khruschev, adopted a new policy. They realised that it was impossible, without plunging the Soviet Union into complete chaos, to launch into a new purge, which would have affected tens of millions of people. The Soviet Union, in the world situation which existed, did not dare face a prospect of that sort. In addition to which, the Russian working class was far stronger than before, and the bureaucracy was not prepared to risk a tremendous clash. The significance of Malenkov***, Khruschev, Kosygin and Co, is that that they have stood for *a policy of reform from the top in order to prevent revolution from the bottom.* The whole policy of the

---

*In January 1953, nine Professors of Medicine were 'unmasked' as being agents of the British and American Secret Services. Unlike previous purges, which had listed living associates of Stalin as the 'intended victims', this time the only 'victims' were dead. The implications of this shook the bureaucracy and could well have led to Stalin's assasination by others in the Politbureau.
**Leading Russian bureaucrats. Nikita Khruschev was Prime Minister 1958-64, Kliment Voroshilov was President 1953-60, Laurent Beria was head of the Secret Police 1958-63, and Zhukov was second in command (after Stalin) of the Russian forces at the end of the war.
***Aleksei Kosygin, Russian Prime Minister 1964-80, Georgi Malenkov, Prime Minister 1953-5.

bureaucracy in the Soviet Union is orientated to a defence of their privileges against the working class and to try by various reforms and concessions to prevent the working class from overthrowing them.

Trotsky, in predicting the *political revolution* in the Soviet Union, had indicated the way in which the demands of the working class for a restoration of soviet democracy would proceed. In the Hungarian revolution in 1956 there were Hungarian workers who had never read Trotsky, but had read Lenin. They nevertheless put forward exactly the demands which Trotsky had worked out. This was no accident. The demands which they put forward were for the four conditions we have mentioned earlier. They demanded, in addition, the right of all parties which accept state ownership and a plan to put forward their positions. Never again were the Hungarian workers prepared to tolerate the totalitarian dictatorship of any one party.

Whereas it could be argued that in the early days of the Russian revolution, the Bolsheviks were forced to adopt a repressive regime, now, at a time when the Soviet Union can produce 91 million tons of steel, when capitalism has been weakened throught the world, when the bureaucrats allege that socialism has been realised in the Soviet Union, not even the elementary principles of the dictatorship of the proletariat as worked out by Lenin and Marx exist in the Soviet Union.

Why is it that the bureaucracy cannot introduce democracy? Why is it that they cannot allow workers' organisations the freedom to exist? Let us look at the bourgeois revolution. In the early stages of such revolutions, as under Cromwell for example, the bourgeoisie was compelled to take dictatorial measures against feudal reaction. But at a later stage, after the bourgeois had established themselves, they had no objection to reaction putting forward the programme of a return to the 'good old days' —back to feudalism in effect —because the idea was ludicrous and reactionary. Yet in the Soviet Union, at a time when there are sixty million workers, when only democracy can really permit the full development of the potential of the Soviet state, the bureaucracy still continues with its totalitarian measures. And measures against who? The bourgeoisie has long since ceased to exist. The peasantry is supposed to be, according to our friend Clifford, the dearest ally of the proletariat (and we would certainly say that the peasants would not want to go back to the old system if they were offered an alternative by the working class of the Soviet Union). The measures of the bureaucracy are directed *against the workers*, as more and more they realise that they, the bureaucracy, are an impediment upon production.

The reason why the bureaucracy is now compelled to fool around with capitalist 'incentives', to give the managers an incentive in the production of their factories, is precisely because they are completely incapable of appealing to the masses themselves. To do this would mean destroying the privileges of the bureaucracy. This is the problem from which stem the zigzags of the bureaucracy over the past ten to fifteen years, under Stalin, under Malenkov, under Khruschev and now Brezhnev and Kosygin.

The bureaucracy first of all *centralised* the enterprises −500,000 of them, run by a handful of people −which idea was absolutely crazy. Khruschev *de*centralised and, as the Trotskyists at the time said would happen, from one centralised bureaucracy controlling industry, sixteen bureaucracies appeared and proliferated, laying new burdens of chaos, red tape and difficulties before the Russian economy. The original impetus given to industry by the regionalisation turned into its opposite. Now they are *re*centralising and at the same time trying to decentralise! The one thing they cannot do, and which the material base has been created for now, is to permit the creative intervention of the masses, because that would mean the end of their privileges and power. That is the one reason why −unlike the bourgeoisie, whose system was based on private ownership, and who could allow the development of democracy −the Stalinist bureaucracy in the Soviet Union cannot allow any form of democracy. It is impossible, for that matter in China or in any other of the deformed workers' states.

Comrade Clifford has mixed up (consciously or unconsciously) two fundamentally different questions: the Theory of the Permanent Revolution and the dictatorship of the proletariat. We have defined the dictatorship of the proletariat, what it means and how it works.

We will now take up the Theory of the Permanent Revolution. Very simply, the theory can be explained in this way. In the period of the modern development of capitalism there is, first of all, what Trotsky calls the law of combined development: superimposed on feudal or semi-feudal remains, we have the development of modern industry −as we had in Russia, to a certain extent in China and in other countries of the so-called underdeveloped or backward areas of the world. Because of the period in which we live, the bourgeoisie in the backward countries is incapable of playing the role that was played by the bourgeoisie in the revolutions of the past, for example in the English revolution or the great French revolution of 1789. Trotsky's Theory of Permanent Revolution bases itself on the idea of Marx −and this they held in common with Lenin −that under modern conditions *the bourgeoisie is quite incapable of carrying through the bourgeois democratic revolution.* The reason for this is the linking up of the interests of the landowners with the bourgeoisie, and in the colonial countries the linking up of both of these together with imperialism. Therefore, *the problem was posed of a new class coming on the scene and carrying through the programme of the bourgeois democratic revolution.*

To understand this clearly we can take the development of the Russian revolution itself. What were the various positions and conceptions in relation to the revolution? The Mensheviks, echoing Plekhanov in this regard, said that we are facing a bourgeois revolution in Russia, therefore we must make an agreement with the liberal bourgeoisie. We will come to an agreement with the liberal bourgeoisie, they argued, Tsarism will be overthrown, then over a period of decades democracy will be developed in Russia and *then* will come the question of the socialist revolution.

The Menshevik spokesman Martynov* wrote on the eve of the 1905 revolution:

> The coming revolution will be a revolution of the bourgeoisie; and that means that...it will only, to a greater or lesser extent, secure the rule of all or some of the bourgeois classes. If this is so, it is clear that the coming revolution can on no account assume political forms against the will of the whole of the bourgeoisie, as the latter will be the master of tomorrow. If so, then to follow the path of simply frightening the majority of the bourgeois elements would mean that the revolutionary struggle of the proletariat could lead only to one result −the restoration of absolutism in its original form...(A Martynov, *Die Dikatury*, Geneva, 1905, pp 57-8)

Martynov's implied conclusion is that the working class should impose self-restraint on itself so as not to 'frighten' the bourgeoisie; but at the same time he states that it should persistently press the bourgeoisie to lead the revolution:

> The struggle to influence the course and outcome of the bourgeois revolution can be expressed simply in the proletariat's exerting revolutionary pressure on the will of the liberal and radical bourgeoisie, the more democratic 'lower' section of society compelling the 'higher' section to agree to lead the bourgeois revolution to its conclusion.

Similarly, the Menshevik paper *Iskra*** wrote at the time:

> When looking at the arena of struggle in Russia, what do we see? Only two powers: Tsarist autocracy and the liberal bourgeoisie, the latter organised and of tremendous specific weight. The working classes are split and can do nothing; as an independent force we do not

*Leading Menshevik at the time of the 1901 split in the RSDLP.
***Iskra* was established by Lenin in 1900 to lay the foundations for an all-Russian Revolutionary Party. However, soon after the split at the 1903 Congress, a majority of the *Iskra* editorial board sided with the Mensheviks for whom the paper became a mouthpiece.

exist, and therefore our task consists in the support of the second force
— the liberal bourgeoisie; we must encourage it, and on no account
frighten it by putting forward the independent demands of the
proletariat. (Quoted by G Zinoviev, *Istoriia Rossiiskoi Kommunisticheskoii
Partii (Bolshevikov)*, Moscow-Leningrad, 1923, p 158.)

Lenin's Position

Lenin's position was somewhat different to this. Lenin took the
position that they were facing a bourgeois democratic revolution.
But, he said, echoing the words of Marx, the further East one goes,
the more corrupt, the more rotten, the more venal is the
bourgeoisie and the more incapable it is of playing a progressive
role. We are facing a bourgeois revolution, he said, in agreement
with the Mensheviks, *therefore some of our main blows must be struck
against the bourgeoisie itself; we must have absolutely no confidence in, we
must give absolutely no support whatsoever to the liberal bourgeoisie.* Lenin
put forward the idea of an alliance of the proletariat and the
peasantry, of the 'democratic dictatorship of the workers and
peasants'.

He said that the bourgeoisie was linked to Tsarism, and to the
landowners; and that therefore *we would have to have in the early
stages a bourgeois democratic dictatorship of the proletariat and
peasantry.*

Lenin and the Bolsheviks said that the revolution would be
bourgeois in character and that its aim would not overstep the
limits of a bourgeois revolution. 'The democratic revolution will
not extend beyond the scope of bourgeois social-economic
relationships...' wrote Lenin. And again, '...this democratic
revolution will not weaken, but will strengthen the domination of
the bourgeoisie.' He returned to the theme again and again.

Lenin accentuated and emphasised that the democratic
dictatorship of the proletariat and the peasantry was to be a
bourgeois dictatorship. And on the basis of the bourgeois
revolution —and here we see the internationalism of Lenin
— Russia *would provoke the socialist revolution in Europe and then on the
basis of the socialist revolution in Europe, the socialist revolution would be
carried to Russia and we would have a proletarian revolution in Russia.*

One can see this point in all of Lenin's writings and pamphlets up
to 1917 and Lenin always emphasised this point.

Trotsky's Conception

What was wrong with the conception of Lenin, as Trotsky would
express it, was that he put forward an *algebraic formula,* leaving history

and the actual course of development to fill in the unknown. Trotsky said that if you have a dictatorship of the proletariat and peasantry, the question arises: which is to be the dominant force? If there is to be a dictatorship of the proletariat and peasantry, then it is obvious that the *proletariat has to be the dominant force* and get the support of the peasantry by supporting the aims of the peasantry.

As Trotsky pointed out, all history has demonstrated that the peasants, and the petit bourgeoisie in the towns, can play no independent role as a class. Under modern conditions they support the bourgeoisie or they support the proletariat. Marx explained this many times. Lenin explained it. Trotsky explained it. The only people who never understood this were Stalin, Mao Tse Tung and their hangers-on or would-be hangers-on.

Trotsky's theory put the issue in a different way to Lenin. He agreed with Lenin as against the Mensheviks, and quoted many figures to support this view, showing how the landlords were linked with the banks, how the banks were linked with the bourgeoisie, how the bourgeoisie was linked with the landlords. The bourgeoisie had investments in the land; the landlords had investments in industry. Both were linked to Tsarism. Therefore, the bourgeoisie, because of these links, because of the belated character of the revolution and because of the links with foreign capital, could not carry through the bourgeois democratic revolution.

Therefore, Trotsky said, the revolution would *begin* as a bourgeois revolution, with democratic slogans, with the slogan of the eight hour day, with the slogan of the land to the peasants and so on. Where he differed with Lenin on this question, was in that he said that because the bourgeoisie was incapable of carrying through the bourgeois democratic revolution, *the proletariat would have to come to power in Russia in order to carry through the tasks of the bourgeois democratic revolution.* And how, in a bourgeois democratic revolution, could they come to power without the support of the peasantry, without the support of the petit bourgeoisie? The idea is absolute nonsense.

But, Trotsky said, the proletariat, having come to power and having carried through the bourgeois democratic tasks (having overthrown the monarchy, given land to the peasants, unified Russia, given freedom to the oppressed nationalities, and so on) would not stop at this; but having obtained power through the bourgeois democratic revolution, in order to carry through the bourgeois democratic revolution, would then go on to the socialist tasks of the revolution. Having carried through the socialist revolution —and obviously Russia could not carry it through on its own —the revolution would then expand to the countries of the West.

This is what is meant by the Permanent Revolution —that beginning as a bourgeois revolution, it becomes a socialist revolution. Having become a socialist revolution in one country it then expands to other countries. In other words, *the revolution assumes a permanent character.*

Let us make clear that as far as Lenin, Trotsky and all the Marxists at that time were concerned, the question of socialism in one country could not be raised. It could not have been raised by Stalin, Plekhanov or anyone else because it was such a reactionary idea. That was not at all the difference between Lenin and Trotsky before the revolution. It was as to whether the bourgeois revolution could become a proletarian revolution; and on this question Lenin had not taken up a firm position before 1917.

'Socialism in one country' meant revolution in one country

It will be clear from what has been said that today, fifty years after the revolution of 1917, the tasks and problems in Russia have not yet been solved. Because the revolution took place only in one country, inevitably it degenerated into a bureaucratic or deformed workers' state (this was Lenin's description of it in 1923). Bureaucratisation in turn fed upon the continuing isolation. Then, through control of the Comintern, the bureaucracy, under Stalin, became an active and openly counter-revolutionary agent in the communist workers' movement internationally, Because of all this, the task of moving towards socialism still remains in the Soviet Union. The working class in the Soviet Union will have to pay with a new revolution, a political revolution, because of the fact that the revolution remained isolated and therefore degenerated.

Even though Russia has become the second industrial power of the world, it is quite clear that it has not succeeded in solving its problems, and events since the second world war have demonstrated this over and over again. Even if one assumes that in the next five years —and this is entirely possible —the Soviet Union should succeed in overtaking and exceeding the production of America, still they would not have solved the problems that exist. First and foremost, there is the problem of the bureaucracy, which is now clogging up all the creative power of the Soviet Union. Secondly, if one assumes that in the class struggle which is still taking place relentlessly in all the countries of the world, in the advanced countries as well as the backward countries, that the working class were to be defeated, then the fate of the

Soviet Union, as formerly, or even more than formerly, will be decided by the class struggle in the West. The boom that we've seen in the last twenty years, the upswing of capitalism, is bound to change into a downswing. Then it is a question again of war or revolution, as the Marxists have never tired of pointing out.

If we were to assume the defeat especially of the American working class in the titanic struggles that loom ahead, and of which the blacks' struggle is but the first glimpse, and the seizure of power by a totalitarian fascist system, that could mean only one thing —a world war. With modern weapons this means annihilation.

It was the betrayal of the German, French and Spanish workers that led to the second world war. The great potential strength of the working class has in the past twenty years prevented the imperialists attempting another major war. If the working class is defeated in America in the coming struggles, then the question of the H-Bomb being used will really come up, and in an hour everything that has been built up in fifty or sixty years of the labour of the Russian people will be destroyed.

The fate of all countries in the world is bound together, today more than ever before and any attempt to infuse blood and life into the wholly discredited Stalinist and bureaucratic notion of 'socialism in a single country' is an attempt to do a disservice to the revolutionary movement.

The continued existence of imperialism in a number of advanced countries with all the possibilities inherent in that situation; the fact that Stalinism through its misleading of the working class contributed to that situation and continues today from two centres, 'two Romes', to spread its revisionism in the ranks of the workers' movement; the fact that this revisionism can again contribute to victories of reaction with the consequent unleashing of nuclear world war, is the *final irrefutable proof* of the irrelevance and reactionary nature of the 'single country' nonsense. It is the final and irrefutable proof of the purely *national and reactionary* interests of the Stalinist bureaucrats, whether in Moscow, Warsaw, Budapest, Peking or anywhere else. Whether they like it or not, the nationalism of Mao Tse Tung, of Stalin and all the others is tied up with the fate of the class struggle in the imperialist world. In the most reactionary way, all these elements pave the way for the possible annihilation of mankind.

Leninism, and not Stalinism dishonestly dressed up as Leninism, is the only way forward for the working class and for humanity as a whole. Only international socialism, only the international revolution can prevent a nuclear holocaust and guarantee the future.

Theory and Practice in the Russian Revolution

We will now look at how the theories and conceptions put forward by the Mensheviks, by Lenin and by Trotsky worked out in practice in the Russian revolution itself.

What were the positions of all the tendencies in 1917, after the February revolution? The Mensheviks, logically carrying through the programme on which they'd based themselves for two decades, together with the Social Revolutionaries, supported the *bourgeois* Provisional Government which came to power.

What was the attitude, on the other hand, of Stalin, Kamenev, Zinoviev and of all the other 'Old Bolsheviks' at that time? Because of the lack of clarity in the slogans of Lenin —of a democratic dictatorship of the proletariat and peasantry —they failed to understand the situation that existed. Had the revolution depended on Stalin, Zinoviev, Kamenev and all the other 'Old Bolsheviks', it would have been defeated. It would have met the same fate as the Chinese revolution of 1925-7, the German revolution, the Italian and French revolutions, and the revolutions in other countries where the leadership of the proletariat failed.

What was the position taken by Stalin? Stalin's attitude was that the revolution had established the democratic dictatorship of the proletariat and peasantry *and therefore full support should be given to the Provisional Government and to the Mensheviks.* Stalin even said that now that the differences between the Mensheviks and the Bolsheviks had been erased by the revolution itself, they should unite with the Mensheviks into one single united party. When Stalin and Kamenev returned from exile, they found Molotov and some others in control of *Pravda,* the party press. They insisted that the line of the party press was too left; they took over the editorship of the paper and moved in the direction of conciliation and full support for the Provisional Government.

What was the attitude of Lenin? What Lenin explained when he came to Russia in the sealed train was that in so far as a democratic dictatorship of the proletariat and peasantry was to be realised, *the Kerensky regime was the democratic dictatorship of the proletariat and peasantry.* There could be no other, except through the bourgeoisie. And Lenin now patiently explained to the working class that the only solution to the problem lying before the peasants, *the only way to carry through the bourgeois revolution to a conclusion was in the proletarian revolution.* At the same time, of course, for Lenin as for all Marxists of that time and before, any utopian idea of solving the problem on a Russian basis alone was ruled out. No one, no one at all, raised the question of socialism in a single country until Stalin in 1924.

The bourgeois democratic revolution has been in existence in Ireland for forty years. No other democratic dictatorship is possible, apart from that of Fianna Fail — Fine Gael. Only the Irish working class of North and South, of two imperialist-established statelets, can unify the country, can establish the independence of the country. And they will do so on *the basis of a socialist programme, with socialist slogans,* and with the support of elements of the rural and urban petty bourgeoisie.

The Irish bourgeoisie can go no further than they have already gone. The place of the petit bourgeoisie is behind the workers; they must place themselves in alliance with the revolutionary proletarian movement. The working class must aim at the establishment of its own power in order to solve the problems of Ireland — that is the way to winning the support of the Republican workers, of the workers in the Belfast shipyards and the North. The petit bourgeoisie can be won to the support of the workers; the question is how are they to be won? Will they be won by capitulation to the exploiters of the Irish petit bourgeoisie?

They can be won by explaining how their interests are linked with the socialist revolution in Ireland, with the freedom and unity of the country; and again, by explaining how they are linked up with the interests of the British and world working class. This is all the more important when we consider that between one and one and a half million Irish workers have been forced to emigrate to Britain in the last 40 years and that the coming revolutionary struggles in Ireland will have not a small effect in Britain.

Appeal against expulsion. Labour Party Conference

September 1983

COMRADE CHAIR, comrades, this is a sorry day for the Labour Party, that we should be discussing expulsions instead of discussing —as we have been doing and will continue to do in conference —the fundamental way in which we can get rid of the Tories. *(Applause)*

Our crime is allegedly that we are organised. *Solidarity** is organised. This movement has now reached a situation where MPs no longer have a divine right to their seats. They are now accountable to re-selection. *(Applause)* No longer do they have the divine right to elect the leader; the leader is now elected by the whole of the party conference, and that is absolutely correct. But apparently one divine right remains, that is the right of the right wing to be organised. But there is no such right for those who can effectively fight against the right wing.

If we look at our history, we see that it was the traitors of the SDP** —Rodgers, Owen, Williams —who first raised the question of a witchunt in the Labour Party. In fact one of the reasons they gave for leaving the Labour Party was that *Militant* was not expelled from the party. There was an enormous campaign from our enemies, in the press, in the media, by the Tories, Thatcher, Tebbit, Howe and all the rest, demanding that *Militant* should be expelled so that Labour could set its house in order.

Were they grateful when the expulsions took place? On the contrary, they used this to show the disunity in the Labour Party. Is it not an absolute disgrace that four or five NEC meetings before the general election were taken up with discussions about *Militant*,

---

*An organisation with its own members, funds and full time organisers, set up by a section of the right wing in the Labour Party.

**The Social Democratic Party was formed in 1981 as a result of a split led by the three named Labour MP's and Roy Jenkins. All were former Labour Cabinet members.

***Jim Mortimer was then General Secretary of the Labour Party. He was himself expelled in the 1930's for supporting CP front organisations.

Ted Grant appealing against expulsion during the Labour Party's closed session at 1983 Conference. Photography was banned.

instead of with preparing a campaign that would be victorious against the Tories? *(Applause)*

We have it on the word of Jim Mortimer*** himself last November that a large majority of constituency Labour parties were not sympathetic to the exclusion of *Militant*. To those I would add the overwhelming majority of the rank and file of the trade unions. They want unity; they do not want to spend years discussing this question.

If we take the situation that exists, nobody can deny that among the best workers in the general election, among the best workers in the local elections, among the best workers at all times in the Labour Party are the supporters of *Militant*. *(Applause and interruptions)*

We warned the NEC before the Bermondsey by-election that it would be absolute madness to expel us just on the eve of a by-election. We asked that the hearing should be postponed for a week, a month or as long as they liked. The right wing said that if these expulsions took place that would help to gain a victory. We saw the result in Bermondsey. We have seen the result in the general election, the result of witch-hunting.

My final point, comrade chair and comrades. Michael Foot was expelled from this party. Nye Bevan was expelled from this party. *(Interruptions)* Mortimer was expelled from the party. *(Calls of 'no, no')* Yes, it's absolutely true, these were all expelled from the party. Whatever the result of this vote, whether we gain a victory or whether we are expelled, we shall still continue to work for a Labour victory.

We shall still continue to work to make certain that this Tory government is thrown out, and preferably a Labour government with socialist policies returned. Whatever programme is put forward, *Militant*, as it has always done in the past, will continue to work for the victory of this movement. There is no way that Marxism can be separated from the Labour Party. There is no way you will succeed with these expulsions. We will be back. We will be restored, if not in one year, in two or three years. We will be back. At every trade union conference, at every ward, at every GMC, at every shop stewards' committee meeting this question will come up and we will be back. *(Applause)*

The appeal was lost on a card vote: 4,972,000 to 1,790,000.

Index

Names which frequently occur (Hitler, Stalin etc) are only indexed in relation to specific political issues, 'n' after an entry indicates a footnote. Parties are under their country, except Britain. Papers and journals are only referred to when quoted from.

Further Reading Around *The Unbroken Thread*

Because of the wide ranging nature of the book, it is impossible to list all the works available on specific issues or countries — please write for our free comprehensive booklist. Below are some key Marxist works covering broad areas in this book and further material written jointly by Ted Grant with other authors.

Fascism and war

Lessons of Spain. Trotsky *30p*
Spanish Revolution 1931-7. Grant and Taaffe *70p*
On War and Peace. Lenin *30p*
The Struggle Against Fascism in Germany. Trotsky *£7.95*
Fascism — what it is and how to fight it. Trotsky *80p*

Stalinism

Revolution Betrayed. Trotsky *£4.50*
Bureaucratism and Workers' Power. Silverman and Grant *60p*
Gorbachev: Reform or Revolution? Grant *30p*
Stalinism in Crisis. Militant *60p*

The Colonial Revolution

Problems of the Chinese Revolution. Trotsky *£3.50*
Third International After Lenin. Trotsky *£3.50*
Cuba - Analysis of a Revolution. Taaffe *20p*

The Crisis in Britain

Falklands War. Grant *15p*
General Election 1987. Militant *50p*

General

Short History of European Working Class. Abendroth *£4.60*
Origins of Family, Private Property and State. Engels *95p*
History of the Russian Revolution. Trotsky *£8*
Transitional Programme. Trotsky *30p*
Lenin and Trotsky - What They Really Stood For.
Woods and Grant *£1.50*

The above books are available from World Socialist Books, 3/13 Hepscott Road, London E9 5HB. Prices are as at May 1989. Please add 25% for postage on orders under £5, 10% on orders £5 - £10. Over £10 post free. Please make cheques payable to *World Socialist Books.* You can also get the publications of *Fortress Books* (opposite) from us.

Special offers from Fortress Books

Out of the Night
by Jan Valtin

712 pages hardback, £7.95 (cover price £9.95)

A classic socialist autobiography, outlining the struggles of a Communist Party trade union activist and sailor in Germany from 1918-1938.

Germany – From Revolution to Counter-Revolution
by Rob Sewell

96 pages £2 (cover price £2.50) 5 copies for £8.50

A concise and concentrated summary of the events and lessons of the tumultuous events in Germany, from the 1918 revolution to Hitler's rise to power.

Liverpool – A City That Dared To Fight
by Peter Taaffe and Tony Mulhearn

528 pages Hardback £9.95 (cover price £14.95)
Softback £6.95, five copies for £25

Essential reading, rich in lessons for every struggle of the class.
'A fascinating self-portrait...told with imagery redolent of Petrograd 1917.'
The Independent

Month of Revolution
by Clare Doyle

80 pages £1.95 (cover price £2.50) 5 copies for £8

A vivid account of the revolutionary events of France 1968. Based on eyewitness accounts and material from the time.